The Gun Debate

The Gun Debate

An Encyclopedia of Gun Rights & Gun Control in the United States

Third Edition

Glenn H. Utter

Robert J. Spitzer

GREY HOUSE PUBLISHING

PUBLISHER: Leslie Mackenzie
EDITORIAL DIRECTOR: Laura Mars
EDITORIAL ASSISTANT: Jennifer Bossert
PRODUCTION MANAGER: Kristen Hayes
MARKETING DIRECTOR: Jessica Moody

AUTHORS: Robert J. Spitzer, Glenn H. Utter
COPYEDITOR: Marguerite Duffy
COMPOSITION: Lumina

Grey House Publishing, Inc.
4919 Route 22
Amenia, NY 12501
518.789.8700 FAX 845.373.6390
www.greyhouse.com
e-mail: books@greyhouse.com

While every effort has been made to ensure the reliability of the information presented in this publication, Grey House Publishing neither guarantees the accuracy of the data contained herein nor assumes any responsibility for errors, omissions or discrepancies. Grey House accepts no payment for listing; inclusion in the publication of any organization, agency, institution, publication, service or individual does not imply endorsement of the editors or publisher.

Errors brought to the attention of the publisher and verified to the satisfaction of the publisher will be corrected in future editions.

Publisher's Cataloging-In-Publication Data
(Prepared by The Donohue Group, Inc.)

Names: Utter, Glenn H. | Spitzer, Robert J., 1953-
Title: The gun debate : an encyclopedia of gun rights & gun control in the United States / Glenn H. Utter, Robert J. Spitzer.
Other Titles: Encyclopedia of gun control and gun rights. | Encyclopedia of gun control & gun rights in the United States
Description: Third edition. | Amenia, NY : Grey House Publishing, [2016] | Originally published as: Encyclopedia of gun control and gun rights. | Includes bibliographical references and index.
Identifiers: ISBN 978-1-68217-102-8 (hardcover)
Subjects: LCSH: Firearms—Law and legislation—United States—Encyclopedias. | Gun control—United States—Encyclopedias.
Classification: LCC KF3941.A68 U88 2016 | DDC 363.3/3/0973/03—dc23

CONTENTS

PUBLISHER'S NOTE

With public debate of gun violence at an all-time high, this third edition of *The Gun Debate: An Encyclopedia of Gun Rights & Gun Control in the United States* combines history with current events. At issue are fundamental questions of constitutional law and the rights of individuals, opportunities for self-protection, and the control of violence and national security. An additional factor making this topic especially intriguing is that firearms are inherently interesting. Thousands of firearms fans flood gun shows, admiring the craftsmanship and technological expertise that goes into producing them.

The goal of this new edition is to present a balanced and unbiased approach to this controversial issue. With a total of 374 entries, 40 of which are brand new and the rest updated and revised, coverage includes recent gun laws and legislation, mass shootings and gun incidents, and new information from the groups who support gun rights and those who advocate for stricter gun control.

Content and Format

The topics in this publication have been selected, formatted, and written with the needs of non-specialist readers in mind. Emphasis is on the clear representation of facts supported by tables, charts, graphics, and illustrations. Entries range in length from 500 to 3,000 words and are heavily cross-referenced to related topics within the work, and each entry includes a further reading list for additional study.

New entries discuss police shootings, hunting culture, gang violence, the Castle Doctrine, the New York SAFE Act, and recent shootings in Tucson, San Bernardino, and Orlando. Research for this new edition included consulting the many books, periodicals, organization literature, and personally expressed views of individuals with opinions on both sides of the issue.

Special Features

Several features distinguish this title from other works on the topic, and include the following elements:

- Detailed **Introductory Essay** by the authors is a 10-page overview of the gun debate in America, complete with facts and statistics.

- A **Chronology** of the debate spans from the Minutemen's role in 1775 to 2016, when the gun debate loomed large in the U.S. presidential campaign, as gun violence escalated.

- The **Guide to Selected Topics** arranges all 374 entries into 16 major categories, including Court Cases, Firearms & Ammunition, and Individuals Supporting Gun Rights/Gun Control.

- **Primary Documents** includes 25 original documents, most reprinted in their entirety, that support both sides of the gun debate and span more than 200 years. From the *Federalist Papers* and excerpts from the Second Amendment to significant court cases, acts of law, and recent articles from national newspapers and magazines that showcase viewpoints on both sides of the issue, these documents are designed to offer an historical reference point and broader understanding of the complicated issues that surround the ongoing debate.

- Several **Appendices** provide valuable information, including State Constitutional Provisions, State Firearms Laws, and a list of relevant Organizations

- Finally, a comprehensive **Bibliography** and **Index** conclude the work.

Acknowledgments

Grey House Publishing thanks authors Glenn H. Utter and Robert J. Spitzer for their thoroughness and thoughtfulness in making the third edition of *The Gun Debate: An Encyclopedia of Gun Rights & Gun Control in the United States* a substantially improved and much expanded work.

INTRODUCTORY ESSAY

Perhaps with the exception of abortion, gun control is the most controversial issue in American politics, appealing strongly to the emotions of those who support, as well as to those who oppose, further regulation of firearms. Although people take many different positions on the issue, supporting some proposals for control and rejecting others, the more uncompromising on both sides tend to collapse pro- and anti-gun control categories into two. The pro-gun forces see themselves as the supporters of a vital constitutional right to keep and bear arms pitted against the "gun grabbers." Strong advocates of gun control see themselves struggling for a more civilized society against the "gun nuts" and profit-hungry firearms manufacturers and dealers. Like many other subjects, the issue of gun control is preeminently a political question in that the competitors attempting to influence public policy have an intense interest in the ultimate outcome. Therefore, positions tend to harden and proponents of one position tend to deny any merit in the stand taken by others, each side attributing dishonest motives to those with whom they disagree. Scholars who otherwise are meticulous in presenting research results can become as impassioned in their argumentation as the most openly partisan supporter of a fervently held political position.

Supporters and opponents of gun control disagree over the significance of firearms as an independent variable in explaining the high level of violence in the United States. The term "gun culture" is used by both sides in explaining their respective views of the special role firearms have played in American history and continue to play in contemporary society. Gun rights advocates point with pride to the role that average Americans played in the Revolutionary War, especially because of the skill they reportedly demonstrated with firearms against an intimidated British force. Firearms are seen as an important ingredient in the unique ability of Americans to maintain their independence from a potentially oppressive government. Those less impressed with the gun tradition see that the American love affair with firearms has contributed to a violent past and a continuing belief that the presence and use of firearms promise to cut cleanly through a quagmire of social problems. While not denying this predilection for violence, gun supporters note that other cultures not having as extensive a supply of firearms also experience high levels of violence, that some societies with high concentrations of firearms have much lower levels of violence, and that the level of violent crime in the United States did not increase proportionately with a marked increase in the number of firearms available. Gun rights advocates express their position with the popular saying, "Guns don't kill people, people kill people," and claim that those advocating limitations on firearms suffer from hoplophobia, which is defined as an irrational and morbid fear of guns. However, Franklin Zimring and Gordon Hawkins have argued that firearms have had an independent influence on violence in the United States in that the number of violent crimes that lead to serious injury and death are significantly higher in the United States than in other countries. Table 1 indicates that the homicide rate is much higher in the United States, where firearms are easily obtainable, than in the United Kingdom, where firearms are far less available to the general public.

Table 1
Firearm Homicides, England and Wales and the United States, 2013

	United Kingdom	United States
Population (in millions)	64.5	315.0
Firearm Homicides	23	11,208
Rate (per 100,000 population)	.04	3.56
England and Wales to U.S. Ratio	1 to 89	

Source: The table was derived from comparative data on homicides provided by the School of Public Health, University of Sidney, www.gunpolicy.org.

Supporters of an individual right to keep and bear arms rely on two basic arguments to make their case. First, they claim that the right can be defended as a basic natural, or human, right independent of any positive law, or has evolved through a long tradition of common law stretching back in English history and subsequently recognized and protected in the Second Amendment to the U.S. Constitution. The Second Amendment guarantee of the right to keep and bear arms, they insist, is the premier right that must be preserved to protect the remaining rights listed in the Bill of Rights. In recent years, scholars advocating the position that the Constitution protects an individual's right to possess and carry firearms, not just a corporate right of state governments to maintain a militia independent of the federal government, have published a large body of literature, primarily in law journals.

The second major defense of a right to keep and bear arms makes a utilitarian argument, relying on empirical claims that law-abiding citizens can use firearms effectively to protect themselves against law-breakers. Contrary to the gun control position that certain firearms such as handguns have no legitimate use outside their application to certain sports such as hunting and skeet shooting, gun supporters claim that such weapons have a definite defensive use. Researcher John R. Lott concludes that concealed carry laws give the law-abiding citizen a definite advantage over the potential criminal.

A majority of U.S. Supreme Court justices have accepted both of these arguments for an individual right to keep and bear arms in *District of Columbia v. Heller* (2008) and *McDonald v. Chicago* (2010), cases in which municipal ordinances severely restricting firearm ownership were declared to be violations of the Second Amendment right of individuals to keep and bear arms. These two decisions have significantly altered the playing field on which gun control supporters and gun rights advocates will contend for the foreseeable future. For instance, state and local restrictions on concealed carry have been challenged in court, and limits on where concealed weapons may be carried—college campuses, national parks, restaurants and bars, and churches—have in certain cases been lifted.

Although firearms supporters consider the Second Amendment the heart of their defense of gun rights and the most important protection in the Bill of Rights, they often cite other guarantees as important to their cause. The Fourth Amendment protection against unreasonable searches and seizures is considered important to protect gun owners against investigations conducted by government officials enforcing gun control laws. Gun rights advocates believe that such searches often are carried out according to unconstitutional laws and therefore represent inappropriate harassment. The Ninth Amendment, which guarantees individual rights not specifically stated in the Constitution, has been used by firearms supporters to argue for an additional protection for the right to keep and bear arms, which they consider a fundamental right established in natural law, common law, and the American political tradition. Gun rights supporters consider the Fourteenth Amendment important because of the tendency of the U.S. Supreme Court in recent decades to apply specific protections found in the Bill of Rights to the states. They have argued that the

Second Amendment should also be applied to the states, thus limiting state government power to restrict firearm ownership—a position the Supreme Court affirmed in *McDonald v. Chicago*.

Contrary to the gun rights position, gun control supporters argue that the Second Amendment, like any other freedom, is not absolute (a position that the Supreme Court also has supported in recent decisions). Some gun rights advocates agree that the government can institute reasonable firearms restrictions to maintain an ordered society. However, those more suspicious of the motives of gun control advocates hold that any gun control measure represents yet another step down a slippery slope toward banning firearms and in the direction of a national confiscation effort. If any consensus exists on the gun control issue, it is that guns should be kept from particular individuals, such as felons and those who are mentally unstable. However, conflict arises over where to draw the boundary. For instance, should those convicted of misdemeanor domestic violence charges lose their right to possess firearms? May those convicted of more serious crimes ever reclaim their right to possess firearms? The greatest controversy arises over existing laws and proposals that call for regulating and to some extent restricting firearms ownership in the general population rather than focusing primarily on punishing those who have misused firearms.

Beyond the arguments presented by different sides in the gun control debate, groups have made various efforts to influence the decisions of the national and state governments, and the contest among the various participants has been played out in legislative chambers as well as the courts. Modern efforts at gun control began in 1934 with passage of the National Firearms Act, which placed limitations on certain types of weapons, such as machine guns. The National Rifle Association (NRA), established in 1871, had a significant influence on the contents of the legislation. In 1938, Congress passed the Federal Firearms Act, the last major piece of gun control legislation to receive serious consideration for the next 30 years. Following the assassinations of President John Kennedy in 1963 and Martin Luther King, Jr., and Robert Kennedy in 1968, Congress passed the Gun Control Act (GCA) of 1968. However, pro-gun groups strongly criticized the legislation and fought for revisions. The 1986 Gun Owners Protection Act repealed those sections of the GCA that gun interests considered more objectionable. The passage of this act over the objections of police organizations and other opponents resulted in the mobilization of the gun control movement. Handgun Control, Inc., the most influential of the gun control organizations, captured two major allies in James and Sarah Brady. James Brady, President Ronald Reagan's press secretary, had been badly wounded in the assassination attempt on the president in 1981. The Reagan administration's strong opposition to gun control notwithstanding, the Bradys came to the forefront of the pro-regulation movement. After leaving office, Reagan became a supporter of the Brady Bill. In 2001, Handgun Control, Inc., became the Brady Campaign to Prevent Gun Violence, the premier gun control organization.

Passage of the Brady Handgun Violence Prevention Act in 1994 represented a significant shift in the fortunes of the gun control movement. The act established a five-day waiting period so that local law enforcement agencies could conduct background checks on prospective handgun purchasers to determine if they fell into a class of those prohibited from owning a firearm. In 1997, the U.S. Supreme Court, in *Printz v. United States* dealt a minor setback to the Brady Act when it ruled that the provision mandating that local law enforcement agencies run background checks was an unjustified federal intrusion into state affairs. However, the waiting period ended in November 1998, when the computerized National Instant Criminal Background Check System (NICS) went into effect. Therefore, the *Printz* decision had minimal effect on the application of the Brady Act.

The effectiveness of the Brady Act has been a matter of debate. Supporters, including President Bill Clinton, have claimed that thousands of purchases have been prevented because of the background check requirement. However, others note that the act is a limited measure that requires enhancement through passage of additional provisions. Gun rights supporters doubt the effectiveness of the legislation, questioning the accuracy of claims about the prevention of purchases and noting that few prosecutions have occurred under the law. However, gun advocates have perhaps neglected the potential deterrent effect of the law: Most of those who are disqualified from purchasing firearms may not try to make a legal purchase. Gun rights advocates respond that such people receive weapons from persons they enlist to purchase firearms for them (so-called straw purchasers) and from alternative illegal sources, thus nullifying any beneficial effect the legislation might achieve, while still inconveniencing law-abiding citizens. In 2007, due largely to concerns about mentally ill individuals who may be a threat to themselves and others, Congress passed the NICS Improvement Amendments Act, which encouraged states to submit relevant mental health records to the NICS, and also provided a procedure by which those legally determined to be mentally incompetent could have their right to purchase and possess firearms restored.

Some gun control organizations, such as the Violence Policy Center (VPC), are nearly as critical of the Brady Act as gun rights groups, claiming that the legislation is ineffective. They have argued that the best way to limit gun violence is to institute a general ban on handguns, an option that the U.S. Supreme Court in the *Heller* and *McDonald* decisions effectively eliminated. Paul Helmke, president of the Brady Campaign to Prevent Gun Violence, argued that these Supreme Court decisions eliminated the "slippery slope" claim of gun rights organizations that any compromise on gun control will lead inexorably to greater pressure to compromise still further. Therefore, Helmke claimed, the Court's decisions open the door for more moderate gun control policies because gun rights supporters no longer need to fear more extreme proposals and the realization of their greatest nightmare, the confiscation of firearms. However, gun rights organizations, voicing a more general distrust of government, still sound the alarm that moderate measures, which they consider unnecessary, will lead to more extreme policies. Given that gun ownership is considered a basic constitutional right—and to many the premier right—any compromise appears unjustified. Gun rights advocates express concern about the increase in federal firearms legislation, beginning especially in the 1940s.

Gun control advocates have attempted to counter the ways that the law can be circumvented, and therefore concentrate their efforts on controlling the illegal gun trade. For instance, to restrict straw purchases, some gun control supporters have advocated limiting the purchase of handguns to one per month, arguing that no legitimate purchaser needs to buy more than twelve weapons in one year.

Gun control advocates have also focused on the issue of gun safety, particularly to prevent accidents involving unauthorized access to firearms by children. This issue of gun-related injuries and deaths among young people has inspired calls for the mandatory use of locks on handguns and the development and application of technology to produce so-called smart guns that would prevent the use of a handgun by anyone other than the owner. Although pro-gun groups have been somewhat suspicious of such calls for the mandatory sale of a gun lock with each new handgun, the industry has responded to this proposal by developing several types of locking devices. The more skeptical among gun rights supporters question whether the value of a handgun for self-defense can be maintained if they are kept locked, but some companies have advertised their safety products as compatible with keeping the weapon readily accessible in an emergency.

Gun rights groups have cautioned that an emphasis on gun locks and other technology to maintain the safety of firearms neglects the importance of educating the owners of firearms about safe handling and storage, and teaching young people to stay away from firearms when unsupervised. The NRA developed the Eddie Eagle program to teach gun safety to children. However, gun control organizations doubt the ultimate effectiveness of such a program, arguing that keeping firearms out of the home represents the surest way to avoid a tragic accident. Because children, even when instructed, tend to act irresponsibly, the best strategy involves keeping firearms completely inaccessible. Some gun control groups even suspect that the Eddie Eagle program encourages a positive attitude toward firearms among children that promotes future ownership, a charge that the NRA and its supporters readily deny.

With a Republican Congress and the legislatures of several states passing preemption laws preventing local governments from passing gun control ordinances more stringent than state statutes, some gun control organizations and municipal governments shifted their focus to the courts, suing firearms manufacturers and retailers for compensation for the damage done by their products. Such lawsuits instituted by municipal governments in Chicago, Atlanta, New Orleans, and elsewhere resembled the state government lawsuits against the tobacco industry to recover the costs of medical care attributed to the ill effects of smoking. In February 1999, a federal jury in New York raised the concern of the firearms industry by awarding $500,000 to a survivor of a shooting incident. The jury found that 15 of 25 manufacturers named in the lawsuit were responsible for injuries because they had negligently marketed a lethal product. Among the companies found liable were Beretta USA, Colt, and Jennings Firearms. The plaintiffs argued that the companies oversupplied firearms to states with more lenient gun control laws, mainly in the South, because they were aware that the excess guns would ultimately make their way through the black market into the hands of criminals in states such as New York that have instituted more stringent regulations. Firearms companies had argued that their responsibility ended with delivery to distributors. Tables 2 and 3 report domestic firearms production (1986-2012) and imports (2012-2013), respectively. The largest importers of handguns to the United States were Austria, Brazil, and Germany. The largest source of rifle imports were Canada and Brazil. Italy and Turkey led in imports of shotguns and unspecified firearms.

Gun rights supporters feared that lawsuits could bankrupt the firearms industry and claimed that gun control groups were pursuing that outcome as their ultimate goal. Effective lobbying by gun rights groups led to congressional passage of the 2005 Protection of Lawful Commerce in Arms Act, which limited the liability of firearms manufacturers for the illegal use of their products. However, in 2016 parents of the young children shot and killed at the Sandy Hook Elementary School in Newtown, Connecticut, began to sidestep the 2005 law by arguing that Bushmaster Arms International and Remington are liable under the "negligent entrustment" exception in the law. The judge in the case allowed the suit against the gun manufacturers to proceed.

Related to the lawsuit strategy, gun control advocates have called for regulating firearms as consumer products. The firearms industry is essentially self-regulating, setting its own safety standards. So-called Saturday night specials or junk guns, inexpensive handguns that are claimed to be less safe than higher quality firearms, became the focus for much of the concern for consumer protection. The 1968 Gun Control Act prohibited the importation of such weapons, but domestic production expanded greatly to fill the demand. Gun control supporters argued that by requiring high production standards, the manufacture of Saturday night specials could possibly come to an end.

Gun rights groups have attempted to counter the initiatives of gun control organizations, challenging gun laws in the courts and sponsoring legislative initiatives at the national and state levels. When Massachusetts passed a stringent gun control bill in 1998, the NRA quickly began a legal challenge to the law. Pro-gun organizations have supported the liberalization of concealed carry laws, backing "shall issue" provisions that require law enforcement agencies to issue a concealed carry license to anyone not specifically prohibited from owning a firearm. The NRA has also challenged the NICS, questioning the keeping of purchase records by the ATF even for a brief time. Since 2004, with passage of the Tiarht Amendment, background check records may not be kept longer than 24 hours. On the national level, gun groups, with the support of some law enforcement organizations, have lobbied for a reciprocity measure whereby each state would be required to recognize the concealed carry licenses of other states, just as each state recognizes the drivers' licenses of other states. Bills have been introduced in Congress to establish reciprocity among all states, but so far the proposal has not gained approval.

Table 2
Domestic Production of Civilian Firearms, 1986-2012 (In Thousands)

Year	Handguns	Rifles	Shotguns	Miscellaneous	Total Production
1986	1,424	971	641	5	3,041
1987	1,687	1,008	858	7	3,560
1988	1,856	1,145	928	35	3,964
1989	2,033	1,407	936	42	4,418
1990	1,842	1,212	849	57	3,960
1991	1,835	883	828	16	3.562
1992	2,139	1,002	1,018	17	4,176
1993	2,656	1,174	1,145	81	5,056
1994	2,591	1,317	1,255	11	5,174
1995	1,723	1,411	1,174	9	4,317
1996	1,486	1,424	926	18	3,854
1997	1,407	1,251	916	20	3,594
1998	1,285	1,536	1,037	25	3,883
1999	1,331	1,570	1,107	40	4,048
2000	1,282	1,583	898	30	3,793
2001	947	1,285	680	21	2,933
2002	1,089	1,515	741	22	3,367
2003	1,121	1,430	726	31	3,308
2004	1,023	1,325	732	20	3,100
2005	1,078	1,431	709	23	3,241
2006	1,406	1,497	715	36	3,654
2007	1,611	1,611	645	55	3,922
2008	2,041	1,735	631	93	4,500
2009	2,415	2,249	753	139	5,556
2010	2,817	1,831	743	68	5,459
2011	3,171	2,318	862	190	6,541
2012	4,155	3,168	949	306	8,578
Totals	**45,296**	**37,121**	**22,453**	**1,111**	**114,559**

Source: Bureau of Alcohol, Tobacco, Firearms, and Explosives, www.atf.gov/resource-center/docs/
firearmscommerceannualstatisticalreport2014pdf/download

Table 3
Firearm Imports, 2012-2013

Firearm Type	2012	2013
Handguns	2,627,201	2,095,528
Rifles	1,243,924	1,507,776
Shotguns	973,465	936,235
Total Imports	4,844,590	5,539,539

Source: Bureau of Alcohol, Tobacco, Firearms, and Explosives,
www.atf.gov/resource-center/docs/firearmscommerceannualstatisticalreport2014pdf/download

The participation of health care professionals in firearms research has created a good deal of controversy. Health care researchers, concerned about the number of people killed and injured by firearms each year, employ the epidemiological model in their research on firearms, the same procedure used in studying the progression of a disease. The use of this methodology raised suspicions among some gun rights supporters that these researchers had prejudged firearms, like a disease, as something bad that deserves to be eliminated. Those more sympathetic to gun ownership claimed that this research fails to meet the standards of good social science methodology. Arthur Kellermann's finding that a firearm kept in the home is far more likely to be used to harm a family member or friend than to fend off an attack by an intruder has been challenged by those more sympathetic to gun ownership. They argue that the use of firearms to harm others is more likely to occur among those with criminal histories. For their part, health care researchers have criticized research indicating that carrying concealed weapons (CCW) laws at the state level have a measurable deterrent effect on crime, and question the methodology employed, the assumptions made, and the conclusions reached.

The controversy over appropriate research methodologies and objectives reached the political realm in 1997 when gun rights groups lobbied Congress successfully to cut the budget for the Centers for Disease Control's (CDC) National Center for Injury Prevention and Control (NCIPC) in order to limit NCIPC-sponsored research on firearms, which was claimed to be politically motivated, biased, and, hence, "unscientific." Doctors for Integrity in Policy Research (DIPR), a pro-gun rights organization that was active in the 1990s, led the criticism leveled at the CDC.

In response to calls for additional gun control, gun rights advocates argue that existing legislation covers virtually any illegal action committed with a firearm. They recommend the more judicious application of existing statutes, but also raise doubts about the possibility of keeping firearms out of the hands of criminals. Some researchers have focused on the illegal gun trade, attempting to trace the typical routes of firearms from manufacturers to those who use them in illegal activities. Gun control advocates suggest that registration of firearms would assist in tracing firearms used in criminal activity back to their original purchasers. Such a plan would place greater legal responsibility on gun owners for the safe and secure storage of firearms. Some states already have instituted child access prevention (CAP) laws holding gun owners responsible if young people harm themselves or others with weapons to which they have gained access.

In 1994, responding to gun control advocates' contentions that semi-automatic weapons with large capacity ammunition clips were being used disproportionately in criminal activity, Congress passed an assault weapons ban. However, some gun researchers and gun rights advocates argued that the banning of specific weapons represented a distinctly ineffective way to limit firearms violence because other types of firearms could easily be substituted for the prohibited models. Firearms not classified as assault weapons could have as much, or more, destructive effect as the banned guns, and manufacturers modified proscribed models sufficiently to legally avoid the ban. In 2004, Congress failed to renew the assault weapons ban, a definite victory for gun rights groups. Following mass shootings in 2015 and 2016, gun control supporters in Congress introduced bills to reinstate an assault weapons ban and a restriction on the capacity of ammunition magazines, but the Republican majority in both the House and the Senate defeated the proposals.

In the political struggle over gun control, gun control groups are at a definite disadvantage, given the large membership in gun rights organizations and the many popular publications dealing with firearms. Table 4 provides circulation figures for these major periodicals. In the last decade, the print circulation of most of these publications has declined, as has that of magazines and newspapers, mainly due to the increased influence of the Internet. Such magazines as *Guns and Ammo*, *Guns Magazine*, *Women and Guns*, *American Handgunner*, *Shooting Times*, and the NRA's *American Rifleman* still provide colorful descriptions of new firearms along with articles highly critical of gun control measures and supportive of gun rights, but undoubtedly many people access the magazines online rather than via the print medium. Each magazine hosts a Web site where they provide information about firearms and gun rights. *Soldier of Fortune* distributed the magazine's final print issue in April 2016 and now is available exclusively online. Gun control advocates have attempted to counteract this advantage by enlisting the support of public relations firms to produce public service advertisements that caution the public about the dangers of firearms in the home. In 2014 Michael Bloomberg, former mayor of New York, pledged $50 million in support of the newly created Everytown for Gun Safety and other gun control organizations. Such campaigns have included television announcements, billboards, and special marches to raise concern about firearms-related violence, especially among youth. Michael Moore's movie, *Bowling for Columbine*, revolved around the 1999 shooting at the Littleton, Colorado, high school in which two students shot and killed 12 fellow students and one teacher and wounded several others before killing themselves.

Table 4
Major Commercial Gun Publications: Circulation, 2008

Publication	Circulation
American Rifleman (National Rifle Association)	1,334,095
American Hunter (National Rifle Association)	910,291
North American Hunter (North American Hunting Club)	825,313
Guns and Ammo	456,943
America's First Freedom (National Rifle Association)	407,689
Barrett Tactical Weapons	180,000
Shooting Times	174,659
American Handgunner	115,063
Handguns	112,145
Shotgun News	104,523
Guns Magazine	89,278
Combat Handguns	83,000
Gun World	71,124
Gun Digest	66,779
Women and Guns	38,000

Source: The Standard Periodical Directory, 31st edition (New York: Oxbridge Communications, 2008).

The focus on guns and young people includes a concern for students who carry firearms to school. Estimates are that several thousand young people take a gun to school each year. Reasons for carrying a weapon include the desire to impress others and the belief that a weapon will guarantee personal safety. In 1994, Congress passed the Gun-Free Schools Act, a measure geared to deter such behavior. The highly publicized school shootings in 1997, 1998, and 1999 continued to raise concerns about firearms in schools. However, some more avid gun rights supporters argued that firearms in schools—in the hands of authorized persons—would likely deter such shooting incidents.

The emphasis that gun control campaigns have placed on youth is especially troubling for gun interests. They believe that discouraging youth interest in firearms threatens a tradition that has been passed from father to son for generations. The sporting industry is concerned that the demand for their products, which in the past depended on generational transfer, may be headed for a decline because the next generation may not become as firmly tied to the sporting tradition. When Charlton Heston began a public relations campaign for the NRA in 1997, he focused his attention on transmitting positive attitudes about gun ownership to a new generation. Trade associations encourage such transfer, recommending that fathers take not only their sons but also their daughters on hunting trips. Gun control organizations disapprove of such attempts because they consider firearms a clear threat of injury and death to youth. Animal rights groups also oppose the continuation of the hunting culture.

Gun control advocates are especially critical of what they consider the efforts of the firearms industry to increase sales by manipulating the emotions of women. They claim that gun manufacturers, finding that the male market had been saturated, decided to develop a new market among women to maintain demand for their products. They charge that gun interests focus on women's fears of being attacked by a stranger to encourage them to become firearms owners. Gun rights supporters respond that women have the same rights as men to protect themselves and charge that the women's rights movement is inconsistent in demanding equal rights for women, but at the same time objecting to women's possession of firearms for self-protection. Gun control advocates note that the most probable threat of violence that women face is not from a stranger, but from people that women know, such as husbands and boyfriends. In any event, gun ownership among women lags considerably behind that for men.

The question of militia groups lies at the periphery of the gun control debate. Militia supporters argue that their organizations are protected by the Second Amendment and believe that the amendment provides the opportunity to defend individual freedom against a tyrannical government. This position involves what many consider the curious argument that the Constitution guarantees a right to revolt against the governmental structure that it established: The governing document plants the seeds of its own destruction. (At least one state constitution—that of New Hampshire, recognizes a right to revolt.) Supporters of the militia idea contend that the protection of liberties against a powerful government must include the possibility of violent resistance. Therefore, gun control legislation is viewed with special apprehension because it is seen as denying the ability to take the ultimate step to defend freedom against tyranny. Those less skeptical of the government respond that freedom ultimately depends on a legal order and a strong government that is able to defend citizens against the encroachment on the rights of some by others in society.

One of the more extreme arguments against gun control, made by such organizations as Jews for the Preservation of Firearms Ownership, involves the charge that restrictions on firearms ownership have often accompanied genocide. Examples such as the nineteenth-century attempt to disarm Native Americans, the effort to keep African Americans disarmed in the South following Reconstruction, and the Nazi gun control policies that preceded the Holocaust are often mentioned to emphasize the dangers of gun control. Such disarmament is thought to put the people at the mercy of an oppressive government. Stephen P. Halbrook's book, *Gun Control in the Third Reich* (2013), offers a detailed argument about the potential consequences of gun control and gun confiscation. Those more sympathetic to gun control conclude that such arguments are historically inaccurate and less than persuasive, especially given that black youth are particularly prone to suffer injury and death from firearms that appear to be readily available, a limited form of genocide in itself. Therefore, it is not surprising that groups representing minorities often support measures intended to limit minority youth access to firearms. For instance, the National Organization of Black Law Enforcement Executives (NOBLE) has taken positions in favor of various gun control legislation, as has African-American Representatives John Conyers, (D-MI) and John Lewis (D-GA).

Rather than limiting their activities to defending gun interests against additional gun control proposals, gun rights groups have pursued an aggressive strategy intended to weaken already existing firearm laws and to extend gun rights. Since 2003, Justice Department appropriations have included the so-called Tiahrt amendment (named for Representative Todd Tiahrt, who introduced the measure), which prohibits the use of appropriated funds to disclose information contained in the Firearms Trace System database. This measure was intended in part to protect firearms manufacturers from litigation. In 2004, Congress failed to renew the Assault Weapons Ban law, thus allowing the sale once more of these previously prohibited weapons. In 2005, Congress approved the Protection of Lawful Commerce in Arms Act, which limited the liability of firearms manufacturers for the criminal use of their products. In 2008, a conservative majority on the U.S. Supreme Court ruled that the Second Amendment protects the right of individuals to possess firearms, and in 2010 the Court decided that the Second Amendment applies to state and local governments as well as to the federal government. By 2010, 37 states had passed laws permitting the carrying of concealed weapons with a permit (three additional states—Alaska, Arizona, and Vermont—allowed concealed weapons carrying without a license) and by 2016 all 50 states had adopted some form of concealed carry; 44 states had instituted firearms law preemption legislation (four additional states had instituted such a measure through judicial rulings) that prohibit local jurisdictions from passing firearms ordinances more restrictive than laws at the state level; and 34 states had enacted Castle Doctrine provisions, which allow citizens to defend themselves with deadly force in their homes and eliminate the "duty to retreat." By 2016 at least 23 states had expanded the Castle Doctrine to public spaces. These so-called stand-your-ground laws provide greater immunity from prosecution for individuals who use deadly force in self-defense.

Given the successes of pro-gun individuals and organizations over the last decade, the probability of enacting additional gun control measures in the foreseeable future appears to be slight. Organizations advocating gun control have supported proposals to close the so-called gun show loophole (those without a federal firearms license may legally sell firearms at gun shows without purchasers having to pass a criminal background check) and to make more effective the system of tracking illegal firearms. In addition, these organizations have taken a defensive position by opposing, for instance, the adoption of the Thune amendment, proposed by Senators John Thune and David Vitter, that would establish national reciprocity among the states with regard to concealed carry laws: If persons are permitted to carry a concealed weapon in their home state, every other state would be required to recognize that permit. The future success of gun control measures may depend upon partisan control of Congress, possible shifts in public opinion resulting from shooting incidents, the perceived danger of armed terrorists within the United States, and general shifts in the public mood regarding the role of the government in American society. In January 2010 at a political rally in Tucson, Arizona, a gunman, using a Glock pistol that he had legally purchased, shot and killed six individuals, including U.S. district court judge John Roll, and wounded a dozen others, including U.S. Representative Gabrielle Giffords (D-AZ). Giffords received a gunshot wound to the head but survived. In June 2016, a lone gunman entered a gay nightclub in Orlando, Florida, killing 49 and injuring at least 50 others in the deadliest one-person shooting in U.S. history. In the nationwide debate that followed these and other shooting incidents, some noted that the Assault Weapons Ban, which Congress allowed to expire in 2004, limited the capacity of ammunition magazines to 10 rounds. Calling for a reintroduction of the ban, they argued that if the restriction were still in place, lives could have been saved. Others more sympathetic to gun rights went so far as to suggest that members of Congress should be permitted to carry firearms on the floor of the House and Senate.

In January 2016, President Barack Obama, frustrated at what he perceived as lack of congressional action on proposed legislation, announced a series of executive actions, including tightening the definition of who is engaged in the business of selling firearms in order to expand the background check requirement to a greater number of purchasers, adding mental health records from the Social Security Administration to the NICS, and instructing government agencies to review the state of smart gun technology. Such actions, although applauded by those supporting more stringent gun control measures, were likely to have minimal effect on gun-related crime.

CHRONOLOGY

1775   Colonial militia, called the minutemen, defend a store of arms in Lexington, Massachusetts, against an attempt by British troops under the command of General Thomas Gage to confiscate weapons. The minutemen take on a reputation far beyond their contribution to the fight for independence, becoming a crucial ingredient in many Americans' positive attitudes toward firearms.

1789   James Madison fulfills a promise to submit 12 constitutional amendments in the first session of the new House of Representatives; the amendments are to constitute a Bill of Rights to the recently adopted U.S. Constitution. Although initially holding that a Bill of Rights is unnecessary, Madison agrees to support the idea to attain ratification of the Constitution. One of Madison's proposed amendments originally reads: "The right of the people to keep and bear arms shall not be infringed; a well-regulated militia being the best security of a free country: but no person religiously scrupulous of bearing arms shall be compelled to render military service in person." The amendment is revised to exclude a religious exemption and is submitted to the states as: "A well regulated Militia, being necessary to the security of a free State, the right of the people to keep and bear Arms, shall not be infringed." This Second Amendment to the U.S. Constitution is ratified on December 15, 1791.

1792   Congress passes the Militia Act, which establishes an organized militia and an enrolled militia composed of all free white males, who were expected to provide their own muskets, firelocks, and ammunition. The act is never truly implemented by the states.

1846   In *Nunn v. State*, the Supreme Court of Georgia overrules a lower court decision convicting Hawkins Nunn of carrying a pistol in violation of an 1837 state statute. The court finds that both the U.S. and Georgia state constitutions guarantee the right to keep and bear arms and traces the historical roots of the right, calling it "one of the fundamental principles, upon which rests the great fabric of civil liberty, reared by the fathers of the Revolution and of the country."

1857   The U.S. Supreme Court, in *Scott v. Sanford*, rules that the Bill of Rights does not apply to blacks. Chief Justice Roger Taney argues that if blacks were given full citizen status with free white men, they would have the right of free speech and the right "to keep and carry arms wherever they went."

1871   Colonel William C. Church and George W. Wingate, former Union army officers, collaborate in establishing the National Rifle Association (NRA). The NRA hopes to encourage rifle practice so that Americans will be better prepared militarily for any future conflict. New York State provides funds to purchase land on Long Island to establish a rifle range for NRA members.

1876   The U.S. Supreme Court, in *United States v. Cruikshank*, rules for the first time on the basis of the Second Amendment, declaring that the amendment applies to the national government only, and not to private groups. Among other charges, the defendants were originally indicted for preventing two African Americans from exercising "the right to keep and bear arms for a lawful purpose." The Court decided that only the states have the authority to protect citizens against such violations of their rights by private persons.

1881   A gun-wielding attacker assassinates President James Garfield, the second president to be killed in office.

1886   In *Presser v. Illinois*, Herman Presser, the appellant, appealed his state conviction for violating the Military Code of Illinois to the U.S. Supreme Court. Presser led a contingent of 400 armed men in a Chicago parade, himself carrying a cavalry sword, without receiving a license from the governor to parade as part of the state militia. The Supreme Court rules that the section of the Illinois statute banning armed parades without authorization does not violate the right of the people to keep and bear arms.

1901   President William McKinley is assassinated by a gunman.

1903   Congress passes the Dick Act, which repeals the Militia Act of 1792. The Dick Act is an attempt to revive state militias based on voluntary recruitment and greater national government control over the organization and operation of the National Guard.

1911   Responding to the outcry against street violence in New York City, the New York State legislature enacts the Sullivan Law, the most stringent gun legislation of the time. The statute requires a license to possess or carry a concealable weapon. One provision of the law forbids aliens to possess firearms in public.

1924   Congress passes the Mailing of Firearms Act, which prohibits sending pistols and other firearms that can be concealed on the person through the United States Post Office.

1934   Congress enacts the National Firearms Act, which focuses on limiting access to weapons commonly thought to be used primarily by gangsters. Over-the-counter sale of machine guns is prohibited, and automatic weapons, short-barreled rifles, and sawed-off shotguns must be registered.

1938   Congress passes the Federal Firearms Act, which is intended to regulate the interstate sale of firearms. Those wishing to manufacture, sell, or import firearms and ammunition must receive a license from the federal government's Internal Revenue Service (IRS), which is responsible for collecting the license fees.

1939   In *United States v. Miller*, the U.S. Supreme Court rules on a challenge to the National Firearms Act of 1934 that by prohibiting the transportation of a sawed-off shotgun across state lines the law violates the Second Amendment. The Court rejects the appeal, ruling that the Second Amendment does not protect the possession of a sawed- off shotgun, which has no relation to the preservation of a well-regulated militia.

1948   The Federal Aviation Act prohibits the carrying of firearms on commercial aircraft.

1963   President John F. Kennedy is assassinated by a gunman using a mail-order rifle.

1966   Following the shooting incident at the University of Texas at Austin, in which 12 people are killed and 33 others wounded by a lone gunman, President Lyndon Johnson urges legislators to take action on gun control legislation before Congress.

1968 In separate incidents, Dr. Martin Luther King, Jr., and Senator Robert F. Kennedy are assassinated by gunmen.

Congress passes the Gun Control Act. Among its provisions, the law strengthens the firearms licensing process to limit foreign and interstate transport of firearms, prohibits the interstate shipment of pistols and revolvers to private individuals, and forbids certain criminals, the mentally incompetent, and drug addicts from shipping or receiving weapons through interstate commerce, and firearms dealers are prohibited from knowingly selling weapons to these categories of people.

1972 The Internal Revenue Service's Alcohol, Tobacco, and Firearms Division receives bureau status in the Department of the Treasury, but does not receive status as an independent regulatory agency, leaving it more open to political attacks.

1980 In *Lewis v. United States*, the U.S. Supreme Court upholds a lower court conviction under a provision of the Omnibus Crime Control and Safe Streets Act of 1968, which prohibits any person convicted by a federal or state court of a felony from possessing a firearm. The Court rules that Congress acted reasonably when it determined that a convicted felon should be prohibited from dealing in or possessing firearms, even if the conviction occurred without the benefit of counsel.

1981 The Village of Morton Grove, Illinois, receives national attention when it passes an ordinance to regulate the possession of firearms "and other dangerous weapons." No person may possess a handgun, unless it has been made permanently inoperative.

In *Quilici v. Village of Morton Grove*, a U.S. Circuit Court affirms the constitutionality of the Morton Grove ordinance. The court rules that local governments with home rule charters have the right to govern their own affairs.

1982 Inspired by the firearm ban enacted in Morton Grove, Illinois, in 1981, the city council of Kennesaw, Georgia, a small town north of Atlanta, passes an ordinance to require residents to keep firearms in their homes.

1986 President Ronald Reagan signs the Firearms Owners Protection (McClure-Volkmer) Act, which limits various provisions of the Gun Control Act of 1968. The act permits the sale of ammunition through the mail, allows weapons dealers to resume the interstate sale of rifles and shotguns, and relieves ammunition dealers of record-keeping requirements. The Bureau of Alcohol, Tobacco, and Firearms (BATF) is prohibited from centralizing records and from establishing a firearms registration system. Focusing on the misuse of firearms, the law requires mandatory penalties for such misuse.

1988 Congress passes the Undetectable Firearms Act, which bans the manufacture, importation, receipt, and transfer of plastic and ceramic guns that X-ray machines and magnetometers cannot detect. The law requires firearms to contain a minimum of 3.7 ounces of metal to make them detectable.

1989 Following a shooting incident at a Stockton, California, elementary school, in which a man wielding a Chinese-made AK-47 killed several children, the California legislature passes the Roberti-Roos Assault Weapons Act, which is the first statute in the United States to ban the sale, possession, or manufacture of semi-automatic, military style firearms.

1992   A standoff between Randy Weaver and federal government officers occurs at Ruby Ridge, Idaho. After Weaver tries to sell two sawed-off shotguns to a government informant, the Federal Bureau of Investigation (FBI) tries to recruit Weaver as an informant. He refuses. The resulting standoff leads to the death of a U.S. Marshall and Weaver's wife and son. The event heightens the suspicions that more extreme groups have about federal government firearms policy.

1993   Federal agents conduct a raid on the Branch Davidian compound in Waco, Texas, because the members of the religious group are suspected of weapons violations. Four BATF agents and six Branch Davidians die in the initial assault. After a 51-day siege, the compound is assaulted with tanks and tear gas. Seventy-five people, including 20 children, die in a fire apparently set by group members. The incident lowers the prestige of the BATF and increases the hatred some extremist groups have for the federal government.

1994   Congress passes the Brady Handgun Violence Prevention Act, which establishes a temporary five-day waiting period before individuals may purchase a handgun to run a background check to discover if potential purchasers are disqualified from owning a handgun.

Congress passes the Assault Weapons Ban Act, which prohibits the sale, manufacture, importation, or possession of 19 types of assault weapons.

1995   In *United States v. Lopez*, the U.S. Supreme Court affirms an appeals court reversal of a conviction based on the Gun-Free School Zones Act of 1990. Basing its decision on an interpretation of Congress's commerce power, the Court disallows the measure that made it a federal crime to knowingly possess a firearm within a public, parochial, or private school, or in a zone within 1,000 feet of school grounds.

1996   Maryland enacts a one-gun-per-month statute, which limits an individual to purchasing no more than one gun in a 30-day period. The legislative success of the statute inspires gun control advocates to push for a similar law on the national level.

1997   In *Printz v. United States*, the U.S. Supreme Court declares unconstitutional a provision of the Brady Handgun Violence Prevention Act that requires chief law enforcement officers in local jurisdictions to perform background checks on prospective handgun purchasers. Speaking for the majority, Justice Antonin Scalia states that Congress violated the constitutional system of state sovereignty by compelling states to enforce a federal regulatory program.

1998   A National Instant Check System (NICS) goes into effect on November 30, in which gun dealers must consult a computerized background check system to determine whether a prospective handgun purchaser is disqualified from owning a firearm. The National Rifle Association (NRA) quickly files a suit against the operation of the system, claiming that records are being kept illegally.

The Supreme Court rules in *Caron v. United States* that a felon may have the right to own firearms restored under federal law only if a state confers the right to own all types of firearms.

Two boys, aged 11 and 13, are arrested in Jonesboro, Arkansas, for shooting and killing four fellow students and one teacher, and wounding 11 others at the Westside Middle School. The incident sparks renewed debates about gun control.

1999   A jury in New York finds in favor of a handgun victim against several firearms manufacturers. Given the potential significance of the ruling for manufacturers, the decision is expected to be appealed.

Two students, aged 17 and 18, enter their high school in Littleton, Colorado, with automatic weapons, sawed-off shotguns, and homemade bombs, killing 12 students, one teacher, and themselves. The incident and its aftermath receive nationwide coverage, opening a debate over the need for additional gun control measures.

President Bill Clinton proposes several gun control measures, including the reimposition of a waiting period to purchase a firearm, a prohibition on gun ownership for those under 21 years of age, and the establishment of penalties, including imprisonment and fines, for adults who give children access to firearms.

Although the U.S. Senate approves stronger gun control legislation, a coalition of conservative Republicans and Democrats defeat a considerably weakened measure in the U.S. House of Representatives. While rejecting a proposal to require labeling entertainment products with violent content, the House approves a measure allowing the posting of the Ten Commandments in schools and government buildings.

To counter cities such as Boston and San Francisco, which have initiated lawsuits against gun manufacturers and dealers to recover the costs of gun violence, the National Rifle Association lobbies state legislatures to limit the authority of local governments to file such suits.

2000   Pro-gun control activists organize the Million Mom March, a grassroots rally held in Washington DC on Mother's Day to support stronger gun laws. The rally attracts about 700,000 people. The MMM organization works to institutionalize its efforts, but enthusiasm ebbs, and while the MMM organization continues, it is combined with the Brady Campaign to Prevent Gun Violence.

Republican Texas Governor George W. Bush is elected president in the close and disputed 2000 presidential election. Bush defeats Vice President and Democratic nominee Al Gore. Gore supports stronger gun laws, whereas Bush wins the endorsement of the National Rifle Association. Bush proves to be the most gun-friendly president in modern history.

2001   President Bush's Attorney General, former Missouri Republican Senator John Ashcroft, sends a letter to the National Rifle Association in which he endorses the individualist interpretation of the Second Amendment's right to bear arms. The statement represents a change in Justice Department policy extending back to the 1930s accepting the militia-based interpretation of the amendment.

The United States is attacked by Islam extremist terrorists on September 11. The two World Trade Center towers in New York City are destroyed, and the Pentagon is also damaged as nineteen terrorists take over civilian airplanes to use them as missiles against targets. The attacks prompt Americans to purchase more guns in the months after the attack.

A three judge federal panel from the US Court of Appeals for the Fifth Circuit becomes the first federal court in American history to accept the individualist interpretation of the Second Amendment in the case of *United States v. Emerson*. Despite the ruling, the court fails to apply the right to the defendant in the case, who is eventually convicted of violating a federal gun law.

2004   Congress fails to reenact the federal ban on assault weapons, first enacted in 1994. Under the terms of the law, Congress had to act affirmatively for the law's provisions to continue. The lapsing of the law also again makes legal civilian ownership of large capacity ammunition clips.

2005   Congress enacts the Protection of Lawful Commerce in Arms Act, which bars civil suits against gun manufacturers, distributors, dealers, and importers of firearms and ammunition. Enactment of the law had been the top legislative priority of the National Rifle Association.

2006   New York City Mayor Michael Bloomberg and Boston Mayor Thomas Menino form Mayors Against Illegal Guns, organized to track and curtail illegal gun trafficking from states with lax gun laws into urban areas. In four years, the organization attracts over 300 mayors to join the organization.

2007   A mentally unstable graduate student at Virginia Tech State University uses two legally acquired handguns to shoot and kill thirty-two students and faculty before killing himself, making this the worst gun massacre in modern history. The shooting prompted states to improve the accumulation and reporting of data concerning those unqualified to own guns by virtue of mental problems. In a rare moment of bipartisanship, gun control and gun rights groups combine to support enactment of a federal law to fund and more strongly regulate state reporting of data.

2008   The Supreme Court rules 5-4 in the case of *District of Columbia v. Heller* that the Second Amendment's right to bear arms protects a personal or individual right of citizens to possess handguns for personal self-protection in the home. The case arises as a challenge to DC's strict handgun law (DC is under federal control). The ruling reverses past court rulings which interpreted the amendment to protect a militia-based right, and becomes the first time in history that a gun law under federal jurisdiction is struck down as a violation of the Second Amendment.

Five students on the campus of Northern Illinois University are shot and killed and eleven injured by a former student who entered a large lecture class and started shooting. This and the Virginia Tech shootings in 2007 prompt campuses to increase their security measures.

Illinois Democratic Senator Barack Obama is elected president. Gun rights groups oppose his election and spend heavily in support of his opponent, Republican Senator John McCain from Arizona. Despite a past record in favor of stronger gun laws, Obama also voices support for Second Amendment rights. To the dismay of gun control groups, during his administration Obama avoids championing stronger gun measures.

2009   As part of a large spending bill, Congress includes a provision to allow Amtrak train passengers to carry unloaded guns in their luggage, with ammunition to be carried in separate, secure wooden or metal boxes.

Congress approves a measure to allow people to carry loaded weapons in national parks. The measure is enacted in 2010 despite opposition from parks officials, conservationists, and law enforcement.

2010   The Supreme Court rules in *McDonald v. Chicago* that the Second Amendment's right to bear arms now applies to the states through the process of "incorporation," by which portions of the Bill of Rights are applied to the states. This ruling endorses the Court's earlier interpretation of the Second Amendment in the 2008 *Heller* case, and is the product of the same 5-4 vote as *Heller.*

2011   Arizona Democratic Congresswoman Gabrielle Giffords was shot in the head during a constituent "Congress on Your Corner" meet-and-greet in front of a supermarket in Tucson. Giffords survived the shooting, but six others were killed, including a federal judge, and twelve others were wounded. The shooter, Jared Lee Loughner, has a history of mental problems, but legally purchased the handgun he used.

A gunman firing an automatic weapon shot and killed seven people and wounded fifteen others before killing himself at a shopping mall near Amsterdam in the Netherlands. No obvious motive explained the shooting.

2012   An African American teenager, Trayvon Martin, visiting his father in Sanford, Florida was shot and killed by a neighborhood watch volunteer, George Zimmerman, who apparently mistook the teen for a possible thief. In 2013, Zimmerman was acquitted of murder.

A disturbed former graduate student entered a movie theater at a shopping mall in Aurora, Colorado shortly after the start of a midnight showing of the latest Batman movie, *The Dark Knight Rises*, and started shooting with an assault weapon and another gun. He rapidly killed twelve and injured 70. In 2015, the shooter was sentenced to life without parole.

The movie theater shooting briefly pushed the gun issue into the presidential campaign then unfolding between incumbent Democratic President Barack Obama and his Republican challenger, Mitt Romney. By and large, however, guns and gun violence played little role in the election.

In December, a severely disturbed young man entered the Sandy Hook Elementary School in Newtown, Connecticut where he killed 20 schoolchildren and six adult staff members with an assault weapon before killing himself. Before entering the school, he also murdered his mother as she slept. This shooting shocked and outraged the nation in a way few such shootings had. Within days, President Obama convened a task force, headed by Vice President Joe Biden, to produce policy recommendations.

2013   In January, Vice President Biden's task force issued its report, calling for universal background checks for all gun purchases, restrictions on assault weapons and high capacity bullet magazines, mental health and school safety initiatives, and other measures. The proposals were sent to Congress, but were defeated in several floor votes in the Senate (the House of Representatives did not take up the measures). Congress would take up no other gun measures for the balance of Obama's presidency.

In the months after the shooting, over a dozen states enacted tougher gun laws. Over 30 states enacted measures to weaken their existing gun laws.

A civilian contractor entered the Washington, D.C. Naval Yard with a shotgun and proceeded to kill twelve people and injure three others. The shooter, referred to in news reports as "delusional," was killed at the scene.

2014   The "Black Lives Matter" movement becomes a national movement in the aftermath of the police shooting of an unarmed eighteen-year old man, Michael Brown, by a police officer in Ferguson, Missouri. Brown, who had stolen some cigars from a local store, had some kind of encounter with the police officer before he gave Brown chase, resulting in the death of Brown. The officer was found not guilty of wrongdoing.

2015   A young white man who identified with white extremism entered a predominantly African American church in Charleston, South Carolina, and after sitting with a Bible study group for an hour, pulled out a gun and fatally shot nine people.

A husband and wife of Middle Eastern ethnicity entered an office building in San Bernardino, California, where the man had worked, and opened fire on those present, killing 14 and wounding 22. After an intensive hunt, the two were killed in a gun battle by the police. The two had apparently been radicalized, although neither apparently had specific ties to radical Islamist groups.

2016   The gun issue intrudes on the presidential campaign. Democratic contender and former Secretary of State Hillary Clinton expressed support for stronger gun laws and used the issue to criticize her primary opponent, Vermont Senator Bernie Sanders, who had a background of opposing some stronger gun laws. Republican presidential candidates uniformly opposed stronger gun laws.

An American-born man who pledged allegiance to the Middle Eastern terrorist group ISIS entered a predominantly gay nightclub in Orlando Florida where he shot and killed 49 people, and wounded 53 others. After a three hour stand-off, police entered the nightclub, killing the shooter.

GUIDE TO SELECTED TOPICS

This subject guide arranges this edition's entries into the following 16 categories. A number of entries fall into more than one category.

COUNTRIES
FIREARMS & AMMUNITION
FIREARMS RESEARCHERS
GROUPS SUPPORTING GUN CONTROL
GUN CONTROL ISSUES
HISTORICAL INDIVIDUALS & GROUPS
INDIVIDUALS SUPPORTING GUN RIGHTS

LEGISLATORS & GOVERNMENT OFFICIALS

COURT CASES
FIREARMS INDUSTRY ORGANIZATIONS
GOVERNMENT AGENCIES & POLICIES
GROUPS SUPPORTING GUN RIGHTS
HISTORICAL EVENTS
INDIVIDUALS SUPPORTING GUN CONTROL
LEGISLATION & CONSTITUTIONAL
   AMENDMENTS
PUBLICATIONS

Firearms and Ammunition

Firearms Industry Organizations

Firearms Researchers

Government Agencies and Policies

Groups Supporting Gun Control

Groups Supporting Gun Rights

Gun Control Issues

everal colleagues have contributed to the preparation of the first and second editions of this book. At Lamar University, Dr. James Love, professor of criminal justice, provided invaluable help. In several productive discussions, he offered his personal insights from the perspective of a former police officer. Dr. James True, Jack Brooks Chair of Government and Public Service, now retired, assisted with data analysis, and Dr. Terri Davis, assistant professor of political science, conducted legal research. Dr. Larry Osborne, chair of the Computer Science Department, provided practical assistance regarding computer resources, and Dr. Thomas Sowers, associate professor of political science, assisted in the collection of data for the second edition. Colleen Barry, an undergraduate research assistant, conducted bibliographical searches. Provost Stephen Doblin and Dr. Brenda Nichols, dean of the College of Arts and Sciences, provided support for the completion of the project. People on both sides of the gun control question contributed helpful information. They include Richard Aborn, Massad Ayoob, David Kopel, Alan Korwin, Bill McGeveran, Josh Sugarmann, David Hemenway, and Franklin Zimring. Mark A. Hazlip provided much-needed technical expertise in preparing the manuscript for the third edition. Although recognizing the assistance of many people, we accept full responsibility for any errors of judgment or fact.

A

Aborn, Richard (1952–)

As president of Handgun Control, Inc. (HCI) (later renamed the Brady Campaign to Prevent Gun Violence) and the affiliated Center to Prevent Handgun Violence (CPHV) (subsequently renamed the Brady Center to Prevent Gun Violence) from 1992 to 1996, Richard Aborn has been an active supporter of more stringent gun control legislation. Since 1979, Aborn has been involved in the campaign to reduce gun violence. From 1979 to 1984, he worked in the Manhattan District Attorney's Office, investigating and prosecuting homicide and illegal gun distribution cases. After leaving government, Aborn worked as a volunteer for HCI and was elected to the board of trustees in 1988 and to the presidency in 1992. In 1999 the office of the New York City public advocate engaged Aborn to investigate the police department's disciplinary program, which resulted in various reforms to reduce police misconduct.

Aborn worked to implement CPHV's STAR (Straight Talk About Risks) program in New York City public schools. The program, which is aimed at children from prekindergarten through the twelfth grade, is intended to educate youth about the dangers of firearms to reduce injuries resulting from their misuse. Aborn contributed to former New York Governor Mario Cuomo's publication project, *New York State Strategy to Reduce Gun Violence*. He has been a consultant to the Ford Foundation on violence and youth and has worked with a New York task force of public health officials to consider solutions to the problem of violent crime.

Aborn has supported passage of a comprehensive federal gun control bill that would include licensing and registration of handgun purchases and transfers, the limitation of gun purchases to one per month, and a ban on Saturday night specials. He advocates a tax on ammunition, dealers' licenses, and firearms to be used to pay for the medical costs of gun-related injuries. He supports the Brady Campaign position that the organization does not want to ban all guns or interfere in the lawful acquisition of firearms, but instead strives to stop the illegal gun market. Aborn sees no contradiction between gun ownership and gun control.

Aborn notes that illicit gun traffickers acquire firearms in jurisdictions with weak gun control laws and then sell them illegally in jurisdictions with more stringent laws. Aborn holds that Saturday night specials (which he defines as a handgun that has a barrel less than two inches long, is made of nonhomogeneous metal, is unsafe, and cannot pass a drop test from more than five feet) are disproportionately used as crime weapons and have little self-defense use.

Aborn claims that gun control laws already passed have been effective. He cites a U.S. Justice Department estimate that the Brady Handgun Violence Prevention Act, for which he served as the principal lobbyist, prevented over 70,000 felons from purchasing guns from retail outlets during the first year after the law went into effect. In addition, he asserts that the 1994 assault weapons ban, before it expired in 2004, effectively restricted the supply of such firearms.

In an effort to reassure gun owners that the Brady Campaign and other organizations supporting greater regulation of firearms do not intend to ban guns, Aborn states that anyone who wishes to have a firearm for self-defense should be allowed to do so. However, he is careful to indicate that a firearm in the home poses serious risks to the residents. In arguing for more stringent gun control laws, Aborn refers to public opinion polls that have consistently indicated that a majority of U.S. citizens support such legislation. Aborn has continued his activities in the gun control movement, working with PAX and other gun control organizations. In 2001 Aborn advised the New York City Democratic mayoral candidate in developing a comprehensive criminal justice policy. When the opposing candidate, Michael Bloomberg, won the election, Bloomberg implemented Aborn's program. In 2007 Aborn, along with New York Mayor Michael R. Bloomberg, took part in a news conference announcing an advertising campaign, GUNS = PRISON, to publicize a new state law that mandates a three and one-half year prison sentence for anyone caught carrying an illegal, loaded, handgun in the state. In 2009 he made an unsuccessful run in the New York Democratic primary for District Attorney of Manhattan.

Aborn is a partner in the law firm Constantine Cannon and serves as the president of Constantine and Aborn Advisory Services (CAAS), which provides recommendations to police departments and other organizations in the United States and other countries. Aborn is also president of the Citizens Crime Commission of New York City, an organization that deals with criminal justice and public safety issues. Aborn advocates diligence, innovative strategies such as ballistic fingerprinting technology, and energetic law enforcement to reduce the harm caused by illegal guns in the New York area.

See also: Brady Campaign to Prevent Gun Violence; Brady Handgun Violence Prevention Act; PAX; Saturday Night Special.

Further Reading: "Richard M. Aborn Biography," www.bradycampaign.org/about/bio/additional; Citizens Crime Commission of New York City, www. nycrimecommission.org; "Richard Aborn for D.A.: About Richard," www.abornforda. com/index.php/ site/about.

Academics for the Second Amendment (A2A)

Academics for the Second Amendment (A2A) is an organization composed of law professors, political scientists, philosophers, and historians who support an individual's right to keep and bear arms. From the organization's founding in 1992, its members rejected the view held by many academics (but

dismissed by the U.S. Supreme Court majority in *District of Columbia v. Heller*, 2008) that the Second Amendment guarantees only the right of states to maintain militias. The organization attributes this position to a general hostility among academicians toward guns and gun owners.

A2A has sponsored legal, philosophical, and historical analysis that has sought to establish that the right to bear arms applies to individual citizens. To disseminate the results of such scholarship, ASA has conducted professional meetings attended by scholars, lawyers, news reporters, and students.

A2A argues that in the eighteenth century the term "militia" referred not to a formal military organization but to a system of universal military service in which each male citizen of military age was required to possess a firearm for defense against foreign invasion, tyranny, and criminal activity. The organization claims that after the Civil War, debates in Congress regarding the nature of citizenship affirmed the need to protect the individual rights of African Americans in the South to keep and bear arms for self-defense.

A2A contends that, just like the First Amendment rights of freedom of speech and assembly, an individual's right to keep and bear arms guaranteed in the Second Amendment is not absolute. Unlike some other gun rights organizations, ASA believes reasonable people may have genuine differences of opinion regarding the application of the right of gun ownership, thus leaving the door open for "sensible gun laws" that are constitutional.

A2A is headquartered in St. Paul, Minnesota, and Joseph E. Olson, the organization's president, is a professor of business law at Hamline University. He served as administrative law judge for the state of Minnesota and has been a consultant for state legislators and the Minneapolis City Council. Olson served as a member of the board of directors of the National Rifle Association (NRA) and as president of the American Association of Certified Firearms Instructors, and founded Concealed Carry Reform NOW! Olson participated, along with David Hardy and Clayton Cramer, in writing the *amicus curiae* brief submitted to the U.S. Supreme Court on behalf of A2A in *District of Columbia v. Heller* (2008), in which the Court ruled that the Second Amendment to the U.S. Constitution protects an individual's right to possess firearms (particularly handguns) within the home in territory governed by the federal government. A2A also file a brief in

United States v. Lopez, in which the U.S. Supreme Court invalidated the Gun-Free School Zones Act of 1990, ruling that Congress's commerce power did not apply to this law. While those involved in the organization consider their efforts necessary to counteract a fundamental prejudice against firearms among academics, gun control advocates consider the organization as biased in favor of the NRA and other gun rights organizations.

See also: District of Columbia v. Heller (2008); National Rifle Association; Second Amendment.

Further Reading: "Brief of *Amicus Curiae*, Academics for the Second Amendment in Support of the Respondent," www.gurapossessky.com/news/parker/documents/07-290bsacAcademicsforSecond Amendment.pdf; Scott Heller, "The Right to Bear Arms," *Chronicle of Higher Education* 21 (July 1995), "Joseph E. Olson," http://aacfi.com/trainers/JoeOlson; html Robert J. Spitzer, *The Politics of Gun Control*, 6th ed. (Boulder, CO: Paradigm, 2015).

Accidents Involving Guns

Gun control advocates have long considered accidents involving guns a major reason for introducing greater regulation of firearms, including such measures as mandated training for gun purchasers, firearm safety locks, and strict limitations on the ownership of handguns. Opponents of such measures argue that decreases in the number of gun accidents in recent years make any additional legislation unnecessary. Using 1987 data from the Metropolitan Life Insurance Company, Gary Kleck, a leading firearms researcher, estimates that fatal gun accidents (FGAs) amount to less than 5 percent of all gun deaths and just over 1 percent of all accidental deaths. He puts the total number of FGAs each year at less than 1,400. Table 5 presents Kleck's estimates of FGAs from 1933 to 1995, based on data from the U.S. National Center for Health Statistics and the National Safety Council. Data for the years 1999 to 2014 are also provided in the table, which indicate that unintentional firearm deaths have continued to fall after Kleck published his results. Employing data gathered by the Consumer Product Safety Commission in 1980–81, Kleck observes that guns ranked as the thirty-sixth most common cause of nonfatal accidents. Although Kleck concludes that the general level of

Table 5
Fatal Gun Accidents, United States, 1933–1995, 1999–2007

Year	Total	FGAs per 100,000 Resident Population
1933	3014	2.40
1935	2799	2.20
1940	2390	1.80
1945	2454	1.84
1950	2174	1.43
1955	2120	1.28
1960	2334	1.30
1965	2344	1.21
1970	2406	1.18
1975	2380	1.10
1980	1955	0.86
1985	1649	0.69
1990	1416	0.57
1991	1441	0.57
1992	1409	0.55
1993	1521	0.59
1994	1356	0.52
1995	1225	0.47
1999	824	0.30
2000	776	0.28
2001	802	0.28
2002	726	0.26
2003	730	0.25
2004	649	0.22
2005	789	0.27
2006	642	0.22
2007	613	0.20
2008	592	0.19
2009	554	0.18
2010	606	0.20
2011	591	0.19
2012	548	0.17
2013	505	0.16
2014	586	0.18

Source: Reprinted with permission from Gary Kleck, *Targeting Guns: Firearms and Their Control* (New York: Aldine de Gruyter, 1997), pp. 323–24. Copyright © 1997 by Walter de Gruyter, Inc., New York. 1999–2007 data from Centers for Disease Control, National Center for Injury Prevention and Control, http://webappa.cdc.gov/cgi-bin/ broker.exe.

gun ownership is ostensibly unrelated to fatal gun accident rates, David Hemenway (2004) notes that people living in states having higher rates of gun ownership have an increased chance of dying in gun accidents.

Kleck notes that the rate of FGAs declined by 33 percent from 1967 to 1987. He attributes the decline in part to improved medical treatment of gunshot wounds and possibly to the increasing number of so-called Saturday night specials, small-caliber handguns with lower power. Another possibility is that the gun control movement's warnings about the dangers of firearms, particularly handguns, may have reached many gun owners. In more recent years, gun rights organizations such as the National Rifle Association (NRA) have placed greater emphasis on firearm safety through such initiatives as the Eddie Eagle program. Another possible contributor to the decline in the number and rate of unintentional firearm deaths is a decrease in the proportion of homes where firearms are kept. Although agreeing that there has been a genuine decline in accidental gun deaths, Hemenway claims that a portion of the reduction in fatal gun accidents resulted from a change in the categorization of gun deaths that occurred in 1968—many deaths that before 1968 would have been labeled accidental were now placed in an "undetermined intention" category.

Recent gun control initiatives have been defended as ways of preventing gun accidents involving children. However, Kleck estimates that the probability of a gun accident in gun-owning households involving a child from 0 to 14 years old to be approximately 1 in 58,000, and for handgun-owning households, 1 in 60,000. Hemenway, who estimates that two to three accidental firearm deaths occur each day, claims that the number of nonfatal gun accidents far surpasses the fatal accidents: More than 30 people are injured each day in nonfatal gun accidents, and additional people suffer from other effects of firearms, including lead poisoning and hearing loss. Although keeping guns locked away is the most effective method of preventing gun accidents involving children, people often have handguns in the home for self-protection and many believe that an unloaded gun or a gun kept in a locked place defeats the purpose of having the weapon.

Kleck associates the probability of gun accidents with age, sex, and racial groups. Blacks and males aged 15 to 24 have higher accident rates than the general population. For instance, the National Center for Injury Prevention and Control reports that the 2007 fatality rate for whites was 0.19 per 100,000 population while the rate for blacks was 0.32. In addition, Kleck notes that gun accidents are related to social class: Lower-income people are more likely to have gun accidents, just as they are more likely to have accidents in general. These are just the people that gun safety programs are less likely to reach. Some evidence also indicates that gun accidents are related to the characteristics of individual gun owners. Kleck notes that a large proportion of gun accidents are related to reckless behavior. Accident-prone owners are more likely to be impulsive, alcoholic, or willing to take risks, and more likely to have a flare for the sensational.

To further decrease the number of accidents involving guns, various groups have advocated mandatory training and proficiency tests to receive a permit to purchase a firearm, although gun rights organizations are less likely than gun control groups to support such measures. Training, which may help reduce accidents due to lack of knowledge and appropriate skills, would have little effect on incidents involving intentional, or semi-intentional, reckless activity. Greater attention to possible safety flaws in particular guns may reduce some types of gun accidents. For instance, particular models may be prone to firing when dropped. Trigger locks or other devices, such as loaded-chamber indicators, magazine safeties, and firing pin blocks, could be mandated to protect against accidental firing.

While gun control supporters suggest various measures that may help reduce firearm accidents and other causes of gun deaths and injuries, gun rights advocates quickly become wary of any restrictions on the right to own a firearm. In addition, some gun rights supporters question the effectiveness of existing gun control legislation in reducing gun accidents. Even with recent reductions in the numbers of gun accidents, which to some extent could be attributed to gun control legislation, calls for further measures will continue as long as highly emotional incidents (especially involving children) occur.

The National Shooting Sports Foundation (NSSF) attributes the decline in the rate of firearm injuries and fatalities to its educational efforts as well as those of the National Rifle Association and state-affiliated hunter education programs. The NSSF also attributes the decline to the voluntary initiative of firearms manufacturers to include free firearm locking devices with sales of new firearms and technological advances in firearm design. David Hemenway and Sara J. Solnick analyzed data from the National Violent Death Reporting System for 16 states from 2005 to 2012 and determined that there was an average of 110 unintentional firearm deaths year among children aged 0 to 14. They emphasized the importance of keeping guns away from children, siblings, and friends. Pediatricianss continue to consider firearms in the home a serious threat to the safety of children.

See also: American Academy of Pediatrics; Eddie Eagle; Fatalities; Hemenway, David; Kleck, Gary; National Center for Injury Prevention and Control; National Rifle Association; Saturday Night Special; Trigger Locks.

Further Reading: Susan Glick and Kristen Rand, eds., *Kids Shooting Kids: Stories from Across the Nation of Unintentional Shootings among Children and Youth* (Washington, DC: Violence Policy Center, 1997); David Hemenway, *Private Guns, Public Health* (Ann Arbor, MI: University of Michigan Press, 2004); Gary Kleck, *Point Blank: Guns and Violence in America* (New York: Aldine de Gruyter, 1991); National Center for Injury Prevention and Control, http://webappa.cdc.gov/cgi-bin/broker.exe; National Shooting Sports Foundation, "Firearms-Related Injury Statistics" (2015). www.nssf.org/PDF/research/IIR_InjuryStatistics2015.pdf; American Academy of Pediatrics, "Periodic Survey No. 86—Firearm Injury Prevention" (2013), www.aap.org/en-us/Documents/surveys_research_exec_summary_ps86_firearms.pdf; David Hemenway and Sara J. Solnick, "Children and Unintentional Firearm Death," Injury Epidemiology 2 (October 2015): 26.

African Americans and Guns

Researchers indicate that African Americans face a far greater risk of being victims of gun violence than the American population as a whole. African American males in their teens and early 20s are especially prone to suffer from gun violence. In 2000, it was estimated that while the overall homicide rate associated with firearms was 4 per 100,000 population, the rate for African American males was 27 per 100,000, nearly seven times as great.

"Black-on-black" violence remains a significant problem. In 2001, in homicides in which the offender could be identified, 94 percent of cases with white victims involved a white offender, and 86 percent with African American victims involved an African American offender. Black youths are considerably more likely to be threatened or shot with a firearm. The 2000 homicide rate per 100,000 population for blacks aged 15 to 24 was 41.8, but the rate for whites was 4.7.

In contrast to homicide, African Americans have a lower rate of suicide than do whites. Among white males in 2000, the suicide rate per 100,000 population was 12, but the rate among black males was 6. Comparable figures for white and black females were 6 and 1.7, respectively. The difference in rates between white and black youths is considerably smaller than the overall difference between whites and blacks. Data from 2000 indicate that among those aged 15 to 24, the white suicide rate was just 30 percent higher than the black rate. A somewhat higher percentage of African Americans in that age category used firearms (64 percent versus 57 percent). Gun control advocates point to the increasing availability of guns as one important factor in explaining the differences in homicide and suicide rates between blacks and the population as a whole. The African American population appears to have arrived at the same conclusion, for surveys indicate that African Americans support gun control at higher rates than whites.

Despite such data, gun rights advocates argue from a broader historical perspective. African Americans from the time of slavery to the present suffered from discrimination that, among other restrictions, prevented them from possessing firearms they could have used to defend themselves against racially motivated violence. They argue that despite Fourteenth Amendment (ratified in 1868) guarantees of equal protection under the law for all Americans, blacks were denied basic rights, particularly in the South, and thus were reduced to a status inferior to whites. Although in *United States v. Cruikshank* (1876) the Supreme Court refused to allow the national government to intervene to protect the rights of blacks to keep and bear arms, numerous tales are told of blacks who used firearms to protect themselves during the dark days of racial segregation and intimidation.

Lynchings of blacks by whites and other acts of intimidation led some blacks to acquire firearms for self-defense. Although at times blacks took collective action to arm themselves, southern states established legal policies intended to disarm them.

Firearms laws did not ban the possession of guns, but made it more difficult for African Americans to acquire firearms. Gun rights advocates note that even during the height of nonviolent opposition to discrimination during the 1960s, some southern blacks decided to protect themselves by owning firearms. For instance, in 1964, a group of armed blacks in Jonesboro, Louisiana, formed the Deacons of Defense and Justice, vowing to resist any racist attacks. The organization established chapters in Louisiana, Mississippi, and Alabama to deter the violent attacks conducted against civil rights workers.

Gun rights advocates argue that today the crucial violence problem for African Americans cannot be solved by more stringent gun control efforts in the minority community, but rather by blacks exercising their right to keep and bear arms because government has demonstrated an inability to provide adequate protection. When applied to African Americans, gun rights supporters label gun control a racist policy, based on the long history of attempts to prevent blacks from exercising what is considered a basic civil right of self-defense. Gun control advocates respond to the claimed racist history of gun control measures by arguing that African Americans have suffered historically and are still experiencing the harmful effects of a society inundated with firearms. In any event, data indicate that blacks are at greater risk of being victims of firearm-related violence, and generally are more likely to support gun control measures.

A Pew Research Center poll conducted in in 2015 indicated increasing support among African Americans for gun rights. The survey reported that 60 percent of blacks interviewed still supported gun control measures over gun rights, but that level of support represented a 14 percent decline from the 1993 finding that 74 percent of blacks interviewed supported gun control measures. The 2015 mass shooting at the Charlston, South Carolina, African Methodist Episcopal Church, in addition to well-publicized police shootings of Africans Americans has added to the increasing of government, especially the police, which is generally associated with support for gun rights and a belief in the need for self-protection.

See also: Black Codes; Black Panther Party; Congress of Racial Equality; Fatalities; Fourteenth Amendment; State Laws, Appendix 2; Suicide; *United States v. Cruikshank* (1876).

Further Reading: Gregg Lee Carter, *The Gun Control Movement* (New York: Twayne, 1997); Robert J. Cottrol and Raymond T. Diamond, "The Second Amendment: Toward an Afro-Americanist Reconsideration," in David B. Kopel, ed., *Guns: Who Should Have Them?* (Amherst, NY: Prometheus, 1995); David Hemenway, *Private Guns, Public Health* (Ann Arbor, MI: University of Michigan Press, 2004); Tariro Mzezewa and Jessica DiNapoli, "African-Americans Still Favor Gun Control But Views Are Shifting" (July 15, 2015). Reuters.com/article/us-africanamerican-guns-idUSKCNOPP2N320150715.

AK-47

With the sixtieth anniversary in 2007 of the AK-47, the most successful assault rifle ever made, several books were published celebrating its great worldwide popularity. As many as 100 million AK-47s have been produced since its development. The AK-47, or Avtomat Kalashnikov 1947, is celebrated for its exceptional reliability, highly accurate semi-automatic fire, and controllable automatic burst fire. Mikhail Kalashnikov was a sergeant in the Soviet army in 1947 when he developed the relatively simple, but deadly, weapon. Kalashnikov developed the weapon in the highly secretive atmosphere of the Stalinist regime, basing the design on a German assault rifle, or *Sturmgewehr,* used during World War II. The assault rifle met the criteria set by the Soviet military establishment of the time: simplicity of manufacture and operation, reliability, and firepower. For his accomplishment, the Russian sergeant received a monetary reward and gained recognition as a Hero of Socialist Labor.

Because the AK-47 proved relatively inexpensive and required little sophistication to produce, underdeveloped countries, especially those associated with the former Soviet Union, became major sources of the weapon. The AK-47 was used throughout the world in various guerrilla wars supported by the Soviet Union. Other countries, including China, Finland, Israel, North Korea, South Africa, and Eastern European nations then under Soviet control, produced versions of the weapon, and additional nations produced weapons based on the AK-47 design. Norman Benotman, a former Islamist militant, commented to Fareed Zakaria in an interview on CNN news in October 2010, "I do respect my AK-47."

In 1959, the AK-47 was even further simplified, thus reducing its costs of production. The revised weapon was called the AKM. Countries within the Soviet bloc, which produced their own weapons, standardized parts for the assault rifle. The United States failed to develop a similarly efficient system of small arms production. Many argue that the more technically sophisticated weapons produced by American and European manufacturers were no more effective than the AK-47 and were considerably more expensive.

American forces first faced the legendary Soviet assault rifle in Vietnam, where the AKM was generally judged more reliable than the American M-16. Unlike the M-16, the AKM withstood the harshest conditions, further increasing the weapon's reputation for dependability. The AKM could also be used to great effect by relatively untrained soldiers, an important feature in a guerrilla war.

Nations outside the Soviet bloc, including Israel, South Africa, and Finland, also produced variations of the AK-47, which retained the basic features of the Soviet weapon with certain additions, such as a bipod stand, carrying handle, folding stock, or grenade launcher. Semiautomatic versions of the AK-47 have been available to private citizens in the United States. The call for a ban on assault rifles gained momentum in the 1990s in part due to the reputation of the Kalashnikov and similar automatic and semiautomatic weapons. Their widespread availability throughout the world and the mystique that developed around them made these weapons an attractive possession and a valued commodity in illegal foreign trade. The AK-47 and its variations remain popular weapons among those involved in insurgencies and terrorist activities. An estimated 50 to 75 million AK-47s have been produced, in addition to 100 milliion riles influence by the AK-47 design.

See also: Assault Weapons Ban; Israel; Stockton, California, Shooting.

Further Reading: Virginia Ezell, "The 50th Anniversary of the AK-47: A Visit to the Izhevsk Machine Plant," *Small Arms Review* 1 (April 1998), 42–48; Michael R. Gordon, "Russians Honor Inventor of AK-47 Assault Rifle," *New York Times* (March 13, 1997); Michael Hodges, *AK-47: The Story of a Gun* (MacAdam/ Cage, 2008); Larry Kahaner, *AK-47: The Weapon that Changed the Face of War* (New York: Wiley, 2006); Joe Poyer, *The AK-47 and AK-74 Kalashnikov Rifles and Their Variations*, 2nd ed. (North Cape Publications, 2006); Military Factory, "Since 1949, the Timeless Kalashnikov AK-47 Assault Rifle Has Found Many Homes—and Users" (August 9, 2016), militaryfactory.com/smallarms/ detail.asp?smallarms_id=19.

Aliens

In February 1997, following the shooting at the Empire State Building in New York City, in which an alien who had been in the United States for just five weeks killed one person and wounded several others with a firearm he purchased in Florida, Senators Richard J. Durbin, Democrat from Illinois, and Edward M. Kennedy, Democrat from Massachusetts, introduced the Empire State Building Counter-Terrorism Act. The bill was intended to amend the Brady Handgun Violence Prevention Act by prohibiting the purchase or possession of a firearm or ammunition by an alien admitted to the United States under a nonimmigrant visa. The Bureau of Alcohol, Tobacco, Firearms, and Explosives (ATF) defines "nonimmigrant aliens" as persons lawfully admitted to the United States "who are tourists, students, business travelers, and temporary workers who enter the U.S. for fixed periods of time."

The bill contained exceptions for aliens admitted to the United States for legitimate hunting or sporting purposes and for official government representatives, "distinguished foreign visitors," and foreign law enforcement officers of governments friendly to the United States. According to the provisions of the proposed legislation, a person admitted into the country under a nonimmigrant visa could receive a waiver by submitting a petition to the U.S. attorney general indicating that foregoing the prohibition "would be in the interests of justice" and "would not jeopardize the public safety." Gun rights organizations reacted negatively to the bill, arguing that such proposals demonstrated an antiforeign bias and could deny individuals the needed means for self-defense.

The Durbin-Kennedy bill was approved as part of the Omnibus Appropriations Act for fiscal 1999. In November 1998, an official of the Bureau of Alcohol, Tobacco, and Firearms (ATF) announced at the National Association of Sporting Goods Wholesalers show in Tampa, Florida, that the new federal restrictions on the sale of firearms to aliens included in the Durbin-Kennedy bill were being instituted. Individuals included in the ban are those traveling temporarily in the country, those attending school in the country but maintaining a residence abroad, and certain foreign employees. In addition to aliens admitted to the United States for lawful hunting or sporting purposes, the prohibition does not apply to official representatives of a foreign government accredited to the U.S. government or to an international organization with headquarters in the United States.

ATF Form 4473, which was revised in October 1998 to accommodate the National Instant Check System, was altered in early 1999 to provide for a declaration regarding alien status. However, questions arose regarding the effectiveness of a system that depends on a statement by the purchaser and an instant check system that may not have the required information to flag an alien with a nonimmigrant visa. In addition to federal restrictions, several states have instituted various limitations on alien possession and carrying of firearms. For instance, Arkansas will not issue handgun licenses to noncitizens; noncitizens in California are prohibited from transporting handguns in automobiles; and Louisiana forbids an "enemy alien" from possessing firearms or other weapons.

See also: Brady Handgun Violence Prevention Act; Bureau of Alcohol, Tobacco, Firearms, and Explosives; Empire State Building Shooting; Gun Shows; National Instant Check System.

Further Reading: Bureau of Alcohol, Tobacco, Firearms, and Explosives, "Nonimmigrant Aliens," www.atf.gov/firearms/faq/nonimmigrant-aliens. html (accessed October 18, 2010); Bureau of Alcohol, Tobacco, Firearms, and Explosives, "Questions and Answers—Revised ATF F4473 (April 2012 Edition)," www.atf.gov/resource-center/docs/non-immigrant-alienspdf/download; Durbin-Kennedy Empire State Building Counter-Terrorism Act of 1997 www. thomas.loc.gov/cgi-bin/query/z?c105:S.380; Robert M. Hausman, "ATF Announces New Gun Restrictions for Aliens," *Gun Week* 33 (December 20, 1998), 3; "U.S. State and Federal Gun Laws for Non-Citizens," www.vrolyk.org/guns/aliens-laws.html.

Amendment II Democrats

The Web site for Amendment II Democrats described the organization as "an informal confederation of liberal, progressive, moderate, and conservative Democrats and like-minded individuals who are dedicated to fighting for a free and armed America." The organization supports maintaining streets safe not only from "armed robbers, murderers, rapists, and gangsters," but also from "those in our government who abuse the public trust instead of serving it," supposedly by supporting legislation that limits the right to own a firearm. Amendment II Democrats states that, although some of its members also are members of the National Rifle Association (NRA), the organization receives no financial or other support from the NRA and claims to have the goal, in common with the Brady Campaign to Prevent Gun Violence, of creating a society in which people are free from the threat of firearm violence. The organization also supports sensible and firm regulation of the firearms industry.

Amendment II Democrats differ with organizations supporting gun control measures in that the organization advocates the right of individual citizens to gain access to firearms not only for hunting and sports but also for personal protection, and opposes calls for limitations on firearm ownership based on arguments for crime reduction and public health. The organization asserts that firearm ownership accords with the principles of the Democratic Party, assuming that the party supports the understanding that the Second Amendment protects an individual's right to possess firearms. As do supporters of the First Amendment protection of freedom of speech, the organization argues that the pursuit of security should not be used to accept the limitation of a right.

In opposing the extension of the 1994 assault weapons ban in 2004, Amendment II Democrats presented what the organization termed as ten myths about the ban and asserted that, rather than classifying as criminals a group of otherwise law-abiding citizens because of the type of firearms they possess, police should focus their efforts on apprehending the "real criminals" who misuse all types of firearms.

During the 2010 election campaign, Amendment II Democrats submitted a list of questions to Democratic candidates for Congress that dealt with firearms ownership. For instance, candidates were asked "Do you support Federal legislation that would restrict or even outlaw private ownership of semiautomatic firearms by law-abiding citizens?" "Do you support legislation that would allow ownership and/or carrying of firearms by law-abiding students and/or faculty on college campuses?" and "Do you believe that the United States should support and enforce United Nations agreements that contain measures that would infringe upon the Second Amendment rights of Americans?" The organization placed the responses of specific candidates on its Web site.

Although the organization's Website has suspended operation, Amendment II Democrats continues a presence on Facebook. Among its recent policy positions, the organization opposes attempts to restrict civilian ownership of semi-automatic firearms, to prohibit civilian ownership of large capacity ammunition clips, to limit the number of firearms a person may purchase "during an arbitrary time period," and to employ "a faulty and secretive 'watch list'" to prevent firearm possession or purchases without legal due process.

See also: Academics for the Second Amendment; Brady Campaign to Prevent Gun Violence; National Rifle Association.

Further Reading: Amendment II Democrats Facebook page, www.facebook.com/amendmentiidemocrats

American Academy of Pediatrics (AAP)

The American Academy of Pediatrics (AAP), concerned with what it considers an unacceptable level of firearm-related deaths and injuries among children and adolescents, has taken a strong stand against the possession of firearms in the home. Two groups within the organization—the committee on injury and poison prevention and the committee on adolescence—have made extensive policy recommendations to reduce the number of deaths and injuries among children and adolescents due to firearms. Although AAP has supported model state legislation that would prohibit the manufacture, sale, distribution, or ownership of handguns, the U.S. Supreme Court decisions in *District of Columbia v. Heller* (2008) and *McDonald v. Chicago* (2010) have severely restricted the possibility of enacting this gun control proposal.

The organization expresses concern that no safety regulations exist for handguns, which are considered potentially deadly consumer products. AAP notes that the American culture, including the mass media, encourages dangerous gun use. Firearm safety programs are considered of questionable worth, given that children and adolescents often lack good judgment and tend to act impulsively. The organization cautions that some gun education programs may actually encourage or promote firearm use among children and recommends that schools and local groups choose such a program with care. The Academy supports a collective interpretation of the Second Amendment, claiming that it was intended to prohibit the national government from interfering with state militias. The organization concludes that, recent Supreme Court decisions notwithstanding, the Second Amendment is no barrier to legislation geared to reduce the availability of handguns to children.

AAP asserts that the most dependable way of reducing firearms-related deaths and injuries among children is to remove handguns from their environment. To accomplish this end, restrictions should be placed on the private purchase of handguns and on their possession in the home. As another strategy for reducing the danger handguns pose to children, AAP suggests reducing the destructive capability of ammunition. The Academy recommends that pediatricians and other health care providers inform parents about the dangers of handguns in the home and calls for reducing the romantic portrayal of guns in the media.

The Academy estimates that 20 percent of fatalities among older youth are due to firearms, three-quarters of teenage homicides involve the use of firearms, and 80 percent of child accidental firearm deaths occur among youth aged 10 to 19. In 1997, 22.5 percent of injury deaths among children and adolescents aged 1 to 19 involved firearms. Health care providers are asked to identify adolescents who may be at greater risk of firearm violence, and provide appropriate counseling.

AAP has called for the formation of coalitions of health care professionals, parents, schools, police, the media, and others to work to reduce firearm injury and death. Educational programs would involve curricula that cover such topics as coping skills, conflict management, and risk awareness. The organization advocates research to increase understanding of those variables related to firearm injuries and to arrive at additional policies to reduce gun violence.

The Academy has distributed a pamphlet that recommends always keeping guns unloaded and locked away. It advises keeping ammunition locked in a separate location and making sure that children do not have access to keys. For families that do not have a firearm, the pamphlet recommends that parents tell their children to stay away from guns when at their friends' homes. Although parents who possess guns are urged to unload them and lock them away from children, the brochure emphasizes that the safest way to prevent gun accidents is not to keep a gun in the home. Parents are asked to tell their children that movie and television violence is not real and that guns could seriously hurt them. Parents should also counsel their children in nonviolent ways of settling arguments. In addition, the brochure cautions against allowing children to participate in shooting activities.

In 2015, AAP joined with six other societies representing physicians, along with the American Bar Association, to call for action on firearm-related violence, such as improving access to mental health care and instituting appropriate laws requiring physicians to identify patients likely to cause harm to themselves or others.

See also: Academics for the Second Amendment; Accidents Involving Guns; *District of Columbia v. Heller* (2008); Health Care Professionals; *McDonald v. Chicago* (2010); Media Violence; Second Amendment; Trigger Locks.

Further Reading: American Academy of Pediatrics, "Firearms and Adolescents," *Pediatrics* 89 (April 1992), 784–87; American Academy of Pediatrics, "Firearm Injuries Affecting the Pediatric Population," *Pediatrics* 89 (April 1992), 788–90; American Academy of Pediatrics, *Keep Your Family Safe from Firearm Injury*, brochure (n.d.); American Academy of Pediatrics, Committee on Injury and Poison Prevention, "Firearm-Related Injuries Affecting thePediatric Population," *Pediatrics* 105 (April 2000), 888–95; Catherine A. Okoro, David E. Nelson, James A. Mercy, Lina S. Balluz, Alex E. Crospy, and Ali H. Mokdad, "Prevalence of Household Firearms and Firearm-Storage Practices in the 50 States and the District of Columbia: Findings from the Behavioral Risk Factor Surveillance System, 2002," *Pediatrics* 116 (2005), 370–76, www.pediatrics.org/cgi/content/full/116/3/e370; American Academy of Pediatrics Council on Injury, Violence, and Poison Prevention Executive Committee, "Firearm-Related Injuries Affecting the Pediatric Population" (2012), www.pediatrics.aappublications.org/content/130/5/e1416.

American Bar Association (ABA)

The American Bar Association (ABA) recognizes that gun safety is a major public concern, citing data that identify firearms as the most often used instrument in homicides. Referring to the more than 32,000 deaths attributed to firearms each year, the ABA notes that the overall homicide rate in the United States far exceeds that of other industrialized nations. The organization considers gun violence among youth a serious public policy problem. Citing a United Nations report, the ABA notes that 9 out of 10 killings of youth in industrialized nations occur in the United States.

The ABA was formed in 1878 and subsequently became the primary representative of the legal profession in the United States. In 1936, the House of Delegates was created as the organization's major policy-making body. In 1997, the House of Delegates had 525 members, including, among others, delegates from the states, state and local bar associations, and affiliated organizations. Members of the Board of Governors are also members of the House of Delegates. The Board acts and speaks for the ABA, following the direction of the House.

Among its stated goals, the ABA promotes improvements in the justice system and the law, serves as the legal profession's national representative, and supports the interests of the membership. Approximately half of American lawyers are members. The organization informs members, policy makers, and the general public about its recommendations on various issues, including gun control.

In the past, the ABA focused on possible legal strategies to keep firearms away from youth and adult criminals. More recently, the organization has entertained proposals originating with public health professionals and community leaders. While recognizing the legitimacy of gun ownership, especially in a nation with a long tradition of firearms possession, the ABA supports efforts to control illegal or unauthorized access to firearms to reduce the death rate from suicides, accidents, and homicides related to firearms.

The ABA supports policies geared to regulate firearms sales and transfers to ensure that minors are prevented from gaining access to guns, and supports legislation establishing consumer safety standards for firearms. Such a measure would effectively ban the domestic manufacture of Saturday night specials, which are handguns generally considered of inferior quality. Such standards would include a mandate that each new firearm sale to a private individual include a safety lock and a device to indicate if a weapons contains ammunition. The organization recommends such safety features to ensure that teenagers and children cannot inadvertently fire a gun.

In 2004 the ABA House of Delegates approved a resolution from the Special Committee on Gun Violence and other committees, which advocated stronger implementation and enforcement of existing gun control laws at the national, state, and local levels, including full implementation of the National Instant Criminal Background Check System, and the enactment of legislation requiring the retention for 90 days of background check records on gun purchases. In 2008 the ABA created a new Standing Committee on Gun Violence, which replaced the Special Committee. The ABA's official position on gun control notwithstanding, the organization's Web site contains information from various sides of the firearms debate.

In 2008, following the U.S. Supreme Court decision in *District of Columbia v. Heller*, ABA president William H. Neukom released a statement commenting that although the decision recognizes an individual right to own firearms for such legitimate purposes as defending the home, the decision also acknowledges an interest the public has in regulating the safe ownership and use of firearms. Neukom emphasized that the Court's decision should not be regarded as a warrant for eliminating reasonable limitations on firearm ownership.

In 2011 the ABA expressed opposition to "shall issue" gun license laws that require officials to grant a permit to anyone meeting minimum requirements. The organization instead supported broad discretion to law enforcement authorities in issuing a permit or license. In 2012 the ABA expressed opposition to government action that limits the right of physicians to ask patients whether they have guns in the home and how those weapons are secured, and also the right of to counsel patients about the dangers of firearms in the home. In 2015 the ABA joined with seven professional societies representing physicians, calling for universal background checks on prospective gun purchasers, limits on the production and sale of military-style weapons, and additional research on methods of reducing firearm-related death and injuries.

See also: Accidents Involving Guns; Lawyer's Second Amendment Society; Legal Community Against Violence; Saturday Night Special; United Nations.

Further Reading: American Bar Association Web site, www.abanet.org; *District of Columbia v. Heller* (2008); William H. Neukom, "Issues Statement on Supreme Court Gun Control Decision," http://abanet.org/abanet/media/statement/statement.cfm?releaseid=37; Rhonda McMillion, "ABA Joins Medical Organizations in Advocating Steps to Curb Gun Violence," *ABA Journal* (June 1, 2015), www.abajournal.com/magazine.article.aba_joins_medical_organizations_in_advocating_steps_to_curb_gun_violence.

American Civil Liberties Union (ACLU)

On many civil liberties issues, the American Civil Liberties Union's (ACLU) positions coincide closely with those of gun rights groups such as the National Rifle Association (NRA). The ACLU, like the NRA, calls for greater accountability of federal law enforcement procedures, especially in light of such events as the Ruby Ridge standoff in 1992 and the raid on the Branch Davidian compound in Waco, Texas, in 1993. Each organization believes that additional authority should not be granted to law enforcement agencies until procedures have been established to secure every person's constitutional rights. For instance, both the ACLU and the NRA have expressed concern that the rights of citizens not be violated in the federal government's war on drugs. On subjects such as the Fourth Amendment protection against unreasonable searches and seizures, the Fifth Amendment guarantee against self-incrimination, and other safeguards in the Bill of Rights, the two organizations tend to agree.

In 2013 the ACLU expressed concern about proposed legislation to institute universal background checks for gun buyers, claiming that background checks on private transfers could lead to extended record-keeping of such transfers, and possibly a "national gun registry." The ACLU takes a similar stand to that of the NRA on whether those who have been placed on the terrorist "no fly" watch list should also be prevented from purchasing or possessing a firearm. Both organizations oppose such legislation, arguing

The American Civil Liberties Union holds positions similar to those of the National Rifle Association on many gun rights issues, but denies that the Second Amendment guarantees an unlimited right of individuals to own firearms. *www.ACLU.org*

that the prohibition would lack due process of law protections guaranteed in the Fifth Amendment. The distinction between the two organizations is that while the NRA is a single-issue group concerned almost exclusively with an individual's right to keep and bear arms, the ACLU has broader concerns for the privacy rights and civil liberties of individuals. However, on the Second Amendment, which is of greatest importance to the NRA and other gun rights groups, the ACLU holds a significantly different interpretation. Due to that difference, the relationship between the ACLU and the NRA is sometimes amicable, but often uneasy. Many libertarians who hold that the Second Amendment recognizes a right equal in importance to other rights listed in the Bill of Rights, which the ACLU avidly defends, disagree with the ACLU on the issue of gun rights.

The 500,000-member ACLU is headquartered in Washington, D.C., but has offices in all 50 states, as well as staffed affiliate offices in major cities and more than 300 chapters in smaller towns. The organization maintains regional offices in Denver and Atlanta. Anthony Romero has served as executive director since 2001, and Susan Herman, Centennial Professor of Law at Brooklyn Law School, has been president since 2008. An 84-member board of directors governs the organization. The ACLU's approximately 100 staff attorneys, along with 2,000 volunteer lawyers, handle nearly 6,000 cases each year. The ACLU has had significant influence in many civil liberties areas, including the rights of prisoners, children, voters, workers, and women.

The ACLU has adhered to a collectivist interpretation of the constitutional right to keep and bear arms. The national board, after much discussion, agreed that the original intention of the Second Amendment was to guarantee the right of states to establish militias to protect their security and freedom against national government intrusion. According to the ACLU, this intention is "somewhat anachronistic" in the contemporary world because its implementation would logically require possession of weapons far more deadly than handguns or rifles. While many gun rights advocates argue that circumstance should have no bearing on an absolute right protected by the Constitution, the ACLU maintains that the Second Amendment does not guarantee an unlimited right of individuals to own firearms and other weapons, and that such measures as licensing and registration constitute reasonable restrictions.

The organization believes any reasonable person will conclude that the right to bear arms does not apply to such modern weapons as bazookas, torpedoes, missiles, and submachine guns. If government has the right under the Constitution to restrict arms, then there must be a determination of what constitutes a reasonable restriction, which may include regulations that do not violate any of the other rights guaranteed by the Bill of Rights.

Following the U.S. Supreme Court decision in *District of Columbia v. Heller* (2008), the ACLU expressed the organization's disagreement with the Supreme Court majority, and continued to maintain that the Second Amendment refers to a collective, rather than an individual, right of firearm ownership and use. The ACLU noted that the decision left unresolved several issues, including what regulations are allowable and the ownership of what specific weapons can be deemed protected by the Second Amendment.

See also: District of Columbia v. Heller (2008); National Rifle Association; Ruby Ridge; Second Amendment; Waco, Texas, Raid.

Further Reading: ACLU, "Guardian of Liberty: American Civil Liberties Union," briefing paper, 1997; ACLU, "Gun Control," ACLU library resource,1996; ACLU, "Heller Decision and the Second Amendment," www.aclu.org/2008/07/01/heller-decision-and-the-second-amendment; David Iaconangelo, "Why the NRA and ACLU Take Same Side of 'No Fly' Gun Debate," *Christian Science Monitor* (June 24, 2016), www.csmonitor.com/USA/Justice/2016/0624/why-the-NRA-and-ACLU-take-same-side-of-no-fly-gun-debate.

American Firearms Institute (AFI)

Evin Daly established the American Firearms Institute (AFI) in 2009 as a private corporation in Florida and primarily as a Web site to provide information about the right to keep and bear arms and to counter the arguments of pro-gun control individuals and groups. At the time the organization was established, Daly predicted that the first-year membership would reach 100,000 (individuals can become members free of charge). Among those said to be members are law enforcement and military personnel, lawyers, firearm collectors, lawmakers, researchers, and concealed weapon carry permit owners. The organization states that it is privately funded, but has no affiliation with the National Rifle Association (NRA). The AFI has three stated missions: "To recognize and promote the right to keep and bear arms as proclaimed and ratified by the Second Amendment," "To provide the American gun-owners and general public with information and opinions about firearms and firearms ownership," and "To support our members through [the organization's] four cornerstones, which are Safety, Education, Responsibility, and Knowledge." The AFI also states two goals: "To publicize and support the right to keep and bear arms" and "To provide easy communications access to our membership."

The AFI zealously objects to any claimed connection between firearm ownership per se and criminal intent; guns and legal gun owners do not cause gun crimes. An estimated 300 million firearms are owned legally in the United States, but the number of illegal guns can only be estimated. The AFI notes that there are three categories of firearm owners: military and law enforcement officials ("the government"), private citizens, and criminals. Members of the last category existed before firearms had been developed and used such weapons as knives and clubs. The type of weapon has no special relation to crime except that a criminal is using it. The organization identifies three sources of firearm violence. First, such violence occurs most frequently in urban areas where poverty and the illegal drug trade are prevalent, and consequently where young people are caught up in the cycle of violence and firearms become a tool of the trade and a means of self-defense. Second,

violent criminals use firearms to prey upon the rest of society. Finally, those with mental health problems, often associated with alcohol and drugs, at times become violent and turn to firearms as their instrument of destruction.

The AFI claims that, rather than focusing on these three sources of gun violence, many target the firearms that are instruments used by the disadvantaged, criminals, and the mentally ill. Those advocating gun control supposedly are driven by fear and a need to control others—in this case law-abiding firearm owners. Such people, the AFI insists, should instead concentrate on ways of changing society in order to eliminate the three causes of gun violence instead of focusing on the firearms used by violent criminals, but also possessed by millions of law-abiding citizens. The energy focused on control should be redirected toward establishing effective educational and vocational programs, promoting family values, and demanding parental responsibility.

AFI's Web site contains a history of the development of firearms from c.e. 142 to the present; rules for firearm safety; data on firearms-related crime; a list of firearm manufacturers; and a "Communications Center" where individuals can consult various sources of information, such as legislative information from the Library of Congress, and contact their state representative, U.S. House representative, and U.S. senators about firearms issues.

See also: Instrumentality Effect, National Rifle Association, Youth and Guns, Zimring, Franklin E.

Further Reading: American Firearms Institute Web site, www.americanfirearms.org.

American Jewish Congress (AJC)

The American Jewish Congress takes a strong pro-gun control position on several firearms-related issues, holding that more stringent legislation is required. In May 1998, following a series of school shootings, the Congress announced that it was initiating a campaign in the Jewish community to mobilize support for more effective gun control laws. In the announcement, AJC President Jack

Rosen and Executive Director Phil Baum stated that firearms "have exacted a terrible toll on American life," and asserted that those opposing gun control do not represent the majority position. They labeled absurd the claim that "rapid-firing assault weapons are designed for personal use," rejected assertions about gun rights based on "specious constitutional arguments," and called foolish the pro-gun slogan "guns don't kill people, people kill people." Rosen and Baum pointed to "the unspeakable killings of children by children," claiming that gun violence in the United States kills 16 young people each day. The announcement noted that the president of AJC's Northern Pacific Region was among eight people who were shot and killed in 1993 by a gunman in San Francisco.

In June 1997, the Congress reacted against the U.S. Supreme Court ruling in *Printz v. United States* that a provision of the Brady Handgun Violence Prevention Act requiring background checks of prospective gun purchasers by local law enforcement officers violated the constitutional separation of powers between the federal and state governments. AJC President David V. Kahn and Executive Director Baum issued a statement criticizing the Court's narrow interpretation of federal power. Kahn and Baum asserted that the Court was adhering to an outdated eighteenth-century conception of federalism and urged Congress to find alternative ways of dealing with the problem of handguns and their relation to criminal activity.

In September 1997, Baum issued a statement on behalf of the Congress regarding assault weapons. Baum supported Senator Dianne Feinstein's request that Israel cease exporting assault weapons to the United States and expressed the hope that Israel would comply. However, Baum claimed that the ultimate fault did not lie with Israel, stating that "it is problematic to call upon another country to exercise restraints on behalf of the people of the United States which the people of the United States have been unwilling to impose upon themselves." Baum pledged that the AJC would cooperate with Senator Feinstein to enhance legislation prohibiting the importation of assault weapons "so that the door to them will be closed firmly, once and for all."

The AJC has a petition on its Web site for people to send to their representative and senators, asking them to support gun control legislation to deal with the gun violence that occurs each year. Among the recommendations, the petition requests that gun dealers be required to register firearms with the federal government so that law enforcement agencies can determine the owner of any weapon thought to be involved in a crime. In addition, gun manufacturers should be required to include safety features on firearms in order to reduce the likelihood of gun accidents.

The AJC joined other organizations in support of the District of Columbia ban on handguns by filing an *amicus curiae* brief to the U.S. Supreme Court in *District of Columbia v. Heller.* Following the Court's 2008 ruling, in which the majority interpreted the Second Amendment as guaranteeing an individual right to possess firearms, the AJC declared that the decision was "bad law and even worse public policy." The AJC president claimed that the decision would result in more people dying as a result of increased gun violence.

Following the June 2016 mass shooting in Orlando, Florida, in which a gunman killed 49 people and wounded 53 others, AJC president Jack Rosen issued a statement condemning the act of terror as senseless and barbaric, expressed the organization's condolences to the victims' families, and called for national unity in resisting terrorism.

See also: Assault Weapons Ban; Brady Handgun Violence Prevention Act; *District of Columbia v. Heller* (2008); Feinstein, Dianne; Israel; *Printz v. United States* (1997).

Further Reading: American Jewish Congress Web site, www.ajcongress.org.

American Revolution

For gun rights advocates, the causes and conduct of the American Revolution are a vital support for their understanding that the Second Amendment guarantees an individual right to keep and bear arms. According to this view, the British maintenance of a standing army in the American colonies threatened the basic rights of colonists, who, in any event, had learned through necessity the value of arming themselves against the elements, the Indians, and, ultimately, a tyrannical foreign power. Key moments in the revolution stand out in this interpretation. In March 1770, the "Boston Massacre," a confrontation between British soldiers and an unruly mob of Bostonians, ended in bloodshed as the troops shot into the unarmed crowd. Five men were killed and the soldiers responsible were placed on trial. Gun supporters also focus on the April 19, 1775, battles of Lexington and Concord, which marked the true beginning of the war. British forces attempting to regain control of munitions taken by the colonists suffered moderately heavy losses at the hands of militia bands. At the Battle of Bunker Hill two months later, the British suffered losses of 228 killed and 826 wounded.

According to gun rights advocates, Americans can derive a fundamental lesson from the revolutionary experience: The ultimate defense of individual and nation against tyranny depends upon a citizenry willing and able to take up arms, not upon an organized standing army that can easily become the instrument of oppression. Therefore, any attempt to limit an individual's right to keep and bear arms must be vigorously resisted because it may foreshadow attempts to tyrannize the population.

Despite this pro-gun interpretation, the revolutionary experience with arms contains mixed lessons. Notwithstanding the antipathy that many colonists had toward a standing army, the British army had come to the defense of the colonies during the French and Indian War. In May 1775, members of the Second Continental Congress, realizing that dependence on militias alone could not achieve their objective, sought to devise a more effective military strategy. They overcame the strong aversion to a standing army and created an American military force to improve the chances of victory against the professional British army. As the war proceeded, the standing Continental army became the most important military instrument for the Americans. In winter 1778, Baron Friedrich Wilhelm von Steuben, a Prussian army officer serving with General George Washington at Valley Forge in Pennsylvania, molded American troops into an effective fighting force.

The American Revolution was not a clear conflict pitting the united colonists against the tyrannous British, but was to some extent a civil war. According to historians, the American population divided into three groups roughly equal in size: the pro-independence faction, those who remained loyal to Great Britain (Tories), and those who were neutral, prudently supporting one side or the other depending upon the fortunes of war. The revolutionaries struggled not only with the British, but with the Loyalists, a significant segment of the population composed of a varied group of small farmers, large landowners, and professional people.

Some argue that marksmanship contributed significantly to the ultimate American victory. Living on the edge of the wilderness, Americans had a long experience with firearms, which many colonists learned to handle at an early age. Revolutionary forces attempted to impress and intimidate the British with their proficiency in firearms. British General William Howe, commenting on his enemy's prowess, once referred to the "terrible guns of the rebels." To reinforce this image, General George Washington ordered his troops to wear hunting shirts, symbolizing the adeptness of the riflemen. However, a lack of arms presented a serious problem for the American army. Historians estimate that in the summer of 1776 one-fourth of Washington's troops had no guns. British confiscation was not the only source of difficulty. Although local gun makers worked feverishly to produce weapons, and contracts were signed with foreign producers, gun-making was slow and tedious in this preindustrial age. The French helped the Americans acquire desperately needed arms to continue the struggle, contributing an estimated 100,000 firearms by 1781.

Alexander Rose (2010) criticizes historians who have questioned the marksmanship of militia members in the early days of the Revolution. Rose argues that militiamen were well trained in the use of their weapons, and that these arms "were working, effective, [and] well-maintained." He contends that at the battles of Lexington and Concord and the Battle of Bunker Hill, nearly all men had their own firearm, and that, given the state of firearm development at the time, the militiamen were "proficient shooters" who overcame the limitations of their handmade weapons. Rose estimates that American militiamen were 12 times more accurate in their rifle shots than were the British and European soldiers.

Many factors contributed to the final American victory formalized in the 1783 Treaty of Paris, including the transition from militia units to regular troops, French assistance, and British difficulties in supporting and supplying troops. However, following the war, Americans focused on the role of a militia composed of citizen soldiers, and continued to venerate the abilities of the individual marksman. Although Washington wished to maintain at least a limited standing military force following the end of hostilities, the Continental Army was allowed to dwindle to less than 100 soldiers. Fear of centralized government, combined with suspicion of a standing army, resulted in a postwar emphasis on militias. The Second Amendment, whether interpreted as a right to keep and bear arms guaranteed to Americans individually, or as a right granted to states in the formation and maintenance of their respective organized militia units, arises out of this historical context.

See also: Minutemen, Revolutionary; Native Americans; Second Amendment; United Kingdom.

Further Reading: Lee Kennett and James LaVerne Anders, *The Gun in America: The Origins of a National Dilemma* (Westport, CT: Greenwood, 1975); Wayne R. LaPierre, *Guns, Crime, and Freedom* (Washington, DC: Regnery, 1994). Alexander Rose, "Marksmanship in 1775: Myth or Reality?" *American Rifleman* (July 2010), 45–47, 70.

American Rifleman

The official journal of the National Rifle Association (NRA), the *American Rifleman* contains articles on such topics as new handguns and rifles, hunting and shooting techniques, the history of firearms in the United States, and the activities and meetings of the Association. Of all the gun magazines, the *American Rifleman,* in its 125th year of publication in 2010, stands as the primary voice for pro-gun interests. Each issue contains material on the politics of gun ownership, focusing on the protection of what the NRA has long argued is the Second Amendment's guarantee of the individual's right to keep and bear arms. Members of the organization receive the magazine, which is published 11 times per year.

Several regular features advocate the rights of gun owners. "The Armed Citizen" offers several accounts of gun owners who were able to defend themselves against crime because they had access to a firearm. Wayne LaPierre, NRA executive vice president, writes a regular column about the status of gun rights in the United States and abroad. LaPierre has dedicated the organization to electing a pro-gun president, maintaining support for gun rights in Congress, and educating a pro-gun generation. During the 2016 presidential campaign, LaPierre and the NRA endorsed Republican candidate Donald Trump. LaPierre reports on legislative proposals to regulate gun sales and ownership, and focuses on perceived threats to gun

rights from within the U.S. government or from international organizations.

Another feature of the magazine, "ILA Report," offers detailed news of legislative activities from the NRA's Institute for Legislative Action (ILA). The ILA provides members with information about the progress of NRA-backed legislative proposals and reports on state legislative action, such as the passage of versions of the NRA-ILA's model Crime Victims' Protection Act. "ILA Report" also publishes the names of those who have made monetary contributions to the Institute.

"NRA Woman's Voice," a column written by women active in the NRA, offers information about the special place of women in the organization and the problems they sometimes face in acquiring training in the use of firearms. The "NRA Regional Report" includes news about NRA activities from around the nation, including legislative activity at the state level, training workshops, shooting events, law enforcement activities, and a schedule of gun shows. Each issue contains at least one feature article relevant to the NRA's position on the Second Amendment.

See also: Clinton, William Jefferson (Bill); Gun Shows; Institute for Legislative Action; LaPierre, Wayne; National Rifle Association; Second Amendment; United Nations; Women and Guns.

Further Reading: *American Rifleman* (National Rifle Association, Fairfax, VA).

American Shooting Sports Council (ASSC)

Founded in 1989, and merged in 2000 with the National Shooting Sports Foundation, the American Shooting Sports Council (ASSC) was the trade association of the firearms industry, conducting lobbying activities on legislative and legal issues. The organization represented all parts of the industry, including firearms, ammunition, and various accessory producers. Approximately 2,000 firearms, ammunition, and accessory manufacturers and importers belonged to the organization, plus several hundred wholesale distributors, over 25,000 retailers, and several thousand industry representatives, such as salespeople, suppliers, and trade and consumer publications. The ASSC campaigned against what the organization considered unreasonable limitations on the right to keep and bear arms. The group constituted a large lobbying force in Washington, D.C., and the state capitals. From 1992, ASSC members rallied in Washington, D.C., meeting with their representatives and senators and their staffs and with government officials in federal agencies involved in regulating the firearm industry. At the Annual Wild Game Banquet, the Council presented a favored legislator with the Congressional Leader of the Year Award. In 1997, Republican Representative Bob Barr of Georgia received the award, and in 1998 the recipients were Republican Senator Jeff Sessions of Alabama and Democratic Representative John Tanner of Tennessee.

Along with gun rights organizations, the ASSC strongly disagreed with those who claimed a close relationship between guns and crime, contending instead that firearms do not play a major independent role in illegal activities. The Association claimed that American citizens owning firearms contribute significantly to individual and collective security. Contrary to charges that the industry's products are an inherently unsafe product, ASSC Executive Director Richard Feldman asserted that "our industry markets safety," and argued that firearms, when used "properly and responsibly," are inherently safe and protect law-abiding citizens from criminals.

The ASSC strove to protect the industry from national or state government actions that would limit the possession of firearms. In January 1998, Feldman announced that the Council had taken legal action against Massachusetts Attorney General Scott Harshbarger, who had intended to institute new restrictions on gun ownership in the state. Feldman charged that the Massachusetts attorney general had acted unilaterally, ignoring input from the ASSC; Feldman stated that his organization was willing to work with the state on "feasible, rational solutions." Fearing that new regulations in the guise of consumer safety would include a ban on handgun sales in Massachusetts, the ASSC charged Attorney General Harshbarger with attempting to achieve gun prohibition by issuing regulatory orders without the appropriate interest group and constituent input. Although enforcement of the Massachusetts attorney general's regulations was halted temporarily due to a firearms industry lawsuit and an appeal by Harshbarger, a strict new Massachusetts gun control law went into effect in October 1998.

On the national level, the ASSC disputed Handgun Control, Inc.'s claim that a significant number of prosecutions have resulted from passage of the Brady Handgun Violence Prevention Act. According to Feldman, crime rates had declined because more Americans purchased firearms and many states enacted provisions allowing citizens to carry concealed weapons, not because of the Brady Law's provisions. Like other gun rights groups, the Council was concerned by calls from various international organizations for a cross-national gun control policy. Representing the ASSC at the Americas Regional Workshop on Firearm Regulation in São Paulo, Brazil, in December 1997, Feldman cautioned the representatives that they must respect the right to possess a firearm in nations, such as the United States, that recognize such a right. Feldman also declared that the ASSC supported efforts to obstruct illegal arms trading and the criminal misuse of firearms, but strongly objected to any efforts to prevent law-abiding citizens from owning guns.

Although having a common interest in the right to possess firearms, the NRA and the ASSC, because they represented different groups of people, disagreed on some firearms issues. The NRA represented firearms consumers, but the ASSC represented firearms manufacturers and retailers. Although the NRA advocated the ready availability of federal firearms licenses (FFLs), the ASSC preferred more limited accessibility in order to protect the business interests of its members. Also, the ASSC, along with most of the larger firearm manufacturing companies, supported the policy of providing trigger locks with the purchase of handguns. The disagreements between the NRA and ASSC undoubtedly contributed to the demise of the Council.

See also: Barr, Bob; Brady Handgun Violence Prevention Act; Concealed Carry Laws; Handgun Control, Inc; Massachusetts Gun Violence Prevention Law.

Further Reading: Richard Feldman, "From the Capital: Pro Safety or Anti-Gun?" *Guns and Ammo* (September 1997), 34–35; Richard Feldman, "America's Regional Workshop on Firearm Regulation," American Shooting Sports Council statement (December 1997); Richard Feldman, *Ricochet: Confessions of a Gun Lobbyist* (Hoboken, NJ: John Wiley and Sons, 2008).

Americans for Democratic Action (ADA)

Americans for Democratic Action (ADA), a liberal organization founded in 1947 by such noted individuals as Eleanor Roosevelt, Walter Reuther, Arthur Schlesinger, Jr., Reinhold Niebuhr, and Hubert Humphrey, has taken a consistently pro-gun control stand. ADA members include professionals, businesspeople, labor leaders, educators, political leaders, and other persons who subscribe to a liberal political ideology. The 65,000 members in several state and local chapters work to elect liberal candidates and to lobby for progressive measures at the state and local levels.

The national organization, headquartered in Washington, D.C., maintains a political action committee, ADA/PAC, which makes campaign donations to liberal candidates seeking seats in the U.S. Congress. Since 2010, former member of Congress Lynn Woolsey (D-CA) has served as the organization's president. Woolsey did not seek re-election to Congress in 2013.

ADA takes a strong position against the use of weaponry of any sort, particularly when the use of force is perceived as threatening the democratic political process. The organization advocates decreasing the national military budget by at least 50 percent and using the funds for development programs in the United States and other countries. Believing that demilitarization and democracy are closely linked, the organization advocates an American foreign policy that encourages other nations, particularly developing countries, to reduce the political role of their armed forces, thereby stimulating progress toward freedom of speech, fair elections, and the elimination of human rights abuses. ADA supported passage of the Brady Handgun Violence Prevention Act and advocates its maintenance in the face of court challenges, noting that the legislation has been effective in preventing illegal firearms purchases. The Lautenberg Amendment, which prohibits firearms sales to those previously convicted of a misdemeanor involving domestic violence, also received ADA support. The group has opposed attempts in the U.S. Congress to limit the ability of gun violence victims to sue gun manufacturers for damages, has supported passage of state consumer protection laws to protect the consumer against low-quality firearms, and has opposed proposals to allow the importation of surplus military weapons. To protect children from the misuse of handguns, the ADA advocates measures mandating the use of trigger locks and safety courses for gun owners.

While urging the strict enforcement of existing gun control legislation, the ADA advocates the passage of additional measures to limit the harmful effects of firearms. The organization supports control of firearms trafficking, especially among youth, noting that the Bureau of Alcohol, Tobacco, Firearms, and Explosives (ATF) has insufficient authority to trace weapons. The ADA also advocates a policy that would hold gun owners responsible for failing to store firearms properly if children who gain access to the weapons use them to injure or kill others. The organization supports bans on Saturday night specials and recognizes the need for greater safety in schools against the possibility of gun violence. The ADA's overall approach to the problem of violence is to advocate the implementation of policies, such as improved educational opportunities, drug and alcohol treatment and job training programs, and the pursuit of greater economic security, that the organization claims will reduce the incidence of crime.

In a resolution adopted in 2001 and reaffirmed in 2007, ADA called for a general ban on the sale of assault weapons, the prohibition of concealed weapons, stricter gun registration requirements, holding adults responsible for juvenile misuse of firearms, and vigorous enforcement of current handgun laws. Gun rights advocates claim the ADA has taken inconsistent positions by refusing to recognize the individual right to keep and bear arms, which gun rights supporters hold is protected by the Second Amendment.

ADA has posted a petition on its Website stating in part that there has been almost one school shooting per week since the December 2012 mass shooting at the Sandy Hook Elementary School in Newtown, Connecticut, and that an average of seven children aged 0 to 19 die each day from gun-related violence, concluding: "We demand meaningful gun reform in America now. We need laws that will restrict and regulate access to firearms and save lives."

See also: Brady Handgun Violence Prevention Act; Bureau of Alcohol, Tobacco, Firearms, and Explosives; Lautenberg Amendment; Saturday Night Special; Second Amendment; Trigger Locks.

Further Reading: Americans for Democratic Action Web site, www.adaction.org; "ADA Resolution on Handgun Control," www.adaction.org/pages/issues/all-policy-resolutions/politics-amp-government/251-handgun-control.php (accessed October 18, 2010); Steven M. Gillon, *Politics and Vision: The ADA and American Liberalism* (New York: Oxford University Press, 1987).

Americans for Responsible Solutions

The consequences of gun violence were brought shockingly to the attention of Democratic Congresswoman Gabrielle Giffords (AZ) when a deranged gunman attempted to kill her during a constituent "meet and greet" in her home district city of Tucson, Arizona, in January 2011. Rep. Giffords suffered a gunshot wound to the head, but made a remarkable recovery. Two years later, she and her husband, former astronaut and Navy Captain Mark Kelly, formed a new gun safety organization, Americans for Responsible Solutions (ARS). While the devastating attack against Giffords was an impetus, the catalyst for their foray into politics was the December 2012 Sandy Hook Elementary School shooting, when twenty schoolchildren and six staff people were killed by a lone gunman.

In forming this group, Giffords and Kelly note that they support Second Amendment rights. Both own and use guns, and want to make sure that gun rights are protected, including the ability to collect guns, use them recreationally, and for self-protection. But they also support policy solutions to prevent gun violence. Organized as a 501(c)(4) advocacy organization and political action committee, it seeks to counterbalance what they see as the overweening influence of gun groups like the National Rifle Association by raising and spending money for political campaigns, engaging in education activities, and building a national base of supporters. Both Giffords and Kelly have been outspoken on the gun issue in testimony before Congress and in many public venues, although Giffords' head injury has impeded her ability to speak, leaving Kelly to be their chief public spokesperson.

According to Open Secrets (opensecrets.org), the ARS-PAC spent over $19 million during the 2014 election cycle. Much of that money went to seven U.S. Senate races and four House races to buttress the candidates' pro-gun safety agendas.

The money went to television advertisements, direct mail, and digital communications. ARS's activities parallel those of another recently formed gun safety interest group, Everytown for Gun Safety, in that they both seek to raise and spend significant sums of money to counter-balance the traditional spending advantage of the National Rifle Association, and to build grassroots bases of support to the same end. In 2016, the group reported a membership of over 800,000.

In 2016, ARS merged with the Law Center to Prevent Gun Violence, a gun safety research organization known as a resource for legal expertise and information on state and federal firearms laws. It was founded in 1993.

Recommended Readings: Gabrielle Giffords and Mark Kelly, *Enough: Our Fight to Keep America Safe from Gun Violence* (New York: Scribner, 2014); Robert J. Spitzer, *The Politics of Gun Control* (Boulder, CO: Paradigm Publishers, 2015); http://americansforresponsiblesolutions.org/

Americans United for Safe Streets (AUSS)

Established in 2009, Americans United for Safe Streets (AUSS), with headquarters in Washington, D.C., is a nonpartisan organization dedicated to instituting effective strategies to lower the incidence of violent crime in U.S. communities. AUSS's Website lists Alex Howe as the organization's spokesperson. Although recognizing that a substantial decrease in the crime rate occurred in the United States in the 1990s, the organization observes that more recently the crime rate has begun to climb once more, noting that Federal Bureau of Investigation (FBI) data report a 3.5 percent increase in violent crime, a 4.8 percent increase in the murder rate, and a 10.9 percent increase in robberies since 2004. AUSS also cites FBI data indicating that the number of police officers fatally shot rose 20 percent in 2007.

AUSS advocates policies to counter violent crime in the United States. First, the organization supports greater funding for law enforcement in order to increase the number of police officers patrolling the streets and to make more efficient the information sharing among communities. Second, the organization encourages the implementation of new crime-fighting technology to identify those committing crimes as well as to clear those mistakenly accused of criminal offenses. Finally, AUSS urges the establishment of more effective policies, such as closing the so-called gun show loophole, to deny firearm ownership to people who are more likely to commit a violent crime, such as those convicted of a felony.

In addition to requiring criminal background checks for all firearm purchases at gun shows, AUSS advocates the elimination of the Tiahrt Amendment, which instituted restrictions on access to gun crime data that local law enforcement agencies could use to identify gun traffickers and firearm dealers that may be selling guns illegally.

AUSS has conducted a mail campaign to inform constituents about the unwillingness of their congressional representative to support measures in the U.S. Congress to close the gun show loophole and eliminate the Tiahrt Amendment that restricts the amount of time that the federal government can keep Brady criminal background check information.

See also: Background Checks; Brady Handgun Violence Prevention Act; Gun Show Loophole; Tiahrt Amendment.

Further Reading: Americans United for Safe Streets Web site, www.americansunitedforsafestreets.org.

Antiterrorism and Effective Death Penalty Act

In 1996 Congress passed the Antiterrorismand Effective Death Penalty Act in response to the 1993 bombing of the World Trade Center and the 1995 bombing of the Oklahoma City federal building. The act introduced several changes in federal firearms laws. According to the act, anyone who knowingly provides "material support or resources," including firearms, to a foreign terrorist organization, or conspires to do so, is subject to a fine or to imprisonment for a term of up to 10 years. The act also made it a crime to provide, or hide, firearms, knowing or intending that they be used to commit a crime.

The act directed the U.S. attorney general and secretary of defense to conduct a joint study of the "number and extent of thefts from military arsenals (including National Guard armories) of firearms, explosives, and other materials that are potentially useful to terrorists." Referring to acts of terrorism beyond the nation's borders,

the law declared that an act of terrorism includes the use of a firearm to assault any person in the United States if the assault involves "conduct transcending national boundaries," and if the offense involves one or more of the following: the use of the mail or interstate or foreign commerce or has an effect on interstate or foreign commerce; the victim is employed in the federal government or the military; any federally owned building or property is damaged; or the offense occurred in a U.S. territorial jurisdiction. Nonlethal assault with a firearm can result in a maximum sentence of 30 years. The law also provides penalties for threatening or conspiring to commit an assault with a firearm.

The act significantly increased the penalty for carrying a firearm onto an airplane. Punishments are provided for anyone who kills or attempts to kill an officer or employee of the federal government, including any member of the armed forces while engaged in official duties. This provision also applies to former government personnel. The definition of a deadly weapon includes a weapon "intended to cause death or danger" but that fails to operate due to a defective component.

The act directed the secretary of the treasury to conduct a study of tagging explosive materials "for purposes of detection and identification," to explore the possibility of making inert those chemicals commonly used to manufacture explosives and the feasibility of controlling "certain precursor chemicals used to manufacture explosive materials," and to investigate state licensing requirements for the purchase and use of commercial high explosives. At the request of firearms organizations, the act excluded black or smokeless powder from the mandated study.

Also mandated was a Treasury Department study of law enforcement officer deaths and serious injuries over the preceding decade, including felonies and accidents, shootings, the type of firearm involved, whether officers were shot with their own firearms or with other officers' firearms, and instances in which bullet-resistant vests or helmets were penetrated by armor-piercing ammunition. In the examination of ammunition, the study was to determine the effect a ban on particular calibers would have on uses for civilian self-defense and sports. The act authorized up to $10 million for the National Institute of Justice Office of Science and Technology to develop technologies to be employed to combat terrorism, including detection devices for weapons, explosives, and chemicals, and to evaluate technologies to assist state and local law enforcement agencies in efforts to resist terrorism. As with the subsequent USA PATRIOT Act of 2001, the act has been criticized for what are perceived as provisions that threaten civil liberties.

See also: Taggants.

Further Reading: David Cole and James X. Dempsey, *Terrorism and the Constitution: Sacrificing Civil Liberties in the Name of National Security*, 3rd ed. (New York: New Press, 2006); Alan Korwin, with Michael P. Anthony, *Gun Laws of America* (Phoenix: Bloomfield, 1997).

Armijo v. Ex Cam, Inc. (1987)

Armijo v. Ex Cam, Inc. (656 F. Supp. 771, 1987) raised the question of whether a manufacturer of a gun that is used in a murder or assault can be held liable for damages to a victim of the crime. The U.S. District Court for New Mexico granted the defendant's motion to dismiss, stating that the New Mexico courts would not recognize any cause for action except under existing theories of liability accepted in the state.

On April 3, 1983, Dolores Armijo's brother, Steven, shot and killed James Saulsberry, Dolores's husband. Steven turned the gun on Dolores and her daughter, but it misfired. Ex Cam, Inc., had imported and distributed the gun used in the shooting. Dolores sued the company, employing various bases for liability, including the special product liability argument for Saturday night specials articulated in the Maryland case, *Kelley v. R G. Industries, Inc.*, which had established a special area of liability for gun manufacturers.

The court enunciated the doctrine of liability under New Mexico law, indicating that the plaintiff must demonstrate five conditions: the product was defective; the product was defective when it left the defendant and reached the consumer in the same condition; the defect made the product dangerous to the user; the consumer was injured; and the defect in the product was the immediate cause of the injury. The court concluded that the handgun performed as it was intended, and therefore could not be considered defective under the laws of New Mexico.

As to the potential criminal misuse of the firearm, the court indicated that New Mexico case law does not support any such theory. Any gun purchaser could reasonably recognize that it might be used as a murder weapon, just as a knife, an axe, or a bow and arrows. The court also disallowed the plaintiff's contention that marketing handguns should be labeled "ultrahazardous." The plaintiff attempted to establish a negligence standard for liability, claiming that the manufacturers failed to exercise reasonable care in selling a product that involved a significant risk of its use in criminal activity. The court rejected the prospect that New Mexico courts would recognize such an obligation on a manufacturer under existing liability statutes.

All firearms may be used in criminal activity, but in *Kelley v. R.G. Industries, Inc.*, the Maryland Court of Appeals ruled that manufacturers of a particular type of handgun could be held liable for its misuse. Therefore, the New Mexico court argued that an unusual circumstance resulted in Maryland: Only victims shot by Saturday night specials are able to recover damages; those shot by any other weapon lack any basis for a liability suit, even though the more expensive guns are agreed to be more deadly and accurate. The court concluded that the New Mexico courts could not adopt such a doctrine.

See also: Kelley v. R.G. Industries, Inc. (1983); Saturday Night Special.

Further Reading: *Armijo v. Ex Cam, Inc.,* 656 F. Supp. 771 (1987).

Arming Women Against Rape and Endangerment (AWARE)

Arming Women Against Rape and Endangerment (AWARE), headquartered in Bedford, Massachusetts, strives to make women aware of the possibility of being a victim of crime, assists women in avoiding violence through education and training, and provides women with information about dealing with unavoidable violent situations. AWARE claims that "defending yourself is okay," that fighting back is the best strategy because women who resist attacks suffer fewer injuries and stop attacks more successfully. According to AWARE, its name implies that a woman should be armed "with courage, spirit, knowledge, and determination, whether or not one is armed with an extrinsic weapon." The organization recognizes firearms as one possible means of self-defense that women may wish to consider.

AWARE provides information and advice about such criminal threats as rape, carjacking, purse snatching, stalking, domestic abuse, and attempted or threatened murder. In addition, the organization provides advice about protecting children from violence. With regard to firearms, AWARE refers to the National Rifle Association's (NRA) Eddie Eagle warning: "don't touch it, leave the area immediately, tell an adult." Unlike organizations such as the Violence Policy Center that are critical of the NRA's Eddie Eagle training program, AWARE recommends the program highly and offers information about obtaining available materials from the NRA.

AWARE provides advice regarding various methods of fending off an attack. Although the martial arts are good for exercise and building confidence, they are considered of limited value to women for self-defense. Personal alarms and rape whistles are not recommended as a primary defense because they depend on the assumption that someone else will come to a woman's defense.

AWARE does not recommend the use of stun guns, which they consider overrated by manufacturers. Experience indicates that stun guns hurt but do not always incapacitate, and they require actual contact with the attacker. The organization cautions that chemical defensive sprays, such as pepper spray (oleoresin capsicum), which cause vision impairment, a burning sensation to the skin, and difficulty in breathing if inhaled, may not be effective against some violent people and results depend on appropriate use.

Although AWARE takes no explicit political stand on gun control and recognizes that many women object to the use of firearms, the organization supports the option of firearms as a means of self-defense. The organization has commented that "whatever you might think of the NRA, they have created excellent introductory courses." AWARE maintains a program in self-defense training, including courses in Basic Pistol, Basic Shotgun, Defensive Handgun, and Responsible Use of Lethal Force, and offers the opportunity for individualized instruction. The organization recommends the magazine *Women and Guns* as a source of information on the selection of firearms and self-defense. AWARE board members contribute articles to the magazine. AWARE no longer maintains an active Website, but Lyn Bates, the organization's vice

president, continues to write a column for *Women and Guns*.

See also: Eddie Eagle; National Rifle Association; Women and Guns; *Women and Guns* Magazine.

Further Reading: Arming Women Against Rape and Endangerment Web site, www.aware.org.

Assault Weapons Ban

In the late 1980s and early 1990s, an intense political struggle occurred between the pro- and anti-gun control forces over passage of an assault weapons ban, a measure to prohibit the sale of certain military-style semiautomatic firearms. After more than five years in which such a proposal came to a floor vote six times in the Senate and six times in the House of Representatives, a ban was placed in the Violent Crime Control and Law Enforcement Act (P.L. 103-322, 108 Stat. 1796) that finally became law in September 1994.

Much controversy continued to rage over the definition of an assault weapon and the significance of such a definition in categorizing a particular type of firearm. Assault weapons include semiautomatic firearms that fire a single round of ammunition with each pull of the trigger. Among other characteristics, they have large ammunition clips that can hold up to 30 rounds or more; are compact; have barrels less than 20 inches long; weigh from 6 to 10 pounds; are made for military use; and have pistol grips.

The 1993 assault weapons ban, which expired in 2004, prohibited the sale and possession of various types of firearms, such as this Uzi pistol. *www.wikipedia.org*

Opponents of a ban challenged the method of defining assault weapons. They insisted that the original definition included the ability to fire several rounds with one pull of the trigger, thus making assault weapons synonymous with machine guns. Because machine guns had been under strict federal government regulation since passage of the National Firearms Act in 1934, opponents saw no need for additional legislation. Referring to the 1939 Supreme Court decision in *United States v. Miller*, opponents argued that the military character of these weapons placed them under Second Amendment protection as just those types of firearms crucial to the maintenance of a militia. Relying on their interpretation of the militia's purpose, opponents maintained that assault weapons could prove especially useful should citizens find themselves resisting a tyrannical government.

Opponents further noted that the number of assault weapons used in crimes was small, claiming that just 4 percent of the nation's homicides involved any type of rifle at all. Employing Bureau of Alcohol, Tobacco, and Firearms (ATF) data, opponents observed that just 1 percent of military-style semiautomatic weapons are "misused." Supporters of a ban responded that drug traffickers and urban gangs were using such weapons in increasing numbers, and that Congress should take steps to limit their distribution before they became more widespread. The weapons' offensive and destructive capabilities and their lack of legitimate hunting and sporting uses added to the need for a ban. On the other hand, opponents of a ban insisted that gun control advocates had decided to target assault weapons because of a few cases of their misuse and because of their ominous appearance.

Two events spurred the introduction of an assault weapon ban in Congress: the January 1989 schoolyard shooting in Stockton, California, that left five children dead and 29 others wounded; and the Killeen, Texas, cafeteria shooting in which 22 people were killed and 23 others wounded before the shooter took his own life. Republican President George H. W. Bush, who had previously rejected calls for regulating assault weapons, reversed his position in March 1989 with an executive order instituting a temporary ban on the importation of some assault weapons. He soon extended the import ban to include several more weapons, and ultimately made the ban permanent. Democratic President Bill Clinton expanded the ban in 1993 to include assault-type handguns.

Proposals to institute a ban were introduced in Congress in 1989, 1990, and 1991, but failed to gain approval in both houses. In November 1993, the Senate passed a ban on the manufacture of 19 assault weapons, and in spring 1994 the House began to consider the measure, with President Clinton actively lobbying for the bill. In April, the House Judiciary Committee approved the measure, although the committee chair, Jack Brooks of Texas, vehemently opposed it. After approval in the full House, the assault weapons ban, as part of a larger bill, went to conference committee to resolve differences between the House and Senate. In August, after long discussions leading to compromises, the bill was returned to both chambers for final approval. However, opposition to the bill remained strong in the House, where it was defeated on a close floor vote, due largely to Republican concern for proposed expenditures of $33 billion, and both Democratic and Republican opposition to the assault weapons measure. Despite the defeat, President Clinton, with the backing of police organizations and congressional leaders, insisted on continuing the effort to pass the bill. After intense negotiation, the House approved the measure, with support from 46 Republicans. When the revised bill went to the Senate, supporters succeeded in mustering sufficient backing to win procedural votes, thus paving the way for final approval.

The assault weapons ban outlawed the sale and possession of 19 types of weapons, along with several replica models sharing certain characteristics, for a period of 10 years. Gun clips holding more than 10 bullets were also prohibited. The measure exempted over 650 sporting rifles as well as existing assault rifles. Determining the effect of the restriction proved difficult, in part because firearm manufacturers could alter features of the weapons in order to circumvent provisions of the ban. Therefore, the ban came under criticism from both gun rights supporters as well as gun control advocates. In 2004 the Republican-controlled Congress failed to renew the assault weapons ban. President George W. Bush had expressed his support for the renewal, but did not campaign actively for extending the assault weapons ban.

In recent years, as mass shootings have continued to make headlines, gun control supporters and their advocates in Congress, such as Senator Dianne Feinstein, have attempted to reintroduce an assault weapons ban and restrictions on large capacity magazines, but a Republican-controlled House and Senate, along with Democratic colleagues who support gun rights have prevented passage of new restrictions on assault weapons.

See also: Bureau of Alcohol, Tobacco, Firearms, and Explosives; Bush, George H. W.; Clinton, William Jefferson (Bill); National Firearms Act of 1934; Stockton, California, Shooting; *United States v. Miller* (1939).

Further Reading: Alan M. Gottlieb, *Gun Rights Fact Book* (Bellevue, WA: Merril, 1989); Jeffrey A. Roth and Christopher S. Koper, "Impacts of the 1994 Assault Weapons Ban: 1994–96," *National Institute of Justice Research in Brief* (March 1999), 1–12; Robert J. Spitzer, *The Politics of Gun Control*, 6th ed. (Boulder, CO: Paradigm, 2015).

Aurora, Colorado Movie Theater Shooting, 2012

On July 20, 2012, 24-year-old James Holmes entered a shopping mall Century 16 movie theater through a rear door he had earlier propped open in Aurora, Col. about 18 minutes after the start of its midnight showing of the latest Batman movie, "The Dark Knight Rises." In the darkened movie theater, Holmes tossed a tear gas canister, and then opened fire, rapidly killing twelve and injuring 70. He was dressed in tactical gear, and had dyed his hair orange-red. He also wore a ballistic helmet, a gas mask, black gloves and protective gear for his legs, throat and groin. Some in the audience said later that they initially thought his actions were part of the movie before realizing that he was firing live rounds.

Holmes possessed four legally purchased guns: an AR-15-type semi-automatic assault rifle with an attachable 100-round drum magazine; two .40-caliber Glock handguns (each of which held large-capacity bullet magazines); and a Remington 12-gauge pump-action shotgun. In all, Holmes purchased 6000 rounds of ammunition through anonymous Internet purchase. Within minutes of the shooting, he was arrested without resistance in the parking lot outside of the theater. The previous year, Holmes suffered what some called a "psychotic break" around the time he dropped out of graduate school. Reports at the time of his arrest were that Holmes's mother said "you have the right person" when first told of the assault (she later denied making the comment). Holmes's significant emotional problems in the months before the attack either preceded or roughly coincided with his gun-buying binge. After his arrest, police who went to his apartment found it filled with explosives rigged to detonate when someone entered. It took police two days to remove the explosives.

The prosecution sought a sentence of death for Holmes; the defense argued for a plea of not guilty by reason of insanity. In 2015, Holmes was found guilty of 24 counts of first-degree murder (two for each person killed), and sentenced to life imprisonment. He was also convicted of 70 counts of attempted murder. The sentence was one of the longest ever handed down by an American court. This shooting was one of several during this time

Memorial across the street from the Century movie theater in Aurora, Colorado. *www.wikipedia.org*

period that outraged Americans and accelerated calls for stricter gun laws.

Recommended Readings: Steve Almasy, "James Holmes Sentenced to Life in Prison for Colorado Movie Theater Murders," CNN, August 8, 2015, at http://www.cnn.com/2015/08/07/us/james-holmes-movie-theater-shooting-jury/; Robert J. Spitzer, *The Politics of Gun Control,* 6th ed. (Boulder, CO: Paradigm Publishers, 2015).

Australia

Like the United States, gun control measures in Australia were avidly pushed following well-publicized multiple killings involving firearms. U.S. politicians, including President Barack Obama and Hilary Clinton, have referred to the gun laws of Australia as an example for that the United States should consider. In December 1987, eight people were killed; in August 1991, seven people lost their lives; and in 1996, the most serious of all shooting incidents occurred in Port Arthur, where a shooter used two semiautomatic weapons to kill 35 people. John Howard, the newly elected prime minister, succeeded in having parliament pass the National Firearms Agreement, which introduced much stricter controls on firearms. The new law introduced gun licensing and registration, and required gun purchasers to submit to a 28-day "cooling-off period" before taking possession of a firearm to allow for a background check for criminal offenses. The new law prohibited—except in special cases—ownership of automatic and semiautomatic assault rifles and pump shotguns, established stringent licensing requirements, created a national gun registry, and introduced a temporary gun buy-back program, which reportedly collected 20 percent of firearms in private hands. Also, the ownership of what were considered especially dangerous weapons was restricted. In 1997, a national gun buyback program was instituted in which the government purchased nearly 650,000 of the guns that recently had been prohibited.

The parents of two children who were killed by guns in 1968 and 1970 dedicated themselves to strengthening the gun laws in Australia. They established the Council to Control Gun Misuse in 1981. Following the 1987 killings, the movement gained new momentum and in 1988 Gun Control Australia was formed. The organization began to distribute books on social, ethical, and legal issues regarding firearm use. The organization used the occurrence of multiple gun-related killings, which it called "gun massacres," in its lobbying efforts for more stringent gun control. In the 10-year period beginning in 1987, three such events occurred each year, leaving an average of five people dead. Gun Control Australia observed that only in the United States does the "massacre rate" exceed Australia's.

The Australian Labor Party (ALP) supported uniform gun control legislation. The party conceded that sporting shooters, hunters, collectors, and people in hazardous occupations have legitimate reasons for owning firearms, but considered high-caliber firearms and automatic weapons too dangerous to be possessed by the civilian population.

Gun Control Australia claimed that the new gun control legislation had serious weaknesses. The Australian Clay Target Association (ACTA) was granted an exemption from the prohibition on the use of semiautomatic and pump action shotguns. The requirement that hunters must receive written permission from landowners to shoot was weakened by offering a lifetime approval. The organization contended that guns used in hunting are the most dangerous, when stored in the home, because they are "available for domestic impropriety." Most disturbing for Gun Control Australia was that the granting of gun ownership and use to members of gun clubs led to increased membership in these organizations. Gun Control Australia believed that new firearms legislation had not altered the number of guns in homes, 25 percent of which were estimated to contain at least one weapon. The organization also held that storage requirements for guns kept in the home must be improved to reduce the probability of accidents.

Pro-gun organizations, such as the Sporting Shooters Association, vehemently resisted the push toward stricter gun control. In 1993, the Association formed a lobbying arm called the Institute of Legislative Action. Proposals were made to allow semiautomatic weapons to be used at shooting ranges, to allow target shooting on private property, to permit some people to carry guns in urban areas, to allow unlicensed minors to shoot pistols at approved shooting ranges, and to exempt existing gun owners from the cooling-off period before purchasing another weapon.

In 2008 Australian researchers Samar McPhedran and Jeanine Baker concluded that the 1996 firearm restrictions had not reduced gun-related deaths; firearm homicides had been decreasing before 1996, and that trend simply continued. Others noted that whereas there had been eleven mass shootings in Australia in the decade before 1996, there had been none after passage of the restrictive legislation. However, McPhedran and Baker responded that such events are too rare to draw any statistical conclusions. The intentional gun death rate did fall about one-third from 1986 to 1996, but the rate of decline increased from 1996 to 2006, decreasing by approximately 60 percent. In 2013 the rate of gun-related homicides and suicides was 0.87 deaths per 100,000 residents, compared to 2.71 deaths per 100,000 in 1996.

See also: Canada; Switzerland; United Kingdom

Further Reading: Australian Labor Party Web site, www.ssaa.org.au/alpolicy.html; Gun Control Australia Web site, http://home.vicnet.net.au/~guncontrol; David B. Kopel, *The Samurai, the Mountie, and the Cowboy* (Buffalo, NY: Prometheus, 1992); Daniel Williams, "Australia's Gun Laws: Little Effect," *Time* (May 1, 2008), www.time.com/time/world/ article/0,8599,1736501,00.html; Austin Ramzy, Michelle Innis, and Patrick Boehler, "How a Conservative-Led Australia Ended Mass Killings," *New York Times* (December 4, 2015), www.nytimes/2015/12/05/world/australia-gun-ban-shooting.html?_r=0.

Aymette v. The State (1840)

In *Aymette v. The State* (21 Tenn. 154-162, 1840), a Tennessee court of appeals ruled on the constitutionality of an 1837 Tennessee statute that prohibited any person from wearing "any bowie knife, or Arkansas tooth-pick [dagger], or other knife or weapon in form, shape or size resembling a bowie knife or Arkansas tooth-pick under his clothes, or concealed about his person." The court determined that this provision did not conflict with the first article of the state constitution that stated that "the free white men of this State have a right to keep and bear arms for their common defense." The court emphasized the qualifying phrase "for the common defense" in allowing restrictions on arms bearing, ruling that the state constitution did not guarantee the right to keep and bear weapons that have no recognized military use. Nearly 100 years later, in 1939, the U.S. Supreme Court in *United*

States v. Miller followed a similar line of reasoning regarding the Second Amendment right to keep and bear arms.

In 1839, William Aymette was indicted for violating the statute prohibiting the carrying of a concealed Bowie knife. He went in search of a person with whom he had argued earlier in the day, issuing verbal threats and brandishing the knife. The jury found Aymette guilty and the court sentenced him to three months imprisonment and fined him $200. Aymette appealed the verdict, claiming that the law violated the state constitution.

In rendering its decision, the appeals court investigated the purpose for which citizens are granted the right to bear arms. Referring to Great Britain under the rule of James II in the late seventeenth century, the court noted that Protestants had been denied the right to bear arms in defense of their rights against the government: "The grievances to which they were thus forced to submit, were for the most part of a public character, and could have been redressed only by the people rising up for their *common defence* to vindicate their rights." The court noted that the provision of the Tennessee constitution was adopted "in reference to these historical facts."

The court emphasized that the words "bear arms" refer to the military use of weapons and do not apply to wearing arms on the person "as part of the dress." For the purpose of defense, citizens do not need weapons that are used primarily in "private broils" and that have little value in warfare: "They could not be employed advantageously in the common defence of the citizens."

The court declared that although the right to keep and bear arms for the common defense must be zealously preserved, the state constitution does not prohibit the legislature from enacting legislation to regulate the manner in which weapons may be used. For the court to deny the legislature the authority to pass legislation regarding the use of arms would be "to pervert a great political right to the worst of purposes." An individual may legitimately be prevented from carrying weapons "merely to terrify the people, or for purposes of private assassination." While the court was willing to suggest that the right to *keep* arms was unqualified, the right to *bear* arms could be limited according to the purpose for which arms were carried, which must ultimately involve maintaining the common defense.

The Tennessee court respectfully dissented from a Kentucky court's decision in *Bliss v. Commonwealth* in 1822. That court had ruled that a similar statute in Kentucky was contrary to the state constitution and hence void. The Tennessee court argued that a legitimate distinction could be made between a law prohibiting the right to bear arms and a law that regulated the manner in which a weapon may be carried. Given the relation of bearing arms to the common defense, the Tennessee court refused to regard such activities as carrying a dagger or a pistol under clothing as examples of bearing arms. Applying the practical criterion of usefulness during war or for the defense of citizens, the court declared that such weapons simply did not meet this qualification for protection and therefore could be restricted.

See also: Bliss v. Commonwealth (1822); State Laws, Appendix 2; *United States v. Miller* (1939).

Further Reading: *Aymette v. The State* (21 Tenn. 154-162, 1840); "*Aymette v. The State* (1840)," in Robert J. Cottrol, ed., *Gun Control and the Constitution: Sources and Explorations on the Second Amendment* (New York: Garland, 1994), pp. 2–10.

Ayoob, Massad (1948–)

Massad Ayoob, director of the Lethal Force Institute, a self-defense training program for police officers and civilians, has been a vocal advocate of the right to carry firearms for self-defense. He is considered an expert in self-defense techniques and firearms training. Ayoob is a contributing editor for *Gus Magazine* and writes the handgun column. He has contributed to other firearms periodicals, including *American Handgunner, Gun Week, Guns and Ammo,* and *Combat Handguns.*

Early in his career as a self-defense expert, Ayoob concentrated on hand combat, writing for such martial arts journals as *Black Belt, Official Karate,* and *Karate Illustrated.* In 1979 Ayoob, concerned about the legal problems faced by individuals who use force in self-defense, published *In the Gravest Extreme: The Role of the Firearm in Civilian Self-Defense.* In 1981 he established the Lethal Force Institute to offer instruction in self-defense. An expert pistol shooter, Ayoob created an intensive training course that includes actual combat shooting as well as lectures, video presentations, and discussion. One course, titled "Judicious Use of Deadly Force," deals with such topics as the legally permissible circumstances for using a firearm in self-defense, the selection of firearms and ammunition, shooting stances, street gun-fighting tactics, psychological preparation for violent encounters, and choosing an attorney for defense in court.

In 1987 Ayoob was named national director of firearms and deadly force training for the American Society of Law Enforcement Trainers. Although not himself a lawyer (he received a bachelor of science degree in business from New Hampshire College in 1970), Ayoob has served as co-vice chair of the Forensic Evidence Committee of the National Association of Criminal Defense Lawyers. He has served as a senior research associate for the Center for Advancement of Applied Ethics at Carnegie-Mellon University and as a part-time police officer for over 23 years. He is also a certified prosecutor. Ayoob has been called on a number of occasions as an expert witness, testifying for police officers who have used deadly force.

In the book *The Truth about Self-Protection,* Ayoob offers advice on avoiding violent crime, covering such topics as mental alertness, alarms, martial arts, firearms, and auto security. He adheres to the basic premise that it is morally superior to resist evil action than to acquiesce to it. In *The Ayoob Files: The Book,* Ayoob describes several shooting incidents and suggests what the reader might do in similar circumstances. In *Deadly Force: Understanding Your Right to Self Defense,* (2014), Ayoob elaborates on the presentation he made in *In the Gravest* Extreme, discussing in detail the basic principles of self-defense and the legal principles of using deadly force. Ayoob has produced several DVDs, including *Shoot to Live,* in which he provides strategies for surviving a gunfight and advice about where to shoot an assailant for maximum effect. *Cute Lawyer Tricks* is a video intended to prepare police officers and civilians for the techniques lawyers use in the courtroom.

Ayoob has staunchly defended the individualist interpretation of the Second Amendment. He argues that the gun control issue is closely associated with civil rights, and claims that policy proposals such as needs-based licensing of firearms and increased taxes on guns and ammunition discriminate against the poor and minorities. He contends that any ban on particular weapons would require that the government pay fair market value to gun owners under the provisions of eminent domain. Such compensation would require billions of dollars that Ayoob maintains would be better spent for medical research or housing for the homeless. He argues that women should have the same rights of self-protection as men. Holding that affordable handguns give disadvantaged women the opportunity to protect themselves, Ayoob singles out women's groups for special criticism because they discourage women from acquiring firearms for self-defense.

See also: Gun Week; Guns Magazine; Second Amendment; Self-Defense; Women and Guns.

Further Reading: Massad Ayoob, *The Gun Digest Book of Concealed Carry* (Iola, WI: F+W Media, 2008); Massad Ayoob, *The Truth about Self-Protection* (Concord, NH: Police Bookshelf, 1999); Massad Ayoob, *The Ayoob Files: The Book* (Concord, NH: Police Bookshelf, 1995); Massad Ayoob, *In the Gravest Extreme: The Role of the Firearm in Civilian Self-Defense* (Concord, NH: Police Bookshelf, 1980); Massad Ayoob and the Lethal Force Institute Website, www.ayoob.com.

B

Background Checks

The Brady Handgun Violence Prevention Act (Pub. L. 103-159, 107 Stat. 1536), which President Bill Clinton signed on November 30, 1993, following seven years of effort by gun control advocates to have Congress approve the legislation, went into effect on February28, 1994. It mandated background checks of those intending to purchase a handgun from a federally licensed firearms dealer. From March 1, 1994, when the act required background checks to begin in most states, through December 1996, the Bureau of Justice Statistics estimated that approximately 7,782,000 presale checks were performed on people applying to purchase a handgun from federally licensed firearms dealers. Of that total, 173,000, or 2.2 percent of the total number of applicants, were not allowed to purchase a handgun. Nearly 68 percent of the rejections were associated with a felony conviction or current felony indictment. While gun control supporters lauded the results of checks, gun rights advocates focused on what they considered a small percentage of rejections. From 1999 to 2005, the number of background checks per year varied from 8.5 million to just over 9 million. In 2006, the number of checks rose to more than 10 million, and continued to rise in 2007, reaching 12.7 million in 2008.

The Gun Control Act of 1968 specified that the following individuals be denied the opportunity to purchase a handgun:

1. juveniles (under 18 years old)
2. fugitives from justice
3. persons under indictment for, or already convicted of, a crime punishable by imprisonment for more than one year
4. persons unlawfully using controlled substances
5. persons legally determined to be mentally defective or committed to a mental institution
6. aliens illegally in the United States
7. persons dishonorably discharged from the armed forces
8. persons who have renounced U.S. citizenship
9. persons subject to a court order restraining them from harassing, stalking, or threatening an intimate partner or a child
10. persons convicted of a felony or misdemeanor related to domestic violence

Thirty-two states were originally covered by the Brady law while the 18 remaining states (called Brady-alternative states) had their own legislation mandating background checks. By the end of 1996, nine additional states had enacted their own legislation, creating 23 Brady states and 27 Brady-alternative states. The Bureau of Justice Statistics reported that during 1996, the 32 original Brady states had a rejection rate of 3.6 percent while the original Brady-alternative states rejected 1.9 percent of applications, a statistically significant difference. The 23 current Brady states had a rejection rate of 3.1 percent while the current Brady-alternative states had a 2.5-percent rate, which was not statistically significant.

After felony indictment or conviction, the reasons for rejecting an application included being a fugitive from justice (6.0 percent), violating a state law prohibition (5.5 percent), being under a restraining order (3.9 percent), having been judged mentally ill or suffering from a mental disability (1.5 percent), addicted to drugs (1.2 percent), and violating a local law prohibition (0.7 percent). The remainder were rejected for a variety of reasons, including applications by illegal aliens, juveniles, those dishonorably discharged from the military, and those convicted of domestic violence.

Through 1996, background checks were conducted under the interim provisions of the Brady Act, which required a five-day waiting period to allow time for chief law enforcement officers (CLEOs) at the state and local levels to conduct the investigation of each applicant. In 1997, the Supreme Court, in *Printz v. United States*, disallowed the federal provision in the Brady Law requiring CLEOs to conduct background checks. Therefore, supporters of background checks anxiously awaited the completion of a national computerized instant check system. In November 1998, the Federal Bureau of Investigation (FBI) initiated the National Instant Criminal Background Check System (NICS), a computerized procedure allowing federal firearms officials to run an immediate background check on potential firearms purchasers. Because background checks apply only to federally licensed firearms dealers selling new handguns, a potentially vast market in handguns continues without any limitation on purchasers who would otherwise fall into one or more of the prohibited categories. Gun control advocates call for more restrictive background check laws, such as closing the so-called gun show loophole (unless prohibited by state law, people who are not federal firearms dealers can sell firearms at gun shows without running a background check), and improving NICS access to mental health records as well as felony and domestic violence restraining order records. Background check supporters also urge that the use of straw purchases— someone who purchases firearms for others who cannot pass the background check—be more closely monitored and restricted. The Brady Campaign to Prevent Gun Violence reports U.S. Department of Justice data indicating that since 1994, the Brady Law has prevented 1.8 million firearm purchases by people who have failed the background checks due to criminal backgrounds or for other reasons.

In 2007 Congress approved the NICS Improvement Amendments Act which, according to William J. Krouse (20013), "amends and strengthens a provision of the Brandy Handgun Violence Protection Act . . . that requires federal agencies to provide, and the Attorney General to secure, any government records with information relevant to determining the eligibility of a person to receive a firearm for inclusion in databases queried by NICS." Of major concern was the encouragement of states to provide information about those who, for mental reasons, are likely to be a danger to themselves of others. Groups on both sides of the gun control issue tended to disagree about the merits of the legislation. The National Rifle Association (NRA), after successfully amending the bill, supported its passage, but other gun rights organizations such as Larry Pratt's Gun Owners of America opposed the bill. The Brady Campaign reluctantly supported passage, but the Violence Policy Center and other groups opposed the legislation, considering it to be too great a compromise with the NRA.

Gun control supporters continue to push for an expansion of the NICS to include all private sales and transfers except those between close family members. Such legislative proposals were made in 2016 following the San Bernardino, California, and the Orlando, Florida, mass shootings, but the Senate rejected the proposed legislation.

See also: Brady Campaign to Prevent Gun Violence; Brady Handgun Violence Prevention Act; Gun Control Act of 1968; Mayors Against Illegal Guns; National Instant Check System; *Printz v. United States* (1997); State Laws, Appendix 2; Straw Purchases.

Further Reading: Donald A. Manson and Darrell K. Gilliard, "Presale Handgun Checks, 1996," *Bureau of Justice Statistics Bulletin* (September 1997); Mayors Against Illegal Guns, "Inside Straw Purchasing" (April 2008), www.mayorsagainstillegalguns.org/downloads/pdf/inside-straw-purchases.pdf; Regional Justice Information Service, St. Louis, Missouri, *Survey of State Procedures Related to Firearm Sales, 1996* (Washington, DC: Bureau of Justice Statistics, 1997).

Bailey v. United States (1996)

In *Bailey v. United States* (516 U.S. 137, 1996), the U.S. Supreme Court ruled on what the term "use" meant in the context of a federal statute [18 U.S.C. section 924 (c) (1)] that established a minimum five-year sentence for anyone found guilty of using or carrying a firearm "during and in relation to any crime of violence or drug trafficking crime." The Court established a narrow interpretation of "use," thus spurring a move by gun control advocates in Congress to expand the term's definition to include instances the Court did not recognize as being covered under existing legislation.

In May 1989, police stopped Roland Bailey's automobile when they noticed the vehicle lacked a front license plate and an inspection sticker. After officers ordered Bailey to leave the vehicle, they discovered he had no driver's license and their search of the car revealed plastic bags containing 30 grams of cocaine. When officers discovered a 9-mm. pistol in the trunk, violation of 18 U.S.C. 924 (c) (1) was added to several other charges. A jury, informed by the prosecution that drug dealers often carry firearms for self-protection and to safeguard their drugs and money, found Bailey guilty on all charges. On the weapons charge, the defendant received a five-year prison term.

Bailey appealed his conviction to the Court of Appeals for the District of Columbia Circuit, which upheld the lower court decision. The court interpreted the notion of "use" broadly, stating that the statute applied in this case because the jury could reasonably conclude that the firearm found in the trunk of Bailey's car had aided drug transactions, having been used to protect the illegal drugs and the money received from sales.

Meanwhile, in another drug case, Candisha Robinson was arrested for selling crack cocaine to an undercover officer. When police officers found an unloaded .22-caliber Derringer stored in a trunk she kept in her apartment, Robinson was charged with a firearm violation under section 924 (c) (1) and subsequently found guilty. However, the Court of Appeals in this case reversed the conviction, ruling that the evidence showing a gun close to the drugs was insufficient to establish a violation of the "use" provision of the firearms statute. Given the conflicting outcomes of the Bailey and Robinson cases, the District of Columbia Circuit Court of Appeals combined the two cases for a consistent ruling. A majority of the court, by deciding that evidence in each case was adequate to uphold conviction under the firearms statute, established a proximity and accessibility test for determining when a firearm has been "used," thus reversing the original appeals court decision in the Robinson case and affirming Bailey's conviction.

The defendants in each case argued that "use" should be interpreted in the narrow sense of "active employment of a firearm." On appeal, the Supreme Court agreed with the appellants that the proximity and accessibility test provided a too-broad interpretation of use, concluding that this test offered virtually no limitation on the type of possession to be considered criminal. The Court declared that the government must demonstrate "active employment of the firearm," that the statute requires actual, not merely intended, use. The Court also indicated that the active meaning of "use," includes "brandishing, displaying, bartering, striking with, and most obviously, firing or attempting to fire, a firearm." The "inert presence" of a firearm, such as its storage, does not justify prosecution under the statute.

Recognizing that its interpretation of congressional intent restricted the statute's range of application, the Supreme Court noted that the government may charge offenders under the "carry" provision of the statute. Because the District of Columbia Court of Appeals did not consider the defendants' liability under the "carry" provision, the Supreme Court returned the Bailey and Robinson cases to the trial courts for reconsideration of the convictions on that basis.

See also: Firearm Sentence Enhancement Laws.

Further Reading: *Bailey v. United States*, 516 U.S. 137 (1996).

Barr, Bob (1948–)

When Republican Congressman Bob Barr entered the U.S. House of Representatives in January 1995, he quickly established himself as a major opponent to new gun control proposals and existing gun legislation and as a strong supporter of the individualist interpretation of the Second Amendment. Having serious reservations about the power of federal law enforcement agencies, Barr worked for the elimination of the Bureau of Alcohol, Tobacco, and Firearms (ATF), for downsizing other federal law enforcement agencies, and for the repeal of the Brady Handgun Violence Prevention Act and the assault weapons ban.

A native of Iowa, Barr received a B.A. from the University of Southern California in 1970, an M.A. from George Washington University in 1972, and a law degree from Georgetown University in 1977. While a student in Washington, D.C., Barr worked for the Central Intelligence Agency (CIA) as an intelligence analyst. After completing his law degree, Barr moved to Georgia to practice law. From 1986 to 1990, he served as a U.S. attorney. In 1992, he sought the Republican nomination for a seat in the U.S. Senate, but lost in a runoff. Two years later he won the Republican nomination for a seat in the U.S. House of Representatives and defeated the five-term incumbent in a nationwide conservative tide. Gun control supporters point out that the new congressman received $5,000 from the Georgia Gun Owners' Political Action Committee during the primary, and an additional $4,950 from the National Rifle Association (NRA) during the general election campaign.

When House Speaker Newt Gingrich established a Republican task force on firearms, he chose Barr to head the group. In that capacity and as a member of the Judiciary Committee, Barr attempted to revise a domestic and international terrorism bill. Voting against the bill as it was reported from the committee in June 1995, Barr worked with committee chairman Henry J. Hyde, Republican of Illinois, to develop an alternative that would be more appealing to House conservatives. In March 1996, Barr proposed an amendment to the bill that eliminated a section allowing the introduction of evidence obtained through illegal wiretaps and a provision facilitating prosecution of those who sell guns subsequently used in a crime.

Barr successfully opposed the reintroduction of the excluded measures in the House-Senate conference committee. He insisted that federal law enforcement officers did not need the increased authority that the deleted provisions would provide. The bill became law in April 1996. Despite subsequent terrorist acts, including the bombing at the Centennial Olympic Park in Atlanta, Georgia, Barr's home state, the congressman remained unwilling to support a more stringent antiterrorism measure, objecting to any quick reaction to a specific criminal act.

Barr proposed repealing the 1994 ban on particular types of assault weapons. He argued that longer prison sentences were a better deterrent to crime than attempting to ban weapons. Tanya Metaksa, executive director of the NRA's Institute for Legislative Action, commended Barr for his efforts to schedule a House vote on the repeal, which occurred in March 1996. Neal Knox, then first vice president of the NRA, also credited Barr for his efforts to repeal the assault weapons ban. The measure included a provision to increase sentences for committing violent or drug-related crimes. Although the bill passed in the House by a vote of 239-173, it failed in the Senate. In March 1999, Barr introduced legislation to limit the liability of firearms manufacturers for the criminal use of their products, but the bill died in committee. He also supported legislation to limit federal asset forfeiture authority. Barr reluctantly supported the 2001 USA PATRIOT Act, but subsequently became a strong critic of the antiterrorism legislation because, he argued, it violated the governmental system of checks and balances and threatened citizen liberties.

In August 2002, in a reception in his honor, Barr inadvertently fired an antique .38-caliber pistol that Georgia lobbyist Bruce Widener had handed to him. No one was injured, but the accident underscored Barr's subsequent loss in his 2004 reelection bid to the House of Representatives, largely due to congressional redistricting. From 2003 to 2008 he served as the 21st Century Liberties Chair for Freedom and Privacy at the American Conservative Union. As the Libertarian Party presidential candidate in 2008, Barr championed libertarian causes, including the right to keep and bear arms. However, some libertarians complained that Barr had not maintained a 100 percent support rating on gun rights while in Congress. Barr now writes a weekly column for the *Atlanta-Constitution* newspaper. In a July 2010 piece, he praised the U.S. Supreme Court's decision in *McDonald v. Chicago*, in which the Court majority ruled that no state or municipality can deny an individual the right to possess a firearm. Barr considered Justice Clarence Thomas's concurring opinion claiming a substantive right to keep and bear arms to be preferable to the majority opinion's reliance on a due process argument.

In 2012 Barr returned to the Republican Party, which he had abandoned in 2008 to become the Libertarian Party's presidential candidate. In March 2013 Barr announced that he would run for a seat in the U.S. House of Representatives from Georgia's eleventh congressional district and received the NRA's endorsement, but he lost a runoff election in the Republican primary. Barr continues to practice law in Atlanta, Georgia, where he has a consulting firm, Liberty Strategies. Barr heads Liberty Guard, an organization devoted to protecting individual liberty, and also serves on the boards of the Law Enforcement Education Foundation and the Law Enforcement Education Organization. Since 1997 he has served on the board of directors of the NRA, and in 2013 was elected to a sixth three-year term.

Following the December 2015 mass shooting in San Bernardino, California, Barr commented that the right to keep and bear arms should not be further restricted and that the government should no limit the amount of ammunition individuals may possess.

See also: Assault Weapons Ban; BradyHandgun Violence Prevention Act; Bureau of Alcohol, Tobacco, Firearms, and Explosives; Civil Forfeiture; Knox, Neal; Legal Action Project; Metaksa, Tanya K.; National Rifle Association.

Further Reading: Bob Barr Web site, www.bobbarr. org; Robert Dreyfuss, "Uzi Does It," *Mother Jones* 21 (September/October 1996), 46–47; Philip D. Duncan and Christine C. Lawrence, *Politics in America: The 105th Congress* (Washington, DC: CQ Press, 1997).

Barrett .50-Caliber Sniper Rifles

The controversy over civilian ownership of Barrett .50-caliber sniper rifles and equivalent firearms reflects the controversy between gun control advocates, who contend that certain weapons, designed for military use, should be prohibited from private ownership, and gun rights advocates, who insist that government should not determine what type of weapons law-abiding citizens may own. The Federal Firearms Act of 1938 was based on the premise that certain weapons are too dangerous for civilian ownership and are primarily used in criminal activity, and therefore the legislation restricted the sale and ownership of automatic machine guns, sawed-off shotguns, and hand grenades. Gun control advocates argue that .50-caliber rifles should be added to that list. An issue both sides of the firearm debate face is the possible consequences that technological development of firearms may have for the willingness to allow private citizens the freedom to possess advanced firearms with great destructive capacity.

Ronnie Barrett, founder and chief executive officer of the Barrett firearms company of Murfreesboro, Tennessee, developed the Model 82 semiautomatic .50-BMG rifle in the early1980s, a weapon that can hit a target from more than a mile away and has the ability to pierce reinforced armor. Barrett based a profitable firearms company on manufacturing these rifles, as well as ammunition, optics, and other firearm accessories, for the U.S. military, the military establishments of more than 60 governments, law enforcement agencies, and civilians in the United States. The U.S. Army adopted Barrett's original Model 82A1 .50-caliber rifle as the M107 rifle. In 2007 the Army selected the M107 as one of the top ten military inventions. In 2010, the National Rifle Association (NRA) publications *American Rifleman*, *American Hunter*, and *Shooting Illustrated* presented to Barrett the Golden Bullseye Pioneer Award that since 2007 has been bestowed on individuals who have made commendable achievements in "the development, introduction, and promotion of equipment that has made a profound and enduring impact on the way Americans shoot and hunt."

The Violence Policy Center (VPC) has argued that the Barrett .50-caliber sniper rifle should be included among the weapons prohibited under the 1938 Federal Firearms Act. The organization called it an especially attractive firearm for terrorists, citing a finding of a 2004 RAND corporation report that snipers with .50-caliber rifles potentially could destroy aircraft on the ground. The NRA responded that those calling for restrictions on private ownership engage in "fear-mongering because they rely on speculations about possible future events rather than what actually has occurred." The NRA, using the "slippery slope" argument, has claimed that the VPC's goal transcends the call for restricting private sales of the .50-caliber rifle and ultimately involves the objective of severely limiting or even banning all firearms ownership. The NRA has argued that .50-caliber rifles are simply too expensive and too large for

Gun control advocates want to ban civilian ownership of .50 caliber rifles like the one shown above. *www.wikipedia.org*

"run-of-the-mill lowlifes" to use in robberies or to settle disputes over the illegal drug trade. In response to the NRA's claim that .50-caliber rifles are not used in criminal activity, the VPC provided a list of numerous instances in which the weapon was related to criminal activity.

The VPC and other gun control groups continue to warn that terrorists could use the weapon to hit various strategic targets, while the NRA rejects the "military-only" use for the weapons, and claims that most of those who own .50-caliber rifles use the firearm legitimately for target shooting. In any event, the NRA has succeeded in preventing congressional passage of federal legislation that would regulate .50-caliber sniper rifles in the same way that machine gun ownership is restricted.

See also: American Rifleman, Assault Weapons Ban; Violence Policy Center.

Further Reading: Barrett Company, www.barrett. net; Impact Guns, www.impactguns.com/store/ barrett_50_rifles.html; Modern Firearms, "Barrett 'Light Fifty' M82A1 M82A2 M82A3 (USA)," www. world.guns.ru/sniper/sn02-e.htm; Robert Spitzer, *The Politics of Gun Control,* 6th ed. (Boulder, CO: Paradism, 2015); Violence Policy Center, "Information on 50 Caliber Anti-Armor Sniper Rifles," www.vpc. org/50caliber.htm.

Barrett v. United States (1976)

In *Barrett v. United States* (423 U.S. 212, 1976), the U.S. Supreme Court ruled on a provision of the Gun Control Act of 1968 [18 U.S.C. 992 (h)] that prohibited a convicted felon, among other categories of individuals, from receiving "any firearm or ammunition which has been shipped or transported in interstate or foreign commerce." The major issue to be decided was whether the provision applies more broadly to a person who makes an intrastate purchase of a firearm that has been transported in interstate commerce from the manufacturer to a distributor and ultimately to a dealer, or whether the law can be interpreted more narrowly as having application only to direct interstate sales or acquisitions.

In 1967, a Kentucky state court convicted Pearl Barrett of housebreaking, imposing a two-year sentence. In April 1972, Barrett purchased a .32-caliber revolver from a federally licensed

firearms dealer. The firearm, which had been manufactured in Massachusetts, was shipped to a distributor in North Carolina and then to the Kentucky dealer. Within an hour of the purchase, a county sheriff stopped Barrett for driving while intoxicated and discovered the fully loaded firearm lying on the floorboard. At his trial on the charge of having violated section 922 (h), Barrett moved for a directed verdict of acquittal, arguing that the statute did not apply to his receipt of a firearm because the purchase was in no way associated with the interstate transfer of the weapon. The judge denied the motion and Barrett was found guilty. The Court of Appeals, in a divided opinion, affirmed the verdict.

Because of the significance of the issue and a contradictory decision by another Court of Appeals, the Supreme Court decided to accept the appeal. Barrett admitted that Congress has the authority under the Commerce Clause of the Constitution to regulate interstate firearms trafficking, but argued that Congress intended the legislation to apply to interstate trafficking alone, not to transfers within a state that have no connection to interstate commerce. In response, the Court noted that while the prohibited action ("to receive any firearm") is in the present tense, the statute's reference to interstate commerce is stated in the present perfect tense ("has been shipped or transported"), which indicates that the interstate transfer has been completed before acquisition by the purchaser. If Congress had intended to restrict the statute to direct interstate receipt, it would have explicitly stated the limitation. The Court disagreed with the charge that the statute was ambiguous and therefore rejected the call to decide the case more charitably.

According to the Court, the structure of the Gun Control Act indicated that Congress "did not intend merely to restrict interstate sales but sought to keep firearms away from the persons Congress classified as potentially irresponsible and dangerous." For instance, section 922 (d) prohibits a federally licensed dealer from "knowingly selling or otherwise disposing of any firearm . . . to the same categories of potentially irresponsible persons." The Court noted that other sections of the Act, such as licensing provisions, apply both to exclusively intrastate as well as interstate actions. Therefore, 922 (h) can be consistently interpreted, with the intent of the entire act, to apply to intrastate retail firearms sales. To decide otherwise, the majority opinion concluded, would eliminate the statute's application to the typical circumstance—a felon purchasing or receiving a firearm from a local dealer.

The Supreme Court declared that the narrow interpretation in *United States v. Tot* (1942) of a similar provision limiting interstate transactions that was included in the Federal Firearms Act of 1938 had no relevance to the Court's task of determining Congress's intentions in the *Barrett* case. The justices concluded that nothing in the legislative history of the Gun Control Act argued persuasively that Congress intended to apply the limited interpretation presented in the *Tot* decision.

See also: Federal Firearms Act of 1938; Gun Control Act of 1968; *United States v. Tot* (1942).

Further Reading: *Barrett v. United States*, 423 U.S. 212 (1976).

Barron v. Baltimore (1833)

The U.S. Supreme Court case *Barron v. Baltimore* (32 U.S. 7 Pet. 243, 1833) established the principle that the Bill of Rights of the U.S. Constitution only limited the actions of the national government and did not apply to the states. Although subsequent constitutional history resulted in much of the Bill of Rights being applied to state and local governments, the Second Amendment until recent decisions remained under the precedent set by the Barron case. Gun rights advocates have finally been successful in calling for a court ruling applying the Second Amendment to the states.

In the 1830s, when the City of Baltimore, Maryland, under the authority of the Maryland legislature, diverted the flow of some streams, Barron's wharf became useless for shipping due to deposits of silt. Barron argued that the state legislature and the actions of the city had divested him of his property without just compensation, a violation of the Fifth Amendment of the U.S. Constitution. Chief Justice John Marshall, speaking for the Supreme Court, stated that the provision of the Fifth Amendment regarding just compensation for property taken for public use limited the power only of the national government and was not applicable to state laws and actions. He claimed that the limitations generally established in the Constitution applied only to the government created by that document, noting that during ratification proceedings for the Constitution calls were made for a bill of rights to protect the people

specifically against possible encroachments by the national government.

Gun rights supporters long contended that the Supreme Court ruling in *Barron v. Baltimore* no longer applied, given the long series of Supreme Court rulings establishing that most of the provisions within the Bill of Rights limit the states via the Fourteenth Amendment. They claimed that the logic of Supreme Court rulings indicated that the Second Amendment protection of the right to keep and bear arms applied to the states as well as to the national government. However, gun control supporters, arguing that the Second Amendment established a state right to maintain militias independent of the national government, denied that the Barron case and subsequent decisions applying portions of the Bill of Rights to the states ever had any potential applicability to the Second Amendment. In *District of Columbia v. Heller* (2008), the Supreme Court majority interpreted the Second Amendment as guaranteeing an individual right to keep and bear arms, and in *McDonald v. Chicago* (2010) ruled that the Amendment applies to states and cities as well as the federal government.

See also: District of Columbia v. Heller (2008); Fourteenth Amendment; *McDonald v. Chicago* (2010); Second Amendment.

Further Reading: *Barron v. Baltimore*, 32 U.S. 7 Pet. 243 (1833).

Beecham v. United States (1994)

In *Beecham v. United States* (511 U.S. 368, 1994), the U.S. Supreme Court dealt with the issue of a convicted felon's eligibility under federal law to own firearms. Federal legislation was intended to keep firearms away from those considered most likely to misuse them, but there remained the difficult question of how a convicted felon's right to possess firearms might be restored. Specifically, does the removal of felony status by a state also apply to felony status resulting from a federal conviction? The Court ruled that for persons convicted of a felony to receive relief from provisions of the Gun Control Act of 1968, the federal statute that prohibits a convicted felon from possessing a firearm [18 U.S.C. 922 (g)], "they must have had their civil rights restored under federal law."

The Court ruled simultaneously on cases involving two defendants, Beecham and Jones, who had both been found guilty of violating the federal statute prohibiting firearm ownership to convicted felons. In 1979, Beecham had been convicted in Tennessee of a federal firearms violation, and Jones had two West Virginia state convictions and one 1971 federal conviction in Ohio for interstate transportation of a stolen automobile. West Virginia had subsequently restored Jones's civil rights, and Beecham claimed that Tennessee had restored his civil rights. The district courts in the two cases were asked to decide whether these state restorations of civil rights eliminated the application of the gun ownership restriction for the two defendants. The courts had to decide which jurisdiction— state or federal—determines whether the restoration of civil rights applies to a prior federal conviction.

Although the district courts determined that state restoration removed the imposed disabilities under federal law, the Fourth Circuit Court of Appeals reversed the lower court rulings, concluding that state restoration of civil rights did not free a convicted felon from restrictions resulting from a federal conviction. The Supreme Court agreed with the Fourth Circuit. Although states had restored the defendants' civil rights, these restorations applied only to the jurisdiction in which the conviction occurred.

Justice Sandra Day O'Connor, arguing for the Court, faced an issue raised by the district courts' original rulings: because no federal process existed for restoring civil rights to a federal felon, Congress must have intended that other jurisdictions, not the federal government, should perform the function. The Supreme Court rejected this interpretation, noting that nothing in the statute sustains the view that felons in all jurisdictions were intended to have access to all the procedures, including pardon, expungement, set-aside, and civil rights restoration. As O'Connor observed, because "some jurisdictions have no procedure for restoring civil rights," a person convicted of a felony in a federal court has no greater disadvantage than someone convicted in the court of a state that has no provision for restoring civil rights. The Beecham decision maintained the federal government's discretion in applying firearm ownership restrictions for convicted felons.

See also: Gun Control Act of 1968.

Further Reading: *Beecham v. United States*, 511 U.S. 368 (1994).

Beecher's Bibles

The term Beecher's Bibles refers to the Sharps rifles that Northern opponents of slavery sent to Kansas after 1854 to assist those who wanted to keep the territory free of slavery. Supporters of gun rights today argue that the events in Kansas during the 1850s are a prime example of the need for the right of individuals to possess firearms to defend themselves against tyranny and oppression. The conflict in Kansas, a prelude to the Civil War, began with Congress's passage of the Kansas-Nebraska Act in May 1854. The act intended to allow the residents of Kansas to decide whether slavery would be legal in the territory; but rather than allowing a peaceful resolution to the conflict by local citizens, the act led to violence that ignited the emotions of both North and South.

Although the bona fide settlers from the North outnumbered the supporters of slavery, slaveowners in Missouri, fearful that a free Kansas would threaten their financial holdings and ultimately their way of life, sent thousands of men into Kansas to coerce the population to favor legalization of slavery. The invasion of Missourians carrying revolvers, shotguns, and other weapons overwhelmed Free State forces. In November 1854, an election was held to select a territorial representative to Congress. Approximately 2,000 Missourians crossed the border to coerce voters and election officials and to cast their own ballots in the election. A proslavery candidate was elected. In March 1855, a second invasion of an estimated 5,000 Missourians led to the election of a pro-slavery territorial legislature in Kansas.

News of the events in Kansas spread through an indignant North, leading many to urge that assistance be provided to anti-slavery forces in "Bleeding Kansas." Many people were encouraged to emigrate to Kansas to serve the anti-slavery cause. As part of this campaign, many individuals and groups donated funds to purchase Sharps rifles for the anti-slavery forces in Kansas. Reverend Henry Ward Beecher, pastor of Plymouth Church in Brooklyn, New York, raised funds among his parishioners. Beecher declared that the rifles served a greater redeeming role for Kansas than the Bible, noting that at times self-defense was a man's religious duty. Due to Beecher's strong appeals for funds, the Sharps rifles became known as Beecher's Bibles.

Charles Robinson, representative for the Emigrant Aid Company in Lawrence, Kansas, formed two military companies and requested rifles and other weapons to arm the groups. The Sharps rifles, highly effective weapons for that time, were early models of the breech loader that could fire up to 10 rounds per minute with a greater range than comparable weapons. For two years, appeals were made in churches throughout the North for funds to purchase these weapons. Due to Beecher's noted success, Plymouth Church became known as the Church of the Holy Rifles. Although prominent individuals made donations, they were fearful of the potential political consequences. The rifles could help the Free Staters defend themselves against southern slaveholding interests, but the donors recognized that they were defying a national government that at least nominally supported the slave position.

Although gun rights supporters see in this historical event a key example of the value of the right to keep and bear arms, historians comment that as soon as the Free State forces, including John Brown, used violence in response to the disruption caused by Missourians, they lost their claim to moral superiority. Both sides shed blood in a mini-civil war that no government sanctioned. Not armed force, but the continued push toward fair elections, proved the more effective strategy. Historian Oswald Garrison Villard (1943) contends that the movement toward freedom for all in Kansas occurred in part because of the "abandonment of the policy of carrying on an unauthorized war, and of meeting assassination with assassination" (p. 307). Historical examples such as Beecher's Bibles do not necessarily present a clear lesson about the value of firearms; at best, they indicate the delicate balance between resisting tyranny with armed force and maintaining a commitment to legal procedure.

See also: American Revolution; Black Codes.

Further Reading: Richard O. Boyer, *The Legend of John Brown: A Biography and a History* (New York: Alfred A. Knopf, 1973); Oswald Garrison Villard, *John Brown* (New York: Alfred A. Knopf, 1943).

Bernethy v. Walt Failor's Inc. (1978)

Bernethy v. Walt Failor's Inc. (97 Wash. 2d 929, 1978) is an example of a tort case (a lawsuit involving a wrongful act, damage, or injury willfully caused). In cases like Bernethy, victims of firearm violence have attempted to establish the legal and financial responsibility of a gun manufacturer or retail outlet for injuries resulting from firearm use. Because gun control advocates believe that dealers should show greater caution about the people to whom they are willing to sell firearms, they regard such judicial actions an important means to keep firearms away from those who are likely to commit acts of violence. Walt Failor, owner of a gun store in Washington state, became the defendant in a wrongful death suit after Robert Fleming, using a 30-30 rifle he had taken from Failor's store, shot and killed his wife, Phoebe, in a tavern where they had been drinking.

On April 11, 1978, Fleming, who had been drinking with his wife and friends at a local tavern, went to Failor's store to purchase a weapon. Although Failor claimed that Fleming demonstrated no significant symptoms of drunkenness, others reported that he was most definitely intoxicated when he entered the store. Fleming told Failor he wished to purchase a rifle for his son. Failor laid the weapon and ammunition on the counter and began completing the necessary forms and processing the credit card sale. At this point, Fleming walked out of the store with the gun and ammunition. When Failor followed him into the street, asking for payment, Fleming threatened the store owner with the gun.

When arrested for killing his wife, Fleming had a blood alcohol level more than twice that accepted in many states for drunk driving. A wrongful death suit was brought against Failor on behalf of Phoebe Fleming's three children, claiming that he had shown negligence in providing the rifle to Fleming. When the court dismissed the case, determining that the store owner was not negligent in providing a firearm to Fleming, even though the purchaser was intoxicated, the case was appealed. In turn, the Court of Appeals requested that the Supreme Court of Washington determine the appropriateness of the original court's summary judgment in favor of the defendant.

Citing a provision within tort law, the Washington Supreme Court indicated that a seller may be found liable for providing a piece of property if the purchaser is evidently incompetent or the seller can reasonably anticipate that the transfer will result in physical harm. Although Failor argued that the principle did not apply in this case because Fleming's actions were ultimately criminal, the court ruled that if "intervening criminal acts" are found to be foreseeable, then a claim of negligence may be made.

Although Failor argued that he did not sell the gun to Fleming, but that the man had in fact stolen the weapon, the court noted that Failor had nearly completed the sale, and that Fleming was able to leave the store with the weapon because Failor had left it within reach. The court ruled that actual liability in Phoebe Fleming's death must be determined in a jury trial. Ultimately important for the gun control question is that the court established the principle of liability of a gun retailer for the actions of the purchaser at least under circumstances where the seller can reasonably anticipate the use to which the purchaser may put the weapon.

See also: Fatalities.

Further Reading: *Bernethy v. Walt Failor's Inc.*, 97 Wash. 2d 929 (1978); Mark A. Siegel, Nancy R. Jacobs, and Carol D. Foster, eds., *Gun Control: Restricting Right or Protecting People?* (Wylie, TX: Information Plus, 1991).

Binghamton, New York, Shooting (2009)

On the morning of April 8, 2009, Jiverly Antares Wong, a 41-year-old Vietnamese immigrant who had become a U.S. citizen, drove to the American Civic Association in Binghamton, New York, where he had been attending English lessons, blocked the rear door of the building with his automobile, entered the front door, and immediately began shooting with two firearms, a 9mm. Beretta and a .45-caliber Beretta. He first shot two receptionists, killing one and seriously wounding the other, before moving on to a classroom, shooting all of the students in the room. Wong ultimately fired a total of 99 rounds: 88 from the 9mm. and eleven from the .45 caliber. After killing 13 people and wounding four others, Wong shot and killed himself. The shooter possessed a pistol permit issued by the state of New York and both handguns were registered. Police discovered two high-capacity magazines for the Beretta, each of which could hold 30 rounds. The Federal Assault Weapons ban, which expired in 2004, had limited magazines to ten rounds.

The gunman had sent a letter, filled with grammatical errors, to a Syracuse, New York, television station in which he offered a rambling explanation for his decision to commit the horrific act. After referring to perceived mistreatment from the police, whom he blamed for his failure to find employment and thus for causing him to engage in the shooting, Wong concluded the letter by writing "and you have a nice day." Wong's poor facility with the English language apparently contributed to his dejection. The package containing the letter also included a gun permit, photos of Wong holding guns, and Wong's driver's license.

Paul Helmke, president of the Brady Campaign to Prevent Gun Violence, called the shooting a "wake-up call reminding us that Americans must do something to stop the gun violence in our country." He referred to other recent firearm-related violence, including the deaths of ten people in Alabama, eight in North Carolina, and ten in California. Helmke criticized government officials for failing to take steps to prevent gun violence. Gun rights supporters responded that no restrictions on gun ownership could have prevented Wong from obtaining firearms and that concealed carry laws in many cases might be a sufficient deterrent to such acts. However, overall, the Binghamton shooting did not produce much response from either side of the gun control debate. Josh Sugarmann of the Violence Policy Center wrote a parody piece in which the reader is invited to fill in the appropriate blanks to fit the most recent firearm shooting incident, perhaps suggesting that such events have become relatively common and therefore have little effect on public policy proposals.

See also: Background Checks; *Bowling for Columbine*; Empire State Building Shooting; Jonesboro, Arkansas, School Shooting; Littleton, Colorado, Columbine School Shooting; Stockton, California, Shooting; Texas Tower Shooting; Virginia Tech Shooting.

Further Reading: *2009 Murders in the United States; Fort Hood Shooting, United States Holocaust Memorial Museum Shooting, Binghamton Shootings* (Memphis, TN: Books LLC, 2010); Peter S. Green, "Shots from Two Guns, Police Say," www.bloomberg. com/apps/news? pid=newsarchive&sid=ajZkPio mE8g4; Paul Helmke, "Today's Mass Shooting in New York Latest Wakeup Call for Nation" (April 3, 2009), www.bradycampaign. org/media/press/ view/1126; Josh Sugarmann, "Mass Shooting Template—Repeat as Necessary" (April 20, 2009), www.huffingtonpost.com/josh-sugarmann/mass-shooting-template—r_b_189054.html.

Black Codes

Those who have argued that the Fourteenth Amendment made the Second Amendment applicable to the states have employed the history of the Black Codes in the post-Civil War South to bolster their position. These Codes, which restricted the rights of formerly enslaved African Americans, were one of the factors that motivated Congress to propose the Fourteenth Amendment to assure that all Americans, regardless of race or color, could enjoy equal rights under the Constitution.

In 1865–1866, the former states of the Confederacy passed a series of laws that established, state by state, the basis of citizenship for newly freed African Americans. The Codes granted certain basic civil rights to blacks, including the right to marry, to own personal property, and to sue in the state judicial system. However, their basic rights were severely limited through such measures as establishing segregated public facilities, limiting the ability to gain work and the right to own real estate, and denying the right to testify in court. To protect the rights of former slaves and prevent what amounted to reenslavement, Congress established the Freedmen's Bureau, an agency that opposed enforcement of the Codes. Radical Republican governments under Reconstruction later repealed this legislation.

Of great concern to those interested in applying Second Amendment protections to the states, the southern states of Alabama, Louisiana, and Mississippi enacted measures that prohibited blacks from owning firearms without first gaining a license, a legal procedure not required of whites. For instance, an 1865 Louisiana statute declared that any black not in military service could not carry a firearm unless granted special permission by an employer and a law enforcement officer. Punishment for violating the statute included forfeiting the weapon and being fined $5. To the dismay of northern Republicans, southern legislation protected the right of former members of the Confederate forces to bear arms while at the same time denying that right to blacks, a group that had demonstrated its loyalty to the Union.

Contemporary Second Amendment supporters contend that when Congress began to debate the substance of the Fourteenth Amendment, southern efforts to disarm blacks played a clear role in their thinking. Specific congressmen are quoted as saying that they believed the new Amendment would apply the Bill of Rights to the states, including the Second Amendment with its guarantee of the right to keep and bear arms.

However, application to the states of the Second Amendment or any of the other provisions of the Bill of Rights did not occur for the remainder of the nineteenth century. The first of the few cases regarding the Fourteenth Amendment and the right to bear arms came before the Supreme Court in 1876. In *United States v. Cruikshank*, William Cruikshank was charged with denying the rights of two black men to peaceably assemble and bear arms. The Supreme Court held that the national government could not protect the rights of citizens against the actions of other private citizens. Because the First and Second Amendments were not applicable in this case, the plaintiffs were required to seek a remedy from state legislatures and state judicial systems.

Not until *McDonald v. Chicago* (2010) did the U.S. Supreme Court declare that the Second Amendment right to keep and bear arms, which the Court two years earlier ruled applies to individual persons, must be respected by state and local governments as well as the federal government. Justice Clarence Thomas, in his concurring opinion, referred to the history of the Fourteenth Amendment, arguing that one of the amendment's original objectives was to ensure that former slaves could be guaranteed the right to keep and bear arms for self-protection.

See also: African Americans and Guns; Fourteenth Amendment; Second Amendment; *United States v. Cruikshank* (1876).

Further Reading: Robert J. Cottrol and Raymond T. Diamond, "The Second Amendment: Toward an Afro-Americanist Reconsideration," in David B. Kopel, ed., *Guns: Who Should Have Them?* (Amherst, NY: Prometheus, 1995); Walter L. Fleming, ed., *Documentary History of Reconstruction: Political, Military, Social, Religious, Educational and Industrial, 1865 to the Present Time* (Gloucester, MA: P. Smith, 1960); *McDonald v. Chicago* (2010).

Black Panther Party

An organization of the late 1960s that gained fame and notoriety far beyond its numbers, the Black Panther Party gave new significance to the notion of a right to bear arms. Two young African

Americans, Bobby Seale and Huey Newton, officially created this self-defense group in Oakland, California, on October 15, 1966. Seale assumed the office of party chairman and Newton took the position of minister of defense. They had read Robert Williams's *Negroes with Guns*, and had resolved to abide by Mao Tse-tung's revolutionary principle that "Power also grows out of the barrel of a gun." Following the lead of another local organization, the Panthers planned to patrol the streets of Oakland, observing arrests and informing those arrested of their legal rights. They also decided to use the novel tactic of carrying firearms. In November 1966, the Panthers began to patrol the streets, harassing the police at opportune moments. Newton discovered a California statute that allowed the carrying of a loaded shotgun or rifle provided that it was not concealed. Newton and Seale subsequently acquired an M-1 rifle and a 9mm. pistol.

In January 1967, Newton, Seale, and fellow Panther Bobby Hutton, all of whom worked for antipoverty programs, used their paychecks to open the first Black Panther Party office in North Oakland. They soon acquired new recruits and new weapons. With money received from selling copies of *Quotations from Chairman Mao Tse-tung*, they purchased additional firearms. The ability to handle handguns and rifles became a prerequisite for membership, and the party leadership ultimately established a six-week training period for recruits.

The Black Panthers received widespread publicity for their new practice of carrying firearms. Their clothing, consisting of a blue shirt and black pants, black leather jacket and black beret, gave the Panthers the look of a militia unit and contributed to the attention they received in the media. However, they also gained the keen attention of law enforcement officers. In April 1967, when state legislator Donald Mulford proposed legislation restricting the carrying of loaded firearms in public places, the Panthers played the role of gun rights advocates. On May 2, a group of Panthers traveled to the state capital of Sacramento, armed with handguns and rifles and accompanied by reporters and cameramen. Those Panthers who were arrested for conspiracy to disrupt a legislative session pleaded guilty to committing a misdemeanor and were sentenced to six months in prison. In July, the state legislature enacted the provision prohibiting the carrying of a loaded firearm.

By early 1968, the influence of the Panthers appeared to be increasing, even though Newton had been convicted of voluntary manslaughter, the result of a gunfight with a police officer the previous October. The officer died in the shootout and Newton was wounded. Another Panther, Eldridge Cleaver, advocated preparation for impending revolutionary violence. In September 1968, he spoke before a group of lawyers in San Francisco, where he stated that the lawyers could help the movement by donating machine guns. Demonstrating the audacity so characteristic of the Black Panthers, Cleaver declared that the Panthers needed to buy guns to kill judges, police, and corporation lawyers.

The Black Panthers hit their peak in 1969, obtaining a nationwide membership of 1,500 to 2,000. As confrontations with the police continued, nearly 350 members were arrested on a variety of charges from murder to bank robbery. In 1970, the membership declined significantly. Increasing disagreements, particularly between Newton and Cleaver, contributed to the party's steady decline.

Following the demise of the Black Panthers in the early 1970s, the party leadership led less than successful lives. In 1989, Newton, who experienced drug problems, was shot and killed outside a crack house. That same year Seale, a recovering alcoholic, pleaded guilty to charges of passing bad checks. Cleaver, who fled the country to live in Cuba and Algeria, returned to the United States. In the late 1980s and early 1990s he also experienced drug problems. In summer 1990, he entered a drug rehabilitation center due to crack cocaine addiction, but was arrested again for cocaine possession in June 1992. He died in 1998.

The history of the Black Panthers demonstrates the complexity of the gun control issue. Ronald Reagan, while president of the United States in the 1980s, strongly opposed any gun control legislation (although after leaving the presidency, he announced his support for the Brady bill). However, while governor of California from 1967 to 1975, he signed the 1967 bill to limit the carrying of firearms, legislation prompted by the activities of a small group of African American revolutionaries in the Black Panther Party.

See also: African Americans and Guns; Brady Handgun Violence Prevention Act; Reagan, Ronald; State Laws, Appendix 2.

Further Reading: G. Louis Heath, *Off the Pigs! The History and Literature of the Black Panther Party* (Metuchen, NJ: Scarecrow Press, 1976); Hugh

Pearson, *The Shadow of the Panther: Huey Newton and the Price of Black Power in America* (Reading, MA: Addison-Wesley, 1994); Robert Franklin Williams, *Negroes with Guns* (Detroit, MI: Wayne State University Press, 1998 [1962]).

Black Talon Bullet

In the early 1990s, the Black Talon bullet came under severe criticism for its destructive capacity. Bills were introduced in Congress to restrict use of the bullet, including a measure supported by Senator Daniel Patrick Moynihan, Democrat of New York, that would have levied a 10,000 percent tax on the ammunition. Originally, the Black Talon was touted as the ideal ammunition to resolve a dangerous situation for law enforcement officers. At times, police cannot stop violent criminals even after shooting them several times. The Black Talon increased the likelihood that incapacitating damage had been done to anyone endangering the life of a police officer. However, Winchester-Olin, the manufacturer of the Black Talon, distributed the ammunition to the general public and by 1993 the bullet gained notoriety when it was used in several violent crimes, including the murder of a Washington, D.C., police officer. The Black Talon came to be known as the "cop-killer" bullet.

In 1987, Marty Fackler, a U.S. army researcher and veteran combat trauma surgeon, had recommended to the Federal Bureau of Investigation that the light and fast ammunition they were using did not penetrate deeply enough or produce sufficient tissue damage. He recommended a heavier cartridge with greater destructive capability. Tom Burczynski, who had been working with hollow-point bullets, developed a bullet with a cone-shaped post in the point, which he called the Hydra-Shok. Federal Cartridge purchased the license to manufacture the new ammunition and in 1989 won a contract with the Federal Bureau of Investigation (FBI) to supply agents with the new bullets. Fackler, not convinced that the Hydra-Shok was the best solution to the problem, tried to improve Winchester's soft copper-jacketed cartridge. Alan Corzine and David Schluckebier finally designed a new bullet, which Winchester christened the Black Talon. The bullet derives its name from the six sharp petals, or talons, that are produced on impact, and from the black oxide coating, included both for cosmetic reasons and to reduce bore friction. The Black Talon retains the soft copper jacket which, after entering the body, peels back to expose the six sharp points. After traveling four inches into the body, the Black Talon expands to nearly three times its original diameter. The devastation produced by the bullet increases as it rotates within the body. Fackler considered it to be the greatest advance in handgun ammunition since the original development of the hollow-point bullet, which is composed of a lead slug with an indentation at the tip to allow for expansion upon impact.

Winchester aggressively marketed the new bullet, introducing it at a gun show in the New Orleans Superdome in January 1992. The company gave demonstrations for law enforcement agencies, and police forces in Baltimore, Dallas, and New York City switched to the new ammunition. The bullets were packaged in black boxes on which the words "deep penetrator" were printed in red. The company provided gun store displays, showing spent bullets with the six distinguishing tines. Hunting magazines praised the new bullet, calling it a "top-flight big-game bullet." David B. Petzal, reviewing ammunition in *Field and Stream*, commented that the Black Talon and bullets like it "penetrate deeply, destroy major organs, break major bones, and exit the far side, leaving a blood trail."

In July 1993, a man used Black Talons to kill eight people in a San Francisco law office before shooting himself. Health care professionals, who witnessed the effects the ammunition had on victims, spoke out against its sale. Some physicians expressed fear of being cut by the sharp barbs as they operated on gun shot wounds. In November 1993, after two bills had been introduced in Congress to ban the Black Talon, Winchester announced it would limit sales to law enforcement agencies On December 7, six people were killed on a Long Island Railroad car by an individual wielding a semi-automatic weapon loaded with Black Talon bullets. Despite the voluntary ban on sales to the general public, the Black Talon remained legal and variations of the bullet without its distinctive characteristics continued to be widely available.

In 2007 Winchester introduced the Ranger SXT, which is the identical bullet but without the Black Talon's special (Lubalox) coating. Remington and other manufacturers offer ammunition with characteristics similar to the original Black Talon.

See also: Fatalities; Gun Shows.

Further Reading: Jonathan Alter, "Curb Violence by Targeting Bullets," *Washington Monthly* 26 (January/February 1994), 45–46; Application Consulting Group, "Black Talon Ammunition—Truth and Myth," www. acg1.net/black_talon.htm (accessed October 18, 2010); Julie Petersen, "This Bullet Kills You Better," *Mother Jones* 18 (September/October 1993), 15; David E. Petzel, "Bullet-In," *Field and Stream* 97 (February 1993), 65–67; Peter Richmond, "The Black Talon," *Gentlemen's Quarterly* 64 (July 1994), 100–05; Martin D. Topper, "The Truth About Hollow Points," *Handguns* 12 (February 1998), 36–38, 40–41, 74–75; Suzanne Wiley, "Black Talon and Today's Best Self-Defense Ammo," *Ammunition* (October 12, 2014), www.blog.cheaperthandirt.com/black-talon-todays-self-defense-ammo.

Bliss v. Commonwealth (1822)

In 1822, a Kentucky state court decision, *Bliss v. Commonwealth* (12 Ky. [2 Litt.] 90, 1822), affirmed the individual citizen's right to keep and bear arms as protected in the Kentucky state constitution. The court regarded such a right in the strongest terms, declaring it absolute and immune from any attempt by the legislature or any other government office either to ban or to regulate the right to bear arms.

Found in possession of a sword in a cane, Bliss was charged under state law with carrying a concealed weapon. The jury in the court of original jurisdiction found him guilty and assessed a fine of $100. Bliss appealed the decision, claiming that the statute under which he was convicted violated article 10, section 23 of the state constitution. The section stated "that the right of the citizens to bear arms in defence [sic] of themselves and the state, shall not be questioned." In contrast, the statute under which Bliss was convicted stated that any person in the commonwealth of Kentucky who wears a pocket pistol, dirk (dagger), large knife, or sword in a cane, "unless when traveling on a journey," shall be subject to a fine of $100 or more.

The court argued that it had the right to declare acts of the legislature contrary to the state constitution. Reminiscent of the U.S. Supreme Court in the 1803 case *Marbury v. Madison*, the state court declared that "it is emphatically the duty of the court to decide what the law is." The court

has the responsibility to compare the law with the constitution, and when the two conflict, decide in favor of the constitution. Although recognizing that deciding such conflicts was a delicate matter, the court affirmed the judicial branch's responsibility to decide in favor of the constitution over any ordinary act of the legislature.

The court referred to a section in article 10 of the Kentucky state constitution, which declared that everything in the article shall forever remain inviolate from government power, and that laws contrary to its provisions shall be void. Foreshadowing justifications used in subsequent cases for limiting the right to bear arms, the state attorney in his argument before the court distinguished between prohibiting the exercise of a right, and simply regulating the way in which the right may be exercised. However, the court responded that any restraints on the full exercise of the right, whether a complete prohibition, or any measure short of complete restriction, violated the provisions of the constitution.

Using an absolutist interpretation of the right to bear arms, the court ruled that the act under which Bliss was convicted failed to agree with the state constitution and thus was void. The absolute right existed at the time the constitution was adopted, limited only by the individual decisions of citizens to bear or not to bear arms. Therefore, restricting that liberty inevitably meant violating the right guaranteed in the constitution. The legislature did not have the authority to prohibit the wearing of weapons that were lawful to wear when the constitution was adopted. The court also ruled that no valid distinction could be made between concealed weapons and weapons carried openly—if one practice was protected under the constitution, so was the other.

See also: State Laws, Appendix 2.

Further Reading: *Bliss v. Commonwealth*, 12 Ky. [2 Litt.] 90 (1822); Earl R. Kruschke, *The Right to Keep and Bear Arms* (Springfield, IL: Charles C. Thomas, 1985).

Bloomberg, Michael R. (1942–)

Considered a major opponent of the National Rifle Association (NRA) and other pro-gun rights organizations, Michael Bloomberg has dedicated significant financial resources in support of the gun

New York City Mayor Michael Bloomberg speaks on gun laws January 24, 2011 at City Hall in New York City. Bloomberg has called for existing gun laws on the books to be enforced more rigorously. *Photo by Chris Hondros/Getty Images*

control cause. In 2014 Bloomberg, whose net worth is estimated at $45 billion, pledged to contribute $50 million to back organizations supporting various gun control and gun safety issues.

Bloomberg served three terms as mayor of New York City, from January 1, 2002, to December 31, 2013. Originally a Democrat, he switched his affiliation to the Republican Party before running for mayor. In 2007, Bloomberg became and Independent, a political migration that highlights his political individualism. Bloomberg tends to take more conservative positions on economic and foreign policy issues but more liberal stances on social issues such as abortion rights, same-gender marriage, and stricter gun control policies. He spoke at the 2016 Democratic National Convention, but his speech reflected this divide in his political thinking between liberal and conservative views.

In 2006, Bloomberg founded, along with Mayor Thomas Menino of Boston, Mayors Against Illegal Guns. After stepping down as New York mayor, he merged Mayors Against Illegal Guns and Moms Demand Action for Gun Sense in America to form Everytown for Gun Safety. In June 2016, Everytown president John Feinblatt, who was Mayor Bloomberg's chief policy adviser, announced that the organization supported Hilary Clinton for the presidency, mentioning Clinton's support for gun control measures and her opposition to the gun lobby. Earlier in the year, Bloomberg reportedly had contemplated a run for the presidency as an independent.

In restructuring Mayors Against Illegal Guns, Bloomberg established a new bipartisan advisory board, which included Tom Ridge, former Republican governor of Pennsylvania and Homeland Security secretary under President George W. Bush; investor Warren Buffett; and Michael G. Mullen, former chairman of the Joint Chiefs of Staff under presidents Bush and Barack Obama. A key goal of Everytown is to elect to national, state, and local offices candidates who will support additional firearm measures. Upon its founding, the organization was expected to follow an NRA policy by submitting a questionnaire to political candidates to determine their positions on firearm-related issues.

In 2013, following the defeat of congressional gun control legislation proposed after the Sandy Hook Elementary School shooting in Newtown, Connecticut, Bloomberg sent a letter to many large contributors to Democratic candidates, asking them not to donate to four Democratic senators who failed to support legislation to strengthen background checks on gun purchasers. Democratic senators criticized Bloomberg's action, concluding that such a strategy could be counter-productive by further alienating such senators from the policy objectives of gun safety proponents, and could lead to the election of candidates who are even less sympathetic to gun control measures. They suggested a more positive strategy that would encourage constituents to persuade their senators to support background checks.

See also: Everytown for Gun Safety

Further Reading: Michael R. Bloomberg, *Bloomberg on Bloomberg* (New York: Wiley, 2001); Michael Confessore and Jeremy W. Peters, "Donors Asked to Shut Wallets Over Gun Votes," *New York Times* (June 12, 2013): A1; Jeremy W. Peters, "For Next Step, Bloomberg Set His Sights on the N.R.A.," *New York Times* (April 16, 2014): A12; Joyce Purnick, *Mike Bloomberg: Money, Power, Politics* (New York: Public Affairs, 2010).

Bowling for Columbine

Michael Moore's 2002 documentary *Bowling for Columbine* was inspired by the 1999 Columbine high school shooting in Littleton, Colorado, in which, to the horror of the local community and the nation, two students carrying legally obtained semiautomatic weapons and sawed-off shotguns killed 12 other students and one teacher before killing themselves. Video tapes from the school's surveillance cameras show panicked students fleeing the two gunmen. The film's title refers in part to the bowling class the two students are said to have attended the morning of the shooting. In typical style, Moore explores the possible reasons why firearm-related deaths in the United States far outpace the rate of such deaths in other countries. The film is as much a witty and impassioned indictment of those who Moore considers responsible for the high rate of firearm violence in the United States compared to other western democracies as it is a disinterested analysis of the

issue. However, gun rights supporters in many cases present their views with minimal comment from Moore, perhaps with the assumption on Moore's part that their convictions in fact serve as supporting evidence for his position on gun violence. For instance, Moore interviews James Nichols, brother of Terry Nichols, who received a life sentence for conspiring with Timothy McVeigh to bomb the Alfred P. Murrah Federal Building in Oklahoma City in April 1995. Out of camera range, James shows to Moore the .44-magnum pistol he keeps in his bedroom.

Claiming to be a lifelong member of the National Rifle Association (NRA) and the winner of an NRA marksman award as a teenager (a claim that likely provides entrance to people that otherwise would not have agreed to speak with him, including then-NRA president Charlton Heston), Moore critiques American society for the high level of firearm ownership and firearm deaths. Ostensibly searching for an explanation for the Littleton shooting as well as more generally for the country's disproportionately high level of firearm violence, Moore asks various people to offer reasons for the violence. To the suggestion that the United States has a unique history of violent behavior, Moore responds that other countries that experienced an equally savage past presently have far lower levels of gun violence. Some place the blame on violent video games, but people in other nations with much less firearm-related violence also enjoy such games.

Moore identifies the U.S. government and corporations as key influences on U.S. attitudes and actions regarding firearms. He speaks with an official at Lockheed Martin, a major Defense Department contractor with production facilities in Colorado, and takes aim at K-Mart because the two Littleton High School shooters purchased their ammunition from one of the company's stores. When Moore takes two of the students who were wounded at Columbine to K-Mart headquarters in Troy, Michigan, to confront the company's policy of selling handgun ammunition, a company representative ultimately announces that within 90 days, K-Mart stores no longer will sell handgun ammunition.

Moore travels to Canada, a country that, according to his portrayal, is far more peaceful than the United States. He compares the level of gun violence in Detroit, Michigan, with that of Windsor, Ontario, just across the Canadian border from Detroit. People he interviews in Canada tell him that they do not settle disputes with violence, and it never occurs to them to lock their doors, which is perhaps an indication of less fear of crime than in the United States. Moore's perhaps exaggerated view of Canadian peacefulness nonetheless provides a stark comparison of two countries with significant differences in the levels of gun violence.

All of the interviews, documentary footage, and a brief cartoon relating the violent history of the nation, culminates in an interview with Charlton Heston (National Rifle Association president from 1998 to 2003) at Heston's home. After the two discuss the possible causes of the high level of firearms violence in the United States, Moore suggests that Heston apologize for holding an NRA rally in Flint, Michigan, soon after a 6-year-old girl was shot and killed by a classmate who had brought a gun to school. As Heston walks away, Moore asks him to look at a photograph of the young girl he is holding. Undoubtedly such emotionally charged scenes speak to those already convinced that firearms and related violence are a serious problem for the country. However, those committed to gun rights find the film unfair to honest citizens who possess firearms. Moore's efforts have not led to successful campaigns to reduced firearm-related violence. If anything, gun rights supporters have won further legislative victories, especially at the state level.

See also: Littleton, Colorado, Columbine School Shooting; Northern Illinois University Shooting; Stockton, California, Shooting; Texas Tower Shooting.

Further Reading (Viewing): Roger Moore, *Bowing for Columbine.*

Boxer, Barbara (1940–)

Barbara Boxer, a Democratic senator from California, outspokenly advocates additional gun control measures. She has initiated legislation to ban domestic manufacture and sales of junk guns, or Saturday night specials, and has authored legislation that would mandate locks for handguns. Her campaign for gun regulation focuses on the danger that firearms present to children and adolescents. In 1998, the final year of her first term in the Senate, Boxer stepped up efforts in support of firearms regulation.

Born in Brooklyn, New York, Boxer earned a B.A. in economics from Brooklyn College in 1962. She became a stockbroker and journalist before entering politics. After serving on the Marin County, California, Board of Supervisors from 1977 to 1983, where she became the first woman board president, Boxer was elected to the U.S. House of Representatives. In 1992, she was elected to the U.S. Senate, and won reelection in 1998 and 2004. In the 111th Congress (2009–2010), Boxer's committee assignments included Environment and Public Works, which she chaired; Commerce, Science, and Transportation; Foreign Relations; and the Select Committee on Ethics, which she also chaired. In addition to gun control, she supported legislation dealing with such issues as the pensions of working people, lower trade barriers, public education, abortion rights, environmental protection, and health care. While Boxer backed legislation to protect the property rights of California computer and entertainment companies, she has challenged the legitimacy of California companies that produce inexpensive handguns.

In January 1997, along with three other senators, Boxer reintroduced a bill, called the American Handgun Standards Act, which would apply production norms to American-manufactured handguns that the Gun Control Act

Senator Barbara Boxer (D-CA) is an outspoken advocate of gun control. *www.wikipedia.org*

of 1968 already imposed on imported weapons. The legislation would have subjected handguns to product safety standards from which they are presently exempt. Boxer argued that the less expensive handguns are at least three times more likely than other handguns to be used in the commission of a crime. Although some gun rights advocates profess that so-called junk guns, or Saturday night specials, can be reliable defense weapons, especially for the less well-to-do, Boxer noted that they are subject to unpredictable firing and inaccuracy, making them poor prospects either for hunting or for self-protection.

When the California legislature began considering a prohibition on junk guns, Boxer urged passage of the measure. Because nearly 40 California municipalities had already approved bans on the sale of junk guns, the chances of passage were considered good. In June 1997, the senator commended the legislature for passing the measure, and publicly encouraged Republican Governor Pete Wilson to sign the bill. When Wilson vetoed the legislation, claiming that junk guns presented no extraordinary danger, Boxer offered to meet with him to present information about their unreliability. Despite Boxer's characteristically aggressive strategy, the governor's veto remained unchanged.

In October 1997, after President Bill Clinton reached an agreement with eight handgun manufacturers to include safety locks with newly manufactured handguns, Boxer sent letters to California manufacturers of inexpensive handguns, urging them to join in the agreement. She recommended that manufacturers select high-quality locks that cannot be opened by a young child, and encouraged companies to make improvements in the guns themselves to meet quality and safety standards imposed on imported handguns. Although recommending voluntary compliance, Boxer also introduced legislation mandating that gun locks be included with the sale of all new handguns. In 1998, Boxer urged newly elected National Rifle Association (NRA) president Charlton Heston to support safety locks. In more recent years, Boxer has opposed legislation to prohibit lawsuits against firearm manufacturers for gun violence committed with weapons they produced, and has supported criminal background checks at gun shows.

In January 2015, Boxer announced that she would not seek re-election to the U.S. Senate in 2016, but stated that she would continue to actively pursue the issues of greatest concern to her through her political action committee. Following several mass shootings, in June 2016 Boxer expressed a continuing obje3ctive of instituting reforms in firearm policy. She supported legislation to prevent individuals on the terrorist (no-fly) list from purchasing a firearm, to prohibit private ownership of military-style weapons, to expand background checks to all gun sales, and to allow individuals to take legal action to prevent family members who they consider are threats to themselves or others from purchasing or possessing a firearm.

See also: Clinton, William Jefferson (Bill); Feinstein, Dianne; Gun Control Act of 1968; Heston, Charlton; National Rifle Association; Saturday Night Special.

Further Reading: Philip D. Duncan and Christine C. Lawrence, *Politics in America, 1998: The 105th Congress* (Washington, DC: CQ Press, 1997); Senator Barbara Boxer Web site, http://boxer.senate.gov; "On the Issues: Barbara Boxer on Gun Control," www.ontheissues.org/domestic/Barbara_Boxer_Gun_Control.htm (accessed September 9, 2010); www.boxer.senate.gov (accessed July 12, 2016).

Brady Campaign to Prevent Gun Violence

Before 2001, the Brady Campaign to Prevent Gun Violence was called Handgun Control, Inc. (HCI). Mark Borinsky, founder of HCI, is a prime example of an interest group entrepreneur—a person who, through individual efforts, creates an organization to further a cause. Borinsky's ordeal of being robbed at gunpoint when he was a student in Chicago inspired him to do something about the gun problem. Some individuals respond to such a situation by buying their own gun for self-protection, but Borinsky took another path. He decided to form an organization dedicated to controlling handgun ownership. After moving to Washington, D.C., in 1974, he ran a newspaper ad inviting like-minded individuals to join him in the fight against handguns. Edward Welles, a retired Central Intelligence Agency (CIA) employee, responded to the call. They opened an office for the newly formed organization, the National Council to Control Handguns (NCCH), the precursor of HCI. Pete Shields, a marketing manager whose 23-year-old son had been murdered with a handgun, joined the organization in 1975. His organizational skills and political abilities opened doors in Washington for the fledgling organization. Subsequently, he became chairman of HCI.

At about the same time Borinsky was establishing HCI, the Board of Church and Society of the Methodist Church founded the National Coalition to Ban Handguns (NCBH), an organization that HCI joined. Originally HCI supported the NCBH's mission to ban the sale of all handgun ammunition. However, public opinion survey results convinced the HCI leadership that while Americans willingly accepted the prospect of licensing and registering handguns and the imposition of waiting periods for their purchase, they tended to reject a total ban. The organization left the alliance with the NCBH and changed its goal to creating controls on the sale of handguns, while accepting them as appropriate possessions if acquired for legitimate purposes. No longer in association with HCI, the NCBH continued to pursue the more ambitious goal of banning handguns.

In its effort to become an effective lobbying instrument for the gun control movement, HCI received assistance from the *pro bono publico* work of two Washington law firms that supported the organization's mission. The firms helped HCI become legally established and develop into an effective legislative lobbying organization. HCI succeeded in enlisting the assistance of sports and entertainment personalities such as Steve Allen, Leonard Bernstein, Ann Landers, and Neil Simon.

In 1976, after establishing a friendly relationship with members of the House Judiciary Committee, HCI appeared on the way to attaining a ban on the manufacture of Saturday night specials. However, when the National Rifle Association (NRA) activated its membership to contact their representatives and senators in Congress, four members of the Judiciary Committee withdrew their support for such a ban. Following the 1981 assassination attempt on President Ronald Reagan that left his press secretary, James Brady, seriously wounded, HCI found a potent ally in Brady's wife, Sarah, who joined the organization in 1985 and ultimately became its chairperson. After an assailant wielding a cheap handgun killed famed singer John Lennon on the streets of New York in 1980, HCI's membership increased 16-fold. In 1983, the organization created an education outreach organization, the Center to Prevent Handgun Violence, which became the Brady Center

to Prevent Handgun Violence in 2001. In 1989, it established the Legal Action Project to push its agenda in the courts.

Gruesome events continued to improve the prospect for HCI's gun control objectives. The January 1989 murder of school children in Stockton, California, by a gunman using an AK-47 rifle spurred a call to ban assault weapons. HCI achieved a major victory when the 1994 Violent Crime Control and Law Enforcement Act included a ban on 19 types of assault weapons. The Brady Handgun Violence Prevention Act, enacted in 1993, went into effect the same year, establishing a five-day waiting period so that a background check could be conducted by local law enforcement officers on those wishing to purchase a handgun. HCI, working with legislative allies, pushed for further measures to curb handgun violence that involved added regulations on gun owners and manufacturers and the taxation of guns and ammunition. However, in the November 1994 election many gun control supporters in Congress were defeated and the mood on Capitol Hill became far less sympathetic to HCI goals.

HCI/Brady Campaign continues to lobby for limitations on gun trafficking and child access to handguns, federal firearms licensing reform, a ban on assault weapons, and maintenance of existing gun laws against attacks from pro-gun groups. At the state level, HCI acts to preserve existing laws and to enact further legislation intended to prevent gun violence. It files *amicus curiae* briefs when gun laws are challenged in the courts, as it did in the cases of *District of Columbia v. Heller* (2008) and *McDonald v. Chicago* (2010). In both instances, however, the Brady Campaign found itself on the losing side, as the Supreme Court majority accepted the individual rights view of the Second Amendment in 2008, and then applied it to the states in 2010. These losses in the courts reflected the larger trend during the first decade of the twenty-first century, when gun rights organizations logged major successes at both the national and state levels.

As part of its recruitment efforts, HCI/ Brady reaches out to those who have experienced gun violence. In 2000, the Brady Campaign lent support to the Million Mom March (MMM), a grassroots organization that organized a massive rally in Washington, D.C. in support of stronger gun laws that drew over 600,000 people. The MMM was not able to maintain its momentum, however, and the following year the MMM organization was rolled into the Brady Campaign, which has continued its grassroots activities in most states. The Brady Campaign derives its greatest support from larger urban areas, with regional offices in Chicago, Los Angeles, San Diego, and San Francisco.

The Brady Campaign continues its lobbying efforts in Congress and supports candidates who approve of their gun control agenda. The Brady Political Action Committee, the political arm of the organization, raises funds to be contributed to the campaigns of candidates who have demonstrated support for gun control. In recent years, the organization has argued successfully in court on behalf of existing gun laws, against gun carrying on college campuses, and pushed for closing the "gun show loophole," which allows handgun purchases from unlicensed, private dealers to occur without background checks at gun shows. Noting that only 60 percent of gun sales are subject to a background check, the Campaign has lobbied for expanding criminal background checks to all firearms sales and transfers. Also, the organization works to reform gun industry practices by challenging the ways in which firearms are marketed. The Campaign hopes to change attitudes toward guns in order their presence in the home and thus further assure child safety.

Dan Gross joined the Brady Campaign in 2012 and serves as the organization's president. Gross co-founded the Center to Prevent Youth Violence (formerly PAX) following the Empire State Building shooting in 1997, during which his brother was wounded.

See also: AK-47; Assault Weapons Ban; Brady, James; Brady Handgun Violence Prevention Act; Brady, Sarah; *District of Columbia v. Heller* (2008); *McDonald v. Chicago* (2010); Million Mom March; National Rifle Association; Reagan, Ronald; Saturday Night Special; Stockton, California, Shooting; Trigger Locks; Washington, D.C.

Further Reading: Brady Campaign, www. bradycampaign.org; Gregg Lee Carter, *The Gun Control Movement* (New York: Twayne, 1997); Kristin A. Goss, *Disarmed: The Missing Movement for Gun Control in America* (Princeton: Princeton University Press, 2006); Robert J. Spitzer, *The Politics of Gun Control*, 6th ed. (Boulder, CO: Paradigm, 2015).

Brady Handgun Violence Prevention Act

The Brady Handgun Violence Prevention Act (Pub. Law 103-159), which became law in November 1993 and went into effect in February 1994, imposed a five-day waiting period so that background checks could be run on those wishing to purchase a handgun. It was the first significant piece of federal gun control legislation to be enacted since 1968. The legislation was named after James S. Brady, press secretary to President Ronald Reagan, who was severely wounded during an assassination attempt on the president in 1981. After the attempt, Brady and his wife Sarah became avid gun control advocates and spearheaded much of the effort for passage of the Brady bill.

The introduction of the bill into Congress in 1987 began a battle between pro- and anti-gun control forces that lasted nearly seven years. Although the National Rifle Association (NRA) had supported a waiting period in the 1970s, the organization became increasingly militant and worked hard to prevent adoption of the measure. The NRA questioned the effectiveness of such waiting periods, arguing that most criminals acquire guns from illicit sources, not from reputable dealers. Therefore, the law supposedly would have little effect on criminals but would unduly inconvenience law-abiding citizens.

The long battle and strong opposition notwithstanding, advocates of the measure were spurred on by an awareness of the huge number of handguns already available in the United States and the support most Americans were expressing for stricter control of handguns. Proponents noted that similar requirements in some states had prevented sales to criminals and had led to some arrests. They argued that the law could also provide for a cooling-off period that would deter crimes of passion committed by such people as angry employees and jealous spouses looking for immediate revenge. The intense efforts to have the bill enacted symbolized the strong feelings on both sides of the issue and became a test of antagonistic political forces. Passage finally came when the Republican leadership (the Republicans then being the minority party in Congress), recognizing strong public support, ended attempts to obstruct a vote on the measure.

The provisions of the Brady law are generally considered moderate. The legislation does not ban any firearms, such as inexpensive handguns, called Saturday night specials, or assault weapons, but imposes a waiting period of five business days before an individual may take possession of a purchased handgun. The waiting period was intended as a temporary measure, remaining in effect for five years to allow the federal government time to institute a national computerized system for instantly checking the backgrounds of handgun purchasers. States that had waiting periods of at least five days to conduct background checks were not subject to the new law. The legislation required gun dealers in states subject to the law to provide local chief law enforcement officers with the names of people purchasing handguns and directed officials to conduct background checks. In this way, felons and the mentally unstable could be prevented from legally purchasing handguns.

Justice Department estimates in 1997 indicated that since the Brady bill became law, at least 250,000 sales of handguns had been prevented. More than 70 percent of these cases involved people convicted or indicted on felony charges. The Justice Department figures also revealed that over 70 federal prosecutions and 52 convictions had occurred since the law's passage. However, pro-gun groups were unimpressed with the figures, noting that the number of aborted sales and convictions were small compared to the total number of checks. However, in 2010, the Brady Campaign presented data from the U.S. Department of Justice that 1.8 million firearm sales to criminals and other groups prohibited from purchasing a gun had been prevented.

A legal challenge led to a 1997 Supreme Court decision invalidating a key portion of the Brady law requiring local chief law enforcement officers to run background checks on handgun buyers. However, other provisions of the law were left intact and the National Instant Criminal Background Check System (NICS) became operational in November 1998, obviating the need for assistance from local law enforcement. In addition, by 1998, 27 states had enacted their own laws requiring a background check.

In 2007 Congress passed the NICS Improvement Amendments Act, which gained the support of the NRA and the Brady Campaign, although other organizations, both pro-gun rights and pro-gun control, opposed the legislation. The purpose of the Act is to enhance the efficiency of reporting ineligible persons to the background check system, especially of those due to mental illness are liable to injure themselves or others.

See also: Background Checks; Brady, James; Brady, Sarah; National Instant Check System; National Rifle Association; *Printz v. United States* (1997); Reagan, Ronald; Saturday Night Special.

Further Reading: Brady Campaign, "Brady Background Checks: 15 Years of Saving Lives," www.bradycampaign.org/studies/views/47; Gregg Lee Carter, *The Gun Control Movement* (New York: Twayne, 1997); Robert J. Spitzer, *The Politics of Gun Control*, 6th ed. (Boulder, CO: Paradism, 2015).

Brady, James (1940–2014)

Since the mid-1980s, James Brady, along with his wife Sarah, has played an important role in furthering gun control policies. Brady, who was shot and seriously wounded during the March 30, 1981, attempt to assassinate President Ronald Reagan, became a strong advocate for more stringent federal and state gun laws. However, he did not join the gun control effort as early as his wife. Officially still on the White House staff until the end of the Reagan administration in 1989, he did not wish to publicly oppose the administration's policy positions. Although confined to a wheelchair and experiencing speech difficulties, Brady traveled with his wife to present what they jovially called a "dog-and-pony show," advocating greater control of firearms, particularly handguns.

Brady entered politics as a campaign manager and in 1980 worked for John Connally in the former Texas governor's bid for the presidency. When that effort failed, Brady joined Ronald Reagan's campaign. Following the Reagan victory, Brady was named presidential press secretary. He was at Reagan's side when an assassin's bullet hit him in the head, reportedly leaving him with only 80 percent of his brain. Although doctors initially did not expect Brady to live, he walked out of the hospital, with great difficulty, eight months later. He will remain largely paralyzed and in pain for the rest of his life. He experienced a slow and onerous recovery. At first Brady had difficulty controlling his emotions, laughing or crying unexpectedly, a condition common to those suffering head injuries. Although he recovered some use of his left side, his left arm remained paralyzed. He could walk, at least a few steps, with the aid of a cane. Just getting in and out of automobiles presented a major challenge. Brady, who continued to have speech and memory problems, was a living example of the damage a handgun can inflict.

After January 1989, Brady decided to join his wife in support of Handgun Control, Inc. (HCI). In November 1989, Brady testified before the Senate Judiciary Committee in favor of proposed legislation that would ultimately be called the Brady bill. Presenting himself as an example of what true inconvenience meant, he asked the committee members if they would continue to satisfy the wishes of special interests who might be inconvenienced by new legislation. Brady said that although he had watched from his wheelchair as the gun lobby opposed "one sane handgun control bill after another," he was no longer going to watch passively. He called on Congress to pass the bill that would mandate a waiting period before purchasing a handgun. Brady noted that members of Congress had "closed their eyes to tragedies like mine" and cited polls indicating that over 90 percent of Americans supported the bill. Although the legislation did not pass that year, Brady continued his active support until final passage in 1993.

Brady described the National Rifle Association as "the evil empire." He had become, in his own words, the gun lobby's "worst nightmare," a living example of the dangers of firearms. Since passage of the bill, Brady has continued to advocate further measures to limit handgun violence, such as instituting education programs, limiting traffic in private transfers of handguns, and defending already existing gun laws. In 2000, the Board of Trustees of Handgun Control and the Center to Prevent Handgun Violence honored James Brady and his wife Sarah by renaming the organizations the Brady Campaign to Prevent Gun Violence and the Brady Center to Prevent Gun Violence. Brady continues to serve as an honorary member of the board of trustees of the Brady Center.

When Brady died in 2014, the medical examiner for Northern Virginia ruled his death a homicide resulting from the gunshot wound he suffered in 1981. The District of Columbia police department was informed of the ruling.

See also: Brady Handgun Violence Prevention Act; Brady, Sarah; Handgun Control, Inc.; National Rifle Association; Reagan, Ronald.

Further Reading: Brady Campaign, "James S. Brady Biography," http://bradycampaign.org/about/bio/jim; Wayne King, "Target: The Gun Lobby," *New York Times Biographical Service* (December 1990), 1156–61; Philip Shenon, "Wife of Aide Cut Down with Reagan Scoring Hits Against the Gun Lobby," *New York Times Biographical Service* (May 1990), 500–01.

Brady, Sarah (1942–2015)

In the 1980s and 1990s, Sarah Brady perhaps contributed more than anyone else to the push toward more stringent gun control legislation. Wife of James Brady, press secretary to President Ronald Reagan who was shot during an attempt on the president's life in 1981, became an ideal spokesperson for the gun control movement. Handgun Control Inc. (HCI) membership doubled after she became the organization's chairperson, a position for which her previous political experience had provided excellent training. Her greatest triumph came with passage of the Brady Handgun Violence Prevention Act in 1994, which required a five-day waiting period and a background check before a potential buyer could take possession of a firearm. She is also credited with assisting in the passage of several state gun control measures.

The daughter of an agent for the Federal Bureau of Investigation (FBI), Sarah Kemp Brady graduated from the College of William and Mary in 1964. She became an assistant to the campaign director for the National Republican Congressional Committee in 1968. From 1970 to 1974, Brady served as administrative aide to Republican Representatives Mike McKevitt of Colorado and Joseph J. Maraziti of New Jersey. She met her future husband, James Brady, at a Republican campaign cocktail party. After the birth of her son Scott, Sarah Brady devoted her time to married life.

When her husband was shot and seriously wounded during the Reagan assassination attempt on March 30, 1981, Sarah Brady began a long and arduous period assisting her husband's partial recovery. She devoted herself to volunteer work with such organizations as the March of Dimes and the Foundation for Critical Care Medicine. An incident that occurred in 1984 while she and her son were visiting James Brady's relatives in Illinois motivated her to become involved in the gun control movement. While driving in a friend's truck, Scott, then five years old, discovered what he thought was a toy pistol under the seat and pointed it at his mother. She became angered by what she perceived to be the laxness of gun laws. Passage of the Firearms Owners Protection Act of 1986, backed by the National Rifle Association (NRA) and other gun rights organizations, convinced Brady of the need to work for maintaining existing laws and initiating stronger controls on gun ownership. When she contacted HCI, the organization's president, Charles J. Orasin put her to work writing letters to senators about repealing the Protection Act. She also spoke to senators personally and wrote to national newspapers about the issue.

As an advocate for the gun control cause, Brady had instant credibility because she spoke from personal experience. Gun rights advocates soon realized they had a formidable opponent. She was constantly on the move, speaking in favor of stricter gun laws, especially the Brady bill, which called for criminal background checks to be conducted on firearm purchasers. She challenged members of Congress to be courageous and defy the NRA by supporting gun control legislation. She expressed her lack of respect for members of Congress, calling them "weak-kneed" and "gutless" for voting with the NRA. Brady called the NRA a "horrible organization," the leaders of which "lie a lot."

During the 1988 presidential campaign, Brady warned aides to Republican candidate George H. W. Bush that she would denounce Bush if he opposed the Brady bill and the waiting period it mandated. Although the bill failed to pass that year, Bush maintained his silence. Gun rights advocates found it difficult to respond publicly to Brady, apparently realizing the sympathy the public had for her and her husband. Magazines with a large proportion of women readers ran articles about the ordeal Brady and her husband endured and reported on her efforts in support of gun control. Brady continued to chair of the Brady Campaign and the Brady Center to Prevent Gun Violence, and served on the organization's board of trustees. That organization's ability to challenge the NRA at the state and national levels was due in large part to the efforts of Sarah Brady, whose name became closely associated with gun control efforts. In 2001 Sarah, once a heavy smoker, announced that she was being treated for lung cancer. She remained chairwoman of the Brady Campaign until her death in 2015, a year after James Brady's death.

See also: Brady Handgun Violence Prevention Act; Brady, James; Bush, George H. W.; Firearms Owners Protection Act; Handgun Control, Inc.; National Rifle Association; Reagan, Ronald; Women and Guns.

Further Reading: Brady Campaign, "Sarah Brady Biography," www.bradycampaign.org/about/bio/sarah; Mary Huzinec, "Brady's Battle," *Ladies Home Journal* 108 (March 1991), 61–62; Wayne King, "Target: The Gun Lobby," *New York Times Biographical Service* (December 1990), 1156–61; Rita Rooney, "Sarah Brady's Fighting Spirit," *McCalls* 114 (November 1986), 150, 153; Philip Shenon, "Wife of Aide Cut Down with Reagan Scoring Hits Against the Gun Lobby," *New York Times Biographical Service* (May 1990), 500–01.

Britain

See UNITED KINGDOM

British American Security Information Council (BASIC)

In 1987, Daniel Plesch founded the British American Security Information Council (BASIC), a nongovernmental organization based in Washington, D.C., and London that conducts research on international security issues, including nuclear disarmament and nonproliferation, and regulation of the legal and illegal distribution of small arms to conflict areas around the world. BASIC claims that legally manufactured and distributed weapons contribute as much to conflict and crime as do weapons that are transferred illegally. BASIC has received funding from various private sources, including the Ford Foundation and Rockefeller Family Associates. The organization claims that light weapons have caused approximately 90 percent of war casualties since 1945. Through its efforts, the Council hopes to increase international security and decrease the probability of armed conflict.

BASIC established the Project on Light Weapons in an attempt to create more effective procedures to control international weapons transfers. The organization provides information to governmental and nongovernmental organizations about weapons sales and disseminates proposals for more effective control. BASIC has explored the relationship between ammunition and armed conflict and researchers associated with the organization have investigated such topics as ammunition production, trade routes for small arms, and the adverse effects of ammunition availability on national and regional stability and security. The organization has explored strategies for controlling the illicit as well as the legal ammunition market that focus on both governmental and private trade. Policies that BASIC recommends include destroying collected weapons, establishing codes of conduct for weapons manufacturers, initiating more stringent domestic gun control, marking and registering firearms, and improving international cooperation among law enforcement agencies.

The Council has published several reports dealing with small arms, including a directory of individuals and organizations involved in limiting such weapons and an overview of the illicit light weapons trade and investigations of light weapons manufacturing in particular countries. The Council warns against focusing too intently on the illicit firearms market while ignoring the spread of small arms through legal transfers and the so-called "gray" market involving sales of guns to legally qualified purchasers, which are ultimately transferred to people involved in criminal activities. Another BASIC report offers information on the various legislative initiatives countries have taken to deal with the light weapons trade.

The Council informs individual and organizational members and others about the outcome of meetings to discuss the control of small arms. The Council has distributed analyses such as David Isenberg's "From the Frying Pan into the Fire: U.S. Arms Sales and Military Assistance to the Persian Gulf and Middle East" (2007). Isenberg argued that prospective U.S. arms sales deals and additional military assistance programs in the Middle East would alter the strategic balance in the region. Isenberg noted that although President George W. Bush had declared that U.S. support for authoritarian regimes would end, the announced arms sales represented a continuation of traditional policy. Isenberg asserted that providing advanced weapons to current allies in the Persian Gulf and Middle East was unwise because there was no assurance that those governments would remain on good terms with the United States. Providing weapons to Arab states and Israel raised the probability that both would become the targets of militant Islamist groups and that the United States would be required to maintain an extended presence in the region. BASIC admonitions notwithstanding, in October 2010 the Barack Obama administration announced a planned arms sale of nearly $60 billion to Saudi Arabia, including 84 F-15 fighter jets and 190 helicopters.

Gun rights advocates have expressed serious reservations regarding BASIC's attempts to institute international small arms control, fearing that any intergovernmental agreements will result in further firearms limitations in the United States, which, they believe, would constitute further violations of the Second Amendment right to keep and bear arms. Although BASIC emphasizes primarily the illegal distribution of small arms worldwide, gun rights advocates are particularly concerned by the organization's support for additional controls on the legal trade in firearms.

See also: United Kingdom; United Nations.

Further Reading: British American Security Information Council Web site, www.basicint.org; David Isenberg, "From the Frying Pan into the Fire: U.S. Arms Sales and Military Assistance to the Persian Gulf and Middle East" (September 2007), www.basicint.org/pubs/Papers/BP55.htm; Matthew Lee, "U.S., Saudi Arabia in Massive Arms Deal," *Houston Chronicle* (October 21, 2010), A16.

Browning, John Moses (1855–1926)

The modern weapons that provide an important part of the context for the heated debate over gun control differ markedly from the firearms available in the early nineteenth century. John Moses Browning, who altered the landscape of firearms production in the late nineteenth and early twentieth centuries, vies for the position of the greatest of all firearms inventors. His innovations contributed greatly to the fortunes of Winchester and other gun manufacturers.

Browning acquired an interest in firearm design from his father, Jonathan, who also manufactured guns. Born in Tennessee in 1805, the elder Browning first encountered a firearm in his early teens when he was given an old flintlock rifle in payment for some farm work. He repaired the gun and sold it back to the previous owner. Working in a blacksmith shop, Jonathan acquired metalworking skills. After converting to the Mormon faith, Jonathan moved to Utah, where Brigham Young selected him as the community's gunsmith.

As a youth, John Moses found himself surrounded by the firearms business. When he

John Browning was one of the most innovative American inventors of firearms in the nineteenth century. *www. wikipedia.org*

made a primitive firearm at the age of 10, the elder Browning, unimpressed, commented that a boy nearly 11 years old could do a better job. In 1878, after examining a rifle, Browning commented to his father that he could improve on the design. Jonathan encouraged his son to try. The son made his first serious attempts at firearm construction, receiving a patent for one of them, a single-shot cartridge rifle. Browning and his brothers produced some 600 of the rifles before he sold the patent to Oliver F. Winchester and the Winchester Repeating Arms Company for an outright payment of $8,000 in lieu of royalties.

As Browning continued to develop new firearms, he built a model by hand, from which he made drawings. In 1884, Browning displayed a well-designed lever-action hunting rifle. A cautious person, he made sure to receive a patent before revealing the innovative design to Winchester. The new rifle became the Winchester Model 1886. Through 1935, Winchester manufactured 160,000 of these rifles. In the late 1880s, Browning designed some of the best firearms of the time,

including a single-shot cartridge rifle, a repeating lever-action rifle, and a repeating shotgun. During this same period, he also developed the idea for a gas-operated firearm that would fire nearly 1,000 rounds per minute.

When Winchester wanted to produce a miniaturized version of the Model 1886, the company offered Browning $10,000 for a model delivered in three months, or $15,000 if forthcoming in two months. Browning responded that he could design the firearm in 30 days if Winchester were willing to pay $20,000 for it. Browning received the $20,000 for developing what became the Model 1892. Had Browning opted for royalties, his return would have been far greater. The company sold over one million of the rifles before discontinuing production in 1941.

In 1902, Browning offered Thomas Bennett, president of Winchester, a newly produced automatic shotgun. However, this time Browning opted for royalties rather than a single payment. When Bennett refused, the 20-year Browning-Winchester collaboration came to an end. Browning explored new business collaborations with other gun manufacturers. Using Browning patents, Colt produced the first American automatic pistol, the Model 1900. Remington manufactured a semiautomatic rifle, the Model 8, from a Browning patented design. Browning, still active, died in 1926 from a heart attack in his son's office in Liege, France. By the time of his death, Browning's innovative work had laid the groundwork for many future developments in the arms industry.

See also: Colt, Samuel; Remington, Eliphalet, II; Winchester, Oliver Fisher.

Further Reading: Sam Fadala, *Great Shooters of the World* (South Hackensack, NJ: Stoeger, 1990); Wayne Van Zwoll, *America's Great Gunmakers* (South Hackensack, NJ: Stoeger, 1992).

Bryan v. United States (1998)

In *Bryan v. United States* (524 U.S. 184, 1998), the U.S. Supreme Court ruled on the meaning of a section of the Firearms Owners' Protection Act (FOPA). The section [U.S.C. 924 (a) (1) (D)] prohibits any person without a federal firearms license from engaging in a business involving firearms dealing. Although widely considered a general weakening of the Gun Control Act of

1968, FOPA clarified provisions of that act, such as providing a definition for the term "engaged in the business." Gun rights advocates were concerned that federal firearms legislation could be used to prosecute individuals who might sell their gun collections, not knowing they were doing anything that could be considered illegal. The Bryan case dealt with the kind of knowledge an individual must possess to be found culpable under the law. Did conviction of violating section 924 require the defendant to have knowledge of the law, or less restrictively, knowledge that he or she was acting unlawfully?

The original prosecution of Sillasse Bryan determined that the defendant, who did not have a federal license to deal in firearms, used other individuals to purchase pistols in Ohio under false pretenses, assuring these purchasers that he would file the serial numbers off the guns. He then resold the handguns in areas of Brooklyn, New York, known for illegal drug activity. The evidence demonstrated that Bryan knew that his actions were unlawful. However, the prosecution presented no grounds for concluding that he was aware of the federal law prohibiting firearms dealing without a license. The judge denied a defense request to instruct the jury that they could arrive at a guilty verdict only if Bryan knew about the federal licensing requirement. The jury subsequently found Bryan guilty of violating federal firearms regulations.

When the Appeals Court affirmed the conviction, the Supreme Court decided to hear the case because an Appeals Court for another circuit had ruled that the government must demonstrate that a defendant was aware of the licensing requirement. The Court rejected the defendant's argument that knowledge of the law is required for conviction because the statute's use of the term "knowingly" regarding the commission of the relevant act "does not necessarily have any reference to a culpable state of mind or to knowledge of the law"; in other words, the term knowingly "merely requires proof of knowledge of the facts that constitute the offense."

Bryan had argued that the Supreme Court, in cases dealing with violations of the tax code, determined that conduct is criminal only when done "willfully"; in other words, the defendant must be aware of the specific provision he is charged with violating. Because certain statutes containing technical provisions may trap people who genuinely believe they are engaged in innocent conduct, the Court employed a more specific sense of "willful," referring to knowledge of the specific statute. However, in the Bryan case the jury found that the defendant knew he was involved in unlawful conduct even though the prosecution did not determine that he was aware of the specific statute prohibiting firearms dealing without a federal license. Therefore, the Court ruled that the Bryan case does not qualify as an exception to the general rule that ignorance of the law is no excuse.

See also: Firearms Owners Protection Act; Gun Control Act of 1968.

Further Reading: *Bryan v. United States*, Docket No. 96-8422 (U.S. Supreme Court, 1998).

Bureau of Alcohol, Tobacco, Firearms, and Explosives (ATF)

The Bureau of Alcohol, Tobacco, Firearms, and Explosives (ATF) is responsible for overseeing compliance with federal policies regarding illegal activities involving firearms and explosives, including terrorist acts, and the illegal sale of alcohol and tobacco products. In 1972 the agency was given bureau status in the Treasury Department as the Bureau of Alcohol, Tobacco, and Firearms (ATF). The Bureau was composed of two sections, one for regulatory enforcement and the other for criminal enforcement. Matters such as gun licensing and tracing, illegal firearms transport and possession, and explosives were the domain of the criminal enforcement section. The political battle over gun control focused on the ATF, with gun control supporters frustrated by an agency they considered ineffective, and gun control opponents expressing concern over what they called a power-grabbing and rights-violating behemoth.

In January 2003, under the Homeland Security Act, the ATF and the agency's law enforcement operations were relocated to the Department of Justice as the Bureau of Alcohol, Tobacco, Firearms, and Explosives. This newly established bureau assumed responsibility for firearms, explosives, and arson, as well as for federal criminal laws dealing with alcohol and tobacco. The taxation and trade functions of the Bureau remained in the Treasury Department as the newly established Alcohol and Tobacco Tax and Trade Bureau (TTB).

The ATF has a long heritage. Its roots extend back to 1791 when Secretary of the Treasury

Alexander Hamilton established a mechanism for collecting a liquor tax. In 1919, with the beginning of Prohibition, a Bureau of Prohibition was created within the Treasury Department. In 1933, when Prohibition ended with ratification of the Twenty-First Amendment, the Bureau of Prohibition was renamed the Alcohol Tax Unit. Having become part of the Internal Revenue Service (IRS), the unit was renamed the Alcohol and Tobacco Tax Division in 1951 and was granted authority to collect a newly created federal tobacco tax. Although the agency first assumed responsibility for gun regulation in 1942 as a result of the National Firearms Act of 1934 and the Federal Firearms Act of 1938, it achieved its current status and title with the Gun Control Act of 1968.

The ATF's capacity to enforce gun control legislation has not been extensive. It issues licenses for gun manufacturers and dealers, but lacks any regulatory authority. The Bureau has limited access to information about the number of guns sold each year. In 1965, just five full-time employees were engaged in enforcing the 1934 and 1938 laws and the Bureau achieved few convictions under these laws. It conducted few firearm investigations and revoked the licenses of just a handful of firearms dealers. In the 1980s, to assist in its legal responsibility of tracking firearms, the agency proposed a plan to computerize records. This proposal prompted the National Rifle Association (NRA) to encourage its membership to write representatives and senators and object to the agency's attempts to make its operations more efficient. In response, the Treasury Appropriations Subcommittee cut funds from the Bureau's budget that would be designated for computerization and the Bureau was denied the authority to expend any funds for the purpose of centralizing records dealing with the acquisition and status of firearms that are maintained by federal firearms licensees. This prohibition became part of the 1986 Firearms Owners Protection Act.

Because the agency lacked independent agency status and did not have the prestige of some federal agencies, it depended on the president and Congress for its continuation. In 1981, the agency escaped President Ronald Reagan's attempt to disband it, but still suffered significant budget cuts. A proposal at that time to shift the Bureau's duties to the Internal Revenue Service was also aborted. The Bureau recouped some of its limited prestige and financial support in the late 1980s due

to successful operations involving investigations of extremist groups. However, the Bureau's mishandling of the 1993 raid on the Branch Davidian compound near Waco, Texas, along with evidence that officials attempted to conceal their mistakes, proved a serious blow to the agency. A committee headed by Vice President Al Gore recommended merging the Bureau into the Federal Bureau of Investigation (FBI), but the plan was not implemented.

The NRA, already a fierce critic, attacked the agency for its performance in Waco as well as for the 1992 assault, in cooperation with the FBI and federal marshals, on the Randy Weaver home at Ruby Ridge, Idaho. Weaver, a white supremacist, lost family members in skirmishes with Bureau agents. Following these events, a new director attempted to improve morale and management within the agency. However, pro-gun groups have continued their attacks on the agency. With the transfer of ATF to the Justice Department, NRA lobbyist Chris Cox expressed caution about an agency that his organization has criticized for many years.

The strong tradition of opposition to the Bureau from gun rights groups notwithstanding, it performs many functions related to the illegal transfer, acquisition, and use of firearms. A major current role for ATF is to reduce the amount of illegal gun trafficking associated with the illegal drug trade. The agency's Project Gunrunner involves curbing the illegal weapons trade across the U.S.-Mexico border and lowering the firearms-related violence on both sides of the border. The Bureau's National Tracing Center (NTC) traces firearms retrieved by law enforcement personnel in order to identify those persons engaged in diverting firearms into illegal trade and to determine various patterns of illegal firearms transfers. ATF investigates violations of the Brady Handgun Violence Prevention Act that involve attempts by prohibited individuals to acquire firearms. The Bureau also monitors provisions of international firearms agreements to which the United States is a party in order to determine if they comply with U.S. laws and policies.

The political nature of ATF came to light once more when gun control organizations noted in August 2010 that President Barack Obama had not yet nominated a candidate for director of the agency, 18 months after he took office. Some suggested that the Obama administration did not wish to deal with a nomination that would likely generate opposition from gun rights groups. However, the ATF suffered a significant setback beginning in October 2009 when the Bureau initiated an ill-conceived sting operation, Operation Fast and Furious, that ultimately ended in a fiasco. In order to track firearms that straw purchasers in the United States had purchased for transport to Mexico, ATF's Phoenix, Arizona, field office allowed the sales to proceed. However, the ATF agents were able to seize only about 100 firearms while losing track of nearly 2,000 guns destined for Mexico. In December 2010, in the Arizona desert, Border Patrol Agent Brian Terry was killed in a gun battle with criminal suspects. Agents found two guns at the scene that the ATF had allowed a straw purchaser to buy earlier in 2010. The event and the loss of illegal weapons led to a congressional investigation and the Auguat 2011 reassignment in the Justice Department of ATF Acting Director Kenneth Melson, who ultimately retired from the Justice Department in September 2012. A July 2012 congressional report blamed Melson as well as ATF Deputy Director William Hoover—who resigned in July—for the failed operation. In February 2016 the inspector general for the Justice Department reported that the Bureau had moved to correct deficiencies that led to the failure.

See also: Federal Firearms Act of 1938; Firearms Owners Protection Act; Gun Control Act of 1968; National Firearms Act of 1934; National Rifle Association; Reagan, Ronald; Ruby Ridge; Waco, Texas, Raid.

Further Reading: Bureau of Alcohol, Tobacco, Firearms, and Explosives Web site, www.atf.gov; James Moore, *Very Special Agents: The Inside Story of America's Most Controversial Law Enforcement Agency—The Bureau of Alcohol, Tobacco, and Firearms* (New York: Pocket Books, 1997); Robert J. Spitzer, *The Politics of Gun Control*, 6nd ed. (Boulder, CO: Paradigm, 2015); Josh Sugarmann, *National Rifle Association: Money, Firepower and Fear* (Washington, DC: National Press, 1992); Eric Lichtblau, "Risks Remain in Gun Investigations, Report Says" *New York Times* (February 11, 2016); Cable News Network, "Operation Fast and Furious Fast Facts" (September 25, 2015), www.cnn.com/2013/08/27/world/americas/operation-fast-and-furious-fast-facts/index.html; Bryan Schatz, "Outgunned and Outmanned," *Mother Jones* (September/October 2016):5-7.

Bush, George W. (1946–)

Georg W. Bush was the forty-third president of the United States, serving two terms from 2001 to 2009. During his political career, the Republican was a strong supporter of gun rights, first as a two-term governor of Texas (1995-2000) and then as president, when he and his administration championed, and advanced, the political agenda of the National Rifle Association.

As Texas governor, Bush twice signed bills to allow citizens to obtain permits to carry concealed weapons. A 1995 law legalized concealed carry statewide (it had formerly been barred), and a 1997 law expanded concealed carry to churches and hospitals. Bush also signed a bill to prevent localities from filing lawsuits against gun manufacturers. During the closely contested 2000 presidential contest, in which he was challenged by Democratic nominee Al Gore, the gun issue proved to be a dividing line between the two. The NRA endorsed Bush in both of his presidential campaigns, and was a co-sponsor of the Republican conventions that nominated him. One NRA spokesman claimed that the organization would

Republican George W. Bush was a strong supporter of gun rights, and he advanced the political agenda of the National Rifle Association during his political career. *White House photo by Eric Draper; www.wikipedia.org*

have unlimited access to Bush as president, and the NRA claimed credit for helping to elect Bush by pushing key states into his column.

After the election, Bush made good on his stated loyalty to the gun rights agenda. He appointed former Missouri Senator, Republican John Ashcroft, as attorney general. Ashcroft had been rated as the most gun-friendly member of the Senate, and in 2001, Attorney General Ashcroft issued a memorandum that reversed decades of Justice Department opinions concerning the meaning of the Second Amendment's right to bear arms. Up until this time, both Republican and Democratic administrations had viewed it as protecting citizen service in a government-organized and regulated militia. Ashcroft changed this position to reflect the view that the amendment instead protected a personal, individual right of citizens to own guns. This policy change proved to be one important step in paving the way for the Supreme Court's ruling in *District of Columbia v. Heller* (2008), when the high court for the first time in history enshrined that right as a personal one rather than as militia-based. The two Bush-appointed Supreme Court justices, John Roberts and Samuel Alito, both supported this view in the court's 5-4 decision. In 2010, the high court extended this right to the states, also by 5-4 vote, in the case of *McDonald v. Chicago*.

Legislatively, the Bush administration engineered the passage in Congress of the NRA's highest priority: a bill to provide special legal protections to the gun industry. In 2005, Congress passed the Protection of Lawful Commerce in Arms Act. This law bars civil suits against gun manufacturers, distributors, dealers, and importers of firearms and ammunition, with an allowance for narrow exceptions in cases of defective guns or expressly criminal behavior. No similar protections are available for other industries or manufacturing concerns.

The Bush administration also took various administrative actions supported by gun rights proponents. It reduced the length of time that the government held on to gun check records from 90 to 180 days to one day. It blocked law enforcement access to gun background check data, excluding even those instances when law enforcement was searching for possible terrorists, a move that raised some eyebrows in the aftermath of the September 11, 2001 terrorist attacks. The administration also cancelled a federal gun buy-back program.

Further Reading: John Ashcroft, *Never Again: Securing America and Restoring Justice* (New York: Hachette Books, 2006); Robert J. Spitzer, "Gun Rights for Terrorists?" *Transformed by Crisis: The Presidency of George W. Bush,* Jon Kraus, Kevin J. McMahon, and David M. Rankin, eds. (New York: Palgrave Macmillan, 2004); Robert J. Spitzer, *The Politics of Gun Control*, 6th ed. (Boulder, CO: Paradigm Publishers, 2015)

Bush, George H. W. (1924–)

George H. W. Bush, Republican president of the United States from 1989 to 1993, was a life member of the National Rifle Association (NRA) until his resignation in 1995 in protest against remarks made by the organization's executive vice president, Wayne LaPierre, in a verbal attack on federal law enforcement agents. The resignation was especially notable because Bush had been a strong supporter of the gun rights movement throughout his political career, and had often received the political backing of gun rights groups.

In 1988, because of his consistent support of gun rights, Bush received the NRA's endorsement for the presidency. The NRA spent $1.5 million during the campaign to support Bush and to oppose the Democratic candidate, Michael Dukakis, who was considered a major enemy of the organization for his advocacy of gun control. In December 1988, the NRA named Bush its "Person of the Year," declaring him to be the only candidate who would defend the rights of gun owners. However, Bush's honored position in the NRA did not last much longer. Although Bush had opposed any ban on assault weapons, in March 1989 he reversed his position following extensive media reporting on the Stockton, California, shooting in which school children were injured and killed by an assailant wielding a Chinese-manufactured Norinco AK-56S, a semiautomatic version of the Soviet AK-47.

William Bennett, Bush's director of the Office of Drug Policy, announced an import ban on five types of assault weapons. Soon afterward, Bush announced an extension of the temporary ban to 24 types of assault weapons. Speaking in favor of the ban, Bush noted that assault weapons were the "guns of choice" for criminals and stated that the ban was meant to keep sophisticated firearms out of the hands of criminals. Bush also announced proposals to double the minimum sentencing for the criminal use of a semiautomatic firearm, to enact a permanent ban on the import of assault weapons, and to prohibit future production and sale of high-capacity ammunition magazines (greater than 15 rounds). Bush opposed the Brady Handgun Violence Prevention bill through the rest of his term, but gave hints that he might approve the legislation as part of an acceptable crime bill. The Brady bill was passed after Bush left office.

Initially, the NRA refrained from blaming Bush for the assault weapons ban, opting instead to focus criticisms on Bennett and the administration in general and to ask the president to reverse the shift in administration policies. However, although Bill Clinton, Bush's Democratic opponent in 1992, was a major advocate of restrictions on firearms, the NRA refused to endorse Bush for reelection or to contribute to his campaign, concluding that Bush had failed the organization by supporting restrictions on the import of assault weapons.

In 1995, Bush reacted strongly against an NRA fund-raising letter distributed just before the bombing of the Oklahoma City federal office building. The letter, signed by Wayne LaPierre, compared federal government agents to Nazis who wore "Nazi bucket helmets and black storm trooper uniforms" and harassed, intimidated, and even murdered law-abiding citizens. In his letter of resignation addressed to NRA President Thomas Washington, Bush stated that LaPierre's comments left him outraged. He considered the verbal attack "a vicious slander on good people." Although Bush admitted that he had long agreed with most of the organization's objectives, the attack on federal agents offended his own "sense of decency and honor" and his "concept of service to country." Bush regarded LaPierre's statements to be a slander on officials "who are out there, day and night, laying their lives on the line for all of us." Bush decided to resign his life membership in the NRA because Thomas Washington had failed to repudiate LaPierre's attack. Washington responded to Bush's letter, defending LaPierre's remarks, but LaPierre ultimately apologized, stating that he

regretted having offended federal law enforcement officials.

When George H. W. Bush's son, George W. Bush, assumed the office of president in 2001, he already had built a pro-gun rights record as Texas governor. Bush opposed the passage of any new gun control legislation, with the exception of instituting more severe penalties for those who use a firearm in committing a crime. He opposed mandatory safety locks for handguns, but supported the distribution of locks for those who wish to use them voluntarily. Bush also supported legislation at the state level to allow individuals to carry concealed weapons. While Texas governor, Bush signed a lawsuit preemption bill passed by the state legislature that prohibited local governments from suing firearm and ammunition manufacturers to recoup the costs of gun violence borne by public agencies. In 2004, President Bush announced his support for renewing the assault weapons ban, which was due to expire in September, but he took no active steps to persuade legislators, and Congress allowed the ban to expire. Bush undoubtedly was unwilling to expend political capital for a policy to which he was not enthusiastically committed.

See also: Brady Handgun Violence Prevention Act; Clinton, William Jefferson (Bill); LaPierre, Wayne; National Rifle Association; Oklahoma City Bombing; Stockton, California, Shooting.

Further Reading: Jack Anderson, *Inside the NRA: Armed and Dangerous* (Beverly Hills, CA: Dove, 1996); Richard Feldman, *Ricochet: Confessions of a Gun Lobbyist* (Hoboken, NJ: John Wiley and Sons, 2008); On the Issues, "George W. Bush on Gun Control," www. ontheissues.org/2004/George_W_ Bush_Gun_Control.htm; Robert J. Spitzer, *The Politics of Gun Control*, 4th ed. (Washington, DC: CQ Press, 2008); Josh Sugarmann, *National Rifle Association: Money, Firepower and Fear* (Washington, DC: National Press, 1992).

C

Canada

Gun rights advocates, such as the National Firearms Association (NFA) of Canada, as well as organizations in the United States, have criticized the adoption of more stringent gun control measures in Canada, arguing that such laws violate an individual's right to bear arms. Given the close geographical proximity of the two countries, gun rights groups in the United States fear that stricter laws in Canada foreshadow similar statutes in the United States. Inspection authority granted to Canadian government officials by the Firearms Act, which went into effect in 1998, is intended to ensure compliance with statutes regarding the safe storage of firearms.

In 1989, following the murder of 14 women at the University of Montreal, additional types of weapons were restricted or banned and tighter standards for acquiring a gun permit were instituted. Canadians wishing to purchase a gun had to undergo evaluation and were required to take a safety course. Automatic firearms and semi-automatics capable of being adapted to automatic fire were banned. Still, millions of firearms remained in private hands, a troubling condition for many Canadian gun control advocates.

In 1994, after a series of highly publicized violent incidents involving firearms, the Coalition for Gun Control, supported by several groups representing such interests as the police, lawyers, teachers, health workers, and women, campaigned for stricter gun control legislation. The Liberal Party, which won the 1993 federal elections, promised to support stronger legislation. The NFA argued that further gun control would restrict Canadians' ability to defend themselves against criminal activity. Opponents of stricter legislation noted that guns were consistently involved in only 32 percent of

homicides, and just 27 percent of all robberies. Gun control supporters responded that the use of handguns in crimes had risen sharply, and the general public strongly supported stricter gun control legislation. In 1993, 86 percent of respondents in a national poll supported registration of all firearms, 84 percent favored a prohibition on assault weapons, and 71 percent wanted to ban all handguns.

The new Firearms Act provides for inspection of businesses, gun collectors, owners of prohibited firearms, and owners with more than 10 firearms. Inspectors must give owners reasonable notice regarding the place to be inspected and must gain the consent of the resident. Police cannot use force to enter a home to conduct a search. Gun owners can be required to show their weapons to the police, but can bring them to the front door of the residence or to a police station.

Like the legal codes of most states in the United States, the Canadian criminal code treats as a separate offense the use of a firearm during the commission of a crime. The Firearms Act specifies minimum sentences for certain crimes, such as manslaughter, kidnapping, hostage-taking, robbery, or extortion, if committed with a firearm. An individual could also be prosecuted for possessing a firearm without being licensed to do so, or for failing to register the firearm. The act increased the Canadian government's authority to prevent firearms smuggling. Canadian residents wishing to import or export firearms must acquire licenses and registration certificates.

Information contained in the computerized registration system is governed by the Privacy Act to prevent unauthorized individuals from acquiring information. Firearms dealers can submit information to the system, but they are unable to access information contained in the system. Data regarding the types and number of firearms owned will not be directly matched with the owner's name and address, but rather with a firearms identification number. All gun owners must be licensed and all handguns and many semiautomatic firearms must be registered. Handguns cannot be carried outside the home unless the owner has received a license to do so, which officials only issue if the person can demonstrate a special need such as employment or a verifiable threat. Receiving a license requires gun safety training and a background check. Firearms must be securely stored and locked.

Supporters of the new registration system expected that it would assist the police in several ways. If weapons are registered and entered in a computerized database, then police can more easily trace the legal owner of a firearm. If all legal owners have registered their firearms, then those failing to register can be charged under the criminal code, thus providing the police with an additional weapon in the fight against crime. If domestic violence in a home appears likely, registration allows the police to determine more accurately how many firearms need to be removed from the premises. Traceability was expected to increase gun owner responsibility for maintaining the security of weapons. Owners may be more likely to report the loss or theft of a firearm and more hesitant to lend firearms to those with whom they are not familiar.

Canadian law classifies firearms into three categories: (1) non-restricted, which mainly include regular shotguns and rifles, (2) prohibited, which involves most handguns, automatic weapons, guns with sawed-off barrels, and military-style rifles, such as the AK-47, and (3) restricted, including non-prohibited handguns, some semi-automatic rifles. Restricted and prohibited firearms must be registered with the Royal Canadian Mounted Police. Purchasing or owning a restricted or prohibited firearm requires additional testing. Stephen Harper of the Conservative Party and prime minister from 2006 to 2015, eliminated the requirement to register non-restricted firearms.

By 2010, the 15-year-old firearm registration system was estimated to have cost the Canadian government one billion dollars, which many considered far too expensive. However, a Royal Canadian Mounted Police estimate places the continuing cost of the registry at less than $4 million per year. The registry particularly of long guns (shotguns and rifles) came under criticism from various groups, including the Canadian Shooting Sports Association, while others, including most police chiefs, labor organizations, physicians, and women's groups, continued

to support it. By August 2010, the Canadian parliament, with the support of Prime Minister Stephen Harper and Conservative members, was considering a bill to end the long-gun registry.

See also: National Firearms Association of Canada.

Further Reading: Al Bohachyk, "Street-Level Police Officers Don't Echo Chiefs' Support," *Edmonton Journal* (August 27, 2010), www.edmontonjournal.com; Marshall J. Brown, "New Canadian Gun Law Faces Budget, Legal Problems," *Gun News Digest* (Summer 1998), 38–39; Canadian Government Web site, canada.just.gc.ca/; "Gun Control," *Economist* 333 (October 29, 1994), 50; Antonia Zerbisias, "The Duel Over Gun Control Pits Law-and-Order Tories Against the Police," *The Star* (August 27, 2010), www.thestar.com.

Caron v. United States (1998)

In *Caron v. United States* (524 U.S. 308, 1998), the U.S. Supreme Court ruled that a felon could have the right to own firearms restored under federal law only if a state conferred the right to own all types of firearms, not just some. If federal authorities discover a convicted felon in possession of specific firearms that the state has granted him or her a right to possess, he or she still may have violated federal prohibitions on the ownership of firearms. The federal government uses state determinations of whether an individual is too dangerous to possess a firearm, but need not follow a state's policies regarding the ownership of specific categories of firearms in applying prohibitions on gun ownership or for enhanced sentencing for a convicted felon who uses a firearm in another crime. The federal statute [921 (a) (20)] states that a previous conviction is not to be considered for enhanced sentencing if the offender's civil rights have been restored, "unless such . . . restoration . . . expressly provides that the person may not . . . possess . . . firearms."

On three separate occasions (in 1958, 1959, and 1963), Gerald Caron had been convicted in Massachusetts state court of attempted breaking and entering. In 1970, a California state court convicted him of assault with intent to commit murder and attempted murder. Subsequently residing in Massachusetts, Caron was allowed under state law to possess rifles or shotguns because his conviction was more than five years old and he had obtained a firearm permit. In 1993 federal agents arrested him for threatening a man and his family with a semiautomatic rifle. Agents seized six rifles and more than 6,000 rounds of ammunition from Caron's home. After conviction, the Federal District Court in Massachusetts enhanced his sentence for having been convicted at least three times as a violent felon.

Taking an appeal from the Court of Appeals for the First Circuit, the U.S. Supreme Court, in a 6-to-3 decision, affirmed the lower court's ruling that the defendant's previous convictions counted toward enhanced sentencing. The Court stated that the phrase "may not . . . possess . . . firearms" can be understood in two "all-or-nothing" ways. The first interpretation, which the government attorneys supported, holds that the phrase applies to all firearms at the federal level when a state *forbids* possession of one or more types of firearms. According to the second interpretation, the phrase does not apply if a state *permits* possession of one or more types of firearms. The Court sided with the government contention that a state limitation on firearms possession, regardless of how extensive, "activates the uniform federal ban on possessing any firearms at all."

The Court declared that the federal government has "an interest in a single, national, protective policy, broader than required by state law," for determining when a convicted felon should continue to be denied the right to possess firearms. States cannot provide the "positive assurance" that an individual no longer presents a risk of danger. Federal law offers that assurance by considering "primary conduct not covered by state law." Because federal law refers to firearms possession generally and not to specific types of weapons, the Court interpreted the relevant statute to establish a more stringent standard for reestablishing the right to possess firearms than states have at times adopted.

See also: Federal Firearms Act of 1938; Gun Control Act of 1968; Lautenberg Amendment.

Further Reading: *Caron v. United States*, 524 U.S. 308 (1998).

Cases v. United States (1942)

On an appeal from the District Court of the United States for Puerto Rico, the U.S. Court of Appeals for the First Circuit in *Cases v. United States* (131 F.2d 916, 1942) reviewed the sentencing

of the appellant, Jose Cases Velazquez, who was found guilty of violating two sections of the Federal Firearms Act (FFA) of 1938, which made it unlawful for anyone under indictment or convicted of a crime of violence to ship or transport any firearm or ammunition in interstate or foreign commerce, or to receive a firearm or ammunition that had been transported in interstate or foreign trade. Firearm or ammunition possession is presumptive evidence that the firearm was transported or received by the individual in violation of the law.

In August 1941, the defendant received 10 rounds of ammunition from a friend who had purchased it for him in a hardware store. Three days later he went to a beach club in the municipality of Carolina, carrying a .38-caliber Colt revolver. He became angry with another patron, shooting him with the revolver. The defendant had been convicted in a Puerto Rican court in 1922 of aggravated assault and battery, thus bringing him under the prohibition of the FFA and making illegal his possession of the weapon and ammunition.

The defendant employed several arguments in claiming that the FFA was unconstitutional. First, he argued that it was an ex post facto law, establishing additional punishment for an act already committed. The court disagreed, ruling that in no sense was the FFA an ex post facto law because no one transporting or receiving a firearm or ammunition prior to passage of the act could be prosecuted under its provisions. With regard to the law instituting additional punishment, the court stated that the statute represented a valid exercise of legislative authority to regulate, even though certain conduct was made dependent on past behavior, including acts committed prior to passage of the legislation. The court focused on the nature of the past behavior in establishing the ineligibility of a person to engage in a future activity. Citing a related Supreme Court ruling, the court indicated that a felony conviction can be used to disqualify a person in the practice of medicine. In the present case, the intention of Congress was to protect the citizenry from those who, by their past conduct, had demonstrated their unfitness to own dangerous weapons.

In response to the appellant's argument that his Second Amendment right to possess a firearm had been violated, the court stated that the right to keep and bear arms is not an individual right and that the sole purpose of the Second Amendment is to prevent the federal government from encroaching on a right that could be established in local legislation. The circuit court cited *United States v. Miller* (1939), in which the U.S. Supreme Court in a limited ruling declared that weapons having no relation to the preservation of a well-regulated militia are not protected by the Second Amendment. The circuit court noted that under a strict interpretation of the Miller decision, the only firearms that could be regulated would be "weapons such as a flintlock musket or a matchlock harquebus." To hold that only antiquated weapons with no relation to a well-regulated militia could be subject to regulation would in effect make the untenable assertion that the Second Amendment right to bear arms is absolute.

The appellant further argued that the FFA denied him equal protection under the law because it did not apply equally to all who were included in the disqualifying category. Crimes used to define the category were differently defined in different states and territories, a potential difficulty that arose because a federal law depended on criminal definitions provided by varying state statutes. The court agreed with this view, but concluded that the definitions of crimes were not sufficiently varied in different states to make the classification unconstitutional. Congress had achieved "practical uniformity" among the states and territories in the application of the act.

The appellant also charged that the ammunition he was accused of having acquired three days before the incident at the beach club was not covered under the act. However, the court determined that the evidence sufficiently indicated that the appellant had no other weapon than the .38-caliber revolver. This fact justified the conclusion that the ammunition acquired was for the .38-caliber weapon and hence satisfied the definition of ammunition within the FFA. Therefore, all objections of the appellant were rejected and the appeals court upheld the district court judgment.

See also: Federal Firearms Act of 1938; Second Amendment; *United States v. Miller* (1939).

Further Reading: *Cases v. United States*, 131 F.2d 916 (1942).

The Castle Doctrine

The American legal tradition has long accepted, with some exceptions, the principle that a person confronted in one's home by violent attack has a right to defend one's self and family, and one's home (from the Middle Ages, one's castle), rather than to retreat. This privilege of non-retreat has given rise to the familiar expression, appearing as early as the 1600s in a British court case, that "a man's home is his castle." The special status accorded the home in this doctrine did not arise from any belief that a person's homestead or possessions were of such value that they merited the use of violence or lethal violence to protect them, but rather because a person's home was the ultimate refuge of someone attempting to escape harm or avoid conflict. Thus, with a person who has "retreated to the wall" (meaning the person has no place left to go) of, in this case, the home, an attack against an aggressor there merited special protection under the self-defense doctrine if necessary to prevent great bodily harm or imminent death. By the early seventeenth century, a British court ruled in Seyman's Case:

> That the house of everyone is to him as his castle and fortress, as well for his defence against injury and violence, as for his repose; and although the life of man is a thing precious and favoured in law so that, although a man kills another in his defence, or kills one *per infortunium* [by misfortune] without any intent, yet it is felony, and in such case he shall forfeit his goods and chattels for the great regard which the law has to a man's life, but if thieves come to a man's house to rob him, or murder, and the owner or his servants kill any of the thieves in defence of himself and his house it is not felony, and he shall lose nothing. . . .

While the British legal tradition played a key role in the development of American law on this and many other subjects, American self-defense law soon diverged in important respects from that of Britain. In the late nineteenth and twentieth centuries, the Castle Doctrine came to be applied in different ways among the states, ranging from a legal standard saying that safe retreat from one's home was a higher priority than mounting a defense against an aggressor within it, to other states where individuals have considerable discretion to apply even lethal force if threatened by an intruder within their homes. In addition, some states provide legal protection to those who seek to meet an aggressor in the home simply to protect it and its possessions (defense of premises), whereas other states place a higher priority on the avoidance of injury or death. Some jurisdictions also distinguish between the use of non-lethal force versus lethal force by the home dweller, where the use of non-lethal force is considered far preferred (and exempted from prosecution) whereas in other jurisdictions both non-lethal and lethal force might be protected.

While the principle of self-defense within the home is widely understood, prosecutors and law enforcement usually find great difficulty in resolving the justifiability of real life claims of self-defense, as real life cases are rarely clear-cut. In the late nineteenth century, American courts began to recognize the idea that individuals might, under certain circumstances, have a right to exercise the castle doctrine in public places – that is, to confront force with force outside of the home rather than safely retreat. This came to be known as the "stand your ground" principle, an idea that was significantly expanded in many states beginning in the first decade of the twenty-first century.

Further Reading: Richard Maxwell Brown, *No Duty to Retreat* (New York: University of Oklahoma Press, 1994); *Seyman's Case,* 5 Co. Rep. 91a, 91b, 77 Eng. Rep. 194, at 195 (K. B. 1603); Robert J. Spitzer, *Guns across America: Reconciling Gun Rules and Rights* (New York: Oxford University Press, 2015).

Center for the Study and Prevention of Violence (CSPV)

The Center for the Study and Prevention of Violence (CSPV), located at the University of Colorado at Boulder, was established in 1992 with a grant from the Carnegie Corporation of New York as an organization dedicated to understanding and preventing violence, including violence involving the use of firearms. Although the Center provides information about the prevalence and prevention of firearms-related violence, it is cautious about identifying firearms as an independent cause of violence and does not focus on gun control policy in sponsored research.

The Center has three basic missions. First, CSPV's Information House, which is the core of the organization, gathers research reports on the causes and prevention of violence, maintains databases, conducts literature searches, and provides information to the public upon request. Second, the Center provides assistance to those

wishing to develop a violence prevention program. Third, CSPV conducts research on the causes of violence and the effectiveness of programs intended to prevent violent behavior.

The CSPV has reported that from 1984 to 1993 handgun homicides among youth aged 15 to 19 increased more than 450 percent. In 1992, 5,262 youths aged 5 to 19 died of gunshot wounds. Among the causes, 62 percent were homicides, 27 percent were suicides, and 9 percent were unintentional injuries. Among children aged 5 to 9, firearm injuries were the fifth leading cause of death, and among those aged 10 to 14, such injuries were the second leading cause of death. The Center also focuses on the availability of guns among youth, citing survey data indicating that 13 percent of respondents in the sixth through twelfth grades had been threatened with a firearm. The Center reports that increasing numbers of children are being exposed to gun violence, which can traumatize young people and disrupt the educational system. The Center cites data indicating that in 1992 the average cost of a violent injury, fatal or nonfatal, was $44,000. That year the total medical cost of violence was estimated to be $13.5 billion. Although the Center reports that the increase in lethal firearm injuries is associated with greater youth access to firearms and less hesitancy to use them, it concludes that the problem of firearms violence must be addressed in a larger social context.

Through funding from the Colorado Trust, CSPV began a study of youth handgun violence in cooperation with the Center for Public-Private Sector Cooperation at the University of Colorado at Denver. The research project involved investigating the extent of the problem, analyzing information gathered from focus groups within Colorado, and identifying prevention or intervention initiatives that demonstrate promise of success. Three violence prevention programs were chosen to participate in the Youth Handgun Violence Prevention Project: The Conflict Center, Project PAVE, and Catholic Charities, each of which initiated a gun violence prevention curriculum into their activities. Each of the three programs targeted primarily inner-city adolescent males.

The CSPV holds that the public health approach to the study and prevention of youth violence is a valuable research tool. According to the Center, the public health approach focuses on searching for ways of preventing disease or injury. According to this primary prevention strategy, researchers should conduct an epidemiological analysis to discover the behavioral and environmental "risk factors" (such as the availability of firearms to youth) that are related to injury. According to the Center, "the public health approach allows one to think about violence not as an inevitable fact of life, but as a problem that can be prevented."

In 2006 the CSPV initiated an ongoing school safety study with the goal of maintaining a hospitable school environment "free of drugs, violence, intimidation, and fear." Researchers at the University of Colorado have developed a randomly selected sample of school districts to participate in the study.

See also: Doctors for Responsible Gun Ownership; Harborview Injury Prevention and Research Center; Johns Hopkins Center for Gun Policy and Research; Pacific Center for Violence Prevention; Violence Prevention Research Program.

Further Reading: Center for the Study and Prevention of Violence Web site, www.colorado.edu/cspv.

Center to Prevent Handgun Violence (CPHV)

See **BRADY CAMPAIGN TO PREVENT GUN VIOLENCE**

Central Conference of American Rabbis (CCAR)

For many years, the Central Conference of American Rabbis (CCAR) has taken a strong stand in favor of stricter gun control measures. In 1975, at its 86th annual convention, delegates adopted a resolution advocating gun control. The preamble to the resolution stated that increasing numbers of handguns in the United States have led to ever greater loss of life, and the resolution asserted that the handgun is the weapon most often involved in "cases of rage and passion" that result in injury or death. The resolution declared that easy access to firearms has increased the number of deaths among young people aged 1 to 19 and that greater numbers of high school students fall victim to handguns each year.

Founded in 1889, the Conference is composed of Reform rabbis ordained at the Hebrew Union College-Jewish Institute of Religion as well as rabbis ordained at liberal European seminaries. The group is an authoritative force for many American Jews on public policy issues, including gun control.

CCAR has resolved that the U.S. Congress and state legislatures should enact legislation to ban the sale of handguns. The ban should not apply to military personnel, police officers, security personnel while on the job, and target shooters who have received licenses from local authorities. The Conference concludes that legislation should provide for the collection of all handguns presently possessed by "citizens, aliens, residents and visitors of the United States." Just compensation would be given to those whose firearms were confiscated. In addition, the Conference resolved that its members would assist those working for passage of legislation. However, with recent U.S. Supreme Court decisions in which the Court majority interpreted the Second Amendment as guaranteeing an individual right to possess handguns for self-protection, the possibility of banning handguns appears extremely remote.

At its 98th Annual Convention in 1987, the Conference approved another resolution regarding the effort to enact more stringent gun control legislation. Noting the organization's continuing support for gun control, the resolution stated that stricter laws are intended to "eliminate the senseless slaughter of humans in our land by those who easily obtain unlicensed hand guns." CCAR declared its opposition to the National Rifle Association (NRA) for its "dedicated pursuit of unlicensed gun ownership." Observing that the NRA contributes to congressional election campaigns, and claiming that legislators' voting records are influenced by these contributions, CCAR urged members of Congress to refuse financial support from the NRA and to support strict gun control legislation.

At its 100th Annual Convention in June 1989, CCAR approved a resolution which noted that firearms and "automatic weapons" continued to proliferate and that deaths and injuries resulting from such weapons were increasing "astronomically." The Conference resolved that local, state, and national officials restrict handgun sales and ban automatic weapons sales to the general public. Because federal law already severely limits the sale of automatic weapons, the Conference likely meant semiautomatic versions of automatic weapons, or so-called assault rifles, which may be converted to automatic use.

At the Conference's 111th Annual Convention in 2000, the rabbis renewed their support for gun control measures. They resolved to urge the members of their congregations to advocate gun control by writing to members of Congress demanding that gun control measures be enacted. Conference members also resolved to invite elected officials to meet with their congregations and explain their positions on gun control, and to become involved in other coalitions that advocate more stringent gun control measures.

In a resolution adopted in August 2015, CCAR reasserted the organization's commitment to it gun violence prevention efforts. CCAR urged law enforcement agencies at all levels of government to use their firearms purchasing power in urging gun manufacturers to develop more reliable relationships with dealers and safer gun technology. In January 2016 Rabbi Denise L. Eger and Rabbi Steven A. Fox, CCAR's president and chief executive respectively, issue a statement in support of President Barack Obama's efforts to reduce gun violence. In June 2016 Eger and Fox declared their support for the families of those killed and wounded in the Orlando, Florida, shooting, and once more urged political leaders to act to end what they called the epidemic of gun violence.

See also: American Jewish Congress; Assault Weapons Ban; Jews for the Preservation of Firearms Ownership; National Rifle Association.

Further Reading: Central Conference of American Rabbis Web site, www.ccarnet.org; Central Conference of American Rabbis Resolution, "Ending Gun Violence" (March 2000), http://data.ccarnet.org/ cgi-bin/resodisp.pl?file=gun&year=2000; CCAR Resolution on Gun Violence (August 2015), www.ccarnet.org/rabbis-speak/resolutions/all/ccar-resolution-gun-violence.

Children's Defense Fund (CDF)

The Children's Defense Fund (CDF), an organization that promotes the interests of poor, minority, and disabled children, has advocated policies to limit youth access to firearms and to hold adults responsible for the illegal use of guns by youth. More broadly, the organization promotes programs to improve the health and education of children and to prevent broken families and youth crime and violence. Although some social scientists

and gun rights advocates have claimed that guns represent a minimal danger to children under 10 years old, organizations like the CDF present powerful emotional arguments in favor of gun control measures.

Marian Wright Edelman, who founded the organization in 1973, worked for the Poor People's March in the late 1960s and subsequently founded the Washington Research Project, a public interest law firm and precursor of the CDF. The Fund receives financial support from foundations, corporations, and individuals. The organization opposes any policy that involves taking primarily punitive actions against juveniles involved in illegal activities. Rather than devoting resources to incarceration after crimes have been committed, the CDF advocates preventive measures to keep youth in school and away from illegal activities. This conviction could have led to a position on firearms closer to that of gun rights organizations, which claim that guns are not dangerous, youth in trouble are dangerous. Instead, the organization recommends locking up guns, not children.

The CDF claims that since the 1980s nearly all the increase in violent crime involving youth can be associated with access to firearms. From 1983 to 1995, gun homicides committed by juveniles tripled, although homicides committed with other weapons declined. Data are cited indicating that child gun deaths have risen from 8 per day in 1983 to 14 per day in 1995. Although the CDF admitted in 1998 that violent crime arrests had declined 12 percent since 1994 and homicide rates among children aged 10 to 17 had decreased 31 percent since 1993, the organization still considered youth violence a major problem, especially because weapons violations doubled between 1985 and 1994. In a 2010 report, the Fund reported that since 1979, 110,645 children and teenagers have been killed by firearms, and that although the number of firearm deaths for white children and teenagers had declined by more than half from 1979 to 2007, the number of deaths of black children and teenagers had risen by more than 60 percent.

The CDF believes that any legislation dealing with youth crime must address the problem of firearms. The CDF supported legislation being considered in the 105th Congress (1997–1999) that would impose penalties for transferring firearms to youths and for assisting young people to make illegal purchases. The organization has advocated a measure that would hold adults accountable if children gain access to guns, and supports collaboration among federal, state, and local law enforcement agencies to trace the sources of firearms that youths use in crimes. Like many other groups, the CDF advocates the introduction of safety locks that are integral to the design of handguns. Although several manufacturers have agreed to include locks, the organization believes that legislative mandates would ensure the maintenance of basic standards.

The CDF supported the 1998 Children's Gun Violence Prevention Act, which was introduced by Representative Carolyn McCarthy, Democrat of New York, a congresswoman whose husband was killed during a Long Island Railroad gun incident. Among its provisions, the bill would mandate studies to determine the most effective means of making guns child-resistant, and would impose a fine and prison sentence for adults who allow their firearms to be used by children to commit acts of violence. The CDF expects further reductions in firearms violence among youth generally with the adoption of legislation to establish adult responsibility for gun safety, and to institute after-school programs that would occupy youth during times when violent acts are most likely to occur.

Following the mass shooting in San Barnardino, California in December 2015, in which a man and woman shot and killed 14 people and wounded 21 others, CDF President Edelman stated that gun violence should be the major health issue in the United States. She urged the establishment of background checks for ammunition sales, a tax on ammunition, a liability insurance requirement for gun owners, and the development of smart gun technology. Edelman called on Congress to remove limitations on firearm-related research conducted by the Centers for Disease Control and the National Institutes of Health. Following the June 2016 mass shooting at the Pulse nightclub in Orland, Florida, in which a gunman killed 49 people and wounded more than 50 others, Edelman urged Congress to institute a "no buy list," which would prohibit those on terrorist watch lists from purchasing a firearm. She also called for universal background checks on firearm purchases and a ban on assault weapons and large capacity ammunition magazines.

See also: Accidents Involving Guns; Clinton, William Jefferson (Bill); Trigger Locks.

Further Reading: Children's Defense Fund Web site, www.childrensdefense.org/; Children's Defense Fund, "State of America's Children 2010 Report—Gun Violence," www.childrensdefense.org.

Citizens Committee for the Right to Keep and Bear Arms (CCRKBA)

The Citizens Committee for the Right to Keep and Bear Arms (CCRKBA) was established in 1971 to affirm that the Second Amendment to the U.S. Constitution guarantees to all citizens the right to own and carry firearms. The organization operates on the principle that "an armed populace is more likely to be a free populace."

The CCRKBA has a staff of 40 to 50 people, a yearly budget of more than $3.6 million, and offices in Washington, D.C., and Bellevue, Washington. The organization is affiliated with groups in all 50 states. Many members of Congress serve on CCRKBA's national advisory committee. Membership comes with a $15 annual donation to the organization. Five-year memberships ($50), lifetime memberships ($150), and patron status ($1,000) are also available. Members receive "action alerts"— bulletins that provide information about proposed gun control legislation and advice on what actions to take to prevent passage. The organization's Web site contains news stories about gun rights and gun control efforts nationwide.

In a 2010 mailing, the organization asked members and other gun rights supporters to sign a petition addressed to then Senate majority leader Harry Reid (D-AZ) that claimed U.S. sovereignty would be threatened by any "anti-gun proposal" emanating from "the international gun grabbers" in the United Nations. The petition stated that the U.S. Senate should reject any U.N. agreement on gun control. In another mailing, the organization asked for a "gun owners whip count" of those opposing a bill (H.R. 45) introduced by "rabid anti-gunner Rep. Bobby Rush (D-IL), a close friend of President Barack Obama." According to the CCRKBA, the bill (which had no chance of passage) would mandate the establishment of a database to be kept in the Justice Department "to record every gun owner, gun sale, and transfer of a firearm and for other purposes to be determined." Recipients were informed that if they did not return a response opposing the bill, they would be recorded as supporting the measure. Such mailings include a request for a donation.

In Washington, D.C., the CCRKBA public affairs staff interacts with public officials and other pro-gun groups to initiate and assist in the passage of pro-gun legislation and to defeat gun control measures. In 1986, CCRKBA cooperated with the National Rifle Association (NRA) and Gun Owners of America (GOA) in an intensive lobbying campaign to gain passage of the Firearms Owners Protection Act. CCRKBA maintains a political action committee (Right to Bear Arms Political Victory Fund) that raises funds to donate to political candidates who support the organization's pro-gun positions. In 2008, The CCRKBA filed an *amicus curiae* brief, written by Bellingham, Washington, attorney Jeffrey B. Teichert, in *District of Columbia v. Heller* in support of the right of individuals to possess and carry firearms.

The Bellevue, Washington, headquarters is responsible for grassroots lobbying in state legislatures. State affiliates monitor the state and local activities of gun control groups. With the assistance of local organizations, the Committee works to defeat anti-gun legislation in states and localities. To achieve its objectives nationwide, the organization informs members about gun issues and encourages them to participate in efforts to protect gun rights.

As part of its educational campaign, CCRKBA maintains a speakers bureau that promotes speaking engagements by pro-gun activists. Committee representatives appear at conferences, schools, gun shows, and on television and radio. The organization supports research to demonstrate the positive impact of guns on society. For instance, a 1996 news release from the organization reported the results of a study indicating that states with laws that are less restrictive in granting the right to carry a concealed weapon have significantly lower violent crime rates than states with more restrictive laws.

When Democrats in the U.S. House of Representatives staged a sit-in on the House floor to demand the consideration of gun control legislation following the June 2016 Orlando, Florida, mass shooting, the CCRKBA chairman

Alan Gottlieb accused the legislators of attempting to restrict the civil rights of citizens, particularly the right to keep and bear arms. At the same time, the Committe3e expressed its strong opposition to Democratic efforts in the Senate to pass gun-related legislation. The Committee opposed the effort to pass legislation to prohibit those on the terrorist "no fly" list from purchasing firearms.

The Committee's chairman, Alan Gottlieb, has published several books, including *Politically Correct Guns* (1996), *Gun Rights Fact Book* (1998), *Gun Rights Affirmed: The Emerson Case* (2001), *America Fights Back: Armed Self-Defense in a Violent Age* (2007), *These Dogs Don't Hunt: The Democrats' War on Guns* (2008), and *Assault Weapons: The Campaign to Eliminate Your Guns* (2009, coauthored with Dave Workman).

See also: Firearms Owners Protection Act; Gottlieb, Alan Merril; Gun Owners of America; National Rifle Association; Second Amendment.

Further Reading: Citizens Committee for the Right to Keep and Bear Arms, "States Allowing Citizens to Carry Concealed Firearms Have Less Violent Crime" (news release, March 27, 1996); CCRKBA Web site, www.ccrkba.org; Alan M. Gottlieb, *Things You Can Do to Defend Your Gun Rights* (Bellevue, WA: Merril Press, 1993); Joe Huffman, CCRKBA Files Amicus Brief in Heller Case, *The View from North Central Idaho* (February 12, 2008), http://blog.joehoffman.org/Trackback.aspx?guid=4c7cce76-11c9-4a17-9495-0be5b77725ff; Alan Gottlieb and Dave Workman, *Shooting Blanks: Facts Don't Matter to the Gun Ban Crowd* (Bellevue, WA: Merril Press, 2011); Alan Gottlieb and Dave Workman, *Dancing in Blood: Exposing the Gun Ban Lobby's Playbook to Destroy Your Rights* (Bellevue, WA: Merril Press, 2014).

City of Las Vegas v. Moberg (1971)

The Court of Appeals of New Mexico, in *City of Las Vegas v. Moberg* (82 N.M. 626, 1971), ruled that any ordinance denying people the right to bear arms violates Article II, section 6 of the state constitution of New Mexico, which states that "The people have the right to bear arms for their security and defense, but nothing herein shall be held to permit the carrying of concealed weapons."

The court decided that while this constitutional provision allows local governments to prohibit the carrying of concealed weapons, ordinances cannot limit the right of persons to carry weapons openly.

When Leland Moberg discovered that his automobile had been burglarized, he went to the booking room of the police department of the city of Las Vegas, New Mexico, to report the crime. When police officers observed that he was carrying a pistol openly in a holster, Moberg was arrested for "carrying a concealed and deadly weapon" and was convicted in municipal court of violating a city ordinance making it unlawful for anyone to carry a weapon, concealed or not, within the city limits of East Las Vegas. The ordinance defined deadly weapons to include guns, pistols, knives with blades longer than two and a half inches, slingshots, sandbags, metallic knuckles, concealed rocks, and "all other weapons, by whatever name known, with which dangerous wounds can be inflicted."

Moberg appealed the conviction to the district court, which granted him a new trial. At this trial, no evidence was presented that the defendant was carrying a concealed weapon. Both the defense and the prosecution dealt with the charge as involving the carrying of a deadly weapon as such. The district court found him guilty of violating the city ordinance prohibiting the carrying of a deadly weapon, but one which was in plain view and not concealed. Moberg then appealed the conviction to the Court of Appeals of New Mexico, contending that the ordinance under which he was convicted violated his right to bear arms as guaranteed under the state constitution.

The court first established the obvious: an ordinance that denies rights protected in the state constitution is void. Ordinances that specifically prohibit the carrying of *concealed* weapons are considered a proper exercise of the police power because they do not deprive citizens of the right to bear arms but simply regulate that right. The constitution specifically provides for this exception. However, the court noted that the Las Vegas ordinance prohibited the carrying of all weapons, whether concealed or not, thereby denying to citizens the constitutionally guaranteed right to bear arms. Therefore, that portion of the Las Vegas ordinance that prohibited the carrying of weapons openly was determined to violate the state constitution.

See also: Concealed Carry Laws.

Further Reading: *City of Las Vegas v. Moberg*, 82 N.M. 626 (1971).

City of Salina v. Blaksley (1905)

In 1905, the Supreme Court of Kansas, in *City of Salina v. Blaksley* (83 P. 619, 72 Kan. 230, 1905), ruled that there was no absolute right to possess or carry a handgun for self-defense. The court declared that the state constitution did protect an individual's right to bear arms, but the right belongs only to the people collectively when associated with membership in authorized military groups. The court ruled that the state could restrict possession of weapons to those employed in "civilized warfare."

James Blaksley was arrested for carrying a revolver within the Salina city limits while under the influence of alcohol. After he was found guilty in the city police court, the defendant appealed the conviction to the district court, which upheld the original verdict. Blaksley then appealed to the Kansas Supreme Court, claiming that section 1003 of the General Statutes of 1901 violated the state constitution. The statute stated that "The [city] council may prohibit and punish the carrying of firearms or other deadly weapons, concealed or otherwise." Section four of the bill of rights within the state constitution declared that "The people have the right to bear arms for their defense and security; but standing armies, in time of peace, are dangerous to liberty, and shall not be tolerated."

In response to Blaksley's contention that the constitution limited the legislature's power to prevent an individual from possessing or carrying arms, the court concluded that the provision in the bill of rights regarding the bearing of arms refers to the people collectively rather than to the rights of individual persons. The court believed that the expression of concern for standing armies and their threat to liberty established the relationship between the right to bear arms and the nature of the military establishment. Therefore, the framers did not intend to establish a right of individuals independent of a concern for military organization. Article eight of the state constitution clarified the way in which the people could exercise the right to bear arms. In preserving the general security, all able-bodied citizens between the ages of 21 and 45 were to serve in the militia. In time of peace, the militia would serve as the sole means for maintaining security. However, no one had the right to assume that responsibility without the sanction of the legislature through the authority of the constitution.

The court also focused on the Second Amendment to the U.S. Constitution in support of its position that the right to bear arms applied only to membership in the state militia or other legitimate military organization. Similar to the state constitution, the objective of the national document was, the court argued, to maintain security by guaranteeing to people, as members of a well-regulated militia or other legally sanctioned military organization, the right to bear arms. According to the court's interpretation of the exercise of this right, the defendant could not satisfy the condition of membership in an organized militia or any other legal military organization that would sanction the bearing of arms. His carrying a weapon was not covered under the state bill of rights and therefore no constitutionally protected right was involved.

See also: Bliss v. Commonwealth (1822); Second Amendment.

Further Reading: *City of Salina v. Blaksley*, 83 P. 619, 72 Kan. 230 (1905); Earl R. Kruschke, *The Right to Keep and Bear Arms* (Springfield, IL: Charles C. Thomas, 1985).

Civil Forfeiture

Civil forfeiture refers to government confiscation of property, including such things as automobiles, trucks, airplanes, sea vessels, cash, and real property that in some way has been involved in a crime. Although federal, state, and local governments have generally used forfeiture to discourage the drug trade, the procedure applies to many other unlawful acts, such as transporting illegal aliens, violating conservation laws, counterfeiting, sale of obscene materials and contraband cigarettes, and illegal gambling. Gun rights advocates fear that the procedure may be used more extensively against gun owners who have in some way inadvertently violated a firearms statute. Although civil forfeiture has been upheld by the U.S. Supreme Court, many have expressed concern that the federal program grants extensive powers to government officials.

The Controlled Substances Act, in Title 21, section 881, provides for a forfeiture program aimed primarily at drug smugglers and dealers. The acquittal of a defendant on criminal charges may not end civil action. Although no criminal guilt may be established, property can still be confiscated because the courts require a less demanding level of proof in civil forfeiture than in criminal proceedings. While criminal cases employ "beyond reasonable doubt" as the standard of proof, civil forfeiture cases employ "probable cause." Although a forfeiture could be challenged in court, those concerned about the process, including gun rights advocates, have noted that the claimant might not have the right to counsel, a jury trial, or the opportunity to confront witnesses or informants. Those troubled by the civil forfeiture process have claimed that law enforcement agencies may demonstrate great zeal in confiscating property even when a criminal conviction seems unlikely, given the lower burden of proof and the incentive of monetary gain. Although forfeiture statutes contain exemptions for property owners who are ignorant of any illegal use, the courts have upheld forfeitures even when the owner most likely was innocent of any involvement or collaboration in criminal activity.

In 1999 Congress passed the Civil Asset Forfeiture Act, a measure introduced by Representative Henry Hyde (R-IL). The legislation required that the federal government prove a relationship between the seized property and a crime; allowed for an "innocent owner" defense so that owners who are not aware that their property is involved in criminal activity may regain their possessions; provided an appointed counsel for indigent defendants; and established the "preponderance of the evidence" standard that the federal government must reach in order to effect a forfeiture. Nonetheless, civil forfeiture remains a legal weapon the federal government can use to discourage illegal activity. The Department of Justice pursues three major goals: 1) punishing and deterring criminal activity by denying persons the property used in or obtained through illegal activities; 2) improving collaboration among federal, state, and local law enforcement agencies by sharing recovered resources, and 3) accumulating revenues to be used in further law enforcement operations involving forfeiture. The last goal includes providing legal training for law enforcement officers engaged in the civil forfeiture process. The Treasury Department reported that the Treasury Forfeiture Fund acquired more than $483 million in 2009, $600 million in 2010 and $526 million in 2011.

Gun rights advocates are most concerned about the possible forfeiture authority of the

Bureau of Alcohol, Tobacco, Firearms, and Explosives (ATF). Congress provided the ATF with seizure authority, specifically with regard to customs violations, in the Gun Control Act of 1968. However, the Firearms Owners Protection Act of 1986, for which the National Rifle Association (NRA) and other gun rights organizations lobbied extensively, limited that authority. ATF agents may seize only those firearms actually used in a specific illegal activity. Any other property owned by the accused cannot be seized. To confiscate a weapon, the owner must have been charged with a "willful or knowing" violation of firearms laws. Confiscation also requires a higher burden of proof: clear and convincing evidence. If acquitted, the gun owner must have his or her weapon returned. California, Connecticut, Indiana, and New York allow law enforcement officers to seize firearms without a warrant if it is determined that the owner is in a questionable mental state or is likely to commit a crime.

The more limited firearms forfeiture rules notwithstanding, gun rights advocates express concern that Congress and the president may be willing to establish more extensive forfeiture authority, especially in relation to bans on certain firearms such as assault rifles. The nightmare scenario for gun advocates is an ATF granted the authority to confiscate, on the word of a confidential informant, guns and possibly other property for "minor" violations of firearms laws. Such fears may lead gun rights groups to lobby for additional weakening of existing forfeiture statutes.

See also: Bureau of Alcohol, Tobacco, Firearms, and Explosives; Firearms Owners Protection Act; Gun Control Act of 1968; National Rifle Association; *United States v. One Assortment of 89 Firearms* (1984).

Further Reading: May Ferguson Bradford, *Asset Forfeiture* (Beaumont, TX: United States Attorney's Office, Eastern District of Texas, n.d.); Department of the Treasury, "Treasury Forfeiture Fund Accountability Report, Fiscal Year 2009," www.ustreas.gov/offices/enforcement/teoaf/publications/FY_2009_ACCOUNTABILITY_REPORT%20Treasury%20Forfeiture%Fund.pdf; Diane Cecilia Weber, "Civil Forfeiture: The 'War on Drugs' Could Become the 'War on Gun Owners,' " *Guns and Ammo* 42 (June 1998), 16, 18–19; 42 (July 1998), 12, 14, 96; U.S. Department of the Treasury, "About Forfeiture," http://ustreas.gov/offices/enforcement/teoaf/about-forfeiture.shtml (accessed September 13, 2010).

Clinton, William Jefferson (Bill) (1946–)

Democratic President Bill Clinton was a major supporter of more stringent gun control, and consequently became a major target of gun rights groups such as the National Rifle Association (NRA). During his administration, Clinton signed into law the Brady Handgun Violence Prevention Act and a ban on assault weapons. At the signing ceremony for the Brady Act, Clinton reminisced about his boyhood experiences with guns, stating that "I live in a place where we still close schools and plants on the first day of deer season." However, he claimed that this aspect of American life had been transformed into "an instrument of maintaining madness. It is crazy."

The 1992 Democratic platform on which Clinton first campaigned for the presidency contained an explicit endorsement for additional gun control legislation. The platform supported a waiting period for handgun purchases and a ban on assault weapons, advocated increased penalties for crimes committed with firearms, called for a halt to the illegal gun market, and backed severe punishment for those selling firearms to youths. However, Clinton's platform stated that no restrictions should be placed on firearms used for "legitimate hunting and sporting purposes."

The Brady bill languished in Congress during the Republican administrations of Ronald Reagan and George H. W. Bush, but when Clinton became president in January 1993 the measure gained a major advocate. On November 30, 1994, Clinton signed the bill into law. A more difficult fight for Clinton was passage of the assault weapons ban. In 1993, he expanded the import ban instituted by President George H. W. Bush, issuing an executive order that included assault-style handguns. In 1994, Clinton supported an assault weapons ban being considered by the U.S. House of Representatives as part of the crime bill. Although the bill was initially defeated in a House vote, Clinton stated that the fight was not over. He obtained the support of police organizations in a public relations campaign. Although many who backed the crime bill asked

Clinton to remove the assault weapons ban, the president refused. A compromise bill, which included decreased spending, passed the House in August, gained Senate approval, and was signed by the president in September. Unpopular among gun rights advocates, the ban came under attack in 1996 in the new Republican-controlled Congress. In March, a repeal was approved by the House, but not by a sufficient margin to survive a Clinton veto, and the Senate never took up the measure. In 1998, Clinton further expanded the ban on assault weapons, announcing a permanent prohibition on the importation of 58 additional firearms.

Although a national instant background check system for purchasing a handgun was inaugurated on November 30, 1998, to replace the five-day waiting period imposed by the Brady law, Clinton stated that he would ask Congress to institute a new waiting period. In a speech given shortly after the new system went into effect, Clinton praised the instant check, stating that in the first four days of operation, 100,000 prospective firearms sales were examined and 400 purchases were stopped. In August 2000, the Clinton White House announced that up to March of that year, 10 million background checks had been conducted, and approximately 179,000 illegal guns sales had been prevented. Clinton continued to argue that a waiting period would provide a "cooling-off" interval to prevent purchases made in anger or desperation and would allow for a more thorough check of records that are not yet computerized. Clinton criticized the NRA for initiating a lawsuit against the instant check system.

In addition to reestablishing the waiting period, Clinton announced that he would ask Congress to impose a lifetime prohibition on gun ownership for juveniles convicted of violent crimes. Under current law, the criminal records of youths are disregarded after they turn 21. In addition, Clinton asked Attorney General Janet Reno and Treasury Secretary Robert Rubin to propose strategies to require people who purchase firearms at gun shows to undergo background checks. With Republican control of Congress, these measures were not enacted.

See also: Assault Weapons Ban; Brady Handgun Violence Prevention Act; Bush, George H. W.; Gun Shows; Littleton, Colorado, Columbine School Shooting; National Rifle Association; Reagan, Ronald; Reno, Janet.

Further Reading: Alice Ann Love, "Clinton Eyes Handgun Waiting Period," Associated Press (December 5, 1998), *Yahoo!* News Web site, http://dailynews. yahoo.com/headlines/ap/a.../?s=v/ap/19981205/ ts/clinton_radio_4.html; Jack Nelson, "Clinton to Introduce Gun Control Measures, Challenge NRA Lobby," *Los Angeles Times* (November 19, 1993); Robert J. Spitzer, *The Politics of Gun Control*, 2nd ed. (New York: Chatham House, 1998). On the Issues, "Bill Clinton on Gun Control," www/ontheissues.org/ celeb/Bill_Clinton_Gun_Control.htm.

Coalition to Stop Gun Violence (CSGV)

The Coalition to Stop Gun Violence (CSGV) works to reduce gun-related violence by engaging in research projects and advocating policies intended to prevent firearm violence. The CSGV's sister organization, the Educational Fund to Stop Gun Violence, filed an *amicus curiae* brief in the U.S. Supreme Court case *District of Columbia v. Heller* (2008), defending the District's ban on handguns. However, when the Supreme Court ruled in favor of an individual's right to possess firearms, the CSGV began to emphasize less ambitious measures. Even when advocating a ban on handguns, the organization did not call for a similar ban on shotguns and rifles used for hunting because they are not considered a serious threat to public safety.

The CSGV was established in 1974 as the National Coalition to Ban Handguns. Initially operating in collaboration with Handgun Control, Inc. (HCI), the CSGV soon separated from its partner organization because of disagreements about the basic strategy to pursue. In 1990 the organization assumed its present name. The CSGV is a coalition of 47 associations, including religious, child welfare, social justice, public health, and educational groups. In 1993 and 1994, the CSGV joined with broadcast networks like MTV and Nickelodeon and with several movie studios to produce a media campaign against violence.

The CSGV advocates what it considers "intermediate steps" to limit the level of violence, including closing the "gun show loophole" that allows prohibited persons such as felons to purchase firearms from unlicensed dealers at gun shows; tightening the qualifications for concealed carry licenses; requiring the use of microstamping technology that earmarks an expended cartridge with a gun's serial number; and reinstituting the assault weapons ban. Observing that in 1994 over half of the guns used in crimes that the Bureau of Alcohol, Tobacco, Firearms, and Explosives (ATF) could trace originated with federally licensed firearms dealers, the CSGV calls for measures to limit the availability of federal licenses for firearms dealers. The organization observes with approval that from 1994 to 1996 the number of licensed dealers declined from over 245,000 to 142,000. The 1994 Brady Handgun Violence Prevention Act had increased the three-year license fee from $30 to $200.

The CSGV advocates restrictive licensing and registering of gun owners and opposes attempts on the state level to liberalize laws allowing for the carrying of concealed weapons. The organization has expressed concern over the costs of treating victims of firearm violence, most of which are passed on to the taxpayer. The organization estimates that while 35,000 to 40,000 firearms-related deaths occur each year, the number of injuries are three times as great, with medical costs approximately $300,000 per injury. Therefore, the CSGV supports measures to increase taxes on handguns and ammunition, with the revenues to be earmarked for health care costs. The organization also supports legislation to establish strict liability for firearms manufacturers and dealers. A related measure would allow for regulating firearms as consumer products that must meet certain safety standards.

Banning Saturday night specials, or "junk guns," has been one of the organization's longstanding objectives. Citing ATF data, the CSGV identifies junk guns as a major culprit in crime. Although the Gun Control Act of 1968 banned import of such weapons, domestic production has continued. The organization hopes to stop manufacturers from producing the weapons, or at least to convince manufacturers to set higher production standards. Hoping to limit the illegal transfer and use of handguns, the CSGV supports a national one-handgun-a-month limit on purchases. Although the Educational Fund no longer maintains the Firearms Litigation Clearinghouse, the organization continues to offer legal assistance to victims of firearms violence and their attorneys. The organization believes that greater controls on legal gun owners and dealers, called the "gatekeepers" of firearms used in crimes, will result

in lowered gun violence. Until the *Heller* decision in 2008, the CSGV rejected the argument that the Second Amendment guarantees an individual right to keep and bear arms, relying on the decision in *United States v. Miller* (1939), in which the Supreme Court held that firearm possession is not a right protected by the Constitution unless related to the maintenance of a well-regulated militia. In 2010, the Coalition reacted strongly against U.S. Senators John McCain (R-AZ) and John Tester (D-MT), and Representatives Travis Childers (D-MS) and Mark Souder (R-IN) when they introduced the "Second Amendment Enforcement Act," a bill reportedly drafted by the National Rifle Association that would further weaken gun control measures in the District of Columbia.

Responding to the claim that handguns offer an effective method of self-defense, the CSGV has cited data indicating that suicides are five times more likely, and homicides are three times more likely, to occur in homes with firearms. The CSGV emphasizes the extremely restricted instances in which a firearm may be used legally against another person. The organization strongly opposes the stand-your-ground laws—which terms "shoot first" laws—that many states have passed in recent years. Such laws eliminate the so-called duty to retreat in a public space before a person can justifiably use force against another person. The CSGV holds that stand-your-ground laws will lead to an increase in the use of force in public places. Following the mass shooting in Orlando, Florida, in June 2016, the CSGV urged supporters to become single-issue voters by pledging to vote only for candidates who will support stronger gun control measures. The organization asks supporters to contact their member of Congress and contribute time and other resources to further gun violence prevention.

Joshua Horwitz, executive director of the CSGV, coauthored with Casey Anderson *Guns, Democracy, and the Insurrectionist Idea* (2009), in which the authors challenge the idea that the right to possess firearms can be based in part on the need for protection against government oppression. Horwitz and Anderson argue that insurrectionism—the belief that an armed citizenry is necessary to limit an overweening government—is the true threat to freedom.

See also: Brady Handgun Violence Prevention Act; Bureau of Alcohol, Tobacco, Firearms, and

Explosives; Gun Control Act of 1968; Handgun Control, Inc.; Saturday Night Special; Second Amendment; *United States v. Miller* (1939).

Further Reading: Coalition to Stop Gun Violence Web site, www.csgv.org; CSGV, "'Second Amendment Enforcement Act' a Farce in Name and Purpose" (April 28, 2010), www.csgv.org/media-web/press-releases/197-second-amendment-enforcement-act-a-farce-in-name-and-purpose; Robert J. Spitzer, *The Politics of Gun Control* (Washington, DC: CQ Press, 2008).

Collectors

Gun collectors have been a sticking point in discussions of firearms regulation proposals, given their concern that such measures could threaten hobbies and economic enterprises. According to Roland Docal, "[The gun collector's] focus is on the beauty, craftsmanship, rarity, and profit potential that accompany the possession of firearms. While the collector usually sides with pro-gun forces, he does so to ensure the continued legality of his activity and to protect the value of his investment." Gun control supporters often express sympathy for the concerns of gun collectors, realizing that to be successful, they cannot afford to alienate a potentially influential group that does not have the same overriding concern with the Second Amendment that gun rights organizations have.

The number of collectors burgeoned during the twentieth century. In 1939, there were an estimated 50,000 collectors in the United States. Twenty years later, that estimate had increased to 650,000 and has continued to increase. Fascination with the art and technology of firearms and the expectation of rising values have contributed to the enterprise. Since 1979, the National Rifle Association (NRA) has published *Man at Arms*, one of the major magazines devoted to historical guns, swords, and related collectable items, and there are several other publications and Web sites devoted to collecting.

The assault weapons ban of 1994, known as the Public Safety and Recreational Firearms Use Protection Act, while making it unlawful "to manufacture, transfer, or possess a semiautomatic assault weapon," made exceptions, including "any firearm that (i) is manually operated by bolt, pump, lever or slide action; (ii) has been rendered permanently inoperable; or (iii) is an antique firearm." This attempt to accommodate gun collectors notwithstanding, some collectors remained pessimistic regarding the future prospects for firearms restrictions, especially given the general public sentiment in favor of further controls.

Collectors contend that any measure banning the manufacture, sale, and possession of particular firearms would be a violation of the Fifth Amendment protection against being deprived of property without just compensation. Ronald Docal estimated that the "fair market value" of the millions of privately owned firearms in the United States is $66.6 billion. However, he noted that this figure represents less than 5 percent of the annual federal budget, and therefore is seen as a realistic amount for gun control advocates to recommend paying to confiscate firearms.

Docal expresses apprehension about so-called "practical confiscation," legal requirements that stop short of actual confiscation but effectively eliminate firearms from a jurisdiction. For instance, a statute could offer several alternatives to gun owners, such as selling their firearms, keeping them outside a given jurisdiction, or surrendering them to authorities. Any of these options is less than palatable to gun collectors whose major concern is not with the use to which a firearm may be put, but primarily its possession as an object of value. Although opposing the U.S. Supreme Court decision in *District of Columbia v. Heller* (2008), the Brady Campaign to Prevent Gun Violence has suggested that those supporting gun rights—such as gun collectors—should be less concerned about moderate gun control measures now that the Court has recognized an individual's right to keep and bear arms. Calls for instituting background checks at gun shows undoubtedly concerned collectors who occasionally trade in firearms but do not rise to the status of a federally licensed firearms dealer, as well as President Barack Obama's executive decision in January 2016 to expand the definition of a licensed gun dealer and thus weaken an exception in the law that state that only those "engaged in the business" of dealing in firearms must complete background checks on purchases. However, attorney general Loretta Lynch state that the exception for legitimate collectors would remain in effect.

See also: Assault Weapons Ban; Gun Shows; National Rifle Association; Second Amendment.

Further Reading: Ronald Docal, "The Second, Fifth, and Ninth Amendment—The Precarious Protectors of the American Gun Collector," *Florida State Law Review* 23 (Spring 1996), FSU Web site, www.law. fsu.edu/journals.lawreview/frames/234/docatxt.html; Lee Kennett and James La Verne Anderson, *The Gun in America: The Origins of a National Dilemma* (Westport, CT: Greenwood, 1975); "Links to Arms Collector Groups," http://armscollectors.com/clublist. htm (accessed September 13, 2010).

Colorado Springs, Colorado Planned Parenthood Shooting, 2015

On November 27, 2015, 57-year-old Robert L. Dear, Jr. entered a Planned Parenthood clinic in Colorado Springs, Colorado, and began shooting with a semi-automatic rifle, and wearing hunting gear. He killed three and injured nine. One of those killed and five of the wounded were police officers. After a five hour standoff, police talked him out of the building. Propane tanks were found next to Dear's car, which authorities thought Dear planned to shoot in order to explode them. Dear's former wife reported that he had long expressed antipathy toward Planned Parenthood, extending back over twenty years, and had once put glue in the door locks of a Planned Parenthood clinic. She also said that he had a history of violent behavior, and that he claimed to be an evangelical Christian.

In courtroom appearances, Dear expressed anti-abortion and anti-Planned Parenthood sentiments and said he was a "warrior for the babies." He also said he was guilty. He was ordered to undergo a mental health examination by the court. The clinic reopened in February 2016. Over the years, other Planned Parenthood facilities have been the target of threats and violent attacks, as have medical personnel, and many more have been the site of non-violent protests by those opposed to abortion. According to the pro-choice group the National Abortion Federation, since 1993, 11 murders and 26 attempted murders have resulted from anti-abortion violence.

Further Reading: Nina Liss-Schultz, "The New, Ugly Surge in Violence and Threats Against Abortion Providers," *Mother Jones,* November 28, 2015, at http://www.motherjones.com/politics/2015/11/violence-abortion-clinics-planned-parenthood-colorado-springs-shooting; Violence Statistics, National Abortion Federation, at http://prochoice.org/education-and-advocacy/violence/violence-statistics-and-history/

Colt, Samuel (1814–1862)

Samuel Colt, an inventive gunsmith and astute businessman, made the repeating handgun a common possession in the United States. He called his six-shooter "the peacemaker," a description with which contemporary gun supporters would agree, for it coincides with the view that a gun can play a crucial role in maintaining security and tranquility among people by keeping at bay those who would threaten the safety of the community.

Although his guns are most often associated with the winning of the West, Colt was born in Hartford, Connecticut. Colt lived in the East, where he established his firearms manufacturing plants. His interest in guns began at the age of 7, when he was given a horse pistol. After Colt's mother died when he was 11 years old, his father sent him to live on a farm—where he was expected to contribute to the daily chores—and then to Amherst Academy. However, Samuel's fascination with explosives resulted in his ouster when an explosion

Samuel Colt was a nineteenth-century gunmaker whose sixshooter, the "peacemaker," made the repeating handgun a common possession in the United States. *www.wikipedia. org*

rocked the school. At age 16, Colt found himself aboard a sailing vessel where he served a one-year stint as a sailor. Colt then returned to Hartford and put himself to work making two model pistols, neither of which proved successful. His father advised Colt to abandon the project.

Despite his father's counsel, Colt continued to develop his repeating pistol. Muzzle loaders placed settlers at a disadvantage in confrontations with Indians because reloading was laborious and potentially dangerous, involving several complex steps. An Indian with a bow and arrow could shoot far more quickly than a pioneer with a muzzle loader, and with deadly effect. For four years, Colt, who was still in his teens, abandoned his firearm project, traveling around the country as "Dr. Coult" and entertaining audiences, at times passing himself off as a healer of sorts. By the mid-1830s, Colt returned to his revolver and improved it sufficiently to obtain patents in England and France. In February 1836, at the age of 21, he received a U.S. patent for the revolving breech pistol, which granted him a 20-year monopoly on the production of revolvers. That same year he opened the Patent Arms Manufacturing Company in Paterson, New Jersey, and maintained a showroom in New York City.

Colt's repeating handgun, while not an innovation, encompassed the best of prevailing ideas. However, the first model had several disadvantages. At times it malfunctioned due to fouling or broken parts, and it was relatively expensive. Although the gun sold slowly, Colt, with a knack for advertising, made the public aware of his product by taking part in an advertising tour. His sales efforts notwithstanding, Colt was unsuccessful in interesting the federal government in his weapon. His financial situation grew worse because he tended to spend profits before they were made, and in 1842, Colt was forced to close the Paterson plant.

War ultimately saved Colt's business. When the United States declared war on Mexico in 1846, the national government placed an order for 1,000 revolvers. Colt reached an agreement with Eli Whitney, Jr., to produce a new revolver Colt had developed in collaboration with Samuel Walker, a .44-caliber weapon that came to be called the Colt Walker. Colt resolved to improve the design of his successful revolver and opened his own manufacturing plant in Hartford. By 1850, his plant was operating successfully. That same year, the Connecticut State Militia commissioned him as a lieutenant-colonel, a title he used in promotional efforts targeted at government and military officials.

Colt traveled to Europe several more times to establish a market for his product, and opened a firearms manufacturing plant in London. A generous man who also knew how to promote his revolver, Colt presented several noted individuals with commemorative models, including Prince Albert, husband to Queen Victoria of Great Britain; Presidents Zachary Taylor and Franklin Pierce; the Prince of Wales, heir to the British throne; and Czar Nicholas I of Russia. These gifts helped spread the Colt name to many nations. Colt continued to improve his handgun, replacing the Walker with newer models. When the Crimean War broke out in Europe in the 1850s, demand rose once again for Colt firearms.

As the American Civil War approached in 1861, Colt anticipated the increased demand for weapons. During the war, Colt's factory operated around the clock. Pushing himself too hard, Colt died in January 1862 at the age of 48. At the time of his death, his company was worth more than $11 million. It has been said that "God made men, [but] Sam Colt made them equal." Colt's innovation made possible the production of repeating firearms through mass production methods, thus making these weapons available to people of all stations around the world.

See also: Browning, John Moses; Remington, Eliphalet, II; Ruger, William Batterman (Bill); Whitney, Eli; Winchester, Oliver Fisher.

Further Reading: Sam Fadala, *Great Shooters of the World* (South Hackensack, NJ: Stoeger, 1990); William N. Hasley, *Colt: The Making of an American Legend* (Amherst: University of Massachusetts Press, 1996); Wayne Van Zwoll, *America's Great Gunmakers* (South Hackensack, NJ: Stoeger, 1992).

Commonwealth v. Davis (1976)

The Supreme Judicial Court of Massachusetts, in *Commonwealth v. Davis* (369 Mass. 886, 1976), ruled that a state statute imposing penalties for the illegal possession of a shotgun with a barrel less than 18 inches long, does not violate either the Massachusetts Declaration of Rights or the Second Amendment to the United States Constitution. The court was guided in its ruling by the precedent of past federal appeals court decisions, such as *United*

States v. Tot (1942), *United States v. Miller* (1939), and *Cases v. United States* (1942).

In January 1974, while conducting a search, with a warrant, of an apartment for narcotics, police discovered firearms and ammunition in the possession of Hubert Davis. Indicted for possession of a shotgun with a barrel less than 18 inches long, Davis was tried and found guilty. Moving for a new trial, Davis argued that the statute under which he was convicted violated his right to bear arms under both the Massachusetts and U.S. constitutions.

Article 17 of the Massachusetts Declaration of Rights states that "The people have a right to keep and to bear arms for the common defence [sic]. And as, in time of peace, armies are dangerous to liberty, they ought not to be maintained without the consent of the legislature; and the military power shall always be held in an exact subordination to the civil authority, and be governed by it." The court ruled that the intention of Article 17 was not to guarantee individual ownership or possession of weapons, but rather arose from a distrust of standing armies and the decision to rely instead on a militia. Thus, the right guaranteed in the article refers to the provision for the common defense and citizen participation in an organized militia.

Although the court ruled that the statute in question, which limits the possession of arms by individuals, might at one time have interfered with the operation of the militia because weapons were provided by individual citizens, today the militia, or National Guard, is equipped by public moneys. The court further ruled that even in the distant past regulation of the possession or carrying of firearms, so long as it did not involve a blanket prohibition, would not have been considered an unconstitutional limitation on individual liberty or a restriction on the militia.

Deciding that the Massachusetts constitution did not support Davis's claim regarding the right to keep and bear arms, the court also rejected the claim that the statute was beyond the police power, arguing that a sawed-off shotgun, because it is a dangerous weapon and can be concealed, is reasonably subject to regulation. Therefore, the state legislature can justifiably treat such a weapon as related to violent crime and make it subject to rigorous licensing and even a ban.

The court considered the claim that the statute violated the Second Amendment to the U.S. Constitution. Making reference to the precedent established by previous Supreme Court decisions, especially in *United States v. Miller*, the court argued that the amendment resulted from the apprehension during the time the Constitution was being debated that the power of the national government over the state militias established in Article I, section 8, clauses 15 and 16, could have a deleterious effect on state militia organizations. The court interpreted the amendment as a declaration that the militias may be protected from national government action. Therefore, the amendment limits only the national government, not the states.

The court at the time saw little likelihood that the Second Amendment might someday be interpreted as limiting the states as well as the national government, because, unlike other provisions in the Bill of Rights, the Second Amendment does not focus on guaranteeing the rights of individuals, but protects state militias against national government interference. Even if the Supreme Court should one day decide that the amendment applies to the states, the states would still have the ability to exercise their regulatory authority in the realm of firearms.

See also: Cases v. United States (1942); *District of Columbia v. Heller* (2008); *McDonald v. Chicago* (2010); Second Amendment; *United States v. Miller* (1939); *United States v. Tot* (1942).

Further Reading: *Commonwealth v. Davis*, 369 Mass. 886 (1976).

Concealed Carrying on College Campuses

The mass shooting on the Virginia Tech State University campus in 2007 and a similar shooting on the Northern Illinois University campus in 2008, when a deranged former student shot and killed five people and wounded eighteen in a large lecture class before killing himself, fanned calls by some for students, faculty, and other employees to be allowed to carry guns on college campuses.

The first state to so act was Utah in 2004, although court challenges prevented implementation of the law until 2006. Since then, seven other states have enacted laws to allow campus concealed carry on public campuses whether campus leaders object or not. Those states include Colorado, Idaho, Kansas, Mississippi, Oregon, Texas, and Wisconsin. These states, however, impose various conditions or qualifications. For example, the Kansas law says gun carrying must be allowed unless campus buildings have adequate safety measures. Mississippi limits carrying to those with special training. Oregon allows carrying in public spaces, but not buildings. Wisconsin allows its campuses to exempt buildings if they post signs barring gun carrying; such signs are indeed now posted on every campus. As of this writing, 19 states ban concealed weapons on campuses, and in 23 states campuses can decide for themselves whether to bar or allow concealed carry. Overwhelmingly, campuses have opted to bar firearms. Campus law enforcement agencies are not affected by these restrictions; most campus police nationwide carry firearms.

The arguments on behalf of allowing civilian concealed carry parallel those supporting gun carrying in society. First, advocates say that an armed civilian on campus could confront a shooter or other serious threat to either deter or stop an attack more quickly than campus or local police. Second, they argue that concealed carrying reduces crime by its deterrent effect on would-be criminals. Third, they argue that criminals can easily enter campuses, which are normally not gated, to wreak mayhem. Such gun-free areas may invite predators to exploit such an environment. Fourth, the Supreme Court's 2008 and 2010 rulings establishing a personal right to have a gun for personal self-protection provide a constitutional basis for campus carrying. A student group supported by gun rights groups, Students for Concealed Carry on Campus (concealedcampus.org), lobbies for concealed carry on campuses and in state legislatures around the country. An opposing group, Keep Guns Off Campus (keepgunsoffcampus.org), lobbies against such efforts.

Campus administrators, faculty, campus law enforcement agencies, and most students have opposed such measures. Opponents note, first, that despite a handful of horrifying mass shootings, college campuses are very safe places. For example, a study comparing campus crime rates with those in society from 1997-2010 found that rates of violent crime on campuses were about 10 percent of those in society during this period. It also noted that crime rates continued to drop throughout this period. The odds of a campus homicide in 2010 were one In 875,000, far lower than in society. Second, campuses have increased security measures in recent years, including the hiring of more campus police, better lighting and

patrolling practices, safety awareness training for students and staff, installation of notification systems and cameras, and implementation of campus lock-down plans. Third, students who live on campuses live in densely populated dormitories and are mostly young adults subject to periods of intense stress, impulsive behavior, and alcohol and drug use. All of these factors invite problems when firearms are also present in the form of gun suicides, thefts, out-of-control altercations, and accidents. Fourth, the Supreme Court's two rulings establishing gun rights carved out specific exceptions for long-standing laws against gun carrying and possession, specifically listing such places as schools and government buildings. Fifth, college campuses are places of learning, and gun carrying is viewed as incompatible with that mission.

Recommended Readings: "Guns in Schools Policy Summary," *Law Center to Prevent Gun Violence*, at http://www.ncsl.org/research/education/guns-on-campus-overview.aspx; Robert J. Spitzer, *The Politics of Gun Control,* 6th ed. (Boulder, CO: Paradigm Publishers, 2015).

Concealed Carry Laws

Concealed carry laws provide for the issuance of carrying concealed weapons (CCW) licenses, which allow individuals to bear loaded, hidden weapons on their persons. Some state legislatures have enacted measures that completely prohibit carrying concealed weapons. Other states have "may-issue" provisions that allow local law enforcement agencies the discretion of approving or denying applications for a CCW license after investigating an applicant's record and confirming the need to carry a weapon. The largest group of states has instituted "shall-issue" laws that direct law enforcement officials to issue CCW licenses to anyone who applies, unless the person is disqualified for some designated reason, such as having been convicted of a felony.

Many advocates of the right to carry a concealed weapon claim that the right to bear arms is nearly absolute and therefore no demonstration of need should be established as a criterion for carrying a concealed weapon. They contend that a major benefit of a lenient CCW law is to reduce crime generally. Proponents argue that if those contemplating crime realize that a targeted victim may be armed, they are less willing to risk the physical danger to themselves of carrying out the assault.

In 1996 the Citizens Committee for the Right to Keep and Bear Arms (CCRKBA) issued the results of a study of data from the FBI's *Uniform Crime Reports* for 1994 to demonstrate that crime rates in states that have instituted CCW provisions are significantly lower than rates in states lacking such provisions. The organization claimed that states with restrictive concealed carry laws had murder rates nearly 99 percent higher than nonrestrictive states. The CCRKBA data summary indicated that the robbery rate in restrictive states was 109 percent higher than the rate for nonrestrictive states, and the aggravated assault rate for restrictive states was 65 percent higher than for nonrestrictive states. The Committee concluded that concealed carry laws should receive major credit for the differences in crime rates among the various states. Other researchers, such as David Hemenway (2004), claim that there is insufficient evidence to conclude either that CCW laws deter crime, or lead to higher levels of violence.

CCW advocates have been successful in gaining acceptance of concealed carry provisions in all 50 states. Eight states (California, Massachusetts, Connecticut, Rhode Island, New Jersey, Delaware, Maryland, and New York) have "may-issue" provisions. Five states (Alaska, Arizona, Kansas, Vermont, and Wyoming) allow concealed carry without a license. The remaining 37 states have "may-issue" provisions. Many states have instituted reciprocity provisions with other states that allow individuals eligible to carry a concealed weapon in the home state to do so in other states. Measures introduced in the U.S. Congress to establish concealed carry nation-wide have so far been unsuccessful. Courts have rejected challenges to "may-issue" CCW laws. For instance, in June 2016 the U.S. Court of Appeals for the Ninth District in San Francisco upheld a California law that requires CCS applicants to establish "good cause" (such as being employed in a position where there is a security threat) for carrying a concealed weapon.

Although CCW advocates argue that when citizens carry weapons, society becomes safer and more "polite," opponents claim that this position demonstrates a cynical view of human relationships and is basically untrue. They argue that because the United States already has more than 240 million firearms owned by private citizens, we should

already have the safest and most polite society in the world. However, in the United States the death rate attributed to firearms remains high. The anti-CCW advocates also argue that the primary beneficiaries of such provisions are gun manufacturers, who, they claim, look upon concealed carry laws as an opportunity to bolster sales.

Opponents of CCW provisions also argue that law enforcement officers face greater danger with liberalized concealed carry laws. Police confront a greater chance that the persons they stop on the highway or meet in other potentially volatile situations may be carrying a concealed firearm. Opponents, noting that the FBI's *Uniform Crime Reports* indicate that almost one-third of all murders result from arguments, contend that such encounters, which otherwise would end in shouting matches or fistfights, are more likely to result in serious injury when guns are present. They also claim that suicides, criminal homicides, and gunshot accident deaths are far more likely to occur than homicides resulting from legitimate self-protection efforts.

Contrary to the findings of researchers that CCW laws reduce crime, Ian Ayres and John J. Donohue's (2009), analysis of available data from the states lead them to conclude, first, that previous research has failed to control for other variables, such as rates of incarceration, the crack cocaine trade, and general measurement error that bias their findings; and second, that CCW laws are positively associated with increased levels of aggravated assault, and possibly with higher rates of murder and robbery. (Inconsistent findings fail to establish a relationship with rape or auto theft.) Researchers undoubtedly will continue the debate over CCW laws and their possible relationship to crime rates, as pro-gun rights and pro-gun control groups advocate their contrasting positions on the issue of concealed carry laws.

Following mass shootings on college campuses—most notably the 2007 shooting at Virginia Tech University in which a gunman killed 33 people and wounded 17 others—gun rights supporters began to push for concealed carry on university campuses. By 2016 eight states (Colorado, Idaho, Kansas, Mississippi, Oregon, Texas, Utah, and Wisconsin), either by legislation or court rulings, had initiated varied policies allowing carrying concealed weapons at institutions of higher learning. The organization Students for Concealed Carry on Campus continues to advocate the right of students to carry concealed weapons on college campuses, while many students have registered their opposition to concealed carry.

See also: Brady Campaign to Prevent Gun Violence; Citizens Committee for the Right to Keep and Bear Arms; Concealed Weapons Detectors; Lott, John R., Jr.

Further Reading: Massad Ayoob, *The Gun Digest Book of Concealed Carry* (Iola, WI: F+W Media, 2008); Ian Ayres and John J. Donohue III, "More Guns, Less Crime Fails Again: The Latest Evidence from 1997–2006," *Econ Journal Watch* 6 (May 2009): 218–238; Dan Baum, "Happiness Is a Worn Gun: My Concealed Weapon and Me," *Harper's Magazine* (August 2010): 29–38; Citizens Committee for the Right to Keep and Bear Arms, "States Allowing Citizens to Carry Concealed Firearms Have Less Violent Crime," (Bellevue, WA, 1996); Jonathan J. Cooper, "Arizona House Approves Concealed Weapons Bill," *Houston Chronicle* (April 9, 2010): A8; Susan Glick, *Concealed Carry: The Criminal's Companion* (Washington, DC: Violence Policy Center, 1995); Susan Glick, *Concealing the Risk: Real-World Effects of Lax Concealed Weapons Laws* (Washington, DC: Violence Policy Center, 1996); David Hemenway, *Private Guns, Public Health* (Ann Arbor, MI: University of Michigan Press, 2004); Mike Stuckey, "Record Numbers Licensed to Pack Heat" (June 24, 2010), www.msnbc.msn.com/id/34714389/ns/us_news-life; Robert J. Spinks and Michael C. Powell, "Concealed Carry of Firearms on University Campuses," in Glenn H. Utter, ed., *Guns and Contemporary Society* (Santa Barbara, CA: Praeger, 2016): vol. 3, 19-58; National Conference of State Legislatures, "Guns on Campus: Overview" (May 31, 2016), http://ncsl.org/research/education/guns-on-campus-overview.aspx; Adam Nagourney and Erik Eckholm, "A Federal Appeals Finds No Right to Carry a Concealed Weapon," *New York Times* (June 10, 2016): A11.

Concealed Weapons Detectors

In 1995, the U.S. Justice Department provided $2.15 million for a project to develop test models of concealed weapons detectors. The Department's National Institute of Justice (NIJ) was granted supervision over the project, which has involved work at three laboratories. The purpose of the project was to produce an instrument capable of identifying and describing a concealed weapon from a distance of 12 feet that an individual is carrying in his or her clothing. The hope is that the distance at which a weapon may be identified can be increased.

Especially following the September 11, 2001, terrorist attacks, the goal has been the development of a concealed weapons detector that can determine the presence not only of a firearm but also of suicide vests, knives, and other weapons. Airports around the world are testing full-body scanners to determine their effectiveness in detecting concealed weapons. Also, in October 2010, Homeland Security officials announced the development at the Los Alamos National Laboratory of a magnetic resonance device that can determine a liquid's molecular structure as a means of discovering whether the liquid is an explosive. When the scanning device is put into service at airports, passengers may no longer be limited to small liquid containers.

Law enforcement agencies may find new technology useful, especially if installed in police vehicles. By pointing the instrument from the window, police could be able to determine if someone on the street is carrying a firearm. Those who support the development of such devices indicate that liberalized concealed carry laws may make the ability to detect firearms a crucial factor in effective policing. Although the Fourth Amendment guarantee against unwarranted searches and seizures, a right that gun advocates take very seriously, limits standard frisking without reasonable suspicion that a person may be armed, a detector might avoid such legal restrictions. If a detecting device could identify the presence of a concealed weapon without a search, then a subsequent frisk and confiscation may be legally justifiable.

The projects granted funding have investigated different methods of detection. One method involves the measurement of irregularities in the human body's natural electromagnetic waves caused by the presence of a firearm. Another method, similar to radar, measures the reflection of an emitting pulse. A third procedure attempts to detect irregularities in the earth's magnetic field caused by a firearm. Each method includes a monitor and a computer system that, with sufficient sophistication, could even identify the type of firearm being detected.

With regard to the politics of gun control, improved technology potentially has the advantage of avoiding many of the traditional issues that divide the opponents and proponents of firearms restrictions. David Van Biema reported that the prospect of improved technology that allows the development of concealed weapons detectors has gained the support of liberal as well as conservative politicians. Although civil liberties issues may arise regarding the use of the new technology, at least one spokesperson for the American Civil Liberties Union (ACLU) has expressed cautious acceptance, perhaps due in part to the ACLU's willingness to entertain the constitutionality of gun control legislation. However, gun rights advocates may not support the ability of potentially oppressive government agents to ferret out the firearms of law-abiding citizens. Nonetheless, the development and of such detection technology has continued, and commercial detectors have reached the market, such as Thermal Matrix VSA's ACT system, which the company claims can detect from a distance not only concealed guns but also explosives, knives, and liquids. The system does not invade personal space.

See also: American Civil Liberties Union; Concealed Carry Laws; Fourth Amendment.

Further Reading: David Van Biema, "Peekaboo: The New Detector," *Time* 145 (March 27, 1995), 29; Susan Montoya Bryan, "Liquid Scanner Aims for Safer Air Travel," *Houston Chronicle* (October 14, 2010), A3; A. Trent De Persia, Suzan Yeager, and Steve Ortiz, eds., *Surveillance and Assessment Technologies for Law Enforcement* (Bellingham, WA: International Society for Optical Engineering, 1997); Department of Energy, "Bannock County Courthouse to Be 'Secure' Using INEEL Technology," *Department of Energy News* (April 22, 1997); Chris Tillery, "Detecting Concealed Weapons: Directions for the Future," *National Institute of Justice* (October 2007), www.ojp.usdoj. gov/nij/journals/258/detecting-concealed-weapons. html; Bhavna Khojone and V. K. Shandilya, "Concealed Weapon Detection Using Image Processing," *International Journal of Scientific Engineering Research* 3 (June 2012), www.iser. org/researchpaper%5cconcealed-weapon-detection-using-image-processing.pdf; Thermal Matrix, "Advanced and Reliable Concealed Weapons Detection Systems," www.thermalmatrix.com.

Congress of Racial Equality (CORE)

The Congress of Racial Equality (CORE), a civil rights organization that has taken a position on

gun control sympathetic to the National Rifle Association (NRA), was established in 1942 by James Farmer. CORE maintains a national headquarters in New York City and has local affiliates and chapters throughout the United States and in parts of Africa, Central America, and the Caribbean. The organization prides itself on striving for equal rights for all and works to achieve self-determination and self-government. CORE believes all people should have the right "to decide for themselves what social and political organizations can operate in their best interest."

Initially, CORE worked to desegregate restaurants and other public accommodations in Chicago. The organization sponsored nonviolent sit-ins at segregated public places in the South and sponsored the interracially supported Freedom Rides through the southern states, a strategy intended to end segregation on interstate bus routes. CORE helped sponsor the 1963 civil rights march on Washington, D.C., and subsequently engaged in black voter registration efforts in southern states and improvement in slum housing and police conduct.

In the 1980s, the NRA began to collaborate with CORE and its leader, Roy Innis, on crime prevention strategies. In 1984, Innis and the NRA initiated a campaign to liberalize handgun laws in the state of New York. Innis, who had two sons who were victims of gun violence, declared that some way was needed to "bring some kind of fear into a criminal" and to "make the street safe for citizens and unsafe for criminals." CORE continues a Crime Victims/Witness Program and maintains a "Good Samaritan" fund to help those who confront crime to bear the resulting medical and legal costs. In 1986, the NRA joined with CORE in developing the National Crime Fighters' Crusade. Josh Sugarmann, director of the Violence Policy Center, has reported that the NRA donated $5,000 to CORE to conduct the initiative. NRA representative Richard Feldman declared that the intentions of CORE and the NRA were to "let decent citizens know how to lawfully obtain firearms." Sugarmann claims that at the opening of the crusade, New York State Rifle and Pistol Clubs "demonstrated gun safety techniques and handed out handgun permit applications." In 1986, the NRA continued its support for CORE, contributing more than $4,000 to Innis's unsuccessful bid for a seat in the U.S. House of Representatives.

CORE is considered a more moderate civil rights organization that emphasizes the need for self-help. The gun rights perspective found a comfortable home with the organization's overall philosophy. For instance, Project Independence, the organization's welfare reform and job training program, focuses on alleviating the costs of welfare, unemployment, and the criminal justice system by providing workforce training and "welfare-to-work" assistance. The organization strives to instill in individuals technical skills, work values, and self-esteem. Recognizing the importance of personal security, CORE has been willing to join forces with the NRA to achieve that end.

In *District of Columbia v. Heller* (2008), CORE submitted an *amicus curiae* brief, and in *McDonald v. Chicago* (2010) CORE joined in a brief to support the right of individuals to possess firearms for self-protection. In *Heller*, the brief, written by Stefan Bijan Tahmassebi, Robert Cottrol, and Raymond T. Diamond, emphasized that *prima facie* neutral gun control laws actually disproportionately affect the poor and minorities, partly because enforcement efforts tend to target these groups, which can result in illegal searches and seizures. The brief in *McDonald*, written by David B. Kopel, argued that guns, when used for self-defense, can save lives. Kopel claimed that, because "defensive arms" are frequently present in U.S. homes, the burglary rate of occupied homes is much lower in the United States than in other countries. In addition, he noted that a sizable increase in crime compared to other U.S. cities occurred following the passage of the 1982 Chicago ban on handguns.

In 2015 CORE expressed to the Florida state legislature its support for permitting the concealed carry of firearms on university campuses. In 2016 CORE joined a California coalition to oppose a proposed ballot initiative, the Safety for All Act, which would require background checks for purchasing ammunition and would ban possession of large capacity ammunition magazines.

See also: Kopel, David B.; National Rifle Association; Violence Policy Center.

Further Reading: Congress of Racial Equality Web site, www.core-online; David B. Kopel, *McDonald v. Chicago amicus curiae* brief (2010), http://abanet. org/publiced/preview/briefs/pdfs/09-10/08-1521_ PetitionerAmCuInternationalLawEnforcement EducatorsAndTrainersAssociation.pdf; Josh Sugarmann, *National Rifle Association: Money,*

Firepower and Fear (Washington, DC: National Press, 1992); Stefan Bijan Tahmassebi, Robert Cottrol, and Raymond T. Diamond, *District of Columbia v. Heller amicus curiae* brief (2008), www. abanet.org/publiced/preview/briefs/pdfs/07-08/07-290_RespondentAmCuCongrRacialEqualitynew.pdf.

Constitutional Accountability Center

In 2008 the Constitutional Accountability Center (CAC) became the successor organization to the Community Rights Counsel, which was established in 1998 to promote "constitutional principles to defend laws that make our communities environmentally sound and socially just." The organization focuses much of its efforts on attempting to influence the decisions of the U.S. Supreme Court and other federal and state courts by filing *amicus curiae* briefs. The CAC is described as "a think tank, law firm, and action center" attempting to achieve the "progressive promise" of the Constitution and the document's history. Elizabeth B. Wydra, was the organization's chief counsel from 2008 to 2016, when she became the Center's president. Judith E. Schaeffer is vice president and chief operating officer for the Center.

The CAC has taken positions on various issues from a perspective that views the Constitution as a governing document that is conducive to a liberal political agenda. For instance, CAC founder and president Douglas Kendall (1964-2015) opposed Arizona's immigration law that authorized law enforcement officers to check the immigration status of those stopped for other offenses and who are suspected of being undocumented. CAC lawyers filed an *amicus* brief in the case *United States v. Arizona*, arguing that the new Arizona law violated the U.S. Constitution, the history of its drafting, and the federal structure it established. According to the brief, the founders of the Constitution stipulated that the federal government solely had authority to establish immigration policy. The CAC also defends the constitutional status of environmental regulations, and holds that the thirteenth, fourteenth, and fifteenth amendments, ratified following the Civil War, provide a firm basis for the federal government to assure civil rights against violations by state governments.

Doug Pennington, who served as CAC's press secretary from 2010 to 2016, when he became the organization's director of communications, previously served as the director of communications for the Brady Campaign to Prevent Gun Violence, and reportedly managed the gun control organization's reaction to the Virginia Tech shooting as well as the media campaign surrounding the U.S. Supreme Court cases *District of Columbia v. Heller* (2008) and *McDonald v. Chicago* (2010). The Brady Campaign responded to the *Heller* decision somewhat optimistically, contending that the Court, in recognizing an individual's right to own firearms, left open the possibility that the Second Amendment did not signify an absolute right to own firearms and therefore allowed certain limitations on that right. Accepting the Supreme Court's decision in *Heller* that the Second Amendment guarantees the right of individuals to keep and bear arms, the CAC filed an *amicus curiae* brief in *McDonald* arguing that the Second Amendment protects this individual right from state and local government violation based on the Privileges or Immunities Clause of the Fourteenth Amendment ("No State shall make or enforce any law which shall abridge the privileges or immunities of citizens of the United States").

Adam Winkler, law professor at the University of California at Los Angeles and one of the eight academics who wrote the brief, commented that an individual's right to bear arms, which the organization understands as part of a right to bodily autonomy, conforms to a "living Constitution." When the Supreme Court justices agreed to review the decision of the Seventh Circuit Court in *McDonald v. Chicago* regarding a Chicago, Illinois, ordinance prohibiting the possession of handguns, Douglas Kendall announced his approval, and expressed his hope that the Court would "restore the precise constitutional text" mandating that states abide by the protection of fundamental rights. Kendall noted that the CAC is concerned not just with gun rights, but with the general objective of firmly establishing the protection of substantive rights and liberties via the Fourteenth Amendment's Privileges or Immunities Clause, which the organization hopes will support liberal arguments in favor of federal government enforcement of due-process protections at the state level.

See also: Brady Campaign to Prevent Gun Violence; *District of Columbia v. Heller* (2008); Fourteenth Amendment; *McDonald v. Chicago*; Second Amendment.

Further Reading: Ben Adler, "Gun Rally: Liberals and the NRA Have Found Common Cause in a Pending Supreme Court Case," *Newsweek* (March 8, 2010): 44–45; Constitutional Accountability Center Web site, www.theusconstitution.org; Constitutional Accountability Center *Amicus Curiae* brief, *McDonald v. City of Chicago*; www.theusconstitution. org/upload/filelists/285_McDonald_v_Chicago. pdf?phpMyAdmin=TzXZ 9IzqiGqj5tqL1t06F; "Statement by Doug Kendall, President and Founder, Constitutional Accountability Center Hailing the Decision of the Supreme Court to Review *McDonald v. City of Chicago*"; (September 30, 2009), www.theusconstitution.org/page_module. php?id=28&mid=32; Constitutional Accountability Center, "Where Will the Second Amendment Revolution Lead?" (June 3, 2016), www.theusconstitution.org/think-tank/crossroads. where-will-second-amendment-revolution-lead.

Consumer Product Safety

Gun control advocates note that no federal agency has been granted the authority to regulate the consumer product safety of firearms. Although Congress authorized the Bureau of Alcohol, Tobacco, Firearms, and Explosives (ATF) to regulate commerce in guns and ammunition, that agency has little authority to oversee the safety of firearms as consumer products, nor does any other agency of the federal government. Supporters of consumer gun safety claim that firearms satisfy the basic conditions for legitimate regulation because they are obviously dangerous and exact a high yearly death toll. The law places on the list of exceptions to consumer products subject to regulation "any article which, if sold by the manufacturer, producer, or importer, would be subject to the tax imposed by section 4181 of the Internal Revenue Code of 1986." Section 4181 applies to firearms and ammunition.

Consumer product safety advocates have suggested that the ATF be granted the same authority that three other federal regulatory agencies already have to determine product safety. The Consumer Product Safety Commission (CPSC), established in 1972, regulates more than 15,000 varied consumer products. When Congress originally passed legislation creating the CPSC, firearms and ammunition were exempted from its control.

The CPSC relies on a series of about 90 hospital emergency rooms, called the National

Electronic Injury Surveillance System (NEISS) to record injuries associated with consumer products. This reporting system allows the agency to respond to potentially hazardous products. The two other regulatory agencies are the National Highway Traffic Safety Administration (NHTSA), which was established under the National Traffic and Motor Vehicle Safety Act of 1966 to regulate automobile safety, and the Environmental Protection Agency (EPA), which was given the authority under the Federal Insecticide, Fungicide and Rodenticide Act (FIFRA) of 1947 to regulate the manufacture, sale, and use of pesticides, and manages the enforcement of the Toxic Substances Control Act (TSCA) of 1976, which limits the use of harmful chemicals.

Gun control advocates argue that if various other potentially dangerous products are regulated by federal agencies, firearms are a reasonable candidate for such consumer safety regulation. Although this regulation might be considered best handled by an independent regulatory agency, the ATF has long experience with regulating firearms. The agency would need the authority to set firearms safety standards, to be able to oversee compliance, and have the capability to order recalls of defective weapons. However, the ATF, long a target of severe criticism by gun rights groups, would have to receive significantly increased powers from Congress to act as a consumer agency. In addition, the Homeland Security Act of 2002 divided the functions of the agency between two departments; the tax and trade roles remained in the Treasury Department while the enforcement functions were transferred to the Department of Justice.

According to gun control supporters, the ATF should be given the authority to limit the availability of especially hazardous firearms and to order an end to selling firearms that present an immediate danger to the public. They also contend that air and pellet guns, presently under the jurisdiction of the CPSC, should be transferred to the ATF. If given powers similar to other product safety agencies, the ATF would have the ability to gather data regarding injuries and deaths associated with firearms. Prior to marketing, if a firearm presents a serious risk to consumer safety, the ATF could prevent the weapon from being offered to consumers.

The call by some gun control groups to ban handgun sales, more than any other proposal, led gun rights advocates to conclude that the ultimate purpose of applying consumer product safety policy to firearms was to take guns away from law-abiding American citizens. Although gun control advocates argue that safety devices such as loaded chamber indicators, magazine safeties that prevent a gun without an ammunition clip from firing, "drop-safe" firearms, and personalized, so-called smart guns should be mandatory, gun rights supporters, holding to the maxim that guns do not kill people, people kill people, tend to attribute injuries to the malicious or incompetent use to which firearms are put. They conclude that firearms, like automobiles, are inherently dangerous products and that safety can best be ensured not through prohibition but by effective consumer training in their use.

See also: Bureau of Alcohol, Tobacco, Firearms, and Explosives; Product Liability Lawsuits.

Further Reading: Wayne R. LaPierre, *Guns, Crime, and Freedom* (Washington, DC: Regnery, 1994); Robert Longley, "Defective Firearms Greater Threat Than Thought" (February 2005), http://usgovinfo.about.com/od/consumerawareness/a/badguns.htm?p=1; Josh Sugarmann and Kristen Rand, *Cease Fire: A Comprehensive Strategy to Reduce Firearms Violence* (Washington, DC: Violence Policy Center, 1997); Joseph Sanderson and Norman Silber, "Unsafe at Any Range: Treat Guns Like the Consumer Products That They Are," *Huffington Post* (June 29, 2013), huffingtonpost.com/norman-i-silber/guns-consumer-regulation_b_3174972.html.

Conyers, John (1929–)

U.S. Congressman John Conyers, liberal Democrat from Detroit, Michigan, has consistently advocated more stringent gun control measures. In 1985, he supported the ban on armor-piercing ammunition; in 1986, he opposed passage of the Firearms Owners' Protection Act, which allowed for the interstate sale of rifles and shotguns and the easing of record-keeping for firearms transactions; in 1988, he supported the ban on the production and importation of firearms that could not be detected by X-ray machines and metal detectors; in 1993, he voted in favor of the Brady Handgun Violence Prevention Act; in 1999 he voted against reducing the waiting period before purchasing a firearm from three days to one; and in 2003 and 2005, Conyers opposed a bill to prohibit lawsuits against gun makers and dealers for the misuse of their products.

His positions on gun-related issues are consistent with his generally liberal stand. The National Rifle Association has given Conyers a score of "F" for his positions on firearms.

The son of a Detroit auto worker, Conyers attended Wayne State University, where he received a B.A. in 1957 and a law degree in 1958. He first won election to the U.S. House of Representatives in 1964 from a newly created black majority district. In 2006 Conyers became the chair of the House Judiciary Committee. When Republicans held a majority in the House of Representatives, he was often at odds with the Judiciary Chairman Henry Hyde (R-IL), especially over the Republican anti-crime bill during the 104th Congress, and gained a reputation for offering firm opposition to the Republican majority. Conyers believed that the Republicans were attempting to federalize too many crimes, in contradiction to their program of returning authority to the states. Throughout the impeachment hearings for President Bill Clinton in 1998, Conyers remained one of the staunchest opponents of Republican-drafted impeachment articles.

During the Democratic-controlled 103rd Congress (1993–1994), Conyers played an important role in crafting President Clinton's crime bill. He lobbied with the Democratic leadership to maintain an assault weapons ban, as well as crime-prevention funding, in the bill. Conyers also supported a provision to direct the attorney general to gather data on incidents of police brutality. However, some members to the Black Caucus, which Conyers helped found, were not satisfied with the bill. To resolve the discrepancy between his commitment to the Black Caucus and his responsibility as a senior Democrat to support the party's legislative agenda, Conyers voted twice to have the crime bill considered on the House floor, but then opposed final passage. In the 105th Congress (1997–1998), Conyers continued to support gun control, proposing an amendment to federal firearms statutes that would "prohibit the transfer of a firearm to, and the possession of a firearm by, a person who is intoxicated."

Following the December 2015 mass shooting in San Bernardino, California, in which a man and woman killed 14 people and wounded 21 others, and the June 2016 mass shooting at the Pulse nightclub in Orlando, Florida, in which a lone gunman killed 49 people, Conyers joined with other members of the U.S. House of Representatives in a sit-in on the House floor. He called the sit-in a call to action, challenging the Republican majority to schedule votes on proposed legislation that would prevent people on the terrorist "no fly" watch list from purchasing firearms, and that would expand criminal background checks to those purchasing firearms online, at gun shows, and from private persons.

See also: Assault Weapons Ban; Brady Handgun Violence Prevention Act; Clinton, William Jefferson (Bill); Firearms Owners Protection Act.

Further Reading: Congressman John Conyers Web site, www.house.gov/conyers; Philip D. Duncan and Christine C. Lawrence, *Politics in America, 1998: The 105th Congress* (Washington, DC: Congressional Quarterly, 1997). On the Issues, "John Conyers on Gun Control," www.ontheissues.org/MI/John_Conyers_Gun_Control.htm.

Cook, Philip J. (1946–)

Philip J. Cook has conducted research on firearms and violence for more than 30 years. Cook is a professor in the Sanford School of Public Policy and the departments of Sociology and Economics at Duke University. He has published more than fifty articles dealing with weapons and violent crime, including such topics as implementation of the Brady Handgun Violence Prevention Act, causal links between gun control ordinances and levels of crime, the effect of gun availability on robbery and murder committed during robbery, state programs for screening handgun buyers, the effect of gun availability on violent crime patterns, defensive gun uses, and regulating gun markets. He concludes that the availability of firearms has an independent effect on the seriousness of crime. With regard to suicide rates, he has concluded that the availability of deadly instruments can affect the resolve to complete the act. Therefore, depriving suicidal persons of the means, including firearms, to complete the act of self-destruction can save lives.

Cook received a B.A. from the University of Michigan in 1968 and a Ph.D. in economics from the University of California at Berkeley in 1973. In the latter year, he went to Duke University as an assistant professor and in 1984 became professor of public policy and economics. In 1992, Cook attained the position of professor of public policy, economics, and sociology, and in 1994, he was named to his current position as ITT/Terry Sanford Professor of Public Policy Studies. He served as chair of the Public Policy Studies Department from 1997 to 1999. Cook has held several visiting positions, including Schelling Visiting Professor of Public Policy at the University of Maryland (2008–2009). He has received several research grants, including support from the Harry Frank Guggenhein Foundation (1993–94) to examine markets for stolen guns, and from the Joyce Foundation (1997–99 and 2000–03) to investigate the costs of gunshot wounds and community gun prevalence and crime.

In 1996 Cook served as editor for a symposium on youth, firearms, and public policy. Among the motivations for organizing the symposium was the observation that violent crime among youth had increased significantly in recent years. The participants at the symposium investigated more promising policies to discourage potentially violent youths from acquiring, carrying, and employing firearms. The symposium concluded that firearms have made youth violence more lethal and gun use has been transmitted among youth groups in a fashion similar to the spread of an infectious disease. Although keeping guns away from youth will not solve the more basic causes of violence, the symposium participants reasoned that a focus on restricting access to firearms could save lives and reduce fear.

Cook and coauthors Jens Ludwig and David Hemenway (1997) have criticized the widely disseminated claim that citizens use firearms 2.5 million times each year for self-defense. Reanalyzing the data from which that claim was derived, Cook concluded that some survey respondents must have misreported self-defense incidents and suggested that many "false positive" reports occur when attempting to measure a rare event in a large population. He claimed that medical researchers in epidemiology employ screening methods to avoid the problem of false positives, but social surveys still ignore this threat to validity. In "The Social Costs of Gun Ownership" (2005), Cook and coauthor Jens Ludwig presented a statistical analysis of the consequences of household gun prevalence (measured indirectly by the proportion of suicides committed with a handgun). They found that "gun

prevalence is positively associated with overall homicide rates but not systematically related to assault or other types of crime." The study results suggested that as gun prevalence increases, criminal violence becomes more lethal.

Cook, along with James A. Leitzel (1996), has responded to the major arguments against gun control. Noting the limits of punishing crime after the fact, Cook supports measures to preempt the violent use of firearms. In response to the argument that gun control laws are ineffective in keeping firearms from criminals, Cook claims that regulations, such as a tax on guns, may ultimately affect the illegitimate market. Cook argues that, contrary to belief, guns are scarce goods and can be made scarcer through law enforcement policy. For instance, in the coauthored article "Underground Gun Markets" (2007), Cook focused on Chicago's restrictive firearm legislation (which the U.S. Supreme subsequently declared unconstitutional in the 2010 decision *McDonald v. Chicago*), concluding that the transaction costs for sellers and purchasers of illegal firearms are sufficiently large to diminish somewhat the underground gun market even as the drug trade has continued apace. In suggesting various policies to control the level of gun-related violence, such as an increased sales tax on ammunition and licensing with annual permit fees for firearm owners, Cook holds that any right to keep and bear arms is not absolute and therefore is subject to reasonable limitations to guarantee public safety.

In 2014 Cook, along with Kristin Goss, published *The Gun Debate: What Everyone Needs to Know*, which provides basic information about the current state of firearms and firearm policy in the United States. In 2015 Cook co-authored the article "Sources of Guns to Dangerous People: What We Learn by Asking Them," a report on a survey of 99 inmates at the Cook County, Illinois, jail. Among the findings, Cook and colleagues concluded that the respondents reported obtaining most of their firearms through social networking and personal acquaintances.

See also: Accidents Involving Guns; Center for the Study and Prevention of Violence; Hemenway, David; Ludwig, Jens Otto; Suicide.

Further Reading: Thomas B. Cole and Philip J. Cook, "Strategic Thinking about Gun Markets and Violence," *Journal of the American Medical*

Association 275 (June 12, 1996), 22; Philip J. Cook, "The Technology of Personal Violence," in Michael Tonry, ed., *Crime and Justice: An Annual Review of Research* (Chicago: University of Chicago Press, 1991); Philip J. Cook and James A. Leitzel, "Perversity, Futility, Jeopardy: An Economic Analysis of the Attack on Gun Control," *Law and Contemporary Problems* (Winter 1996); Philip J. Cook and Jens Ludwig, *Gun Violence: The Real Costs* (New York: Oxford University Press, 2000); Jens Ludwig and Philip J. Cook, editors, *Evaluating Gun Policy: Effects on Crime and Violence* (Washington, DC: Brookings Institution Press, 2003); Philip J. Cook and Jens Ludwig, "The Social Costs of Gun Ownership," *Journal of Public Economics* 90 (2006), 379–91; Philip J. Cook, Jens Ludwig, and David Hemenway, "The Gun Debate's New Mythical Number: *How* Many Defensive Uses Per Year?" *Journal of Policy Analysis and Management* 16 (Summer 1997), 463–69; Philip J. Cook, Jens Ludwig, Sudhir Venkatesh, and Anthony A. Braga, "Underground Gun Markets," *Economic Journal,* 117 (November 2007), 588–618; Philip J. Cook and Kristin A. Goss, *The Gun Debate: What Everyone Needs to Know* (New York: Oxford University Press, 2014); Philip J. Cook et al., "Some Sources of Crime Guns in Chicago: Dirty Dealers, Straw Purchases, and Traffickers," *Journal of Criminal Law and Criminology* 104 (2015): 717-760; Philip J. Cook, S. T. Parker, and H. A. Pollack, "Sources of Guns to Dangerous People: What We Learn by Asking Them," *Preventive Medicine* 79 (2015): 28-36.

Cox, Christopher (Chris) W. (1978–)

In 2002 the National Rifle Association (NRA) appointed Chris Cox the organization's chief lobbyist and the principal strategist for the organization's Institute for Legislative Action. He first joined the NRA in 1995, prior to which he served as a senior legislative aide in Congress, focusing on judicial, criminal justice, and firearms policy. Cox also serves as chairman of the NRA's Political Victory Fund (NRA-PVF), the organization's political action committee, which contributes funds to the election campaigns of candidates who share the NRA's commitment to individual gun rights. Born in west Tennessee, where he was raised in the tradition of hunting and fishing, Cox earned a B.A. degree in history with

a minor in business administration from Rhodes College in Memphis, Tennessee.

Cox oversees the organization's advertising efforts and administers direct mail operations. The NRA attributes Congress's failure in 2004 to renew the assault weapons ban to Cox's lobbying efforts. According to the NRA, in 2014, 90 percent of candidates in federal elections that the organization endorsed were successful in winning election. The NRA attributes this high level of success to Cox's efforts to mobilize voters at the local level and to organize an aggressive media campaign.

Cox advances the NRA's interests not only in the election of public officials, but also in the selection of Supreme Court justices and judges of other courts in order to achieve a favorable legal interpretation of the Second Amendment. For instance, Cox and the NRA strongly opposed President Barack Obama's U.S. Supreme Court nominations of Sonia Sotomayor in 2009 and Elena Kagan in 2010. In August 2010, Cox announced that the NRA would not support Senate majority leader Harry Reid (D-NV) for reelection because of Reid's support for Sotomayor and Kagan. However, Cox did not say that the NRA would support Reid's opponent in the November election. Although Reid had developed a close relationship with the NRA during his tenure in the U.S. Senate and the organization recently had made a donation to the Reid campaign, strong reaction from rank and file members, who directly attacked Cox, apparently led to the decision not to make an endorsement. Cox, along with other NRA officials, undoubtedly find it necessary to accommodate the views of the more uncompromising members of the organization. However, Cox emphasizes that the NRA is a single-issue group concerned almost exclusively with the right to bear arms. The organization does not make decisions about which candidate to support on the basis of party affiliation, but will support candidates from both parties based on their record of support for the organization and for the Second Amendment.

In 2016 Cox announced the NRA's opposition to Merrick Garland, President Barack Obama's nominee to the U.S. Supreme Court to replace conservative Justice Antonin Scalia, who had died that year. Given the close division on the Court demonstrated in the *District of Columbia v. Heller* (2008) and *McDonald v. Chicago* (2010) decisions in which, by 5-to-4 majorities, the Court proclaimed an individual right to possess firearms for self-defense in the home, Cox asserted that Scalia's death could lead to "the end of individual gun ownership in the United States." He argued that Garland, as a member of the U.S. Court of Appeals for the District of Columbia Circuit, demonstrated that he failed to support the individualist interpretation of the Second Amendment.

See also: District of Columbia v. Heller (2008); *McDonald v. Chicago*; National Rifle Association.

Further Reading: "Chris Cox Biography," www.nraila.org/News/Read/NewsReleases.aspx?id=5476; "Statement from NRA-PVF Chairman Chris W. Cox on the 2010 Nevada U.S. Senate Race" (August 27, 2010), www.nravf.org/news/Read.aspx?ID=14170&T=1; Christopher W. Cox, "NRA: Why We Oppose Merrick Garland's Supreme Court Nomination," *Washington Post* (March 18, 2016), www.washingtonpost.com/opinions/nar-why-we-oppose-merrick-garlands-supreme-court-nomination/2016/03/18/1ea4c9d0-ac5b-11e5-60fd-073d5930a7b7_story.html.

D

Diaz, Tom (1940–)

Tom Diaz, a former member of the National Rifle Association (NRA) and a competitive shooter, became a major advocate for gun control measures, including instituting a limitation on large-capacity detachable ammunition magazines and lifting congressionally-established limitations on the Bureau of Alcohol, Tobacco, Firearms, and Explosives (ATF) and the Justice Department that prohibit these agencies from sharing gun-related crime data with law enforcement agencies.

Diaz graduated from the University of Florida and the Georgetown University Law School. He has worked for the Violence Policy Center, an organization dedicated to reducing the level of gun violence in the United States.

Diaz has written numerous opinion pieces for newspapers and has appeared on television and radio news programs to present his views on the dangers of firearms and to suggest policy changes to reduce the level of gun violence. Diaz has published two book dealing the firearms industry's attempts to increase demand for its products. In Making a Killing: The Business of Guns in America (1999), Diaz faults the gun industry for resisting passage of laws to regulate the safety of firearms. Federal legislation dealing with consumer product safety exempts the industry firearm industry from the requirement to introduce safety components to firearms. Diaz argues that, instead of focusing on gun safety issues, the industry has introduced increasingly lethal firearms to the civilian market that contain greater ammunition capacity, larger caliber, and increased concealability. In his second book, The Last Gun–How Changes in the Gun Industry Are Killing American And What It Will Take to Stop It (2013), Diaz attributes the troubling number of

mass shootings as well as the daily toll of deaths and injuries from gun-related violence, accidents, and suicides, to the firearm industry's marketing of more lethal guns that originally were designed for military use. Diaz recommends that citizens "stop accepting excuses from politicians" and embrace realistic solutions to gun-related violence. Citizens also should demand that the federal government create databases from information that now is restricted from general use. He recommends that data should be gathered about the use of specific weapons in violent crime, and the gun industry's distribution of these weapons. Diaz also urges Americans to learn from the experiences of other developed countries that have far lower levels of gun-related violence.

See also: National Rifle Association; Product Liability Lawsuits; Violence Policy Center.

Further Reading: Tom Diaz, *Making a Killing: The Business of Guns in America* (New York: New Press, 1999); Tom Diaz, *The Last Gun: How Changes in the Gun Industry Are Killing Americans and What It Will Take to Stop It* (New York: New Press, 2013).

Dick Act

The Dick Act, or Militia Act, of 1903 repealed the Militia Act of 1792. The act revived state militias, or, as they had come to be called, National Guard units, based on voluntary recruitment and greater national government control over their organization and operation. The national army gained some control over the militia and was granted the authority to create a reserve force under its own supervision. Gun control advocates argue that the modern militia, beginning with the Dick Act, eliminated any notion of universal citizen membership in the militia and with it the claim that citizens in general have a right to bear arms as members of at least the "unorganized militia." Gun rights advocates contend that the National Guard as established under the Dick Act does not satisfy the constitutional reference to an organized militia.

The Militia Act of 1792 never operated well in maintaining a militia force in each of the states. The inadequacies of American military preparedness during the Spanish American War of 1898 prompted Republican President William McKinley's secretary of war, Elihu Root, to begin an inquiry into possible strategies for modernizing and rationalizing the military organization. Noting that the militia system was still operating under the 111-year-old Militia Act and recognizing the value of an effective reserve system, Root asked Colonel William Sanger, inspector general of the New York National Guard, to investigate the citizen reserve systems in other nations. In 1900, following a tour of Europe, Sanger submitted a report on the English and Swiss systems.

Sanger developed the legislation in collaboration with Ohio Congressman Charles Dick, who was a major general in command of the Ohio National Guard, president of the National Guard Association, and chairman of the House Committee on the Militia. In 1902, Dick presented a plan to the annual meeting of the National Guard Association. Supporters of militia reform, including local militias, desired not only greater funds for state organizations, but also greater recognition for the militia's role in the national military system. Republican President Theodore Roosevelt strongly supported reform, as did the regular army.

Meanwhile, the War Department proposed its own reform bill, which included a measure that, although rejected, had a significant impact on the final version of the act. Section 24 of the failed reform bill would have mandated the creation of a national reserve force of up to 100,000 men with prior military service. This force would have had no relationship to any state. Although the House passed the bill, the Senate refused to concur. However, the Senate quickly passed the bill when Root agreed to withdraw Section 24. States' rights advocates, who had strongly opposed the national force, supported the revised bill even though it established significant national government supervision over the state militias. Not until after World War II did state militias protest expansion of

national supervision, but by then such objections were too late to force a policy change.

According to Elihu Root, the Dick Act would not simply replace state with national funds, but create an effective training ground for volunteer soldiers. The act required states to meet national standards to receive grant-in-aid funds. Funds were contingent upon a state having at least 100 militiamen for each senator and representative the state had in Congress. A state's militia units had to drill at least 24 times each year with at least two-thirds of its strength, and attend a five-day summer camp. Summer maneuvers had to be held jointly with regular troops, and could not occur unless federal inspectors certified that the militia was prepared. Federal inspections of all units were to be held annually and any deficiencies corrected. State governors were required to request additional arms before the War Department would provide them. Congressional appropriations for state militias increased from $3.5 million in 1903 to $5 million in 1908, while states collectively contributed from $5.8 to $9 million each year. The act succeeded in achieving one of its major objectives: to bring states with inadequate militia organizations up to national minimum standards.

Whatever anyone might argue about the purpose of state militias in opposing a possibly tyrannous national government, the Dick Act essentially placed militias (by 1903 commonly referred to as the National Guard) under federal control. Rather than representing a force potentially opposed to the national government, the National Guard and the regular army served as complementary organizations with a common objective. However, some gun rights advocates insist that if the National Guard, which they are not willing to equate with the militia as designated in the Constitution, is the first line of defense held in reserve, then another constitutionally protected force is the unorganized militia, potentially composed of all adult citizens armed with weapons they provide for themselves through the Second Amendment right to keep and bear arms. The practicality of such an interpretation does not matter so much to them as the asserted constitutional relationship between militia service and an individual's right to possess firearms.

See also: Militia Act of 1792; Second Amendment.

Further Reading: John K. Mahon, *History of the Militia and the National Guard* (New York:

Macmillan, 1983); William H. Riker, *Soldiers of the State: The Role of the National Guard in American Democracy* (Washington, DC: Public Affairs Press, 1957).

Dickerson v. New Banner Institute, Inc. (1983)

The U.S. Supreme Court decision in *Dickerson v. New Banner Institute, Inc.* (460 U.S. 103, 1983) dealt with Title IV of the Gun Control Act of 1968 [18 U.S.C. 922 (g) (1) and (h) (1)], which prohibits any person convicted of a crime punishable by more than a year in prison from shipping, transporting, or receiving any firearm or ammunition in interstate commerce. The case involved the annulment of a guilty verdict in state court and whether this state action exempted the defendant from the relevant provisions of the Gun Control Act. Although the Court ruled in 1983 that it did not, in 1986, Congress passed the Firearms Owners Protection Act, a provision of which overruled the decision by indicating that a state law governed a state conviction.

David Kennison, chairman of the board and shareholder of the New Banner Institute, Inc., had pleaded guilty in an Iowa state court to a charge of carrying a concealed handgun. Although the conviction could have brought a fine and imprisonment for up to five years, Kennison was placed on probation. After completion of the probationary period, his record of deferred judgment was expunged. In May 1976, he applied to the Bureau of Alcohol, Tobacco, and Firearms (ATF) for licenses to manufacture, deal in, and collect firearms and ammunition, but failed to reveal his guilty plea in the Iowa case. Although Kennison received the license, it was later withdrawn when the ATF discovered the Iowa conviction. The case ultimately reached the U.S. Court of Appeals for the Fourth Circuit, which ruled that Kennison could not be denied a federal firearms license because the conviction had been dismissed under Iowa's deferred judgment procedure. The Supreme Court agreed to hear the case to resolve conflicting decisions rendered by other Courts of Appeals.

The Supreme Court first noted Kennison's guilty plea to a state charge punishable by more than one year in prison, which it considered equivalent to a conviction. Whether Kennison actually received a prison term was considered

irrelevant; the statute simply referred to violations punishable by imprisonment for more than a year. Therefore, the Court considered that Kennison had been convicted according to the language of the relevant provision within the Gun Control Act.

The Court referred to other provisions within federal gun control legislation to support its conclusion that Congress did not intend dismissal of a state conviction to remove any legal prohibition regarding firearms. Noting that the secretary of the Treasury was granted the authority to issue exemptions to such prohibitions, the Court declared that Congress likely did not intend to allow this grant of authority to the secretary "to be overcome by the vagaries of state law." The Court noted that a search of the legislative history of Title IV and related federal firearms statutes resulted in no support for state annulment as a method of removing the disabilities of 922 (g) (1) and (h) (1).

The Court emphasized Congress's intention to establish a uniform national policy to deter illegal firearm use and observed that Congress used state convictions to activate federal prohibitions. But by employing state court convictions, Congress did not intend "to tie those disabilities to the intricacies of state law." Rather, state convictions were conducive to identifying those considered at risk for committing violent crime. The Court concluded that "the circumstances surrounding the expunction of his conviction provide little, if any, assurance that Kennison is a person who can be trusted with a dangerous weapon."

See also: Bureau of Alcohol, Tobacco, Firearms, and Explosives; Concealed Carry Laws; Firearms Owners Protection Act; Gun Control Act of 1968.

Further Reading: *Dickerson v. New Banner Institute, Inc.*, 460 U.S. 103 (1983).

District of Columbia v. Heller (2008)

In *District of Columbia v. Heller* (554 U.S. 570, 2008), the U.S Supreme Court handed down the first decision based on an interpretation of the Second Amendment since *United States v. Miller* (1939). Many lower court decisions prior to 2008 had concluded that the Second Amendment established a corporate right of states to maintain militias against encroachment from the federal government, and the *Miller* decision was generally understood to maintain this collective interpretation. If then the collective interpretation prevailed, the *Heller* decision overturned the precedent by ruling that the Second Amendment does indeed recognize the right of individuals to possess firearms.

In 1975, the District of Columbia instituted the Firearms Control Regulations Act, which prohibited the possession of handguns as well as loaded rifles and shotguns in the District. In the year the law was enacted, more than 50 percent of murders, 60 percent of robberies, and 26 percent of assaults involved handguns. Twenty years later, the District's violent crime rate had not declined due to the firearms restrictions, but had actually increased. Many attributed the continuing gun violence within the District to the more lax firearms laws in neighboring states, where guns were acquired and brought into the District. Although gun control supporters conjectured that the violent crime rate would have been even higher without the strict gun law, gun rights supporters emphasized the value of firearms (especially handguns) for self-protection in an area with high rates of violent crime.

Dick Heller was one of several District of Columbia residents who challenged the handgun ban and other firearm restrictions. Heller, a special police officer in the District of Columbia, applied for a registration certificate to keep a handgun at home, but District officials refused his request. Heller filed a lawsuit in the Federal District Court for the District of Columbia to direct the District of Columbia not to enforce the prohibition on the registration of handguns, the requirement prohibiting the possession of a firearm in the home without a license, and the stipulation that weapons in the home be disassembled and unloaded, or fitted with trigger locks. Heller argued that the District's gun law violated the Second Amendment's guarantee of a right to keep and bear arms. When the district court dismissed the suit, Heller appealed to the U.S. Court of Appeals for the D.C. Circuit, which, in a 2-to-1 ruling, reversed the dismissal and invalidated provisions of the Firearms Control Regulations Act, arguing that the act violated the Second Amendment. The District of Columbia appealed the decision to the U.S. Supreme Court, which agreed to hear the case.

In his majority opinion, Justice Antonin Scalia argued that the Second Amendment essentially recognizes a preexisting right of individuals to possess and carry firearms, and interpreted the *United States v. Miller* decision in that light: in upholding the conviction of two men "for transporting an unregistered short-barreled [sawed-off] shotgun in interstate commerce," in violation of the National Firearms Act the 1939, the Court ruled that "the *type of weapon at issue* was not eligible for Second Amendment protection," not that the defendants were not bearing arms for military purposes.

The handgun, Scalia noted, is considered "the quintessential self-defense weapon. . . . It is easier to store in a location that is readily accessible in an emergency; it cannot easily be redirected or wrestled away by an attacker; it is easier to use for those without the upper-body strength to lift and aim a long gun; it can be pointed at a burglar with one hand while the other hand dials the police." Noting that few gun control laws have been as restrictive as the D.C. law, Scalia concluded that it "fail[s] constitutional muster."

Gun rights supporters were elated by the decision and felt vindicated in their long crusade to have a constitutionally protected right of individuals to possess firearms for sporting purposes as well as for self-protection. The Legal Action Project of the Brady Campaign to Prevent Gun Violence in its response disagreed with the basis for the decision—that the Second Amendment recognizes an individual right to keep and bear arms—but saw a bright spot for gun control advocates. The Brady Campaign's proposals to institute universal background checks and to limit the illegal trafficking in firearms might now have greater prospects for success in that the Supreme Court decision had removed gun control as a divisive "wedge issue." Gun rights supporters hopefully would not be as opposed to "sensible gun laws" now that the Supreme Court has recognized a constitutional right to own firearms.

See also: Brady Campaign to Prevent Gun Violence; *United States v. Miller* (1939); *United States v. Tot* (1942).

Further Reading: Stephen Breyer, "On Handguns and the Law," *The New York Review of Books* (August 19, 2010), 18, 20; *District of Columbia v. Heller* (554 U.S. 570, 2008); Legal Action Project of the Brady Center to Prevent Gun Violence, "Unintended Consequences: What the Supreme Court's Second Amendment Decision in *District of Columbia v. Heller* Means for the Future of Gun Laws" (October 20, 2008), www.bradycenter.org/xshare/ pdf/ heller/post-heller-white-paper.pdf; National Rifle Association, "The Second Amendment" (July 15,

2008), www.nraila.org/Issues/FactSheets/Read.
aspx?id=177; Nicholas J. Johnson, "*Heller* as *Miller*:
Court Decisions Dealing with Firearms," in Glenn
H. Utter, *Guns and Contemporary Society* (Santa
Barbara, CA: Praeger, 2016): vo.1,83-102.

Doctors for Responsible Gun Ownership (DRGO)

Doctors for Responsible Gun Ownership (DRGO),
a program of the Claremont Institute located
in Claremont, California, was established in
1994 to respond to health care professionals and
organizations that were supporting further gun
control policies by taking an epidemiological
approach to firearms and gun violence. Founded
in 1979, the Claremont Institute encourages a
return to what it considers the nation's founding
principles: a limited government held accountable
to the people, respect for private property, stable
family life, and a strong national defense. Adhering
to the principles of the parent organization, DRGO
promotes individual freedom and responsibility
against government intervention. Sister programs
supported by the Institute include the Salvatori
Center for the American Constitution, Americans
for Victory Over Terrorism, the Center for
Constitutional Jurisprudence, and the Investment
Security Program. DRGO has worked with other
organizations in an attempt to discredit the research
findings of medical professionals who claim that
gun ownership represents a serious threat to public
health.

DRGO states that its membership includes
"experts on public health, firearm technology,
gun safety education, and tactical medicine."
The organization associates with various gun
rights organizations, including the National Rifle
Association (NRA), the Second Amendment
Foundation (SAF), and the Citizens Committee
for the Right to Keep and Bear Arms (CCRKBA).
Timothy Wheeler, a head and neck surgeon
practicing in Fontana, California, heads the
organization. Employing a medical analogy
similar to those it criticizes pro-gun control
health professionals for using, DRGO claims to
be the "antidote" to what it considers dishonest
research and mistaken ideological positions of
pro-gun control groups. The organization contends
that an alternative body of research conducted
by criminologists and other social scientists
demonstrates that firearms owned by law-abiding

citizens deter crime and prevent far more deaths
and injuries than they cause.

DRGO especially opposes the so-called
public health approach to gun violence. The
organization claims that major medical groups
such as the American Medical Association (AMA)
and the American Academy of Pediatrics, have
a political agenda that involves "deep-seated
prejudice against gun owners." DRGO claims that
firearms are a major health benefit in that private
ownership of guns help prevent violence crime.
The organization supported Congress's decision in
1997 to prohibit the Centers for Disease Control
and Prevention (CDC) from using federal funds
to conduct firearms research. DRGO also has
strongly criticized physicians who ask patients
about whether they keep firearms in the home.
The organization recommends various gun safety
instruction programs, but does not appear to take a
position on whether training should be mandatory
for obtaining a concealed carry permit.

DRGO participated with two other
organizations, Doctors for Integrity in Policy
Research (DIPR) and the Lawyer's Second
Amendment Society (LSAS), in an *amicus
curiae* brief submitted to the U.S. Supreme
Court, supporting a challenge, based on the Tenth
Amendment, to the Brady Handgun Violence
Prevention Act. Filed in 1995, the brief argued
that extensive benefits are derived from firearms
ownership and that gun control legislation,
especially the Brady law, has been ineffective
in controlling crime. DRGO and the other
organizations participating in the brief challenged
the claim that the Brady law had prevented over
60,000 illegal handgun purchases. The brief
contended that the Brady law had cost more lives
than it saved because citizens were being denied
the right to defend themselves and their families.

Although raising objections to any limitations
on what the organization considered an individual's
right to keep and bear arms and a right of self-
defense, the brief stated that if the Supreme Court
allows "an infringement of the right to keep and
bear arms," the limitation should be as minimally
intrusive as possible. Therefore, an "instant check"
system was supported as a replacement for the five-
day waiting period. However, the brief urged that
this system be voluntarily adopted by the states, not
mandated by the Brady law, which would constitute
a violation of the Tenth Amendment guarantee of
state powers. DRGO also submitted an *amicus
curiae* brief to the U.S. Supreme Court in *District*

of Columbia v. Heller (2008), in which authors Don B. Kates and Marc Ayers challenged the research findings that the District of Columbia used in defending its restrictive gun control ordinance.

See also: Brady Handgun Violence Prevention Act; Health Care Professionals; Lawyer's Second Amendment Society; National Center for Injury Prevention and Control; National Instant Check System.

Further Reading: Claremont Institute Web site, www. claremont.org; Steven A. Silver, "Amicus Brief on Behalf of Doctors for Integrity in Policy Research, Doctors for Responsible Gun Ownership, and The Lawyer's Second Amendment Society in Support of Petitioner Sheriff Richard Mack" (Encino, CA: Lawyer's Second Amendment Society, 1996); Timothy Wheeler, "The Bully Pulpit and the Right of the People," *Pasadena Star News* (June 26, 1997).

Dodd, Thomas J. (1907–1971)

Although Democratic Senator Thomas J. Dodd played a major role in the negotiations that ultimately led to passage of the 1968 Gun Control Act, he was an unlikely leader on the gun control issue. He hailed from Connecticut, a major gun manufacturing state; he had a penchant for alcohol that became widely known among his colleagues; and he came under investigation by the Senate for misappropriation of campaign funds that ultimately resulted in a censure vote by his senatorial colleagues.

Dodd began his political career with a sterling reputation. Before World War II, he spent a year working in the Federal Bureau of Investigation (FBI). As a special assistant to a U.S. attorney, he prosecuted southern public officials for civil rights violations at a time when the issue had little national saliency. During the war, he brought to justice leaders of the German-American Bund, a pro-Nazi group supporting the German war effort, and prosecuted officials of the Anaconda Wire and Cable Company for supplying defective telephone wire to the military. At the Nuremberg war crimes trials following the war, Dodd served as executive trial counsel. In 1952, he withstood the Republican presidential and congressional victories to become the only Connecticut Democrat to be elected to Congress. In 1958, Connecticut voters elected him to the

U.S. Senate. During the Cold War era, he was a moderate Democrat with strong anti-Communist credentials.

Like fellow senators from Massachusetts and Connecticut, who wished to protect the domestic firearms industry, Dodd attempted but failed to add riders to bills that would ban importation of military firearms. In 1963, Dodd developed a new strategy, focusing the fight on the claim that cheap imported guns contributed to violent crime, especially among youth. At least initially, Dodd did not alienate the major American firearms manufacturers because he concentrated his investigations on inexpensive mail-order guns and the surplus military weapons imported from abroad. In January 1963, Dodd, as chairman of the Senate Subcommittee on Juvenile Delinquency, opened the Hearings on Interstate Traffic in Mail-Order Firearms. Gun dealers testified about current practices, police officials related the tragic results of firearms reaching the hands of juveniles, and private citizens told stories about the misuse of firearms, especially by youth.

In August 1963, with the support of the National Rifle Association (NRA), Dodd introduced a bill that was referred to the Committee on Commerce, where it languished until President John F. Kennedy's assassination by a gunman using an Italian-made Mannlicher-Carcano rifle purchased through a mail-order firm. The assassination gained nationwide publicity for Dodd's legislative agenda. Originally, Dodd proposed to ban mail-order handgun purchases, but he agreed to expand the bill to include rifles and shotguns. Strong opposition from gun interests blocked the new legislation, despite support from New England firearms manufacturers. In 1965, Dodd again failed to get a bill out of committee. The following year his censure by the Senate severely limited the senator's ability to push the gun control bill. However, Dodd insisted on maintaining his leadership on the firearms issue, negotiating with the NRA for support of his proposed legislation. Frank Orth, executive vice president of the NRA, was willing to back Dodd's call to include rifles in the bill, but he did not necessarily represent a majority of the organization's board of directors.

Gun control legislation continued to be debated extensively for the next four years. Dodd became frustrated by the NRA, which promised its support privately, but voiced strong opposition in the pages of the organization's publications. In 1968,

the assassinations of Robert Kennedy and Martin
Luther King, Jr., opened the way to passage of
the Gun Control Act. Two years later, Dodd failed
to gain reelection. Although the NRA claimed
responsibility for defeating Dodd and other public
officials who supported gun control, in Dodd's
case, the Senate censure reduced his chances for
reelection. If someone other than the beleaguered
Dodd had led the fight for gun control, the 1968 act
might have contained more extensive provisions.

See also: Gun Control Act of 1968; National Rifle
Association.

Further Reading: Bill R. Davidson, *To Keep and
Bear Arms* (New Rochelle, NY: Arlington House,
1969); Robert Sherrill, *The Saturday Night Special*
(New York: Charterhouse, 1973).

Drive-By Shootings

In the 1970s, drive-by shootings began to replace
the traditional rumble, or gang fight, as the
characteristic violent interchange among street
gangs. The combination of two technologies—the
firearm and the automobile—made the drive-
by shooting a favored strategy of gangs. Gang
researcher William B. Sanders (1994) reports that
the percentage of San Diego, California, gang
assaults that were drive-by shootings increased
from 23.7 in 1981 to 40.8 in 1988. In many
American cities in the late 1980s, the crack cocaine
trade and related drive-by shootings had become
extensive. Such shootings contributed to the large
number of adolescent firearms victims, especially
innocent bystanders, and consequently to increased
calls for additional gun control legislation.

Sanders states that a drive-by shooting occurs
"when members of one gang drive a vehicle into a
rival gang's area and shoot at someone." The drive-
by shooting, or foray, is contrasted with the melee
or rumble, where rival gang members meet at a
specific time and place to fight. The introduction of
firearms altered this strategy because mass shoot-
outs were an impractical alternative to the rumble.
Instead, youths ventured into a rival gang's territory
for a brief encounter, and returned quickly to
home territory. Initially, in more densely populated
areas on the East Coast, with neighborhoods
close together, forays would occur on foot or on
bicycle. On the West Coast, with neighborhoods
geographically dispersed, the automobile became

the primary mode of transportation. After a
shooting, gang members could quickly return to
their home neighborhood located miles from the
incident.

According to Sanders, gangs develop
mythologies about rivals, labeling them dangerous
people deserving of violent attack. Revenge for
the past misdeeds of rivals plays an important
role. Because forays are considered dangerous for
the perpetrators, involving the risk of arrest and
of becoming a target themselves, participation
demonstrates the appropriate virtues of gang
membership, including heart, courage, and
honor. The drive-by is equivalent to a tactic in
warfare. Just as in combat, innocents are not
intentionally targeted, but they may become
victims nonetheless. In part because they consider
themselves engaged in warfare against a dangerous
enemy, gang members generally demonstrate little
remorse over the injury or death of innocents,
including young children.

Innocents can become victims if a drive-by
targets a party held by a rival gang. Although
women are usually not targets, they may become
so simply by being present at a gathering. For
instance, in March 2010, in the District of
Columbia, nine young people—six men and three
women—were shot in a drive-by shooting, and four
of the victims died. The gunman apparently aimed
randomly into a crowd. If a house is the focus of
an attack, a gang member's family can become
victims. No group norms appear to prohibit the
wounding or killing of family members. The injury
or killing of innocents in drive-by shootings has
led to calls for further gun control measures. Gun
rights supporters tend to conclude that attempts to
restrict access to firearms are ineffective because
the use of weapons in this way is already illegal
and subject to severe penalties. However, gun
control advocates argue that instituting various
strategies to reduce the availability of firearms can
reduce the frequency of drive-by shootings. For
instance, David Hemenway (2004) recommends
that the following five policies be instituted:
allowing a national one-gun-per-month limit on
gun purchases; requiring all firearm purchases
to be made with background checks through
licensed dealers; granting to the Bureau of
Alcohol, Tobacco, Firearms, and Explosives (ATF)
greater authority to trace guns used in crimes;
manufacturing personalized guns to discourage
theft; and licensing firearms owners and registering
handguns.

In January 2012 a law went into effect in California that defined a drive-by shooting—legally called "discharging a firearm from a motor vehicle. The law makes it illegal for someone to allow a passenger to bring a firearm into their car, to allow a passenger to fire a gun from the car, to fire a gun in the car, or to shoot at someone from the car. Drive-by shootings continue to occur. In May 2014 a lone shooter, driving his car in an area near the University of California at Santa Barbara, shot and killed six people and injured seven others at several sites. The driver became the seventh fatality as police approached the gunman's crashed vehicle and discovered that he had shot and killed himself.

See also: Violent Crime Rate; Youth and Guns.

Further Reading: CBS News, "D.C. Drive-By Shooting Kills 4," www.cbsnews.com/stories/2010/03/31/national/main6349061/shtml (accessed 9/16/10); David Hemenway, *Private Guns, Public Health* (Ann Arbor, MI: University of Michigan Press, 2004); William B. Sanders, *Gang-bangs and Drive-Bys: Grounded Culture and JuvenileGang Violence* (New York: Aldine de Gruyter, 1994).

Dueling

The decline of dueling as a method of resolving disputes represents an area in which gun control and the control of other deadly weapons was successful, at least in limiting a particular use. Dueling reached its peak in the United States between 1770 and 1860, but could not be declared extinct until the early decades of the twentieth century. However, gun control advocates wonder if many contemporary altercations involving the use of firearms are a throwback to the time when gentlemen defended their honor, one-on-one, on the field of combat.

Dueling originated in Europe during medieval times as a means of resolving judicial disputes. Judicial combat, where the two sides to a disagreement resorted to arms to arrive at a settlement, was based on the belief that the victory would go to the person who had God on his side. During the Middle Ages, thousands of men lost their lives in this form of conflict resolution. Although the Roman Catholic Church and, subsequently, various Protestant denominations condemned dueling, and several European monarchs banned the practice and imposed severe punishments for disobedience, dueling continued largely unabated. The inability of legal sanctions to end the practice of dueling is echoed in contemporary pronouncements by gun rights defenders that gun control legislation simply does not keep firearms away from those who truly want them for criminal purposes.

European colonists brought the tradition of dueling to the New World. Practices similar to dueling occurred among Native Americans, although some historians argue that these were copied from the Europeans. The first recorded duel in America occurred in 1621 between two servants in Plymouth, Massachusetts. Fighting with daggers, the two men succeeded in wounding each other, but no one suffered any lethal injury. The community reacted with disapproval, not so much because of the duel itself, but because the participants were servants. Only gentlemen were thought to have the privilege to engage in the practice. Most Americans never approved of dueling, including Benjamin Franklin, who once remarked that dueling allowed each person to assume the position of judge for his own complaint, and to act as the jury and ultimate executioner. Popular opinion notwithstanding, laws prohibiting the practice were either ineffective or nonexistent. Prior to 1850, several states had no statute making dueling illegal. Even the District of Columbia had no law banning dueling until 1838. In 1849, the first California state constitution outlawed dueling, but some of the members of the constitutional convention who sought to eliminate dueling subsequently became duelists themselves. In February1861, Joseph Sadoc Alemany, the first Roman Catholic bishop of California, expressed his concern about the coming military conflict by writing a pastoral letter in which he condemned the disastrous effects of dueling. Archbishop Alemany condemned the practice as contrary to divine and natural law as well as to social progress.

Historians have suggested various explanations for the ultimate disappearance of dueling. The passage and enforcement of stringent laws certainly had its effect. In addition, people became more aware that dueling over relatively minor affronts resulted in the squandering of human life. School children today learn about the famous duel in 1804 in which Aaron Burr shot and killed Alexander Hamilton, a signer of the Constitution, a member of President George Washington's cabinet, and one of the most brilliant statesmen in American history. Burr, who was vice president under President Thomas Jefferson, never regained his stature in national politics. The appalling loss of such talent to the shot of a pistol did not bode well for a practice increasingly labeled as barbaric.

A change in the conception of a man's honor occurred in the last half of the nineteenth century. No longer were gentlemen willing to risk their lives over a slight offense. The spread of the democratic ideology throughout American society undoubtedly contributed to this change. Rather than resorting to mortal combat, men increasingly viewed a fistfight (later still a lawsuit) as the appropriate response to a crude comment. Contemporary gun control advocates oppose concealed carry laws in part because, they claim, when guns are readily available, the offhand remark can quickly escalate into the use of deadly firepower, thus harking back to a time when the duel, in a more formal way, led to the same consequences.

By the mid-nineteenth century, the practice of dueling came under increasing derision, which contributed to its extinction. Even at its height, the press and the general public often reacted to an announced duel with taunting, mockery, and even contempt. A practice intended to defend a gentleman's honor could not survive for long under public ridicule.

See also: Jefferson, Thomas; Native Americans.

Further Reading: Robert Baldick, *The Duel: A History of Dueling* (New York: Clarkson N. Potter, 1965); Hugh Barbour, "On Dueling, Divorce, and Red Indians," *Chronicles* (February 2010): 15–18; Hamilton Cochran, *Noted American Duels and Hostile Encounters* (Philadelphia, PA: Chilton, 1963).

E

Eddie Eagle

In 1988, the National Rifle Association (NRA) selected Eddie Eagle, a cartoon character in the form of an eagle, as the mascot for the organization's Firearms Safety for Children program. The program involves a school-based curriculum for children in preschool through the sixth grade. Despite the asserted civic virtue of the program, Eddie Eagle created the same sort of controversy in the gun control debate that Joe Camel prompted in the dispute over cigarette smoking. While the NRA stated that the cartoon character added to the appeal of the safety program, gun control advocates claimed that it attracted young children to essentially unsafe products and diverted attention away from more effective ways of ensuring the protection of children from firearms. The NRA has responded that the program, which includes student workbooks, a short animated video, an instructor guide, and student reward stickers, does not show or promote firearms and never mentions the NRA. The program instructs children on what to do if they discover a gun: "Stop! Don't touch. Run away. Tell a grown-up." Lisa Monroe, early childhood curriculum specialist at the University of Oklahoma, created the instructor guides for the program.

NRA President Marion Hammer began the Eddie Eagle program in Florida in response to state legislative efforts to enact child access prevention (CAP) legislation that would establish criminal penalties for adults who failed to keep firearms away from children. Hammer argued that the best way to protect children from firearms was to educate them about the potential dangers of guns. Although the bill ultimately passed the Florida legislature, Hammer was able to include an amendment that required the Florida Department

of Education to generate a framework for a gun awareness program to be introduced in the Florida public schools. The Dade County school system passed over the Eddie Eagle program and funded a Center to Prevent Handgun Violence (CPHV) gun violence prevention program. However, Hammer succeeded in having the Eddie Eagle materials included along with the CPHV program.

The NRA has campaigned for the introduction of its firearm safety program as a substitute for CAP legislation that would initiate penalties for unsafe storage of weapons. For instance, in February 1997 the Indiana General Assembly replaced a CAP bill with an amendment mandating an Eddie Eagle program. Proponents of CAP legislation argue that the NRA substitute inappropriately relieves the gun owner of responsibility for firearm storage and in effect places that responsibility on children.

The NRA noted that the Eddie Eagle program had received the National Safety Council's (NSC) Silver Award of Merit in 1995 for initiating the training program for children. Opponents of the program quickly noted that the president of the National Safety Council informed Hammer that the NRA had improperly cited the award issued to the organization by the Council's Youth Activities Division when lobbying against a bill requiring trigger lock safety devices, a bill that the National Safety Council endorsed. The organization requested that the NRA stop referring to the NSC or the safety award in their lobbying campaign.

Paul Helmke, then president of the Brady Campaign to Prevent Gun Violence, called for the end of what he called "this misguided excuse for gun safety education." He cites studies indicating that even though a small sample of children memorized the advice that Eddie Eagle presents—they should not touch the gun, run away from it, and tell and adult—the children were likely to ignore the warning when placed in an actual situation where they discover a gun. Rather than placing the responsibility of gun safety with children, Helmke advocated mandatory adult safety training programs and laws such as safe storage requirements.

See also: Brady Campaign to Prevent Gun Violence; National Rifle Association.

Further Reading: *Joe Camel with Feathers: How the NRA with Gun and Tobacco Industry Dollars Uses Its Eddie Eagle Program to Market Guns to Kids* (Washington, DC: Violence Policy Center, 1997); Paul Helmke, "NRA's 'Eddie Eagle' Doesn't Fly or Protect," *Huffington Post* (September 16, 2010), www.huffingtonpost.com/paul-helmke/nras-eddie-eagle-doesn't-f_b_572285.html; National Rifle Association, "Eddie Eagle," www.nrahq.org/safety/eddie; Margie Sanfilippo, "Why the NRA's Repackaged Eddie Eagle Program Still Doesn't Reach Kids" (June 18, 2015), www.bradycampaign.org/blog/why-the-nras-repackaged-eddie-eagle-program-still-doesnt-reach-kids.

Educational Fund to Stop Gun Violence

See COALITION TO STOP GUN VIOLENCE

Emanuel African Methodist Episcopal Church Shooting

On June 17, 2015, a young white man who was a stranger to the members of the Emanuel African Methodist Episcopal Church in Charleston, South Carolina, entered the building asking to see the minister. Members welcomed him and invited him to him to attend a Bible study taking place in the basement of the church. After members had sung hymns and prayed for about an hour, the young man, Dylann Roof, took out a .45 caliber pistol and began shooting, killing nine people, including Clementa C. Pinckney, the church's pastor who also was a Democratic state legislator. Three individuals survived the shooting. When authorities took the shooter into custody after the senseless carnage, Roof expressed hatred toward African Americans and, as a motive for the shooting, reportedly said that he hoped to incite a race war in the United States.

One year after the shooting and within days of the shooting in Orlando, Florida, various pastors and politicians attend a memorial service of congregations in the region to mark the tragic event. John Tecklenburg, mayor of Charleston, spoke in support of legislative action to limit the availability of assault weapons and to institute more effective background checks on gun purchasers.

Since the shooting, much discussion of gun policy revolved around closing the so-called Charleston loophole: allowing buyers to purchase a firearm if a background check has not been completed after three business days. In Roof's case, he would have been prohibited from purchasing the gun he used in the shooting if the background check had been completed within the time limit because he had been charged in a drug arrest. Supporters of closing the loophole have called for a policy of delaying a purchase until the Federal Bureau of Investigation's National Instant Criminal Background Check System (NICS) has been able to complete the criminal background check.

The shooter in the Charleston case faced state and federal charges, including the commission of a hate crime and for committing murder while obstructing religious freedom. The trial, scheduled for early 2017, could result in the death penalty.

Many church members around the nation debated the topic of security and how to protect the congregation against such attacks. Some called for security guards and possibly allowing some members of the church to be armed and ready to defend against an active shooter.

See also: Background Checks; African Americans and Guns

Further Reading: Associated Press, "Religious Congregations Are Stressing Safety After a Season of Violence," *New York Times* (December 20, 2015): 27. Chris Dixon, "November Trial for Suspect in Church Shooting," *New York Times* (June 8, 2016): A11; Jason Horowitz, Nick Corasaniti, and Ashley Southall, "Nine Killed in Shooting at Black Church in Charleston," *New York Times* (June 17, 2015). www.nytimes.com/2015/06/18/us/church-attacked-in-charleston-south-carolina.html?_r=0.

Empire State Building Shooting

Like other acts of violence involving firearms, the February 23, 1997, Empire State Building shooting evoked renewed calls for more stringent gun control legislation at the national, state, and local levels. Other voices, more sympathetic to gun rights, emphasized the self-protection value of firearms. The incident began when Ali Abu Kamal, a 69-year-old Palestinian from Ramallah in the West Bank, who had arrived in the United States just five weeks before, opened fire on a group of approximately 100 tourists on the observation deck of the Empire State Building. New Yorkers were shocked by the shooting, in which one tourist from Denmark was killed, several people were wounded, and others were injured in the resulting panic. Abu Kamal died of a self-inflicted gunshot wound to the temple.

Many public officials and citizens were troubled to discover that a loophole in existing gun control legislation allowed Abu Kamal to purchase a .380-caliber semi-automatic Beretta handgun from a gun shop in Melbourne, Florida. Kamal had lost his life's fortune and blamed Zionists and Zionist sympathizers for his financial troubles. Apparently realizing that the New York City gun laws, which required fingerprinting and a background check, a process that could take from six months to a year, would make it extremely difficult for him to purchase a firearm locally, Abu Kamal traveled to Florida to acquire a weapon. Although Florida had a five-day waiting period in compliance with the Brady Handgun Violence Prevention Act, nothing on the form required a statement of length of residence in the United States. A 1994 federal law prohibited gun purchases by anyone who had been in the country for less than 90 days. Abu Kamal acquired a picture identification card from the Florida Department of Highway Safety and Motor Vehicles, which proved sufficient identification to purchase a handgun.

Almost immediately after Abu Kamal's brief shooting spree, public officials began to call for gun control reform. Three days after the shooting, the Clinton administration announced that gun purchase forms would be reworded to notify gun dealers that a 90-day residency in the United States was required to purchase a gun. The administration also indicated that ways were being explored to combine FBI records with those of the Immigration and Naturalization Service. On February 28, Democratic Senators Edward M. Kennedy of Massachusetts and Richard J. Durbin of Illinois announced they were introducing legislation that would prohibit foreign visitors from buying and carrying firearms. Noting that the United States was a potential terrorist target, Durbin stated that the nation should not permit guns to be placed in the hands of "would-be terrorists." Kennedy commented that there was no justifiable reason to allow temporary visitors to the nation to purchase and carry a firearm. The legislative proposal would hold gun dealers liable for knowingly selling a firearm to a foreigner not qualified to own a weapon. Gun purchasers would have to certify that they were not foreigners prohibited from buying firearms.

On March 5, President Bill Clinton, at a ceremony attended by James S. Brady, the presidential press secretary who was shot and seriously wounded during an assassination attempt on President Ronald Reagan in 1981, announced that he had ordered the Bureau of Alcohol, Tobacco, and Firearms (ATF) to apply more rigorously the law requiring legal immigrants to prove that they had been a resident in the United States for at least 90 days. The president also declared his support for the Durbin-Kennedy bill, which ultimately was passed as part of the Omnibus Appropriation Act for fiscal 1999. In addition, he took the opportunity to announce a legislative proposal to ban armor-piercing bullets, and stated that federal agencies had been directed to require trigger locks on every handgun issued to law enforcement agents.

While gun control supporters were advocating various legislative measures, including federally imposed national uniformity in gun control policy to prevent out-of-state purchases of handguns, the National Rifle Association (NRA) cautiously announced its opposition to any new legislation. Chip Walker, a spokesman for the organization, stated that Clinton's proposals were inappropriate because one incident of gun violence involving an alien should not lead to a denial of gun ownership to peaceful and productive foreign visitors who, just like American citizens, have the right of self-protection. Given the equal protection guarantees of the Fourteenth Amendment, Walker doubted that the courts would support gun ownership restrictions based solely on citizenship.

See also: Aliens; Brady Handgun Violence Prevention Act; Brady, James; Brady, Sarah; Bureau of Alcohol, Tobacco, Firearms, and Explosives; Clinton, William Jefferson (Bill); Fourteenth Amendment; National Rifle Association; Reagan, Ronald; Trigger Locks.

Further Reading: *New York Times*, February 24, 1997 (A1, B4); February 25, 1997 (A26, B5); February 26, 1997 (B3); February 27, 1997 (A22); February 28, 1997 (B3); March 6 (B3).

Everytown for Gun Safety

Unlike most other organizations advocating gun control measures, Everytown for Gun Safety has a handsome source of funding. Former mayor of New York Michael Bloomberg initiated the organization in 2014 as a merger of two groups—Mayors Against Illegal Guns, which Bloomberg, along with Boston Mayor Thomas Menino, founded in 2006, and Moms Demand Action for Guns Sense in America, which Shannon Watts initiated in 2012 immediately following the mass shooting at Sandy Hook elementary school in Newtown, Connecticut, and which Bloomberg supported financially.

Everytown states that its purpose is to inform policy makers, the mass media, and citizens about the problem of gun violence, and to work for the adoption of policies to prevent criminals from gaining access to firearms. From its inception, the organization has strived to become a major voice on the issue of gun violence, to provide representation for those concerned about gun safety, and to offer effective opposition to the National Rifle Association (NRA) and other pro-gun rights organizations. At the time of the organization's founding, Bloomberg pledged to contribute $50 million to the organization and to the cause of gun control.

Everytown supports federal legislation that specifically targets gun trafficking and that establishes severe penalties for engaging in the illegal firearm trade. The organization also advocates laws requiring the safe storage of firearms and the introduction of new technologies to prevent access to firearms by children and to deter unauthorized use of firearms. Everytown also has advocated legislation to prevent domestic abusers from owning firearms.

Everytown has followed a moderate agenda, attempting to gain limited political victories. In the 2014 election, the organization supported a ballot initiative in Washington State that would extend background checks for purchasing a firearm to most gun sales—by federally licensed gun dealers as well as private citizens. Everytown contributed $3.5 million to the campaign to pass the initiative, which voters approved by a comfortable margin. In Oregon, the organization successfully supported three Democratic candidates for the state legislature, giving Democrats a majority in the state legislature. The following year, the legislature passed a measure that established background checks for all firearm sales.

However, Everytown has experienced failure in other campaigns. In 2015, despite an advertising effort by Everytown, the legislature of Maine approved legislation permitting the concealed carry of weapons without a permit. In the November 2015 elections in Virginia, Everytown failed in its attempt to help Democrats win a majority of seats in the state senate despite spending $2 million in the campaign.

Given its more moderate approach to gun control, Everytown is willing to bypass certain legislative efforts. For instance, in 2016 the organization decided not to support a ballot initiative targeting assault weapons, including a ban on large-capacity magazines. Leaders of other pro-gun control organizations have questioned the more centrist approach of Everytown, concluding that such tactics fail to ignite enthusiasm for gun safety measures, even though the stated purpose of Everytown is to establish a grassroots organization to rival the NRA.

See also: Bloomberg, Michael; Mayors Against Illegal Guns

Further Reading: Jeremy Peters, "For Next Step, Bloomberg Sets His Sights on the N.R.A.," *New York Times* (April 16, 2014): A12; Leon Neyfakh, "Whatever Happened to Michael Bloomberg's Anti-Guns Crusade?" *Slate* (July 2016). www.slate.com/articles/news_and_politics/crime/2016/07/everytown_for_gun_safety_michael_bloomberg_s_anti_gun_group_is_taking_on.html.

F

Farmer v. Higgins (1990)

The case of *Farmer v. Higgins* (907 F.2 1041, 1990) concerned a challenge to restrictions on the right to make or own a machine gun, an area of gun control that for years has troubled the more uncompromising defenders of the right to own firearms, especially those who engage in gun collecting. Although the Firearms Owners' Protection Act of 1986 generally weakened federal gun control legislation, one provision of the act prohibited private individuals from owning machine guns unless they had possession of the weapons prior to May 19, 1986. Except for more avid gun rights supporters, the prevailing view is that because machine guns lack sporting value and are extremely deadly weapons, private ownership should be strictly regulated.

In October 1986, J.D. Farmer, Jr., a gun collector, applied to the Bureau of Alcohol, Tobacco, and Firearms (ATF) for authorization to make and register a machine gun. The ATF refused Farmer's request, referring to the new firearms law as the basis for its ruling. Farmer challenged the decision in court, claiming that the ATF had misinterpreted the intent of the law. Farmer's argument depended on the meaning of the phrase "under the authority" because the law stated that the prohibition on the transfer or possession of a machine gun does not apply to "a transfer to or by, or possession by or *under the authority* of, the United States or any department or agency thereof or a State, or a department, agency, or political subdivision thereof." Farmer argued that by applying under the National Firearms Act of 1934 to manufacture a machine gun, he satisfied this provision of the 1986 law. He claimed the ATF was legally obligated to grant him permission to manufacture a machine gun.

A Federal District Court upheld Farmer's claim. However, the U.S. Court of Appeals for the Eleventh District overruled the lower court decision, concluding that the intent of Congress was clear. The court referred to section 922 (o)(2)(B) of the statute, which stated that the prohibition on transferring or owning a machine gun did not apply to "any lawful transfer or lawful possession of a machine gun that was lawfully possessed before the date this subsection takes effect." The court ruled that if Congress had not intended to alter the 1934 legislation, then this clause exempting from the prohibition any owners prior to May 19, 1986, would lack any meaning. The court further determined that the phrase "under the authority" of a government agency had a delimited application that did not cover Farmer's interpretation. The phrase referred to machine guns manufactured for the military, for police forces, or under government jurisdiction for export to a foreign nation. On January 15, 1991, the U.S. Supreme Court refused to hear the appeal, thus letting stand the Appeals Court ruling.

See also: Bureau of Alcohol, Tobacco, Firearms, and Explosives; Firearms Owners Protection Act; National Firearms Act of 1934.

Further Reading: *Farmer v. Higgins*, 907 F.2 1041 (1990); Mark A. Siegel, Nancy R. Jacobs, and Carol D. Foster, *Gun Control: Restricting Rights or Protecting People?* (Wylie, TX: Information Plus, 1991).

Fatalities

The rate of fatalities from firearms varies according to age, race, and gender, and specific circumstance (homicide, suicide, or accident). The observation of overall trends in firearm fatalities has contributed to the call for further efforts to restrict access to guns, particularly among youth. In *Gun Control: An American Issue* (1997), Nancy Jacobs, Mark Siegel, and Mei Ling Rein provide a summary of data regarding firearm-related fatalities compared to other causes of death. In 1995, firearm injuries were the second leading cause of accidental fatalities in the United States (24 percent), behind motor vehicle traffic injuries (29 percent).

In 1995, 13 percent of all deaths among children aged 10 to 14 were attributed to firearms, the second leading cause of death for this age group. The death rate from firearms increased significantly from 1980 to 1994.

In 1980, the number of deaths per 100,000 population for those aged 15 to 19 attributable to motor vehicle accidents was 42.5, while the rate for firearms was 14.8. In 1994, the rate for motor vehicle accidents had declined to 29.1 but the firearm rate had increased to 28.4. Although the Centers for Disease Control and Prevention (CDC) predicted that firearms would become the leading cause of injury by the year 2000, falling crime rates, including homicide, appear to have invalidated that projection. Table 6 compares the number of firearm deaths in 2007 to those in 2014.

In 1994 the firearm death rate among males aged 15 to 24 exceeded that for motor vehicle accidents (54 and 41 per 100,000, respectively). The death rate from firearms among males aged 15 to 24 was eight times higher than that for females in that age group. The firearm-related murder rate was twice as high as the suicide rate from firearms. For those aged 25 to 64, males were five times more likely than females to die from firearm injuries. Among all males in the United States, the firearm death rate was considerably higher than for other developed countries (averaging 11-12 per 100,000 in Canada, Israel, and Norway, and 1 per 100,000 in The Netherlands, England, and Wales).

The increase in firearms-related fatalities in the 1980s was most pronounced among African American males. In 1980, the death rate among black males aged 15 to 19 was 46.7 per 100,000 population, which was more than three times the rate for the total population in that age group. By 1994, the rate for all youth aged 15 to 19 had nearly doubled while for black males the rate more than tripled. The rate for black males stood at 152.7, more than five times the rate for all youth aged 15 to 19. Among white males, the rate increased from

21 per 100,000 population in 1980 to 30.6 in 1994. For white females, the rate increased only slightly from 4.2 in 1980 to 4.8 in 1994. In 2007, with the decline in overall rates of firearm-related fatalities, the National Center for Injury Prevention and Control reported 70.8 firearm-related deaths per 100,000 population for black males, a significant reduction from 13 years earlier. However, that rate far outpaced the 2007 white male level of 12.56. The black female and white female rates were 5.49 and 2.01, respectively.

Older Americans are more likely to die from disease than either automobile accidents or firearms. Of those aged 45 to 64 who died from firearm injuries in the 1990s, suicide was the cause of death two to four times more often than homicide. For persons at least 65 years old, firearms caused 14 percent of injury deaths, compared to 23 percent for falls and 22 percent for motor vehicles. Nearly 90 percent of firearm deaths in this age group were suicides. Males aged 65 to 74 were 11 times more likely to die from firearm suicides than were females. For the oldest Americans, firearm suicide was primarily a male phenomenon. The suicide rate for males more than 85 years old was 45.7 per 100,000, compared to 1.2 for females.

Jacobs, Siegel, and Rein report CDC estimates of potential years of life lost to firearm-related fatalities. From 1980 to 1991, firearms ranked fourth among the causes of potential life lost before age 65, behind unintentional injuries from causes other than firearms, cancer, and heart disease. In that same time period, the potential years lost increased 13.6 percent for firearm-related deaths, but decreased by 25.2 percent for non-firearm related unintentional injury deaths, declined 18.1 percent for heart disease, and remained the same for cancer. Table 6 compares the number of firearm-related deaths in 2007 to those in 2014 by age categories. Overall, there were 2,405 more fatalities in 2014 than in 2007. However, dividing the fatalities into two age categories reveals that there were just 242 fewer deaths of those aged 0-44 in 2014 than in 2007, but 3,267 more deaths of those over 44 years of age. The declining crime rate in the mid-1990s and a continuing lower rate into the 2000s may have contributed to a consistently lower fatality rate in the younger age group. Given that younger people are more likely to engage in violent crime, any fall in the crime rate could influence more markedly the firearm death rate in the younger age category. One possible explanation

Table 6
Firearm Deaths (Unintentional, Homicide, Legal Intervention, and Suicide), 2007 and 2014

Age	2007	2014
0-4	85	78
5-9	69	75
10-14	244	307
15-19	2,669	2,089
20-24	4,233	4,051
25-29	3,389	3,472
30-34	2,813	2,903
35-39	2,505	2,495
40-44	2,615	2,394
45-49	2,553	2,512
50-54	2,308	2,779
55-59	1,888	2,551
60-64	1,450	2,021
65-69	1,085	1,616
70-74	853	1,418
75-79	990	1,043
80-84	726	894
85 +	638	924
Unknown	11	4
Total	**31,224**	**33,629**

Source: National Center for Injury Prevention and Control.

for the greater number of firearm deaths in 2014 than in 2007 among those aged 45 and older is the great number of gun suicides for this age group in 2014 (9,521) than in 2007 (6,135).

See also: Accidents Involving Guns; Canada; Israel; Suicide; United Kingdom; Violent Crime Rate.

Further Reading: Nancy R. Jacobs, Mark A. Siegel, and Mei Ling Rein, eds., *Gun Control: An American Issue* (Wylie, TX: Information Plus, 1997); National Center for Injury Prevention and Control, http://webappa.cdc.gov/sasweb/ncipc/mortrate10_sy.html.

Federalist Papers

From 1787 to 1788, Alexander Hamilton, James Madison, and John Jay, under the collective pseudonym "Publius," wrote and published the *Federalist Papers*, a series of newspaper articles advocating the ratification of the new U.S. Constitution. Although their arguments possess no official status, they have often been used to interpret the intent of the constitutional framers. Publius did not discuss the idea of a right to bear arms, for the Second Amendment was not proposed until the Constitution had been ratified and the first Congress had convened. However, Hamilton and Madison did investigate the merits of militias in the several states, which are relevant to the right to bear arms because the Second Amendment refers to "a well regulated Militia being necessary to the security of a free State," as opposed to a standing army.

However, contrary to the belief that standing armies should not be allowed under the new constitution, Hamilton in *Federalist* No. 24 noted that only two state constitutions contained prohibitions on the formation of standing armies in peacetime and that the Articles of Confederation imposed no limitation on the ability of the U.S. government to form a standing army. In addition to arguing that there was no precedent for denying the new national government the authority to establish a standing army, Hamilton claimed that the nation required the services of such a military force even in peacetime. Small garrisons on the Western frontier would provide defense against the "ravages and depredations of Indians," and a professional military would ward off any possible aggressive actions by the British or Spanish. Militias, he argued, could not meet these defense needs, for citizens would constantly be dragged from their private occupations for military service. The loss to society of their labor and the burden such service would represent for these men demonstrated that a permanent army paid by the government could better fulfill the nation's defensive needs.

In *Federalist* No. 25, Hamilton argued for the natural superiority of a standing army over a militia force. He questioned the argument that a militia was primarily responsible for the American victory in the war for independence, stating that "the liberty of [the militiamen's] country could not have been established by their efforts alone, however great and valuable they were." Although Hamilton admitted in *Federalist* No. 28 that a minor disturbance in part of a state could be handled adequately by the militia, sometimes a more extensive military force would be necessary to preserve peace and maintain the authority of the laws against insurrection and rebellion. A national standing army would at the same time guarantee that state governments did not exceed their authority.

In *Federalist* No. 29, Hamilton defended the new Constitution's provision for national control over militias, especially in periods of insurrection and invasion when a common authority would become vital to the maintenance of defense: "This desirable uniformity can only be accomplished by confiding the regulation of the militia to the direction of the national authority." Thus, if an insurrection or invasion occurred in one state, the proper action would be for the militia in a neighboring state to come to its aid against a common enemy, under the control of the national authority.

Despite Hamilton's conclusion that a regular army can outperform a militia, Madison in *Federalist* No. 46 assured Americans that a regular army under the control of the national government would pose no serious threat because the people and their state governments could stave off the threat. State militias composed of nearly a half-million men could not be defeated by a much smaller regular army. As evidence to support this contention, Madison referred to the recent war for independence and the fact that Americans, unlike citizens of most other nations, were well armed. These citizens, joined by their state governments, would form a "barrier against the enterprises of ambition, more insurmountable than any which a simple government of any form can admit of."

Madison was surely in favor of a significantly stronger national government and believed that the new Constitution would accomplish this objective. However, for the states to ratify the document, many had to be convinced that the new national government would not pose a threat to the integrity of the states and to individual liberties. Therefore, Madison's argument can be seen as an attempt to allay fears rather than an endorsement of the notion that states, with the aid of a militia composed of citizen soldiers, could back an insurrection against a repressive national government.

See also: American Revolution; Militia Act of 1792; Second Amendment.

Further Reading: Alexander Hamilton, James Madison, and John Jay, *The Federalist Papers* (New York: Mentor, 1961); Robert J. Spitzer, *The Politics of Gun Control*, 6th edition (Boulder, CO: Paradigm, 2015).

Feinstein, Dianne (1933–)

Dianne Feinstein, Democratic Senator from California, has gained the ire of gun rights organizations for her avid support of gun control measures. In 1994, the Senate passed two bills she supported, the assault weapons ban and the Gun-Free Schools Act. Although generally considered a liberal who supports abortion rights (in 2005 the liberal organization Americans for Democratic Action gave her a 95 percent approval rating while the American Conservative Union rated her at 0 percent), Feinstein has supported the death penalty and advocated a constitutional amendment prohibiting desecration of the U.S. flag. Throughout her public career, Feinstein has maintained an interest in criminal justice issues, and considers gun control a major priority in the campaign to limit violence.

Feinstein received a B.A. in history from Stanford University in 1955. She was a member of the California Women's Parole Board from 1960 to 1966 and in 1968 served as a member of the San Francisco Committee on Crime. In 1969, she was elected to the San Francisco Board of Supervisors, serving as president in 1970–71,

Senator Dianne Feinstein (D-CA), an advocate of gun control, supported both the assault weapons ban and the Gun-Free Schools Act. *www.wikipedia.org*

1974–75, and 1978. When San Francisco Mayor George Moscone and fellow Board member Harvey Milk were assassinated (an event that influenced her subsequent position on gun control), Feinstein succeeded to the office of mayor.

In 1979 Feinstein was elected mayor in her own right, a position she held until 1989. During her tenure as mayor, Feinstein focused on public safety and improving the efficiency of the police force. In 1990, Feinstein lost the California gubernatorial election to Pete Wilson, but subsequently won the U.S. Senate seat formerly held by Wilson, defeating Wilson's personally chosen replacement in a special election to fill the remaining two years in Wilson's senate term. In 1994, she won election to a full term. Feinstein serves on the Judiciary Committee; the Appropriations Committee; the Committee on Rules and Administration; and is the vice chair of the Select Committee on Intelligence.

Feinstein's assault weapons ban proposal was included in the 1994 Crime Bill, which called for the prohibition of the manufacture, transfer, and possession of 19 specific types of semiautomatic assault weapons, such as the Uzi and the M-11 Submachine pistol. Arguing in favor of passage, Feinstein advocated what was called commonsense legislation to stop the distribution of military-style assault weapons. She was careful to emphasize the legitimate use of firearms for home defense, hunting, and recreation. When a fellow senator who opposed the ban suggested that Feinstein had insufficient knowledge of weapons, she related a very personal experience with firearms, telling of her attempt to find Harvey Milk's pulse after he had been shot. In 2013, when the Senate Judiciary Committee was considering an assault weapons ban, Feinstein responded similarly to freshman Senator Ted Cruz's (R-TX) questioning of her regarding the First and Second Amendments to the U.S. Constitution.

Feinstein, along with Senator Byron Dorgan (D-ND), sponsored the Gun-Free Schools Act, which mandated that schools enforce a gun-free policy or face the loss of federal funding. Claiming that 100,000 guns are brought to school each day, she declared that schools should be "safe havens" for children, a place where they can be protected from the violence too often present in the world. Because state and local policies regarding students who take guns to school vary widely, Feinstein argued that uniform national guidelines were necessary.

In 1998 Feinstein sponsored an amendment to an appropriations bill to ban the importation and sale of high-capacity ammunition magazines. She intended the legislation to fill a gap left by the 1994 Crime Bill. Although the 1994 legislation prohibited the future manufacture and sale of ammunition clips with a capacity more than 10 rounds, it allowed the importation and sale of clips manufactured prior to enactment of the ban. The senator claimed that such ammunition magazines had no legitimate sporting purpose and represented a serious threat to public safety. She pointed to the Jonesboro, Arkansas, school shooting, in which two young boys killed four students and one teacher and wounded 11 others, to illustrate the dangers of such large ammunition clips. The intent of the proposed legislation was to prohibit the further importation of clips and to prevent the sale of present stocks. Those already legally possessing high-capacity clips could keep them, but could not transfer them to another person. In July 1998, the Senate voted to table Feinstein's amendment.

Feinstein's concern for public safety proceeded in areas complementary to her interest in gun control policy. In April 1998, the senator announced her support for a proposed constitutional amendment that would protect the victims of violent crime. The Victims' Rights Amendment would guarantee various rights to crime victims, including the right to attend any judicial proceedings, to be heard in the legal process, to receive restitution from the convicted offender, and to be provided safety from any future action by the offender.

In 2008 Feinstein criticized the George W. Bush administration for instituting a new policy allowing the carrying of concealed weapons in national parks. She noted that the Ronald Reagan administration had established regulations prohibiting loaded weapons in national parks, calling it "a consistent and uniform standard aimed at protecting public safety." In 2009, Feinstein introduced legislation that would prevent people who had been convicted of a felony or domestic violence in a foreign country from owning firearms in the United States. A person whose foreign conviction was determined to be invalid would be exempted from the ban. Also in 2009, given the increase in violence near the U.S. border with Mexico related to the drug trade, Feinstein, along with Senator Richard Durbin, asked the Senate Foreign Relations Committee to take action on the Inter-American Convention against illegal arms trafficking. Although the Convention had been negotiated in 1997, the U.S. Senate had not yet ratified it. Feinstein mentioned that close to 90 percent of the firearms used by Mexican drug cartels are acquired in the United States. The National Rifle Association and other gun right groups oppose such international agreements, calling them threats to the right of Americans to possess firearms.

Following the 2015 mass shooting in San Bernardino, California, Feinstein introduced legislation to prevent persons on the federal government's terrorist watch list who are prohibited from flying on commercial airlines from purchasing a firearm, but the bill was defeated. After the 2016 Orlando, Florida, mass shooting in which a gunman killed 49 people, Feinstein introduced another bill that would prevent individuals on the broader Terrorist Identities Datamart Environment (TIDE) list from purchasing a gun. She argued that the prohibition would affect about 5,000 people within the United States, and that those prohibited from making a gun purchase would have administrative and judicial appeals available to have their names removed from the list. Feinstein insisted that he proposal addressed a national security issue, not a gun control issue. Her measure, along with three other proposals, were defeated in the Senate.

See also: Assault Weapons Ban; Boxer, Barbara; Gun-Free Schools Act; Jonesboro, Arkansas, School Shooting.

Further Reading: Philip D. Duncan and Christine C. Lawrence, *Politics in America: The 105th Congress* (Washington, DC: CQ Press, 1997); "Senators Launch Effort to Ban High Capacity Ammunition Clips," *News from Senator Dianne Feinstein* (March 31, 1998); Dianne Feinstein Web site, www.senate. gov/~feinstein; Carolyn Lochhead, "Senate Votes Down Gun Control Measures, Including Feinstein Bill" (June 20, 2016), www.SFGATE.com/nation/ article/The-Senate-refused-to-budge-votes-down-four-gun-8314001.php.

Feldman, Richard (1951–)

Richard Feldman, founder and president of the Independent Firearm Owners Association, served as regional political director for the National Rifle Association (NRA) and as a lobbyist for the firearms industry, and as executive director of the American Shootings Sports Council. Feldman takes a more moderate position on firearms policy, demonstrating a willingness to compromise, at least when the more basic right to keep and bear arms is not at issue. He negotiated an agreement with the President Bill Clinton administration in 1997 to have firearm manufacturers voluntarily provide a gun lock with each new firearm purchase. The NRA and other gun rights organizations opposed the agreement. Feldman later claimed that the NRA's opposition to such reasonable compromises could be explained by that organization's focus on fund-raising, which requires the portrayal of the Second Amendment as constantly imperiled by any attempt to regulate firearms.

In the debates over gun rights, gun control, and gun safety, Feldman urges rational discussion and civility. He comments that no reasonable person approves the negligent misuse or intentional criminal use of firearms or access to guns by psychologically deranged individuals. Feldman states that the rights of law-abiding citizens to keep and bear arms, as well as the rights of mentally ill persons to have as much liberty as possible within the reasonable bounds of public safety, should be preserved. Feldman supports a competent and efficient Bureau of Alcohol, Tobacco, Firearms, and Explosives (ATF) that has the financial resources and technology to trace guns used in crimes back to suspects. He also supports extending criminal background checks for gun purchases to gun shows.

Feldman calls for a national firearm safety awareness campaign that would encourage gun owners to keep firearms safe and secure, although he expresses scepticism about the feasibility of so-called smart guns that, either through fingerprint recognition or some other electronic means, could be used only by an authorized person. He calls for both the freedom to possess firearms as well as the responsibility that accompanies firearm ownership. Existing firearms laws should be enforced more effectively in order to reduce the criminal use of guns as well as tragic gun accidents.

Feldman maintains a speaker program, titled "Behind Enemy Lines." He lectures on such topics as the politics of gun control, the ATF, Second Amendment issues, and cultural aspects of guns in the United States. He also writes a column for various periodicals, including the online journal Huffington Post and comments on gun-related issues in the broadcast media.

See also: American Shooting Sports Council; National Rifle Association; Trigger Locks.

Further Reading: Richard Feldman, *Ricochet: Confessions of a Gun Lobbyist* Hoboken, NJ: Wiley, 2008); Richard Feldman, "Seeking Common Ground: Perspective of a Gun Rights Supporter," in Glenn H. Utter, editor, *Gun Control and Contemporary Society* (Santa Barbara, CA: Praeger, 2016): 251-263.

Firearm Sentence Enhancement (FSE) Laws

Firearm Sentence Enhancement (FSE) laws at the state and national levels establish minimum sentences or mandate additional prison time for felonies committed with firearms. For instance, the Gun Control Act of 1968 prohibited the possession or employment of a firearm in the commission of a federal violent crime, and established a minimum penalty in addition to any sentence dispensed for the principal offense. As an example of such laws on the state level, in 2013 the New York state legislature and governor enacted the controversial Secure Ammunition and Firearms Enforcement (SAFE) Act following the Sandy Hook Elementary School shooting in Newtown, Connecticut, in which a gunman killed twenty young children and six adult, and the murder of two firefighters in Webster, New York. The act includes among its provisions augmenting sentences for crimes committed with a firearm, as well as increasing the offense of possessing a firearm on school property from a misdemeanor to a felony.

Both pro- and anti-gun control advocates tend to support such laws, as does the general public. Those supporting sentence enhancement laws argue that the threat of greater punishment deters crime and that longer sentences keep violent offenders in prison where they cannot victimize even more people. However, researchers have raised serious questions about the effectiveness of longer sentences for crimes committed with a firearm.

Wayne R. LaPierre, executive vice president of the National Rifle Association (NRA), supports mandatory prison sentences for those who are convicted of using a deadly weapon in the commission of a felony. LaPierre advocates "real-offense sentencing," which mandates that a judge consider the fact that a defendant used a firearm or other weapon, or caused bodily harm in the commission of a crime, even though the official charge does not reflect that fact. Further, LaPierre advocates a mandatory life sentence with no chance of release for anyone convicted a third time for a violent felony.

In January 1997, Congresswoman Sue Myrick, Republican from North Carolina, introduced a measure, titled the Mandatory Minimum Sentences for Criminals Possessing Firearms Act, which would amend the existing federal criminal code regarding mandatory additional sentences for crimes committed with firearms. The bill was meant to clarify the intentions of Congress in previous legislation establishing sentence enhancement for criminal firearm use. In 1995, the Supreme Court had ruled that a person committing a crime had to fire or brandish a weapon before enhanced or minimum penalties became applicable. The bill provided for imprisonment for an additional 10 years beyond the sentence imposed for the violent crime if the accused person possesses a firearm in carrying out the criminal act. Anyone who brandishes a firearm would be sentenced to 15 years imprisonment in addition to the original sentence for the crime of violence. The bill defined "brandishing" to mean "to display all or part of the firearm so as to intimidate or threaten, regardless of whether the firearm is visible." Finally, anyone who fires a gun during a crime of violence shall receive an additional 20-year sentence. In February 1998, the House passed the bill and referred it to the Senate, which took no action.

Although firearm sentence enhancement laws have proven to be popular, serious questions have been raised regarding their effectiveness. For instance, in a 1995 article in *Criminology*, Thomas Marvell and Carlisle Moody analyzed the effects of such laws in the states that had passed sentence enhancement or minimal sentencing measures. They noted that measuring consequences is complicated by alternative social theories that offer conflicting predictions: Sentence enhancement statutes can arguably both increase and reduce prison populations, crime rates, and the use of firearms in the commission of crimes. Marvell and Moody concluded that FSE laws generally do not reduce crime rates or gun use nationwide.

Available data indicate that only a small proportion of state FSE laws are significantly associated with decreased crime or gun use, and that a corresponding proportion of laws are associated with increased levels of violent crime. Various other factors, including judges who find ways to bypass mandatory sentencing, the minimal deterrent value of additional sentencing, the limited capacity of existing prison facilities, and criminals' increased ability to evade arrest for gun crimes may militate against the effectiveness of FSE laws.

See also: Bailey v. United States (1996); LaPierre, Wayne; National Rifle Association.

Further Reading: Dan Carney, "Crimes Committed with Guns May Carry Higher Penalties," *Congressional Quarterly Weekly Report* 55 (September 13, 1997), 2149; "Governor Paterson Introduces Legislation to Enhance Gun Laws," www.state.ny.us/governor/press/060210gunlawlegislation.html; Wayne R. LaPierre, *Guns, Crime, and Freedom* (Washington, DC: Regnery, 1994); Thomas B. Marvell and Carlisle E. Moody, "The Impact of Enhanced Prison Terms for Felonies Committed with Guns," *Criminology* 33 (1995), 247–78; Sue Myrick Website, www.house.gov/myrick.

Firearms Coalition

Neal Knox established the Firearms Coalition in 1982 following his removal from the National Rifle Association's (NRA) Institute for Legislative Action. Initially called the Neal Knox Hard Corps (the organization still distributes a semimonthly newsletter titled the "Knox Hard Corps Report"), the Coalition functions as a rallying point for those members of the NRA who take a more hardline position on the issue of gun control. The organization refers to the "sacred right" of self-defense that "should be limited in only the most extreme circumstances." In 1984, Knox became a registered lobbyist for the Coalition. On the organization's membership application, the contribution was called a "retainer" for Knox's services as a Washington lobbyist. Josh Sugarmann, head of the Violence Policy Center, estimated that the Coalition receives approximately $100,000 per year in contributions.

The organization provided Knox with a base from which to further his anti-gun control agenda within the NRA. Coalition supporters, many of whom were NRA members, opposed more moderate elements in the NRA who were considered too willing to compromise on gun control measures. When Charlton Heston was elected NRA president in 1998, the Coalition reported his support for the Gun Control Act in 1968, claiming that the new president's views on gun control had not changed noticeably since then. The Coalition participated in controversies over rules within the NRA, particularly those dealing with the nomination of candidates to the board of directors.

Wishing to activate gun owners politically, the Coalition keeps members and others interested in gun rights regularly informed about the activities of Congress regarding proposals related to firearms policy. The Coalition maintains the Online Bulletin as a means of communication among pro-gun advocates. In December 1998, with the National Instant Check System scheduled to begin, the Coalition paid close attention to legislative proposals in order to prevent federal government agencies from keeping a file of those who applied for a firearm purchase. The Coalition emphasized that the Brady Handgun Violence Prevention Act prohibits the retention of information on the subjects of background checks who were found to be qualified to purchase a firearm.

Although the Coalition recognizes that there are more pro-gun Republicans in Congress than pro-gun Democrats, it recommends that gun owners not become overly committed to a political party. The Coalition criticized Heston for supporting the Republican opponent of a pro-gun incumbent Democratic congressman who had received the endorsement of the NRA's Institute for Legislative Action (ILA) and a contribution from the ILA's Political Victory Fund. Although a Republican-controlled Congress is much more likely to support the interests of gun owners, the Coalition holds that the actions of Republicans as well as Democrats must be monitored closely so that no politician takes support from gun rights groups for granted.

In 1998 the Coalition opposed a measure to mandate the sale of trigger locks with new handguns and it objected to a proposal to require the safe storage of firearms, calling it "one of the most far-reaching 'gun control' laws pushed in recent years." Congress did not pass either measure. The Coalition supported a measure to allow law enforcement officers and civilians with concealed weapons permits in their home states to carry concealed firearms in other states. The organization strongly criticized President Bill Clinton and his administration for supporting additional gun control legislation.

Following Neal Knox's death in 2005, his son Jeffrey (Jeff) became head of the Coalition. Under the younger Knox's leadership, in 2008 the Coalition established www.GunVoter.org, a Website that provides information to gun rights advocates and allows the sharing of information among like-minded people. Through this site, the organization attempts to mobilize pro-gun rights voters. The Coalition also publishes an electronic newsletter, FCalerts. The Coalition urges those concerned about gun rights to be cautious about candidates for public office who support "reasonable restrictions" on gun ownership, calling such restrictions "clear violations of the Second Amendment." The Coalition continues to demonstrate a critical but comradely regard for the NRA. In 2016, as the NRA elections for the board of directors approached, Jeff Knox once again criticized the NRA's election process, but urged all NRA members to participate.

See also: Clinton, William Jefferson (Bill); Concealed Carry Laws; Gun Control Act of 1968; Heston, Charlton; Institute for Legislative Action; Knox, Neal; National Instant Check System; National Rifle Association; *Shotgun News*; Trigger Locks; Violence Policy Center.

Further Reading: Firearms Coalition Web site, http://firearmscoalition.org; www.GunVoter.org.

Firearms Owners Against Crime (FOAC)

Firearms Owners Against Crime (FOAC) is one of many state organizations dedicated to arguing for the preservation of a constitutional right to keep and bear arms. The organization was established by several people who had worked unsuccessfully to defeat a 1993 ordinance in Pittsburgh, Pennsylvania, that banned certain firearms and ammunition. FOAC became a political action committee in 1994, focusing on electoral politics in an attempt to influence government policy toward firearms. Kim Stolfer, who co-founded the organization, is the chairman. Stolfer has written several pieces of state legislation, including Castle Doctrine and preemption enhancement laws.

FOAC evaluates candidates for statewide as well as local and national offices each election cycle and urges like-minded voters to support candidates friendly to gun rights and to help persuade others to do the same. Although gun control legislation has been enacted, the organization holds that "laws can be repealed,

bureaucracies abolished, judges impeached, and jurisdiction limited."

FOAC monitors the state legislative agenda and the voting records of elected officials and publishes a voting guide that it distributes to the constituents of state legislators. The FOAC holds that a vote choice should never be one between two evils. If no candidate for a particular office has demonstrated sufficient support for the interests of firearms owners, the organization will not make a recommendation to voters. FOAC welcomes one-time or monthly donations, but does not set a specific membership fee.

FOAC holds to a fundamental principle: "In a free society, no citizen should ever have to justify the assertion of a fundamental right." Gun control advocates might well agree with that assertion, but deny that the right to keep and bear arms qualifies as an absolute right. The organization also holds the position that government is best when it governs least. FOAC believes that, contrary to this basic principle, government bureaucracy is intruding into the lives of private citizens more than at any other time in the nation's history. If violent crime is a problem with which government must deal, FOAC believes that it must enforce laws already in existence to punish and deter criminal acts before considering additional legislation that would infringe on the rights of law-abiding citizens to keep and bear arms. The organization complains about what it considers the high-handed activities of federal officers, such as agents of the Federal Bureau of Investigation (FBI).

Thomas J. Ridge, Republican governor of Pennsylvania from 1995 to 2001 (and subsequently Assistant to the President for Homeland Security from 2001 to 2003, and the first U.S. Secretary of Homeland Security from 2003 to 2005), came under attack for his support of gun control proposals. He was accused of initiating "the most striking anti-individual rights campaign in history" by attacking "almost every amendment in the Bill of Rights in the U.S. Constitution as well as the Declaration of Rights in the Pennsylvania Constitution." The governor was criticized for supporting a state law establishing an instant check system for those wishing to purchase a handgun and making the seller of a firearm responsible for the criminal use of the weapon. FOAC also expressed opposition to a measure allowing the confiscation of firearms from individuals under psychiatric treatment who have been declared threats to themselves and to others.

On its Website, the organization maintains a "watch list" that allows supporters to track proposed legislation at the state and federal levels and to send messages to their legislators. Following the 2016 mass shooting in Orlando, Florida, when the U.S. Senate was considering legislation to prevent persons on the terrorist "no fly" watch list from purchasing a firearm, FOAC strongly opposed the proposals, claiming that such bans would not have prevented the Orlando tragedy.

See also: Second Amendment; National Instant Check System.

Further Reading: Firearms Owners Against Crime Website, www.foac-pac.org.

Firearms Owners Protection Act (FOPA)

The first piece of significant national firearms legislation since 1968, the Gun Owners Protection (McClure-Volkmer) Act, which became law in 1986, was in fact a measure that weakened many of the provisions of the Gun Control Act of 1968. The leadership of the National Rifle Association (NRA) lobbied intensely for the act's adoption, while police organizations were either ambivalent toward, or actively opposed to the legislation.

In the early 1980s, the Gun Control Act of 1968 came under intense criticism from gun rights advocates, who claimed that the act unnecessarily limited the freedoms of law-abiding citizens while failing to keep firearms out of the hands of criminals. The Bureau of Alcohol, Tobacco, and Firearms (ATF), the government agency given responsibility for enforcing the law, was singled out as a major violator of individual rights. Senator James A. McClure (R-ID) and Representative Harold L. Volkmer (D-MO) were the bill's chief sponsors. McClure argued that the provisions of the 1968 act were vague and imprecise, allowing abuses that must be remedied. Volkmer expressed concern that the law branded as criminal the perfectly legitimate actions of individual citizens.

Senator McClure proposed amendments to the 1968 act that were intended to eliminate the perceived abuses. His amendments dealt with such subjects as the law's restrictions on the interstate sales of firearms, the alleged harassment of citizens by the ATF and other government agencies, and the forfeiture of property for violations of the act's provisions. He called for limiting such seizures only to those weapons actually used in the commission of a crime.

Referring to various guarantees of individual rights within the Constitution (the Second Amendment guarantee of the right to bear arms, the Fourth Amendment prohibition against illegal searches and seizures, the Fifth Amendment due process declaration, and the Tenth Amendment reservation of powers to the states and to the people), the new Firearms Owners Protection Act declared that it was not the intention of Congress to restrict unnecessarily the rights of American citizens who acquired, possessed, or used firearms for such lawful purposes as hunting, target shooting, or personal protection.

The act permitted the sale once again of ammunition through the mail. Weapons dealers were allowed to resume the interstate sale of rifles and shotguns, although a provision to permit the sale of mail-order handguns was deleted from the bill. Ammunition dealers were no longer held to stringent record-keeping regulations. Violations of record-keeping requirements for weapons dealers were reduced from a felony to a misdemeanor and more stringent criteria were established to prove guilt. Officials must be able to demonstrate the intentions of dealers, determining whether they knowingly or willingly violated the law. The act also established time limitations for officials administering provisions of the legislation. The ATF was prohibited from centralizing the records of firearms dealers or from establishing a firearms registration system. The act also restricted the authority of ATF officials to inspect dealer records, and allowed an individual wishing to reclaim a firearm seized by law enforcement agents to shift defense attorney fees to the prosecuting agency.

The McClure-Volkmer bill emphasized that gun ownership by itself constituted no legitimate reason for limiting the rights of citizens. The law focused instead on the misuse of firearms, requiring minimum and mandatory penalties for such misuse. Those engaging in drug trafficking who carry a firearm were subject to additional penalties. The bill also banned the future production of machine guns for sale to individuals, and prohibited the importation of barrels for Saturday night special handguns.

See also: Bureau of Alcohol, Tobacco, Firearms, and Explosives; Fourth Amendment; Gun Control Act of 1968; McClure, James Albertas; National

Rifle Association; Saturday Night Special; Second Amendment; Volkmer, Harold Lee.

Further Reading: Gregg Lee Carter, *The Gun Control Movement* (New York: Twayne Publishers, 1997); Earl R. Kruschke, *Gun Control* (Santa Barbara, CA: ABC-CLIO, 1995); Josh Sugarmann, *National Rifle Association: Money, Firepower and Fear* (Washington, DC: National Press, 1992).

Fourteenth Amendment

Gun rights advocates have looked to the Fourteenth Amendment as the vehicle by which the Second Amendment, which they have ardently claimed protects an individual's right to keep and bear arms, limits the power of state governments as well as the national government to control firearms. When first adopted in 1789, the Bill of Rights was understood to limit only the powers of the national government against encroachment on the rights of citizens. States had their own bills of rights to protect citizens against the power of these subordinate governments within the federal system. However, ratification of the Fourteenth Amendment in 1868 began a slow and halting process (called "selective incorporation") by which the Supreme Court in many cases over time interpreted various rights guaranteed in the Bill of Rights as applying to states as well as to the national government.

Section 1 of the Amendment states that "All persons born or naturalized in the United States, and subject to the jurisdiction thereof, are citizens of the United States and of the State wherein they reside. No State shall make or enforce any law which shall abridge the privileges or immunities of citizens of the United States; nor shall any State deprive any person of life, liberty, or property, without due process of law; nor deny to any person within its jurisdiction the equal protection of the laws." The full significance of this provision did not become established until many decades later, when the Supreme Court decided, in many separate cases, that selected rights guaranteed in the U.S. Constitution limit states as well as the federal government. For instance, in *Gitlow v. New York* (1925), the Supreme Court ruled that the First Amendment freedoms of speech and press are protected, via the Fourteenth Amendment, against state limitation. However, early Supreme Court decisions—including rulings on the right to keep and bear arms (*United States v. Cruikshank*

[1876] and *Presser v. Illinois* [1886]) as well as the First Amendment freedoms of speech, press, and religion, the Fourth Amendment guarantee against unreasonable search and seizure, and the Fifth Amendment protection from self-incrimination—determined that the Bill of Rights still applied only to the federal government.

The consistent refusal of the Court to apply the Bill of Rights to the states began to crumble in 1925 when the Supreme Court, in *Gitlow v. New York*, ruled that the First Amendment right of freedom of speech applied to the states. Since then a long list of decisions has selectively incorporated portions of the Bill of Rights into the Fourteenth Amendment. Those portions that the Supreme Court has so far not applied to the states include the Third and Seventh Amendments, and the indictment by grand jury requirement of the Fifth Amendment. Not until the *McDonald v. Chicago* decision in 2010 did the Supreme Court rule that the Second Amendment, which the Court previously had decided (in *District of Columbia v. Heller* in 2008), guarantees an individual right to keep and bear arms, applies to state and local governments via the Fourteenth Amendment. Gun rights advocates, arguing in favor of Second Amendment incorporation, argued that one of the primary purposes of the Fourteenth Amendment was to protect the right of African Americans to own and carry firearms, one of many rights threatened by the so-called Black Codes that Southern states enacted immediately following the Civil War in order to limit the freedoms of former enslaved persons. Gun rights advocates claim that senators considering the proposed amendment were especially concerned by the denial of the right to own firearms. Whether or not this right played a major role in proposing the Fourteenth Amendment, the Supreme Court for more than 130 years declined to incorporate the Second Amendment within the Fourteenth. In the meantime, gun rights advocates argued that there is no clearer guarantee within the Bill of Rights to be protected against state encroachment.

Gun control advocates responded that the Supreme Court misinterpreted the Second Amendment in ruling that it includes an individual's right to keep and bear arms instead of a collective right of individual states to form and maintain armed militia units. Following Supreme Court decisions in *Heller* and *McDonald*, gun control advocates argued that the right to keep and bear arms is not absolute, just as the protection of free speech in the First Amendment does not preclude any and all limitations on free speech, as in cases of libel, slander, and pornography. Those on both sides of the gun control debate expected many more challenges to gun control legislation in the years to come.

See also: African Americans and Guns; Black Codes, Fourth Amendment; Gottlieb, Alan Merril; *McDonald v. Chicago* (2010); *Presser v. Illinois* (1886); Second Amendment; State Laws, Appendix 2; *United States v. Cruickshank* (1876).

Further Reading: Alan M. Gottlieb, *The Rights of Gun Owners* (Bellevue, WA: Merrill, 1991); William E. Nelson, *The Fourteenth Amendment: From Political Principle to Judicial Doctrine* (Cambridge, MA: Harvard University Press, 1995).

Fourth Amendment

Gun rights supporters consider the Fourth Amendment protection against unreasonable searches and seizures to be a significant supplement to their arguments, based on the Second Amendment, against gun control legislation at the state and national levels and in opposition to the efforts of police officials to enforce such legislation. Gun rights supporters contend that many of the searches and seizures conducted against gun owners violate the rights of law-abiding citizens.

The Fourth Amendment states that, "The right of the people to be secure in their persons, houses, papers, and effects, against unreasonable searches and seizures, shall not be violated, and no Warrants shall issue, but upon probable cause, supported by Oath or affirmation, and particularly describing the place to be searched, and the persons or things to be seized." Under standard circumstances, police officials must demonstrate "probable cause" before a judge or other magistrate will issue a search warrant. This order specifies the place to be searched and objects that may be seized. If officials can demonstrate that the situation did not allow time, securing a warrant may not be essential to the legality of a search to acquire incriminating evidence. However, if the court rules that the evidence was not obtained legally, the "exclusionary rule" may apply, that is, evidence obtained by illegal or unreasonable means cannot be admitted in either a federal or state criminal

trial. The courts in effect must decide between the presence of probable cause and an individual's right to privacy in determining the appropriateness of a search warrant in a given circumstance.

The meaning of "unreasonable" has been subject to interpretation. More recently, the Supreme Court has tended to allow greater leeway for the police in conducting searches and seizures. More general searches, such as administrative inspections for health or safety reasons, and blanket searches such as those conducted at airports, potentially pose troubling questions regarding citizen rights because the wording of the Fourth Amendment usually is taken to refer to suspicion directed at an individual person.

With regard to the Fourth Amendment, gun rights advocates may be arguing one of two points. First, they can claim that police officials, in their zeal to ferret out illegal firearms, in fact violate citizen rights under the constitutional protection against unreasonable searches and seizures. When police officers search a home, an automobile, or an individual, they may conduct the search in such a way as to violate the reasonableness proviso. On the other hand, gun rights advocates may contend that because gun control laws are, from their perspective, clearly unconstitutional, any searches and seizures of weapons involve harassment of law-abiding citizens who have been made criminals by unconstitutional laws. The very conduct of a search violates a gun owner's protection against unreasonable searches and seizures because such searches have been conducted to enforce an unconstitutional law.

Gun control supporters would not necessarily have any difficulty with the first position, in that all searches and seizures, whether involving illegal firearms or the illegal use of them, or any other violation of the law, must be conducted within the boundary of the Fourth Amendment protection, although each side may draw the line at different places. However, to the extent that the second argument is invoked, gun control advocates reject the claim that gun laws are un-constitutional and hence that the Fourth Amendment should be employed to limit enforcement.

See also: Fourteenth Amendment; Gottlieb, Alan Merril; Second Amendment.

Further Reading: George Anastapol, *The Amendments to the Constitution: A Commentary* (Baltimore: Johns Hopkins University Press, 1995);

Alan M. Gottlieb, *The Rights of Gun Owners* (Bellevue, WA: Merrill, 1991); Robert J. Spitzer, *The Politics of Gun Control* 6th ed. (Boulder, CO: Paradigm Press, 2016).

Fraternal Order of Police (FOP)

In 1993, the Fraternal Order of Police (FOP), along with several other law enforcement organizations, supported passage of the Brady Handgun Violence Prevention Act. Gun control advocates saw this support as weakening the relationship between police organizations and the National Rifle Association (NRA), which opposed the Brady Act. The national FOP organization, called the Grand Lodge, continues to support the Brady Act, and other gun control measures, as a means of preventing criminals from acquiring firearms. In addition, the Grand Lodge supported the assault weapons ban, enacted in 1994 (the law lapsed in 2004, and was not renewed, despite support from police organizations). The organization supports a ban on "cop-killer" bullets, ammunition capable of penetrating the body armor used by police officers.

The FOP has voiced opposition to the Lautenberg Amendment, also known as the Domestic Violence Offender Gun Ban. The 1994 law, which prevents those convicted of domestic violence misdemeanor charges from purchasing or owning a firearm, has been applied to police officers around the country. According to the FOP, the law has forced police departments to dismiss veteran officers with good records for a misdemeanor offense that occurred many years ago. The Fraternal Order initiated an unsuccessful judicial challenge to the Lautenberg Amendment, claiming that the provision was unconstitutional because it applied retroactively to convictions that occurred prior to passage.

With regard to other firearms-related measures, the FOP supports the imposition of greater penalties for those who use body armor while committing a crime. Another measure the organization favors would increase criminal penalties for those who use laser sights on firearms when committing a crime. The organization has expressed its opposition to the proposed one-gun-a-month legislation that would limit individuals to purchasing no more than one firearm in a 30-day period.

The FOP supports a mandate to federal law enforcement agencies to issue locks to gun-carrying employees and legislation requiring the sale of a gun safety lock with each purchase of a new firearm. Following the Empire State Building shooting in February 1997, which was committed by a recent immigrant to the United States, the organization expressed its support for the more effective enforcement of a statute that would not allow resident aliens to purchase a firearm until they have lived in a state for at least 90 days. The organization also advocates a requirement that federally licensed firearms dealers post notices in gun stores informing customers that it is a federal offense for a juvenile to possess a handgun, advising customers that handguns are a major cause of death among youth, and recommending safe storage and locking devices as the means for preventing firearms accidents.

As an organization representing law enforcement officers, the FOP supports legislation that would exempt presently employed officers in good standing and retired officers from state and local prohibitions on carrying concealed firearms. Such legislation would permit officers to carry concealed firearms when traveling in jurisdictions other than their own. According to the FOP, such a provision would accomplish two major objectives. First, officers with the appropriate knowledge and training would have the means of enforcing the law and keeping the peace if called on to do so when not on active duty. Second, law enforcement officers may become the targets of criminals they helped to convict and therefore have special requirements for self-protection that should supersede state and local regulations. In 2013, the FOP expressed support for gun measures then before Congress, including expanded background checks for gun purchases, greater power and resources for the Bureau of Alcohol, Tobacco, Firearms and Explosives, expanded law enforcement access to mental health records in connection with firearms acquisition, and more funding for law enforcement.

See also: Assault Weapons Ban; Brady Handgun Violence Prevention Act; Bureau of Alcohol, Tobacco, Firearms and Explosives; Empire State Building Shooting; Lautenberg Amendment; National Rifle Association; Trigger Locks.

Further Reading: Fraternal Order of Police Web site, www.grandlodgefop.org.

G

Gang Violence and Guns

Gang violence results in many of the gun-related deaths and injuries each year. Although social science researchers have long established the correspondence of gang activity and gun-related violence, many have disagreed about whether the violence is due to gang attitudes or the guns such groups possess.

Although federal, state, and local officials have not agreed on a definition of what constitutes a gang (also referred to as a street gang, youth gang, or criminal street gang) certain criteria are often use to determine whether a group of individuals comprises a gang. Gangs usually include at least three individuals aged 12 to 24. The members identify with a name and possibly other symbols, and regard themselves as a gang. The group has a certain level of organization and persists over time. Importantly, the group engages in frequent criminal activities, which often involve violence and the presence of firearms.

The National Youth Gang Survey (NYGS) reports that gangs exist in roughly 30 percent of local jurisdictions in the United States, but are concentrated in urban areas. The only available measure of gang-related offenses is the number of homicides associated with gang activity, about which, unlike other offenses, most law enforcement agencies provide data. In 2012, the NYGS recorded 2,363 gang-related homicides. During the previous five years, the Survey indicated that the number of gang-related homicides varied from 1,700 to 2,100 each year. Thus gang-related homicides amounted to about 15 percent of the approximately 13,000 murders each year, a relatively small but still significant figure. Gang-related homicides occurred primarily in large municipalities, with a small number of cities contributing to the increase in recent years.

Gang violence is mentioned as one of the possible factors—along with the heroin epidemic and hard economic times—for the recent increase in homicides in some cities, including Chicago, Illinois; Dallas, Texas; Las Vegas, Nevada; Jacksonville, Florida; Los Angeles, California; and Memphis, Tennessee. Although the number of homicides in Chicago is much lower than in the early 1990s, when officials reported more than 900 murders in some years, the recent increase has raised serious concern among local officials.

Government officials, researchers, and political commentators have debated what steps can be taken to reign in gang-related violence, including tougher law enforcement tactics against gang members, discovering and eradicating the sources of illegal firearms, taking steps to approach potential gang members to discourage their joining gangs, and more long-term strategies to improve the economic prospects of young people.

See also: Youth and Guns; Youth Crime Gun Interdiction Initiative.

Further Reading: Monica Davey, "Killings Rising, Chicago Braces For Even More," *New York Times* (March 19, 2016): A1; Evan De Filippis and Devin Hughes, "Do We Have a Gang Problem or a Gun Problem?" *Huffington Post* (June 3, 2014). www.huffingtonpost.com/evan-defilippis/do-we-have-a-gang-problem_b_5071639.html; Eric Lichtblau and Monica Davey, "New Data on Homicide Rates Rekindles a Debate," *New York Times* (May 14, 2016): A11; National Gang Center. http:nationalgangcenter.gov/About/FAQ. Accessed June 23, 2016; Federal Bureau of Investigation, National Gang Report 2015. www.fbi.gov/file-repository/stats-services-publications-national-gang-report-2015.pdf/view.

German Firearms Laws, 1920s-1930s

During the 2016 presidential campaign, Republican presidential aspirant Dr. Ben Carson made a statement concerning guns, the Holocaust, and Jewish people that bought to the fore an often-repeated argument on behalf of arming civilians. When asked about his position on gun laws and gun ownership, Carson was quoted as saying that, "I think the likelihood of Hitler being able to accomplish his goals [in Nazi Germany] would have been greatly diminished if the people had been armed." This statement echoed the persistent comments of some in the gun community who have long argued that governmental tyranny in authoritarianism in nations around the world, including Nazi Germany, the Soviet Union, Communist China, and elsewhere, could have been forestalled or even defeated, if the people in those countries had been armed. Further, they argue, one of the first steps taken by dictators to gain or consolidate power is to enact strict gun control laws. The implication is that stricter gun laws in the U.S. might also foreshadow an American government becoming tyrannical, and that an armed citizenry and weak gun laws can prevent tyranny. These arguments as they pertain to Nazi Germany found voice in a book written by National Rifle Association lawyer and writer Stephen P. Halbrook, *Gun Control in the Third Reich* (2013). Halbrook argues that German and Nazi laws restricting gun ownership among civilians were key to Hitler's rise to, and consolidation of power, and that they were central to the persecution of Jewish people in Germany, who were barred by law from owning guns. Halbrook's writing is based on his research of German gun laws spanning the German Weimar Republic (1919-1933) and the post-Weimar Nazi era in the 1930s.

While this argument continues to hold sway among many, it found no favor among historians of the Weimar-Nazi era, who noted at the outset that the vast literature on this era lends no support for the idea that gun control laws played any role in the rise of Nazism or the oppression of groups like the Jews, Gypsies, gay people, or others. In addition, Adolph Hitler became German Chancellor in 1933, but the Nazi regime enacted no new gun laws until 1938 (referred to as its Waffengesetz), when the law was changed to require police permission for civilian handgun ownership. An order barring Jews from owning weapons came at the end of 1938, after the infamous nationwide violent crackdown on Jewish people called Kristallnacht. According to Nazi-era historian, Alan Steinweis, it is "preposterous" to say that Jews, who amounted to less than one percent of Germany's population, could have mounted any kind of armed resistance to the Nazi government which was a large, popular, and well-armed regime. A lone instance of a Jew killing a low-level Nazi diplomat in Paris shortly before Kristallnacht provided an important pretext to justify the event. Even before Hitler's rise to power, his paramilitary forces relied heavily on force and violence to combat its opponents. Any effort to somehow spread guns to the civilian population would have found the Nazi groups to be the chief beneficiary, given their willingness to use lethal force and the relative weakness of the Weimar regime.

Further Reading: Stephen P. Halbrook, *Gun Control in the Third Reich* (Oakland, CA: The Independent Institute, 2013); Bernard E. Harcourt, "On Gun Registration, the NRA, Adolph Hitler, and Nazi Gun Laws," *Fordham Law Review* 73(November 2004); Alan E. Steinweis, "Ben Carson Is Wrong on Guns and the Holocaust," *New York Times,* October 14, 2015.

Gottlieb, Alan Merril (1947–)

Alan Gottlieb has played a central role in the campaign for recognition of a constitutional right of individuals to keep and bear arms and has worked vigorously to defeat measures that would impose more stringent gun control. Before entering a career as a gun rights advocate, Gottlieb served in the Army National Guard, entering as a private in 1968 and leaving as a Specialist Fourth Class in 1974. In 1971, he received a B.S. from the University of Tennessee. A political conservative, Gottlieb served as the national director of Young Americans for Freedom in 1971–72 and has been the national treasurer of the American Conservative Union. In 1974, Gottlieb established the Citizens Committee for the Right to Keep and Bear Arms (CCRKBA) to proclaim his interpretation of the Second Amendment and to serve as a source of information for individuals with the same goal. At the same time, Gottlieb founded the Second Amendment Foundation (SAF), the research and education affiliate of CCRKBA. He also heads the Center for the Defense of Free Enterprise.

Gottlieb has authored or coauthored numerous books dealing with the rights of gun owners, including *The Gun Owner's Political Action Manual* (1976); *The Rights of Gun Owners* (1981); *The Gun Grabbers* (1986); *Gun Rights Fact Book* (1988); *Things You Can Do to Defend Your Gun Rights* (1993); and *More Things You Can Do to Defend Your Gun Rights* (1995), both coauthored with David Kopel; *Guns for Women* (1988), coauthored with George Flynn; *Gun Rights Affirmed: The Emerson Case* (2001); *Assault on Weapons: The Campaign to Eliminate Your Guns* (2009), coauthored with David Workman, and *Shooting Blanks: Facts Don't Matter to the Gun Ban Crowd* (2011). Gottlieb owns Merril Press, which publishes his books. Much of Gottlieb's publications offer practical advice to those who want to further the gun rights cause. For instance, *Things You Can Do to Defend Your Gun Rights* contains information about ways to influence government, including registering to vote, writing letters to elected officials, circulating petitions, visiting public officials personally, working for political candidates who take pro-gun rights stands, and testifying at public hearings. He gives advice on ways to gain publicity for the gun rights movement.

Gottlieb and Flynn's *Gun Rights for Women*, which is dedicated to Annie Oakley, the famous trick-shot artist, offers practical advice to women who wish to purchase a handgun (a disclaimer at the beginning of the book states that the authors are not recommending the purchase of a handgun, but are simply offering guidance for those who have already made the decision to buy a weapon). A chapter titled "Armed Citizens" provides 100 accounts of women who used a firearm to save their own or others' lives. Other chapters describe handgun features and specific makes and models, offer tips about firearm safety, and present the names and addresses of organizations that the reader might wish to join.

Gottlieb has received several recognition awards for his active support of gun rights, including the Good Citizenship award from the Citizens Home Protective Association (1978); the Good Citizen award from the Hawaii Home Protective Association (1978); the Cicero award from the National Association of Federally Licensed Firearms Dealers (1982); the Top Ten Outstanding American Handgunners award from the American Handgunner Award Foundation (1984); and the Kentucky Freedom Fighter award, presented by the Kentucky House of Representatives (1985).

Gottlieb's tenure as chairman of the CCRKBA has not been entirely smooth. In May 1984, he pleaded guilty to a federal charge of income tax evasion for failing to report income in 1977 and 1978 from his company, Merril Associates, a consulting firm for direct mailing clients. He was sentenced to one year in jail and a $5,000 fine. Gottlieb served eight and a half months of the sentence before being released. He claimed that the indictment was part of the Treasury Department's strategy of targeting gun rights groups.

In another incident, members of the CCRKBA who complained about his handling of the organization's affairs were excluded from the group. These individuals launched a court challenge, but Gottlieb maintained his leadership position.

Gottlieb has continued to campaign for gun rights, publishing various periodicals for the CCRKBA and SAF, including *Gun Week* and *Gun News Digest*, a quarterly publication. Gottlieb has also made appearances on many news programs, including *Good Morning America*, *The News Hour*, *Piers Morgan Live*, and *PBS Late Night*. Gottlieb's combative dedication to the Second Amendment has kept him at the forefront of the anti-gun control forces.

See also: Citizens Committee for the Right to Keep and Bear Arms; *Gun Week*; Kopel, David B.; Second Amendment; Second Amendment Foundation; Women and Guns.

Further Reading: Alan M. Gottlieb and David Workman, *Assault on Weapons: The Campaign to Eliminate Your Guns* (Bellevue, WA: Merril Press, 2009); Josh Sugarmann, *National Rifle Association: Money, Firepower and Fear* (Washington, DC: National Press, 1992); www.saf.org.

Gritz, James (Bo) (1939–)

In the 1980s and 1990s, James "Bo" Gritz, a Vietnam-era Green Beret colonel and a leader in the Patriot Movement, played a prominent role in far-right fringe and paramilitary survivalist groups, combining an appeal to patriotism with conservative Christian beliefs. Gritz has maintained associations with such Christian Identity figures as Pete Peters. He has identified an enemy composed of "seditious bankers" and "satanic globalists" led by the United Nations. Gritz is an avid opponent of gun control legislation, counseling supporters to resist any federal government attempt to confiscate their firearms. In the 1980s, Gritz made unsuccessful attempts to find American prisoners of war allegedly still held in Southeast Asia. In 1988, he joined Populist Party presidential candidate David Duke, a former Ku Klux Klan Imperial Wizard, to run for vice president, but resigned from the ticket to make an unsuccessful bid for the Republican nomination for a U.S. House seat from Nevada. In 1992, Gritz became the Populist Party presidential candidate. Comparing his campaign to a second American revolution, Gritz promised to restore states rights, reject global government, and safeguard personal liberty.

In 1992, Gritz gained national publicity during the standoff at Ruby Ridge between Randy Weaver and federal authorities in which Weaver's wife and son and a U.S. marshal were killed. Gritz served as an intermediary, helping Weaver, a fellow Green Beret veteran, surrender to authorities. In 1996, he persuaded Federal Bureau of Investigation (FBI) agents to permit him to mediate a standoff with the Freemen of Montana, but he was unable to convince them to surrender. The standoff ultimately ended peacefully. In 1998, he led a group into the rural North Carolina woods to try to persuade accused abortion clinic bomber Eric Rudolph to surrender. Gritz ultimately condemned federal agents for the handling of the Randy Weaver situation, as well as the Waco, Texas, Branch Davidian raid in 1993.

Gritz offers a military training regime called SPIKE (Specially Prepared Individuals for Key Events) Delta Force Training. The training is said to provide "classified, secret information so that you will never be a victim again." Among the topics covered are gun control, counterterrorist driving, medical emergencies, and lock-picking. Gritz offers the training on over 70 hours of videotapes.

In 1994, Gritz established a Christian Covenant Community in Kamiah, Idaho, on land purchased from a Native American reservation. The community was intended to serve as a haven where patriotic Americans could survive the anticipated devastation. He called the land Almost Heaven, and began selling lots to families wishing to move to the remote Idaho site. By 1996, the community had not developed as quickly as expected and some residents became critical of Gritz for failing to commit more completely to the community.

Gritz continued to maintain an organization in Sandy Valley, Nevada, called the Center for Action, broadcasting a shortwave radio show, "Freedom Calls." In September 1998, after his wife had filed for a divorce, Gritz was found lying by a remote road in rural Idaho, suffering from a self-inflicted gunshot wound. He survived the incident. In 2001, he attempted to assist the Indianapolis Baptist Temple, an organization that refused to accept federal authority, in its standoff with federal authorities after a federal court authorized the federal government to seize church lands. Fearing that Gritz's presence might inflame the situation, church leaders asked him to leave. The matter was resolved peacefully. Gritz also attempted, unsuccessfully, to intervene in the Terry Schiavo right-to-die case in 2005. Gritz remains active through his Web site and an Internet radio program, "Freedom Call."

See also: Ruby Ridge; United Nations; Waco, Texas, Raid.

Further Reading: Aaron Delwiche, "Propaganda Examples: James Bo Gritz," www.carmen.artsci. washington.edu/propaganda/gritz.htm; "Extremism in America: Bo Gritz," Anti-Defamation League, www. adl.org/learn/ext_us/gritz.asp?xpicked=2&item=5; Bo Gritz Web site, www.bogritz.com; *The Militia Watchdog*, "Patriot Purgatory: Bo Gritz and Almost Heaven," www.militia-watchdog.org/gritz.htm.

Gun Buyback Programs

Gun buyback programs have been established in some cities to decrease the number of firearms, reduce gun-related criminal activity, and prevent gun accidents, particularly involving children. Such programs have gained support in the international community as a way of decreasing tensions in nations facing civil unrest. Gun rights supporters have responded to gun buyback programs with skepticism about their effectiveness and with concern that a political message is being conveyed that guns, independent of the human beings who use them, are evil. Although gun buyback programs appear to have had little impact on the level of crime and violence, and gun rights supporters object to the program's assumption that firearms are themselves dangerous and possibly worthy of confiscation, supporters hope to have some impact, however minimal, on what they consider to be a serious social problem, and to raise general public awareness of the problem of gun violence.

Gun buyback programs have been attempted in such cities as Houston, Dallas and Fort Worth, Los Angeles, Buffalo, and Boston. In 1994, a program in Baltimore, Maryland, offered $100 for each working handgun surrendered. One thousand guns were gathered during the first day of the offer, depleting funds devoted to the buyback program. The city continued the buyback program after a private citizen donated additional funds, but decreased the offer to $50 per gun.

In November 1995, Texans Against Gun Violence conducted a gun buyback program in Houston, called "Operation Safe and Secure." Participants could exchange a firearm for a gift certificate worth a minimum of $50 in merchandise at two local retail outlets. Residents at participating apartment complexes could receive a voucher for $100 toward their rent. Those turning in firearms also received tickets to a Houston Aeros hockey game. This in-kind payment avoided the criticism leveled at cash payment programs because the funds could not be used to purchase drugs or additional firearms. For instance, a program in Baton Rouge, Louisiana, offered cash for guns, which, according to some reports, encouraged some participants to purchase inexpensive firearms and redeem them for more than their value. Supporters believe that even though some cheating may occur, the programs have led participants to turn in guns kept in the home that could result in accidental shootings.

The Houston buyback program, which was funded by donations from local businesses, collected 133 weapons, including small-caliber handguns, rifles, and shotguns, some of which were reported to have sawed-off barrels. Civilian volunteers conducted the operation, in part to assure participants that they would not be arrested for illegal possession of a firearm. Organizers of the program indicated that weapons would be melted down to prevent them from reentering society. Since the mid-1990s,

many cities around the country have funded such programs.

In 1999, the Bill Clinton administration funded gun buyback programs through the Department of Housing and Urban Development. It spent $15 million in a two-year effort that eliminated 20,000 guns in 1999 and 2000. The program was canceled by the George W. Bush administration in 2001, claiming that the program was ineffective.

See also: Help Network; Project Lifeline.

Further Reading: "Bush Halts HUD Gun Buyback Program," About.com: U.S. Government Info, http://usgovinfo.about.com/library/weekly/ aa073101a. htm, July 31, 2001; Cindy Holden, "Los Angeles Gun Buyback Takes Over 2500 Firearms Off the Streets," *California Newswire*, May 11, 2010, http://californianewswire.com/2010/05/11/ CNW7360_174951.php; Mike Tolson, "Program Collects 133 Weapons: Houston's First Gun Buyback Also Draws Group of Protestors," *Houston Chronicle* (November 19, 1995), 42A.

Gun Control Act of 1968

The Gun Control Act of 1968 was the first major piece of gun control legislation to be enacted since the Federal Firearms Act of 1938. The act was contained in two statutes: Titles IV and VII of the Omnibus Crime Control and Safe Streets Act (82 Stat. 225, 236), and the Gun Control Act (82 Stat. 1213). The act placed controls on those people engaged in the sale of firearms and essentially replaced the Federal Firearms Act of 1938.

The effort to pass a new gun control law began in 1963 when the Senate Judiciary Committee considered a bill prohibiting mail-order sales of handguns to minors. The long trail of events leading to final passage in 1968 included several assassinations. After President John Kennedy was shot and killed in November 1963, supporters expanded the bill to include a ban on mail-order sales of shotguns and rifles. However, the lobbying efforts of anti-gun control forces, headed by the National Rifle Association (NRA), were successful in keeping the bill locked in committee.

Growing concern over violence led several states and municipalities to enact legislation of their own, which proved to be another impetus toward national action. The assassinations of

Martin Luther King, Jr., and Robert Kennedy in 1968 provided the crucial momentum toward congressional action. The legislation, the result of considerable compromise, pleased few. Those opposing gun control finally accepted the bill, fearing the possibility of even more rigorous provisions, and supporters were disappointed that stronger restrictions were not included.

Among its provisions, the legislation strengthened the firearms licensing process to limit foreign and interstate transport of firearms to legitimate manufacturers, dealers, and importers. The act prohibited the interstate shipment of pistols and revolvers to private individuals. Gun buyers could only purchase a handgun in the state in which they resided. The licensing fee for federal firearms dealers was increased from $1 to $10 and minors were forbidden from receiving a license. Dealers could not sell rifles, shotguns, or ammunition to anyone under 18, or pistols and ammunition to anyone under 21. Dealers and collectors were required to keep more complete records. The legislation prohibited importation of foreign military surplus firearms, except those used in hunting, and extended the National Firearms Act of 1934 by requiring registration and a transfer tax on such "destructive devices" as antitank guns, bazookas, and mortars.

Focusing on criminal activity, the act forbade convicted felons, the mentally incompetent, and drug addicts from shipping or receiving weapons via interstate commerce, and licensed dealers could not knowingly sell weapons to these categories of people. Anyone who used a firearm to commit a crime that involved breaking a federal law was subject to additional punishment, which included a minimum of one year in prison. Although the legislation represented a significant step forward for those advocating gun control, the measure failed to meet Democratic President Lyndon Johnson's primary objective: to require national registration and licensing of firearms.

See also: Dodd, Thomas J.; Federal Firearms Act of 1938; Firearms Owners Protection Act; National Firearms Act of 1934; National Rifle Association.

Further Reading: Lee Kennett and James La Verne Anderson, *The Gun in America: The Origins of a National Dilemma* (Westport, CT: Greenwood, 1975); Earl R. Kruschke, *Gun Control* (Santa Barbara, CA: ABC-CLIO, 1995); Robert J. Spitzer, *The Politics of Gun Control*, 6th ed. (Boulder, CO: Paradigm, 2015).

Gun Culture

The term "gun culture" has been used to refer to the strong American attraction to firearms. Proponents of gun control have used the term pejoratively to explain what they consider the extremely serious problem of firearms violence in the United States and to offer a reason for the strong resistance to effective firearms legislation, while gun rights supporters use the term to indicate what they consider the long and honorable American tradition of firearms ownership. In 1970, historian Richard Hofstadter identified the origin of the American gun culture in the history of the nation. Early settlers who expanded the frontier westward needed firearms to shoot wild game and farmers used guns to shoot vermin and predatory animals. Hofstadter noted that in 1675-76 Indians "damaged half the towns of New England, destroyed a dozen, and killed an estimated one out of every sixteen males of military age among the settlers." In such a dangerous environment, the firearm became a necessity of life.

By the time of the American Revolution, Americans had become adept at the use of firearms and that experience contributed significantly to the colonists' success in revolutionary battles. According to Hofstadter, British troops became so fearful of the hunter's marksmanship that General George Washington asked his troops to dress in hunting shirts to terrorize the enemy. Although Washington had little faith in the militia and preferred to rely instead on the regular army, Americans became convinced that the minutemen had demonstrated their military superiority over the professional soldiers upon which the decadent nations of Europe relied.

Despite the popular view that developed about the use of firearms during the Revolution, historians have noted that Americans in the early nineteenth century were often uninterested in gun ownership and unacquainted with gun use. In the early years of the nation, the federal government largely failed in its efforts to increase citizen participation in militias and to encourage gun ownership. Following the Civil War, Union soldiers were allowed to keep their firearms and, with declining gun prices that followed decreased government demand, weapon ownership in the civilian population became far more common.

In addition to the influence of the Civil War on the development of an American gun culture,

Hofstadter claimed that before the development of the entertainment industry and organized competitive sports, hunting and fishing became major pastimes. For many American youth, receiving their first real rifle symbolized passage to manhood. However, while some have argued that the gun is so important to Americans because it is a symbol of masculinity, Hofstadter responded that this claim does not explain why men in other societies did not come to associate firearms with masculinity.

Although the percentage of the nation's population engaged in farming declined markedly, the gun remained a prevalent feature in American life. Hofstadter attributed this phenomenon partially to basic political beliefs: the fear of a standing army as a threat to liberty and a continuing "faith in the civic virtue and military prowess of the yeoman." The firearm, which played such a crucial role in settling the West and defending settlers against the Indian, entered popular culture through novels, movies, and, ultimately, television. Hofstadter observed a unique tendency in the United States to prefer "the isolated, wholly individualistic detective, sheriff, or villain," and to resolve conflicts through "ready and ingenious violence." The Second Amendment came to be regarded as guaranteeing a basic individual right to keep and bear arms, despite the fact that courts interpreted the amendment in terms of the need for a well-regulated militia until 2008, when the Supreme Court established a Second Amendment-based right to citizen handgun possession for self-defense in the home in the case of *District of Columbia v. Heller*.

Hofstadter identified as a component of the gun culture the belief that access to firearms served as an important deterrent to tyranny. In 1970, Hofstadter disputed an argument gun rights advocates have used more recently—that gun control laws in Nazi Germany contributed to the establishment of tyranny—contending that the Weimar Republic failed to respond decisively to Nazi terror tactics. According to Hofstadter, "It is not strong and firm governments but weak ones, incapable of exerting their regulatory and punitive powers, that are overthrown by tyrannies." Contrary to the prevailing gun culture, which holds that firearms in private hands provide a basic defense of freedom, Hofstadter considered the presence of groups of individuals in possession of arms a threat to public order.

The recognition of underlying cultural beliefs about firearms helps to explain the deep-seated disagreements that exist in the American debate over gun control. While proponents of stronger gun control, such as Hofstadter, identify a disturbing pattern of attitudes toward the use of firearms in the United States, gun rights advocates find a similarly emotional belief system among gun opponents. Gun rights supporters claim that gun control advocates want to brand all firearms as evil in and of themselves, regardless of the person using them.

See also: American Revolution; *District of Columbia v. Heller* (2008); Minutemen, Revolutionary; Native Americans; Second Amendment.

Further Reading: Richard Hofstadter, "America as a Gun Culture," *American Heritage* (October 1970), 4–11, 82–85; David Kopel, *The Samurai, the Mountie, and the Cowboy* (Buffalo, NY: Prometheus, 1992); Scott Melzer, *Gun Crusaders: The NRA's Culture War* (New York: New York University Press, 2009); Robert J. Spitzer, *The Politics of Gun Control*, 6th ed. (Boulder, CO: Paradigm, 2015).

Gun-Free Schools Act

Cosponsored by Senators Dianne Feinstein, Democrat of California, and Byron Dorgan, Democrat of North Dakota, the Gun-Free Schools Act was signed by President Bill Clinton in October 1994 as part of the Elementary and Secondary Education Act. The Education Act provided $12 billion in federal funding for public schools for the next five years, the receipt of which was made dependent on a school's adherence to the provisions of the Gun-Free Schools Act. The act was a response to the perception that violence had increased significantly in American schools and that too many students were taking guns to school. It was an attempt to establish national standards for dealing with instances of gun-carrying by students on school property. An earlier version of the law was declared unconstitutional by the Supreme Court in the case of *United States v. Lopez* (1995). The court struck the law down by saying that Congress had exceeded its powers under its ability to regulate interstate commerce.

The provisions of the law require schools to expel for a least one year any student found carrying a firearm. In addition, each school is required to report to their state education agencies any incidents involving a student carrying a gun. Schools are to include in their reports the number of occurrences and the types of guns involved. Although state and local governments may have their own policies regarding gun-carrying in schools, the federal law provides a minimum standard for such policies. Although the law requires public schools receiving federal funding to abide by its provisions, individual schools may alter the expulsion policy in response to local circumstances. Table 7 provides data on gun deaths in public schools from 1992 to 2010. Gun use is extremely rare in public schools (given a public school population of over 50 million), and generally in decline since the early 1990s.

Americans have traditionally preferred a decentralized system of public education. Not only have states assumed the primary role in school policy, but in some states, local school districts enjoy considerable autonomy. In 1994, when the Gun-Free Schools Act was approved, all states had some form of expulsion guidelines for their school districts. These policies ranged from suspension for being caught with a gun at school to a one-year expulsion. Some states had no express policy regarding the discovery of weapons at school, or had not specified a period of expulsion. The Los Angeles Unified School District had formulated an expulsion policy, but with no stated minimum length of time. Maryland allowed county boards to establish suspension, expulsion, and other disciplinary policies on a county-by-county basis. New York authorized the board of education of each school district to enact provisions for suspension and expulsion. Texas law provided for a student's expulsion for, among other things, possessing a firearm, an illegal knife, or other prohibited weapons while present at school or attending a school-sponsored event. By the end of the first decade of the twenty-first century, however, gun bans in schools were commonplace across the country, as was a "zero-tolerance" policy that required expulsion for any violation.

While supporters of the legislation believe its merits are obvious, some proponents of the defensive use of firearms contend that gun-free schools become easy targets for those wanting to harm students and teachers. However, it is not clear what the consequences might be of a policy that allowed people other than trained security officers to carry guns at school. Whether because of the

Table 7
Public School Shooting Deaths, 1992–2014

Year	Shooting Deaths
1992–1993	45
1993–1994	41
1994–1995	16
1995–1996	29
1996–1997	15
1997–1998	36
1998–1999	25
1999–2000	16
2000–2001	19
2001–2002	4
2002–2003	14
2003–2004	29
2004–2005	20
2005–2006	5
2006–2007	16
2007–2008	3
2008–2009	10
2009–2010	5
2010-2011	8
2011-2012	15
2012-2013	32
2013-2014	13
TOTAL	416*

*Deaths by guns at schools amounted to 74% of all violent public school deaths. Total public school violent deaths from all other causes from 1992–2010 was 120. The second leading cause across this time period was stabbing/slashing (67 deaths).

Source: National School Safety Center's Report on School Associated Violent Deaths, www.schoolsafety. us.; John Light, et al., "Guns in America After Newtown," *Moyers and Company,* June 10, 2014, http://billmoyers. com/2013/05/03/gun-violence-since-newtown/. Some data also examined at "List of School Shootings in the United States," Wikipedia.org

law or not, gun shootings and deaths at schools have generally declined from the 1990s through the end of the first decade of the twenty-first century, according to the National School Safety Center. See Table 7.

See also: Clinton, William Jefferson (Bill); Feinstein, Dianne; Lott, John R., Jr.; *United States v. Lopez* (1995).

Further Reading: Dianne Feinstein, "Gun-Free Schools Act," *Fact Sheet*, Washington, DC, 1998, A14; Dianne Feinstein Web site, http://feinstein.senate. gov/public/; National School Safety Center, www. schoolsafety. us/; Beth Sinclair, Jennifer Hamilton, Babette Gutman, Julie Daft, and Dee Bolick, *Report on State Implementation of the Gun-Free Schools Act— School Year 1996–1997*, Final Report (Washington, DC: U.S. Department of Education, 1998).

Gun Journal

Since 1991, the Collector Arms Dealers Association (CADA) has sponsored the *Gun Journal*, which is published monthly by Blue Book Publications, Inc. The CADA is headed by David Carroll. The magazine appeals to serious gun collectors. The editor encourages readers to join firearms organizations, attend gun shows, read about gun collections, keep their own gun collections in good condition, stay abreast of the classified ads, and check the Web sites for information about antique firearms. The magazine contains a list of firearms sites on the Internet. The bulk of the publication includes classified advertisements for various categories of antique firearms, providing a wealth of information for the collector. The editors often publish articles on the history of guns in the United States and worldwide.

In addition to the extensive classified column, the magazine contains advertisements for Blue Book Publications, including books dealing with combat shotguns, Colt firearms, single-shot rifles, and Spencer repeating firearms. Another section titled "Auction Update" reports on recent auction sales of antique arms. The sale prices, which range from a few thousand dollars up to more than $20,000, provide incentives for collectors to be on the watch for especially valuable finds. Also included are several pages of advertisements for gun shows around the nation at which antique arms and other gun products can be purchased or traded.

In the March 1998 issue, Chris Wolf, in an article titled "How Bad Can It Get?," warned of the imminent confiscation of all firearms in the United States. He compared government policy toward guns to laws regulating smoking and predicted that just like cigarettes, guns will be branded a health hazard. Wolf argued that just as the government has determined to control the loss of lives and wealth related to smoking,

the same will be done with firearms. The author associated the anti-gun crusade with liberalism, but quickly tied that more moderate ideology with communism. In explaining and criticizing the desire to control guns, he used such terms as democratic socialism, liberalists, liberal moralist dictatorship, and moralist puritanism. Wolf stated that he fears a puritanical regime that will ban all firearms in the United States, following the pattern he saw occurring in Canada, Great Britain, and Australia. A Canadian himself, Wolf expressed his displeasure with the Royal Canadian Mounted Police, who are enforcing the new gun control provisions in Canada. He predicted that firearms periodicals will disappear as they are subjected to pressures to be "politically correct" and fail to gain advertising. He predicted that the whole economy would be adversely affected by government restrictions on the manufacture and sale of firearms.

Articles on gun control take fervent stands against laws that limit the right to possess firearms. *Gun Journal* portrays collectors' interests in guns to be far removed from any criminal activity and strongly opposes government regulation or restrictions on collectors' activities. The magazine presents the image of antique gun collectors as enthusiastic participants in a hobby and business who wish that the government would leave them alone in their honest and peaceful activities. The publication considers government interference by such agencies as the Bureau of Alcohol, Tobacco, Firearms, and Explosives to be not only inconvenient but illegitimate.

See also: Australia; Bureau of Alcohol, Tobacco, Firearms, and Explosives; Canada; Colt, Samuel; United Kingdom.

Further Reading: www.bluebookofgunvalues. com; www.dcarroll.net/; *Gun Journal* (Blue Book Publications, Inc., Minneapolis, MN).

Gun Owners

To determine their most likely sources of support, both gun rights and gun control groups need to identify those groups with the highest and lowest levels of gun ownership. According to the results of a 2015 survey reported in Table 8, more men (32 percent) than women (12 percent) own firearms. A considerably larger percentage of whites and those identified as multiracial own firearms (both 25 percent) than do Hispanics (16 percent) or blacks (14 percent). The highest gun-owning age group includes those over 60 years old, an indication that gun ownership nationwide continues to decline as younger age groups fail to retain the gun tradition. Those with some college education have a higher rate of gun ownership (26 percent) than either college graduates or those with less than a high school education.

Firearm ownership increases with income, with those having incomes greater than $100,000 reporting the highest level of ownership. Gun ownership is highest in rural areas (33 percent), and lowest in urban areas (15 percent). Military service is highly correlated with gun ownership (44 percent of veterans compared with 19 percent non-veterans). Those who grew up with guns were far more likely to own them (35 percent) than those who did not (9 percent). See Table 8 for more data on gun ownership in the United States.

See also: Collectors; Gun Culture.

Further Reading: Gary Kleck, *Targeting Guns: Firearms and Their Control* (Hawthorne, NY: Aldine De Gruyter, 1997); Robert J. Spitzer, *The Politics of Gun Control*, 6th ed. (Boulder, CO: Paradigm Publishers, 2015).

Gun Owners' Action League (GOAL)

The Gun Owners' Action League (GOAL), formed in 1974, is the state firearms association of Massachusetts, the state with possibly the most stringent firearms legislation. The organization describes itself as "an association of law-abiding citizens who believe in the basic right of firearms ownership for competition, recreation, and self-protection." GOAL, a strong critic of state gun control provisions, initiated a legal challenge to the Massachusetts Gun Violence Prevention Law in October 1998, the day the provision went into effect. Michael Yacino, executive director of GOAL, declared that the Massachusetts statute is "too vague to understand, too obscure to enforce, and too unintelligible to obey." The organization expressed its concern regarding what it

considered "fuzzy descriptions" of assault weapons, large capacity firearms, and feeding devices. Due to vagueness in the law, GOAL claimed that Massachusetts firearms owners could not be sure if they are complying with its provisions.

GOAL's headquarters, located in Northboro, Massachusetts, has a full-time staff. The executive director oversees the organization's various activities, including fund-raising, publishing, and legislative work, and manages the office. A board of directors, elected by the membership, establishes organization policy. GOAL emphasizes various educational programs and advocates teaching children safety and responsibility in handling firearms. Members have encouraged use of the National Rifle Association's (NRA) Eddie Eagle Gun Safety Program in Massachusetts elementary schools. GOAL provides firearms training courses for older youths. Organization representatives speak at schools about firearms ownership and the association makes available information packets to students. GOAL provides information to adults about national, state, and local firearms laws and distributes a booklet about Massachusetts gun regulations.

Association members receive a directory of state legislators and information on candidates for public office and their positions on firearms policy. Candidates are invited to speak to organization members in their districts to express their views on firearms issues. Each year the organization conducts a Firearms Safety and Education Day for state legislators, assistant district attorneys, media people, and administration officials who are offered personal instruction in safe firearms handling. GOAL has a professional lobbyist at the state capital to monitor the progress of firearms-related legislation and court cases.

GOAL presents its views on firearms issues to the general public through the dissemination of literature and videotapes. The organization maintains a speakers bureau for presentations before various civic groups. GOAL publishes a monthly newsletter, *The Outdoor Message*, which contains information about politics and legislative activities as well as sporting news and advertisements for products. The newsletter contains a calendar of shooting competitions, sporting events, gun shows, and firearms courses. GOAL supports a weekly radio program, The GOAL Line, which deals with firearms issues, hunting topics, and various sports subjects.

Table 8
Demographic Characteristics of Gun Owners
Percentage who own a firearm, 2015

		Any firearm	Handgun only	Long gun only	Both
All		22	6	5	11
Age	18-29	13	3	4	6
	30-44	21	6	4	10
	45-59	24	6	5	13
	60+	25	6	5	14
Sex	Male	32	7	8	18
	Female	12	5	2	5
Race	White	25	5	6	13
	Hispanic	16	6	3	7
	Black	14	8	1	5
	Multi-racial	25	4	6	15
Community	Urban	15	6	3	7
	Suburban	19	6	4	10
	Rural	33	5	9	19
Education	Less than h.s.	11	4	3	5
	High school	23	6	5	12
	Some college	26	6	5	15
	College	20	5	5	10
Annual income	Less than $25,000	13	4	3	6
	$25,000-$59,999	22	6	5	11
	$60,000-$99,999	24	7	4	12
	$100,000+	25	5	6	14
Military service	Veteran	44	10	9	25
	Non-veteran	19	5	4	10
Grew up w/ gun	Yes	35	7	8	20
	No	9	4	2	3
	Don't know	17	9	4	4

Source: "The Stock and Flow of US Firearms: Results from the 2015 National Firearm Survey," *The Guardian*, September 19, 2016, https://www.theguardian.com/us-news/2016/sep/19/us-gun-ownership-survey

See also: Eddie Eagle; Gun Shows; Massachusetts Gun Violence Prevention Law; National Rifle Association; State Laws, Appendix 2.

Further Reading: Gun Owners Action League Web site, www.goal.org; "Suit Challenges Massachusetts Gun Law," *Gun Week* 33 (November 10, 1998).

Gun Owners of America (GOA)

Established in 1975 by California state senator H. L. "Bill" Richardson, Gun Owners of America (GOA) strives to preserve and extend individual gun rights. The organization was formed because the nation's largest gun organization, the National Rifle Association, was considered to be not tough enough in its defense of gun rights. GOA identifies its membership as "patriotic Americans working together to preserve the right to keep and bear arms, protecting and safeguarding our Constitutional freedoms for future generations," and prides itself on being the most uncompromising anti-gun control organization in the United States. The organization claims to have invested more money than any other group in the successful fight to pass the Firearms Owners' Protection Act of 1986, and takes credit for being the only organization to have fought to repeal the Brady Handgun Violence Prevention Act's background check requirement. GOA also advocates the right of law-abiding citizens to carry a firearm without a permit. It also supports the arming of teachers in public schools to confront school violence, a position not embraced by other gun groups like the NRA. Larry Pratt has served as the GOA's executive director since 1984.

Three other organizations are associated with the GOA. Gun Owners of America Political Victory Fund is the GOA's political action committee. This organization raises funds to be donated to candidates for public office at all levels of government who support the right of gun ownership. Also associated with the GOA is Gun Owners of California, an entity that is active only in the state of California. It was founded by Bill Richardson to deal with any issues concerning firearms that arise in that state. Gun Owners Foundation is the nonprofit educational arm of the GOA to which supporters can make tax deductible contributions. The Foundation organizes seminars that are intended to inform the media, government officials, and the general public about Second Amendment issues, and is a source of books and other publications dealing with gun issues.

The GOA publishes a bi-monthly newsletter, called *The Gun Owners*, that includes articles about current legislation being considered at the national, state, and local levels. Sample headlines from the newsletter indicate the concerns of the organization: "ATF Declaring War on Honest Gun Owners" (March 28, 2011), "UN Arms Treaty Threatens Gun Rights" (September 27, 2011), and "VA Abuses Highlight Dangers of Health Care Database—Bill to repeal Veterans Disarmament Act now moving" (March 22, 2010). The organization's general theme is that the right to privacy of law-abiding citizens is threatened by gun laws, and that these citizens face unwarranted arrest and imprisonment simply for trying to defend themselves. The newsletter reports the votes

Gun Owners of America is one of the country's leading pro-gun rights groups. *www.gunowners.org*

of senators and representatives on measures of concern to the organization.

The GOA interprets any measure to control firearms as an attempt to take away the guns of law-abiding citizens. For instance, when Congress passed the Brady Background Check Law in the 1990s, GOA warned that giving bureaucrats the ability to screen law-abiding gun owners would lead to severe abuses. In recent years, GOA has frequently cited a Congressional Research Service report which now indicates that Brady background checks have resulted in roughly 140,000 military veterans losing their gun rights, because ailments like PTSD make them supposed "mental defectives."

The GOA engages in a number of activities to further its objective of preventing the passage of gun control legislation. The organization conducts surveys of the membership, the results of which are sent to congress people and the president to inform them about the attitudes of gun owners. A GOA fact sheet argues for the self-defense value of firearms ("Guns save more lives than they take; prevent more injuries than they inflict"), claims that the Brady law has been unsuccessful, and insists that licensing or registration of firearms leads inevitably to confiscation.

The GOA provides its membership with Candidate Rating Guides each general election year, in which candidates are rated on their support of gun owners. At the local level, the organization works with activists who attend town meetings and state legislative sessions where gun control measures may arise. In this way, the Washington, D.C., headquarters of the GOA can be kept informed of any proposals that local gun control groups are attempting to have passed. The GOA also maintains a Legal Defense Program that provides assistance to gun owners who find themselves involved in a legal action with the government. Although a smaller organization with about 300,000 members, the GOA has played an active role in opposing gun control legislation. It is based in Springfield, Virginia.

See also: Brady Handgun Violence Prevention Act; Bureau of Alcohol, Tobacco, Firearms, and Explosives; Firearms Owners Protection Act; Pratt, Larry; Second Amendment.

Further Reading: Robert J. Spitzer, *The Politics of Gun Control,* 6th ed. (Boulder, CO: Paradigm, 2015); Josh Sugarmann, *National Rifle Association: Money, Firepower and Fear* (Washington, DC: National Press, 1992); Gun Owners of America "Firearms Fact-Sheet" (membership brochure); Gun Owners of America Monthly Newsletter, http://gunowners. org/goa-newsletter.htm; Gun Owners of America Web site, www.gunowners.org.

Gun Rights Policy Conference (GRPC)

The Gun Rights Policy Conference (GRPC) is an annual meeting of firearms rights activists representing national and state gun organizations and scholars who support the right to keep and bear arms. Begun in 1986, the Conference is sponsored by the Second Amendment Foundation (SAF) and the Citizens Committee for the Right to Keep and Bear Arms (CCRKBA) and includes such major pro-gun advocates as Alan Gottlieb, Wayne LaPierre, Joseph Tartaro, Don Kates, and David Kopel. Conference presentations deal with the major political issues confronting the gun rights movement, including mandatory trigger locks and other gun safety proposals, challenges to shooting ranges, the National Instant Check System to determine eligibility to purchase a firearm, the treatment of gun advocates in the media, and reciprocity for state concealed carry laws.

The twenty-fifth annual meeting of the GRPC was held in San Francisco, California in September 2010, a location not considered generally friendly to the gun rights movement. Various gun-related organizations and companies, such as the American Firearms Council, the American Shooting Sports Council, Heckler and Koch, North American Arms, Smith and Wesson, and Beretta USA provided financial assistance for holding the conference.

Among the themes stressed by more than fifty speakers at the convention were criticisms of the United Nations' efforts to limit international arms trafficking, and information about ongoing court challenges to gun laws in the light of the 2010 Supreme Court ruling in *McDonald v. Chicago,* in which the high court extended an individual right to bear arms to the states. The annual meetings strive to coordinate a nationwide gun agenda for the year to come. *See also:* Citizens Committee for the Right to Keep and Bear Arms; Clinton, William Jefferson (Bill); Concealed Carry Laws; Gottlieb, Alan Merril; Kates, Don B.; Kopel, David B.; LaPierre, Wayne; *McDonald v. Chicago* (2010); National Instant Check System; National Rifle Association; Second Amendment Foundation; Trigger Locks; United Nations.

Further Reading: Gun Rights Policy Conference Web site: https://www.saf.org/grpc/

Gun Show Loophole

The term "gun show loophole" refers to the sale of some guns at gun shows that do not include background checks of the purchasers. Under the terms of the Brady Handgun Violence Prevention Act, background checks are to be performed on prospective gun buyers by federally licensed gun dealers. The purpose of such checks is to weed out those individuals who are barred from gun ownership, including individuals with criminal backgrounds and those who have been judged mentally incompetent. In many states, however, gun shows allow both licensed dealers and unlicensed private sellers to buy and sell guns. Unlicensed private individuals are able to make gun sales without the required checks because they are not licensed dealers. The Brady Campaign to Prevent Gun Violence cites the example of Eric Harris and Dylan Klebold, the two students who shot up Columbine High School in Littleton, Colorado in 1999. Because the two were under age, they asked an older friend, Robyn Anderson, to purchase guns for them, who bought three of the four guns used in the shooting from an unlicensed seller at a Colorado gun show. Anderson said later that she would not have made the purchases if she had been subject to a background check.

Thirty-two states make no provision for background checks for private gun sales. Eighteen states impose at least some background check provisions for gun shows. Of those, eight states require background checks for all gun purchases regardless of location, and four require background checks for all handgun purchases.

Gun rights supporters argue that the gun show loophole is not a loophole at all. The purpose of the law, they argue, is to regulate the activities of commercial dealers whether at a gun show or elsewhere, not the actions of private citizens who may wish to sell a gun to a friend or relative, and who are not engaged in gun dealing as a business. It is foolish, they argue, to hold private individuals to the same standard as licensed dealers. Further, most gun show sales are from dealers, and fewer than one percent of guns involved in crimes are obtained at gun shows. Such added regulations are, if anything, a backdoor means to impose greater gun control.

Supporters of closing the loophole cite other studies that note regular illicit gun trafficking from unregulated gun show sales. The Bureau of Alcohol, Tobacco, Firearms, and Explosives (ATF) found gun shows to be a major source of illicit gun trafficking. Over one 17-month period alone, the ATF tracked over 25,000 illicitly traded guns from gun shows. A 2009 Government Accountability Office study of gun trafficking by Mexican drug cartels found that in the previous five years, 87 percent of guns seized by authorities were acquired in the United States, at least some of which came from gun shows. An undercover sting operation conducted through the City of New York of gun shows in Nevada, Ohio, and Tennessee (results released in 2009) found that 63 percent of private gun sellers sold guns to people who said that they probably could not pass a background check. A 2015 study by Harvard researchers found that about 40 percent of those studied had obtained guns without first undergoing a background check. In 2014, Washington State held a referendum on a proposal to implement uniform background checks for all gun sales and transfers. The measure passed by a wide margin.

See also: Background Checks; Brady Handgun Violence Prevention Act; Bureau of Alcohol, Tobacco, Firearms, and Explosives; Littleton, Colorado, Columbine School Shooting.

Further Reading: City of New York, "Gun Show Undercover: Report on Illegal Sales at Gun Shows," October 2009, Everytown for Gun Safety, Everytown.org; National Rifle Association, "The Gun Show Myth," November 7, 2008, www.nraila. org/issues/ factsheets/; www. stategunlaws.org; "Universal Background Checks," Law Center to Prevent Gun Violence, http://smartgunlaws.org/ universal-gun-background-checks-policy-summary/

Gun Shows

In recent years, the United States has experienced a proliferation of gun shows, also called sportsmen shows, expos, arms shows, or weapons fairs. Several thousand gun shows, large and small, are held throughout the United States annually. This number is an underestimate because it does not include events in smaller towns and cities. Usually occurring on the weekend, these shows attract large numbers of people who, for a relatively small admission fee, can view a wide variety of products. The National Rifle Association (NRA) often has a booth established in or around the arena. About 40 percent of nationwide gun sales occur at gun shows annually.

Gun shows display a wide variety of handguns, rifles, and shotguns, both new and used. The participant can find in one place a vast display of firearms that far exceeds the inventory of any one gun shop. By purchasing a used handgun, a buyer can avoid the Brady Act's background check because only new weapons are covered under the statute. In addition, in many states, nonlicensed dealers may sell guns at gun shows, and these sales do not require that background checks occur. This so-called "gun show loophole" has raised the ire of gun control advocates, who argue that such sales should also include background checks. Collectors of antique firearms also congregate at these shows, trading, purchasing, or selling weapons. A show may also include an auction of collectable firearms.

Other items on display include knives and military memorabilia, especially German equipment from World War II, and political literature. Booths offer a wide variety of literature to attendees, including used books and magazines. In addition to standard treatments of firearms, books and pamphlets deal with such topics as converting a semiautomatic weapon to fully automatic, with the disclaimer that the activity is forbidden by federal law. Gun safe manufacturers also exhibit at these shows. Booths offering merchandise less directly related to firearms, such as jewelry, clothing, and popular art, can also be found at gun shows. Other defense items besides firearms are available, including pepper spray and other nonlethal weapons.

Gun shows are large economic enterprises, and the National Association of Arms Shows (NAAS), the official organization representing businesses and individuals promoting weapons fairs, has a strong interest in the survival of gun shows and their continued operation unhampered by official limitations. Members of NAAS meet annually and deal with issues of concern to gun show promoters. NAAS officials make presentations on such topics as obtaining favorable press coverage for gun shows and taking part in legislative lobbying and relevant court cases. Participants share information about the difficulties encountered from national, state, and local governments when attempting to organize and conduct shows.

See also: Brady Handgun Violence Prevention Act; Bureau of Alcohol, Tobacco, Firearms, and Explosives; Collectors; Gun Show Loophole; National Rifle Association.

Further Reading: Joan Burbick, *Gun Show Nation* (New York: The New Press, 2006); Kristen Rand, *Gun Shows in America: Tupperware Parties for Criminals* (Washington, DC: Violence Policy Center, 1996); NAAS Web site, http://naasgunshows.com/index.html.

Gun Trafficking

When speaking of gun trafficking, public officials are referring to the illegal transport and sale of firearms that have been diverted from the legal market to individuals who would not pass a background check. Gun trafficking is also referred to as a black market in firearms. The administrative and political dangers of attempting to thwart gun trafficking appears in the case of Operation Fast and Furious, a Bureau of Alcohol, Tobacco, Firearms, and Explosives (ATF) plan to allow illegal purchases in order to monitor the path of firearms from the United States to Mexico. ATF agents lost track of hundreds of weapons, one of which was subsequently recovered at the location where a U.S. border patrol agent was killed.

The ATF has reported that some unlicensed dealers in firearms, claiming to be collectors of hobbyists, actually traffic firearms to felons and others prohibited from purchasing a firearm. Another source of illegal guns is a small number of corrupt licensed dealers, which is considered a major avenue for marketing illegal guns. Research on trafficking indicates that less than 20 percent of firearms tied to crimes were legally obtained.

Evidence from recent research indicates that recently purchased new guns are often recovered from crime scenes. Studies also indicate that certain federally licensed firearm dealers are disproportionately identified as sources of guns used in crimes. In addition, many private party gun sellers, who are not required to run background checks but nonetheless are prohibited by law from knowingly transferring a firearm to a person who does not qualify to purchase or own a firearm, often participate in illegal gun sales.

Studies report that about one-third of guns used in crime originates in the local community, another third comes from within the state, and a final third is transported from other states. The transportation route from the Southeast to the Middle Atlantic and Northeast is referred to as the Iron Pipeline. An ATF report issued in 2000 identified as the major sources of gun trafficking negligent firearms dealers allowing "straw man" purchases—guns legally acquired that are intentionally transferred or sold to those who cannot pass a criminal background check. Studies conclude that from one-fourth to one-third of guns used in crimes originated with licensed dealers.

Those concerned with the international trafficking in small arms identify a variety of sources of firearms, which can contribute to destabilizing the social and political order of nations. Government agents may grant export licenses in return for bribes, or they may simply fail to monitor transfers of arms. Government-held arsenals may be looted in politically unstable countries, and weapons held in insecure locations may be subject to theft. Weak national laws dealing with the sale and ownership of firearms can result in weapons being diverted to the black market, a situation that gun control advocates argue is the case in the United States.

The United Nations Small Arms Treaty, adopted in 2013, is an attempt to stem the flow of small arms internationally. However, gun rights organizations in the United States oppose the treaty because they fear it may ultimately be used to limit the Second Amendment right to keep and bear arms, and because groups in other countries that oppose oppressive regimes will find it more difficult to obtain the weapons needed to further their cause.

Those supporting limitations on gun trafficking in the United States recommend various actions to restrict the illegal flow of firearms. First, they call for extending background checks to purchases between private individuals as well as from federally licensed firearm dealers. Second, it is recommended that Congress make gun trafficking per se a crime. Currently, gun traffickers can be prosecuted only for conducting a business of firearms sales without a license or for making false statements on ATF Form 4473 when purchasing a firearm—in other words, acting as a straw purchaser. In addition, it is recommended that Congress and state legislatures increase the legal penalties for weapons violations. Coordination between federal law enforcement agencies— primarily the ATF—and state and local agencies would more efficiently expose cases of gun trafficking. Such recommendations focus on what is called a supply-side approach that is intended to reduce the transfer of firearms to criminals.

See also: Background Checks; Bureau of Alcohol, Tobacco, Firearms, and Explosives

Further Reading: Anthony A. Braga and Peter L. Gagliardi, "Enforcing Federal Laws Against Firearms Traffickers," in Daniel W. Webster and Jon S. Vernick, editors, *Reducing Gun Violence in America* (Baltimore, MD: Johns Hopkins University Press, 2013): 143-154; Rachel Stohl, Matt Schroeder, and Dan Smith, *The Small Arms Trade* (Oxford: Oneworld, 2007); Don B. Kates, "The Hopelessness of Trying the Disarm the Kinds of People Who Murder," *Bridges* (Fall/Winter 2005): 313-330; Jason C. Sides, James M. Vanderleeuw, and Joanna Melissa Joseph, "The Failure of 'Operation Fast and Furious' and the Complexity of Firearms Trafficking," in Glenn H. Utter, editor, *Guns and Contemporary Society* (Santa Barbara, CA: Praeger, 2016).

Gun Week (GW)

Established in 1966, *Gun Week (GW)* magazine is a vocal advocate of gun rights and an avid opponent of attempts to institute gun control measures. The Second Amendment Foundation (SAF) publishes *GW* 24 times per year. Some of its articles are also available online at its Web site, www.gunweek. com.

Typical of other gun magazines, *GW* carries articles on new weapons, especially handguns, but contains less advertising. The magazine contains advertisements for gun shows and provides lists of events that will occur during the next month. Those conducting gun shows are invited to list the event free of charge in the pages of *GW*. Advertisements for various literature, as well as other gun magazines, appear in *GW*. such topics as the selection of federal judges, the Bureau of Alcohol, Tobacco, Firearms, and Explosives, state and federal court rulings, and congressional policy on the gun trade.

See also: Bureau of Alcohol, Tobacco, Firearms, and Explosives; Gun Buyback Programs; Gun Shows; National Rifle Association; Second Amendment Foundation.

Further Reading: *Gun Week,* www.gunweek.com/.

Gun World

Regular features include industry news that cover reports on occurrences in gun manufacturing, including corporation mergers and the introduction of new products, such as laser sighting systems, new handgun hunting ammunition, and innovative firearms. *GW* prints brief news stories for hunting enthusiasts, reporting on hunting activities in the various states. It also has a classified advertising section. Books dealing with various firearm subjects are regularly reviewed.

A large portion of each issue is devoted to the politics of gun control, including legislative developments, government regulations, and other political developments. Gun supporters are encouraged to make their views known to their congresspeople, and encourages readers to meet with their representatives in district offices. Attempts to thwart gun control measures at the state level are detailed. Reports of the internal politics of the National Rifle Association (NRA), including battles over the leadership of the organization, appear in the pages of *GW*. Legislators supporting the right to bear arms are given the opportunity to present their views. *GW* reports on attempts to institute gun control measures, usually emphasizing what the magazine considers the folly of such proposals. It also carries a regular column, "The Weekly Bullet," the reports on gun crimes, accidents, and other gun-related news from around the country. Other articles deal with Published monthly by Y-Visions Publishing, *Gun World* contains articles and columns that support the right of gun owners against attempts to enact gun control legislation. *Gun World* covers subjects that typically appear in gun magazines, including various hunting topics, reports on new gun products, and stories on various aspects of the gun industry, such as holster making and locking mechanisms. Reports on a wide variety of gun and gun-related products, appear throughout the magazine. In the past, regular gun writers, including David Kopel and NRA officials, have contributed to the publication.

In 2010, *GW's* longtime editor, Jan Libourel, stepped down, raising some uncertainty as to the publication's future in the face of difficulty filling the position and competition from many other gun magazines.

See also: Concealed Carry Laws; Kopel, David; National Rifle Association; Saturday Night Special; Second Amendment; Washington, D.C.

Further Reading: *Gun World,* www.gunworld.com/.

Guns and Ammo (G&A)

Like *American Rifleman*, each issue of *Guns and Ammo (G&A)* contains articles that support the right to bear arms and oppose initiatives to regulate gun purchases, ownership, and use. Beginning its fifty-third year in 2010, *G&A* is published monthly by the Petersen Publishing Companies, Inc. While not as obviously political as *American Rifleman*, the magazine contains regular features concerning gun policy. Most articles deal with topics related directly to firearms, including reports on new weapons, technical advances, tips for better shooting, and antique weapons, especially those used in the "Old West." The magazine is divided into sections by type of firearm: handgun, rifle, and shotgun. Interspersed among the articles are advertisements for handguns, rifles and rifle scopes, ammunition, collectible guns, knives, gun safes, and other paraphernalia related to firearms. *G&A,* along with *Handguns Magazine, RifleShooter Magazine, Guns & Ammo TV*, and *Personal Defense TV*, are all part of the Guns & Ammo brand, organized under the online provider, gunsandammomag.com.

"Armed Response," a column similar to a feature in the *American Rifleman*, contains accounts submitted by readers relating their "use of a firearm to prevent a crime or save a life." Typically, the column describes an innocent citizen who succeeds in defusing a dangerous situation

by relying on a handgun. Many of the stories involve the value of concealed carry laws. While not dealing overtly with gun control issues, articles dealing with personal security assume that law-abiding citizens live in a dangerous world and therefore need to take appropriate steps to ensure self-defense.

The magazine also deals with questions of firearms and gun rights from the perspective of law enforcement officers. Unlike many police organizations that have in recent years backed such gun control measures as the Brady Act, the magazine regards guns as an inappropriate target in the attempt to determine the causes of crime.

See also: American Rifleman; Boxer, Barbara; Brady Handgun Violence Prevention Act; Handgun Control, Inc.; National Instant Check System; National Rifle Association; Pratt, Larry; Second Amendment.

Further Reading: *Guns and Ammo* (Petersen Publishing, Los Angeles, CA), www.gunsandammo.com/.

Guns Magazine (GM)

Guns Magazine (GM) contains articles opposing gun control measures and advocating the self-defense value of firearms. The magazine, which appears monthly, is a product of the Publishers Development Corporation. While opposing gun control legislation, *GM* prints a disclaimer informing readers that "Products mentioned or advertised may not be legal in all states or jurisdictions." The warning also states that "Firearms are dangerous and if used improperly may cause serious injury or death." Most publication space is turned over to information about guns and accessories.

Each issue contains a letters column that includes communications from those who protest various gun control proposals in the United States and other nations. Although pro-gun interests generally oppose any suggestion of making gun locks mandatory, writers also express enthusiasm for new gun locks on the market. *GM* and other gun magazines also carry advertisements for such gun locks.

Advertisements in *GM* include a wide variety of products and services, including knives, ammunition, concealed carry holsters, souvenir pistols (for instance, "The Audie Murphy Tribute .45,"), books and book clubs (for instance, the Military Book

Club), gun security safes, rifle scopes, bulletproof vests, night-vision viewers, gunsmith schools, and firearms training schools. Each issue contains classified advertisements, including sections for accessories, ammunition, books, collectibles, fireworks, guns and gun parts, knives and swords, military surplus, and police equipment. A "New Products" section presents brief descriptions of recently marketed items, such as pistol grips, ammunition, gun cases, holsters, and knives.

GM contains articles critical of proposed gun control measures that present research findings supporting the position of anti-gun control groups and questioning the findings of pro-gun control researchers.

See also: Concealed Carry Laws; Trigger Locks.

Further Reading: *Guns Magazine* (San Diego, CA), www.gunsmagazine.com.

Gunshot Detection Technology (GDT)

Gunshot detection technology (GDT) may contribute to limiting illegal gun use without initiating additional gun control legislation. GDT involves the placement of sensors in urban areas to detect the sound of gunshots. Transmitters send information to a police dispatch center where a computer receives and reports the messages, indicating the location of the gunshot. On the basis of this information, a decision can then be made whether to send a police unit to the spot of the report. The sensors may be contained in boxes mounted on telephone or light poles or camouflaged as birdhouses or roof vents.

In 1997, a GDT study was conducted by the Center for Criminal Justice Research at the University of Cincinnati. In *Using Gunshot Detection Technology in High-Crime Areas* (1998), Lorraine Green Mazerolle, director of the Center, reported on the research findings. The Center conducted field trials involving two systems, Trilon Technology's ShotSpotter, which was tested in Redwood City, California, and Alliant Techsystems's System for Effective Control for Urban Environment Security (SECURES), tested in Dallas, Texas. The ShotSpotter, which employs a triangulation method, was deployed in a one square mile area divided into 319 sectors. The system was accurate 80 percent of the time in detecting gunshots, and in 72 percent of

instances was able to determine the location of the gunshot within 25 feet. Accuracy varied according to the weapon fired. During the two months of the test, the SECURES system reported 182 firearm shots, 151 of which were not reported by citizens. More recent technological developments allow cameras to zoom in on the location of shots within a second of firing, often capturing those discharging the firearms in the act, thereby facilitating law enforcement response. According to the company Safety Dynamics, the technology has resulted in a 60 percent drop in illegal shootings in cities where it has been deployed.

In the last decade, GDT technology has been deployed in cities around the country. The technology has improved, reducing the number of "false positives." In 2016, ShotSpotter technology detected 165,531 gunshots in 62 urban areas around the country. In Canton, Ohio, a city of 73,000, 772 bullet shots were detected in 2015, helping law enforcement identify high crime areas. Gunfire that year resulted in eight gun homicides, 11 suicides, and gun 25 injuries. The technology has also been purchased by the American military.

Researchers concluded that gunshot detection systems potentially can serve three purposes. First, if a police department has a rapid response policy, the new technology could enhance response time. Second, gunshot detection could also serve as a problem-solving tool, allowing for the identification of areas with many incidents of gunshots, determination of the demographic characteristics of such areas, and evaluation of responses to the problem. Third, gunshot detection systems may act as a deterrent to crime.

Crime reduction would depend on publicizing the introduction of electronic detection, and on whether the presence of detection systems in fact leads to the apprehension of those who fire guns. Sensing devices could be moved randomly to various locations, thereby reducing the cost of the system. As accuracy increases, gunshot detection systems could become a valued instrument for local law enforcement in controlling one aspect of illegal firearms use.

See also: Drive-By Shootings; Violent Crime Rate.

Further Reading: Lorraine Green Mazerolle, *Using Gunshot Detection Technology in High-Crime Areas* (Washington, DC: National Institute of Justice Research Preview, June 1998); Safety Dynamics, www .safetydynamics.net/; ShotSpotter, www. shotspotter.com/.

Halbrook, Stephen P. (1947–)

Stephen P. Halbrook has focused his Fairfax,
Virginia-based law practice on cases dealing with
firearms legislation and Second Amendment issues.
He has worked for and with the National Rifle
Association to advance the individual rights view
of the Second Amendment. He has specialized in
litigation against the Bureau of Alcohol, Tobacco,
Firearms, and Explosives, federal mandates to
the states (such as the Brady Handgun Violence
Prevention Act requirement that local law
enforcement officers run background checks on
prospective handgun purchasers), and civil and
criminal litigation at the state and local levels
regarding firearms prohibitions, license and permit
practices, and product liability lawsuits. He has
authored three books on gun rights, including a
guide for attorneys involved in firearms cases. One
of Halbrook's most noted cases is *Printz v. United
States* (1997), in which he represented Sheriff Jay
Printz before the U.S. Supreme Court regarding the
Brady background check. He argued successfully
that the background check violated the Tenth
Amendment and the principle of separation of
powers between state and national governments.

Halbrook received a B.S. in business in 1969
and a Ph.D. in philosophy in 1972 from Florida
State University. He received a law degree from
Georgetown University Law Center in 1978. From
1972 to 1981, he taught philosophy at Tuskegee
Institute, Howard University, and George Mason
University. In addition to cases involving firearms
regulations, Halbrook represented Virginia in a
challenge to the federal mandate to states contained
in the National Voter Registration (Motor-Voter)
Act. On several occasions, Halbrook has testified
before congressional committees concerned with
firearms issues and advised NRA officials in their

testimony and on other legal matters. He also
defended the NRA's position in the Supreme Court
cases that established an individual right to gun
ownership for home self-protection in *District
of Columbia v. Heller* (2008) and *McDonald v.
Chicago* (2010).

In *That Every Man Be Armed: The Evolution
of a Constitutional Right*, originally published
in 1984, Halbrook examines the philosophical,
historical, and legal roots of the right to bear arms.
Beginning with Plato and Aristotle in ancient
Greece, he examined the historical treatment of
statements about arms: Cicero in ancient Rome,
Machiavelli in Renaissance Italy, English common
law, the American revolutionaries and the framers
of the Constitution, pre–Civil War writers, the
Fourteenth Amendment, Supreme Court decisions,
and state court rulings.

In *A Right to Bear Arms: State and Federal
Bills of Rights and Constitutional Guarantees*,
Halbrook detailed the provisions in the first state
constitutions that dealt with the right to bear arms.
Halbrook's *Firearms Law Deskbook: Federal and
State Criminal Practice*, first published in 1995,
provides information about previous firearms
decisions for lawyers and litigants involved in
legal cases. Halbrook treats federal prosecutions
initiated by the ATF and provides detailed
information about pretrial proceedings, jury trials,
sentencing procedures, and appeals. He analyzes
the congressional intent of the Gun Control Act
of 1968 and the National Firearms Act of 1934;
presents the various regulations pertaining to
the sale, manufacture, transfer, transportation,
licensing, importation, and possession of firearms;
summarizes state gun control laws; and explains
the extent of ATF authority. Halbrook also suggests
litigation strategies, including advice about
challenging recently enacted laws, particularly

on the grounds of excess vagueness. Halbrook provides regular updates to the book. His *The Founders' Second Amendment* builds on his previous written work to make the case that the Second Amendment provides an individual's right to own guns. In 2013, Halbrook published *Gun Control in the Third Reich*, which argues the gun control was key to the rise of Nazi Germany.

See also: American Revolution; Brady Handgun Violence Prevention Act; Bureau of Alcohol, Tobacco, Firearms, and Explosives; *District of Columbia v. Heller* (2008); Fourteenth Amendment; Gun Control Act of 1968; *McDonald v. Chicago* (2010); National Firearms Act of 1934; National Rifle Association; *Printz v. United States* (1997); Second Amendment; State Laws, Appendix 2.

Further Reading: Stephen P. Halbrook, *The Founders' Second Amendment* (Chicago: Ivan R. Dee and the Independent Institute, 2008); Stephen P. Halbrook, *Firearms Law Deskbook: Federal and State Criminal Practice* (Eagan, MN: Thomson/West, 2009–10); Stephen P. Halbrook, *A Right to Bear Arms: State and Federal Bills of Rights and Constitutional Guarantees* (Westport, CT: Greenwood, 1989); Stephen P. Halbrook, *That Every Man Be Armed: The Evolution of a Constitutional Right* (Albuquerque: University of New Mexico Press, 1984); Stephen P. Halbrook, www.stephenhalbrook.com ; Alan E. Steinweis, "Ben Carson is Wrong on Guns and the Holocaust," *New York Times,* October 14, 2015.

Handgun Control, Inc. (HCI)

See BRADY CAMPAIGN TO PREVENT GUN VIOLENCE

Handguns Magazine

Although not as explicitly political as other publications, *Handguns* magazine, which has been in print for over 50 years, has been published since 1986 by Petersen Publishing Company in Los Angeles, California, and is aimed at handgun enthusiasts. While focusing on new handguns, related products and technology, the publication also emphasizes the defensive use of firearms by law-abiding citizens, one of the major themes of pro-gun groups that defend the right to keep and bear arms.

Regular features include featured handguns, tactics and training, ammunition, accessories, and gun-related news, including information about gun shows, sales, new products, and political news. The print magazine is published monthly.

Gun advocate and lawyer Don B. Kates, Jr., writes regularly for the publication and its Web site on many legal and political issues related to guns, including such topics as recent gun-related court cases, concealed carry laws, public opinion about guns and law, and gun laws in other nations. Regular articles also address the defensive use of firearms, the concealed carry and open carry movements, which focus on civilian handgun carrying. Yet the publication's overwhelming focus is on gun technologies for the handgun enthusiast.

See also: Concealed Carry Laws; Kates, Don B., Jr.

Further Reading: Jim Supica, *Handguns* (San Diego, CA: Thunder Bay Press, 2010); www.handgunsmag.com.

Harborview Injury Prevention and Research Center (HIPRC)

Founded in 1985, the Harborview Injury Prevention and Research Center (HIPRC) seeks to develop injury prevention strategies by conducting studies of the causes and nature of the injuries people suffer. Located in Seattle, Washington, the Center is associated with the University of Washington. It is one of twelve injury-control centers supported by the Centers for Disease Control (CDC) in the country. It retains about 40 full-time employees. Similar to other organizations that investigate injuries from an epidemiological perspective, the Center includes firearms injury prevention as one of its many research topics. Center researchers have conducted research involving injury prevention, including injuries caused by firearms.

HIPRC Director Dr. Monica S. Vavilala researches traumatic brain injury and pediatric trauma, specifically linking treatment of acute care with long term outcomes. She has been principal investigator in recent studies examining changes in systemic hemodynamics, cerebral blood flow and cerebral autoregulation after pediatric traumatic brain injury. The Center is involved with several injury prevention projects, including the development of a motor vehicle trauma surveillance system in cooperation with General Motors.

Pedestrian safety, especially for older adults, has also received the Center's attention. The Center has also studied the protection of abused women and the efficacy of court orders in preventing future violence and injury. The study results included recommendations for altering the nature of police, court, and health care intervention in cases of domestic violence.

The Center cooperates with the Seattle Police Department to evaluate aspects of the city's Domestic Violence Unit, including comparison of the Unit with other cities, examination of recidivism rates, possible impediments to police intervention, and data collection and management practices. These studies are indirectly related to firearms violence because guns are sometimes used in domestic violence, and women threatened with violence are often encouraged to purchase a firearm for self-protection.

The Center has conducted initiatives directly related to firearms. The HIPRC entered an agreement with the Washington State Department of Health to appraise a firearms injury surveillance system (FISS), which gathers information about deaths and injuries caused by firearms to provide a more reliable source of information from which to draw conclusions about firearm safety. Another initiative involves the development and evaluation of a community-based project to provide information about the safe storage of handguns. The project enlisted the assistance of health care providers and public health workers, law enforcement agencies, the broadcast and print media, and public schools to disseminate information.

See also: Accidents Involving Guns; Fatalities; Health Care Professionals; Pacific Center for Violence Prevention; Suicide; Women and Guns; Youth and Guns.

Further Reading: Harborview Injury Prevention and Research Center Web site, http://depts.washington.edu/hiprc/.

Harder, Chuck (1944–)

A heavy-set man with a melodious voice, Chuck Harder established himself as a prominent figure in the talk-radio business. He has added to the gun control debate by claiming that, like many other activities, gun control policy initiatives are geared to deny the American people a basic right, in this case, the right to keep and bear arms. Harder used to broadcast on the Peoples Radio Network, based in Florida. He expanded his radio station outlets from just a few in 1987 to nearly 300 in 1995, placing second only to Rush Limbaugh, who broadcast on over 600 stations. Harder's stations were located primarily in the South and Southwest. His radio program contained a strong antigovernment message. In one program, he was quoted as saying, "We have a government, ladies and gentlemen, that is lying to the people, raping the people, defrauding the people. . . . These [federal officials] are very power hungry and, in my opinion, evil people. They want all the marbles."

Harder portrayed a federal government in partnership with large corporations, which he claimed threatened the freedom and well-being of the average American. He said that "New York power brokers," "New York bankers," and "the global elite" have nearly succeeded in gaining control of the American government.

After suffering a serious accident in 1999 that left his legs paralyzed, and changes in the radio industry led to ever-more consolidation, the number of affiliates carrying his program began to decline, until his broadcast became available only on shortwave radio station WHRI, and then on WWCR until 2007, when that broadcast ended. By 2009, his broadcast could only be heard through Internet streaming. In 2010, he ceased broadcasting, but returned in 2011, and continued for several more years.

See also: Clinton, William Jefferson (Bill); Michigan Militia; Russia; Waco, Texas, Raid.

Further Reading: Morris Dees, *Gathering Storm: America's Militia Threat* (New York: HarperCollins, 1996); www.chuckharder .com/; www.museumstuff. com/learn/topics/Chuck_Harder::sub::Network_Declines_And_Goes_Silent.

Health Care Professionals

A large number of health care workers and health care institutions have taken stands in favor of more stringent gun control legislation. Motivated by the large number of gun-related injuries and deaths they regularly face, physicians have produced a body of literature criticizing the widespread availability of firearms in American society. Health care professionals have adopted the epidemiological model to describe the distribution of firearms in American society, describing guns as something akin to a virus causing an epidemic of injuries and death. Many in the medical profession look upon guns not as inanimate objects that may be used for good or ill, but as a distinctly dangerous and harmful product. To reduce the number of gun deaths and injuries, guns should be subject to much more strict regulation. For most health care professionals, the presence of guns causes far more harm than benefit.

The disease metaphor—comparing guns to a virus—contains a psychiatric component. The very presence of guns, called the "weapons effect" or "weapons instrumentality effect" is claimed to encourage violent behavior, or escalate the degree of violence. Findings from several social psychological experiments suggest that the presence of guns can lead to the commission or escalation of violent acts that otherwise would not occur. To the extent that violent actions are impulsive rather than planned, these experiments indicate that the presence of firearms may increase the likelihood of assaults and of harm. The possibility of a weapons effect has been used to argue in favor of more stringent gun control measures that would limit the availability of firearms.

Closely related to the claimed weapons effect is the assertion that many people who participate in violent incidents involving guns are not criminals. Law-abiding citizens have no trouble with the law until they engage in an argument that escalates into violence. If firearms are available, they either magnify the violent confrontation, or increase the probability of serious injuries.

Critics of pro-gun control medical professionals argue that such assertions conceal additional information regarding the characteristics of violent persons. They note that approximately 75 percent of murderers have adult criminal records. In addition, they assert that in 90 percent of homicides committed in the home, police were called to the same address one or more times in the previous two years, indicating a pattern of violent behavior.

In 1979, the Public Health Service announced a goal of reducing the number of privately owned handguns by 25 percent by 2000. The medical profession's view of guns appears similar to its view of cigarettes. Health professionals wish to disseminate information stigmatizing guns as

a socially unacceptable health hazard, just as smoking cigarettes became a widely recognized health hazard. In their campaign against guns, health professionals target not only homicides and other crimes committed with guns, but also suicide, especially among youth.

Critics, who are often social science researchers, point out that violence has many causes. Rather than focusing on the availability of firearms, they identify what they consider more plausible causal factors such as persistent poverty, especially among certain ethnic minority groups; a feeling of hopelessness; a lack of education and promising employment opportunities; the prevalence of the drug trade; and inadequate prison facilities that lead to early release of repeat offenders. Critics reject the weapons effect touted by medical professionals, arguing that law-abiding citizens do not increase the risk of becoming criminals simply through the possession of firearms. This alternative research argues that there is no significant relationship between the availability of firearms and the incidence of homicide, suicide, assault and rape, robbery, or burglary. Critics assert that more radical gun control involving widespread denial of gun ownership would prevent the ordinary citizen from exercising his or her personal choice to own firearms for protecting self, home, and family. They fault health care professionals for failing to provide the average citizen with any reasonable recommendations for protection against crime.

Social science researchers critical of the medical professionals' position on gun control note that a series of existing laws already makes it illegal for felons, those convicted of acts of violence, and those convicted of drug crimes, from possessing guns. Arguing, however, that these laws have proved ineffective, the researchers doubt the value of additional gun control statutes. Once more, in the view of critics, law-abiding citizens are the ones most likely to obey firearms laws, thereby limiting their capacity for self-defense.

Critics claim that publications of the health care profession are far more likely to include articles that support the anti-gun position. The New England Journal of Medicine, for example, has faced severe criticism for a long-standing anti-gun policy, consistently choosing to publish research articles on the various negative aspects of gun ownership while at the same time ignoring research that fails to discover statistically significant relationships between the level of gun possession and rates of violence. Health care professionals respond that critics display the same bias they claim to have discovered in pro-gun control advocates. Health care professionals also claim that their research techniques are superior to those used by social scientists.

See also: Doctors for Responsible Gun Ownership; Fatalities; Physicians for Social Responsibility; Suicide; Violent Crime Rate; Youth and Guns.

Further Reading: Harborview Injury Prevention and Research Center Web site, http://depts.washington. edu/hiprc/; Don B. Kates, Henry E. Schaffer, John K. Lattimer, George B. Murray, and Edwin H. Cassem, "Bad Medicine: Doctors and Guns," in David B. Kopel, ed., *Guns: Who Should Own Them?* (Amherst, NY: Prometheus, 1995); Physicians for Social Responsibility Web site, www.psr.org.

Heartland Institute

The Heartland Institute, a libertarian "think tank" located in Chicago, Illinois, takes a resolute stand against gun control and other legislation intended to impose regulations on the behavior of citizens. Among other publications, the organization distributes *Intellectual Ammunition*, a bimonthly public policy magazine in which anti-gun control articles appear. The board of directors includes individuals from major corporations, such as Altria (formerly Philip Morris), Amoco, and Procter and Gamble. The members of the board of policy advisers hail largely from the academic community. The organization has a staff of eight and a budget of over $1 million.

The Institute claims status as "the first think tank in the nation to focus on free-market solutions to state and local public policy problems." In its various analyses, the Institute maintains the overarching theme that government is the problem, not the solution. With regard to gun control, the Institute opposed such measures as the Brady Handgun Violence Prevention Act. The Institute also filed an *amicus* brief in the 2008 Supreme Court case of *District of Columbia v. Heller* and the 2010 Supreme Court case of *McDonald v. Chicago* in which they argued that strict handgun laws are ineffective, and hobble the ability of law-abiding citizens to defend themselves. The Institute brief was coauthored by conservative law professor Eugene Volokh.

The Institute has sponsored or published gun-related policy studies by such pro-gun writers as Gary Mauser, Don B. Kates, John Lott, and David Kopel. One study by Daniel D. Polsby and Dennis Brennen presented what the authors term 10 myths about gun control. The authors emphasize not only the inability of gun control legislation to prevent crime, but the limitations such legislation places on citizens to protect themselves. Employing the findings of such researchers as Gary Kleck, Polsby and Brennen conclude that no credible relationship exists between the number of guns available in society and increases in crime. In response to the claim that gun control laws prevent friends from killing friends, the authors assert that most murderers and homicide victims have criminal records. They argue that waiting periods imposed for the purchase of a handgun could actually increase killings because many criminals will substitute more deadly weapons, such as rifles and shotguns, which are not covered by such laws. Gun accidents provide a weak justification for gun control laws, the authors claim, because the number of accidents has been declining in recent years. Finally, referring to the work of David Kopel, the authors assert that legal scholarship has conclusively determined that the Second Amendment was intended to protect an individual's right to possess arms.

The Heartland Institute notes that several judicial rulings have determined that the police cannot protect everyone, nor do they have the legal responsibility to do so. Attempting to give law enforcement officials a duty to protect all individuals would result in a huge police force likely to endanger liberty. The Institute contends that the carrying of concealed firearms offers an effective means of self-protection, and that a national concealed carry law would act as a significant deterrent to violent crime. Citing data that citizens often use firearms to kill and wound criminals, the Institute concludes that guns are an excellent means of self-defense.

See also: Accidents Involving Guns; Brady Handgun Violence Prevention Act; Concealed Carry Laws; *District of Columbia v. Heller* (2008); Health Care Professionals; Kates, Don B., Jr.; Kleck, Gary; Kopel, David B.; *McDonald v. Chicago* (2010); Second Amendment.

Further Reading: Heartland Institute Web site, www. heartland.org.

Helmke, W. Paul, Jr. (1948–)

Longtime Republican politician Paul Helmke has become a leading voice in support of gun control as president of the Brady Campaign to Prevent Gun Violence, a position he held from 2006 to 2011. Helmke sought to bring a more conciliatory tone to the job, noting at the time of his appointment that "there should be at least some room for agreement" on the otherwise contentious issue of guns. Helmke succeeded former Maryland Democratic congressman Michael D. Barnes. Helmke was succeeded by Daniel Gross, cofounder and executive director of the Center to Prevent Youth Violence.

The Indiana native grew up in Fort Wayne, graduated from Indiana University in 1970, and earned a law degree from Yale Law School in 1973. Helmke won election as mayor of Fort Wayne in 1987, defeating the Democratic incumbent. He was reelected in 1991 and 1995. (He declined to seek another term in 1999.) Helmke also served as president of the U.S. Conference of Mayors from 1997–1998. Helmke ran unsuccessful campaigns for the U.S. Senate in 1998 and for the House of Representatives in 2002. After working in private legal practice, Helmke was tapped to serve as president of the Brady Campaign.

In media appearances, writings, and speeches, Helmke is sharply critical of the harm posed by guns, and of his organization's archopponent, the National Rifle Association (NRA). Writing for the *Huffington Post* in 2010, for example, Helmke charged that the NRA has supported legislation, titled the Reform and Modernization Act, which would make it more difficult for the Bureau of Alcohol, Tobacco, Firearms, and Explosives to prosecute rogue gun dealers who are responsible for selling large numbers of guns that wind up in the hands of criminals. Helmke cited the example of former NRA board Member Sandy Abrams, owner of Valley Gun in Baltimore, which was cited for over 900 gun law violations, as an example of the NRA's close ties to lax gun dealers. Helmke was sharply critical of the Tea Party movement and its endorsed candidates running for office in 2010 for supporting such measures as gun carrying in Walmart stores, the repeal of assault weapons ban laws in several states, and of Republican U.S. Senate candidate from Nevada, Sharron Angle, for proposing a "Second Amendment solution" to political problems (implying the use of gun violence against political opponents). Helmke

has also been critical of President Barack Obama for failing to take stronger measures to stem the tide of guns flowing from the United States into the hands of Mexican drug cartels. According to Helmke, a single gun store in Houston, Texas, sold 339 guns to cartel buyers over a 15-month period. After leaving the Brady Campaign, Helmke took a position as a professor of practice at Indiana University's School of Public and Environmental Health in 2013, where he directs the Civic Leader Center.

See also: Brady Campaign to Prevent Gun Violence; Bureau of Alcohol, Tobacco, Firearms, and Explosives; National Rifle Association.

Further Reading: Paul Helmke, "NRA Campaigns to Protect Corrupt Gun Dealers," *The Huffington Post*, September 9, 2010, www.huffingtonpost.com/paul-helmke/nra-campaigns-to-protect_b_710496.html; Andrew Jarosh, *Son of a Son of a Politician: Paul Helmke: Behind City Hall Doors* (Bloomington, IN: IUniverse, 2002).

HELP Network

The HELP Network, or Handgun Epidemic Lowering Plan, was established in 1993 to assist in reducing firearm-related violence. The organization, located at the Violent Injury Prevention Center (VIPC) of the Children's Memorial Medical Center in Chicago, brought together an international coalition of medical, public health, and related organizations. It ceased formal organizational activities in 2006. Like other health care organizations, the Network has taken an epidemiological approach to gun violence, regarding it as a disease to be investigated in the same way medical researchers treat standard illnesses. The Network supported legislation mandating child safety locks for handguns and liability laws that allow victims of gun violence to sue firearms manufacturers.

HELP expressed four major policy objectives: (1) to develop procedures for tracking handguns and firearm injuries; (2) to support the research activities of the National Center for Injury Prevention and Control (NCIPC); (3) to reduce the availability of especially dangerous handguns to civilians; and (4) to restrict minors' access to firearms. The organization particularly emphasized the need to establish an effective nationwide system for monitoring nonfatal firearms-related injuries, noting that less than half of the health departments in the nation collect information on such injuries. The Network believed that data on injuries is crucial to the public health approach to preventing firearm injuries.

Katherine Kaufer Christoffel served as chair and medical director of the HELP Network. Christoffel is a professor of pediatrics and preventive medicine at Northwestern University School of Medicine and an attending pediatrician at Children's Hospital in Chicago. In addition to firearms-related injuries, she has conducted research on motor vehicle injuries, consumer product-related injuries, and child abuse. She notes that just as the federal deficit cannot be controlled without reducing health care costs, health care costs cannot be controlled without lowering the costs of treating firearm injuries, which number as many as 100,000 each year. Christoffel claims that a firearm injury can cost more than $1,000,000 over the life of the victim. She argues that the only way to lower the monetary and personal costs of firearm-related deaths and injuries is through preventive strategies.

Network membership included over 100 organizations, including the American Academy of Pediatrics, the American Medical Association, the American College of Physicians, and such gun control organizations as the Center to Prevent Handgun Violence (CPHV) and Cease Fire, Inc. Individual members included health care professionals, especially trauma doctors.

The Network advanced the idea that firearms make domestic violence especially dangerous and argued that guns are not the solution for women seeking greater security, stating that "once a gun is brought into [a woman's] home, it puts her and her family at increased risk of gun homicide, suicide, or unintentional shooting." To assist in the removal of firearms from the home, the Network printed and distributed *The HELP Handgun Disposal Handbook: A Prescription for Safety* to health organizations, violence prevention groups, and the general public. The handbook presents information about ways to dispose of a handgun and provides advice for those interested in initiating a community program to prevent handgun injury. The organization has produced a brochure for patients presenting the dangers of handguns in the home. HELP's activities as an independent organization ceased in 2006.

See also: Accidents Involving Guns; Health Care Professionals; National Center for Injury Prevention and Control; Trigger Locks; Violent Crime Rate; Women and Guns; Youth and Guns.

Further Reading: Christoffel, Katherine Kaufer, "Firearm Injuries: Epidemic Then, Endemic Now," *American Journal of Public Health* 97 (April 2007), 626–29.

Hemenway, David (1945–)

David Hemenway, director of the Harvard Injury Control Research Center and professor at the Harvard School of Public Health, conducts research on firearms from a public health perspective and has published extensively on the subject. His work has been criticized by those who conclude that firearms are an important means of defense against crime, a position Hemenway rejects. Hemenway's research interests include the costs and benefits of gun ownership, gun use among adolescents, the use of guns in self-defense, guns on college campuses, the relationship between firearm availability and completed suicide, and National Rifle Association (NRA) membership characteristics.

Hemenway founded the New England Injury Prevention Center in 1986, where he assumed responsibility for injury prevention training programs. He chairs the Injury Prevention Council of the National Association for Public Health Policy. He has conducted research and written journal articles on a number of subjects, including motor vehicle crashes, falls, fires, suicide, and child abuse. At the Harvard Injury Control Research Center, Hemenway supervises the scientific and administrative staff and is responsible for budget and fund-raising activities and the completion of research projects.

In a coauthored article titled "Firearms and Community Feelings of Safety," which appeared in a 1995 issue of the *Journal of Criminal Law and Criminology*, Hemenway reported the results of a study indicating that gun ownership imposes psychic costs on others in society. Eighty-five percent of non-gun owners surveyed stated they would feel less safe if gun ownership increased in their community. Only 8 percent reported that they would feel safer. Paul Gallant and David Kopel, writing for the Independence Institute, a pro-gun organization, have criticized the study, claiming that psychic costs are "imaginary" and that non-gun owners actually receive advantages from increased gun ownership. Citing studies by such researchers as John R. Lott, they claim that burglars tend to avoid dwellings that appear occupied for fear the owner may be armed.

In a coauthored 1995 *Journal of the American Medical Association* article, Hemenway focused on the risks of keeping a firearm in the home. The article was based on a survey of 800 randomly selected gun owners. He concluded that guns kept for protection and handguns generally are more likely to be stored loaded or both unlocked and loaded. Twenty-nine percent of those surveyed reported keeping a loaded gun in the home and 21 percent responded that they kept a firearm loaded and unlocked. Contrary to the claims of gun rights advocates that training is the key to firearm safety, Hemenway discovered that owners who had received training were almost twice as likely to keep a loaded and unlocked firearm in the home. The study results suggest that residents would be far safer not having guns in the home.

Hemenway has questioned the claim, originating with firearm policy researcher Gary Kleck, that there are 2.5 million cases of defensive firearm use in the United States each year, a figure that has been used to argue against restrictions on firearm ownership. Hemenway claims that the type of survey on which the figure is based tends to overestimate the occurrence in the population of a reported activity, such as defensive gun use. Hemenway does not accept the conclusion that if the legitimate uses of firearms outnumber criminal uses, then extensive firearm ownership contributes to overall public safety.

In 1997, Hemenway received a health policy research grant to conduct a three-year public health study of firearms policies in the United States and to determine approaches to decrease the level of lethal violence. Among the topics Hemenway has investigated are gun-carrying practices, gun storage, the use of firearms for self-defense, and gun brandishing. The research includes an examination of the public health literature and a survey of college students and adults. In 2004, Hemenway published a book encapsulating his many years of research on gun issues, *Private Guns Public Health*.

See also: Cook, Philip J.; Health Care Professionals; Independence Institute; Kleck, Gary; Kopel, David B.; Lott, John R. Jr.; Ludwig, Jens Otto; National Rifle Association; Suicide; Trigger Locks.

Further Reading: Philip J. Cook, Jens Ludwig, and David Hemenway, "The Gun Debate's New Mythical Number: How Many Defensive Uses Per Year?" *Journal of Policy Analysis and Management* 16 (Summer 1997), 463–69; Paul Gallant and David Kopel, "The 'Psychic Cost' of Holiday Gift-Giving" (Golden, CO: Independence Institute opinion editorial, n.d.); David Hemenway, *Private Guns Public Health* (Ann Arbor: University of Michigan Press, 2004).

Henigan, Dennis (1951–)

Lawyer Dennis Henigan has been one of the nation's most prominent advocates for stricter gun laws in the courts and in public debate through his service at the Brady Center to Prevent Gun Violence, where he began in 1989. From 2007 to 2012 he served as vice president for law and policy at the Brady Center. He left the organization in 2012 to become Director of Policy Analysis and Research at the Campaign for Tobacco-Free Kids. Henigan was the founder of Brady's Legal Action Project (LAP), and was legal director for the Brady Campaign, based in Washington, D.C. The LAP provides pro bono legal assistance to gun violence victims, and argues in court on behalf of gun laws. The LAP has won millions of dollars in damages for gun violence. The LAP has also represented municipalities seeking to recover costs attributable to gun violence. In 2004, Henigan was recognized by *Lawyers Weekly* magazine as one of ten "Lawyers of the Year." Prior to joining the Brady Campaign (formerly Handgun Control, Inc.) in 1989, Henigan was a partner in the legal firm of Foley & Lardner, where he worked for eleven years. Henigan received his B.A. from Oberlin College in 1973, and his law degree from the University of Virginia in 1977.

Henigan is also a prolific author on gun issues, having published articles in law journals, as well as regular public commentary for newspapers, magazines, and Web sites like the *Huffington Post*. Henigan argues that the Second Amendment's right to bear arms was designed to protect a militia-based right related to gun ownership, not a personal right to guns. He submitted briefs in such prominent Supreme Court cases as *District of Columbia v. Heller* (2008) and *McDonald v. Chicago* (2010).

In both instances, the court majority adopted the individualist view of the Second Amendment. Henigan argues that, even in the face of these rulings, existing gun laws at the federal and state level do not infringe on this newly established individual right.

In 1995, Henigan coauthored a book on the meaning of the Second Amendment, with E. Bruce Nicholson and David Hemenway, *Guns and the Constitution*. It examined the right to bear arms from legal, political, and public health perspectives. In 2009, Henigan published *Lethal Logic: Exploding the Myths That Paralyze American Gun Policy*. The book examines the pro-gun "bumper sticker logic" arguments against gun regulation, arguing that this pro-gun sloganeering distorts the truth at the core of the gun debate—that gun laws save lives without infringing on the ability of law-abiding gun owners to get and use guns for legitimate purposes.

Henigan was critical of the Barack Obama administration for failing to effectively enforce existing gun laws, delays in nominating a permanent head of the Bureau of Alcohol, Tobacco, Firearms, and Explosives, and for yielding to what Henigan considers the strong-arm tactics of the National Rifle Association.

See also: Brady Campaign to Prevent Gun Violence; Bureau of Alcohol, Tobacco, Firearms, and Explosives; *District of Columbia v. Heller* (2008); *McDonald v. Chicago* (2010); National Rifle Association.

Further Reading: Dennis Henigan, *Lethal Logic: Exploding the Myths That Paralyze American Gun Policy* (Washington, DC: Potomac Books, 2009); Robert J. Spitzer, *The Politics of Gun Control,* 6th ed. (Boulder, CO: Paradigm, 2015).

Heston, Charlton (1924–2008)

In the 1990s, actor Charlton Heston's public comments in favor of gun rights made his name virtually synonymous with the National Rifle Association (NRA). While he was widely recognized by the American public, he was not treated as seriously as he might have been because of his association with a number of film epics. In 1997, in an effort to rescue the NRA from reported financial difficulties, Heston invited members to join him in raising $100 million in the following

three years for a media campaign to present the pro-gun position. In June 1998, after serving a term as NRA first vice president, he was elected to a three-year term on the board of directors and was chosen as the organization's president.

Heston, born Charles Carter, had a long and successful career in the movies. Early in his career, he became typecast as a historical hero. He starred in a series of epics, including *The Ten Commandments* (1956), *Ben-Hur* (1959, for which he won an Academy Award), *El Cid* (1961), and *The Agony and the Ecstasy* (1965). In addition, the public remembers him in such popular movies as *Planet of the Apes* (1968), *The Omega Man* (1971), and *Soylent Green* (1973). In the 1980s, Heston began to support various conservative causes, including gun rights.

Heston referred to the Second Amendment as "America's First Freedom" because, he said, it protects all other freedoms contained in the Bill of Rights: It is "the first among equals." Heston stated that just as the First Amendment protects tabloid newspapers despite most people's dislike of them, so the Second Amendment protects assault weapons. In his effort to assist the pro-gun movement, Heston wrote a column for *Guns and Ammo* titled "From the Capitol," in which he reported on the politics of gun control in the United States and other countries. Heston's defense of gun rights contained an element of nostalgia, harkening back to an America where people could "pray without feeling naive, love without being kinky, sing without profanity, be white without feeling guilty, own a gun without shame." He was

National Rifle Association (NRA) President Charlton Heston holds up a rifle during his address at the 131st NRA convention at the Reno-Sparks Convention Center in Reno, Nevada, April 27, 2002. *Photo by Candice Towell/Getty Images*

criticized for broadening the struggle for gun rights into a cultural warfare in which white, middle-class, Protestant values are preferred.

Heston's election as president of the NRA was opposed by a faction in the organization led by Neal Knox. Opponents within the gun rights movement as well as gun control advocates publicized Heston's early support for the Gun Control Act of 1968. Documents uncovered at the Lyndon Baines Johnson Library at the University of Texas revealed that Heston, along with other actors, supported an expansion of the bill to ban the interstate sale or transfer of rifles and shotguns. Following the assassination of Robert Kennedy, Heston appeared with four other actors on a television talk show to make a nationwide appeal for passage of the Gun Control Act. A 1968 *American Rifleman* column identified Heston as one of several film stars who were staunch supporters of gun control.

In response to the revelations about his past support for gun control, Heston stated that this was one of the mistakes he made. However, Knox claimed that Heston had not changed his views on gun control substantially since supporting the 1968 act, pointing to a May 1997 statement in which Heston commented that some guns were inappropriate for private ownership. Such revelations notwithstanding, Heston and his allies succeeded in gaining leadership positions at the 1998 NRA meeting, even though Knox's opposition indicated that Heston did not represent the most uncompromising stance within the gun rights movement. After being elected NRA President in 1998, Heston was reelected annually, eclipsing the organization's two-term limit, until he retired in 2003, after having been diagnosed with Alzheimer's disease the year before. He died in 2008 owing to complications arising from the disease. Heston's service, stature, and high public profile did much to rehabilitate the NRA's tarnished image from the 1990s.

See also: American Rifleman; Assault Weapons Ban; Gun Control Act of 1968; *Guns and Ammo*; Knox, Neal; National Rifle Association; Second Amendment.

Further Reading: Emilie Raymond, *From My Cold, Dead Hands: Charlton Heston and American Politics* (Lexington, KY: University Press of Kentucky, 2006); Robert J. Spitzer, *The Politics of Gun Control* (Washington, DC: CQ Press, 2008).

Huddleston v. United States (1974)

In *Huddleston v. United States* (415 U.S. 814, 1974), the U.S. Supreme Court dealt with a provision of the Gun Control Act of 1968 [18 U.S.C. (a) (6)] that makes unlawful the making of a false statement "in connection with the acquisition . . . of any firearm . . . from a . . . licensed dealer." The Court was asked to determine whether this provision applied to the redemption of a firearm from a pawnshop.

In 1965, William C. Huddleston, Jr., was convicted in a California state court of the felony charge of writing checks without sufficient funds. Under the Gun Control Act, the conviction precluded him from acquiring a firearm. In 1971, Huddleston pawned three rifles belonging to his wife. The pawnshop owner was a federally licensed firearms dealer. When Huddleston redeemed the rifles, he was asked to complete Treasury Form 4473, "Firearms Transaction Record," which contained the following question: "Have you been convicted in any court of a crime punishable by imprisonment for a term exceeding one year?" The question was derived from 18 U.S.C. 922 (d) (1), which prohibits selling or otherwise disposing of a firearm to someone who "has been convicted in any court of . . . a crime punishable by imprisonment for a term exceeding one year." Huddleston responded "no" to the question and signed each of three forms, certifying that he had answered the questions truthfully and accurately and that he was aware of the penalty for making a false statement.

When Huddleston was charged for violating 922 (a) (6), he moved to dismiss the indictment, arguing in part that the statute was not intended to apply to the redemption of a pawned firearm. The district court denied the motion and found the defendant guilty. The U.S. Court of Appeals for the Ninth Circuit affirmed the conviction.

In an appeal to the U.S. Supreme Court, Huddleston argued that the legislative history and language of the statute demonstrated that Congress did not intend that "acquisition" apply to redemption from a pawnshop. He further argued that even if Congress did have that intention, the ambiguity of the statute required a decision favoring the defendant. The Court concluded that while a redemption is not a sale, it can be included under some "other disposition" of a firearm, a situation it determined is covered under the statute. The Court noted that Congress did not make an explicit exception for a pawnshop redemption and that it was reasonable for Congress to view a pawn transaction as different from a situation in which a firearm is returned to the owner after being repaired. The Court noted that the terms "acquisition" and "sale or other disposition" are closely associated. A pawnbroker could "dispose" of a firearm through a "redemptive transaction." The Court declared that the statute's legislative history supported this interpretation, observing that Congress intended the legislation to deter crime by keeping "firearms out of the hands of those not legally entitled to possess them because of age, criminal background, or incompetency." To enforce the legislation, a person making a false statement regarding eligibility to acquire a firearm from a licensed dealer was subject to criminal penalty. The statute channeled weapons sales through firearms dealers to limit sales to those who did not present a threat to the public interest. To achieve this broader objective, it is reasonable to conclude that Congress intended pawnshop redemptions to be covered by the statute.

The Court perceived no underlying constitutional questions at issue. No claim was made on Second Amendment grounds, and the Court rejected the claim that Huddleston's property had been taken without just compensation as well as the argument that the defendant's Treasury form responses had been coerced.

See also: Gun Control Act of 1968; Second Amendment.

Further Reading: *Huddleston v. United States*, 415 U.S. 814 (1974).

Hunting Culture

Throughout American history, hunting has remained an important aspect of subsistence, sport, and recreation. As the nation became more urbanized, the number of people who engaged in hunting declined considerably, but for a significant proportion of the population, it remains an esteemed activity that many consider a vital part of their lives as well as the nation's tradition and heritage.

Hunting advocates cite what they consider the positive contributions of hunting, beyond the provision of food and clothing that marked the key factors in early hunting. First, they view the activity of hunting as a basic human biological drive in which individuals should be allowed to engage. Second, hunting represents a valuable part of the nation's cultural heritage that includes a spiritual element; it approaches being a religious experience and is crucial to maintaining traditional American values. Third, hunters help to manage the balance of nature by both supporting the maintenance of natural habitats and eliminating the excess population of animals that the environment is unable to support. Fourth, hunting allows people otherwise trapped in modern society to experience and appreciate the natural world and escape the debilitating effects of mass culture.

The division between pro-hunting and anti-hunting advocates reflects the contrast between rural and urban, tough and soft, and at least traditionally between male and female. With regard to the latter, although more women in recent years have been encouraged to participate in hunting and have come to appreciate its benefits, traditionally hunting has been a male-dominated enterprise, with the transference of customs from father to son and the observance of rites of passage into manhood. Therefore, not surprisingly, pro-hunters tend to characterize anti-hunters, as a group, as female. According Simon Bronner (2016), pro-hunters portray anti-hunters as "pet-owning urban women who have little awareness of animals in the wild."Anti-hunters then are naive city dwellers who demonstrate lack of familiarity with the fundamental characteristics of nature.

The views the hunting advocates have of anti-hunters and animal rights supporters resembles the perception that gun rights advocates have of gun control proponents; they are unschooled in the characteristics of guns and heedless of the positive uses to which firearms are put, not only for hunting but also for other sporting activities such as competitive shooting, and for self-defense in a society in which gun rights advocates believe criminal predators are constantly lurking.

As for opponents of hunting and animal rights advocates, they argue that hunting today involves the deliberate killing, for not beneficial end, of a living being, and hence results in a desensitization to the taking of life that may be extended to the use of firearms to kill human beings. From the anti-hunting perspective, mass shooters might be viewed as a type of hunter who is seeking game in the form of other human beings that have become targets of the hunt. Hunting opponents claim that the shooting of animals in the wild has moved from a goal-oriented activity—the acquisition of food and raiment—to gratuitous killing. In like manner, the mass shooter hunts other human beings with no other object than to kill another human being who has been depersonalized.

The divide between the hunting culture and the anti-hunting and animal rights position will continue, with each side representing irreconcilable views of nature, society, and human values. Those on one side of the divide firmly believe in protecting the family and preserving a traditional view of the land and the nation, while those on the other emphasize a more egalitarian society, especially between men and women, but may also defend animal rights.

See also: Gun Culture.

Further Reading: Simon J. Bronner, "Ritual and Controversy at Deer Camp," in Glenn H. Utter, editor, *The Past, Present, and Future of Firearms and Firearm Policy* (Santa Barbara, CA: Praeger, 2016): vol. 2,185-262; Marti Kheel, "The Killing Game: An Ecofeminist Critique of Hunting," *Journal of the Philosophy of Sport* 23 (1996): 30-44.

Hutaree Militia

In March 2010, police arrested nine members of a Michigan-based Christian militia, called "Hutaree," a name said to mean "Christian warrior," on charges that its members were planning to kill at least one police officer, and then set off roadside explosives during the funeral procession of the dead officer. The attack, they hoped, would set off a widespread uprising against the government around the country. The extremist militia group was antigovernment in its ideology, believing that the government itself was the Antichrist. The organization's leader, David Brian Stone, and his wife, Tina, lived in Clayton, Michigan, where they were arrested. Other members were arrested in Ohio and Indiana. The organization was reportedly centered in Michigan's Lenawee County. Like other privately organized militias, whether violent or not, they are not militias as defined in law, as only the government possesses the authority to organize militias. The Hutaree group had no direct affiliation with the Michigan Militia, a private militia group that cooperates with law enforcement authorities.

The emergence of the Hutaree group coincided with an upsurge in extremist, antigovernment groups. According to the Southern Poverty Law Center, the number of such groups nationwide grew from 149 in 2008 to 512 in 2009. This increased activity was attributed to the nationwide economic downturn, and the election of an African American president, Barack Obama. According to the now-inactive Hutaree Web site, "Jesus wanted us to be ready to defend ourselves using the sword and stay alive using equipment." The Hutaree emblem includes crossed spears, a sword, and the letters "CCR," which stand for "Colonial Christian Republic." Central to the Hutaree belief is the fear of a conspiracy to create a one-world government, possibly arising from the United Nations, that would overtake the United States. The nine were arraigned in federal court on charges including sedition and weapons charges. In 2012, seven of the nine were acquitted of the most serious charges, with the federal judge concluding that the evidence against them was largely circumstantial. Two others were convicted of illegal machine gun possession, but sentenced to time served.

See also: Michigan Militia; Obama, Barack H.

Further Reading: Nick Bunkley and Charlie Savage, "Militia Plotted to Kill Police, Charges Say," *New York Times,* March 30, 1020, A1; Southern Poverty Law Center, *The Second Wave: Return of the Militias,* August 2009.

I

Independence Institute

The Independence Institute is a conservative public policy research organization that takes a fervent pro-gun rights position, providing a voice for an essentially libertarian perspective on firearms and the criminal justice system. Located in Golden, Colorado, the Institute was founded in 1985 by David S. D'Evelyn and John Andrews. The Institute conducts studies of various public policy issues, organized around eight policy centers that cover the areas of health care, gun control, education, residential planning, fiscal policy, property rights, transportation, the environment, and criminal justice and violent crime. Largely through the efforts of Second Amendment Project director, David Kopel, the Institute has focused much of its attention on firearms issues. The organization has a free-market, proindividual freedom perspective and emphasizes private-sector, community-based solutions to policy problems.

The Institute publishes research reports, offering recommendations from a profreedom perspective, and distributes to the media regular commentary on current events that emphasizes civil liberties and economic freedom. The Institute broadcasts a weekly television program, *Devil's Advocate*, from a Denver television station, along with other public affairs programming. The organization sponsors public debates and conferences at the Institute headquarters.

The Institute regards itself as a primary source of research on the right to keep and bear arms. It has published many reports on gun control and solutions to crime that respect civil liberties. People associated with the Institute have treated many issues on the gun control agenda from an anti-gun-control point of view. The entrance of medical professionals into the gun control movement is regarded as an attempt to use professional status to influence the debate in a procontrol direction. The effort to ban particular types of firearms has come under investigation. Banning of weapons by type, such as assault rifles, is rejected as unconstitutional because banned guns cannot be rationally distinguished from other weapons. The Institute rejects the claim that firearms should not be kept in the home for self-protection because they are too dangerous.

Institute reports defend state laws permitting carrying concealed handguns, claiming that permit holders are in fact more law-abiding than the general population. Papers defending the Second Amendment have been issued, including an analysis of the Supreme Court's ruling in *United States v. Miller* (1939), the major twentieth-century decision on the right to keep and bear arms. It also produced publications arguing for the individualist view of the Second Amendment's right to bear arms, a view that found favor with the U.S. Supreme Court in *District of Columbia v. Heller* (2008). Other projects include investigations of gun control laws in other countries, including the former Warsaw Pact countries and Japan. Other topics of investigation include evaluations of the success of existing gun control laws, guns as defensive tools for women, biblical and other religious authorizations for the use of arms in the defense of the innocent, and the reliability of media polls that often report significant public support for gun control. Other criminal justice topics closely related to the question of firearms policy, such as media violence, the federalization of criminal law, and sentencing policy, have received the Institute's attention.

See also: Assault Weapons Ban; *District of Columbia v. Heller* (2008); Health Care

Professionals; Kopel, David B.; Japan; Media Violence; Second Amendment; *United States v. Miller* (1939); Women and Guns.

Further Reading: Independence Institute Web site, www.i2i.org.

Institute for Legislative Action (ILA), National Rifle Association

An organization established in 1975 within the National Rifle Association (NRA), the Institute for Legislative Action (ILA) concentrates on lobbying members of the U.S. Congress and state legislatures. Since its foundation, the ILA has become an influential voice within the parent organization, having become skillful at influencing members of the national and state legislatures. The ILA has been successful in mobilizing membership support for its policy stands. The organization's activities absorb 25 percent of the NRA's yearly budget, which in 1992 amounted to nearly $29 million. In the 2000 election cycle, the ILA raised and spent an estimated $30 million. In 2008, it spent about $40 million. In 2012, its outside spending totaled almost $20 million; in the 2014 election cycle, it spent about $28 million.

The ILA conducts mailings to NRA members that include legislative alerts informing the rank and file regarding the organization's efforts to protect gun rights in the national and state legislatures. In addition to warning members about upcoming gun control efforts, the ILA has conducted mass mailings and extensive e-mailing to raise funds to support the organization's activities. Such fund-raising mailings alert the membership to gun control measures proposed in the national and state legislatures. The ILA supervises the Political Victory Fund (PVF), which is the NRA's political action committee. The PVF raises money to be donated to political candidates who have taken a supportive stand on the gun control issue.

The ILA actively supports pro-gun legislation, such as a measure that would institute reciprocity among states having laws allowing the carrying of concealed weapons. The ILA has lobbied in state legislatures to pass versions of the NRA-ILA model Crime Victims Protection Act intended to prevent those convicted of crimes from suing victims who inflicted injuries on them, thus protecting those gun owners who use their weapons in self-defense. In one of its most significant victories, the ILA spearheaded Congress's enactment of the Protection of Lawful Commerce in Arms Act of 2005, which provided legal immunity from civil lawsuits to gun manufacturers, distributors, importers, and dealers, giving them unique protection among American companies and businesses.

The Institute keeps track of other activities that may threaten pro-gun interests and publicizes the opinions of public officials who support its position on the right to keep and bear arms. The Bureau of Alcohol, Tobacco, Firearms, and Explosives (ATF) is a consistent focus of attention because it implements federal gun laws and regulations. The ILA has reported on ATF activities that the ILA claims amount to harassment of gun dealers and private citizens. The National Center for Injury Prevention and Control of the Centers for Disease Control (CDC) has come under attack for labeling gun ownership a "health hazard." The ILA led a successful effort to strip gun research funding out of the CDC's budget. The ILA has been critical of the United Nations' firearms regulation proposals, expressing concern that U.S. policy might be dictated by the international organization.

The ILA has provided publicity for the NRA-ILA program titled "Crime Strike" and publicizes the success of the "Keep Killers in Prison" campaign. At the invitation of murder victims' families, Crime Strike assists these families in their efforts to prevent paroles for convicted murderers. The ILA welcomes support from those legislators opposing gun control.

See also: Bureau of Alcohol, Tobacco, Firearms, and Explosives; Clinton, William Jefferson (Bill); Concealed Carry Laws; Health Care Professionals; National Rifle Association; Protection of Lawful Commerce in Arms Act of 2005; State Laws, Appendix 2; United Nations.

Further Reading: "ILA Report," *American Rifleman* (monthly); Institute for Legislative Action Web site, www.nraila.org; Robert J. Spitzer, *The Politics of Gun Control,* 6th ed. (Boulder, CO: Paradigm, 2015).

Instrumentality Effect

Advocates of gun control claim that the weapons instrumentality effect is a significant factor in determining the seriousness of intentionally inflicted injuries. The instrumentality effect states that the presence of guns increases the probability of more serious injuries and fatalities. As Philip J. Cook has asserted, "case fatality rates for assaults, robberies, and other violent encounters are much higher when the assailant uses a gun than a knife, club, or bare hands." Although Marvin Wolfgang, in a study conducted in the 1950s, concluded that the unavailability of firearms would have little effect on the number of firearms-related homicides because other weapons are readily at hand, Franklin Zimring in the 1960s determined from his study of gun and knife assaults in Chicago that gun assaults led to fatalities five times as often as knife fights.

Attempting to explain his results, Zimring offered an ambiguity hypothesis, suggesting that in many cases, the assailant does not clearly intend to kill the victim. Because firearms are more deadly than other weapons, the chance that an attack will lead to death increases markedly when a gun is used. If the attacker does not have a clear intent to kill the victim, the attack may not be sustained beyond the first blow. Therefore, the lethality of the weapon may be a crucial factor in whether the attack will result in a fatality. Zimring also discovered that the fatality rate increased with the caliber of firearm used, a finding that appeared to support the instrumentality effect. A possible alternative explanation for lower fatality rates with other weapons and lower caliber firearms is that, counter to Zimring's ambiguity of intent hypothesis, those using firearms and higher caliber firearms have a greater intention to inflict harm and choose weapons accordingly. However, a large proportion of the knife attacks could be categorized as serious, leading to the conclusion that had attackers used firearms instead, a higher percentage of injuries would have resulted in death.

In the 1980s, Cook conducted a study to test the weapon instrumentality effect in robbery. He hypothesized that if the type of weapon is an independent causal factor in the probability of death, then there should be a positive relationship between a city's gun robbery rate and the robbery murder rate. Examining changes in robbery and robbery murder in 43 cities from 1976 to 1983, Cook discovered that for each additional 1,000 gun robberies, there occurred 4.8 murders, but every 1,000 non-gun robberies resulted in only 1.4 murders. Cook concluded that the murder and robbery rates are related and that the outcome depends at least in part on the type of weapon used in the robbery.

Research suggests an instrumentality effect with regard to the successful completion of a robbery: Success for cases involving guns is higher than for other weapons. Although the chance that violence will occur is less with firearms, if such violence does occur, the presence of a gun increases the chance that injuries will be more serious. Some have argued that stricter control of handguns would lead to criminals substituting more lethal long guns. However, others observe that handguns are disproportionately used in crime, even though they are more difficult to obtain and are rarer than long guns, and that handguns are preferred because they are more easily concealed. Therefore, those advocating stricter controls on handguns reject the substitution argument, contending that handgun control will result in fewer firearms being involved in crime.

Cook has concluded that "if violent people did not have access to guns, there would still be as much violence in the United States as there is now, or more, but it would be much less deadly." Gun control advocates extend this conclusion, proposing that the presence of firearms in various conflict situations increases the probability that serious injury or death will occur. Contrary to this conclusion, those more supportive of the gun rights position argue that the presence of firearms among citizens acts as a deterrent to crime because criminals fear that their intended victims are armed.

See also: Cook, Philip J.; Fatalities; Violent
    Crime Rate; Zimring, Franklin E.

Further Reading: Philip J. Cook and Jens Ludwig, *Gun Violence: The Real Costs* (New York: Oxford University Press, 2000); Philip J. Cook and Kristin A. Goss, *The Gun Debate* (New York: Oxford University Press, 2014); Daniel W. Webster and Jon S. Vernick, *Reducing Gun Violence in America* (Baltimore, MD: The Johns Hopkins University Press, 2013).

International Association of Chiefs of Police (IACP)

The International Association of Chiefs of Police (IACP), which labels itself "the world's oldest and largest nonprofit membership organization of police executives," has actively opposed efforts on the state and federal levels to enact liberalized carrying concealed weapons (CCW) laws and has objected to proposals to institute a federal law that would establish a more uniform national right to carry concealed weapons by preempting, or superseding, state concealed carry laws. The organization has also supported a variety of gun safety measures, including restrictions on armor-piercing bullets, an assault weapons ban, and uniform background checks for gun purchases. By taking these positions on CCW laws and other measures, the IACP has come into conflict with many gun rights organizations. Established in 1893, the IACP has over 20,000 members from 89 countries. The organization has its headquarters in Alexandria, Virginia, and maintains a professional staff of over 50 people. An advisory board representing international, federal, state, and local law enforcement agencies oversees the professional staff and establishes policy for the organization. The organization produces a monthly magazine, *Police Chief*.

The IACP's concern about civilian gun carrying is illustrated by its president's testimony before Congress in 1997, when then-president Darrell L. Sanders testified regarding proposed CCW legislation before the Subcommittee on Crime of the U.S. House of Representatives Committee on the Judiciary. Sanders declared that his organization opposed preemption of local law enforcement discretion in issuing CCW permits. He observed that no adequate studies had been conducted that would support a decision to federalize a concealed weapons policy. Such laws differ widely from state to state, reflecting the varied wishes of citizens in different states. Sanders was concerned with a provision in proposed legislation allowing current or retired police officers to carry concealed weapons in any jurisdiction. Federal legislation would impose a uniform national standard and thus deprive state and local jurisdictions of the right to maintain their own qualifications for police officers and policies for off-duty carrying.

In part because of the failure of the IACP and other organizations to block the spread of CCW laws in the states, it pressed Congress to enact legislation to make it easier for police (whether on duty or off-duty) and honorably retired police to carry their guns nationwide. Congress responded in 2004 by passing the Law Enforcement Safety Act.

IACP members are encouraged to lobby for strict CCW license revocation policies for such criminal activity as stalking and domestic abuse, to call for CCW laws to be approved by referendum election, and to work for the inclusion of a provision requiring reauthorization after a limited number of years. CCW laws could also contain a requirement that permit applicants to show proof of gun liability insurance. The IACP is especially concerned with maintaining some local police discretion in processing applications for CCW licenses.

See also: Concealed Carry Laws; State Laws, Appendix 2.

Further Reading: International Association of Chiefs of Police Web site, www.iacp.org; *Police Chief Magazine*.

International Brotherhood of Police Officers (IBPO)

The International Brotherhood of Police Officers (IBPO), one of the largest police unions in the nation, representing over 50,000 law enforcement personnel, has supported several gun control initiatives. Priding itself on a militant advocacy of the rights of police officers, the organization maintains a professional lobbying staff in Washington, D.C., and works aggressively for the passage of legislation to benefit it members. The Brotherhood has lobbied for legislation that would prohibit mail-order sales of body armor so that police officers would be less likely to face violent criminals who are well armed and well protected. The IBPO also maintains the Committee on Political Education (COPE), a political action committee that solicits voluntary contributions to support the organization's political and policy objectives.

Established in 1964, the IBPO grew out of a controversy over the firing of seven police officers in Cranston, Rhode Island. As a result of the controversy, the Rhode Island legislature passed the Police Officers Arbitration Act, which granted to police officers the right to organize and negotiate. The organization has defended its members in many court cases and labor relations hearings and before Civil Service commissions.

The IBPO has endorsed proposals such as requiring trigger locks on all new handgun sales. David Holway, the organization's national president, noted that a difficult job for police officers is to enter a home where a child has been injured or killed by an unsecured gun.

Citing Centers for Disease Control (CDC) data indicating that more than one million children have unsupervised access to loaded and unlocked firearms, the organization has supported gun locks legislation.

The IBPO has supported legislation to establish a permanent waiting period for purchasing a handgun. The Brady Handgun Violence Prevention Act provided for a temporary five-day waiting period that was replaced by a National Instant Check System (NICS) in November 1998, when the waiting period was phased out. Reimposition of a minimum three-day waiting period for purchasing a handgun is supported because of the belief that such a waiting period would help prevent impulsive purchases of handguns in crisis situations and allow for a more thorough background check than the instant check system.

The IBPO supports several other gun control initiatives. Firearms dealers should be made more accountable by a policy of revoking the license of any dealer who knowingly sells a gun to a minor. Two forms of identification should be required to purchase a firearm. Steps should be taken to improve the ability to trace firearms and ammunition used in crimes committed by juveniles. Firearms manufacturers should be required to improve safety features on their products. The Brotherhood has supported measures to keep guns away from young people, and also repeal of the Tiahrt Amendment, which restricts law enforcement access to gun trace data.

The IBPO objected to the 1996 Lautenberg Amendment that bans firearms possession for anyone convicted of a misdemeanor related to domestic violence. The organization holds that the legislation is "extreme in its scope" and "shortsighted" because it does not include an exception for weapons possession by government personnel in the performance of their duties. Arguing that police officers often face threats while performing their official duties, the organization supports legislation that would permit active and qualified retired officers to carry a firearm in any jurisdiction.

See also: Brady Handgun Violence Prevention Act; International Association of Chiefs of Police; Lautenberg Amendment; National Instant Check System; Tiahrt Amendment; Youth and Guns.

Further Reading: International Brotherhood of Police Officers Web site, www.ibpo.org.

International Defensive Pistol Association (IDPA)

The International Defensive Pistol Association's (IDPA) emphasis on defensive shooting reflects the growing perception that handguns serve as highly useful defensive weapons for the average citizen. The organization was established in 1996, based in Berryville, Arkansas, by a group of individuals dissatisfied with the United States Practical Shooting Association, which they claim "has lost touch with the original principles of practical shooting and has become just another shooting game." Viewing pistol shooting competition as a simulation of defensive tactics, the IDPA wishes to "create a level playing field for all competitors to test the skill and ability of the individual, not his equipment or gamesmanship." The organization claims more than 17,000 members in 50 countries.

Competition supported by the IDPA involves defensive pistol shooting in realistic self-defense situations. Competitors must use practical handguns, full-charge service ammunition, and holsters that are considered appropriate for self-defense use. The IDPA encourages close range shooting at moving targets. Shooting distances are usually under 15 yards. Shooting stages often begin with the pistol in the holster and concealed. Among its goals, the Association promotes safe and competent use of firearms and equipment intended for self-defense, provides shooters with courses that simulate "potentially life-threatening encounters," and tests skills required for surviving such situations. Competitors in IDPA matches must use service type pistols or revolvers, 9 mm./.38 Special or larger caliber. Holsters must be of the concealed carry type. Matches are open to anyone who can legally own a handgun. Competition is divided into four divisions: stock service pistol, enhanced service pistol, custom defensive pistol, and service revolver.

The IDPA emphasizes safe firearms use, suggesting that the more often persons handle a gun, the more likely they will have a "negligent discharge." The first IDPA pistol competition rule states that any competitor who handles a firearm unsafely will be disqualified from the match. Bill Nottingham, who is associated with the organization, has presented his version of "The Four Laws of Gun Safety" that are meant to decrease the probability of a tragedy occurring if a gun owner experiences "brain-fade," a momentary lapse in safe handling.

While many gun control supporters advocate limitations on the use of firearms to prevent tragedy, Nottingham suggests basic rules to minimize the results of a negligent discharge. According to the first rule, assume that a gun is always loaded. This tenet calls for constantly inspecting a firearm to determine if it contains ammunition. The second rule states, "Never point a gun at something you're not prepared to destroy." Always aim a firearm in a safe direction. The third rule mandates making sure of the target and what is behind it. Firearms users should be aware of the penetrating power of their weapons and aim only at a bulletproof backstop. According to the fourth rule, shooters should keep their finger off the trigger until the sight is on the target: "The finger should not touch the trigger until the instant you are prepared to fire." Nottingham concludes that firearms should be kept from children, those not trained in their use, and "especially thieves."

See also: Concealed Carry Laws; United States Practical Shooting Association.

Further Reading: International Defensive Pistol Association Web site, www.idpa.com.

Israel

Gun rights advocates point to Israel as a nation with a high gun density in the population but with a low murder rate (40 to 60 murders each year in a population of less than 5 million), thus dismissing any claim of a relationship between the availability of firearms and the level of violence. Robert W. Lee, a gun rights advocate, notes that in April 1984 three terrorists began shooting in a Jerusalem café with automatic weapons. They killed just one individual before being shot by Israelis armed with handguns. Lee concludes that certain mass murders in the United States could be prevented if gun carrying were as widespread as in Israel.

However, gun control advocates note that the distribution of firearms in Israel is strictly regulated, and that it is a nation that has been in a state of virtually perpetual war with its neighbors since its founding. Anyone wishing to carry a firearm must demonstrate a valid reason for doing so, although any person without a criminal record may fairly easily acquire a permit. The Interior Ministry must issue a special permit, which requires the approval of the police. The permit contains basic information about the gun owner and the type of gun possessed. The owner of a weapon is legally responsible for it. If it is lost or stolen, the owner must inform the police within 24 hours, but still may be prosecuted on the misdemeanor charge of negligence.

In the article "Israel Has a Successful Gun Control Policy" (1992), Abraham Tennenbaum, a former Israeli police lieutenant, noted that the United States and Israel differ according to the reasons citizens own firearms. In Israel, although guns are owned for hunting and target shooting, their main function is military defense and protection against terrorism. Tennenbaum found that most firearms in Israel are owned not by private citizens who carry them, but by the army, the police, or other authorities. Due to a system of universal military service, most citizens are issued firearms to take home with them. If school children take a trip, they are accompanied by armed guards, who are often parents and teachers. The local police station assigns them firearms that are returned after the trip. The Civil Guards, a volunteer group operated by the Israeli police, conduct armed night patrols of neighborhoods. Firearms are issued at the start and returned at the completion of each patrol.

Tennenbaum attributed the high concentration of firearms in Israel to the special security needs of the country. The basic policy is to distribute firearms generally to those not specifically prohibited from possessing arms. Although criminals can acquire firearms, it is a more difficult task than in the United States and the punishment can be severe. Illegal weapons are either stolen from private citizens or taken from the army. Tennenbaum noted that because the army is a source of illegal weapons, explosives and automatic weapons are used more often in murders. The case of Israel demonstrates that there is no simple relationship between the prevalence of firearms and acts of violence. Cultural factors may play a role in the low incidence of gun-related violent crime, as do serious attempts to keep weapons out of the hands of known criminals. Israeli gun control policy toward Arab residents would likely not be accepted by gun rights advocates in the United States. In 1996, Israeli firearms laws were modified to permit all civilians who have served in army combat units to carry guns. This policy generally excluded Arab residents from firearm possession.

See also: Switzerland; Mexico.

Further Reading: Robert W. Lee, "Gun Control Would Not Reduce Crime," in Charles P. Cozic, ed., *Gun Control* (San Diego: Greenhaven Press, 1992), pp. 50–58; Abraham N. Tennenbaum, "Israel Has a Successful Gun Control Policy," in Charles P. Cozic, ed., *Gun Control* (San Diego: Greenhaven Press, 1992), pp. 248–51.

Izaak Walton League of America (IWLA)

Although the Izaak Walton League of America (IWLA), one of the nation's oldest conservation groups, usually does not take part in the gun control debate, the organization has on occasion supported gun rights groups. The organization's hunting membership influences its position on this issue. Given the organization's prestige in the area of conservation, it has at times been a useful ally, along with other groups concerned with wildlife preservation and resource conservation.

In 1922, 54 sportsmen, concerned about the deterioration of the nation's fishing streams, formed the organization to fight water pollution. Named after a seventeenth-century English fisherman and conservationist, the League today has 50,000 members and attempts to protect not only the nation's waterways, but also its soil, forests, and wildlife. Among its many projects, the League campaigned for the creation of the Land and Water Conservation Fund, a revenue source for acquiring land for parks and recreational facilities.

Since its founding, the IWLA has been active in outdoor recreation activities, including hunting and fishing. In 1937, the organization backed the Pittman Robertson Act, which imposed an excise tax on the sale of sporting firearms and ammunition. Money raised by this tax was to be used for wildlife projects. In the 1950s, as millions of Americans took up the sport of hunting, the League began a program to improve hunter behavior. This program continued through the 1970s, and in 1980 the League sponsored the first National Conference on Outdoor Ethics.

In the 1960s, gun rights groups were able to elicit expressions of support from the Izaak Walton League, along with other wildlife and conservation organizations. When Senator Thomas Dodd, a Connecticut Democrat, expanded his gun control proposals to include regulation of the sale of rifles and shotguns, sporting and conservation groups such as the IWLA sensed a potential threat to the interests of their membership, many of whom were hunters. Pro-gun interests argued that the formulation of any reasonable and effective firearms legislation should include input from groups like the League. Pro-gun groups recognized that the prestige of the IWLA, a longtime conservation group that has gained the respect of hunters, could lend significant support to the gun rights position. In 2006, all IWLA chapters with shooting ranges also became members of the National Shooting Sports Foundation (NSSF). In 2010, the IWLA operated 111 shooting ranges across the country.

In recent years, the League has continued to support outdoor ethics conferences, in which hunters and other outdoor enthusiasts participate. Those engaged in outdoor recreation are urged to take responsibility for preserving and protecting resources. The League's wide interests, including promotion of energy efficiency and lowering greenhouse gas emissions, soil conservation and preservation of agricultural wetlands, and educational projects dealing with natural resource maintenance, assure the organization a respected place in the area of environmental protection.

See also: Dodd, Thomas J.; Gun Control Act of 1968; National Shooting Sports Foundation.

Further Reading: Bill R. Davidson, *To Keep and Bear Arms* (New Rochelle, NY: Arlington House, 1969); Izaak Walton League of America Web site, www.iwla.org.

J

Japan

Japan has strict gun control laws, few guns, and a low crime rate. The nation experiences approximately 200 gun-related violent crimes each year, which, compared to the United States, is extremely low. The robbery rate in Japan is 1.4 per 100,000 population, compared to 220.9 in the United States. Analysts disagree about the nature of the relationship between Japanese gun control policy and that nation's crime rate. While some advocate the introduction of similarly stringent legislation in the United States to curb crime, others observe that the success of Japan's gun control policies cannot be separated easily from Japanese traditions that emphasize social control.

Japanese law prohibits ownership of handguns and rifles. Sportsmen are allowed to own shotguns for hunting and other gun-related sporting activities, but acquiring such a weapon requires undergoing a prolonged licensing process. Applicants must attend classes, take a written examination, and pass a shooting test. They must undergo mental testing and submit an affidavit to police certifying their mental competence to own a firearm. Police run background checks on applicants and their relatives to make sure they have committed no crimes. Police officials are granted extensive discretion to deny a license to anyone they suspect of being a danger to others. As of 2007, only .6% of Japanese homes have guns.

Firearms owners are required to store weapons in a locker and to inform police of its precise location in the home. Ammunition must be kept locked in a separate place. In 1971, the Japanese government prohibited any transfers of rifles, but allowed current licensed owners to keep their weapons. When an owner dies, relatives must surrender the rifle to police. Violation of the handgun prohibition can result in severe punishment. The maximum penalty for possessing a handgun is 10 years in prison and a fine roughly equivalent to several thousand dollars. Even though shotguns and air rifles remained legal, the number of licensed weapons declined by nearly a quarter during the 1980s.

While most analysts admit that Japanese gun control policies have been successful, they have attributed that success to several causes. The police, who generally are held in high regard, have been granted extensive search and seizure powers. Twice each year police make visits to all Japanese homes to gather various types of information. They check on gun licensees to determine if a gun has been stolen, how securely the gun is stored, and the emotional stability of the owner. The Japanese justice system does not ensure protection against police searches, and the right of habeas corpus is not nearly as stringently enforced as in the United States. Police are efficient in clearing criminal cases. Due to this efficiency, no compelling need exists for Japanese citizens to own firearms for self-defense. For instance, Tokyo has been labeled the safest city in the world.

Historically, gun ownership in Japan was limited to a relatively small elite. Unlike the United States, where over 280 million firearms are privately owned, few guns are in private hands. Firearms were introduced into Japan during the sixteenth century and quickly came into use as weapons of warfare. However, largely through the influence of the samurai warrior nobility, which preferred to rely on the sword, firearms distribution was severely limited. Firearms manufacturing never became a significant economic enterprise for private distribution.

Because the Japanese people, traditionally very law-abiding, comply voluntarily with gun control laws, police officials are not required to expend much time or effort enforcing the laws. However, officials have become concerned about even the small rate of violent crime. In 1995, just 34 gun-related homicides occurred in Japan. In 2003, there were 39 gun homicides. In 2008, there were 11 gun homicides; in 2013, there were 12. Still, officials worried that a population exposed to Western popular culture and increasingly concerned about confronting criminals wielding firearms might find gun ownership an attractive option.

Further Reading: Joel Alpert. "93 Gun Deaths in Japan vs. 36,000 in America," *AAP News* 15 (June 1999), 6; David B. Kopel, *The Samurai, the Mountie, and the Cowboy* (Buffalo, NY: Prometheus, 1992).

Jefferson, Thomas (1743–1826)

Gun rights advocates cite the views of such noted early American statesmen as Thomas Jefferson to support their claim that the Constitution guarantees an individual's right to keep and bear arms. Jefferson, in the Declaration of Independence, offered a defense of the right of revolution that for over 200 years has inspired those who oppose tyranny. Those supporting gun rights deduce from that defense that the right to bear arms against an oppressive government stands as a major bulwark against the abuse of power.

Gun advocates use several of Jefferson's statements to support the view that he understood the Second Amendment as guaranteeing a fundamental right to bear arms. For instance, National Rifle Association (NRA) executive vice president Wayne LaPierre notes a quote from Italian criminologist Cesare Beccaria that Jefferson "copied . . . in longhand into his own personal compilation of great quotations." The quote declares that laws forbidding the carrying of arms to avoid a "trifling inconvenience" disarms "those only who are neither inclined nor determined to commit crimes." Second Amendment Foundation president Alan Gottlieb quotes Jefferson from a letter written in 1811 commenting that state militias, which could oppose a national dictatorship, would be composed of every citizen capable of bearing arms. Gottlieb quotes Jefferson as recommending the use of a gun as an exercise to develop a strong body and strong mind. The gun, according to Jefferson, should be "the constant companion of your walks."

After taking part in the drafting and signing of the Declaration of Independence, Jefferson returned to Virginia to take part in writing the new state constitution. He proposed the inclusion of a provision to guarantee "a freeman's right to use arms while forbidding standing armies." During the state convention debates over ratification of the national constitution, Jefferson expressed his own preferences for a bill of rights. He urged that such a document should guarantee freedom of religion, freedom of the press, protection against a standing army, freedom of commerce against the restrictions of monopolies, the right of habeas corpus, and trial by jury. He expressed intense concern, as he had with the Virginia state constitution, with a standing army, which he declared a dangerous instrument against the rights of the nation that places the people at the mercy of the government.

In *The Constitutional Thought of Thomas Jefferson* (1994), David Mayer suggested that Jefferson's influence can be seen in the Second Amendment's guarantee of the right to keep and bear arms. However, others argue that the concerns he expressed pertained to citizen militia service, lending support to the militia-based interpretation of the Second Amendment rather than the individualist view emphasizing a personal right to have guns.

To soften the national government's power to maintain an army, the Second Amendment placed the control of militias solidly in the hands of the states. Therefore, although Jefferson may have supported the right of citizens to bear arms, his preference may not be directly reflected in the Second Amendment. *See also:* American Revolution; Gottlieb, Alan Merril; LaPierre, Wayne; National Rifle Association; Second Amendment.

Further Reading: Alan M. Gottlieb, *Gun Rights Fact Book* (Bellevue, WA: Merril, 1994); David N. Mayer, *The Constitutional Thought of Thomas Jefferson* (Charlottesville: University Press of Virginia, 1994).

Jews for the Preservation of Firearms Ownership (JPFO)

In 1989, Aaron Zelman founded Jews for the Preservation of Firearms Ownership (JPFO) to counter the pro-gun control position of the Anti-Defamation League. Zelman continues to serve as executive director. Based in Hartford,

Wisconsin, the JPFO holds to an absolutist interpretation of the Second Amendment and always puts the term gun control within quotation marks to emphasize complete rejection of its legitimacy. The organization applies lessons from the Holocaust to current debates over gun control, coming to the conclusion that horrible things can happen to people who surrender their right to own firearms. The JPFO recommends that all law-abiding citizens own firearms. The organization supports carrying concealed weapons laws as a method of deterring criminal activity and advocates firearms safety courses in public schools. Those who misuse firearms should undergo severe penalties.

The JPFO maintains that because Jewish law requires self-defense, gun control subverts God's command. Although the organization focuses primarily on activating Jewish gun owners to vocalize their opposition to gun control, non-Jewish members are welcomed. Zelman estimates that 25 percent of JPFO members are not Jewish. While the organization cooperates with other gun rights groups and offers them the results of JPFO investigations, it claims to be the only group that truly understands the importance of the issue. It contends that gun control has historically been an intimate part of genocide campaigns that have led to the deaths of millions of people.

The JPFO promotes a cartoon character similar to the National Rifle Association's (NRA) Eddie Eagle. Gran'pa Jack, who appears in the comic book, *"Gun Control" Kills Kids*, criticizes gun control efforts and tells children that firearms save lives. The character encourages children to make sure their parents own firearms and know how to use them. The comic books are intended for use in school systems.

The organization holds that the Gun Control Act of 1968 is based on a Nazi gun law passed in Germany in 1938. Both laws determine the legality of firearms on the basis of function, contain provisions limiting importation only to those guns judged suitable for sporting purposes, and grant to an unelected bureaucracy the authority to determine the meaning of sporting purpose. The JPFO claims that during the twentieth century, 59 million people were killed worldwide as a result of gun control laws that left them defenseless. However, in contrast to Nazi Germany, the United States has a Constitution that, according to the JPFO, guarantees individuals an absolute right to own firearms.

Consistent with its absolutist stand on gun control, the JPFO opposes the instant background check system, which in 1998 replaced the federal five-day waiting period for purchasing a handgun. The organization claims that the instant check database is equivalent to national gun registration. According to the JPFO, the Nazi model of gun registration will lead to further citizen acceptance of federal government interference in their lives, the classification of gun owners as a dangerous class of people to be watched with suspicion (just as Jews were stigmatized in Nazi Germany), and ultimately confiscation of firearms.

Although gun control supporters have used various mass shootings, including those at schools, in campaigns advocating more stringent regulations on firearms ownership, the JPFO asserts that gun control allows such incidents to occur in the first place. Teachers and school officials are unable to defend students because gun control laws leave them unarmed. A prospective terrorist or anyone wishing to gain publicity knows that schools are an undefended target. The organization recommends enactment of the policies followed in Israel, where PLO terrorist attacks on schools are deterred because teachers and parents carry firearms. In 2009, the JPFO filed a brief in the Supreme Court case of *McDonald v. Chicago* (2010), arguing for applying the Second Amendment to the States.

See also: American Jewish Congress; Central Conference of American Rabbis; Concealed Carry Laws; Eddie Eagle; Gun Control Act of 1968; Israel; *McDonald v. Chicago* (2010); National Instant Check System; National Rifle Association; Second Amendment; Youth and Guns.

Further Reading: "Interview with Aaron Zelman," *Guns and Ammo* (April 1996), 10–13; Jews for the Preservation of Firearms Ownership Web site, www.jpfo.com.

John Birch Society (JBS)

The John Birch Society (JBS), an ultraconservative organization that gained much publicity during the 1960s for its strong anticommunist stand, is a firm supporter of an individual's right to keep and bear arms. Society members believe that the American system of government, which they call a constitutional republic, is "the finest yet developed by man." The Second Amendment, as part of the revered governing document, is understood to guarantee the right of free individuals to possess firearms. Members believe that this right to keep and bear arms must be defended against those who would limit the freedoms of Americans. The Society views the Constitution as a document that should not be amended, in that it has opposed calls for a constitutional convention to amend the document, even when the organization supports the intent of the proposed changes.

Robert Welch founded the Society in 1958 following a meeting of business friends at which he presented his plan to fight collectivism and what he considered treasonous activities in American government. Welch named the organization after an American missionary to China who aided the Chinese in their struggle against the Japanese. Birch was killed by the new communist regime that came to power in China in 1949. For over 50 years, the Society has operated to warn Americans against what it considers ever-expanding government power and socialist tendencies in American government. In addition to gun control, the organization opposes proposals for national health care, a national school curriculum and teacher certification, government-mandated food and vitamin labeling, and any other measure that would result in greater government control over the lives of citizens.

The Society has expressed its opposition to the Brady Handgun Violence Prevention Act, claiming that the law has inconvenienced many law-abiding citizens without demonstrating any positive benefit for fighting crime. Robert W. Lee writes a regular column for the organization's bimonthly publication, *The New American*, in which he reports on the gun rights issue. In response to school shootings in the 1990s in Arkansas, Kentucky, and Mississippi, Lee rejected the conclusion that firearms in the hands of youth are always dangerous. He recounted cases in which young people employed guns successfully to defend themselves against criminal attacks.

In 1998, when Charlton Heston was being considered for the presidency of the National Rifle Association (NRA), Lee raised doubts about Heston's commitment to gun rights, discussing Heston's support for passage of the Gun Control Act of 1968. Heston was described as a "gun control diehard" for maintaining his commitment to a gun control organization led by actor Tom Laughlin after many other actors had dropped away from the group. Lee expressed concern regarding

Heston's expressed intention to move the NRA to a more moderate position.

The Society has supported several items on the gun rights agenda, including state concealed carry statutes, which require local law enforcement officers to grant a license to carry a concealed weapon to anyone who is not expressly forbidden to do so. The Society emphasizes that concealed carry laws have not resulted in increased homicides among normally law-abiding citizens. The organization notes with approval that women are increasingly assuming the right to bear arms for self-defense.

See also: Brady Handgun Violence Prevention Act; Concealed Carry Laws; Gun Control Act of 1968; Heston, Charlton; National Rifle Association; Second Amendment; State Laws, Appendix 2; Women and Guns; Youth and Guns.

Further Reading: John Birch Society Web site, www. jbs.org; Robert W. Lee, "Heston, For the Record," *The New American* (April 13, 1998), 15–16; Robert W. Lee, "Guns in the Right Hands," *The New American* (August 17, 1998), 33–34.

Johns Hopkins Center for Gun Policy and Research

The Johns Hopkins Center for Gun Policy and Research was established in 1995 through funding from the Joyce Foundation. The Center labels gun violence a health issue and strives to reduce gun violence by providing research results to policy makers, organizations, the mass media, and the general public on subjects such as firearms-related injuries and the consequences of various gun policies. The Center takes a pro-gun control stance and questions the value of research conducted by social scientists who conclude that firearms possession can be an effective means of personal defense. Stephen P. Teret was the founding director of the Center. John S. Vernick and Daniel W. Webster now serve as codirectors. The Center employs additional faculty members and collaborates with gun policy researchers at other universities and foundations.

The Center has developed a model handgun safety standard act that state and local governments may use as a guide to revising firearms policy. The model law calls for establishing a commission that will determine an appropriate handgun safety performance standard. Each handgun should be equipped with technologically sophisticated devices that prevent it from being fired by anyone but the owner. The technology must be integral to the gun's design and not an addition to it, and the personalized component should not be subject to easy alteration. The law would mandate that a manufacturer submit a model of a personalized handgun to an independent laboratory where its compliance with the performance standard will be determined.

The model legislation provides for specific exemptions, including handguns that are categorized as antiques, manufactured before the effective date of the law, acquired by law enforcement officers and members of the armed forces, or attached to a federal agency. Although exempted weapons may not be sold, traded, shipped, or distributed by dealers after the law has gone into effect, sales and transfers among private individuals would be allowed.

Law enforcement officers would be authorized to confiscate any handgun not covered by an exemption that fails to meet the performance standard, as long as they comply with constitutional restrictions on searches and seizures. Attorneys general of the various states would have the authority to take legal action against those failing to comply with the regulations. A violation of the law would constitute a felony punishable by fine and imprisonment. If an owner of a handgun or an unauthorized person fires the weapon, causing personal injury to another person, the owner could be held liable for damages.

The Center has criticized research conducted by social scientists such as John R. Lott and David B. Mustard of the University of Chicago, who conclude that allowing those without criminal records or histories of mental illness to carry concealed handguns can provide a higher level of personal safety. The Center claims that the University of Chicago researchers used a discredited methodology, disregarded established theories within criminology, ignored the possible effects of gun laws other than "shall issue" statutes, failed to observe precise dates when laws went into effect, and used an ambiguous definition for "shall issue" laws, which require law enforcement officers to issue a license to carry a concealed firearm to any applicant not specifically prohibited from doing so.

See also: Concealed Carry Laws; Lott, John R., Jr.

Further Reading: G. Hu, D.W. Webster, and S. P. Baker, "Hidden Homicide Trends in the U.S., 1999–2004," *Journal of Urban Health* 85(2008), 597–606; Daniel W. Webster and Jon S. Vernick, *Reducing Gun Violence in America* (Baltimore, MD: The Johns Hopkins University Press, 2013); Johns Hopkins Center for Gun Policy and Research Web site, www.jhsph.edu/gunpolicy/.

Jonesboro, Arkansas, School Shooting

The 1998 Jonesboro, Arkansas, school shooting involved two adolescents, one 11 and the other 13, who were arrested for killing four fellow students and one teacher, and wounding 11 others at Westside Middle School. The shooting followed a series of other gun incidents at schools around the country. When the Jonesboro shooting occurred, the news media and the nation were already sensitized to the troubling repetition of firearms violence committed by adolescents a little older than children. President Bill Clinton, on a tour of African nations, took time to comment publicly that he and his wife were "deeply shocked and heartbroken." The incongruous image of two young boys employing firearms with such deadly effect shocked many around the nation, especially when the news media reported that under Arkansas law the two boys had only limited responsibility for their actions. They had missed school that day to prepare for the shooting. One of the boys pulled the fire alarm and then took a position with the other, taking aim from a wooded area as the unsuspecting students and teachers exited the school building. Wearing camouflage outfits and carrying a Ruger .44-caliber rifle and a 30.06 hunting rifle, they began firing at their classmates and teachers.

The press reported that the stepfather of one of the boys charged in the incident had trained his son in the use of rifles and shotguns and had begun training the boy in a handgun shooting competition involving moving targets. He was also an official in a local gun club. A club member commented that the boy had been taught firearm safety and was a good student of gun handling.

The Jonesboro shooting set the stage for another round of debates over gun control. Many news programs and talk shows discussed the possible causes of the incident and the potential consequences. The Violence Policy Center (VPC) quickly issued a press release about the "massacre of children by children" that should focus national attention on "America's youth gun culture." The organization strongly implied that such gun groups as the National Rifle Association (NRA) and the National Shooting Sports Foundation (NSSF) were partly responsible for the gun culture, given that they "court America's children and actually encourage the use and possession of guns by kids." The VPC claimed that gun organizations intend to create future customers for the firearms industry and to recruit supporters for the pro-gun movement. The organization cited the NRA youth magazine *In Sights* and the 1997 Browning firearms catalog, which displays a photograph of a child wearing a Browning cap and playing with spent shotgun shells.

Gun control critics responded that firearms did not cause the Jonesboro incident. The troubled youth, who were intent on doing harm to their fellow students, could just as well have used the vehicle in which they had intended to escape,

driving it into the school and achieving a similarly deadly effect. Gun supporters balance what they perceive as the benefits of exposing young people to guns against the occasional tragedy caused for reasons other than the simple availability of firearms. In the meantime, pro-gun control groups continued to cite such incidents in their call for more stringent controls on the sale and possession of firearms in the United States.

See also: Clinton, William Jefferson (Bill); Gun Culture; Littleton, Colorado, Columbine School Shooting; National Rifle Association; National Shooting Sports Foundation; Ruger, William Batterman (Bill); Stockton, California, Shooting; Violence Policy Center; Youth and Guns.

Further Reading: *New York Times* (March 25, 1998), A1; Violence Policy Center, "Arkansas School Shooting Focuses New Attention on Youth Gun Culture," March 26, 1998.

K

Kates, Don B., Jr. (1941–)

For over 30 years, Don B. Kates, Jr., has served as one of the more avid spokespersons for an individual's right to keep and bear arms. Kates has developed arguments about the meaning of the Second Amendment, rejecting the collective view in favor of the individualistic interpretation of the right to keep and bear arms. He contends that the word "people" used in the Second Amendment has the same referent as it does in other amendments, indicating individual persons. Aside from the constitutional arguments regarding firearms ownership as an individual's right, Kates claims that gun control fails to produce the results its proponents profess. He asserts that such measures as banning handguns would have little effect on the level of violence in society. Instead, violence can be reduced only through changes in social and economic institutions and in the basic beliefs and values of the population.

Kates received a B.A. from Reed College in Portland, Oregon, and a law degree from Yale University. In the 1960s, he was a civil rights worker, assisting such civil rights lawyers as William Kunstler. Helping with the federal War on Poverty program, Kates focused on civil rights and police misconduct cases. He began carrying a firearm for self-protection during the more violent period of the civil rights movement. After teaching constitutional law and criminal procedure at St. Louis University Law School, Kates opened a private law practice in San Francisco.

In an article published in 1976, Kates explained why he, a civil libertarian, opposed gun control. He explained that a civil libertarian must not trust the military and the police, who have a monopoly on armament, with the authority to decide who may possess firearms. Kates adhered to the replacement hypothesis: those who want to commit violence will do so, whether with a gun, knife, or other device. A firearm simply serves as one instrument for criminal activity.

In the 1990s, Kates focused on the public health researchers who were employing an epidemiological approach to investigating firearms and violence. He accused such researchers—whom he called "health sages"—not only of conducting bad science, but of intellectual dishonesty, "systematically inventing, misinterpreting, selecting, or otherwise manipulating data to validate preordained political conclusions." Questioning the integrity of health care researchers, Kates charged them with "fraudulent omission of material fact" and "overt misrepresentation of facts." He accused these researchers of suppressing information about declines in accidental gun fatalities and accidental child gun deaths, and misrepresenting the relationship between gun ownership and the homicide rate. Kates objected especially to the assumption that ordinary law-abiding citizens are more likely to commit murder simply because they own firearms, citing evidence indicating that murders are most often committed by those who already have a criminal history. He concluded that little can be gained by denying the average citizen the right to own a firearm.

While accusing health professionals of bias due to their close relationship to gun control lobbying groups, Kates himself is closely related to pro-gun organizations. For instance, the National Rifle Association (NRA) has retained him to represent firearms owners in lawsuits, and he writes regularly for gun publications. In a 1998 article entitled "Trigger Points," Bob Thompson noted that while Kates might be correct in his claim that public health research on firearms is biased, he may have made the effort to discover the truth about the issue more difficult with his lawyer's tendency to impeach the credibility of the opposition as forcefully as possible.

See also: Health Care Professionals; National Rifle Association; Second Amendment.

Further Reading: Don B. Kates and Gary Kleck, *The Great Gun Debate: Essays on Firearms and Violence* (San Francisco: Pacific Research Institute for Public Policy, 1997); Don B. Kates, Henry E. Schaffer, John K. Lattimer, and George B. Murray, "Guns and Public Health: Epidemic of Violence or Pandemic of Propaganda," *Tennessee Law Review* (1995), 513–96; Bob Thompson, "Trigger Points," *Washington Post Magazine* (March 29, 1998), 12–16, 23–24, 26–27.

Kellermann, Arthur (1955–)

Arthur Kellermann is a physician who has conducted research suggesting that the presence of firearms contributes independently to a higher level of violence. The claim often made in the media that "a gun in the home triples the risk of a homicide in the home" originated in Kellermann's research reports. Kellermann has been strongly criticized by gun rights researchers and organizations that have concluded that firearms can serve as effective instruments of self-defense. Kellermann is often portrayed as the pro-gun control movement's equivalent to Gary Kleck, the researcher who has concluded that firearms are used for self-defense much more often than they cause injuries to the innocent. Kleck has criticized Kellermann for failing to recognize that violence may lead to increased ownership of firearms for self-defense, thus reversing the suggested cause–effect relationship.

Kellermann received an undergraduate degree in biology from Rhodes College and a masters degree in public health from the University of Washington. He graduated from the Emory University School of Medicine in 1980. Kellermann became chief of emergency medicine at the University of Tennessee at Memphis, medical director of the emergency department at the Memphis County Hospital, and medical director to the Memphis Fire Department and Emergency Medical Services Bureau. In 1993, the Rollins School of Public Health at Emory University recruited Kellermann to establish and serve as director of the Center for Injury Control. He is also

founding director of the Center for Injury Control at Rollins School of Public Health, a collaborating center of the World Health Organization. He has conducted clinical research on various subjects dealing with emergency medicine and has published papers on emergency treatment of asthma, cardiopulmonary resuscitation, defibrillation methods, and emergency department drug screening.

Kellermann first became concerned about firearms violence in 1984 while a graduate student at the University of Washington. The shooting death of soul singer Marvin Gaye, who was killed by his own father, motivated Kellermann to examine the criminological and medical literature on firearms. When he discovered that little relevant research had been conducted, he decided to begin his own work on the question. Along with King County medical examiner Donald Reay, Kellermann studied gunshot deaths in the Seattle area. Kellermann and Reay determined that there occurred "43 suicides, criminal homicides, or accidental gunshot deaths involving a gun kept in the home for every case of homicide for self-protection." In 1986, these research results were published in the *New England Journal of Medicine*, thus giving wide circulation to Kellermann's contention that guns should be considered an independent variable in explaining violent behavior.

In 1988, Kellermann published a paper that summarized the results of his research, which was partially funded by the Centers for Disease Control (CDC), comparing crime rates in Seattle and the neighboring Canadian city of Vancouver. Kellermann reported that while the two cities' crime rates were similar, firearm-related assaults were seven times greater in Seattle. Other researchers were especially critical of this study, focusing their attacks on the methodology Kellermann employed.

Continuing the investigation of the effects of keeping firearms in the home, Kellermann and nine colleagues conducted a six-year study employing the case control method, which, according to Kellermann, was designed to eliminate other potential causes of violence in the home besides the presence of firearms. In 1993, the *New England Journal of Medicine* published the study in which Kellermann concluded that the presence of firearms in the home was "strongly and independently associated with an increased risk of homicide." Kellermann and colleagues have published dozens of studies on the links between guns and violence.

Kellermann has moved on to investigate the implementation and evaluation of various methods of violence prevention, as well as health services research, cardiac care, and injury prevention.

See also: Accidents Involving Guns; Fatalities; Kleck, Gary; Violent Crime Rate.

Further Reading: Arthur Kellermann and Donald Reay, "Protection or Peril? An Analysis of Firearm-Related Deaths in the Home," *New England Journal of Medicine* (June 12, 1986), 1557–60; Arthur Kellermann, et al., "Suicide in the Home in Relation to Gun Ownership," *New England Journal of Medicine* 327 (August 13, 1992), 467–72; John D. Thomas, "Accidents Don't Happen: Arthur Kellermann Addresses Gun Violence and Injuries as Preventable Public Health Problems," *Emory Magazine* (Summer 1995); Rollins School of Public Health Web site, www.sph.emory.edu/; Bob Thompson, "Trigger Points," *Washington Post Magazine* (March 29, 1998), 12–16, 23–24, 26–27.

Kelley v. R.G. Industries, Inc. (1983)

The Court of Appeals of Maryland, in *Kelley v. R.G. Industries, Inc.* (304 Md. 124, 1983), dealt with the question of whether a manufacturer or marketer of handguns could be found liable for injuries caused by one of its handguns during the commission of a crime. In consciously revising common law, the court decided that although standard liability claims did not apply in this case, a claim based on the predictable use of a so-called Saturday night special was appropriate under Maryland law.

An assailant shot and wounded Olen J. Kelley, a grocery store clerk, during an armed robbery. The handgun was a Rohm Revolver, assembled and sold by R.G. Industries, Inc., of Miami, Florida, a subsidiary of Rohm Gesellschaft, a German company. Kelley subsequently sued R.G. Industries, employing several theories of liability. R.G. Industries, in a motion to dismiss, argued that the handgun was not defective in that it performed as expected, and that the company could not be held responsible for the actions of the assailant.

The court rejected Kelley's first two claims of strict liability—that the manufacture and marketing of handguns is an "abnormally dangerous activity" and that handguns are "abnormally dangerous products." The court rejected the applicability of

the doctrine of liability in this case because when a handgun injures an individual toward whom it is aimed, it performs just as intended and the product has no flaw. The court concluded that the misuse of handguns by others cannot justify, under Maryland law, imposing strict liability on the manufacturers of handguns for resulting injuries. A handgun cannot be ruled defective simply because it can be used in criminal activity. Hence, Kelley's argument confused the normal function of a product with a defect in design or manufacture.

Nonetheless, the court identified a possible avenue still open for determining liability. Saturday night specials, defined as poorly made, inexpensive, lightweight, easily concealed handguns that are inaccurate and unreliable, have no legitimate uses in law enforcement, sport, or for personal protection, but are primarily weapons employed by criminals. The court argued that this type of handgun has been appropriately and officially branded unique from all others in its lack of use except in criminal activity. The court referred to testimony before Congress that labeled the Saturday night special dangerous to intended victims and bystanders, subject to backfire, and extremely inaccurate except at close range. Disparaging comments toward the Saturday night special made by Maxwell Rich, executive vice president of the National Rifle Association (NRA), made during testimony before the U.S. Senate, were quoted in the decision. The court concluded that both the U.S. Congress and the Maryland General Assembly had established that Saturday night specials are a unique type of handgun distinct from all others.

Referring to the Gun Control Act of 1968, the court noted the ban on the importation of any firearm that fails to qualify for use in law enforcement, the military, or sport. Also noted during congressional hearings were references to Saturday night specials as "bellyguns" and "manstoppers," indicating what the court concluded was the true purpose of such handguns. Their major value is limited to criminal activity due to their concealability and low cost.

After establishing that the Saturday night special is a unique weapon distinct from all other handguns, the court asserted that the manufacturer or sellers of a Saturday night special should know that the product in which he or she is dealing has primarily a criminal utility. Such uses can be clearly foreseen by manufacturers and marketers. Therefore, the court concluded that holding manufacturers and sellers of Saturday night specials strictly liable to persons who suffer injuries from their criminal use is consistent with established public policy on the state and national levels. The court thereby established a limited area of strict liability for the misuse of handguns of a particular type. If a court establishes that the weapon used to cause injury can be classified as a Saturday night special, the manufacturer or anyone engaged in the sale of the weapon may be held liable. The wrongful act involved is marketing such guns to the public with the knowledge that they have "little or no legitimate use."

The court determined whether, in the present case, the Rohm Revolver could be categorized as a Saturday night special. Citing a handgun identification study, the weapon was placed in the category of the least expensive handguns of poorest quality, and therefore the general basis for liability was established in this specific case.

See also: Gun Control Act of 1968; National Rifle Association; Saturday Night Special.

Further Reading: *Kelley v. R.G. Industries, Inc.*, 304 Md. 124 (1983).

Kennesaw, Georgia

In 1982, Kennesaw, Georgia, a small town on the northern outskirts of Atlanta, gained nationwide publicity when its city council unanimously passed an ordinance that required residents to have a firearm in their homes. The ordinance read in part: "To provide for and protect the safety, security, and general welfare of the city and its inhabitants, every head of household residing in the city limits is required to maintain a firearm, together with ammunition." A member of the city council indicated that Morton Grove, a village in Illinois that had banned the possession of handguns by all residents, was a major reason for Kennesaw's mirror-image ordinance.

Darwin Purdy, mayor of Kennesaw, stated that the measure's purpose was to ensure the safety of the local population. He did not think that the ordinance would have the effect of increasing gunshot wounds among the 7,000 residents, but suggested that the rate of injury to criminals might well increase. Police Chief Robert Ruble claimed that the crime rate had risen 16 percent

in Kennesaw from 1980 to 1981, thus spurring passage of the new legislation. However, when broken down into actual categories, that estimate did not appear nearly as significant for a small town with a population of 7,000. Armed robberies had increased from one in 1980 to four in 1981, and the number of homicides decreased from two in 1980 to none in 1981. These figures suggest that reaction to the Morton Grove ordinance played a major role in the decision to pass the Kennesaw measure.

The Kennesaw City Council established a minimal fine for violation of the ordinance ($50) and exempted certain groups within the population, including those with disabilities that would prevent them from using a firearm, those who oppose the use of firearms due to religious beliefs, and convicted felons. Police Chief Ruble suggested that the Morton Grove police department send to the Kennesaw police department all the guns that they had confiscated. Morton Grove officials declined the offer. The nationwide publicity led to some sympathetic response among gun rights supporters. The Kennesaw police chief received offers from groups in New York, California, Texas, and Oklahoma to send weapons to the small town. The chief of police indicated that he intended to accept all donations.

Before the ordinance could go into effect, the city council wanted to establish firearm safety classes. The council delayed the effective date twice to have a firing range prepared for those citizens who wished to undergo training in the use of a firearm. When the ordinance finally took effect June 1, 1982, the mayor indicated that most residents already were in compliance. On June 1, the American Civil Liberties Union (ACLU) challenged the new ordinance as unconstitutional, but made little headway in the courts.

Although no attempt was made to enforce the gun law, city officials estimated that 85 percent of residents were in compliance. Two years after passage, the police reported a decline in house burglaries. However, with a significant growth in the town's population, the burglary rate began to increase once more. New Chief of Police Dwaine L. Wilson reported that in 1987 the burglary rate was 4.3 per 1,000 residents whereas the year before it had been 3.8 per 1,000. Given the small population, these figures do not amount to a large number of burglaries (39 in 1987). The police chief attributed the growing incidence of crime to the increased population and the fact that burglars were taking advantage of residents who worked during the day. Firearms cannot deter crime when home owners are not there to use them. This time the town responded to the increased crime rate by initiating a Neighborhood Watch program. The 1982 ordinance is still in effect, but not stringently enforced.

See also: American Civil Liberties Union; Morton Grove, Illinois.

Further Reading: David McDowall, Brian Wiersema, and Colin Loftin, "Did Mandatory Ownership in Kennesaw Really Prevent Burglaries?" *Sociology and Social Research* 74 (October 1989), 48–51.

Klanwatch Project

An affiliate of the Southern Poverty Law Center, the Klanwatch Project was founded in 1980 to accumulate data about the activities of the Ku Klux Klan and convey that information to government officials and the general public. The organization employs the legal system to sue those responsible for intimidating other citizens and to pass legislation that protects those groups that have been the target of Klan attacks. In the 1980s and 1990s, Klanwatch enlarged its campaign to include various militia groups it believed were influenced by racist elements. Although the organization recognizes the right of citizens to lobby against gun control legislation peacefully and to take part in various firearms sports, it observes that some gun rights advocates tend to use their opposition to gun control legislation as an excuse to form militia organizations that pose a threat to others.

In the 1980s, Klanwatch filed various lawsuits against the Ku Klux Klan and neo-Nazi groups. In 1984, the organization confronted Glenn Miller and his organization, the Carolina Knights of the Ku Klux Klan, which had been coercing minority groups in that area. After Klanwatch filed a lawsuit, Miller agreed to a settlement that required him to cease harassing blacks and to discontinue militia activities. However, two years later Miller began a militia organization called the White Patriot Party, an organization dedicated to establishing a "White Republic" in the American South. Klanwatch discovered that Miller had accumulated a large stash of stolen military weaponry and had engaged present military personnel to train the militia in the use of various military arms. The militia leader was arrested, tried, found guilty, and sentenced to

prison. When set free on bond, Miller announced a personal declaration of war on the government and minorities. The Federal Bureau of Investigation (FBI) finally arrested Miller in Springfield, Missouri, in a van loaded with weapons. Because of this sort of incident, Klanwatch has supported the enforcement of federal gun control legislation to limit the potential for violence on the part of militia groups tinged with racist ideologies.

Three years after filing suit against Miller and his militia group, Klanwatch sued Klan groups that had attacked civil rights marchers in Georgia. The suits severely hampered the operation of such groups. Two years later, in Portland, Oregon, Klanwatch sued Tom Metzger, leader of the White Aryan Resistance (WAR), who had provided for the training of the skin-head group responsible for the violence. The multimillion-dollar judgment against Metzger shut down his operation. In 1994, observing increased activity among militia organizations, Klanwatch established the Militia Task Force to monitor the activities of white supremacists who were attempting to gain control of militia organizations. Klanwatch feared that combining arms with racial hatred was an explosive combination.

In the 2000s, Klanwatch has gathered information and issued reports about the resurgence and activities of various private militia groups, militant opponents of gun control, and those with racist motivations that expanded their activities in the aftermath of the election of Barack Obama as president in 2008. Klanwatch has also focused on groups that insist on bearing arms as a protection against what they consider a tyrannical government, activities given fuel by the "Tea Party" movement founded in 2009. Klanwatch has looked approvingly on the enforcement of gun control legislation to check the development of such groups.

See also: Ku Klux Klan; Michigan Militia; Militia of Montana; Militia Watchdog.

Further Reading: *Intelligence Report: Meet the "Patriots,"* 138 (Summer 2010); Klanwatch Web site, www.klanwatch.org.

Kleck, Gary (1950–)

In the early 1990s, Gary Kleck, professor of criminology and criminal justice at Florida State

University, became a controversial figure in the gun control debate. Kleck's studies of gun control set the standard for social science research on the question and he assumed near-legendary status among gun rights advocates for suggesting that firearm ownership could contribute to a reduction in violent crime. His research publications produced claims that firearms are used defensively as many as 2.5 million times each year. Reputedly once a gun control advocate, Kleck has become skeptical about the potential success of gun regulations. Although he makes clear that he is affiliated with no gun rights organizations and that he is concerned solely with objective scientific investigation, various pro-gun groups see him as a major proponent for their cause.

Kleck received a Ph.D. in sociology from the University of Illinois at Urbana in 1979. Since then he has published two books and many articles and book chapters on various sociological topics, including questions related to firearms, self-defense against crime, and gun control. He has been interviewed numerous times on television and radio and is a contact person for such publications as *Newsweek*, *Time*, *U.S. News and World Report*, the *New York Times*, and the *Washington Post*. Kleck's research has been concerned with determining the costs versus the benefits of firearms ownership and gun control, the number of lives lost to the criminal use of firearms versus the number of lives saved by the defensive use of firearms, and the number of robberies or assaults involving a firearm versus the number of such events deterred by potential victims who own firearms. In 1993, Kleck's book, *Point Blank*, won the Michael Hindelang Award of the American Society of Criminology for the best book in criminology.

Several of Kleck's conclusions have been subject to criticism. Some question his claim that as many as 2.5 million defensive gun uses occur each year. In *The Politics of Gun Control* (2008), Robert J. Spitzer noted that Kleck began in 1991 by estimating between 606,000 and 960,000 defensive uses, but rounded that figure up to one million. Spitzer observed that by 1994 Kleck's estimate had increased to 2.4 million. Spitzer claimed that Kleck failed to distinguish between actual and imagined instances of self-defense uses of firearms. He concluded that "the numerous problems with Kleck's data are ironic in the light of his harsh criticism of the methodologies of those with whom he disagrees." Kleck, in a revised version of *Point Blank*, titled *Targeting Guns*, reported additional

findings derived from a National Self-Defense Survey to provide evidence of 2.5 million defensive gun uses. This number was also criticized because it was based on an extrapolation from telephone interviews conducted by Kleck where the statistical likelihood of actual defensive gun uses was actually far less than 2.5 million.

Kleck's investigations have led to the conclusion that not only can firearm ownership have significant positive results, its negative impact is not nearly as severe as previously assumed. Contrary to the assertions of many groups advocating more stringent gun control, Kleck states that fatal gun accidents seldom involve preadolescent children. He suggests that limitations on a specific group of firearms, such a handguns, would lead to the substitution of other, perhaps more lethal, types of weapons. In the case of suicide, Kleck concludes that limitations on the accessibility to firearms would lead to the substitution of other methods. Critics counter that suicide by gun is both more lethal than any other method, and is easier than any other method, meaning that a suicidal person who cannot find a gun is less likely to complete the act.

Responding to criticisms of his work on gun control that claim to find flaws in his data and methodology, Kleck states that scholars "are never entitled to ignore or discount strong and relevant evidence merely because it is flawed, for the simple reason that all evidence is flawed." He recommends that his critics employ more constructive strategies rather than engage in "scholarly misconduct" and apply the same level of skepticism to their own investigations of firearms.

Further Reading: Gary Kleck, *Targeting Guns: Firearms and Their Control* (Hawthorne, NY: Aldine de Gruyter, 1997); Robert J. Spitzer, *The Politics of Gun Control*, 6th ed. (Boulder, CO: Paradigm, 2015).

Knox, Neal (1935–2005)

For over two decades, more hardline gun rights elements in the National Rifle Association (NRA) and other organizations have looked to Neal Knox for leadership. He has headed some of the more aggressive campaigns against gun control. A former newspaperman, Knox first came to prominence in the NRA in 1977 when he led a revolt by members who were dissatisfied with the organization's apparent willingness to compromise on gun control issues and concerned about lags in the membership roles. That year, at the annual meeting in Cincinnati, Ohio, the organization selected Harlon Carter, also an uncompromising opponent of gun control, as the new executive vice president. Carter appointed Knox to head the NRA's lobbying organization, the Institute for Legislative Action (ILA).

Knox wanted to weaken the Gun Control Act of 1968. He strongly supported passage of the McClure-Volkmer firearms decontrol bill (also known as the Firearms Owners Protection Act), which Congress enacted in 1986. This law altered major provisions in the 1968 legislation. In addition, Knox focused the NRA's attention on the Bureau of Alcohol, Tobacco, and Firearms (ATF), the federal agency responsible for enforcing national firearms legislation. When Republican Ronald Reagan became president in 1981, Knox led an NRA campaign to weaken the ATF. At congressional hearings, a proposal arose that would place gun regulation authority in another governmental agency. However, Knox expressed reservations about such a move and finally opposed it. One possible reason for Knox's opposition to this proposal was concern that another government agency might prove far more efficient in executing gun control legislation. Although the agency was not destroyed, Congress limited its funding and authority.

Knox's uncompromising position on gun control led to the alienation of some police organizations from the NRA. In the early 1980s, when moves first began to limit armor-piercing, so-called "cop-killer," bullets, Knox was quoted as saying that there is no such thing as a good bullet or a bad bullet. Police organizations did not appreciate what they considered an antipolice position on the issue. In 1981, when the communist leadership imposed martial law in Poland, Knox placed advertisements in newspapers titled "An Open Letter to all Polish Americans" in which he stated that Poland had exactly the firearms laws that the NRA had prevented from being enacted in the United States and that the Second Amendment guarantee of the right to keep and bear arms, if observed, would prevent similar events from occurring in the United States.

In 1982, Knox was ousted from his position as director of the Institute for Legislative Action. In response, he established the Firearms Coalition, which operated from his consulting firm, Neal Knox Associates. In July 1984, he became a registered lobbyist representing the Coalition. In 1991, Knox campaigned to reestablish his position in the NRA. He informed members that the NRA was losing members and that J. Warren Cassidy, the current executive vice president, was responsible. He accused Cassidy of bad management practices and claimed that the organization faced bankruptcy under current leadership. At the 1991 annual meeting, Knox and 22 supporters won 23 of the 26 seats up for election on the board. The election results indicated that the NRA once again was moving toward a more hardline policy. Knox continued to write his column, "Knox's Notebook," for the NRA's *American Rifleman* and *Shotgun News*. In more recent years, his column dealt with such topics as President Bill Clinton's call for trigger locks, the defense of Saturday night specials or "junk guns," gun shows, the activities of the ATF, and various legislative proposals.

At the 1997 NRA annual meeting in Seattle, Knox lost his position on the board of directors, indicating that political struggles among factions in the NRA continue. Knox maintained a faithful following among pro-gun activists and remains a vocal advocate in the gun rights movement. Knox was a vocal critic of NRA president Charlton Heston and subsequent NRA leaders.

See also: American Rifleman; Bureau of Alcohol, Tobacco, Firearms, and Explosives; Clinton, William Jefferson (Bill); Firearms Coalition; Firearms Owners Protection Act; Gun Control Act of 1968; Heston, Charlton; Institute for Legislative Action; National Rifle Association; Reagan, Ronald; Saturday Night Special; Second Amendment; *Shotgun News;* Trigger Locks.

Further Reading: Firearms Coalition Web site, www.nealknox.com; Robert J. Spitzer, *The Politics of Gun Control* (Washington, DC: CQ Press, 2008).

Kopel, David B. (1960–)

David B. Kopel, research director since 1992 for the Colorado-based Independence Institute, has written extensively on the issue of gun control. He has criticized various proposals to restrict firearm ownership, including waiting periods and bans on semiautomatic assault weapons. He emphasizes that the Second Amendment guarantees the right to possess firearms for defense against the lawless as well as the government, and that the

David B. Kopel, research director since 1992 for the Colorado-based Independence Institute, has written extensively on the issue of gun control. *www.wikimedia.org*

amendment's reference to a militia assures the right of individuals to own military-type weapons.

In 1982, Kopel received a B.A. in history from Brown University and graduated magna cum laude from the University of Michigan Law School in 1985. He was assistant district attorney for the borough of Manhattan and assistant attorney general for Colorado where he represented state agencies in the enforcement of environmental laws. In addition to his position at the Independence Institute, Kopel is an associate policy analyst at the Cato Institute, a technical consultant for the International Wound Ballistics Association, and an adjunct professor at New York University Law School. Kopel has conducted research in many policy areas, including hazardous waste law, abortion, media violence, and criminal sentencing.

In 1992, Kopel published *The Samurai, the Mountie, and the Cowboy: Should America Adopt the Gun Controls of Other Democracies?* The book is an exploration of gun control policies in Japan, Great Britain, Canada, Australia, New Zealand, Jamaica, and Switzerland. Kopel looked at the broader historical, political, and cultural contexts of firearms policies in these varied countries, investigating the possibility of introducing into the United States the programs these countries have followed. Two later chapters deal with American

culture and the prospects for the success of gun control in the United States. He declared that the proliferation of firearms in the United States is not directly related to a high crime rate. Countering a fundamental assumption of pro-gun control forces that firearms are an independent cause of greater levels of violence, Kopel argued instead that "America's crime has much more to do with the absence of internal social controls than with the absence of statutory gun controls."

In response to the Stockton, California, school shooting committed by a lone gunman using an assault weapon, Kopel cautioned against outlawing such weapons. He claimed that the core of the Second Amendment is the militia, not hunting. The constitutional guarantee of a popular militia ensures the existence of a force "capable of overthrowing a domestic tyrant, or of resisting an invasion by a foreign one." In response to gun control groups that contend the idea of a militia is obsolete, Kopel argued that citizen forces were still important to defense against invasion or during times of internal disruption.

Kopel predicted that any additional controls, including waiting periods and background checks, would have little effect on criminals' acquisition of firearms. He compared the situation to the restrictions on ownership of automatic weapons that have been in place since enactment of the National Firearms Act of 1934, claiming that "the system is a total failure" because such weapons are "readily obtainable, even by teenage gang members." Kopel concluded that the only control that could have prevented the Stockton killings was keeping the shooter in prison when authorities had the opportunity.

In 1997, Kopel coauthored with Paul H. Blackman *No More Wacos: What's Wrong with Federal Law Enforcement, and How to Fix It*. Kopel viewed the federal law enforcement agencies as increasingly militaristic, violent, and lawless. In addition to the Waco standoff, Kopel discussed the Randy Weaver shooting and other cases of the use of federal law enforcement agents. Kopel made several proposals for altering federal law enforcement agencies, including reforming forfeiture laws and revising arrest procedures, which would contribute to the maintenance of an individualistic interpretation of the right to keep and bear arms. In 2009, Kopel published *Aiming for Liberty*, a critical look at the history of gun control.

See also: Assault Weapons Ban; Australia; Canada; Gun Culture; Independence Institute; Media Violence; National Firearms Act of 1934; National Instant Check System; Ruby Ridge; Second Amendment; Stockton, California, Shooting; United Kingdom; Waco, Texas, Raid.

Further Reading: David B. Kopel, *The Samurai, the Mountie, and the Cowboy: Should America Adopt the Gun Controls of Other Democracies?* (Buffalo, NY: Prometheus, 1992); David B. Kopel and Paul H. Blackman, *No More Wacos: What's Wrong with Federal Law Enforcement, and How to Fix It* (Buffalo, NY: Prometheus, 1997); David B. Kopel, *Aiming for Liberty* (Bellevue, WA: Merril Press, 2009).

Ku Klux Klan

Gun rights supporters refer to the American experience with the Ku Klux Klan to illustrate the fundamental advantages of gun ownership to maintaining rights of self-protection. They cite the Klan's objectives during the post–Civil War Reconstruction era to disarm blacks in the former slave states of the South. They also cite other incidents, running from the early postwar years through the civil rights movement of the 1960s, where blacks were successful in warding off Klan violence by possessing firearms and demonstrating a determination to use them if needed. Gun control supporters viewed the Klan's terrorist activities as an example of the use of guns by private individuals to terrorize and murder innocent people as the kind of lawless violence gun control is designed to prevent and punish.

The original Klan was established by former Confederate soldiers who opposed the imposition of Reconstruction on the defeated southern states. The organization was founded in Pulaski, Tennessee, in May 1866, and the following year Nathan Bedford Forrest, a noted Confederate cavalry officer, assumed the position of Grand Wizard. In 1869, apparently concerned about the violent tactics of local Klan organizations, Forrest ordered that the Klan disband and stepped down as the organization's Grand Wizard. However, the Klan continued, determined to use violence and intimidation to keep blacks from voting or taking part in other political activities. Klan members adopted a wardrobe that included a flowing white robe, a white mask, and skulls on their saddle horns.

The original Klan subsided after the end of Reconstruction, but underwent a resurgence in 1915 when William J. Simmons established a second Klan organization. The revived Klan endorsed a wider agenda, including anti-Catholic and anti-Jewish bias and a nativist platform reminiscent of the "Know-Nothing" party in the 1850s. In the 1920s, the Klan reached a reported nationwide membership of 4 million. However, by 1930 the total number of Klansmen had declined to around 30,000. State laws forbidding the wearing of masks and the hard economic times brought on by the Great Depression contributed to the organization's demise. The Klan has had at least two resurrections since then, including Samuel Green's attempt to revive the organization in Georgia after World War II and Robert Shelton's efforts in Mississippi during the civil rights movement of the 1960s.

Although gun rights supporters suggest that citizens can resist oppression best if they possess the tools to protect themselves, some historians indicate that blacks after the Civil War faced significant handicaps in the effective use of firearms. The weapons they owned were usually shotguns, which did not match up against the Winchester rifles and the handguns that Klan members carried. Black military experience generally paled in comparison to Klansmen who had participated in the Civil War. Even when blacks had gained military experience, they were usually outnumbered by hostile whites who generally were well trained in the use of arms. Even when blacks successfully deterred Klan assaults, there was often a price to pay. The greatest problem facing blacks in the South was that the local white-dominated government sided with the Klan, and the federal government ceased providing protection when federal troops withdrew in the 1870s.

Although many blacks armed themselves for self-defense and organized themselves into militia groups, hostile whites often responded with great indignation, increasing violence, and greater numbers. At times, opponents of Reconstruction took extreme measures to ensure white dominance in southern states. In certain parts of the South, it became apparent that any blacks who confronted the Klan with firepower would suffer dire consequences. In most instances, blacks found themselves in an unenviable dilemma: Radical Republican officials usually hesitated to take measures to resist the Klan, and efforts at organized self-defense could result in intensified violence.

In Arkansas and Texas, where the legal order supported the black community, greater success was achieved in resisting the Klan. Arkansas Governor Powell Clayton employed the state militia, composed of blacks and whites loyal to the Republicans, to arrest suspected Klan members. A few were executed and many fled the state. In Texas, Governor Edmund J. Davis organized a state police force in which 40 percent of the membership was black. From 1870 to 1872, blacks were provided with effective protection as the state police suppressed the Klan, arresting over 6,000 suspected members. The success that Clayton and Davis experienced against the Klan indicated that a willingness to employ organized force sanctioned by the government could be an effective tool against what otherwise appeared to be an unbeatable organization. However, the use of such force could backfire, as it did in North Carolina, where Governor William W. Holden's administration fell after his use of the state militia produced sympathy for the Klan.

Although contemporary gun rights advocates argue strongly in favor of upholding the right of self-protection, the example of the Ku Klux Klan suggests that individual resistance may produce complex consequences that limit the possibility of success, or even increase the probability of escalating the level of violence and death.

See also: African Americans and Guns; Black Codes; Klanwatch Project.

Further Reading: Robert J. Cottrol and Raymond T. Diamond, "The Second Amendment: Toward an Afro-Americanist Reconsideration," in David B. Kopel, ed., *Guns: Who Should Have Them?* (Amherst, NY: Prometheus, 1995); Barry A. Crouch, *The Freedmen's Bureau and Black Texans* (Austin: University of Texas Press, 1992); Eric Foner, *Reconstruction: America's Unfinished Revolution: 1863–1877* (New York: Harper and Row, 1988); Ku Klux Klan Web site, www.kukluxklan.org.

L

LaPierre, Wayne (1950–)

In 1991, the National Rifle Association (NRA) board of directors elevated longtime pro-gun activist Wayne LaPierre to the position of executive vice president. LaPierre, director since 1986 of the NRA's lobbying arm, the Institute for Legislative Action (ILA), had gained a reputation for the resolute support of gun rights and firm opposition to gun control measures. Although LaPierre appeared to lack some of the aggressive qualities of past presidents, his strong credentials for uncompromising stands on gun control led the nominating committee to submit his name alone to the board of directors. LaPierre promised a continuing fight against new proposals for firearms legislation.

LaPierre began his career with the NRA in 1978 at the age of 28 as a lobbyist in the state and local affairs division of the ILA. By 1986, he was serving as the director of federal affairs. When the NRA board removed G. Ray Arnett as executive vice president, LaPierre rose to the position of executive director of the ILA. Guiding the NRA's fortunes in the political arena, he pushed to have public officials favorable to the organization's agenda elected to office. For instance, in 1988, he informed NRA members that if Democratic presidential candidate Michael Dukakis won the election, the liberal president would use his influence over the Justice and Treasury Departments to ban guns in the United States. In 1989, when President George H. W. Bush's director of the Office of Drug Policy, William Bennett, declared that the Bureau of Alcohol, Tobacco, and Firearms (ATF) would prohibit the importation of five types of assault weapons, LaPierre quickly met with White House chief of staff John Sununu regarding the proposed action.

Blaming the press for the fear of assault weapons, the NRA held that such a ban would prevent law-abiding citizens from using the weapons for legitimate sporting purposes.

As executive vice president, LaPierre has maintained the NRA's tenacious stand against any measures intended to limit the possession or carrying of firearms. He has warned the membership about the perceived intention of Democratic Presidents Bill Clinton and Barack Obama to limit the rights of firearms owners. LaPierre has called for unity in the NRA to oppose gun measures at the national level through grassroots organizing and lobbying. He urges gun owners to join in protecting the Second Amendment against attacks that, he claims, could lead to more restrictive gun legislation, as occurred in Australia and the United Kingdom. LaPierre labels various proposed gun control measures as efforts to

NRA executive vice president Wayne LaPierre speaks during the NRA-ILA Leadership Forum at the 2015 NRA Annual Meeting & Exhibits on April 10, 2015 in Nashville, Tennessee. *Photo by Justin Sullivan/Getty Images*

"disarm the innocent," leaving citizens exposed to criminal attack. To oppose such measures, LaPierre has called for the election of a pro-gun president, keeping a pro-gun Congress, and educating a pro-gun public. In 1997, he enlisted the assistance of actor Charlton Heston, recruited to serve as NRA first vice president, to assist in a public relations campaign to publicize the NRA's positions on gun rights and gun control. Heston was subsequently elected president of the organization as LaPierre's preferred candidate. LaPierre's recruitment of Heston was a key political move within the NRA to head off a more extremist element within the NRA. Heston's popularity and high visibility succeeded in thwarting more extremist challenges with the organization, and consolidated LaPierre's power within the NRA. In the post-Heston NRA, LaPierre has retained his power base and influence within the organization, and has become its most visible spokesperson.

LaPierre has continued to be the most public face of the NRA. Shortly after the Sandy Hook elementary school shooting in December 2012, LaPierre gave a press conference, televised nationally, in which he argued against new gun laws and for putting armed guards in every public school.

See also: Australia; Bureau of Alcohol, Tobacco, Firearms, and Explosives; Bush, George H. W.; Clinton, William Jefferson (Bill); Heston, Charlton; National Rifle Association; Sandy Hook elementary school shooting; Saturday Night Special; Second Amendment; United Kingdom.

Further Reading: Wayne LaPierre and James Jay Baker, *Shooting Straight: Telling the Truth about Guns in America* (Washington, DC: Regnery, 2002); Robert J. Spitzer, *The Politics of Gun Control,* 6th ed. (Boulder, CO: Paradigm, 2015).

Large Capacity Ammunition Magazines (LCAMs)

Following several high-profile mass shootings in recent years (for instance, the 1999 Columbine high school shooting, the 2009 shooting at Fort Hood, Texas, the Aurora, Colorado, theater shooting, the 2015 San Bernardino, California, shooting, and the Orlando, Florida, shooting) in which the gunmen used large capacity ammunition magazines, gun control supporters have called for a renewal of the federal limitation on the ammunition capacity of firearms.

In 1994 Congress passed, and President Bill Clinton signed, the Violent Crime Control and Law Enforcement Act, which contained a ban on certain so-called semi-automatic assault weapons as well as a prohibition on the transfer or possession of large capacity ammunition feeding devices that were not owned prior to passage of the legislation. The law defined a prohibited magazine as one that had a capacity of more than ten rounds of ammunition. Anticipating the ban, manufacturers increased production in the months prior to the law's enactment and thus the magazines continued to be available to consumers. The law had a time limit of ten years, and so when its expiration approached in 2004, Congress failed to renew the assault weapons ban and its accompanying prohibition on large capacity ammunition magazines.

However, eight states along with the District of Columbia have instituted their own bans on large capacity magazines. Three states—Hawaii, New Jersey, and New York—and the District of Columbia prohibit the possession of LCAMs acquired prior to the ban, and thus require such magazines to be destroyed or transferred to law enforcement authorities or other appropriate recipients. Although Connecticut does not ban pre-law magazines, the state requires that lawful owners register them with the State Department of Emergency Services and Public Protection. Colorado and Massachusetts do not require registration of pre-ban magazines. Although California and Maryland do not prohibit possession of pre-ban magazines, they ban their manufacture and transfer. In 2013 the California legislature banned the use of kits that allow the construction of large capacity magazines.

Following the San Bernardino shooting in which a man and woman killed 14 people and wounded 21 others, gun control advocates urged Congress to reinstate a ban on LCAMs. However, bills in the Senate were defeated and the House of Representatives failed to consider such legislation. Gun rights organizations opposed the reintroduction of a ban, arguing that a prohibition would not impede a mass shooter but would restrict the rights of law-abiding citizens who want to possess large capacity magazines for sporting purposes and for self-defense.

See also: Assault Weapons Ban; Feinstein, Dianne; San Bernardino, California, Shooting; Orlando, Florida, Shooting.

Further Reading: Law Center to Prevent Gun Violence, "Large Capacity Magazines." smartgunlaws.org/gun-laws/policy-areas/classes-of-weapons/large-capacity-magazines. Accessed June 16, 2016; Jacob Sullum, "The Threat Posed by Gun Magazine Limits" (January 16, 2013). www.reason.com/archives/2013/01/16/the-threat-posed-by-gun-magazine-limits.

Lautenberg, Frank R. (1924–2013)

U.S. Senator Frank Lautenberg, a liberal Democrat from New Jersey, was a major supporter of gun control legislation. He was most well known in relation to gun control for the Lautenberg Amendment, which he attached to the fiscal 1997 Omnibus Appropriations bill. This amendment prohibited anyone convicted of domestic violence against a spouse or child from owning a firearm. A member of the President's Commission on Aviation Security, Lautenberg successfully attached the proposal to the fiscal 1997 transportation appropriations bill that funded President Bill Clinton's request for airport security. In 1997, Lautenberg proposed additional firearms legislation. Along with Senator Joseph Biden, Democrat of Delaware, he called for regulations to increase security at gun shops, stating that "incredible as it may seem, there are no federal minimum standards for security of premises and merchandise at gun shops." The bill provided for the secretary of the Treasury to formulate regulations establishing minimum gun safety and security requirements for federally licensed firearms dealers. He stated that from 1994 to 1997 over 30,000 firearms were stolen from gun dealers.

The son of an immigrant silk mill worker, Lautenberg served in the U.S. Army during World War II and received a B.S. degree from Columbia University in 1949. He amassed a personal fortune in private business and became a major supporter for Democratic candidates, but never ran for public office before competing successfully for the U.S. Senate in 1982. Beginning in the 105th Congress in 1997, Lautenberg became the ranking Democrat on the Senate Budget Committee. Lautenberg was willing to work with committee chairman, Pete Domenici, and other Republican leaders in developing an agreement with the Clinton administration that promised to balance the federal budget by 2002. His ability to work with the Republican majority contributed to the success of his gun control amendment.

Lautenberg has gained the enmity of tobacco interests and pro-gun groups alike. In 1989, the senator, formerly a heavy smoker, backed a smoking ban on domestic airline flights. In 1993, he sponsored an amendment banning smoking in federal buildings. Lautenberg's reform efforts have extended into the environmental arena, where he fought against reductions in funding for environmental protection and advocated continued appropriations for cleanup efforts. From 1994 to 1996, Lautenberg was a member of a bipartisan task force to establish new guidelines for gifts from lobbyists. He objected to the political access that lobbyists were receiving from congresspeople that ordinary citizens do not have.

Lautenberg had his appropriations bill amendment passed despite strong resistance from the National Rifle Association (NRA), arguing that the provision would save the lives of many abused wives and children. While the NRA and other gun rights groups portray Lautenberg as a misguided individual who does not understand the true meaning of the Second Amendment and the defensive value of firearms, the senator regards gun organizations as major stumbling blocks to social reform. Gun control groups have a strong supporter in Lautenberg, but in February 1999 he announced that he would not run for a fourth Senate term in 2000. But in 2002, he came back from retirement at the behest of state Democrats, and again won election to the Senate. He was re-elected in 2008, but passed away in 2013 while still holding office.

See also: Clinton, William Jefferson (Bill); Lautenberg Amendment; National Rifle Association; Second Amendment.

Further Reading: "Antis Push Gun Shop Security Legislation," *Gun News Digest* (Winter 1997–1998), 9; *CQ's Politics in America: The 111th Congress* (Washington, DC: CQ Press, 2009).

Lautenberg Amendment

In 1996, a gun control measure called the Lautenberg Amendment after Democratic Senator Frank Lautenberg of New Jersey, was attached to a continuing resolution approving federal spending. The measure is also called the Domestic Violence Offender Gun Ban. The legislation prohibits anyone convicted of committing an act of domestic violence against a spouse or child from purchasing or owning a firearm. Despite opposition from the National Rifle Association (NRA), other gun rights organizations, and Republicans in the House of Representatives, gun control advocates successfully included the amendment, which received little public notice.

Gun control supporters argued that the measure was necessary to close a loophole in existing legislation. Although laws prohibited convicted felons from purchasing firearms, no statute dealt with misdemeanor convictions. Because domestic violence and child abuse are often prosecuted as misdemeanors, those convicted of such acts remained free to purchase and possess firearms. The gun control measure prevents anyone who has been convicted of a misdemeanor in a domestic violence episode from owning, carrying, or transporting a gun. Supporters of the measure hoped that it would lessen the probability of family conflicts escalating into firearm-related violence.

The Senate passed the legislation in July 1996, but the Republican leadership prevented its approval in the House of Representatives. In September, the Senate again passed the measure by a vote of 97-2. However, still opposed to the original proposal, House Speaker Newt Gingrich of Georgia and other House Republicans formulated an alternative version of the bill that would exempt any individual convicted for a domestic violence misdemeanor by a judge rather than a jury. Because a large proportion of misdemeanor cases are tried before a judge rather than a jury, many found guilty of domestic violence would have avoided the restriction on gun ownership. When Democratic President Bill Clinton and Senator Lautenberg refused to compromise on the measure, Speaker Gingrich and the House Republican leadership finally agreed to accept the original bill. Republicans did not want to be held publicly responsible for delaying the budget agreement between Democrats and Republicans, which was the major focus of the bill.

Soon after President Clinton signed the bill, the National Association of Police Organizations and other police unions protested the gun control measure, claiming that it was unenforceable in the general public and would deny many police officers their jobs. Several police officers in major American cities discovered that they were disqualified from carrying a firearm because they had at some time in the past been convicted of a misdemeanor involving a domestic violence charge. By December, some had already surrendered their guns and been told that they were reassigned to desk duty and could lose their jobs. In Minneapolis, Minnesota, four officers were reassigned to desk duty or put on paid leave. Trying a different strategy, the sheriff's department in Denver, Colorado, requested that deputies who had been convicted of misdemeanor convictions surrender their firearms before leaving work. The federal government began an honor system, asking all employees who carry weapons to state in writing that they had never been convicted of a misdemeanor involving domestic violence. Questions also arose regarding the application of the new legislation to military personnel.

While supporters of the measure argued that police officers should be able to meet a high standard of conduct on the job and off, opponents charged that the legislation amounted to an ex post facto law that punished individuals for crimes committed before the law was passed. They also argued that the law did not allow for the possibility that people who committed a misdemeanor years ago might have altered their behavior since the offense. Several congresspeople called for an amendment that would make the law apply only to new cases, while gun rights groups, such as Gun Owners of America (GOA) advocated its complete repeal. The Clinton administration announced its opposition to any changes in the legislation and it remains in effect.

In 2016, the Supreme Court ruled on a constitutional challenge to the amendment. In the case of *Voisine v. U.S.*, the high court turned aside a challenge to the law, based partly on the Second Amendment, ruling that domestic abusers convicted of minor (misdemeanor) domestic-violence charges are not entitled to keep their right to own guns just because their crimes were merely reckless, as opposed to premeditated. This was the third such challenge to the law heard by the court since 2009.

See also: Clinton, William Jefferson (Bill); Gun Owners of America; Lautenberg, Frank R.; National Association of Police Organizations; National Rifle Association.

Further Reading: *New York Times* (October 1, 1996), 24; Larry Reibstein and John Engen, "One Strike and You're Out," *Newsweek* 128 (December 23, 1996), 53.

Law Enforcement Alliance of America (LEAA)

In 1989, the organization Law Enforcement for the Preservation of the Second Amendment was formed; in 1990, the group became the Law Enforcement Alliance of America (LEAA). The LEAA describes itself as a legislative advocacy organization comprised of law enforcement and corrections officers, private law enforcement personnel, crime victims, and "concerned citizens." It also gives as its mission fighting competing groups that "want to ban our guns, raid our privacy, and sully the U.S. Constitution." The organization maintains its headquarters in Falls Church, Virginia. The founders of the LEAA received financial support from the National Rifle Association (NRA) to establish the organization. The LEAA has taken a strong position in opposition to additional gun control legislation, campaigning against the Brady Handgun Violence Prevention Act and bans on assault weapons. The Alliance has backed a national legislative proposal to allow police officers to carry weapons outside their jurisdictions, and various state proposals to liberalize carrying concealed weapons (CCW) laws.

The LEAA maintains that most police officers do not support gun control, which the organization defines as "restricting the rights of, and disarming, peaceable citizens." The organization maintains that, unlike other police organizations, it represents officers' views on gun control, contending that the "real cops" oppose "any and all efforts to erode Second Amendment rights." The only form of gun control the organization supports is keeping firearms away from violent felons, including habitual criminals, drug users, drug dealers, and those who arm themselves with illegal or altered firearms. The LEAA advocates severe penalties for those who use a firearm in the commission of crimes.

The LEAA claims that present federal firearms legislation provides sufficient legal measures to deter individuals from using firearms while committing crimes. James J. Fotis, executive director of the LEAA, notes that legislation bars convicted felons, illegal aliens, those dishonorably discharged from the armed forces, and those judged insane from purchasing, owning, selling, or using any firearm. Fotis observes that using a firearm during the commission of a crime can result in an additional five-year sentence and a $250,000 fine. He believes that such stiff penalties certainly will "catch the attention of even the most dense-skulled underworld neanderthal."

Unlike the LEAA, other law enforcement organizations, such as the Police Executive Research Forum, the International Association of Chiefs of Police, and the National Sheriffs Association, have supported gun control proposals, particularly the Brady law, and opposed efforts to liberalize concealed carry laws. The LEAA explains its position by claiming that these organizations have received millions of dollars from the Justice Department in return for their support for gun control measures. The LEAA asserts that the rank-and-file members of other police organizations do not support the official pro-gun control positions of the leadership.

See also: Assault Weapons Ban; Brady Handgun Violence Prevention Act; Concealed Carry Laws; International Association of Chiefs of Police; National Rifle Association; Police Executive Research Forum; Second Amendment.

Further Reading: Peter Harry Brown and Daniel G. Abel, *Outgunned: Up Against the NRA* (New York: The Free Press, 2003); Law Enforcement Alliance of America Web site, www.leaa.org; Robert J. Spitzer, *The Politics of Gun Control* (Washington, DC: CQ Press, 2008).

Law Enforcement Officers Protection Act

The Law Enforcement Officers Protection Act of 1986, which banned the sale of armor-piercing ammunition (so-called "cop-killer" bullets), had political significance beyond the immediate provisions of the legislation. Police organizations such as the International Association of Chiefs of Police found themselves on the opposite side of the issue from the National Rifle Association (NRA), which for four years opposed efforts to have Congress ban bullets that could pierce body armor that police wear for self-protection. NRA opposition to the legislation allowed Handgun Control, Inc., the leading gun control organization, to forge alliances with police organizations that ultimately proved valuable in the effort to pass the Brady Handgun Violence Prevention Act in 1993.

Armor-piercing bullets, also referred to as KTWs after their inventors, three individuals named Kopsch, Turcus, and Ward, are composed of hard metals such as tungsten alloys, steel, brass, bronze, iron, beryllium, copper, or depleted uranium. When first developed, the ammunition was considered to be of value to police officers for stopping automobiles used in a crime because the bullets could pierce engine blocks. Police departments ultimately discovered that the ammunition was impractical because it represented a significant risk of harm to innocent bystanders. When police officers discovered that the bullets could be used against them, they called for banning the sale of such ammunition to the general public.

The struggle for legislation to prohibit the manufacture and sale of armor piercing bullets began in 1982. An initial test of political strength came at the local level when the Brookhaven, Long Island, Town Board considered an ordinance to outlaw KTW bullets for handguns. The NRA opposed this local action and sent telegrams to members encouraging them to attend the meeting called to consider adoption of a ban. James Baker, a lobbyist for the NRA, presented the basic position of the organization: No amount of legislation can alter human behavior by attempting to control physical objects.

Although police officers expressed concern regarding their safety, the NRA made the controversial claim that no police officer wearing a bulletproof vest had been wounded or killed by an armor-piercing bullet. The organization argued that the move to ban a type of ammunition represented just another tactic by gun control advocates to limit the right to keep and bear arms. Two top NRA officials, Neal Knox and J. Warren Cassidy, insisted that bullets by themselves are neither good nor bad and that the crucial factor is how they are used. Legislation banning ammunition would only limit law-abiding citizens and could not control criminal behavior.

A bill to ban KTW bullets was introduced into the U.S. Senate by Daniel Patrick Moynihan, Democrat of New York, and in the House by Mario Biaggi, Democrat of New York, a longtime veteran of the New York City Police Department. The initial bills defined armor-piercing handgun ammunition in terms of their ability to penetrate at least 18 layers of Kevlar, the material used to manufacture bulletproof vests. The NRA objected that this criterion was far too broad and would ban many types of rifle as well as handgun ammunition.

In 1986, the NRA, concerned about gaining support for passage of the Gun Owners Protection Act and faced with the intense push by law enforcement organizations for legislation regulating ammunition, communicated its willingness to compromise. The compromise definition shifted the criterion from degree of penetration to the hard-metal content of ammunition. The NRA removed its objections to the bill and it was passed by Congress and signed by Republican President Ronald Reagan in August 1986. The legislation outlawed the manufacture, import, or sale of KTW bullets, but exemptions were allowed for the manufacture of bullets for long guns used in hunting that are designed to meet federal and state environmental standards. Such ammunition must be marked and packaged with a label identifying it as armor piercing. Anyone violating the law was made subject to a five-year mandatory sentence.

See also: Brady Handgun Violence Prevention Act; Firearms Owners Protection Act; Handgun Control, Inc.; International Association of Chiefs of Police; Knox, Neal; National Rifle Association; Reagan, Ronald.

Further Reading: Earl R. Kruschke, *Gun Control* (Santa Barbara, CA: ABC-CLIO, 1995); Robert J. Spitzer, *The Politics of Gun Control,* 6th ed. (Boulder, CO: Paradigm, 2015); Josh Sugarmann, *National Rifle Association: Money, Firepower, and Fear* (Washington, DC: National Press, 1992).

Lawful Commerce in Arms Act of 2005 (PL 109-92; 119 *Stat.* 2095)

From the time of the election of George W. Bush as president in 2000, the National Rifle Association's top legislative priority was to obtain legislation to protect the gun industry and gun dealers from litigation. For several decades sporadic lawsuits had been filed against gun manufacturers and dealers seeking damages to compensate gun crime victims. The legal basis for such actions is the tort law principle that individuals or other entities can be held responsible for selling products that, although legal, needlessly or willfully expose others to great risk of harm. For example, the Ford Motor Company was sued for civil liability in the 1970s for its design and production of the Ford Pinto because the Pinto's gas tank was located in such a way that the car was likely to explode when hit from behind. The poor design feature was not illegal, but Ford executives knew of the defect and sold millions of the cars anyway.

In lawsuits regarding guns, litigants argued that handgun manufacturers knew that, because of their sales and distribution practices, a disproportionate number of their guns wound up in criminal hands (leading to claims of "negligent distribution practices"). In addition, the failure of some companies to install simple and inexpensive safety features yielded additional legal charges.

A case in point was successful litigation against Bushmaster Firearms Inc. of Windham, Maine, and Bull's Eye Shooter Supply store of Tacoma, Washington. In 2002 two men were arrested (and later convicted) for committing ten fatal sniper shootings in the Washington, DC, area. One of the men purchased the gun they used, a .223 Bushmaster rifle (a slightly altered, civilian version of the military M-16), at Bull's Eye. Subsequent investigations revealed that at least 238 guns "disappeared" from the shop—that is, investigators assumed that at least some of the guns had been sold without proper paperwork. Among the 238 missing guns was the one used in the shooting spree. The Tacoma gun store agreed to pay $2 million to eight plaintiffs; Bushmaster agreed to pay $550,000. The gun company's liability was based on the assumption that it could have required the store to implement simple security measures by threatening to withdraw its stock.

Gun control foes decried this litigation, arguing that it was an abuse of the civil justice system that would only bankrupt gun manufacturers and pad lawyers' bank accounts, and that it amounted to back-door gun control. Supporters argued that some in the gun industry were, indeed, culpable and that they should be subject to the same civil law standards as rogue companies in other areas. And they argued against granting any special protection to the gun industry by pointing out that no other business sector enjoyed similar protections. Litigation proponents were emboldened by a similar effort against cigarette manufacturers, who agreed to pay major settlement costs because of a variety of deceptive and improper practices related to the chemical manipulation and marketing practices pertaining to cigarettes. NRA efforts to

legislate gun manufacturer immunity were not limited to Congress. By 2005 thirty-three states had also passed laws barring such lawsuits by localities (called "preemption" laws).

The public had, at best, mixed feelings about such litigation efforts aimed at perceived industry wrongdoing, and Republican leaders highly sympathetic to the gun lobby controlled both Congress and the presidency. In 2003 momentum to provide federal liability protection finally resulted in passage of a bill by the House of Representatives. The Senate was slower to act, but in March 2004 it was poised to approve the same bill. Gun control proponents, however, after failing to block the bill, managed to attach to it amendments to extend the federal assault weapons ban (by a 52–47 vote), slated to expire that September, to require background checks for all gun purchases at gun shows (closing the so-called gun show loophole, added by a 53–46 vote), and to require safety locks to be sold with new handguns (approved 70–27). Infuriated, NRA leaders insisted that the bill be defeated rather than accept the "poison pill" amendments; within hours it failed by a vote of 8–90.

The failure of the 108th Congress to enact the bill was remedied in the 109th. Fortified with an increase in Republicans in both houses, in July 2005 the Senate passed the measure by a 65–31 vote, partly thanks to key support from fourteen gun-sympathetic Democrats, including Democratic Minority Leader Harry Reid of Nevada. Senate majority leader Bill Frist of Tennessee avoided the problems from the previous year by employing a procedural tactic to limit amendments. The measure also got a lift when officials in the American military sent a letter to Congress in July saying that companies providing weapons to the military needed to be protected for national security reasons. The House passed the bill in October by a 283–144 vote. The bill passed with bipartisan support from 223 Republicans and 60 Democrats; voting against were 140 Democrats and 4 Republicans. As passed and signed by President Bush, the Protection of Lawful Commerce in Arms Act of 2005 bars civil suits against gun manufacturers, distributors, dealers, and importers of firearms and ammunition, although it makes an exception for certain cases involving defective guns or expressly criminal behavior by manufacturers or dealers, as, for example, when a gun is knowingly sold to someone not legally entitled to own a gun. The immediate effect of the law was to halt more than a dozen ongoing court cases in states around the country. The law did not affect cases that had already been resolved. The measure also included a requirement that handguns be sold with locks, and it barred the manufacture or importation of armor-piercing bullets. In the aftermath of winning this unique protection for the gun industry, other businesses lobbied Congress to obtain similar immunity.

Further Reading: Robert J. Spitzer, *The Politics of Gun Control,* 6th ed. (Boulder, CO: Paradigm Publishers, 2015)

Lawyer's Second Amendment Society (LSAS)

The Lawyer's Second Amendment Society (LSAS), was small organization of about 200 members that filed *amicus curiae* briefs in court cases involving firearms legislation. The organization held that the Second Amendment affirms a "God-given and individual right" to keep and bear arms. Therefore, any law restricting that right lacks any authority. Noting that most judges denied this understanding of the right to bear arms, the organization worked to alter prevailing judicial interpretations of the Second Amendment. Part of the organization's strategy included opposing judicial nominations of candidates who did not support an individualistic interpretation of the Second Amendment. For instance, the LSAS opposed Senate ratification of President Bill Clinton's federal court nomination of Margaret Morrow, who, as president of the California State Bar in 1993–94, strongly supported a gun control resolution. However, in 1998, the Senate ultimately confirmed Morrow's nomination.

The Society was established in 1994 and incorporated in 1996. As of 2010, the organization was no longer active. It published a bimonthly newsletter, *Liberty Pole*, which had a circulation of 3,000.

The Society identified four basic objectives: (1) to persuade other attorneys that the Second Amendment guarantees an individual right to keep and bear arms; (2) to fund and also engage in litigation to proclaim an individualistic interpretation of the Second Amendment; (3) to offer guidance for attorneys across the country regarding Second Amendment questions; and (4) to serve as a center for research and information

on the Second Amendment. Recognizing that "reasonable limitations" may be placed on any of the rights identified in the Bill of Rights, the LSAS conceded that the right to keep and bear arms could be subject to restrictions.

See also: Brady, Sarah; Bureau of Alcohol, Tobacco, Firearms, and Explosives; Clinton, William Jefferson (Bill); Law Enforcement Alliance of America; National Rifle Association; Second Amendment.

Further Reading: Robert J. Spitzer, *Gun Control: A Documentary and Reference Guide* (Westport, CT: Greenwood Press, 2009).

Legal Action Project (LAP)

Legal Action Project (LAP), an affiliate of the Brady Center to Prevent Gun Violence (formerly Handgun Control, Inc.), was established in 1989 to advocate gun control policies in the courts and to facilitate litigation against gun manufacturers and dealers. LAP defends gun control laws at the national, state, and local levels against challenges initiated by such organizations as the National Rifle Association (NRA). Its founding head was Dennis Henigan. The organization provides legal assistance to victims of gun violence seeking court-awarded damages, and has advanced litigation on behalf of municipalities seeking damages related to gun violence. In addition to participating in litigation, lawyers associated with LAP have challenged the interpretation of the Second Amendment advocated by gun rights organizations. They have published articles and appeared in the media attacking the position that the Second Amendment guarantees an individual right to keep and bear arms.

One of the Project's major goals is the maintenance of previous legislative victories. LAP provides pro bono services to government attorneys who are defending gun control statutes. Among its services, the organization provides attorneys with data supporting gun control statutes, legal briefs that were filed in other cases, the outcomes of recent court rulings, suggestions for expert witnesses, and assistance with legal strategy. The Project files *amicus curiae* briefs to support government defense of firearms legislation. LAP participated in the defense of the temporary five-day waiting period, established in the Brady Handgun Violence Prevention Act in 1994, against NRA-backed lawsuits. The Project has assisted the California attorney general in court defenses of that state's ban on semiautomatic weapons and defended various state and local provisions against the charge that they violate state constitutional provisions regarding the right to keep and bear arms. It also argued on behalf of the militia-based interpretation of the right to bear arms in the Supreme Court cases *District of Columbia v. Heller* (2008) and *McDonald v. Chicago* (2010).

LAP calls for innovations in the design of firearms to reduce the potential danger such weapons present, especially to young people. Guns should include appropriate technology to prevent unauthorized use. Of special concern to the Project is the difficulty in determining whether a firearm has been completely unloaded. In addition to calling for design changes, the Project faults firearms manufacturers for marketing such guns as assault weapons and Saturday night specials that the organization considers only suitable for criminal use. Other products, such as so-called cop-killer bullets and mail-order parts that may be assembled into untraceable guns, are considered to have no legitimate use.

The Project attempts to hold gun dealers legally responsible for sales to individuals who are ineligible to purchase firearms. Open to criticism are dealers who provide inadequate security systems to prevent theft and dealers who take part in bulk purchases that are used to supply guns for criminal activity. LAP has addressed what it considers the serious problem of illegal sales at gun shows. The organization recommends limiting handgun sales to one per month to an individual to prevent "straw-man" sales, prohibiting the sale of firearms at gun shows, and requiring improved security procedures at retail firearms outlets. LAP filed an *amicus curiae* brief in a Florida court case (*Kitchen v. K-Mart*, 1997) in which the state supreme court held that retail gun dealers are legally required to refuse selling a firearm to an intoxicated buyer and may be held liable for any harm resulting from a sale to such a person. In several legal actions, the Project has attempted to hold negligent owners responsible for the misuse of their firearms by others.

The Project has focused its attention on firearm advertising, contending that the firearms industry presents the false impression that a handgun will keep the purchaser safe from criminal attack. The Project makes three recommendations regarding firearms advertising. First, no claims about home and personal security should be made. Second, advertisements should not appeal to "the criminal element or others prone to violent behavior." Finally, no ads should appear in publications aimed at youth.

See also: Assault Weapons Ban; Brady Handgun Violence Prevention Act; Gun Shows; Henigan, Dennis; Legal Community Against Violence; National Rifle Association; Product Liability Lawsuits; Saturday Night Special; Second Amendment; Youth and Guns.

Further Reading: Legal Action Project Web site, www.bradycenter.org/legalaction/.

Legal Community Against Violence (LCAV)

The Legal Community Against Violence (LCAV), based in San Francisco, California, was established in 1993 in reaction to the murder in that city of eight people and the wounding of six others. The organization is a public interest law center committed to reducing gun-related violence through legislative initiatives, participation in litigation, and support for educational programs. The LCAV invites those in the legal profession to assist in drafting model legislation, conducting legal research, and offering pro bono legal assistance to municipal and county governments that have enacted gun control ordinances. The organization maintains information about local government ordinances and legal briefs regarding legal challenges to firearms legislation.

The LCAV offers government officials the legal means to enact firearms policies that the organization believes will save lives. The organization has provided legal assistance to local governments that face challenges from pro-gun groups. At the national level, the LCAV supported passage of the Brady Handgun Violence Prevention Act, the assault weapons ban, and other gun measures. It opposes the extension of concealed carry laws. In California, lobbying efforts have contributed to passage of state laws to deny firearm access to minors, to grant judges the authority to order the confiscation of weapons from individuals subject to restraining orders, and to hold gun owners responsible if minors injure themselves or others with a firearm that was negligently made available to them.

As part of its Local Ordinance Project, the LCAV distributes information such as the publication, "Gun Laws Matter: A Comparison of State Firearms Laws and Statistics," which shows that states with stricter gun laws tend to have lower levels of gun violence. Its publication "America Caught in the Crossfire: How Concealed Carry Laws Threaten Public Safety,"examines the risks to public safety caused by liberal concealed carry laws. It also provides extensive information on Second Amendment case law, and on the effect of recent pro-gun decisions of the Supreme Court on state and local gun laws.

The organization refers to a long series of legal precedents that associate the right to keep and bear arms with membership in an organized state militia, and quotes noted early Americans, such as James Madison and Patrick Henry, to support the position that the intent of the Bill of Rights was to allow states to maintain a military force independent of the national government. Going beyond legal arguments, the LCAV reports opinion poll results indicating that a large majority of Americans support "common sense gun control laws" such as statutes placing stricter controls on handguns.

See also: Assault Weapons Ban; Brady Handgun Violence Prevention Act; Concealed Carry Laws; Gun Shows; Saturday Night Special; Second Amendment; State Laws, Appendix 2; Trigger Locks.

Further Reading: Legal Community Against Violence Web site, www.lcav.org.

Lewis v. United States (1980)

The U.S. Supreme Court in *Lewis v. United States* (445 U.S. 55, 1980) upheld a lower court conviction under section 1202 (a) (1) of Title VI of the Omnibus Crime Control and Safe Streets Act of 1968. This provision states that any person convicted by a federal or state court of a felony shall be prohibited from possessing a firearm. The appellant had been convicted of the disabling charge prior to the Supreme Court decision in *Gideon v. Wainwright* (1963), which held that a state court felony conviction where the defendant did not have counsel and did not refuse counsel is unconstitutional under the Sixth and Fourteenth Amendments to the U.S. Constitution.

In 1961, George Calvin Lewis, Jr., arrested for breaking and entering, was found guilty of a felony in a Florida court upon pleading guilty to the charge. He was not represented by counsel. Lewis served a term in prison. Subsequently, the Supreme Court ruled, in *Gideon v. Wainwright*, that states must provide counsel to defendants who cannot afford legal defense in criminal cases. Lewis never appealed his conviction and it was never overturned. In January 1977, Lewis was arrested in Virginia for knowingly receiving and possessing a firearm in violation of provisions in the Omnibus Crime Control Act. Lewis argued that because he had not been represented by counsel in the 1961 case, that conviction had violated his constitutional rights and therefore should not act against him in the present case.

The court rejected the argument, ruling that the constitutionality of the previous conviction was irrelevant in the present case. Lewis appealed the decision to the U.S. Court of Appeals for the Fourth Circuit, which affirmed the conviction for illegal gun possession. The Supreme Court, hearing the case on appeal from the Circuit Court, investigated the intentions of Congress when writing this provision. The Court found no evidence that Congress intended to allow a defendant to challenge the validity of the prior conviction as a defense of the firearm possession charge. Congress employed "sweeping" language, including no restrictions on the term "convicted." Therefore, the felony conviction clearly results in a prohibition of firearm ownership until the conviction is canceled, or the felon either receives a pardon from the president or a state governor, or obtains permission from the secretary of the Treasury to possess a firearm.

In addition to a possible pardon or permission from the secretary of the Treasury, Lewis could challenge his previous conviction in the Florida state court system, seeking an official reversal of the original conviction. In any event, a defendant must clear his or her record prior to obtaining a firearm, thus complying with the intent of the law to "keep firearms away from the persons Congress classified as potentially irresponsible and dangerous." The Court concluded that Congress's intentions constituted a "rational basis" for legal distinctions and hence were in agreement with the Due Process

Clause of the Fifth Amendment. In addition, the relationship between the right to keep and bear arms and the efficiency of a well-regulated militia stated in the Second Amendment affords Congress the power to regulate firearms. The Court affirmed the ability of Congress constitutionally to prohibit certain activities on the part of a convicted felon and concluded that Congress was acting reasonably when it decided that a convicted felon fell in the category of those prohibited from dealing in or possessing firearms, even if the conviction occurred devoid of counsel.

See also: Fourteenth Amendment; Second Amendment.

Further Reading: *Lewis v. United States*, 445 U.S. 55 (1980).

Libertarian Party

The Libertarian Party, which believes that individuals possess the right to complete sovereignty over their own lives, liberty, and property—as long as they respect the equal rights of others—takes an uncompromising stand against the regulation of firearms. The party deems illegitimate any government interference in the private lives of citizens. Libertarians oppose victimless crime laws and any other government regulation of personal affairs and support private education, protection of property rights, and an unregulated free-market economy. In its commitment to a classical liberal ideology, the party objects to such government activities as foreign aid, welfare, environmental regulations, and consumer protection laws. Because of their uncompromising position on limiting government involvement in the lives of private citizens, Libertarians oppose any government attempts to regulate the possession or carrying of firearms.

In their 2010 party platform, Libertarians embraced the individualist view of the Second Amendment and personal self-defense: "We affirm the individual right recognized by the Second Amendment to keep and bear arms, and oppose the prosecution of individuals for exercising their rights of self-defense. We oppose all laws at any level of government requiring registration of, or restricting, the ownership, manufacture, or transfer or sale of firearms or ammunition."

The party supported repeal of the National Firearms Act of 1934 and the federal Gun Control Act of 1968 and called for the abolition of the Bureau of Alcohol, Tobacco, and Firearms (ATF), the federal agency responsible for enforcing firearms legislation. Laws banning the concealment of weapons also came under attack, as did prohibitions on inexpensive handguns, or Saturday night specials, and semiautomatic assault weapons and magazines. Libertarians also oppose limitations on the use of other self-protection devices such as tear gas and mace, and believe all existing limitations should be eliminated.

The party argues against any gun control measures on theoretical as well as practical grounds. Libertarians contend that gun ownership as such harms no one else and thus is a matter of personal choice. Such ownership cannot justifiably lead to any criminal penalties. Practically, party members argue that gun control, like Prohibition and the present drug laws, is unenforceable. The true victims of gun control laws are honest citizens who have lost the right to defend themselves. The party holds that only if a large proportion of citizens are armed can the nation deter violent crime.

Libertarians support severe penalties for anyone who commits a crime using a gun. Any negligent gun user should be held fully responsible for any harm done to others. However, to the extent that citizens are well-armed and trained in the use of firearms, the party believes that the nation is better protected from crime and the threat of foreign invasion. The Libertarian Party does not indicate whether government should take the responsibility for assuring that firearms owners receive the appropriate training. However, given the party's individualist ideology, it is not likely to support granting this role to government.

See also: Assault Weapons Ban; Bureau of Alcohol, Tobacco, Firearms, and Explosives; Gun Control Act of 1968; National Firearms Act of 1934; Saturday Night Special.

Further Reading: Libertarian Party, National Platform (Washington, DC: Libertarian National Committee, Inc., 2016); Libertarian Party, "Why Libertarians Support Equal Rights for America's Gun Owners," pamphlet (Washington, DC: Libertarian National Committee, Inc., n.d.); Libertarian Party Web site, www.lp.org.

Littleton, Colorado, Columbine School Shooting

The Littleton, Colorado, school shooting at Columbine High School, which occurred in April 1999, followed a series of similar incidents in 1997 and 1998. The shooting galvanized a national debate over what measures might be taken to curb incidents in which armed youth have killed and wounded fellow students and teachers. Soon after the incident President Bill Clinton unveiled several gun control proposals that passed in the U.S. Senate, but were defeated in the House of Representatives. These measures, advanced in the shadow of Columbine, initiated an extensive debate over the effectiveness of additional legislation in preventing gun-related violence.

On April 20, two students armed with semiautomatic weapons, sawed-off shotguns, and homemade bombs, attacked fellow students at Columbine High School in Littleton, a suburb of Denver, Colorado. The two male youths killed 12 students and 1 teacher and wounded several others before killing themselves as SWAT teams attempted to reach them. The national media gave the shootings extensive coverage and precipitated attempts to place blame and discover possible causes, including the ready availability of firearms. The National Rifle Association (NRA), which had scheduled its annual convention in Denver, announced that it would curtail, but not cancel, the meeting. When the NRA met on May 1, 8,000 people gathered to protest the meeting. Two measures to liberalize gun restrictions were removed from the Colorado state legislature's agenda.

President Clinton, who had been planning a series of new gun control proposals prior to the Colorado shooting, decided to make public his gun control agenda one week after the incident. Clinton called for banning gun sales and ownership to anyone under 21 years of age. Background checks would be required for the sale of firearms at gun shows and child safety locks would be mandated for each new firearm sold. Adults who allow children access to firearms would be subject to a prison term of 3 to 10 years and a fine of $10,000. Negligent parents would be held legally responsible if their children committed crimes

The Columbine Memorial in Littleton, Colorado. *www.wikimedia.org*

with guns. Anyone committing violent crimes as juveniles would be subject to a lifetime ban on firearm ownership. In addition, Clinton called for the reintroduction of a waiting period for handgun purchases. The waiting period would be three days with a possible two-day extension if law enforcement officers needed the extra time to complete a check. Another measure would provide for treating explosives sales, including dynamite and blasting caps, the same as gun sales under the Brady Handgun Violence Prevention Act. Senator Charles Schumer, Democrat from New York, proposed allowing only licensed firearms dealers to have Web sites for trading in firearms.

While gun control advocates were proposing additional legislation, gun rights supporters were questioning the need for additional measures restricting firearms sales and ownership. Critics of additional gun control noted that no additional laws would have prevented the Littleton shooting, indicating that other causal factors, such as parental supervision and school security, must be addressed. Advocates of additional restrictions on guns argued that although such measures could not eliminate such incidents, the probability of violence could be minimized.

Stronger gun control provisions passed the U.S. Senate as part of a juvenile justice bill, including such requirements as background checks for purchasing firearms at gun shows, safety devices to be sold with handguns, raising the minimum age for purchasing a handgun from 18 to 21, and a ban on imported high-capacity ammunition clips. However, the U.S. House of Representatives focused attention on other possible causes of violence, such as violence in the mass media, lack of parental supervision of youth, a too lenient juvenile justice system, and lack of respect for moral authority. A compromise gun control bill, proposed by John Dingell, Democrat from Michigan, failed to gain passage. A coalition of conservative Republicans and Democrats, including Dingell, opposed the measure. President Bill Clinton attributed the defeat of strong gun control legislation in the House to the lobbying efforts of the NRA.

See also: Assault Weapons Ban; Brady Handgun Violence Prevention Act; Clinton, William Jefferson (Bill); Jonesboro, Arkansas, School Shooting; National Instant Check System; National Rifle Association; Schools and Guns; Schumer, Charles E.; Stockton, California, Shooting; Trigger Locks; Youth and Guns.

Further Reading: Dave Cullen, *Columbine* (New York: Twelve Publishers, 2009); "Caught in the Cross-Fire: How Gun Control Turned into a Casualty of the Capital Wars," *Newsweek* (June 28, 1999), 31–32; Michael Bane, "A Gun Owner Looks into His Heart: The Tragedy in Littleton, Colorado," *Handguns* 13 (August 1999), 22–23.

Long Gun

Gary Kleck defines a long gun as "a larger firearm with a long barrel and a buttstock, designed to be fired with the buttstock held against the shoulder." Long guns, which include rifles and shotguns, are generally associated with hunting and other sports activities. In contrast, handguns, which include revolvers and semiautomatic pistols, more often bring to mind use in criminal activities. The distinction between handguns and long guns—real and perceived— have resulted in gun control advocates focusing primarily on the control or banning of handguns, while allowing the continued ownership and use of long guns. Americans own twice as many long guns as handguns.

A rifle is a long gun that has a rifled barrel— the inside of the barrel has spiraled grooves. Usually firing one round with each pull of the trigger, rifles may place bullets in the firing position in one of two different methods: cartridges may be placed into position by the mechanical action of a manually operated bolt, lever, or pump, or a semiautomatic mechanism places a new round in the chamber as the gun is fired. Shotguns are constructed with one or two barrels and fire a shell containing many round pellets, or possibly a rifled slug. A shotgun may require reloading after each firing of the barrels, or may have a semiautomatic mechanism that usually holds two-to-five shells, but can contain as many as 20. Older models that require manual reloading may also have hammers that must be cocked for each firing.

Gun control advocates argue that long guns are of less concern for potentially illegal use because they are not nearly as easy to conceal as handguns. Sawed-off versions of long guns are an exception, and have been banned by federal firearms legislation. Also subject to control are assault rifles, which have been defined as rifles with military characteristics that are capable of semiautomatic fire. Critics of current gun control efforts note that in many cases rifles not covered by present legislation actually have a far more destructive effect than handguns or assault rifles.

Critics of the gun control agenda assert that a policy of classifying firearms for purposes of regulation cannot succeed in bringing about reduced rates of firearm use in criminal acts because to ban one type of weapon will lead to substituting others. They claim that far more deadly weapons, such as long guns, will be used more frequently than handguns for illicit purposes should handguns be banned. In addition, critics claim that any weapon that can be used by a criminal to commit a crime can also be valuable to the potential victim for self-defense. Not long guns, but the smaller handgun can be concealed on the person for self-defense when in public, or kept in an available place in the home should the need arise. Gun control advocates argue against the substitution hypothesis by noting that handguns are the preferred choice for those who commit crimes with guns: while there are twice as many long guns as handguns in America, and long guns are easier to obtain, 80 percent of gun crimes are committed with handguns. Further, the very availability of handguns makes them far more dangerous than long guns. For instance, they claim that children are major potential victims of accidents involving handguns. In addition, gun control advocates reject the notion of allowing large numbers of citizens to carry concealed weapons in public places.

See also: Assault Weapons Ban; Kleck, Gary; Sawed-Off Shotgun; Youth and Guns.

Further Reading: David Hemenway, *Private Guns Public Health* (Ann Arbor, MI: University of Michigan Press, 2004); Gary Kleck, *Targeting Guns: Firearms and Their Control* (Hawthorne, NY: Aldine de Gruyter, 1997).

Lott, John R., Jr. (1958–)

John R. Lott, Jr., has gained widespread attention for publishing research results indicating that "shall issue" concealed carry laws contribute to reduced crime rates. He argues that increased gun ownership leads to less, not more crime. Lott has been a visiting faculty member at various institutions, and was attached to the American Enterprise Institute until 2006. Lott no longer has an institutional affiliation; instead, he created the Crime Prevention Research Center, which

he heads. Lott's book, *More Guns, Less Crime*, first published in 1998, elicited a large response from both sides of the gun control debate. The book contains a complex analysis of a huge data set derived from Federal Bureau of Investigation (FBI) yearly crime reports. Many of the findings had already been published in a paper by Lott and David B. Mustard titled "Crime, Deterrence, and Right-to-Carry Concealed Weapons."

Lott received his B.A., M.A., and Ph.D. in economics from the University of California at Los Angeles. Before arriving at the University of Chicago in 1994, Lott held positions at several educational institutions, including Cornell University Law School, the University of Pennsylvania, Rice University, and Texas A&M University. From 1988 to 1989, he was chief economist for the U.S. Sentencing Commission in Washington, D.C.

Lott's study involved crime data for the nation's 3,054 counties for the 14-year period extending from 1977 to 1994 (he later extended his analysis through 2000). He concluded from his analysis that various gun control measures, such as waiting periods, gun buyback programs, and background checks, have little effect on crime reduction. His study proposed that one gun policy yielded significant results: "right-to-carry" laws that allow citizens to have concealed weapons. Lott argued that adoption of shall-issue gun carry laws in 31 states resulted in drops in crimes.

According to Lott, states with concealed carry laws on average reduced the murder rate by 8.5 percent, rapes by 5 percent, aggravated assaults by 7 percent, and robbery by 3 percent. He estimated that if those states without concealed carry laws had permitted concealed handguns in 1992, the number of murders would have been reduced by 1,570, rapes by 4,177, aggravated assaults by 60,000, and robberies by 12,000. Lott claimed that crime rates fall each year a concealed carry law is in effect: murder by 3 percent, rape by 2 percent, and robbery by 2 percent.

Lott concluded that two factors explained the lower rates of violent crime in states with concealed carry laws. First, such laws act as a deterrent to crime. Although a small proportion of the population carries concealed weapons, those contemplating a crime cannot tell who is armed and who is not. Second, those carrying firearms are able to defend themselves if an attack occurs. Lott asserted that a handgun provides women a much greater defensive capability than it does men, measured by the reduction in the murder rate.

A number of researchers who analyzed Lott's data concluded that his analysis did not support the "more guns, less crime" hypothesis. Researchers Dan A. Black and Daniel S. Nagin, for example, analyzed Lott's data and concluded that there was "no statistically significant evidence that RTC [right to carry] laws have an impact on any of the crime rates." Among their criticisms, they note that Lott's model over- or underestimated crime rates in states that adopted concealed carry laws; that Lott's model erroneously assumed "uniform impact" of concealed carry laws across states that enacted them; that when the single case of Florida (a state where crime rates are highly volatile) was removed from the total analysis, all the beneficial consequences Lott attributes to the enactment of concealed carry laws disappeared. Black and Nagin concluded that Lott's model was "inappropriate" for his stated purposes, and that his findings "cannot be used responsibly to formulate public policy." Criminologist Gary Kleck, doubted the veracity of Lott's claims. After discussing the speculative nature of Lott's findings, Kleck concludes: "More likely, the declines in crime coinciding with relaxation of carry laws were largely attributable to other factors not controlled." Researchers Ian Ayres and John J. Donohue published several articles reexamining Lott's data, including Lott's data updates through the 1990s. They conclude that the strongest correlation between the adoption of concealed carry laws and crime rates is an increase in crime in some categories, and no statistically significant correlation between such laws and crime in other categories. They found no support for Lott's hypothesized decline in crime rates.

Lott's reputation also suffered from other revelations, as when he repeatedly said that "98 percent of the time that people use guns defensively, they merely have to brandish a weapon to break off an attack." After first claiming that the number came from national surveys, none of which actually reported such a number, he then claimed that it came from a survey he conducted. Yet he later claimed that he lost the data from the survey, and its existence was never established. In 2003, Lott's critics discovered that a person named "Mary Rosh" who wrote frequent, highly praiseworthy Internet comments about Lott, his written work, and his teaching during the previous three years,

was in fact Lott himself (although he claimed it was actually his teenage son's doing). The last name "Rosh" was derived from the first two letters of the names of two of his four sons (Roger and Sherwin).

See also: Concealed Carry Laws; Gun Buyback Programs; Johns Hopkins Center for Gun Policy Research; Ludwig, Jens Otto; Pacific Center for Violence Prevention; Schools and Guns; State Laws, Appendix 2; Violence Policy Center.

Further Reading: Ian Ayres and John J. Donohue, "More Guns, Less Crime Fails Again: The Latest Evidence from 1977–2006," *Economic Journal Watch* 6 (May 2009), 218–38; Dan A. Black and Daniel S. Nagin, "Do Right-to-Carry Laws Deter Violent Crime?" *Journal of Legal Studies* 27 (January 1998), 209–219; John R. Lott, Jr., *More Guns, Less Crime: Understanding Crime and Gun Control Laws* (Chicago: University of Chicago Press, 2010).

Ludwig, Jens Otto (1968–)

In his academic career, Jens Otto Ludwig has had a prolific research and publication record, including collaborative projects dealing with firearms. As a graduate student, Ludwig worked with firearms researcher Philip Cook at Duke University. He has challenged claims that firearms can be valuable for self-defense and has participated in debates on the issue. In 1998, he appeared as an expert witness before the Committee on Public Safety of the California Assembly, providing testimony on proposed carrying concealed handgun legislation.

Ludwig received a B.A. in economics from Rutgers College in 1990 and an M.A. and a Ph.D. in economics from Duke University in 1992 and 1994, respectively. His primary areas of specialization are econometrics and labor economics. While a professor of public policy at Georgetown University, Ludwig served in 1998 as a visiting scholar at the Northwestern University/ University of Chicago Poverty Center. In 2007, he joined the faculty at the University of Chicago, and is the McCormick Foundation Professor of Social Service Administration, Law and Public Policy at Chicago, where he is also Director of the University of Chicago Crime Lab, and Co-Director of the University of Chicago Urban Education Lab. In addition to his research on firearms, Ludwig has studied education issues, including such subjects as school choice, determinants of academic achievement, and the effects of private schooling on the probability of juvenile criminal involvement. Ludwig has conducted research on the effects of family structure on various forms of youth delinquent behavior.

Ludwig participated in a study titled *Guns in America: National Survey on Private Ownership and Use of Firearms,* which was supported by the U.S. Justice Department's National Institute of Justice (NIJ). The results of the study, which involved a 1994 telephone survey of over 2,500 adults, were released in May 1997. Ludwig observed that fewer people are keeping firearms for hunting and recreational use while the ownership of firearms for self-protection is increasing. The survey results estimated that 42 percent of men and just 9 percent of women own firearms. At the study's release, Attorney General Janet Reno, commenting on the finding that over half of firearms kept in the home are unlocked, advocated legislation to require childproof safety locks on newly sold firearms.

In 1997, Ludwig submitted an affidavit in support of the Canadian Firearms Act, which includes stringent controls on handguns. He has criticized John Lott's research results, which indicate that state laws permitting carrying concealed weapons deter crime. In 1998, Ludwig appeared with Lott in a forum held at Washburn University that was sponsored by the Koch Crime Commission. Ludwig focused his comments on what he perceived to be flaws in Lott's methodology and analysis of the data. He claimed that Lott failed to take account of other variables affecting the violent crime rate, such as gang activity, poverty levels, and the crack cocaine epidemic. Ludwig concluded that there is no compelling evidence that laws permitting

carrying concealed weapons have deterred crime. In response to Lott's contention that concealed carry laws could deter multiple shootings, Ludwig commented that although such events were important from a public health position, they were too infrequent to draw a statistical conclusion.

Ludwig has suggested that a more valid measure of the effects of liberalized concealed carry laws would involve an examination of trends in the gap between adult and juvenile homicide victimization. He argues that because states with concealed carry laws require permit holders to be at least 18 years old, and in many cases 21, the deterrent effect should differentially benefit adults. Therefore, the gap between adult and juvenile victimization rates should be expected to narrow in states with liberalized laws. Ludwig states that his analysis of homicide data at the state level for the years 1977 to 1994 indicate no such effect.

Ludwig also coauthored a book with Philip Cook, *Gun Violence: The Real Costs.* In the book, the authors estimate that the total annual monetary cost for gun violence in America is $100 billion. They also examine the specific categories and consequences of gun violence.

See also: Concealed Carry Laws; Cook, Philip J.; Lott, John R., Jr.; Reno, Janet; Trigger Locks; Youth and Guns.

Further Reading: Philip J. Cook and Jens Ludwig, *Gun Violence: The Real Costs* (New York: Oxford University Press, 2000); Jens Ludwig, "Do Carry-Concealed Weapons Laws Deter Crime?" *Spectrum: The Journal of State Government* 70 (Spring 1997), 29, 31; Daniel W. Webster, John S. Vernick, Jens Ludwig, and Kathleen Lester, "Flawed Gun Policy Research May Endanger Public Safety," *American Journal of Public Health* 87 (June 1997), 918–21.

M

Mailing of Firearms Act (MFA)

Prior to the major push for gun control legislation in the 1930s that ultimately resulted in passage of the National Firearms Act of 1934 and the Federal Firearms Act in 1938, the Mailing of Firearms Act of 1927 (MFA), also known as the Miller Act, was one of the few successes for gun control advocates. The law, which is still in effect today, prohibits sending through the U.S. Post Office pistols and other firearms that could be concealed on the person.

Consideration of the MFA followed soon after the introduction of another gun control bill supported by Senator John K. Shields, Democrat of Tennessee. The Shields bill would have prohibited the interstate shipment of all handguns except service revolvers, the so-called "big pistols" that Shields considered appropriate for home protection. The bill received legislative consideration in 1921, but extensive opposition developed. Because firearms manufacturing companies were highly concentrated geographically, the bill would have had a significant effect on the industry. Representatives of gun interests argued that the bill's restrictions might jeopardize national defense. Senator Frank Brandegee, Republican from Connecticut, a major gun manufacturing state, strongly opposed the bill and kept it from ever leaving the Judiciary Committee. When Shields lost his reelection bid in 1924, the bill died.

Republican Representative John F. Miller experienced greater success in gaining passage of a gun control bill. Miller's constituents in Seattle, Washington, concerned with the mail-order sales of handguns, pressed him to introduce legislation to prohibit mail shipments of handguns. Unlike the Shields bill, Miller's proposal received wide support. An organized letter writing campaign informed Republican President Calvin Coolidge that the availability of pistols through the mail was tempting young people into criminal activity. A resolution from the United National Association of Post Office Clerks supported the legislation. The opposition of gun advocates could not overcome the strong support for the bill. No representatives from small arms manufacturers appeared at the hearings. One witness, a spokesman for the American Reclamation Society of Detroit, presented an argument that would be heard many times in the coming decades: The small number of firearms in Great Britain was responsible for that nation's low crime rate and therefore more stringent gun control legislation was also needed in the United States.

In the debate on the House floor, congressmen from the gun manufacturing states of Massachusetts and Connecticut offered no opposition to the bill. What opposition developed came from congressmen from southern and western states, who objected to the bill because they believed it violated the Second Amendment right to keep and bear arms. At a time when states rights predominated, they argued that the legislation would result in the proliferation of federal officials intent on violating state sovereignty. Congressman Thomas Blanton, Democrat of Texas, offered an anti-gun control argument that continues to be used: Despite the legislation, criminals would acquire guns, while law abiding citizens would have their constitutional rights violated.

Once the bill was approved by both houses, President Coolidge signed it into law in February 1927. His support of the legislation notwithstanding, Coolidge remained skeptical regarding the prospects for success of gun control legislation, especially in view of the miserable experience with federal enforcement of Prohibition.

As the *Saturday Evening Post* observed, "If the Federal government cannot prevent the landing and distribution of shiploads of rum, how can it stop the criminal from getting the most concealed and vital tool of his trade?" The MFA effectively stopped mail shipments of handguns, but the measure had limited scope. In the meantime, firearms manufacturers were successful in opposing other legislation, and were also able to gain protection from foreign competition when Congress passed the Fordney-McCumber Tariff of 1922 and the Hawley-Smoot Tariff of 1930. The legislative battles of the 1920s established the pattern for future political struggles over gun control proposals. *See also:* Federal Firearms Act of 1938; National Firearms Act of 1934; Second Amendment; United Kingdom.

Further Reading: Lee Kennett and James La Verne Anderson, *The Gun in America: The Origins of a National Dilemma* (Westport, CT: Greenwood, 1975); *New York Times* (February 10, 1924), 46.

Martin, Trayvon, and George Zimmerman

In 2005, Florida became the first state to adopt an enhanced "stand your ground" law. Enacted at the behest of intense lobbying efforts of the National Rifle Association, this law expanded a legal protection by codifying two important ideas: the first, already found in some state laws, was that Floridians no longer had a duty to retreat from a dangerous situation in a public place if they had a right to be where they were. Other states require that the person feeling threatened retreat if it is possible to do so safely, as had been the law in Florida until 2005. The second, however, was a significant departure from past similar laws, in that it reversed the burden of establishing guilt or innocence in violent confrontations in public places. The critical provision of the Florida law gives to a person claiming self-defense "an absolute and irrebuttable presumption that an individual who kills or harms another. . .has acted in self-defense and cannot be prosecuted." Law enforcement must thus presume that an individual making a self-defense claim acted out of reasonable fear, a standard met by nothing more than the individual's claim to such a fear.

This law change garnered little public attention until the shooting death of a seventeen-year-old

Young supporters gather during a candelight vigil at a memorial to Trayvon Martin outside The Retreat at Twin Lakes community where Trayvon was shot and killed by George Zimmerman. *Photo by Mario Tama/Getty Images*

African American teenager, Trayvon Martin, by neighborhood watch volunteer George Zimmerman in 2012. Zimmerman was patrolling a local neighborhood in Sanford, Florida on a rainy night in February 2012 when he saw a tall, African-American male wearing a hooded sweatshirt wandering the neighborhood. When Zimmerman called in the sighting, the dispatcher advised him to remain in his vehicle. Instead, Zimmerman left to follow the person he had seen. Zimmerman was armed with a handgun, which he carried legally (although police authorities urge neighborhood watch volunteers not to carry firearms). Within minutes, the two had some kind of encounter, during which Zimmerman shot and killed Martin with a single bullet to the chest at close range. Martin was unarmed; Zimmerman suffered cuts to his head and face. Martin had been visiting his father in the neighborhood where he had been seen wandering, and had gone to a local store to purchase a drink and a bag of candy, but had become disoriented in the darkened, unfamiliar neighborhood. Zimmerman was charged with murder, but was found not guilty in a jury trial in July 2013.

While Zimmerman did not expressly invoke the "stand your ground" defense, the Florida law played a key role throughout the investigation and trial. As a result of the Florida law, because Zimmerman claimed that he acted in self-defense, the police conducted a less thorough initial investigation, nor was he arrested or held. The judge's instructions to the jury were altered because of the stand your ground law, to the advantage of Zimmerman. After Zimmerman's acquittal, the possibility of a civil action against him was all but eliminated because of a near-prohibition of such suits in the law. In addition, some also felt that race had played a role in the shooting, charging that Zimmerman might have responded less aggressively if Martin had not been an African American, and suggesting that public sympathy might also have been greater had the teenager been white. In the years after his acquittal, Zimmerman had a series of run-ins with law enforcement. In 2016, Zimmerman put the gun he used to kill Martin up for sale on the internet, where it reportedly sold for over $120,000.

Further Reading: Richard Maxwell Brown, *No Duty to Retreat* (Norman, OK: University of Oklahoma Press, 1994); Kris Hundley, et al., "Florida 'Stand Your Ground' Law Yields Some Shocking Outcomes Depending on How the Law is Applied," *Tampa Bay Times,* June 1, 2012; Robert J. Spitzer, *Guns across America: Reconciling Gun Rules and Rights* (New York: Oxford University Press, 2015)

Maryland One-Gun-Per-Month Law

Although the U.S. Congress has not enacted a one-gun-per-month statute that would limit an individual to purchasing just one firearm in a 30-day period, Maryland enacted such a law in October 1996. As of 2012, three states, including California, New Jersey, and the District of Columbia had such laws. The Maryland statute provided the opportunity for interests on both sides of the gun control debate to evaluate the effectiveness of the measure. The number of purchases involving two or more handguns at a time declined from 7,569 in the 12 months before the law went into effect to 1,618 during the subsequent 12 months (the law allowed the continuation of multiple sales to gun collectors). Total handgun sales declined in Maryland from 41,726 in 1994 to 21,500 in 1997, and remained relatively low thereafter.

The purpose of a one-gun-per-month statute is to restrict "straw purchases," the practice of buying a large number of guns legally and then selling them on the street to be used for criminal purposes. Democratic Governor Parris N. Glendening, who signed the bill into law, claimed that the provision has been effective in keeping illegal handguns off Maryland streets. Preliminary data support Glendening's claim. From 1995 to 1997, the number of guns sold in multiple sales that were involved in crimes in the District of Columbia declined from 23 to 0, and in Baltimore from 26 to 0. However, studies indicate that Maryland remains the primary source of firearms for the District.

Critics claim that such laws simply cause criminals to substitute other weapons for handguns. The increase in police seizures of long guns relative to handguns lend support to this claim. While the seizure of handguns in Baltimore increased 23 percent from 1995 to 1997, the seizure of long guns increased 63 percent. Data from other locations in Maryland followed the same trend: The rate of increase in long gun seizures outpaced that of handguns, suggesting that those engaged in criminal activities were substituting long guns for handguns.

Lieutenant Governor Kathleen Kennedy Townsend, a Democrat, asserted that in 1997 the new law was responsible for a 9 percent decline in homicides, rapes, robberies, and aggravated assaults in Maryland. However, because the crime rate declined nationwide during the same period, many doubted that the new law could take sole credit for the reduction in Maryland.

One possible unintended consequence of the law might have been an increase in gun shop burglaries. State police reported that in the 18 months prior to passage of the legislation, two gun dealers reported burglaries, while in the 18 months following passage, 13 burglaries were reported. Criminals unable to bypass limitations on acquiring firearms by resorting to straw purchases may have resorted to theft.

While overall sales of handguns declined following the bill's passage, opponents of the measure argued that a general business downturn resulted in reduced sales. In addition, they argued that multiple sales of handguns never were common and that gun stores had not served as major sources of weapons for criminals. While the new law may deter a minor source of illegal handguns, opponents argue it inconveniences legitimate buyers. *See also:* Long Gun; Violent Crime Rate.

Further Reading: Philip P. Pan, "Maryland Handgun Sales Down 25 Percent: Drop Comes Year One-a-Month Buying Limit Was Imposed," *Washington Post* (May 27, 1998), A1.

Maryland v. United States (1965)

The U.S. Supreme Court decision in *Maryland v. United States* (381 U.S. 41, 1965) affects the question of gun control only indirectly, but has more direct significance for the status of state militias. In its decision, the Court commented that the National Guard constitutes the militia reserved to the states in Article I, section 8, clauses 15 and 16 of the U.S. Constitution. Although gun rights advocates argue that so-called "unorganized" militias established by private citizens fall under the claimed Second Amendment guarantee to keep and bear arms, the Court's interpretation of the modern militia leaves little room for informal organizations whose members claim to constitute the militia sanctioned by the Constitution.

The case arose from a collision between a commercial airliner and a Maryland Air National Guard jet trainer. In a suit brought against the United States under the Federal Tort Claims Act by the estates of the pilot and copilot of the commercial plane and the airline company, both parties accepted the trainer pilot's negligence. The main question to be decided was whether the National Guard pilot was acting in his military capacity or as a civilian at the time of the accident. The district court ruled that the pilot had acted as a civilian under the supervision of the federal government and therefore the federal government was liable for his actions. Because two separate district court rulings and subsequent appeals came to different conclusions, the Supreme Court agreed to hear the case.

The Supreme Court ruled that whether the pilot was acting in his military or civilian capacity, he remained an employee of Maryland, not of the United States. The National Guard constitutes the modern equivalent of the militia provided for under Article I, section 8, clause 16 of the Constitution, which reserves to the states "the appointment of the officers, and the authority of training the militia according to the discipline prescribed by Congress." In 1916, to provide state militia organizations with the equipment and training they had previously lacked, Congress passed the National Defense Act. Under the act, the federal government allocated military equipment to militias, with the condition that states "make adequate provision, to the satisfaction of the Secretary of War, for the protection and care of such property."

Even though military members of the National Guard are paid by the federal government and must abide by federal regulations for training and promotion, state authorities appoint them and maintain direct control over personnel. The Court decided that "civilian caretakers" occupy the same status. Even though they have responsibility for maintaining federal property to keep the state militia in readiness, they are immediately responsible to the respective states in performing their duties. The Court declared that Congress intended the caretakers to be employed by the states and that, appointed by each state's adjutant general, they are responsible to state authorities for the performance of their duties.

The Court ruled that the Tort Claims Act did not apply in this case because both military and civilian personnel of the National Guard are considered employees of the states, not the national government. Thus, the decision blocked any legal action by the claimants against the national government. More generally, the case firmly cemented the view that the National Guard constitutes the state militia organizations envisioned by the constitutional framers. Many gun rights advocates maintain that privately organized militia groups, like private citizens, have the right to conduct training operations and to possess firearms. However, gun control advocates claim that court decisions such as the Maryland case contradict the further claim that private militia organizations have some special protection under Article I, section 8 and the Second Amendment to the Constitution. That status has been reserved for organizations established by the respective states and supported by the federal government. This position, argue gun control advocates, contributes to claims for the constitutionality of various restrictions on firearms possession.

See also: Second Amendment.

Further Reading: *Maryland v. United States*, 381 U.S. 41 (1965).

Massachusetts Gun Violence Prevention Law

Gun control advocates labeled the Massachusetts Gun Violence Prevention Law, enacted in July 1998, a model for other states and for Congress. The law's many provisions include increased penalties for the illegal use of firearms, child accident prevention measures, and revised gun licensing regulations. Its introduction into the state legislature initiated an intense lobbying battle between pro- and anti-gun control forces. The final measure, signed by Massachusetts Governor Paul Cellucci, a Republican, is considered one of the most stringent gun control laws in the United States. While Massachusetts Attorney General Scott Harshbarger, a Democrat, called the law "a victory for common sense and for the protection of our children and our neighborhoods," gun rights organizations, extremely unhappy with the legislative outcome, quickly challenged the new law in the courts.

Among its provisions, the Massachusetts law established the responsibility of firearms owners for the safe storage of their guns. Criminal penalties are provided for negligent storage. The law increased penalties for such gun-related crimes as committing a felony with a firearm, illegal gun trafficking, illegal sale of a firearm to a minor, and illegal possession by a felon. Penalties were established for the possession of a firearm while intoxicated. The law prohibits possession or sale of sawed-off shotguns and any firearms that cannot be detected by metal detectors and X-ray machines. Through the codification of consumer protection regulations by the state attorney general, the sale of Saturday night specials, or "junk guns," is prohibited.

The law created a new licensing system for all firearms, making Firearms Identification (FID) Cards renewable every four years, instead of for life as provided under previous regulations. Licenses to Carry (LTCs) are renewable every five years. While FID Cards are issued to any eligible person, LTCs are issued at the discretion of local police chiefs. The legislation provides for a club license that allows the possession of large-capacity weapons for shooting ranges that can stock these weapons for use by members or visitors while on the premises. The statute includes additional bases for rejecting an application for an FID Card or LTC. These include conviction for a violent misdemeanor or the existence of an outstanding warrant against the applicant. Persons convicted of violent crimes or drug or firearms trafficking violations are subject to a lifelong prohibition on obtaining an FID Card.

The law established a firearms Record-keeping Trust Fund that receives half of the licensing fees to finance the conduct of background checks and to maintain the Massachusetts firearms record-keeping system. Firearms dealers are required to verify the validity of FID Cards, LTCs, and purchase permits before they may sell a gun. To ensure better record-keeping, beginning September 1, 1999, gun dealers must operate from a location distinct from their residential address.

Broad policy changes such as the 1998 Massachusetts gun law can create unintended consequences. A provision within the law banning the open carrying of a rifle or shotgun unless while hunting or transporting the weapon in a case inadvertently prohibited veterans from carrying weapons during parades. When veterans' groups protested, the bill's original sponsors declared that their intention was never to prohibit veterans from carrying firearms during parades. The state legislature passed an amendment eliminating the unintended prohibition.

See also: Saturday Night Special; Sawed-Off Shotgun.

Further Reading: Join Together Online Web site, www.jointogether.org.

Mayors Against Illegal Guns

During the administration of Republican President George W. Bush, the federal government enacted measures to restrict access to national gun trace data compiled by the federal Bureau of Alcohol, Tobacco, Firearms and Explosives, even restricting local law enforcement agencies from gaining access to federal gun data. In addition, the Republican-controlled Congress enacted the Protection of Lawful Commerce in Arms Act of 2005, which provided legal immunity to gun manufacturers, dealers, distributors, and importers, from civil lawsuits. Touted as legitimate protections for gun owners and dealers, these measures earned the ire of state and local officials around the country, who felt that urban gun crime owed much of its destructive firepower to illicit gun trafficking from a small number of rogue dealers operating in states with few gun regulations. These frustrations found advocates in New York City Republican Mayor Michael Bloomberg and Democratic Boston Mayor Thomas Menino, who formed a coalition called Mayors Against Illegal Guns (MAIG) in 2006. Beginning with a dozen city mayors from around the country, including the mayors of Dallas, Milwaukee, Philadelphia, Seattle, and Washington,

D.C., the organization had grown to over 1000 mayors by 2014. That same year, Bloomberg launched a new umbrella group, Everytown for Gun Safety, which combined MAIG with another new group, Moms Demand Action for Gun Sense in America. This latter group had been formed in 2013 by an Indiana mother with extensive public relations experience, Shannon Watts.

The organization's stated goal is to combat gun violence in their cities by prosecuting criminals who use guns in crimes to the maximum extent, targeting gun dealers who break the law, opposing government efforts to restrict access to gun data, to support legislation to fight gun crime, and to improve gun identification and tracing technologies. The National Rifle Association has been harshly critical of the Mayors group, and Bloomberg in particular. NRA spokesman Chris Cox called the effort "a taxpayer-funded publicity stunt" that was "an elitist national campaign on the backs of law-abiding gun owners." According to Cox, "Bloomberg's elitist policies . . . don't work (in reducing crime)."

In testimony before the U.S. House Judiciary Committee in 2006, Bloomberg reported that 82 percent of guns used in crimes in New York City were bought outside of the state. He also quoted a 2000 federal report that concluded that almost 60 percent of firearms subject to law enforcement traces were sold by 1.2 percent of licensed gun dealers, underscoring the disproportionately adverse effects of a few dealers on gun crime, and also the difficulty of tracking down and prosecuting these rogue dealers given new federal restrictions. Northeastern states, including New York, have found that many guns used in crimes originate in southern states, which are trafficked north along what police have dubbed the "iron pipeline."

Using city resources, Mayor Bloomberg launched a series of investigations of rogue gun dealers by tracing guns used in city crimes back to their points of origin. During a 2006 sting operation, the city sent private investigators into gun stores in five states that had been the point of origin for over 500 city crimes across a seven-year period. Fifteen dealers were caught making illegal straw purchases (meaning the dealers sold large quantities of guns to undercover agents). The city filed suit against the dealers, seeking money damages and the appointment of "special masters" to monitor the stores' future business activities. It also shared the information with federal authorities. In most instances, the dealers chose to settle with

the city. By 2007, Bloomberg's administration had sued 27 gun dealers, mostly found in southern states.

In 2009, the Mayors group commissioned a study of the attitudes of gun owners, including NRA gun owners that reflected widespread support for some key gun control measures. It reported that 69 percent of NRA members supported closing the gun show loophole; 82 percent supported banning gun sales to those whose names appear on terrorist watch lists, and 69 percent supported the sharing of federal gun trace data with state and local law enforcement agencies. In 2010, the Mayors group launched a new campaign to press states with lax gun laws to impose stricter regulations related to interstate gun trafficking and closing the gun show loophole. At the end of 2013, MAIG merged with a gun safety grassroots group formed in 2012 by Shannon Watts, Moms Demand Action for Gun Sense in America. The new organization was renamed Everytown for Gun Safety. Despite the merger, both groups retained distinct identities.

See also: Cox, Christopher (Chris) W.; Everytown for Gun Safety; Gun Shows; Moms Demand Action for Gun Sense in America; National Rifle Association; Protection of Lawful Commerce in Arms Act of 2005; Watts, Shannon.

Further Reading: Eric Lichtblau, "Study Ties Lax State Gun Laws to Crimes in Other States," *New York Times,* September 27, 2010, A10; Mayors Against Illegal Guns, *Gun Owners: NRA Gun-Owners and Non-NRA Gun Owners,* December 2009; Robert J. Spitzer, *The Politics of Gun Control,* 6th ed. (Boulder, CO: Paradigm, 2015); Everytown for Gun Safety web site: Everytown.org

McCarthy, Carolyn Cook (1944–)

Elected in part as a staunch supporter of gun control, Democratic Congresswoman Carolyn McCarthy represented her Long Island congressional district from 1997 to 2015. Her path to politics and the gun issue were highly personal.

Born in Brooklyn and raised in Mineola, New York, McCarthy was a licensed practical nurse who took little interest in politics until December 7, 1993, when a deranged man, Colin Ferguson, opened fire on a Long Island railroad train with a handgun, killing six people and wounding nineteen others. McCarthy's husband, Dennis, was killed in the attack; her son Kevin was seriously wounded. McCarthy became an advocate for gun control, and in 1996, she won the Democratic nomination for Congress to challenge then-first term Republican Representative Dan Frisa, who had voted to repeal the assault weapons ban that had been enacted by Congress in 1994. McCarthy won the race, and became a champion of stronger gun laws in Congress.

In her first year in Congress, McCarthy introduced a bill to bar the sale of guns to tourists in reaction to a 1997 shooting on the observation deck of the Empire State Building in New York City, and a bill to require trigger locks for all guns. After the 1999 shooting at Columbine High School, McCarthy was a chief sponsor of a measure to close the so-called "gun show loophole" (which allows nondealers to sell guns at gun shows without performing background checks on the purchasers), to make guns child-resistant, and to toughen penalties for gun crimes committed by juveniles. The measure was ultimately rejected in the House. After the federal assault weapons ban lapsed in 2004, McCarthy sponsored a bill to renew it. The bill was never taken up by the full House.

In 2007, she supported a bill to improve state record-keeping for those found to be mentally incompetent, and therefore unqualified to make gun purchases. The measure won rare support from both gun control and gun rights organizations in the aftermath of the Virginia Tech shooting, when a mentally disturbed man was able to buy two handguns legally, even though a judge had ruled him mentally incompetent (Virginia never included his name among those who should have been barred from gun purchases, according to the terms of the Brady law). The measure, signed into law by President George W. Bush in early 2008, provided funding, penalties, and uniform implementation for such record-keeping. Up until this time, many states did not keep proper records or provide names to the national database of those barred from gun purchases because the Brady law provided no penalties for states that did not comply with record-keeping provisions. Aside from gun control, McCarthy has supported abortion rights, efforts to detect and prevent hearing loss, health insurance reform, and federal stem cell research. In 2013, McCarthy announced that she had been diagnosed with lung cancer. The following year, she announced her retirement from Congress.

See also: Assault Weapons Ban; Littleton, Colorado, Columbine School Shooting; Virginia Tech Shooting.

Further Reading: *CQ's Politics in America: The 111th Congress* (Washington, DC: CQ Press, 2009); Robert J. Spitzer, *The Politics of Gun Control,* 6th ed. (Boulder, CO: Paradigm, 2015).

McClure, James Albertas (1924–2011)

James McClure, a former Republican Senator from Idaho, pushed hard during the early 1980s for the adoption of firearms legislation that would amend what he considered the deficiencies of the Gun Control Act of 1968. He, along with Representative Harold L. Volkmer, Democrat from Missouri, sponsored the Firearms Owners Protection Act of 1986, a statute that significantly altered the original provisions of the 1968 act. Gun control advocates claimed that the 1986 act severely restricted the ability of the national government to limit the violent use of firearms. With the lobbying assistance of the National Rifle Association (NRA), the Gun Owners of America (GOA), and the Citizens Committee for the Right to Keep and Bear Arms (CCRKBA), McClure's firearms bill passed the U.S. Senate in 1985.

After serving in the U.S. Navy during World War II, McClure attended the Idaho College of Law, receiving a law degree in 1950. He became the prosecuting attorney of Payette County, a position he held until 1956. He was city attorney for Payette from 1953 to 1966 and served in the Idaho State Senate from 1961 to 1966. McClure campaigned successfully for the U.S. House of Representatives in 1966 and served three terms. In 1972, he was elected to the U.S. Senate, and was reelected in 1978 and 1984. In 1986, McClure, a conservative, received a perfect score from the American Conservative Union for his senatorial voting record. The 1980 election, which brought Republican President Ronald Reagan into office, also gave Republicans control of the U.S. Senate. With a legislative body likely to be more sympathetic to gun rights interests, McClure began his efforts to enact a new firearms law.

While admitting that Congress intended the Gun Control Act of 1968 to restrict violent crime by regulating the sale, transportation, and possession of firearms, McClure claimed that the law had failed to achieve its objectives. He argued that those most affected by the law were not violent criminals, but innocent citizens who did an inadequate job of completing mandated paperwork. Law enforcement agencies, he contended, too often harassed law-abiding gun owners but did little to target dangerous criminals. The proposed legislation was intended to "provide for the legal protection" of citizens against the encroachment of law enforcement agents. He believed that the new legislation would bring firearms statutes in line with the original intent of Congress, "directing enforcement effort away from insignificant paperwork errors and toward willful violations of Federal firearms law."

McClure believed that his proposed bill struck a balance between the necessity of effective law enforcement and preserving the constitutional rights of law-abiding citizens. He emphasized the merits of specific provisions within the bill, including liberalization of interstate sales of firearms when they are legal in both the state of sale and the state of purchase; the necessity of demonstrating criminal intent in the prosecution of federal firearms law violations; clarification of sales procedures for private collectors; establishment of mandatory penalties for using a firearm during a federal crime; limitation of the legal seizure of firearms; provision for the return of seized firearms; and government payment of attorney's fees in frivolous suits. McClure assured skeptics that the legislation would not allow mail-order sales of firearms, permit unlicensed pawnshop gun sales, or restrict "legitimate" inspection of dealer records.

When McClure retired from the Senate in January 1991, the movement was already well under way to strengthen firearms legislation, which he had been instrumental in limiting through the Firearms Owners Protection Act. His efforts to amend the Gun Control Act of 1968 had the unintended consequences of alienating police organizations from the gun rights movement and energizing renewed efforts by gun control advocates to pass various firearms proposals, including what would become the Brady Handgun Violence Prevention Act. McClure founded his own lobbying firm in Washington, D.C., McClure, Gerard, and Neuenschwander. James McClure died in 2011.

See also: Brady Handgun Violence Prevention Act; Citizens Committee for the Right to Keep and Bear Arms; Collectors; Firearms Owners Protection Act; Gun Control Act of 1968; Gun Owners of America; National Rifle Association; Reagan, Ronald; Volkmer, Harold Lee.

Further Reading: James A. McClure, "Should Congress Adopt Proposed Relaxation of Handgun Controls?" *Congressional Digest* 65 (May 1986), 146, 148; Robert J. Spitzer, *The Politics of Gun Control* (Washington, DC: CQ Press, 2008).

McCollum, William (Bill) (1944–)

Republican William McCollum was a U.S. representative from the eighth congressional district of Florida from 1981 to 2001. He served as chairman of the Judiciary Subcommittee on Crime. In that capacity, McCollum took a strong interest in measures to reduce the national crime rate. In that capacity, he earned a reputation as a legislative authority on crime issues. However, the congressman opposed gun control legislation and supported measures to weaken existing gun laws. In 1993, McCollum voted against the final passage of the Brady Handgun Violence Prevention Act, and in 1994 he opposed passage of the ban on assault weapons. Both measures ultimately became law. In 1996, McCollum voted in favor of repealing the 1994 ban on semiautomatic assault weapons, a measure that passed the House of Representatives but failed in the Senate.

McCollum received a B.A. in 1965 and a J.D. in 1968 from the University of Florida. After serving in the Navy from 1969 to 1972, he joined an Orlando law firm, becoming a partner in 1975. McCollum served as Seminole County Republican Executive Committee chairman from 1976 to 1980, when he was elected to the House of Representatives. Among his assignments, he cochaired joint congressional hearings inquiring into the federal government raid on the Branch Davidian compound in Waco, Texas.

In June 1997, following a Supreme Court decision invalidating part of the Brady law that required local law enforcement authorities to conduct criminal background checks on handgun purchasers, the congressman commented that the decision would have little effect because the national instant check system was scheduled for implementation in November 1998. McCollum promised that his subcommittee would closely monitor the Federal Bureau of Investigation's

(FBI) operation of the instant check system. He noted that the background check system does not prevent criminals from acquiring firearms because weapons are available from illegal sources. The congressman concluded that additional measures, especially sentence enhancement laws, are needed to deter criminals from using firearms in violent crimes and drug trafficking.

Although he has opposed specific gun control measures, gun rights advocates might feel uneasy about some of the positions that McCollum has taken on crime policy issues. He supports antiterrorism measures that would grant increased law enforcement powers to federal agents and advocates allowing prosecutors to conduct warrantless searches as long as police officers act "in good faith." Many, including gun rights groups, regard such legislation as being potentially in conflict with Fourth Amendment guarantees against unreasonable searches and seizures.

Although the violent crime rate declined in the mid-1990s, McCollum believes there has not been nearly enough progress in bringing crime under control. He notes that while the number of violent crimes per 100,000 population was 160 in 1960, in 1995 that rate stood at 685. Noting the high crime rates among youths and young adults, McCollum recommended legislation that would assist states in improving their juvenile justice systems. In return for federal assistance, states would be asked to institute such policies as allowing prosecutors to charge as adults anyone who is at least 15 years old and who commits murder, rape, or assault with a firearm. While not rejecting prevention measures, McCollum placed special emphasis on deterrence as a way of combating youth as well as adult crime. After losing his House seat in an unsuccessful effort to win election to the U.S. Senate in 2000, he ran again for the Senate, unsuccessfully, in 2004. In 2006, he was elected attorney general for the state of Florida. In 2010, he sought the Republican nomination for governor, but lost the primary race.

See also: Assault Weapons Ban; Brady Handgun Violence Prevention Act; National Instant Check System; Violent Crime Rate; Waco, Texas, Raid.

Further Reading: Attorney General Bill McCollum Web site, http://myfloridale gal.com/; Robert J. Spitzer, *The Politics of Gun Control* (Washington, DC: CQ Press, 2008).

McDonald v. Chicago (2010)

Following up on its landmark ruling in 2008 in which the Supreme Court established, for the first time in history, a Second Amendment-based personal right to own a handgun for self-protection in the home, the high court ruled in 2010 that this right now applied to the states. In a 5-4 decision, the court majority concluded that a personal right to self-defense was a right fundamental to the concept of ordered liberty, meaning that it was of sufficient importance that it warranted application to the states through a process known as "incorporation."

The *McDonald* case arose as a challenge to the city of Chicago's strict gun law, which effectively banned the possession of handguns to nearly all private citizens in the city. Several city residents, including Otis McDonald, a man in his seventies who lived in a high crime area of Chicago, sought the right to have a handgun for self-protection. While the Supreme Court's 2008 ruling in *District of Columbia v. Heller* established a personal right to civilian gun ownership, that ruling, also by a 5-4 vote, applied only to the national government (the District of Columbia is a federal enclave). The challenge to Chicago's handgun ban, brought with the assistance of gun rights organizations, argued that its law should also be stricken as in violation of the Second Amendment's right to bear arms, and of the Fourteenth Amendment's protection that states shall not deprive persons within their jurisdictions of due process. It is this wording in the Fourteenth Amendment that has been used by the Supreme Court to selectively incorporate or apply parts of the Bill of Rights to the states. The court rejected the alternate argument that incorporation should occur through the Fourteenth Amendment's "privileges or immunities" clause. The incorporation process has occurred in a piecemeal fashion from 1897 until 1969 (the Fourteenth Amendment was added to the Constitution in 1868).

The majority opinion was written by Justice Samuel Alito, with separate concurring opinions authored by Justices Antonin Scalia and Clarence Thomas. The majority opinion said that the qualified right of civilians to own guns set out in the *Heller* case would apply in the same manner to the states. That is, it is not "a right to keep and carry any weapon whatsoever in any manner whatsoever and for whatever purpose." Such measures as "prohibitions on the possession of firearms by felons and the mentally ill," "laws forbidding the carrying of firearms in sensitive places such as schools and government buildings, or laws imposing conditions and qualifications on the commercial sale of arms" would generally be considered allowable.

Like *Heller* before it, the *McDonald* ruling provoked strong criticism and a fierce disagreement from the four dissenters. Rejecting the court majority's assertion in *Heller* and repeated in *McDonald,* that personal self-defense was "the central component" of the Second Amendment right to bear arms, Justice John Paul Stevens' dissent, his final case before retirement, argued that the Second Amendment pertained to the organization and arming of government militias, as the court had noted in its 1939 ruling in *United States v. Miller.* The Second Amendment says, "A well regulated Militia, being necessary to a free State, the right of the people to keep and bear Arms, shall not be infringed." Stevens argued that incorporation was not necessary to resolve the dispute arising from the Chicago law, and that the ruling could have adverse consequences for communities across the country struggling to limit gun violence: "Although the court's decision in this case might be seen as a mere adjunct to Heller, the consequences could prove far more destructive—quite literally—to our nation's communities and to our constitutional structure." He also questioned the majority's equation of firearms with liberty: "firearms have a fundamentally ambivalent relationship to liberty." A second dissenting opinion was authored by Justice Stephen Breyer. In the aftermath of the case, hundreds of lawsuits were filed across the country challenging state and local gun laws.

See also: District of Columbia v. Heller (2008); Fourteenth Amendment; *United States v. Miller* (1939).

Further Reading: *McDonald v. Chicago,* 561 U.S. 742 (2010).

Media Violence

People on both sides of the gun control debate decry the prevalence of media violence, but draw different conclusions regarding its relationship to firearms. Movies, television, and popular music lyrics have come under criticism for their portrayal of violent acts. Gun control supporters tend to identify media violence with the danger of guns,

while gun rights advocates, believing that guns don't kill people, people kill people, blame gun violence not on guns themselves, but on various other possible causes, among which could be the effects of violence in the mass media. For gun control advocates, the media venerate violence *and* guns; for gun rights advocates, the media glorify the *misuse* of guns.

Media critics such as Michael Medved have criticized the increased use of violence in films and television. For example, he reports that in the movies *Die Hard 2* and *Rambo III,* respectively, 264 and 106 people were killed. Current movies not only have far more acts of violence compared to past films, but the violence has become increasingly graphic. Moviemakers appear to be forced to invent ever more explicitly violent acts to shock audiences who are becoming habituated to violent portrayals. Prime-time television programs depict an average of 3.6 crimes per episode, 25 percent of which are murders. Medved has expressed concern that movies increasingly portray violence as comedy. After killing someone, the hero often makes a humorous remark, thereby minimizing the significance of the violent act. Violence becomes entertainment to be enjoyed.

Defenders of the media argue that simply counting the number of violent acts committed in movies or television shows has no particular relevance to making inferences about effects on viewers. Some in the media argue that viewing violent acts can have a cathartic effect, thus actually reducing the probability that the viewer will commit an act of violence. However, several studies dealing especially with the behavior of children suggest that viewing violence encourages aggressive behavior. While media defenders argue that violent acts can be symbolic, representing a deeper lesson beyond the physical act itself, critics respond that an appeal to symbolism cannot erase the portrayal of violence against a human being. In another defense of the portrayal of violent acts, television dramas are described as morality plays in which the "bad guys" receive their just punishment. Critics reject this defense, arguing that younger children cannot always relate an act of violence to the ultimate retribution sometime later in the story.

Media defenders argue that violence in the mass media simply mirrors the actions and values of contemporary society. Therefore, they contend, critics are blaming the messenger, and ignoring the true source of the problem. Critics respond that films exaggerate the nature of physical violence.

Fistfights and gunfights are made to last far longer than is usually the case in reality. In addition, the media exaggerate the frequency with which violent acts occur. Medved reports that a television character has an 8.6 percent chance of becoming a victim of violence, while the average American has a yearly chance of 0.5 percent. The media do not just mirror reality, but vastly overrepresent one aspect of it.

To the extent that the media affect perceptions, people believe they are in greater danger of being victims of violent crime than is in fact the case. The fear of violent crime may affect behavior by, for instance, encouraging citizens to isolate themselves in anticipation of becoming a victim, and to believe that methods of self-defense, such as owning a firearm, are effective responses. However, while gun control advocates argue that perceptions have been distorted by the media, the gun rights supporters contend that the danger of crime is real.

Those people concerned with violence in the media have proposed possible palliatives to the problem of violence in the media. In the late 1980s, Democratic Senator Paul Simon of Illinois encouraged the entertainment industry to develop voluntary guidelines regarding the portrayal of violence, but had little success. Other than adding a computer chip to television sets that allows parents to block certain programs and establishing rating systems for movies and television programs, little has been done, and perhaps can be done, to deal with the problem of violence in the media. In the meantime, the First Amendment will enter the debate, and so will the Second Amendment, at least to the extent that critics associate media violence with the availability of firearms.

See also: National Rifle Association; Second Amendment; Violent Crime Rate; Youth and Guns.

Further Reading: Carl M. Cannon, "Honey, I Warped the Kids," *Mother Jones* (July/August 1993), 17–21; Michael Medved, *Hollywood vs. America* (New York: Harper Collins, 1993); National Research Council, *Firearms and Violence* (Washington, DC: The National Academies Press, 2005).

Mennonite Central Committee (MCC)

The Mennonite Central Committee (MCC), a worldwide ministry of Anabaptist churches, has taken a strong stand in favor of various gun control proposals. The MCC advocates proposals intended to reduce the availability of guns and to regulate their use. The organization, calling itself a "peace church," encourages "people of faith" to surrender any firearms that are kept for self-defense, claiming that such actions will serve as an example to others of a "commitment to nonviolence in a society that has become engulfed by violence." The Committee focuses its concern on handguns, noting that they constitute one-third of all firearms in the United States and are used in 80 percent of all firearm homicides.

The Mennonite Central Committee was founded in 1920 as a relief and development organization within the American Mennonite and Brethren in Christ churches. The MCC sends volunteers to work in approximately 50 countries. These volunteers are involved in various areas of development, including agriculture, health care and maintenance, education, and social services. In the United States and Canada, the organization conducts programs dealing with mental illness, disabilities, job creation, and services to criminal offenders. The organization's basic nonviolent stand has been a major factor in its support for gun control policy.

The MCC has employed poignant symbolism to convey its anti-gun message. In 1997, the Committee dedicated a 16-foot-high sculpture at a plaza located across from the District of Columbia police headquarters. Esther Augsburger and her son Michael, members of the Mennonites, created the sculpture, titled "Guns into Plowshares," using 3,000 guns collected in a gun buyback program by the District of Columbia Metropolitan Police Department.

Mennonites have served in various locations around the world where violence prevails. Carol Rose, a Mennonite worker who has worked in Central America, Thailand, and the Philippines, commented in 1995 after a year's tour of duty in Lancaster, Pennsylvania, that she witnessed more violence during her first year in that American city than during any other tour of duty outside the United States. She attributed the violence to the "easy accessibility to guns."

The MCC backs reenactment of the prohibition on assault weapons, which lapsed in 2004, claiming that such firearms "are part of the culture of death." Saying that these guns are "a favorite among criminals," the Committee supports an extension of the ban on "junk handguns," or Saturday night specials, to include those weapons manufactured in the United States. Additional proposals supported by the Committee include registering firearms, licensing, requiring that gun owners have liability insurance, establishing competency tests for potential gun owners, increasing penalties for misuse of firearms, improving regularized gun transfer procedures, one-handgun-per-month purchase regulations, and establishing gun owners' civil liability for the misuse of weapons. In addition to legislative proposals, the MCC educates people about the dangers of firearms, discouraging the keeping of handguns in the home and offering assistance to victims of gun violence. The organization distributes literature that provides information about firearms violence, gun control laws, the Mennonite position on gun violence, and suggestions for ameliorating the problem of firearm-related violence.

See also: Assault Weapons Ban; Canada; Gun Buyback Programs; Gun Culture; Saturday Night Special.

Further Reading: "Preventing Gun Violence" (Washington, DC: Mennonite Central Committee, 2009); Mennonite Central Committee Web site, www.mcc.org.

Metaksa, Tanya K. (1936–)

Tanya Metaksa, who served as executive director of the National Rifle Association's (NRA) Institute for Legislative Action (ILA) from 1994 to 1998, has been an avid spokesperson and lobbyist for gun rights advocates. Known for her staunch advocacy and libertarian leanings, she adheres to the position that guns themselves are innocent of any wrongdoing; people commit crimes of violence, not the weapons they misuse. As a high official in an organization composed mostly of men, Metaksa represented the new image the NRA was attempting to convey to the American public, even though she proved to be too strident for the NRA, and was pushed out of her leadership position in the organization.

Metaksa has taken strong stands on contemporary issues regarding firearms and gun control. Noting that over 200,000 machine guns are legally in private hands today, she accepts legitimate private ownership and use of such weapons. She denounces attempts to outlaw

assault weapons, a term she claims has come to mean any firearm that gun control advocates want to ban. Metaksa defines an assault weapon more stringently as "a fully automatic firearm used in time of war by the ordinary soldier" and labels as "stupid" the attempt to define assault weapons on the basis of what she considers cosmetic features.

With regard to so-called cop-killer bullets, Metaksa claims that most ammunition can penetrate protective vests. Besides, she has commented, most police officers who have been killed have been shot in the head. Focusing on the individualistic interpretation of the Second Amendment, she admonishes the American Civil Liberties Union (ACLU) for failing to come to the defense of the right to keep and bear arms. She takes a cautious position on requiring the placement of taggants in gunpowder, which are intended to facilitate the tracing of terrorist bombers. She calls for further testing before being willing to accept their inclusion in explosives. However, Metaksa suggests their use be limited to commercial explosives. Those who make ammunition from gunpowder should be exempt.

Metaksa, whose father escaped from Russia after the communist revolution, acquired a strong suspicion of governments, which is reflected in her opposition to any official effort to control private ownership of firearms. She views the organization for which she has labored the "only bulwark of defense" against advocates of gun control. Metaksa graduated from Smith College in 1958, becoming a medical photographer in a New York hospital. She and her husband George settled in Connecticut where Metaksa became a housewife and raised a family. In the late 1960s, she became active in the gun rights cause. She worked for three years as legislative director for Alfonse D'Amato, former Republican Senator from New York.

In 1977, Metaksa became director of state and local affairs in the NRA's Institute for Legislative Action. In 1979, she became deputy executive director of the Institute, but left that position in 1980, apparently over a disagreement with NRA executive vice president Harlon Carter. In 1991, Metaksa returned to a leadership position in the NRA as a member of the board of directors. In 1993, her company, Bullet Communications, was granted a $90,000 contract to create ILA's electronic bulletin board. Although Metaksa received criticism from within the NRA for this no-bid contract, she weathered the storm, and in

1994 rose to head the ILA. In 1998, NRA executive vice president Wayne LaPierre pushed Metaksa out of the ILA, appointing James Jay Baker as the executive director. Metaksa writes and speaks on conservative and libertarian causes.

See also: American Civil Liberties Union; Assault Weapons Ban; Institute for Legislative Action; LaPierre, Wayne; National Rifle Association; Russia; Taggants.

Further Reading: Barbara Grizzuti Harrison, "Cease Fire," *Mother Jones* (March/April 1997), 33–36; Deborah Homsher, *Women and Guns* (Armonk, NY: M.E. Sharpe, 2002); Tanya K. Metaksa, *Safe, Not Sorry* (New York: Regan Books, 1998).

Mexico

Mexico has had an uneasy relationship with the United States with regard to the regulation of firearms. Mexico has stringent gun regulations and does not have an armaments industry. Guns larger than .38 caliber are restricted to military use only. Officials generally associate the carrying of firearms with possible criminal activity. However, the country has a serious and growing problem with violent crime, particularly organized crime syndicates linked to the drug trade, and political unrest at times has resulted in guerrilla uprisings. The Mexican Foreign Relations Ministry reported that from 1995 to 1997 over 1,000 illegal weapons were confiscated each month, 40 percent of which were associated with drug cartels. The Mexican government contends that the large number of firearms available for illegal use originated in the United States. For example, the gun used to assassinate presidential candidate Luis Donaldo Colosio in 1994 was discovered to have originated with a Texas gun dealer.

Just as the U.S. government has complained about the transfer of drugs from Mexico to the United States, Mexico has objected to the flow of illegal weapons from the United States into Mexico, and America's appetite for illicit drugs. Mexican officials claim that thousands of firearms make their way past U.S. Customs Service officials. Over 7,000 gun stores are found on the American side of the U.S.-Mexican border, and escalating gun trafficking from the United States to Mexico has become a major problem for the Mexican government, adding to its concern that lax American gun laws have fueled escalating violence across the border.

In addition, numerous gun shows held near the Mexican border have provided a ready source of guns, as the so-called "gun show loophole" allows anyone to purchase guns from private dealers who are not required to perform background checks on purchasers. From the end of 2006 to April 2010, the Mexican government seized 41,093 assault rifles and 31,946 handguns. Of those that could be traced, 80 percent came from the United States.

Mexican President Felipe Calderón's multi-year effort to use the Mexican army to counter well-armed Mexican gangs has produced escalating violence. Ironically, the military has often found itself out-armed by the gangs. Amnesty International, the organization that monitors government violence against citizens, has protested reported violence against Mexican citizens. Amnesty International has also protested the disappearance of political dissidents and reported incidents of torture. Pro-gun rights groups are suspicious of restrictions on gun ownership in such circumstances, arguing that the right to keep and bear arms is a major defense against an oppressive government.

Further Reading: Brady Center to Prevent Gun Violence, "Exporting Gun Violence," March 2009; U.S. Department of Justice, *Project Gunrunner: Illegal Trafficking of Guns from the United States to Mexico* (2014).

Michigan Militia (MM)

The Michigan Militia (MM) is an organization of people who believe in the right to organize armed military groups to protect themselves against perceived government oppression. Even though it adopts for itself the term "militia," it is not a militia in any legal or constitutional sense, as federal law and court rulings make clear that only the federal or state governments may form militias. The MM is an example of a more extreme element in the anti-gun control movement. The organization's pro-gun position is fueled by the belief that gun control legislation coincides with a much larger plan to enslave the American people.

Norman Olson, a Baptist minister and gun store owner, and Ray Southwell, a real estate agent, established the Michigan Militia in 1994. Southwell approached Olson after losing a struggle

The Michigan Militia is an example of a more extreme element in the anti-gun control movement. *www. michiganmilitia.com*

over educational policy with a local school board. He was concerned that the introduction of a curriculum advocated by the federal government would result in the debasement of the entire education system. To resist federal government intervention into education and other areas, Olson and Southwell formed a militia to defend what they believed to be their constitutional rights.

Olson and Southwell believed that too many state laws had been supplanted by federal restrictions. They saw the Environmental Protection Agency (EPA) as a clear example of such unwarranted intervention. A central issue for them was the preservation of the right to keep and bear arms. The Second Amendment, they argued, is the most important ingredient in the Bill of Rights because the other freedoms could easily be lost without the right to protect them by threat of force against the machinations of "tyrants."

After its founding, the Michigan Militia quickly increased its membership to as many as 7,000. When Mark Koernke joined the organization, he was working as a janitor at the University of Michigan. Not satisfied with the MM, he established the Michigan Militia at Large, considered a more extreme version of the MM. In the evenings, he broadcast an hour-long shortwave radio program, "Intelligence Report," on which he referred to himself simply as "Mark from Michigan." Koernke identified the New World Order as the enemy against which

Americans must defend themselves and claimed that the federal government was involved in an elaborate conspiracy to disarm the American public. Supposedly involved in this conspiracy was a national police force composed of National Guardsmen, Los Angeles street gangs, Nepalese Gurkhas, and Russian troops prepared to take armed control of the United States, all in the name of the United Nations. He foresaw the Federal Emergency Management Agency (FEMA) creating a provisional government in preparation for the New World Order. Koernke produced a videotape, *America in Peril,* which was distributed to militia groups around the country.

Immediately following the Oklahoma City bombing in April 1995, Koernke faxed a brief message to then-U.S. Representative Steve Stockman, Republican of Texas, stating: "Seven to 10 floors only. Military people on the scene." Later he professed no foreknowledge of the bombing, but claimed that in contacting Stockman, he was hoping to get the media to the scene. A few days after the bombing, Koernke claimed that federal agents had given Timothy McVeigh orange clothing so that potential snipers would have a better target.

The MM gained further publicity when leaders of the organization indicated that Terry Nichols, since convicted of complicity in the Oklahoma bombing, had attended meetings, bringing Timothy McVeigh with him to at least one gathering. When federal agents searched the farm of Nichols's brother, they discovered several papers associated with the MM. Olson and Southwell claimed immediately after the Oklahoma bombing that they believed the Japanese were responsible for the attack. These statements led the commanders of the MM to force the two leaders to resign. Claiming that the MM had been captured by moderates, Olson and Southwell formed the Northern Michigan Regional Militia. Interest in private militia organizations like the Michigan Militia declined in the early 2000s, but underwent a resurgence after Barack Obama's election in 2008. The Southern Poverty Law Center noted a 300 percent increase in private militia activity from 2008 to 2009.

See also: Japan; Militia of Montana; Oklahoma City Bombing; Russia; Second Amendment.

Further Reading: Thomas Halpern, David Rosenberg, and Irwin Suall, "Militia Movement: Prescription for Disaster," in Frank McGuckin, ed., *Terrorism in the*

United States (New York: H.W. Wilson, 1997), 51–63; Jonathan Karl, *The Right to Bear Arms: The Rise of America's New Militias* (New York: HarperCollins, 1995); Larry Keller, "The Second Wave: Return of the Militias," Southern Poverty Law Center, August 2009; Michigan Militia Web site, www.michiganmilitia. com; Southern Poverty Law Center Web site, www. splcenter.org/

Militia Act of 1792

According to the Militia Act of 1792, more formally titled "An Act more effectually to provide for the National Defense by establishing an Uniform militia throughout the United States," all free white male citizens, from 18 to 45 years old, were subject to militia duty. Every militiaman was required to furnish a musket or firelock, bayonet and belt, spare flints, knapsack, and a pouch containing not less than 24 cartridges. By establishing these requirements, the Militia Act in effect placed a tax on men 18 to 45 years of age. For 111 years, the act provided the basic structure for the militia system, although it was largely unused for much of that time.

In 1790, President George Washington's Secretary of War, Henry Knox, proposed a plan for an organized militia that called for national government control over military units established in the states. The states disliked the plan because it provided for more national government intervention in state affairs than they were willing to tolerate. In 1792, Congress passed a considerably weakened version of the Knox proposal. While Knox had recommended the organization of the militia into three age classes (18-20, 21-45, and 46-60), with military training appropriate for each class, the final bill called for all eligible men between 18 and 45 to be enrolled in an undifferentiated militia.

Congressional discussions of the Militia Act reveal no evidence that any legislator doubted citizens should have the right to own firearms. Legislators demonstrated a desire that the population should be armed, but at minimal cost to the average citizen. The act reflected the contemporary social conditions and demonstrated racial prejudice, for it prohibited slaves, freed blacks, and Indians from serving in the militia. While the Knox plan included prescriptions for militia organization, the Militia Act only made recommendations. The act intended that the United States would have a uniform militia, with units from the various states being essentially

interchangeable. However, the law qualified this provision by stating "if the same be convenient," which it was not for many states.

As the only uniformity requirement, the act called for each state to have an adjutant general and an inspector for each brigade. The adjutant generals were given the responsibility of maintaining uniformity among the various state militias; each adjutant general was to report the condition of his state's militia each year to the governor and the president of the United States. Beyond this requirement, the act contained no sanctions against state governments or individual officials for failure to comply with its provisions. The potential force to be organized under the act numbered over a half-million men. The states had neither the capacity nor the inclination, given the lack of penalties, to carry out the provisions of the Militia Act.

During the War of 1812, the state militias provided the vast majority of the American forces. The last time the national government made significant use of the militia system was during the Seminole War from 1836 to 1842. In the war against Mexico in 1846–1848, only 12 percent of American forces originated with state militias, and the remainder were national troops. In 1820, Secretary of War John C. Calhoun had recommended an army appropriation that emphasized a professional, national military force, thus focusing on a centralized military system in contrast to dependence on state militias. During the Civil War in the 1860s, less than 50,000 Union troops were derived from state militias. Rather than establishing a militia system according to the recommendations of the 1792 law, states depended on the organization of voluntary companies, a far cry from the universal militia service originally envisioned.

In 1808, Congress established a permanent annual appropriation of $200,000 to purchase muskets that would be distributed to the states in proportion to militia enrollments. A congressional decision in 1855 indicated the failure of the militia system. States that had failed to enroll a militia and therefore were receiving little of the grant money insisted on altering the basis for distribution. Rather than militia enrollments, Congress established a new standard that employed the number of senators and representatives from each state to determine each state's allotment. Ultimately, the Dick Act of 1903 brought an end to the militia system of universal service established in the 1792 act and officially replaced it with a voluntary system of militia service called the National Guard.

See also: Dick Act.

Further Reading: John K. Mahon, *History of the Militia and the National Guard* (New York: Macmillan, 1983); Robert J. Spitzer, *Gun Control: A Documentary and Reference Guide* (Westport, CT: Greenwood Press, 2009).

Militia of Montana (MOM)

Organized in February 1994 by John Trochmann along with his brother and a nephew, the Militia of Montana (MOM) has avidly opposed any gun control measures, considering them to be a violation of the Second Amendment right to keep and bear arms and to organize militia groups for self-protection. Even though it adopted for itself the term "militia," it is not a militia in any legal or constitutional sense, as federal law and court rulings make clear that only the federal or state governments may form militias. MOM established its base of operations in Noxon, Montana, just 50 miles from Ruby Ridge, Idaho, where in 1992 family members of white supremacist Randy Weaver were killed by FBI agents in an armed standoff. Trochmann was present at the police line during the siege of Ruby Ridge. Following the standoff, he joined with others to assist Weaver by forming United Citizens for Justice. Although the organization soon disbanded due to internal strife, it became the base for the Militia of Montana and other paramilitary groups.

MOM established a mail-order business, offering members and interested people books, videotapes, and handbooks that provided advice on forming a militia organization and obtaining military training. Among the items listed in its catalog is a training manual, which contains instructions for the conduct of guerrilla warfare and provides biblical justifications for subversive activity. Among the topics included in the manual are tactics for raiding military armories to obtain weapons and ammunition, the organization of sabotage attacks, and the conduct of domestic terrorism campaigns.

Trochmann associated gun control with his vision of an evil New World Order. To him,

the Brady Handgun Violence Prevention Act represented an initial stage in the plans of those wishing to establish a world government to control American citizens. Ruby Ridge and the standoff at the Branch Davidian compound in Waco, Texas, provided evidence for Trochmann and MOM of a huge conspiracy to take firearms away from citizens. To prevent further incidents and to resist future "gun grabs," Trochmann advocated a coalition of unorganized militias throughout the United States. Simply having guns in the home would not preserve freedom. Citizens must train in military tactics and possess the appropriate equipment to resist with arms any government use of force.

MOM claimed that firearms provided a means to defend a way of life being threatened by government taxation, permissive abortions, and regulation of home schooling. Affirmative action programs came under attack, as well as such trade treaties as the General Agreement on Tariffs and Trade (GATT) and the North American Free Trade Agreement (NAFTA), which were perceived as threats to the livelihood of white American males. The organization saw evidence of a huge government conspiracy to disarm patriotic Americans, institute burdensome taxation, and destroy constitutional rights, all in the name of world government. Trochmann claimed that unorganized militias provided the only way to defend against this conspiracy. Just like the Minutemen of 1775, members of MOM believed they must be prepared to fight in a revolution. To this end, the organization encouraged members to arm themselves with semiautomatic weapons and to learn guerrilla warfare tactics.

MOM holds that the people have a right to arm themselves against their own government. Thus, unorganized militias become the primary line of defense if the government becomes oppressive, as MOM and other militia groups believe it has. With the assumption that government has become the major threat to individual freedom, gun control measures become especially objectionable because they amount to the oppressor disarming citizens and leaving them defenseless. Critics of this view note the incongruity of arguing that a constitution, intended to establish a stable government, would at the same time make provision for the instrument of its own demise. Governments can and do at times violate citizen rights, but one of them is not the right to prepare for revolution.

See also: American Revolution; Brady Handgun Violence Prevention Act; Michigan Militia, Militia Act of 1792; Militia Watchdog; Minutemen, Revolutionary; Ruby Ridge; Second Amendment; Waco, Texas, Raid.

Further Reading: Jonathan Karl, *The Right to Bear Arms: The Rise of America's New Militias* (New York: HarperCollins, 1995); Larry Keller, "The Second Wave: Return of the Militias," Southern Poverty Law Center, August 2009; Militia of Montana Web site, www.militiaofmontana.com.

Militia Watchdog

The Militia Watchdog is a Web site devoted to monitoring the militia movement. It is associated with the Anti-Defamation League (ADL). The Militia Watchdog maintains information on the historical development and legal standing of militia groups and provides information on associations such as the patriot movement, common law courts, and tax resisters that are collaborating to create "an illegal 'shadow' government, heavily armed, answerable to no authority, and motivated by bizarre conspiracy theories." Although the Web site states that it does not take a position on the issues of gun control and the right to keep and bear arms, it does comment that paramilitary groups have "cloaked themselves in the Constitution," which includes an appeal to the Second Amendment to justify not only a right to keep and bear arms, but to organize militia groups to oppose the government itself.

Mark Pitcavage founded the Militia Watchdog as a way of informing the public about the operations of militia groups. The site does not claim to be objective, stating that it believes militia groups present a danger about which citizens must be warned. It wishes to expose what it considers misinterpretations of the history and law of the militia. Along with Sheldon Sheps, a Canadian who has investigated U.S. right-wing/populist movements, Pitcavage developed a list of "Frequently Asked Questions" about the militias that they made available on the Web site. They claim that the militias lack legitimacy and legality, having little in common with the original constitutional and statutory establishment of military groups. Headquartered in Columbus, Ohio, the Militia Watchdog maintains a list of other Web sites and materials, including news items and profiles of individuals in the movement. It welcomes requests for information from individuals, the press, and law enforcement officials, and maintains a mailing list for professionals, including academics, lawyers, and public officials.

According to the Militia Watchdog, the militia movement reemerged in the 1990s, energized by those who perceived that the federal government was about to confiscate firearms. Following the confiscation, the United States would supposedly be overrun by a United Nations-operated "New World Order." The Militia Watchdog identifies common law courts, sovereign citizens (those who recognize only citizenship in a particular state), tax protesters, Christian patriots, and white supremacists as the "vanguard of antigovernment extremism." Among the events leading to the creation of militias are the 1992 Ruby Ridge standoff, the 1993 Waco raid on the Branch Davidian compound, and the passage of the Brady Handgun Violence Prevention Act and the assault weapons ban.

Despite an official disclaimer regarding any position on the gun control issue, Pitcavage provides a critical appraisal of the National Rifle Association (NRA) and other gun rights organizations. He focuses attention on the prevalence of firearms among militia groups and the presence of militia organizations at gun shows. Pitcavage notes that while the Brady waiting period was in effect, many people purchased firearms at gun shows because no waiting period was required to purchase from a private owner. He observes that the NRA has distanced itself from the militia movement, "despite the increasingly erratic actions of leader Wayne LaPierre." In 2000, the Militia Watchdog became the Militia Watchdog Archives when Pitcavage became the Director of Fact-Finding for the ADL. Most of the information on the site covers the period from 1995–2000.

See also: Brady Handgun Violence Prevention Act; Gun Shows; LaPierre, Wayne; Michigan Militia; Militia Act of 1792; Militia of Montana; National Rifle Association; Ruby Ridge; Second Amendment; United Nations; Waco, Texas, Raid.

Further Reading: Militia Watchdog Web site, www.adl.org/mwd/; Mark Pitcavage, "Welcome to a New World (Disorder): A Visit to a Gun Show," *The Militia Watchdog*, www.adl.org/mwd/.

Miller v. Texas (1894)

The U.S. Supreme Court decision in *Miller v. Texas* (153 U.S. 535, 1894) provides an early example of the Court's refusal to interpret the Second Amendment of the U.S. Constitution as limiting the ability of state governments to restrict an individual citizen's right to keep and bear arms. The Court expressly stated that the Second Amendment applied only to the federal government and therefore does not have force regarding the proceedings of state courts. The *Miller* decision occurred prior to the "selective incorporation" process in more recent Court decisions that has made much of the Bill of Rights applicable to the states. The Supreme Court reversed its position on incorporation of the Second Amendment in the 2010 case of *McDonald v. Chicago,* which did apply the Second Amendment to the states.

A Dallas County, Texas, grand jury indicted Franklin P. Miller for a murder that occurred in June 1892. He was convicted in July of that year and sentenced to death. His appeal of the conviction to the Court of Criminal Appeals of Texas resulted in an affirmation of the guilty verdict, whereupon Miller filed a writ of error to the U.S. Supreme Court, claiming that the law under which he was originally arrested violated the U.S. Constitution. He contended that the Texas statute prohibiting the carrying of dangerous weapons infringed his rights as a citizen of the United States and violated the Second Amendment to the U.S. Constitution, noting that the original court had charged the jury that by carrying a pistol on a public street, he was violating the law. Further, he claimed that the arrest without warrant of a person carrying a weapon in violation of the statute violated the Fourth Amendment to the U.S. Constitution, which proscribes unreasonable searches and seizures. Finally, Miller argued that the Texas statute violated the Fifth and Fourteenth Amendments, which provide, respectively, that no person shall be deprived of life, liberty, or property without due process of law, and that no state shall pass any law that abridges the privileges or immunities of citizens of the United States.

The Court's decision did not rely primarily on the substantive claims of the writ of error. The Court noted that no objection involving a federal question was raised either during the trial and before the judgment, or during the original appellate court hearing, but only arose before the appellate court on a motion for a rehearing, which was overruled. Therefore, the writ of error was dismissed because no objection raising a federal question had been introduced during the original trial. However, the Court did speak to the claims made by the defendant in the motion for a rehearing.

With regard to the claim that the Texas statute forbidding the carrying of weapons and allowing for the arrest without warrant of anyone violating this law was in conflict with the Second and Fourth Amendments to the U.S. Constitution, the Supreme Court stated that it could not discover where the defendant was denied any rights provided for in those amendments. Even if the defendant had been denied such protection, the Court ruled that the amendments apply only to the federal government and have no application to state courts. With regard to the Fourteenth Amendment, the Court indicated that the defendant's claim that his rights as a U.S. citizen had been abridged could not be considered because it was not presented in the trial court, and further stated that there had been no denial of due process of law with regard to the ordinary procedures of the court, nor did the Texas statute prohibiting the carrying of dangerous weapons abridge the privileges of citizens of the United States.

See also: Fourth Amendment; Fourteenth Amendment; *McDonald v. Chicago* (2010); Second Amendment.

Further Reading: *Miller v. Texas*, 153 U.S. 535 (1894).

Million Mom March

The Million Mom March is a grassroots movement of women in support of stronger gun laws that staged a massive rally in Washington, D.C., on Mother's Day, 2000. The idea originated with New Jersey mother Donna Dees-Thomases. Outraged by a 1999 shooting at a Jewish community center in California, Dees-Thomases, who also worked part time as a publicist, contacted other like-minded women who eventually established fifty state-based organizations to coordinate a march on Washington styled after the Million Man March held in Washington several years earlier.

The organization identified six policy goals: uniform "cooling-off" periods and background checks for gun purchases; licensing of handgun owners and registration of all handguns; mandatory safety locks for all handguns; one-handgun-per-month purchase limits; strict enforcement of existing gun laws; and enlistment of help from corporate America. Turnout for the march, according to the organizers, exceeded expectations as the daylong event attracted about 700,000 people. Rally speakers included women whose lives had been affected by gun violence, public officials, and celebrities. Smaller rallies were held simultaneously in at least twenty cities around the country. The rally was one of the largest demonstrations ever staged in the nation's capital, and the first large-scale rally on behalf of gun control in modern times.

Much of the impetus for the event, and its resonance among women, arose from the fact that women support gun control in significantly greater numbers than men. During the 2000 elections, polls showed that the gender gap between men and women on the gun issue was greater than for any other issue. For example, a May 2000 Gallup Poll asked the question, "In general, do you feel that the laws covering the sale of firearms should be made more strict, less strict, or kept as they are now?"; to which 52 percent of men responded "more strict" compared to 72 percent of women.

After the march, the organization reorganized itself as the Million Mom March Foundation (MMM), hoping to sustain its momentum and political impact in the way that Mothers Against Drunk Driving influenced drinking-age laws in the 1980s. MMM activities won support from the U.S. Conference of Mayors, the League of Women Voters, the National Parent Teachers Association, and other gun control groups. However, in 2001 the MMM suffered a decline in membership and financial support, and it was never able to recapture its initial groundswell of support. In response, it merged with the Brady Campaign to Prevent Gun Violence (formerly Handgun Control, Inc.). By 2005, about fifty chapters operated in twenty states, engaging in lobbying, electioneering, and public education efforts. By its tenth anniversary, the MMM organization claimed chapters in all fifty states.

A counterdemonstration group was formed in 2000. A group named the Second Amendment Sisters (SAS) sought to rally women in support of gun ownership at what it called the Armed Informed Mothers March. Closely paralleling the National Rifle Association's (NRA) stand on gun issues, it argued that stronger gun laws would infringe on a woman's ability to defend herself. The NRA also launched a parallel advertising campaign to counter the MMM's arguments. The SAS counterdemonstration, held at the opposite end of the Washington Mall in 2000, attracted about 2,000 protestors.

See also: Brady Campaign to Prevent Gun Violence; National Rifle Association; Second Amendment Sisters.

Further Reading: Kristin A. Goss, *Disarmed: The Missing Movement for Gun Control in America* (Princeton, NJ: Princeton University Press, 2006); Caitlin Kelly, *Blown Away: American Women and Guns* (New York: Pocket Books, 2004); Million Mom March Web site (Brady Campaign), www.bradycampaign.org/chapters/.

Minutemen, Modern

The Minutemen, a paramilitary group that operated during the 1960s and early 1970s, was a precursor to the right-wing militia groups of the 1990s and 2000s. Founded in 1960 by Robert Bolivar DePugh, a chemist from Norborne, Missouri, the organization advocated citizen preparedness for a possible communist takeover of the United States. Members of the Minutemen were encouraged to become adept at guerrilla war tactics and to stockpile firearms and ammunition for use in a future conflict to defend the nation against invasion. The emphasis on the acquisition and stockpiling of guns resulted in the arrest and indictment of the organization's leadership for violations of federal firearms laws.

Due to DePugh's fanatical concern for supersecrecy to protect the membership should a communist takeover occur, the group was said to have been organized into squads of up to 25 individuals who supposedly had no knowledge of each other's identities. No membership roles were to be kept and only the state commanders were to know the identity of squad leaders. It is difficult to imagine how any organization could operate effectively under such conditions, and the Minutemen organization itself apparently did not. DePugh's most notable success was his ability to gain headlines, not for what the organization did, but for the violent actions he claimed the organization would take to save the nation.

The total Minutemen membership likely was never very large. DePugh at different times provided membership figures of anywhere from 600 to 25,000. In 1968, J. Edgar Hoover, head of the Federal Bureau of Investigation (FBI), claimed that the organization could not depend on more than 50 individuals as active participants. Others estimated an active membership of no more than 200, with possibly another 400, who donated money to the organization and subscribed to its publications.

Early in its existence, the organization's leaders ran afoul of federal firearms legislation. DePugh, taking his cue from communist strategy, claimed that one of the Minutemen's fundamental objectives was to incite the government into taking repressive measures against citizens to alienate the population from their government. This tactic included a belligerent rhetoric, with references to assassination and terrorism, as well as activities at the edge of the law. Richard Lauchli, for a time one of DePugh's associates, was arrested several times for various violations of firearms laws. In 1960, he was fined $500 for stealing 23 bazookas, and in 1964, he was indicted for allegedly transporting illegal firearms as part of a deal to sell guns to anti-Castro Cubans.

In 1966, DePugh was indicted for possession of bombs, but in March 1967 a judge dismissed the charge. In the meantime, the Minutemen leader was charged with firearms possession while under indictment. DePugh and two associates were convicted of violating the National Firearms Act of 1934 for receiving, transferring, and possessing automatic weapons and silencers. DePugh and another associate, Wally Peyson, were charged with, among other things, illegal possession of a machine gun and failing to pay a $200 tax under the National Firearms Act. In February 1968, DePugh was accused of bank robbery while free on appeal of his sentence of four years, but the charge was ultimately dropped.

At this time, DePugh and Peyson disappeared, prompting a 17-month FBI manhunt. When the two men were captured in Truth or Consequences, New Mexico, in July 1969, they had in their possession a number of homemade bombs, grenades, rifles, and handguns. In February 1970, DePugh was sentenced to four years for his disappearance while under bond. Shortly thereafter, he was convicted of federal firearms violations and in October was sentenced to 10 years in federal prison. He remained imprisoned from 1970 to 1973.

While DePugh languished behind bars, a leadership struggle among his would-be successors tore the Minutemen organization apart. The FBI continued its efforts to infiltrate the organization with informants and to destroy it from within. DePugh was released in May 1973, but his efforts to revive the Minutemen failed. For a time, he tried to coordinate the activities of several right-wing groups, but with little success due to internecine squabbles among the leadership. His final efforts at organization included the formation of the Committee of Ten Million in 1976, which involved holding "Patriots Leadership Conferences" in Kansas City, Missouri. After the organization ceased to exist in 1981, DePugh began a tabloid, *The American Patriot*, but the publication lasted only a short time. This publication marked the end of DePugh's career in radical politics. Far from considering his activism a failure, he claimed to have paved the way for the victory of conservative Republican Ronald Reagan in the 1980 presidential election.

In 1991, DePugh, who was then running a modeling school and agency, was arrested for sexual exploitation of a minor. Officials searched his wife's home back in Norborne and discovered several weapons probably stored there during the active days of the Minutemen. firearms violations and was convicted on three of them. In the 2000s, a new Minuteman group, The Minuteman Project, formed in opposition to illegal immigration across the American-Mexican border. Members took it upon themselves to patrol the border on their own volition, and against the preferences of the federal government.

See also: National Firearms Act of 1934; Reagan, Ronald.

Further Reading: John George and Laird Wilcox, *Nazis, Communists, Klansmen, and Others on the Fringe* (Buffalo, NY: Prometheus, 1992); Harry J. Jones, *A Private Army* (Toronto: Macmillan, 1969); Minuteman Project Web site, www.minutemanproject.com/.

Minutemen, Revolutionary

The revolutionary-era minutemen captured the imagination of generations of Americans who admired the legendary exploits of these revolutionary patriots. Beginning with the 1960s, many extremist groups who have advocated military preparedness of private citizens and engaged in the caching of firearms have used the name to legitimize their own activities, based to some extent on romantic perceptions of the revolutionary minutemen. The minutemen were militia units organized in the early days of the American Revolution in Massachusetts and a few other colonies. In 1774, in Worcester County, Massachusetts, military regiments were reorganized to eliminate officers and members loyal to Great Britain. New members were selected according to their political preferences and became known for their loyalty to the revolutionary cause.

In October 1774, the Massachusetts revolutionary convention designated a portion of the militia that was to be prepared to take up arms at "a minute's notice" when and where needed. These militiamen became known as minutemen, and the revolutionary convention adopted the name. To be prepared for immediate call, each militia member was expected to have a powder horn and bullet pouch, a bullet mold, and extra flints.

The minutemen are most closely associated with the battles of Lexington and Concord, fought on April 19, 1775. During the night, Paul Revere brought the alarm to Lexington that British regulars were on their way to capture a store of weapons. A company of minutemen responded to the urgent message. When no further news came, some of the minutemen returned home and others waited at a local tavern. At dawn the minutemen, under the command of Captain Jonas Parker, gathered again on Lexington Common. When the British troops arrived, the minutemen appeared on the verge of retreat when a musket shot brought a volley from the British. Eight minutemen were killed and ten more lay wounded. The British soldiers then reorganized for a march to Concord.

In Concord, several hundred minutemen had gathered with muskets. Hearing of the events in Lexington, two companies of minutemen began a march to aid their fellow patriots. However, when the group encountered a British column on the road, they decided it was the better part of valor to reverse direction and retreat back to Concord. They in effect led the way for the British along the road to Concord. The minutemen did not engage the British regulars. Instead, as the enemy made its way back to Boston, snipers, hidden in the thick brush beside the road, picked off many of the marchers. At Menotomy (now called Arlington), a group of 1,800 militiamen fired into the British

column, killing a number of the enemy. By the end of the day, 273 British troops out of a total of 1,800 had been killed, wounded, or were missing. Of the minutemen, 49 were killed and 46 were wounded or missing.

Despite the fame that this group of militia attained, they existed for only a short time. The same month as the battles of Lexington and Concord, the Continental Congress decided not to rely solely on militia and minutemen but instead to recruit men for the regular army. Minuteman units continued for no more than six months, and the last units to be formed existed for only a few days. In the overall conduct of the war, the minutemen played a small role. Minuteman units had brief occasions of activity in other states. For instance, the defensive actions of minutemen maintained the American lines against British attack on Long Island. Minutemen were also active in Virginia.

The route of the minuteman march back to Concord leads to Minuteman National Park, which commemorates the storied exploits of this famous group of men. The vision of the minuteman standing watch pervades patriotic memorials. Although the minutemen, the most well-known portion of the militia, played a minimal role in the American Revolution, in the popular mind they were central to the fight for independence. It is not surprising that contemporary groups have attempted to pattern themselves after the image of a personally armed force ready at any moment to defend the community against outside invasion and what they perceive is a tyrannical government.

Further Reading: William J. Casey, *Where and How the War Was Fought: An Armchair Tour of the American Revolution* (New York: William Morrow, 1976); Robert A. Gross, *The Minutemen and Their World* (New York: Hill and Wang, 2001).

Morton Grove, Illinois

In 1981, the Village of Morton Grove, Illinois, gained the attention of the nation when authorities approved an ordinance regulating firearms. Rather than attempting to regulate or ban one or a few guns, the Morton Grove ordinance (No. 81-11) instituted a general ban on firearms. The ordinance contained an especially controversial provision banning handgun ownership within the boundaries of the village. Although the ordinance led to intense debates regarding the appropriate area of activity of a municipality, it was upheld in court, and led the National Rifle Association (NRA) and other pro-gun groups to seek local preemption laws from state legislatures to reserve the making of gun control policy for the states.

Following passage of the ordinance, those council members supporting the measure presented their justification for adopting an ordinance regulating firearms and other weapons. They explained that the regulation of the possession of firearms could be justified by the village's responsibility to promote the welfare of its citizens. While not specifying a specific increase in crime within the corporate limits of the village, they argued that the widespread accessibility of firearms had increased the *possibility* of deaths and injuries related to the presence of such weapons. Narrowing the focus to handguns, the council members observed that these weapons were generally related to assault, armed robbery, and accidental injuries and death.

The ordinance read in part:
No person shall possess, in the Village of Morton Grove the following:

1. Any bludgeon, black-jack, slug shot, sand bag, metal knuckles or any knife, commonly referred to as a switchblade knife . . .
2. Any weapon from which 8 or more shots or bullets may be discharged by a single function of the firing device, any shotgun having one or more barrels less than 18 inches in length, sometimes called a sawed off shotgun or any weapon made from a shotgun . . . or any bomb, bomb-shell, grenade, bottle or other container containing an explosive substance . . .
3. Any handgun, unless the same has been rendered permanently inoperative.

Specific prohibitions did not apply to peace officers, wardens, and superintendents of prisons, and members of the active or reserve armed forces of the United States, the Illinois National Guard, employees of a railroad or public utility who perform police functions, security guards, agents of the Illinois Legislative Investigating Commission authorized to carry weapons, licensed gun collectors, licensed gun clubs, or those possessing antique firearms.

Due in part to the wide sweep of the ordinance, the council found it necessary to define what constituted a firearm: "any device, by whatever name known, which is designed to expel a projectile or projectiles by the action of

an explosion, expansion of gas or escape of gas." A handgun was defined as any firearm that can be fired with one hand, or has a barrel less than 10 inches long, or is small enough to be concealed on the person. The ordinance also included a list of objects that were excluded from the category "firearm," such as any pneumatic, spring, or BB gun; any device the sole purpose of which is to signal; antique firearms; and model rockets.

Although those debating the effectiveness of gun control measures have attempted to use the Morton Grove case as an example, the village did not have a serious problem with crime prior to passage of the ordinance, and did not make a concerted effort to enforce the ordinance once it went into effect. Of significance was a legal action precipitated by the law. In *Quilici v. Village of Morton Grove* (1982), the U.S. Appeals Court for the Seventh Circuit upheld the ordinance. The Supreme Court refused to hear an appeal of the ruling. Pro-gun forces feared that Morton Grove might become a model for other local jurisdictions that would enact a wide variety of limitations on gun ownership within a single state. Due to the efforts of pro-gun groups, 31 states have enacted preemption laws denying localities the power to enact gun control ordinances.

See also: Kennesaw, Georgia; National Rifle Association; *Quilici v. Village of Morton Grove* (1982); Sawed-Off Shotgun.

Further Reading: Gregg Lee Carter, *The Gun Control Movement* (New York: Twayne, 1997); Alan M. Gottlieb, *The Rights of Gun Owners* (Bellevue, WA: Merril, 1991); Robert J. Spitzer, *Gun Control: A Documentary and Reference Guide* (Westport, CT: Greenwood Press, 2009).

Mothers Against Violence in America (MAVIA)

Founded in January 1994, Mothers Against Violence in America (MAVIA) encouraged community activities to protect young people from violence. The organization cooperated with medical, legal, and law enforcement organizations to educate youth and adults about what it considers the potentially devastating consequences of firearms and has supported firearms legislation as part of its campaign to create a safer environment for youth. With headquarters in Seattle,

Washington, MAVIA initially concentrated efforts in its home state, but also established organizations in California, New York, and several other states. Over 32 chapters were organized in Washington and California schools.

Pamela Eakes, an advertising and public relations professional, founded MAVIA. She had served as deputy chief of staff to Tipper Gore, Vice President Al Gore's wife, during the 1992 presidential election campaign. Pam Bartlett, who has years of experience as a speaker and performance coach, chaired the board of directors. Eakes and Bartlett, along with other staff members, utilized their public relations skills to publicize the goals and recommendations of their organization. MAVIA claimed a membership of 4,000.

A typical presentation by group members, titled "Gun Violence Prevention," attempted to explain why so many gun-related injuries and deaths occur each year and offer alternatives to guns for settling conflicts. MAVIA sponsored a "Day of National Concern about Young People and Gun Violence" in Washington state in which thousands of students pledged "never to use a gun to settle a dispute."

In Washington state, the organization supported legislation that raised the legal age for possessing firearms from 14 to 18, and advocated a measure that expanded the sentencing ranges for those convicted of manslaughter. MAVIA focused on the dangers of weapons in homes, advising people to deliberate very seriously before purchasing a firearm, especially if there are children in the home. Recognizing that the debate over the benefits and costs of firearms continues to rage, MAVIA urged that guns at least be securely stored to keep children away from them. By the second decade of the twenty-first century, MAVIA was no longer an active group.

Further Reading: Robert J. Spitzer, *The Politics of Gun Control,* 6th ed. (Boulder, CO: Paradigm, 2015).

Muscarello v. United States (1998)

In *Muscarello v. United States* (524 U.S. 125, 1998), the U.S. Supreme Court dealt with appeals of convictions based on a section of federal firearms statutes that imposes a five-year mandatory prison term for any person who "uses or carries a firearm . . . during and in relation to" a "drug trafficking crime" [18 U.S.C. 924 (c) (1)]. The decision hinged on the meaning of the word

"carry." The Court held that the phrase "carries a firearm" can refer to the possession and conveyance of firearms in a vehicle, even if the firearm is kept in a locked glove compartment or trunk.

The Court combined two cases in its final decision. In the first, Frank J. Muscarello was charged with unlawfully selling marijuana. When police officers searched his truck, they found not only the marijuana, but a handgun locked in the glove compartment. In the second case, Donald Cleveland and Enrique Gray-Santana placed several firearms in the trunk of their car before proceeding to a scheduled drug purchase, intending instead to steal the drugs. When police arrested Cleveland and Gray-Santana, they found both the drugs and the guns. The Courts of Appeals determined that the defendants had carried the guns "during and in relation to a drug trafficking offense." The Supreme Court heard the case on appeal to determine whether guns kept in a locked glove compartment or an automobile trunk constituted "carrying" a firearm under federal statute 924 (c) (1). The defendants argued that carrying meant "bearing" a firearm, or keeping it on the person; the statute did not apply to situations in which a person kept a firearm in a locked glove compartment or car trunk. However, the Court favored the "ordinary English meaning," which included the possibility of carrying in a "wagon, car, truck, or other vehicle that one accompanies."

The Court's decision depended upon what it considered Congress's intentions in using the word "carry." Examining the law's purpose and legislative history, the Court found no support for restricting the word to instances in which a weapon is kept on the person. Given that the law's purpose involved decreasing the probability of violence associated with the illegal drug trade, firearms kept in cars are not less dangerous than guns kept on the person.

The defendants argued that to move beyond an application of "carrying" to keeping on the person made the term equivalent to "transporting." The Court rejected this contention, specifying the basic distinctions in meaning between the two terms. The defendants also referred to the Court's previous narrow interpretation of the phrase "uses . . . a firearm," a related term appearing in the law. The Court responded that the limitation of "use" to "active employment" does not affect the meaning of "carry" which does not necessarily signify a similar active utilization. The Court ruled it could not interpret "carry" in a similarly narrow sense as "uses" without "undercutting the statute's basic objective."

The defendants argued that such a broad reading would expand the instances in which the law applies. However, the Court noted that the statute contains limiting conditions for the application of the carrying provision: A defendant carries a gun "during and in relation to" a drug crime. Circumstances in which a gun is "immediately accessible" and circumstances in which a firearm is carried in a trunk or locked glove compartment are, according to the Court, "logically difficult to distinguish." Finally, with regard to an argument for invoking the rule of lenity due to the ambiguity of statutory wording, the Court responded that ambiguity to some extent characterizes all statutes. Congress's meaning is not "grievously ambiguous" and therefore the Court did not depend on simply guessing legislators' intent.

See also: Bailey v. United States (1996); Firearm Sentence Enhancement Laws.

Further Reading: *Muscarello v. United States* (524 U.S. 125, 1998).

N

National Association of Federally Licensed Firearms Dealers (NAFLFD)

Established in 1973, the National Association of Federally Licensed Firearms Dealers (NAFLFD) represents those individuals who have obtained a license from the federal government to sell firearms (FFLs), and is the oldest such organization. The organization provides its members with information about legislative action important to firearms dealers and disseminates material supporting the gun rights position. The NAFLFD distributes to members production and sales information regarding the firearms industry, descriptions of new products, and advice about conducting a retail business. In addition, the organization gathers data on the import, export, and domestic production of firearms. The Association publishes the *American Firearms Industry*, a monthly magazine that reports on firearms and outdoor sports, cutlery, and archery. The magazine reports on the current political scene with regard to firearms policy, and is also the publication for the Professional Gun Retailers Association (PGRA).

Although officially opposed to further gun control legislation, the organization assists its members in complying with existing rules and regulations in federal firearms law that are administered largely by the Bureau of Alcohol, Tobacco, and Firearms (ATF). The organization sells its members a Firearms Record Book to assist them in keeping accurate records of serial numbers, and the makes and models of firearms in case any are stolen, thus protecting the dealer from possible liability.

The Association supports claims that firearms possession by law-abiding citizens results in less,

not more, crime. The NAFLFD asserts that gun ownership can give women an advantage against an attacker who likely is much stronger than the victim. Further, the claim is made that the number of accidental deaths attributed to firearms is minimal and that lenient state concealed carry laws add little to accidental firearms deaths, while deterring many more acts of violence.

The NAFLFD contests many of the claims of pro-gun control groups. The organization notes that since 1970 fatal gun accidents among children have declined 65 percent even though the number of firearms available to Americans has greatly increased. Citing gun researcher Gary Kleck, the organization disputes the estimate that 135,000 schoolchildren carry guns to school every day. The Association claims that the actual figure is closer to 16,000-17,000. The group also challenges the claim that the leading cause of death among all older teenagers in the United States is guns, claiming instead that this is true only of African American males.

The Association affirms the view that the reduction of street crime in the United States is in the hands of the average, armed citizen. Supporters of gun control, skeptical of such claims, note the financial link between more citizens owning guns and the NAFLFD: Federally licensed firearms dealers would be the source of weapons in a new wave of purchases by private citizens. The Association counters by noting that the "crime-bureaucratic complex" in the United States, composed of lawyers, the courts, insurance companies, and public officials, profit from the existing level of crime.

NAFLFD members believe that the problem of crime in the United States results from a circumstance that allows criminals to get what they want with minimal risk to personal safety or minimal chance of legal punishment. Association members sell a product that they claim is part of the answer to violent crime. Criminals must be deterred from committing criminal acts, and the Association envisions private citizens armed with guns as a key link in crime reduction, along with stiffer sentencing and the more frequent use of the death penalty.

See also: Assault Weapons Ban; Bureau of Alcohol, Tobacco, Firearms, and Explosives; Concealed Carry Laws; Kleck, Gary; Lott, John R. Jr.

Further Reading: *American Firearms Industry* magazine; National Association of Federally Licensed Firearms Dealers Web site, www.amfire.com.

National Association for Gun Rights (NAGR)

The National Association for Gun Rights (NAGR), established in 2005, distinguishes itself from other gun rights organizations as a "no compromise" association regarding the Second Amendment right to keep and bear arms. A key issue focus for the group is "Constitutional Carry:" individuals should not be required to receive government permission before exercising their right possess and carry firearms in self-defense. The NAGR has contributed to the introduction of legislation in several states that would recognize the right to carry a firearm without the requirement of obtaining a license. The organization claims credit for the passage of "Constitutional Carry" in Kansas and Maine in 2015.

Dudley Brown, a gun rights lobbyist since 1993, serves as the organization's president. He established Rocky Mountain Gun Owners in 1996 as an organization strongly opposed to any concession on gun rights, a stance he brought to the NAGR in 2006 as the organization's president. In Colorado, Brown led the successful fight against the concealed carry ban on the Colorado State University campus, the effort to maintain the right to carry a firearm on Post Office property, and the push to block additional gun control legislation following the 2012 mass shooting at the Sandy Hook Elementary School in Newtown, Connecticut.

The NAGR has affiliated organization in more than 13 states and claims more than 4.5 million members and supporters, which apparently includes members of the affiliated groups. Individuals can join the organization for a yearly fee of $35. The NAGR maintains a membership level call Frontline Defenders, which involves making a monthly donation to the organization. Members receive a quarterly newsletter, *The Gun Activist*.

The NAGR states that, like the National Rifle Association (NRA), it is a gun right organization, but that, unlike the NRA, it is completely opposed to any compromise on the gun rights issue. The NAGR faults the NRA for supporting the instant background check system established in the 1993 Brady Handgun Violence Prevention Act and the 1996 Lautenberg Amendment that prohibits the purchase or ownership of a firearm to anyone convicted of domestic violence against a spouse or child. The NAGR also criticizes the NRA for endorsing and supporting financially political candidates whose support for gun rights has proved less than unconditional. According to the organization, the NRA does not support the major position of allowing citizens to carry concealed weapons without requiring a government-issued permit and firearm training, claiming that the NRA instead supports national reciprocity legislation, by which states would be required to recognize the concealed carry permits of other states. The NAGR claims that the NRA benefits financially from offering firearms training programs that are required in most states in order to receive a concealed carry permit.

The NAGR has a staff of more than 60 employees and offers a three-month corporate internship for undergraduate and graduate students in political science, marketing communication, and related fields. Interns participate in various organization activities, including political research, issue advocacy, and grassroots lobbying.

See also: Concealed Carry Laws; Lautenberg Amendment; National Rifle Association; Second Amendment.

Further Reading: National Association for Gun Rights Web site, www.nationalgunrights.org.

National Association of Police Organizations (NAPO)

In 1985, the National Association of Police Organizations (NAPO) joined with several other groups representing police officers in an unsuccessful attempt to prevent passage of the McClure-Volkmer Act, also known as the Firearms Owners Protection Act of 1986. NAPO opposed provisions of the legislation that weakened the Gun Control Act of 1968, believing the law placed law enforcement personnel in greater danger. Since 1985, organization members have continued to pass resolutions on gun control issues. A major motivation on this and any public policy issue has been the safety and rights of organization members.

Representing more than 2,000 police units and associations, 241,000 law enforcement officers, 11,000 retired officers, and more than 100,000 other citizens, NAPO, formed in 1978, represents the interests of law enforcement through legislative lobbying, legal advocacy, and educational and research programs. In 1991, the organization established the Police Research and Education Project (PREP) to "promote the well-being of police officers and their families and to educate the public about the role of law enforcement officers in a democratic society." In cooperation with the National Institute of Justice, PREP has investigated the effects of stress on law enforcement officers and their families. NAPO's National Law Enforcement Officers' Rights Center defends officers' legal and constitutional rights. The Center has assisted police officers and their families by, for instance, filing *amicus curiae* briefs in court cases involving officers.

Among its many issue positions, NAPO has supported legislation to allow qualified active and former law enforcement officers to carry concealed weapons in any jurisdiction in the United States. This measure would limit concealed carrying to current and former law enforcement officers and would not apply to the general population. NAPO supports legislation that would establish the death penalty for killing a law enforcement officer or a federal correctional official. In addition, NAPO backs federal government appropriations to hire additional law enforcement officers nationwide to reach legislatively mandated goals.

NAPO supported the 1994 Violent Crime Control and Law Enforcement Act, which widened the ban on armor-piercing ammunition. Although gun rights groups have expressed doubts about the existence of specifically armor-piercing ammunition, popularly called "cop-killer" bullets, NAPO contends that such ammunition can be distinguished by its ability to penetrate a bulletproof vest. The organization supports legislation banning mail-order sales of bulletproof vests. Calling it "every law enforcement officer's worst nightmare," NAPO is concerned about violent criminals who wear body armor while committing crimes, thus putting police in greater danger of being injured or killed by a criminal's return fire.

NAPO supports legislation that would modify the prohibition on possession or ownership of firearms by anyone, including police officers, convicted of domestic violence misdemeanor charges. The proposal would establish an "official use" exception for law enforcement officers while on duty. A "capable and qualified" officer found guilty of domestic violence would be prohibited from keeping firearms in the home, but could carry a gun while at work. It also has voiced opposition to the growing concealed carry movement that has encouraged civilians to carry guns in public.

See also: Firearms Owners Protection Act; Gun Control Act of 1968; McClure, James Albertas; Volkmer, Harold Lee.

Further Reading: National Association of Police Organizations Web site, www.napo.org.

National Association of School Psychologists (NASP)

The National Association of School Psychologists (NASP) supports gun control measures as a means of protecting the physical and psychological well-being of children, and promotes policies in schools and communities that deal effectively with the possible physical and psychological harm that firearms may cause children. The organization assists policy makers, community leaders, educators, and school psychologists in creating a safe school environment for children. Based in Bethesda, Maryland, NASP collaborates with other organizations, such as the American Psychological Association, in furthering its position on firearms and other issues.

Membership in NASP is open to anyone who works, or is qualified, as a school psychologist, a consultant or a supervisor of psychological services, or is engaged primarily in training school psychologists. NASP has over 26,000 members. Members elect delegates to the Delegate Assembly, which makes policy that is implemented by the Executive Council. The Council is composed of officers, program managers, regional directors, and delegate representatives. The organization publishes a newsletter, the *Communique*, eight times a year, as well as the quarterly *School Psychology Review* and books, monographs, and papers on various subjects, including youth violence and its relation to firearms.

In April 1998, Scott Poland, director of psychological services for a Houston, Texas, school district, represented NASP in testimony before the U.S. House of Representatives Committee on Education and the Workforce. Poland served as a leader for teams of psychologists that were sent to Paducah, Kentucky, and Jonesboro, Arkansas, following school shootings in these cities. Poland claimed that firearms "represent the single greatest threat to education and school children," citing estimates that as many as 270,000 firearms "go to school in America." He told the committee that the availability of firearms to children must be reduced, stating that, "There is a gun in every third home and almost every child can obtain a gun in a few hours." Gun access was cited as one of the predictive factors of youth violence. He questioned the wisdom of gun ownership, asserting that a gun in the home is more likely to kill a family member by accident, homicide, or suicide than to be used in defense against an intruder. Poland stated that he supports legislation that penalizes firearms owners whose weapons are used by children to injure or kill themselves or others.

In an article that appeared in the November 1998 NASP newsletter, Jeremy Shapiro reported on research dealing with attitudes of youth toward guns and violence. Shapiro stated that the number of handguns available in society is directly related to the level of violence, citing Arthur Kellermann's claim that the presence of a firearm in a conflict increases the probability that serious injury and death will occur. Shapiro summarized the results of the Attitudes Toward Guns and Violence Questionnaire (ATGVQ) administered to students in four school systems, concluding that exposure to guns, including witnessing a shooting and having a gun in the home, increased scores on such factors as associating guns and violence with feelings of safety and power and expressing comfortable acceptance of violence. Shapiro noted that the greater attraction of guns and violence in adolescents made them less responsive to "preventive interventions" than younger children. The NASP has continued to speak out against the

problems of guns and youth, decrying in particular school shootings, gun suicides, and other gun-related violence plaguing young people.

See also: Jonesboro, Arkansas, School Shooting; Kellermann, Arthur; Littleton, Colorado, Columbine School Shooting; Schools and Guns; Stockton, California, Shooting; Youth and Guns.

Further Reading: National Association of School Psychologists Web site, www/nasponline.org.

National Center for Injury Prevention and Control (NCIPC)

The Centers for Disease Control and Prevention (CDC) established the National Center for Injury Prevention and Control (NCIPC) in June 1992 to conduct and support research on various causes of injury and possible injury prevention measures. In 1995, the agency came under attack from gun rights organizations such as the National Rifle Association (NRA), which claimed that the firearms research funded by the NCIPC was biased against gun ownership. Critics argued that the NCIPC duplicated the work of other federal agencies and therefore ought to be disbanded. The agency survived such attacks, although with a smaller and restricted budget, but the CDC has been barred from engaging in research "to advocate or promote gun control."

Firearms injuries research historically represents a small portion of the NCIPC's activities. The agency engages in studies of such injury-related factors as falls, fires and burns, drowning, poisoning, automobile accidents, and playground accidents. The NCIPC believes that accidents are not random occurrences and therefore are preventable. Along with health professionals, the agency advocates the same scientific procedures, including the epidemiological approach, employed in research on the causes and prevention of disease. Epidemiology involves investigations of the incidence, geographic and demographic spread, and control of disease. The treatment of firearms injuries from an epidemiological perspective has raised charges that public health researchers judge guns as a causal factor in injuries and therefore as something to be eliminated.

In response to charges of anti-gun bias, the NCIPC claims it is an organization that stands above the debate between gun rights groups and those who wish to institute a ban on firearms. In 1996, Mark Rosenberg, the agency's director, argued that the research the Center supports can offer such beneficial outcomes as improved gun design and better methods of firearm storage. The Center's defenders maintain that the public health perspective should offer the middle ground that will involve more people in discussions about the place of firearms in American society. However, the NRA and other pro-gun groups claim that the Center and health care professionals conducting research on firearms have ignored the findings of firearms researchers who take alternative perspectives. The NRA has gone so far as to claim that NCIPC-funded researchers have provided misleading or false results to support their predrawn conclusions. Center representatives respond that pro-gun groups have reacted so negatively to research results because objective data have not supported the pro-gun position.

In a 1997 publication dealing with fatal firearm injuries from 1962 to 1994, the NCIPC observed that in 1994 firearm injuries represented the ninth leading cause of death, and the second leading cause of death among those between ages 10 and 24. From 1962 to 1994, the number of deaths due to firearms rose from 16,720 to 38,505, a 130-percent increase. The agency estimated that gun assaults on family members and other close acquaintances are 12 times more likely to lead to death than assaults with other weapons. The Center noted that people living in households containing firearms have a five times greater risk of suicide than non-gun owning households.

See also: Concealed Carry Laws; Health Care Professionals; National Rifle Association.

Further Reading: National Center for Injury Prevention and Control Web site, www.cdc.gov/injury/; National Research Council, *Firearms and Violence* (Washington, DC: The National Academies Press, 2005).

National Center for Policy Analysis (NCPA)

In 1983, John Goodman established the National Center for Policy Analysis (NCPA) at the University of Dallas as a nonpartisan, nonprofit public policy research institute. The NCPA opened

an office in Washington, D.C., where its scholars often testify before congressional committees and brief congressional aides on policy issues. The Center has conducted studies in many policy areas, including health care, taxes, Social Security, welfare, criminal justice, education, and environmental regulation. The NCPA, which advocates free market solutions to policy questions, has published commentaries critical of gun control measures and in support of the right of citizens to own and carry firearms for self-protection.

Goodman serves as president of the Center. His areas of expertise include tax, welfare, and Social Security policy and health care reform. Pete du Pont is the policy chairman for the NCPA. He has made presentations on various subjects, including tax reform, economic growth, education, and health care. The NCPA includes centers for health policy studies, tax policy, the environment, and criminal justice.

In its support of the right of individual citizens to possess and carry firearms for self-protection, the NCPA notes that while government has a general duty to enforce laws, it does not have a specific legal obligation to protect individuals. Therefore, to the extent that government denies law-abiding citizens the right to own firearms for self-protection, it denies them the means to protect themselves. The Center notes that each year armed civilians kill almost 3,000 criminals, which is over three times the number killed by police. Civilians wound another 9,000 to 17,000 criminals each year. The organization argues that civilians armed with concealed weapons are a major deterrent to crime.

The NCPA has criticized the call for legislation to require that gun safety locks be provided with each new handgun. Because manufacturers of locks recommend that guns be kept unloaded, the Center contends that locked and unloaded firearms are made less useful for self-defense. While intended to make guns child-safe, gun locks "make homes easier targets for criminals" and can actually increase the number of deaths resulting from crime. Citing surveys in which criminals reported being more fearful of armed homeowners than of the police, the Center places great importance on the ability of private citizens to defend themselves.

The NCPA opposes bans on assault weapons, claiming that these weapons are not functionally different from other semiautomatic firearms, including guns used for hunting and target shooting. The Center notes that since 1934 a special license has been required for a civilian to possess automatic firearms; but "no civilian has ever used a legally owned machine gun in a violent crime." According to the Center, neither automatic nor semiautomatic weapons are used often in the commission of crimes. The NCPA argues that while assault weapons bans have little effect on criminals, they create significant problems for law-abiding citizens who are prevented from owning such weapons for self-defense.

The NCPA has criticized the Brady Handgun Violence Prevention Act, claiming that it has had little effect on the availability of firearms to criminals while it wasted law enforcement resources by requiring background checks. The NCPA has also advocated allowing college personnel to carry concealed handguns on college campuses as a way to thwart campus shootings.

See also: Assault Weapons Ban; Brady Handgun Violence Prevention Act; Concealed Carry Laws; Health Care Professionals; Trigger Locks; Youth and Guns.

Further Reading: National Center for Policy Analysis Web site, www.ncpa.org.

National Crime Prevention Council (NCPC)

The National Crime Prevention Council (NCPC) is a national organization that develops strategies to deter criminal activities, including those involving firearms. The organization was established in 1982 to manage a national advertising campaign featuring McGruff, the "take a bite out of crime" dog, and to coordinate programs for the Crime Prevention Coalition. The NCPC urges Americans to become aware of steps they can take to reduce the chances of being victims of crime and encourages nonviolent ways of resolving conflicts. Among its recommendations, the Council discourages the use of firearms for self-protection.

The NCPC focuses much of its energies on ways of preventing youth violence. In 1998, at the Eleventh National Youth Crime Prevention Conference, NCPC executive director John A. Calhoun referred to recent school shootings and declared that firearms should be considered hazardous consumer products that ought to be subject to strict safety regulation, like children's toys. He noted that gun ownership requires few if any of the standards established for driving

automobiles, including education, competency tests, licensing, and insurance. Calhoun urged his young audience to contact political leaders and policy makers about the personal, economic, and social costs of firearm accessibility, asking "How many more Jonesboros will it take before we stop the killing?" Subsequent school shootings have caused the organization to redouble its efforts.

Although the Council provides recommendations for maintaining a home safe from crime, having a handgun in the home is not considered a viable option for defense. The Council advises people to "think long and hard" about keeping a firearm, citing studies showing that a gun in the home is far less likely to stop a crime than it is to harm or kill a family member or other innocent person, or result in a gun suicide. Other ways of protecting the home are recommended, including improving locks, having a dog, introducing an alarm system, and joining a Neighborhood Watch program.

If there is a firearm in the home, the NCPC recommends that all family members receive instruction in firearm safety. Children should be taught that if they discover a gun they should follow the instructions of the National Rifle Association's (NRA) Eddie Eagle: "Stop, Don't Touch, Get Away, and Tell a Trusted Adult." However, unlike gun rights advocates, who regard firearms as an effective means of home defense, simple education is not considered a sufficient safety measure by itself. Firearms should be safely stored in gun cases or pistol boxes and should be kept unloaded and with a trigger lock. Such measures would decrease the probability that a firearm would accidentally harm a family member, especially a child.

The NCPC has produced public service announcements intended to make the general public aware of the dangers of gun violence. It has also produced a variety of educational lessons and programs aimed at children of various ages to educate them about the dangers associated with guns. It also established the "McGruff Network," named after the cartoon character "McGruff the Crime Dog," to promote self-protection and crime prevention in localities and states. Such efforts are intended to "spur people to take action to reduce the effects of gun violence on children."

See also: Eddie Eagle; Jonesboro, Arkansas, School Shooting; Littleton, Colorado, Columbine School Shooting; National Rifle Association;

Schools and Guns; Stockton, California, Shooting; Trigger Locks; Youth and Guns.

Further Reading: National Crime Prevention Council Web site, www.ncpc.org.

National Education Association (NEA)

Although the National Education Association (NEA) holds that the problem of violence in public schools is not nearly as serious as the mass media suggest and that most schools maintain a safe environment for students, the organization still recognizes school violence and the presence of firearms as real problems that need to be addressed. In 1998, NEA president Bob Chase was quoted as stating, "America's culture of violence has breached the boundaries of the schoolhouse." In 1997, the NEA made the maintenance of school safety one of its major priorities. While primarily advocating school-community alliances to minimize the occurrence of violence, the NEA has also supported legislation at the state and national levels aimed at limiting youth access to firearms, and has opposed efforts to allow public school employees (other than police or security guards) to carry guns in schools.

Founded in 1857, the NEA is the nation's largest organization representing public school teachers. With a membership of about 3.2 million educators at all levels, from preschools to universities, affiliate organizations in all states, and 14,000 local groups, the Association has significant influence on education policy. The NEA's policy positions are set at an annual meeting of the Representative Assembly, which is composed of more than 9,000 delegates from the state and local organizations. Between meetings of the Representative Assembly, the elected Board of Directors and the Executive Committee serve as the decision-making bodies for the Association.

The NEA has declared its concern over the easy accessibility youth have to firearms. Citing data of the number of killings occurring at schools nationwide, the organization has called for responsible gun ownership, including safe storage. The organization has presented data from the U.S. Centers for Disease Control and Prevention (CDC), claiming that 20 percent of high school students surveyed reported carrying a weapon at least once in the last month.

The NEA has called for a "zero-tolerance" approach to firearms in schools: Any student found with a firearm should be expelled immediately and those who sell firearms and other weapons to students should be subject to severe penalties. The Association supports the strict regulation of the manufacture, importation, distribution, sale, and resale of handguns and ammunition. The organization has passed a resolution calling for a ban on the private possession of automatic firearms and semiautomatic assault weapons. The NEA supports the reintroduction of a waiting period before the sale of firearms to allow for a more thorough background check. The resolution also supports educational programs for gun owners that emphasize responsible handling and safe storage of guns.

The NEA's program for violence reduction in public schools extends beyond the elimination of firearms in and around school campuses. Students must feel that they need not arm themselves for self-protection. Various educational strategies are recommended that promote nonviolent resolution of conflicts. Although discipline in the schools plays a crucial role in minimizing violence, the NEA believes the family and the larger community are important sources of violent behavior among students. Therefore, any effective procedure for violence control must include parental and community participation. It has consistently supported the expulsion of students found carrying firearms to schools.

See also: Assault Weapons Ban; Gun-Free Schools Act; Jonesboro, Arkansas, School Shooting; Littleton, Colorado, Columbine School Shooting; Schools and Guns; Stockton, California, Shooting; Youth and Guns.

Further Reading: National Education Association Web site, www.nea.org.

National Firearms Act of 1934

The National Firearms Act of 1934 was the first gun law to have national application. In 1934, congressional hearings were called to consider firearms regulation because the violence related to the gangsterism and organized crime of the Prohibition era, and to the criminal activities of such notorious outlaws as John Dillinger led many to believe that national regulation of firearms was necessary. Democratic President Franklin Delano Roosevelt played a role in the push toward legislation. While governor of New York, Roosevelt had lobbied for handgun licensing laws and the banning of machine guns, and continued that agenda when he became president in 1933. His administration took steps to improve the welfare of the nation, and gun control could be seen as one aspect of that objective. More immediately, an attempt had been made on Roosevelt's life in Miami in 1933 (the killer shot and killed Chicago Mayor Anton Cermak, who was with Roosevelt). The assassination attempt resulted in a call for legislation to limit firearms.

Roosevelt's attorney general, Homer Cummings, was strongly committed to gun control measures, stating at one point, "Show me a man who does not want his gun registered and I will show you a man who should not have a gun." He believed that the sale of machine guns in particular should be regulated and that owners should register with the government, but ultimately held that all firearms should be registered. In 1934, a bill was introduced in Congress that provided for regulation of the sale of machine guns and a requirement to register all handguns.

The National Rifle Association (NRA), whose leadership at this time was not completely opposed to firearms legislation, was nonetheless unwilling to accept handgun registration, regarding it as an unwarranted invasion of the rights of law-abiding citizens. Ironically, the Roosevelt administration's emphasis on gangsterism as the major threat probably contributed to the success of the NRA and other groups in narrowing the bill to gangster-type weapons. The NRA activated those in the sporting community through editorials and press releases to write their congresspeople to oppose national registration. With a deluge of antiregistration mail, the term "all weaponry" in the bill was deleted and replaced with "machine guns and sawed-off shotguns." The NRA supported passage of the amended bill.

The act called for the taxation of the manufacture, sale, and transfer of weapons and associated materials most often connected to gangster activities, including machine guns, sawed-off shotguns, sawed-off rifles, and silencers. Purchasers of weapons covered by the act had to undergo background investigations by the Federal Bureau of Investigation (FBI) and were required to provide a photograph and submit to fingerprinting

to determine past criminal activity. The legislation then required that the weapon be registered. The law imposed a transfer tax of $200 on the seller of the weapon. If someone's application to purchase a weapon were approved, that person was then required to gain the approval of local law enforcement officials to have the weapon in that local jurisdiction.

Although Roosevelt's Justice Department continued to advocate handgun registration, the National Firearms Act represented the last time the president himself took an active role in encouraging such legislation. The legislation was a factor in the NRA's establishment of a legislative division to deal with any further gun related legislation.

See also: National Rifle Association; Sawed-Off Shotgun; Tommy Gun.

Further Reading: Lee Kennett and James La Verne Anderson, *The Gun in America: The Origins of a National Dilemma* (Westport, CT: Greenwood, 1975); Earl Kruschke, *Gun Control* (Santa Barbara, CA: ABC-CLIO, 1995); Robert J. Spitzer, *Gun Control: A Documentary and Reference Guide* (Westport, CT: Greenwood Press, 2009).

National Firearms Association (NFA) of Canada

The National Firearms Association (NFA) of Canada was formed in 1978 by David A. Tomlinson (who served as president until 2007) to defend the right to keep and bear arms in Canada and to "battle for effective and fair firearms legislation." The NFA opposed those political interests that called for more stringent gun control. Holding that gun control and human rights abuses go hand in hand, the Association hopes to protect the rights of Canadian firearms owners. Based in Edmonton, Alberta, the organization claims to represent the interests of 7 million firearms owners in Canada. The Association encourages businesses to become members, a list of which the organization provides on its Web site. The NFA provides detailed information to members about Canadian firearms legislation and the activities of the Canadian Firearms Centre (CFC).

The organization offers advice on various legal matters and offers information to executors of estates with firearms regarding the applicability of the law. The Association makes recommendations to firearms owners about what to do if police arrive with a search warrant, or other potential legal problems. The NFA has provided members with transcripts from favorable court decisions involving charges of unsafely storing firearms, claiming that this information most likely provides sufficient precedent to win acquittal.

The NFA's stated objectives include promotion of firearms safety and education, working for justice by promoting "fair and practical" firearms legislation, and to advance political activities to promote gun ownership and use focused in the Canadian national capital of Ottawa and around the country. The organization provides expert witnesses for firearms-related court cases and lobbies for changes in firearms regulations. It encourages grassroots political activity in all Canadian political parties. Emphasizing that it is nonpartisan, the NFA urges individual members to become involved in the party of their choice. Participation in the selection of nominees for public office is considered especially important.

To attract and retain members, the NFA offers $2 million in liability insurance coverage at a low yearly charge and provides advice over the phone on various matters related to firearms, including shooting range construction, and provides transcripts of court cases dealing with firearms, including NFA legal test cases. The NFA's Patches Program encourages Canadian gun owners to practice gun safety and to undergo training in the use of firearms. The organization also issues bulletins about present firearms regulations and political developments with commentary and analysis. The NFA's official magazine is the *Canadian Firearms Journal*.

Like the National Rifle Association (NRA), the NFA has expressed concern about United Nations (UN) conferences to discuss possible international controls on the small arms trade. The organization has urged its members to support a petition drive to inform the UN and member countries supporting "world disarmament" about the views of firearms owners.

See also: Canada; National Rifle Association; United Nations.

Further Reading: National Firearms Association of Canada Web site, www.nfa.ca.

National Instant Check System (NICS)

The Brady Handgun Violence Prevention Act, enacted in 1993, mandated that a National Instant Check System (NICS) be put into effect by November 1998. The statute initially established a five-day waiting period for purchasing a handgun to allow authorities to check a prospective purchaser's background, and provide for a cooling-off period before a gun purchase. The instant check was intended to replace the waiting period after a national computer system containing federal and state records had been established. Nine categories of individuals are disqualified from purchasing a handgun under federal law: those convicted or under indictment on felony charges, fugitives, those determined to be mentally ill, those dishonorably discharged from the military, those who have renounced U.S. citizenship, illegal aliens, illegal drug users, those convicted of domestic violence misdemeanors, and those under domestic violence restraining orders. While some firearms organizations, such as the National Rifle Association (NRA) supported NICS, other organizations, such as Gun Owners of America (GOA), opposed any check system at all. Gun control supporters doubted the effectiveness of the proposed computer system in conducting background checks on prospective handgun purchasers.

The system involves federally licensed firearms dealers making a toll-free call directly to NICS. Larger retail outlets may use a computerized system that further increases the speed of the check. Each dealer has an identification number and password to access the system. Prior to initiation of the system, the Federal Bureau of Investigation (FBI) estimated that the average check would take approximately two minutes. In cases where delay occurs, the FBI has up to three days to approve or deny the sale. The system operates seven days a week.

As the deadline for NICS to become operational approached, many people expressed concern about the completeness of records. Although Sarah Brady, president of Handgun Control, Inc. (later the Brady Campaign), praised the new instant check system, she raised concerns about the absence of crucial information, such as the records of mental patients, to run a comprehensive background check. In 1992, just 18 percent of complete and accurate state criminal records were available on computer. The percent of state criminal records that were computer accessible increased to 33 percent by 1995, when states started to receive federal funds to improve their records systems. The Justice Department hoped that NICS would be at 50 percent efficiency by the time the system became active. When the system first went into effect, some state and local records involving involuntary mental hospital admissions, domestic violence misdemeanors, and recent arrests not yet computerized were unavailable for the checks. Many states failed to submit proper information regarding mental records until after the Virginia Tech shooting of 2007, when Congress passed new legislation to provide funding for those states that still did not have proper data, and to penalize those states that did not comply. Up until 2007, only twenty-two states submitted mental health data to the NICS system (the Brady law did not include any penalties for states that did not comply).

Before NICS began, Democratic President Bill Clinton expressed his hope that the five-day waiting period would remain in effect to discourage purchases made in the heat of anger. While many pro-gun advocates, such as Wayne LaPierre of the NRA, lobbied strongly for replacement of the five-day waiting system with the instant check, some gun rights activists expressed as much opposition to NICS as they did to the original five-day waiting period. They argued that background checks have failed to reduce crime and violence and claimed that records may be inaccurate, containing initial arrest data but lacking ultimate disposition of many cases, including those in which the suspect was cleared of committing any crime. The FBI stated that it would retain information from checks for 18 months to assist with auditing, to check the system's security, and to track its success. During the George W. Bush presidency, however, Congress enacted legislation to require destruction of the NICS data after 24 hours, and to restrict access to the data by other law enforcement agencies. For some people, any record-keeping at all amounts to a national system of gun registration. From the time of the law's enactment through 2008, about 1.8 million handgun sales were blocked as the result of the law (about 2 percent of all handgun purchases). In 2009, the government passed its 100 millionth background check. By the end of 2014, 2.4 million gun sales had been blocked under the law.

See also: Background Checks; Brady Campaign to Prevent Gun Violence; Brady Handgun Violence Prevention Act; Brady, Sarah; Clinton, William Jefferson (Bill); Gun Owners of America; LaPierre, Wayne; National Rifle Association; Virginia Tech Shooting.

Further Reading: Robert J. Spitzer, *The Politics of Gun Control,* 6th ed. (Boulder, CO: Paradigm, 2015).

National Integrated Ballistic Information Network (NIBIN)

In 1999, the Bureau of Alcohol, Tobacco, Firearms, and Explosives (ATF) established the National Integrated Ballistic Information Network (NIBIN), which is a grant-in-aid program to state and local law enforcement agencies that makes available ballistic imagining technology that allows state and local law enforcement laboratory examiners to compare tool marks on spent cartridges or bullets recovered from crime scenes with digitized images of ballistic evidence in the database.

During the manufacture of firearms, microscopic markings (referred to as tool marks) are left on the firearm, and such markings are transferred to the bullet or cartridge case when the gun is fired. These cartridges and bullets, when collected from crime scenes, can be converted through ballistic imagining technology into digitized images and uploaded to the NIBIN database. The system then searches for matches, called "hits." If matches are discovered, this information is sent to the state or local jurisdiction where an examiner views the match possibilities. If the examiner concludes that there is a match, the examiner can confirm the hit by making an actual comparison under a microscope. If the hit is confirmed, the laboratory sends a report to police investigators.

The NIBIN involves having microscopes attached to computers to view magnified images of spent casings and bullets, and thus recording the distinct and unique microscopic physical features produced by the firing pin and breech face. Confiscated firearms are test fired and the casings are recorded in the database. When a casing from a crime scene is entered into the ATF-maintained database, the software searches for images with similar characteristics and produces a "hit list" of potential matches. These possible matches are then returned to the lab technician for further examination.

Although the NIBIN is considered a highly promising tool for law enforcement in linking crimes committed by the same gun and in discovering overall patterns of firearm-related crime in and across local jurisdictions, its effectiveness has varied due to differential funding and commitment of personnel and other resources to the project.

One limitation of the NIBIN in many states is inadequate communication between police laboratories and law enforcement agencies conducting crime investigations. The system has been referred to as having high potential as a tactical tool in linking crimes committed with the same firearm and identifying suspects.

Gun rights groups have opposed introduction into the system of information on newly manufactured or imported firearms and so Congress has prohibited the ATF from entering ballistic information on any firearms other than those retrieved in criminal investigations.

See also: Bureau of Alcohol, Tobacco, Firearms, and Explosives; Gunshot Detection Technology; Taggants; Youth Crime Gun Interdiction Initiative.

Further Reading: Bureau of Alcohol, Tobacco, Firearms, and Explosives, "Fact Sheet: National Integrated Ballistic Information Network" (March 2016). www.gov/resource-center/fact-sheet-national-integrated-ballistic-information-network; Anastasiya Bolton, "Crime Fighting 2.0: A New Way of Solving Shooting Cases," KUSA 9 News (2015). Www.9news.com/news/crime/crime-fighting-2-0-a-new-way-of-solving-shooting-cases/134409323; William King, William Wells, Charles Katz, Edward Maguire, and James Frank, "Opening the Black Box of NIBIB: A Descriptive Process and Outcome Evaluation of the Use of NIBIB and Its Effects on Criminal Investigations, Executive Summary" (October 2013). www.ncjrs.gov/pdffiles1?grants/243977.pdf.

National Muzzle Loading Rifle Association (NMLRA)

Founded in 1933, the National Muzzle Loading Rifle Association (NMLRA) is composed of individuals who are muzzle loading shooters and hunters. Members have a deep interest in preserving and celebrating the heritage of American firearms. Muzzle loading guns refer to firearms where the projectile and usually the propellant is loaded through the open end of the barrel of the weapon, as opposed to breech-loading firearms, where the ammunition is fed into the firearm from the trigger end. While gun control advocates express concern about the American gun culture that extends back historically to the late eighteenth and early nineteenth centuries, members of the NMLRA consider firearms a crucial part of American history. The organization's purpose is to "promote, support, nurture, and preserve . . . our nation's rich historical heritage in the sport of muzzle loading." It prides itself on defending members' rights to own, shoot, and hunt with muzzle loading firearms. Because the muzzle loading rifle requires the use of black powder or black powder substitutes, members look with suspicion on calls for taggants (a substance introduced in the black powder to make it traceable) in black powder, which they fear may alter the performance of this key ingredient in muzzle shooting.

The organization holds two major types of shooting events. In the first event, the rendezvous, members emphasize historical accuracy, priding themselves on preserving the black powder tradition. They attempt to "re-create the historical and aesthetic qualities of loader shooting," dressing in clothing and using equipment common to the eighteenth and early nineteenth centuries and using targets from that era. The second type of event, the local or national shoot, focuses on shooting skills rather than historical accuracy. The NMLRA conducts the National Shoots each year near the organization's headquarters in Friendship, Indiana. From the beginning of the organization in 1933 to the present, the number of competitors has increased from 100 to over 2,000. Many other matches are held around the nation. The organization's monthly publication, *Muzzle Blasts*, contains articles that describe the frontier heritage, report on shooting events, and provide news items of interest to members.

The fascination with muzzle loader shooting is closely tied to "the pungent aroma of blackpowder smoke, the necessity of making one shot do the job, and the link to history." Many enjoy the challenge of slow ignition times. Others are attracted to the organization because most states grant early or special hunting seasons for primitive firearms. The organization emphasizes that the sport is a highly individualized activity. Rifle owners can mix their own powder, cast their own lead balls or bullets, and determine their own accessories. In shooting matches, participants employ a wide variety of rifles, but must be within the guidelines established in the NMLRA's "Range Rules and Regulations."

With approximately 25,000 members, the NMLRA does not have the political influence of the National Rifle Association (NRA) and other gun rights organizations. However, to the extent that the gun control debate includes a struggle over cultural perspectives, the members of this organization, who through their activities honor the history of firearms, oppose attempts to portray firearms as inherently dangerous instruments that should be subject to further government controls.

See also: Gun Culture; National Rifle Association; Taggants.

Further Reading: *Muzzle Blasts Magazine*; National Muzzle Loading Rifle Association Web site, www. nmlra.org.

National Organization of Black Law Enforcement Executives (NOBLE)

Established in 1976 by African American law enforcement executives attending a conference on crime in urban low income areas, the National Organization of Black Law Enforcement Executives (NOBLE) strives to increase the voice of black law enforcement officers regarding the problems of crime in metropolitan areas. The organization, which represents over 3,000 members, works to have its public policy views made known to public officials and to the general public. Based in Alexandria, Virginia, NOBLE expresses a special concern for African American youths, noting that the rate of murder among young black males is 11 times greater than that among young white males. The organization supports policies, including various gun control measures that it believes will contribute to reducing the level of violence among minority youth. Because handguns are considered a major threat, the organization discourages their use by private citizens and opposes any attempts to weaken federal gun control legislation.

NOBLE lobbies for greater minority participation in the various levels of law enforcement. It has strongly supported the continuation of affirmative action programs,

arguing that only through such policies have greater numbers of minorities entered law enforcement and other professions. It has advocated special recruitment projects at predominantly black colleges to attract more minorities into police work. The organization endeavors to develop greater community cooperation with law enforcement agencies, provides a means of greater communication among minority law enforcement executives, and contributes to the conduct of criminal justice research. The organization expresses special concern for the use of excessive or unnecessary deadly force by law enforcement officers and has developed formal guidelines for law enforcement agencies regarding its use.

Noting that the only use for certain types of ammunition is to kill or wound those wearing body armor, NOBLE supports the banning of armor-piercing bullets. The organization has recommended that the National Institute of Justice (NIJ) be given the responsibility of testing bulletproof vests to determine which ammunition can pierce body armor. The organization has called for the U.S. attorney general to determine which types of ammunition shall be banned. Noting that between 1985 and 1995, 61 law enforcement officers were killed or injured by individuals wielding assault weapons, NOBLE supported the assault weapons ban enacted in 1994 (it lapsed in 2004). The organization has resolved to work toward the elimination of such weapons, which have contributed to "the genocide of our youth."

NOBLE takes a strong stand against the trend in state legislatures to enact measures permitting the carrying of concealed weapons. It has concluded that carrying concealed weapons imperils the safety of citizens and law enforcement officers. Such laws present an especially serious danger because the weapons training required is inadequate for the responsibility involved in carrying a concealed weapon. The organization urges its members, community leaders, and public officials to oppose further attempts to liberalize concealed carry laws. In addition, NOBLE has voiced its concern about the resurgence of the antigovernment "patriot" movement in the 2000s that has expressed itself in part by violence aimed at law enforcement.

See also: African Americans and Guns; Assault Weapons Ban; Concealed Carry Laws; Youth and Guns.

Further Reading: National Organization of Black Law Enforcement Executives Web site, www. noblenational.org.

National Parks Gun Policy

In the waning days of his administration in 2008, the Interior Department under Republican President George W. Bush issued a rule allowing people to carry concealed loaded firearms in national parks and wildlife refuges. The order, enacted at the urging of the National Rifle Association (NRA), altered federal policy dating to the second decade of the twentieth century that barred such carrying. Under the policy the Bush administration sought to overturn, people traveling in parks were required to keep guns "inoperable or packed, cased or stored in a manner that will prevent their ready use." Those found in violation were subject to citation and a fine of up to $150. The 2008 rule came on the heels of failed attempts to change the law through congressional action. Opponents of the new rule, including gun control and environmental activists, halted its implementation by filing suit against the measure in federal court. The logjam was finally broken when Congress passed a provision allowing gun carrying in 2009. Democratic President Barack Obama signed the measure into law in May 2009. The measure took effect in February 2010.

Proponents of the parks open carry law argued that the measure would allow park visitors to protect themselves from wild animals and criminal acts, and that the action was a logical extension of Second Amendment rights. According to NRA lobbyist Chris Cox, "You read stories about people attacked by animals or who stumble upon meth labs or women who are raped in a national park. We don't believe law-abiding citizens should be kept from protecting themselves and their families."

Opponents of the change, including former National Park Service officials, argued that the change was unjustified because crime rates as well as animal attacks in parks are vanishingly small. The introduction of loaded weapons would, if anything, pose a greater threat to the safety of park visitors and would contradict the family-friendly nature of parks. According to a letter written by seven former heads of the Park Service, "There is no evidence that any potential problems that one can imagine arising from the existing regulations [i.e., the ban on gun carrying] might overwhelm the good they are known to do." In addition, park officials and conservationists expressed concern that the measure would lead to an increase in wildlife poaching, and make the illegal hunting of protected species more difficult. Under the non-gun-carry rule, park officials had probable cause to stop anyone seen carrying a gun. Under the new rule, park rangers would have to "see somebody shoot at wildlife or catch them standing over the carcass," according to Association of National Park Rangers President Scot McElveen.

Legislative efforts accelerated in 2009 to legalize park gun carrying. Republican Senator Tom Coburn from Oklahoma spearheaded the effort. To the surprise of many, the Obama administration defended the Bush administration order in court, a clear indication that he would sign such a bill if it crossed his desk. Obama's unwillingness to oppose the measure was seen as a major victory for the NRA, as it had opposed Obama's election for president in 2008. Final enactment was assured when supporters attached the guns in parks measure to a bill that imposed new rules on credit card companies, a top priority for the Obama Administration.

See also: Cox, Christopher (Chris) W.; National Rifle Association; Obama, Barack H.

Further Reading: Carl Hulse, "Bill Changing Credit Card Rules Is Sent to Obama with Gun Measure Included," *New York Times,* May 21, 2009, A16; Kirk Johnson, "Working Out the Details of Guns in National Parks," *New York Times,* May 27, 2009, A12; Jim Robbins, "Rule Change Would Permit Weapons in National Parks," *New York Times*, May 30, 2008, A13.

National Rifle Association (NRA)

While many look to the National Rifle Association (NRA) as the foremost champion of the right to keep and bear arms, others consider the NRA a powerful and uncompromising opponent to reasoned policies to control the violence stemming from the use of firearms, and still others see the organization as far too moderate in its opposition to gun control. Although the NRA is the largest gun rights advocacy group, with a membership of approximately 4 million, other groups, like the Second Amendment Foundation and Gun Owners of America (GOA), with considerably smaller memberships, act as critics of the NRA, arguing

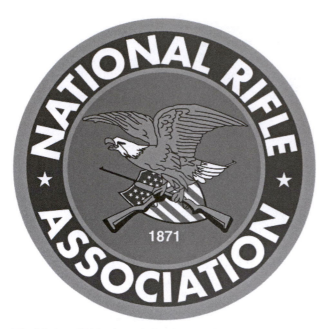

The National Rifle Association is one of the country's leading pro-gun rights groups. *www.nra.org*

that they are keeping its leadership from straying too far from the orthodox anti-gun control stance.

William Conant Church and George Wood Wingate, Union veterans of the Civil War, are recognized as the founders of the NRA. An advocate of military marksmanship, Church called for the establishment of an association, similar to the National Rifle Association of Great Britain, that would encourage systematic training in rifle shooting. In 1871, New York State granted a charter to the newly formed National Rifle Association to encourage rifle practice and target shooting among the militia of New York and other states. The state provided the funds to purchase land on Long Island, called Creedmoor, to construct a site for rifle practice. The early days proved difficult for the fledgling organization, and in 1892 the NRA returned the land to New York and ceased activities. However, eight years later the organization came to life once more, due to increased interest in competitive shooting. In 1909, the NRA increased its board membership to include three appointments by the secretary of war and two from the secretary of the Navy, and directors of the state National Guard units were also added to the board. For many years, the organization benefited from the discount sale of surplus military rifles and ammunition to gun clubs, which proved to be an incentive for people to join the organization.

The NRA's first encounter with gun control occurred in 1911 when it opposed a gun control bill in New York State, which nevertheless became the Sullivan Law. In 1934, the NRA once more took an active role in gun control legislation when Congress considered a measure that ultimately became the National Firearms Act. That same year the organization established a Legislative Division. The NRA lobbied successfully against the inclusion of handgun regulation in the bill. Other measures, such as a proposal to keep on file for identification purposes ammunition fired from all new handguns and machine guns, were defeated. In 1938, when the gun control legislation that would become the Federal Firearms Act was proposed, the NRA successfully opposed more innovative proposals, such as bringing handguns under the provisions of the National Firearms Act. However, the organization failed to have the original provisions of the 1934 legislation altered.

Political assassinations in the 1960s prompted renewed concern for controlling firearms. The NRA took a cautious approach to congressional proposals, but when Democratic President Lyndon Johnson called for a more stringent ban on mail-order shipments of firearms, gun owner licensing, and registration of firearms, NRA president Harold Glassen claimed that such measures would bring an end to shooting sports and ultimately result in disarming Americans. However, NRA officials were willing to entertain a ban on Saturday night special handguns.

The willingness of NRA officials to take a relatively moderate approach to certain gun control measures ended following the 1977 annual meeting in Cincinnati, Ohio. The old leadership, accused of abandoning the Second Amendment, was removed and a more militant contingent succeeded in electing Harlon Carter to the office of executive vice president. Carter committed the organization to an absolutist interpretation of the Second Amendment and appointed Neal Knox, equally as uncompromising on the gun control issue, to head the Institute for Legislative Action (ILA), which was responsible for encouraging the political activity of members and lobbying the national and state legislatures. Carter increased funding for this relatively new office within the NRA. In the 1980s, the NRA focused on two major political objectives: passing the McClure-Volkmer bill, which would weaken many of the provisions of the Gun Control Act of 1968, and limiting the authority of the Bureau of Alcohol, Tobacco, and Firearms (ATF), the federal agency responsible for enforcing federal firearms legislation.

In the 1980s, the NRA began an intense effort to increase membership. By 1984, the organization claimed a membership of nearly three million. Despite political successes, internal conflicts continued. When Carter retired in 1984, the board of directors chose Ray G. Arnett as the new executive vice president. Arnett, a former member of Republican President Ronald Reagan's administration, soon faced a recall effort and in May 1986 the executive committee decided to suspend him without pay. ILA director J. Warren Cassidy replaced Arnett as executive vice president. During Cassidy's leadership, NRA membership declined and the organization faced increasing opposition to the preferred sale of surplus military weapons. Cassidy's willingness to reconsider waiting periods for the purchase of handguns and his unwillingness to endorse those advocating the right to own machine guns eroded his support base. In February 1991, Cassidy announced his resignation. The board of directors selected ILA director Wayne LaPierre to succeed Cassidy as the new executive vice president.

The NRA's initial opposition to such measures as the banning of armor-piercing bullets, plastic handguns, and assault rifles threatened organization support among police organizations. Declining support for the NRA gave impetus for passage of the Brady Handgun Violence Prevention Act of 1994. To regain momentum on the gun control issue, the NRA took steps to mend fences with law enforcement officials and has reached out to a group of potential new members and supporters, establishing the Women's Issues and Information Office in 1990 and in 1993 launching the "Refuse to Be a Victim" program, including a self-defense seminar for women.

The NRA continues to campaign against gun control proposals at the state and national levels. The organization opposed such proposals as required trigger locks on new handguns and a ban on multiple handgun sales. It has consistently opposed a waiting period for a handgun purchase. In 1997, the NRA enlisted the services of actor Charlton Heston as a spokesman and lobbyist for the organization. In 1998, Heston was chosen as the organization's new president, and then its president. Despite some loss of political influence in national and state politics, especially because of its virulent antigovernment rhetoric and financial problems in the early 1990s, the organization's political fortunes revived in the late 1990s and early 2000s. It maintained much of its influence by

supporting candidates politically and financially through its political action committee, the Political Victory Fund. The election of Republican George W. Bush as president in 2000 proved to be a boon for the organization, as Bush was elected with NRA help, and proceeded to be the most pro-gun-lobby president in history. During the Bush presidency, the NRA individualist view of the Second Amendment was adopted as policy by the Justice Department; Congress enacted sweeping new protections for the gun industry to protect them from lawsuits; and in 2008 the Supreme Court embraced the individualist interpretation of the Second Amendment, for the first time in American history, in the case of *District of Columbia v. Heller.* Two years later, this interpretation was applied to the states by the high court in *McDonald v. Chicago.*

In the aftermath of the Sandy Hook elementary school shooting in December 2012, many called for new gun laws, and President Obama offered to Congress a series of measures to strengthen federal law. Within a week of the shooting, however, NRA Executive Director Wayne LaPierre gave a nationally televised speech which rejected the idea of more gun laws, and instead called for armed guards in all public schools. In addition, he emphasized the many dangers faced by Americans from predator criminals and others. During congressional consideration of possible new laws, NRA officials worked behind the scenes with conservative Democratic Senator Joe Manchin (WV) on a compromise bill that included both strengthened protections for gun owners, but also some new gun measures, including a system of uniform background checks for all gun purchases. When word of these efforts reached elements of the gun community, many responded with outrage, claiming that the NRA had sold them out. This prompted the NRA to reverse course and decry the legislation, which failed to win the necessary votes in the Senate.

See also: Assault Weapons Ban; Brady Handgun Violence Prevention Act; Bureau of Alcohol, Tobacco, Firearms, and Explosives; Bush, George H.W; Clinton, William Jefferson (Bill); Eddie Eagle; Federal Firearms Act of 1938; Firearms Owners Protection Act; Gun Owners of America; Heston, Charlton; Institute for Legislative Action; Knox, Neal; LaPierre, Wayne; McClure, James Albertas; National Firearms Act of 1934; Obama's Gun Proposals to Congress, 2013; Reagan, Ronald;

Saturday Night Special; Sandy Hook Elementary School shooting; Second Amendment; Second Amendment Foundation; State Laws, Appendix 2; Sullivan Law; Trigger Locks; United Kingdom; Volkmer, Harold Lee; Women and Guns; Youth and Guns.

Further Reading: Jack Anderson, *Inside the NRA: Armed and Dangerous* (Beverly Hills, CA: Dove, 1996); Peter Harry Brown and Daniel G. Abel, *Outgunned: Up Against the NRA* (New York: The Free Press, 2003); Osha Gray Davidson, *Under Fire: The NRA and the Battle for Gun Control*, expanded ed. (Iowa City: University of Iowa, 1998); *District of Columbia v. Heller* (2008); Wayne R. LaPierre and James Jay Baker, *Shooting Straight: Telling the Truth about Guns in America* (Washington, DC: Regnery, 2002); *McDonald v. Chicago* (2010); National Rifle Association Web site, www.nra.org; Robert J. Spitzer, *The Politics of Gun Control,* 6th ed. (Boulder, CO: Paradigm, 2015).

National SAFE KIDS Campaign

The National SAFE KIDS Campaign, headquartered in Washington, D.C. and founded in 1987, claims to be "the first and only national organization dedicated solely to the prevention of unintentional childhood injury," which the organization states is the major cause of death among children aged 14 and under. Now referred to as Safe Kids USA, the nonprofit organization encourages the safe handling of guns by adults and supports additional legislation to protect children from accidental firearm injuries. Former U.S. Surgeon General C. Everett Koop chairs the Campaign and Vice President Al Gore and his wife Tipper served as honorary chairs. In addition to the national office, there are over 600 state and local chapters in all fifty states. Besides firearms safety, the coalitions develop strategies for injury prevention in such areas as bicycle safety, home fire detection, automobile safety, and burn prevention.

The Campaign labels firearms a "prevalent health hazard," claiming that in 1990 several states had more firearm-related deaths than fatalities caused by motor vehicle accidents. Access to loaded firearms increases the probability of unintentional death and injury to children. The organization believes that many adults underestimate children's ability to gain access to firearms and overestimate children's ability to distinguish real guns from toys

and to handle guns safely and with good judgment. The Campaign reports that every year approximately 1,500 children aged 14 and under receive emergency room treatment for injuries from gun-related accidents, including treatment for injuries caused by such non-powder weapons as BB and pellet guns.

For those who have firearms in the home, the Campaign recommends several safety rules: Keep the gun unloaded and always keep the safety on, even when unloaded. Store firearms in a locked cabinet or drawer and keep ammunition in a separate locked container. Treat all firearms as though they were loaded. Take a gun safety course, teach gun safety in the home, and tell children never to touch a gun. If someone has a history of depression or has discussed suicide, do not keep a firearm in the home.

The organization cites evidence that a gun in the home seldom is used for protection and is much more likely to be used to harm a family member or friend, a claim that is disputed by several firearms researchers and gun rights advocates. The Campaign claims that 30 percent of unintentional firearms fatalities could be prevented if handguns were equipped with gun locks and load indicators and notes with approval that many states have Child Access Prevention (CAP) laws, which hold adults legally responsible for failure to store firearms safely or to use locking devices on guns. The organization claims that the year after Florida passed a CAP law, unintentional firearm fatalities for children aged 14 and under was reduced 50 percent.

The Campaign notes that firearms are unregulated consumer products. No government agency regulates the safety of handguns and most gun laws focus on the gun users, not the firearms manufacturers. The organization cites public opinion surveys showing strong support for regulating the safety design of firearms and for making handguns child-resistant. The organization believes that in addition to saving lives, such measures would be financially prudent, given its estimate that the annual cost of unintentional injuries and deaths of children aged 14 and under that are attributed to firearms exceeds $5 billion.

See also: Accidents Involving Guns; Fatalities; Schools and Guns; Suicide; Trigger Locks; Youth and Guns.

Further Reading: Safe Kids USA Web site, www.safekids.org.

National School Safety Center (NSSC)

In 1984, a directive from Republican President Ronald Reagan created the National School Safety Center (NSSC). Supported by congressional appropriations and based in Oak Park, California, the Center assists public school systems to implement programs geared to eradicate crime, violence, and drug use from schools, and to devise strategies to keep firearms away from school grounds. The NSSC, along with other organizations, monitors the number of school-associated deaths each year. The NSSC offers help in developing programs to deal with student discipline and attendance policy, provides legal and legislative assistance, distributes publications and films, conducts training programs, and provides technical assistance for those in education, law enforcement, and government. Center staff have given testimony before congressional and state legislative committees regarding school safety policy. In April 1998, Ronald D. Stephens, executive director of the NSSC, testified before the U.S. House Subcommittee on Early Childhood, Youth and Families, warning congresspeople about the wide availability of firearms to youth.

The NSSC has identified several causal factors related to the occurrence of violence at schools and has developed an assessment tool composed of 20 items that help to identify those students likely to become violent. An action plan is provided that includes 40 steps that parents, school administrators, and the community can take to make schools safer for teachers and students. In this material, firearms appear as one factor contributing to a higher probability of violence. Two of the 20 items on the assessment tool concern firearms and other weapons. The NSSF has monitored school-associated violent deaths for nearly twenty years. Of the 435 deaths occurring in public schools from 1992 to 2007, 75 percent were from firearms.

Although the Center has not taken explicit positions on gun control issues, it reports that "the easy accessibility of weapons to young people in this country is staggering." The NSSC comments that, due to the availability of firearms, the level of violence has increased over the years. The Center recommends a "zero-tolerance" policy, in which any weapons violation results in expulsion from school. Any charge of weapons possession should lead to immediate investigation and "prompt and reasonable action."

The Center distributes reports on firearms violence prepared by other organizations. For instance, the Center makes available the results of a survey of 2,508 students in 96 public and private schools, grades 6 through 12, sponsored by the Harvard School of Public Health. Fifteen percent of respondents reported having carried a handgun in the month before the survey. Nine percent stated they had shot a firearm at someone, 39 percent reported they knew someone personally who had been killed or injured by a gun, and 59 percent claimed they had access to a handgun.

See also: Jonesboro, Arkansas, School Shooting; Littleton, Colorado, Columbine School Shooting; Reagan, Ronald; Schools and Guns; Stockton, California, Shooting; Trigger Locks; Youth and Guns.

Further Reading: National School Safety Center Web site, www.schoolsafety.us.

National Shooting Sports Foundation (NSSF)

The National Shooting Sports Foundation (NSSF) was established in 1961 to represent the hunting and shooting sports industry. According to the Foundation, its mission is "to bring a positive message about the shooting sports to the news media, to a new generation of shooters and to decision makers on all levels," and to promote active participation in the various shooting sports, especially among those who have not previously participated. More than 5,500 companies are members of the Foundation, including manufacturers, distributors, wholesalers, shooting ranges, and retailers of shooting sports equipment, in addition to other associations related to shooting sports, publishing enterprises, and individuals. The NSSF is closely allied with the National Rifle Association (NRA). Critics say that the NSSF takes political direction from the NRA.

The Foundation recognizes that the shooting sports industry has been supported primarily by the 12 to 14 million Americans who engage in hunting. This group represents two-thirds of the shooting sports market. Although in the past the industry could depend on hunters passing the tradition from one generation to the next, demographic changes such as greater urbanization may result in a significant decrease in the number of hunters. Therefore, the Foundation recognizes the need for more aggressive promotion through the mass media and safety education campaigns to attract new participants. The organization strives to have shooting covered just like any other sport, including shooting-related television programs. Such programs are meant to influence general public opinion about shooting sports and to attract new participants by presenting shooting as an enjoyable activity comparable to biking and skating.

The NSSF emphasizes that shooting is a safe sport, noting that "bowlers receive over seventeen times as many injuries as hunters," but without indicating the relative severity of injuries or differences in number of participants in the two activities. The organization focuses on gun safety and frequently presents basic rules of safe handling, recognizing that a beneficial side effect of education programs can be the development of interest in the sport. The Foundation provides advice to members about attracting new shooters. For instance, a video featuring retired General Norman Schwarzkopf includes "the right mix of command presence and gentle persuasion to communicate a key message: Club members and leaders must treat new shooters in a welcoming and encouraging manner."

Youth, the source of future participants in the shooting sports, are a primary focus for gun safety programs. Young people are encouraged to attend hunter education courses before hunting for the first time. Youth magazines such as *Boy's Life*, *Scouting*, and *New Horizons* (a publication of Future Farmers of America) contain an annual shooting sports section. The organization promotes shooting programs with various youth organizations, including 4-H Clubs, and supports the Team Youth Development Program and the Hunter Education Association, whose estimated 50,000 volunteer instructors train several hundred thousand new hunters each year. The Foundation offers advice to parents taking a young person hunting for the first time. Parents should make sure that clothing is appropriate to the weather, provide an extra change of clothes, and make activities interesting, all geared to ensure that the youth will want to continue participating in the sport.

The NSSC plays an important role as the political voice of the gun industry, but its political activities are generally directed by the NRA. In the late 1990s and early 2000s, the NSSC and the NRA lined up against another trade group, the American Shooting Sports Council (ASSC), when it entered into negotiations involving then-pending liability lawsuits against the gun industry to hold it accountable for guns that wound up in the hands of criminals. When ASSC head Richard Feldman concluded an agreement at the White House with Democratic President Bill Clinton, the NRA pressed for, and won, Feldman's ouster in 1999, and the merging of the ASSC with the NSSC, which stood with the NRA against any compromise to settle the lawsuits.

See also: American Shooting Sports Council; Women and Guns; Youth and Guns.

Further Reading: Peter Harry Brown and Daniel G. Abel, *Outgunned: Up Against the NRA* (New York: The Free Press, 2003); Richard Feldman, *Ricochet: Confessions of a Gun Lobbyist* (New York: Wiley, 2008); National Shooting Sports Foundation Web site, www.nssf.com.

National Tracing Center (NTC)

The Bureau of Alcohol, Tobacco, Firearms, and Explosives (ATF) maintains a National Tracing Center (NTC), which tracks the history of firearms recovered during or following the commission of crimes, from the sources (either manufacturers or importers) through the wholesale and retail enterprises to the persons who ultimately purchased the weapons. The Center can have a potentially significant effect on controlling the illegal firearms trade, both nationally and internationally, depending on its ability to provide useful information to law enforcement officials. However, gun control advocates argue that the strong opposition by gun rights groups to a firearms registration system or long-term record-keeping severely hampers the ability of the NTC to conduct effective traces. The NTC is located in Martinsburg, West Virginia.

Law enforcement agencies at the local, state, national, and international levels can request information from the NTC's Web-based tracing system, called eTrace, which includes information about individuals who have engaged in unlicensed firearms dealing. The eTrace system has registered over 2,800 law enforcement agencies, including 29 in other countries, that can utilize its data. The

Center accumulates information about multiple firearms sales, stolen guns, and firearms with serial numbers that have been eliminated. Multiple sales may indicate "straw purchases," which involve persons acquiring firearms and then transferring them to others to conceal the actual receivers of the weapons.

The Center identifies firearms trafficking "corridors," routes that illegal traffickers recurrently use to transport firearms. Such routes include interstate highways, bus lines, railways, airlines, and such carriers as United Parcel Service and the U.S. mail. A firearms trafficking "gateway" is a location, such as a border crossing point, seaport, airport, or train station, through which illegal traffickers frequently pass during the transport of firearms to final destinations. A market area is any locality where firearms are sold illegally or transferred to criminals and others prohibited from possessing firearms, including juveniles. In addition to conducting firearms traces and identifying illegal sources and transportation routes, the Center has responsibility for maintaining the records of federally licensed firearms dealers who have ceased doing business. It receives an average of 1.3 million out-of-business records per month. A major objective of NTC activities is to identify and eliminate criminals' sources of firearms. The NTC issues many trace analysis reports, including those that provide information about the total number of crime gun trace requests, types of crime guns, information by community, analyses of successful traces, summarization of incomplete traces, and categorization by age of those discovered to possess firearms illegally.

The NTC is affiliated with the ATF's Juvenile Firearms Violence Initiative, which traces firearms found on school grounds or taken from juveniles who used them to commit violent crimes. The Initiative is intended to reduce the number of young people who use firearms in the commission of violent acts, to identify and cut off the sources of firearms for juveniles and other violent users of firearms, and to arrest and prosecute adults who supply firearms to juveniles.

See also: Bureau of Alcohol, Tobacco, Firearms, and Explosives; Youth and Guns.

Further Reading: Bureau of Alcohol, Tobacco, Firearms, and Explosives NTC Web site, https://www.atf.gov/resource-center/fact-sheet/fact-sheet-national-tracing-center.

Native Americans

In their attempt to confirm the liberty-destroying nature of gun control efforts, gun rights advocates argue that any time a government attempts to take firearms from a group, such as Native Americans (American Indians), the intent is ultimately to subjugate the group and to establish tyranny. They note that the conquest of the North American continent and the extermination of Indian tribes was accomplished in large part through the actions of federal government troops. The genocidal programs of such twentieth-century dictatorships as the Soviet Union and Nazi Germany are compared with the federal government's treatment of Native Americans.

However, to be *disarmed*, American Indians first had to be *armed*. Over a long period of time, European settlers provided firearms to Native Americans, even though most colonies enacted laws that barred the sale or transfer of guns to them. Those laws proved largely ineffective. Indians, recognizing the advantages of the new technology, avidly accepted the new weapons and abandoned their bows and arrows. Dutch traders reaped huge profits from trading guns for beaver pelts. Ironically, acceptance of firearms made the Indians dependent on the colonists for lead, powder, and the maintenance of weapons. In the seventeenth century, the British government officially opposed providing Indians with firearms, but the practice became so profitable for traders that by 1650 there was no way to stop the further spread of weapons among native tribes. Such trading somewhat lessened the disparity of weaponry between whites and Indians. Traders surrendered European military superiority and ultimately the lives of colonists for the opportunity to make large profits.

Despite early attempts to discourage gun trading, the French and British, when at war, enlisted the assistance of Indian tribes as allies, providing them with firearms. In Virginia, Indians allied with the English colony were granted the right to firearms and gunpowder. Indian tribes also desired firearms to give them the advantage in their own conflicts with other tribes. An early form of an arms race developed, with the tribe first able to gain modern weapons establishing supremacy over rival tribes. Indians less successful in acquiring the new technology became subordinated not only to the Europeans, but to Indian tribes who possessed firearms. European countries provided several hundred thousand firearms to Indians over a 200-year period. To gain new weapons, Indians efficiently used guns they had already acquired to kill game to trade more furs for additional weapons. In the process, wildlife on the North American continent was significantly reduced.

By the time the 13 colonies became a nation, Native Americans had several hundred years of experience with firearms. Although the Militia Act of 1792 excluded blacks, whether free or slave, and Indians from serving in the militia, the U.S. government followed the tradition established by European nations of providing firearms to the Indians, who could legally acquire rifles under the Indian Intercourse Act of 1834. A government-established factory and trading post system offered Indians firearms in exchange for furs and other goods. The government enticed Native Americans to move westward with the promise of additional firearms and gunsmiths to repair the weapons.

Although American Indians possessed weapons inferior to whites during the first half of the nineteenth century, after the Civil War, many Indians acquired rifles superior to those used by U.S. army soldiers. General George Armstrong Custer, who in 1876 was killed with his whole command by the Sioux and other tribes at the Little Bighorn River in the Dakota Territory (now Montana), once complained sarcastically that Indian warriors were well armed "through the foresight and strong love of fair play which prevails in the Indian Department," which did not effectively limit Indian acquisition of firearms.

History weaves a complex relationship between the firearm and the subjugation of the American Indian. European colonists possessed a major technological advantage over Native Americans when they first arrived bearing firearms. Later, western settlers clamored for federal government protection against Indian attacks. Over hundreds of years Native Americans suffered devastating losses, but far more Indians died from diseases brought across the Atlantic from European settlers than from firearms. In any case, the Indians' plight did not arise from a consistent policy of denying firearms to them. The tragic struggle of Native Americans to resist the increasing waves of European immigration was doomed to failure. That struggle appears to offer no clear generalizations for pro- or anti-gun control groups regarding current laws or proposals.

See also: American Revolution; Militia Act of 1792; United Kingdom.

Further Reading: Alexander DeConde, *Gun Violence in America* (Boston: Northeastern University Press, 2001); Lee B. Kennett and James La Verne Anderson, *The Gun in America: The Origins of a National Dilemma* (Westport, CT: Greenwood, 1975); Carl P. Russell, *Guns on the Early Frontier* (New York: Bonanza Books, 1957).

Ninth Amendment

Some legal scholars have appealed to the Ninth Amendment to claim that the U.S. Constitution guarantees a right to keep and bear arms for self-defense. The amendment states that, "The enumeration in the Constitution, of certain rights, shall not be construed to deny or disparage others retained by the people." Particular rights, if not explicitly mentioned in the Constitution, are not thereby excluded from protection, but remain viable against encroachment by the government. Among those rights considered so protected through the Ninth Amendment is self-protection and the ownership and carrying of firearms for that purpose. In his article "Beyond the Second Amendment: An Individual Right to Arms Viewed Through the Ninth Amendment" (1992), Nicholas Johnson argued that if the amendment is seen as a support for such things as "a right to engage in sodomy," "a right to wear long hair," and "protection against imprisonment in maximum security," it can be persuasively argued to protect a right to bear arms for self-defense. Even if the Second Amendment is interpreted to protect only a collective right of the states to maintain a militia, strong supporters of the right to keep and bear arms, such as Johnson, argue that the Ninth Amendment prevents the government from denying individuals the ability to defend themselves from others.

Johnson claimed that if we recognize that firearms in the United States have been traditionally regarded and still are widely accepted as especially useful tools for self-defense, then "we might view possession of arms for individual defense to be as basic as the right to choose a heavy coat against the cold." Johnson suggested that the common law tradition inherited from Great Britain recognizes a right to bear arms for self-defense, which is implicitly guaranteed by the Ninth Amendment. Similarly, Alan M. Gottlieb, chairman of the Citizens Committee for the Right to Keep and Bear Arms, argued in *The Rights of Gun Owners* (1991) that although the U.S. Constitution does not specifically guarantee the right to armed defense, this traditional common-law right is not nullified, but is protected by the Ninth Amendment.

Appealing to a natural rights view, Johnson suggested that not only do individuals have a right to arms, but that right cannot be restricted by the larger community, even by means of a constitutional amendment. He concluded that the individual's interest in self-preservation cannot be legitimately surrendered to society's interest in order. Pragmatically, the individual cannot always depend on the resources of the collective for personal security. In addition, the government itself may pose a threat to individual security, thereby requiring that people have the ability to resist such misuse of power through the use of force. Human rights principles within international law may be appealed to in establishing Ninth Amendment guarantees. The United Nations Charter recognizes the right of individual and collective self-defense and the Universal Declaration of Human Rights supports the right of individuals to life, liberty, and security.

In arguing for a right to personal protection and the related right to bear arms, Johnson noted that "guns equalize power relationships." The physical strength of an attacker can be resisted if the intended victim has a firearm. If the potential attacker is armed, the person who is the focus of the attack is better off armed, according to the principle that "increasing the cost of violence decreases its likelihood." For government to deny the tools of self-defense to its citizens is to leave them potential victims of the strong and the ruthless. Even though the danger exists that firearms will be misused in an armed society, Johnson concluded that individuals cannot be required to surrender their right to self-protection to benefit collective interests.

Although the argument from natural rights to certain guarantees within the Ninth Amendment may be tenuous, Johnson argued that the de facto resistence of citizens to surrendering the right of self-protection may be a significant affirmation of such a right. He argued against an elitist position, contending that government officials must be equally willing to surrender the right if they expect citizens to do so. Gun control advocates would claim that the argument for the right to bear arms based on the Ninth Amendment, even if valid, does not establish an absolute protection. Although "disarming" citizens may not be constitutionally legitimate, such provisions as requiring registration and licensing, preventing felons from possessing firearms, and banning ownership of certain weapons, such as machine guns, could be considered reasonable precautions taken to ensure an ordered society. The Ninth Amendment argument was undercut by the Supreme Court's 2008 ruling in *District of Columbia v. Heller,* which established a Second Amendment-based personal right to use guns for self-protection in the home.

See also: Fourth Amendment; Fourteenth Amendment; Gottlieb, Alan Merril; Second Amendment; United Kingdom; United Nations.

Further Reading: *District of Columbia v. Heller* (2008); Alan M. Gottlieb, *The Rights of Gun Owners* (Bellevue, Washington: Merril, 1991); Nicholas J. Johnson, "Beyond the Second Amendment: An Individual Right to Arms Viewed Through the Ninth Amendment," *Rutgers Law Journal* 24 (Fall 1992), 1–81.

Northern Illinois University Shooting

Only ten months after the mass shooting on the campus of Virginia Tech State University, a graduate of Northern Illinois University, Steven P. Kazmierczak, entered an afternoon geology lecture class in Cole Hall on the NIU campus in DeKalb and started shooting on February 14, 2008. From 150 to 200 students were in the room at the time. When he was done, five students had been killed by gunfire and eighteen wounded. Kazmierczak then killed himself. The 27-year-old man was a graduate student in sociology at the University of Illinois at Urbana-Champaign at the time of the shooting. He had previously been a graduate student at NIU.

The incident seemed inexplicable to those who knew him. No motive was ascribed to the shooting, and Kazmierczak left no note. Faculty and friends all described him as an excellent and well-liked student. The only clue to motivation was that he had been taking several prescription medications, including an antianxiety drug and an antidepressant, which he had stopped taking about two weeks before the shooting, and the comments of some who knew him who said that he had become somewhat erratic in the days before the shooting, perhaps because he had stopped taking his medications. Some later reports suggested that he had suffered from stress-related problems earlier in his life. Kazmierczak had recently obtained several guns legally, including a 12-gauge shotgun, which he carried into the classroom in a guitar case, and a Glock 9-mm. handgun (both were purchased five days before), and two other handguns—a 9-mm. Sig Sauer and a .380-caliber High Point—purchased the previous year. Kazmierczak had all four guns with him at the shooting.

Kazmierczak's easy acquisition of so much firepower shortly before the shooting again raised concerns among gun control supporters about the ease of access to such weaponry. Police reported recovering 48 bullet casings and six empty shotgun shells at the scene. Gun control opponents bemoaned the tragedy, but emphasized that even stricter laws could not have prevented the shooting, noting that he passed the background checks to which he was subjected when making the purchases. Ironically, the dealer who sold Kazmierczak two Glock bullet magazines and a Glock holster, Eric Thompson, president of TGSCOM Inc., also sold Virginia Tech shooter Seung-Hui Cho a .22-caliber handgun used in that shooting via the Internet, and a Glock 9-mm. magazine and magazine loading apparatus to George Sodini, who shot twelve women (three of whom were killed) at a health club in Pennsylvania in 2009. Thompson expressed sorrow at the deaths, but also noted that he had done nothing illegal.

The incident also fanned the debate over safety on college campuses and efforts by some to liberalize gun policies on campuses. While this and the Virginia Tech shooting seemed to suggest that college campuses had become shooting galleries, national statistics did not support this fear, as serious crime on campuses continued to be vanishingly small. In addition, campuses increased security and warning systems in the eventuality of future serious events. Efforts to increase gun carrying by faculty and students on campuses around the country by gun rights advocates were generally rebuffed.

See also: Background Checks; Virginia Tech Shooting.

Further Reading: Benedict Carey, "Reports of Gunman's Use of Antidepressant Renew Debate Over Side Effects," *New York Times,* February 19, 2008, A20; Susan Saulny and Jeff Bailey, "Grief and Questions after Deadly Shootings," *New York Times,* February 16, 2008, A13.

Nunn v. Georgia (1846)

In *Nunn v. Georgia* (1 Ga. 243, 1846), the Supreme Court of Georgia overruled a lower court decision convicting Hawkins H. Nunn of carrying a pistol, contrary to an 1837 statute. The Supreme Court declared that both the U.S. and state constitutions guaranteed the right to keep and bear arms, anticipating some of the more recent arguments of gun rights supporters, including the appeal to common law and the natural rights tradition.

The state law in question prohibited "any merchant or vender of wares or merchandize in this State, or any other person or persons whatever, to sell, or to offer to sell, or to keep or to have about their persons, or elsewhere, any of the herein-after-described weapons, to wit: Bowie or any other kinds of knives, manufactured and sold for the purpose of wearing or carrying the same as arms of offence or defence; pistols, dirks, sword-canes, spears, & etc., shall also be contemplated in this act, save such pistols as are known and used as horseman's pistols." It then also barred anyone who might "openly wear" weapons including "bowie-knives, dirks, tooth-picks, spears, and which shall be exposed plainly to view." Yet this list failed to include the open carrying of pistols and sword-canes.

Nunn was charged with carrying a pistol in his hand "which was not a horseman's pistol, but a breast pistol." Found guilty in the lower court, Nunn appealed the conviction, arguing that the 1837 statute under which he was convicted violated both the U.S. and Georgia constitutions, and that the indictment did not show that he had carried the pistol secretly. The Georgia Supreme Court, in rendering its decision, provided a broad interpretation of the right to bear arms, concluding that the state legislature had no authority to deny citizens the right to bear a weapon.

The court traced the historical roots of the right to bear arms, stating that "this is one of the fundamental principles, upon which rests the great fabric of civil liberty, reared by the fathers of the Revolution and of the country." The court held that the right antedated the U.S. Constitution, which "only reiterated a truth announced a century before, in the act of 1689." The court further ruled that the Second Amendment applied to both the federal and state governments, arguing that by denying the federal government power to forbid the right to bear arms, the people could not have intended to grant that authority to state governments. Referring to the maintenance of a well-regulated militia, the court noted that the state legislature cannot jeopardize the security of the people by disarming them.

The court called the right to bear arms a natural right and "unlimited," stating that "any law, State or Federal, is repugnant to the Constitution, and void, which contravenes this *right*, originally belonging to our forefathers, trampled under foot by Charles I and his two wicked sons and successors, re-established by the revolution of 1688, conveyed to this land of liberty by the colonists, and finally incorporated conspicuously in our own *Magna Charta*!" However, the court pulled away from an absolutist interpretation of the right by declaring that the law in question was valid to the extent that it "seeks to suppress the practice of carrying certain weapons *secretly*." Only insofar as the law forbade bearing arms openly that portion of the law was contrary to the Constitution and void.

See also: Second Amendment; United Kingdom.

Further Reading: *Nunn v. Georgia*, 1 Ga. 243 (1846).

The New York SAFE Act

The December 2012 mass shooting at Sandy Hook elementary school in Connecticut prompted many efforts to reform gun laws. Efforts in Congress, spearheaded by President Barack Obama, failed, but a dozen states enacted tougher laws, and twice as many states moved to weaken their laws. The first state to enact new gun laws was New York.

In January of 2013, the State Legislature passed the New York Secure Ammunition and Firearms Enforcement (SAFE) Act, at the behest of Democratic Governor Andrew Cuomo. In addition to the Sandy Hook shooting, advocates were also motivated by the murder of two fire fighters in Webster, New York less than two weeks after Sandy Hook by a man who deliberately set a house fire to draw first responders to the scene to then murder them (two others were injured).

The legislature acted rapidly, approving the bill by a vote of 104-43 in the Democratic-controlled Assembly, and 43-18 in the Republican-controlled Senate. The governor signed the bill into law on January 15.

The SAFE Act consisted of what the governor boasted was the toughest set of gun laws in the nation. Chief among its provisions was the imposition of new restrictions on assault weapons. State law first imposed limits on such weapons in 2000, but the new law tightened those restrictions by categorizing assault rifles as those which can accept detachable magazines, and that have at least one additional characteristic (the earlier law specified two characteristics), including a folding or telescoping stock, a protruding pistol grip, a thumbhole stock, a second handgrip or protruding grip, a bayonet mount, flash suppressor, muzzle brake (erroneously spelled "break" in the legislation), a muzzle compensator, a threaded barrel designed to accommodate any of the above features, or a grenade launcher. Semi-automatic shotguns and pistols are also similarly restricted, as was the case with past assault weapons bans. In the case of shotguns, they fall within the terms of the new law if they possess at least one characteristic named in the law, even if the only feature it possesses is a detachable magazine. New Yorkers who already lawfully owned assault weapons considered legal before 2013 under state law, but that would now be restricted under the new law, could keep them, but they had to now register them with the state (the registration must be renewed every five years) by April 2014.

Those who owned an assault weapon as defined by the law that must be registered could also eliminate design features to exempt it from registration by, for example, removing the bayonet lug, or grinding off threading on the barrel. A background check is also run during the registration process, and the state now maintains this information in a database. While the owners of these weapons may keep them for life, they may not transfer or sell them to anyone else, including family members. They can, however, transfer them to authorized sources including the police, a firearms dealer, or to someone out of state for whom ownership is legal in that state. A related new provision now requires Surrogate's courts around the state (each county has one), which handle all probate and estate matters, to inventory a person's firearms separately from other possessions when people die, which will identify the existence of weapons in this category.

The law also imposed new restrictions on high capacity bullet feeding devices (i.e. magazines). Under previous law, those obtained before 1994 of any capacity were grandfathered in (that is, were legal to own). New magazines from 1994 on were limited to those that could hold no more than ten bullets. Under the 2013 law, however, all magazines, including pre-1994 versions, were now illegal to own if they held more than ten bullets; however, they could be loaded with no more than seven bullets. This lower, seven-bullet maximum was stricken from the law when it was challenged in federal court, leaving the ten bullet limit in place. The rest of the law was upheld in federal district court, and in the U.S. Court of Appeals for the Second Circuit, in the case of New York State Rifle and Pistol Association v. Cuomo in 2015. The law also noted that police have no presumptive right to inspect magazines, unless they first have probable cause. Regarding pre-1994 magazines that were formerly legal to own but now illegal to own, the 2013 law has a kind of forgiveness provision saying that if a person believes mistakenly that possession of such a pre-1994 magazine was still legal, they may avoid being charged under the law if they then dispose of it within 30 days. (Ignorance of the law is rarely a basis of avoiding prosecution, but it is in this case.) Non-complying assault weapons and feeding devices more than fifty years old are exempted from these new restrictions as antiques, curios, or relics.

The law also extends background checks, formerly limited to commercial weapons sales, to private gun sales as well as ammunition sales. Under the new procedure, an individual wishing to make a private gun sale may still do so, but must go to a licensed dealer, pay a fee of up to $10, and have the dealer run a background (NICS) check before the sale can be completed. The only individuals exempted from the background check are transfers to immediate family members (spouses, domestic partners, children and step-children). Direct sale of ammunition was barred as of 2014, although such sales can be routed through firearms dealers, as is already true with internet gun sales. Ammunition sale records and checks occur at the state level (not through the NICS system), are required to be purged yearly by the state, and are exempted from freedom of information inquiries.

The SAFE Act also requires pistol permits to be renewed every five years. Formerly, they never had to be renewed. And while information concerning the identification of pistol permit holders is public, permit holders can now, under the new law, file for an exemption from any public disclosure with the state (this provision was challenged in court by newspapers and First Amendment advocates).

The law requires certain categories of mental health professionals to report to state authorities any persons under their care who they believe are "likely to engage in conduct that would result in serious harm to self or others." Those persons are then to be checked to see if they are licensed to own firearms. If so, the State Police are notified and a judgment made as to whether to suspend or revoke their licenses, and then retrieve the guns. Criminal penalties for firearms-related violations were enhanced, including possession or use of firearms while on school property, in connection with drug trafficking, straw gun purchases, and other felonies, including the killing of first responders (e.g. fire fighters). The law also allows those under an order of protection issued by a court to have their gun license suspended or revoked, requires that firearms must be stored safely in homes where others with criminal backgrounds live, and report stolen guns within 24 hours.

The law was criticized by opponents who objected to the strict new assault weapons restrictions, arguing that such weapons are rarely used in crimes, and that the new standard would restrict or bar legitimate hunting weapons. Many questioned the new seven bullet limit on magazines, considering it an arbitrary number that did not readily conform to the capacities of existing magazines. Some in the mental health community objected to the new reporting procedures pertaining to those with mental illness, fearing that the new law would drive gun owners with mental health problems away from treatment for fear of losing their firearms. They also objected to possible violations of patient privacy, and to the substantial new reporting procedures. Opponents also charged that the law violated Second Amendment rights, and that the law would make criminals out of formerly law abiding citizens. Despite these criticisms, numerous public opinion polls in the months after the law's enactment showed that six New Yorkers in ten supported the law.

Recommended Readings: *New York State Rifle and Pistol Association v. Cuomo* (804 F.3d 242; 2nd Cir. 2015); Robert J. Spitzer, "New York State and the New York SAFE Act: A Case Study in Strict Gun Laws," *Albany Law Review* 78:2(2015): 749-87.

O

Obama, Barack Hussein (1961–)

Barack Obama, a Democrat elected the forty-fourth president of the United States, was also the nation's first African American chief executive. Serving from 2009 to 2017, he served at a time when the nation became ever more aware of the divide over guns. Mass shootings and gun violence received ever more attention, yet the call for protecting gun rights also became louder.

Obama served three terms in the Illinois State Senate, and then in 2004 was elected to the U.S. Senate. He wasted little time in beginning a campaign for the presidency, which resulted in his nomination from among a crowded Democratic field and decisive election in 2008. During his Illinois service, Obama was a vocal supporter of stronger gun laws, a fact which gun rights groups used against him in his 2008 campaign. During his presidential campaign, the Democratic party platform endorsed stronger gun measures, but also recognized legitimate gun rights, a position echoed by Obama when he commented on the Supreme Court's 2008 ruling in *District of Columbia v. Heller*, a decision handed down in June during the campaign that established the right of individual citizens to own guns for self-protection in the home. Yet after taking office, Obama took no measurable steps to advance gun regulations. In fact, during his first term, he signed legislation allowing civilian gun carrying in national parks, and allowing Amtrak passengers to bring guns onto trains with them if stowed away in luggage. Both measures were opposed by gun safety organizations. Obama's quiescence on the issue resulted in the gun control group the Brady Campaign awarding him a failing grade of "F" in 2010 for his failure to act on the gun issue. All that changed shortly after his 2012 re-election.

The December 2012 massacre of 20 students and six staff members at Sandy Hook Elementary School in Connecticut horrified the nation as few past mass shootings had. Obama was no less horrified, and he directed Vice President Joe Biden to chair a task force to produce recommendations for new gun laws. The group's recommendations were announced in January 2013, and served as the basis for several pieces of legislation introduced in Congress, which included proposals to establish universal background checks for all gun purchases, restrictions on assault weapons and high capacity

President Barack Obama has made special efforts to speak out against acts of gun violence. *Official White House photo; www.wikipedia.org*

bullet magazines, mental health and school safety initiatives, increased funding for police protection in schools, and stronger measures against straw gun purchasers and trafficking. Obama also issued nineteen executive directives to increase funding on gun research, improve gun trafficking databases, and other steps involving federal agencies. Despite White House pressure and national public support for these measures, they failed to win passage in a series of votes in the U.S. Senate in April. The House of Representatives failed to act. For the balance of his presidency, Obama abandoned further efforts to get Congress to act.

In the final three years of his presidency, Obama made special efforts to speak out against acts of gun violence, especially after succeeding mass shootings, attempting to use the office's "bully pulpit" to rally the public and put pressure on lawmakers. These efforts helped to keep the gun issue in the national spotlight, and it became one of several important issues during the 2016 elections.

Recommended Readings: Michael Eric Dyson, *The Black Presidency: Barack Obama and the Politics of Race in America* (New York: Houghton Mifflin Harcourt, 2016); Robert J. Spitzer, *The Politics of Gun Control,* 6th ed. (Boulder, CO: Paradigm Publishers 2015).

Obama's Gun Proposals to Congress, 2013

The December 2012 mass shooting at Sandy Hook elementary school in Newtown, Ct., in which 20 school children and six staff members were killed, shocked the nation in a way that few past mass shootings had. For President Barack Obama, as for others, this was a watershed moment. During his first term, Obama had largely avoided the gun issue. After a convincing re-election campaign the previous month, bringing with it a renewed electoral mandate, and with his January inauguration and the State of the Union both in sight, Obama decided to move on the issue. Within days of the shooting, Obama appointed Vice President Joe Biden to head a task force to study the gun issue and make recommendations for change. In January 2013, the group presented its report, calling for universal background checks for gun purchases, restrictions on assault weapons and high capacity bullet magazines, mental health and school safety initiatives, increased funding for police protection in schools, and stronger measures to stop straw gun purchases and

gun trafficking. In mid-January, Obama also issued nineteen executive directives to enhance and fund research on gun violence, improve federal gun trafficking databases, examine gun safety measures, and other steps involving federal agencies.

The measures were taken up first in the Democratic-controlled U.S. Senate. Bill supporters hoping that Senate passage of at least some of the bills would pressure the Republican-controlled House of Representatives to at least take up the measure. In March 2013, the Senate Judiciary Committee approved bills to criminalize straw gun purchases, a uniform background check measure, and an assault weapons ban. At about this time, Senator Joe Manchin (D-WV) took up the cause of championing some version of a gun bill, partly at the behest of more liberal Senate leaders who felt that a more conservative sponsor would give the bill greater legitimacy. Manchin was considered one of the most conservative Democrats in the Senate, was a gun owner, and had been endorsed by the NRA throughout his 30-year political career. Manchin was also no new-comer to politics, having served as governor of West Virginia for five years. Yet he eventually broke with the NRA in this effort. He persuaded Pennsylvania Republican Senator Pat Toomey (who had been elected with the help of over a million dollars from the NRA), to co-sponsor the measure. The Manchin-Toomey bill that emerged in April called for universal background checks for gun purchases, including at gun shows and internet sales, excepting transfers to relatives and friends, and it facilitated the gathering of mental health and other relevant data from the states to be submitted to the national background check (NICS) database. Yet it also reduced the gun purchase background check waiting period from 72 hours to 48 hours (if no report came back within that time, the gun sales would go through); made interstate transport of weapons easier; allowed interstate sale of handguns from licensed dealers; made the use of gun records for creating a registry a felony; and established a national commission on mass violence. Throughout this period, bill advocates including Judiciary Committee Chair Pat Leahy (D-VT) and Manchin worked closely with representatives of the NRA; indeed, the provisions added to expand gun access came at the behest of the NRA. While the gun group did not trumpet its involvement, the Manchin-Toomey bill was constructed with, and won the quiet approval of, the NRA.

Almost immediately, however, word of the compromise bill, and the NRA's role, leaked out on gun rights web sites. Gun groups hostile to the NRA like the Gun Owners of America and the National Association for Gun Rights began to pummel the NRA for selling out the cause. Within days, NRA leaders ceased communicating with Manchin; shortly thereafter, they announced their opposition to the bill, vowing to do everything they could to defeat it. Even so, Manchin and Toomey persisted. On April 17, the full Senate voted on seven gun-related measures; each needed to garner 60 votes – not a simple majority of 51 – because at the time, a bill could only proceed if it first received enough votes to end debate (called invoking cloture), 60 votes. The Manchin-Toomey bill thus garnered majority support, but still failed, by a vote of 54 in favor and 46 against. A separate measure to ban assault weapons, championed by Senator Dianne Feinstein (D-CA), failed 40-60; the bill to limit bullet magazine capacity failed 46-54; the straw purchase-gun trafficking bill failed 58-42. The NRA trumpeted the bills' defeat as a great victory for gun rights, but never mentioned to its membership that it had helped craft the bill that it later helped defeat. Bill supporters decried the NRA, noting that public opinion polls consistently showed that 90 percent of Americans supported universal background checks.

Even if the Senate had passed the measure, however, that would have provided no guarantee that the bill would have made its way to the president's desk. As the Senate was working on these measures, House Republican leaders advanced four measures to roll back gun regulations, including provisions to bar the Bureau of Alcohol, Tobacco, Firearms, and Explosives (ATF) from requiring gun dealers to conduct annual inventories of their stock to make sure that guns had not been lost stolen, or improperly sold; to broaden the definition of guns that could be imported into the U.S.; to prevent the ATF from canceling a gun dealer's license for lack of business; and to add a disclaimer to government gun data saying that it could not be used to draw conclusions about gun crimes. Despite President Obama's continued exhortations that Congress take up new gun regulations, Congress took no further action on these measures for the balance of Obama's presidency.

Further Reading: Robert Draper, "Inside the Power of the N.R.A.," *New York Times Magazine,* December 13, 2013; Robert J. Spitzer, *The Politics of Gun Control,* 6th ed. (Boulder, CO: Paradigm Publishers, 2015).

Oklahoma City Bombing

The April 1995 Oklahoma City bombing in which the Alfred P. Murrah Federal Building was destroyed and 168 men, women, and children lost their lives is commonly associated with three events that had occurred in the two years preceding the bombing: the standoff at Ruby Ridge, Idaho in 1992 in which two members of Randy Weaver's family were killed by federal agents; the tragic ending to the confrontation at the Branch Davidian compound just outside Waco, Texas, in 1993; and the passage in 1994 of the Brady Handgun Violence Prevention Act. Each of these events involved federal firearms legislation. Federal officials wanted to arrest Randy Weaver for the illegal possession and sale of two sawed-off shotguns; Branch Davidian leader David Koresh was accused of possessing illegal automatic weapons; and the Brady Act imposed a waiting period and background check on anyone wishing to purchase a handgun. Timothy McVeigh, a gun enthusiast and prime suspect in the bombing, had expressed his extreme dislike for the federal government.

On April 19, 1995, two years to the day after federal agents stormed the Branch Davidian compound, a truck containing a 4,800-pound home-made bomb exploded in front of the Oklahoma City federal building. The building contained several federal offices, including the Bureau of Alcohol, Tobacco, and Firearms (ATF), an agency that many perceive as a major enemy of the right to bear arms. Ninety minutes after the blast, Timothy McVeigh, a 27-year-old former Army sergeant, was stopped by a state trooper for speeding along Interstate 35. McVeigh's automobile had no license plates, and he was carrying an unregistered 9-mm. Glock semiautomatic pistol that was loaded with Black Talon bullets. The trooper arrested McVeigh and transported him to the Perry, Oklahoma, county jail, where he stayed for two days until the Federal Bureau of Investigation (FBI) traced him through his social security number. Using the computer system at the National Crime Information Center, the FBI discovered that their prime suspect was being held in Perry. They contacted the sheriff's office, requesting that McVeigh, who was about an hour away from release, be held for transfer to federal authorities.

In the first days following the bombing, some militia groups claimed that the devastation had been committed by the federal government to lay blame on militia groups, to manipulate Congress

Oklahoma City's Alfred P. Murrah Federal Building two days after a truck bomb ripped the structure apart. *www.wikipedia.org*

into giving law enforcement greater power, and to justify the repression of militia members and gun owners generally. However, the quick arrest of McVeigh and claimed coconspirator Terry Nichols put to rest, for all but the most extreme militia members, claims of federal government involvement. In August 1995, McVeigh and Nichols were indicted by a federal grand jury.

On June 2, 1997, a federal court jury found McVeigh guilty of the Oklahoma City bombing. He was convicted of first-degree murder in the deaths of eight federal law-enforcement officers who were working in the building. The defense had argued that McVeigh was innocent and that the true perpetrators, sponsored by a foreign government, had still not been found. However, the amount of evidence the

prosecution was able to bring forward left any alternative explanation for the crime unconvincing. Before the bombing, McVeigh had told his sister to expect "something big." He had often expressed his hatred for the federal government and the ATF. McVeigh's favorite reading, a right-wing novel titled *The Turner Diaries*, contained a description of a similar bombing event against a government building. Although McVeigh's views gave some hint as to his motives, the conviction rested on the impressive amount of evidence that the prosecution had amassed against the defendant. At the sentencing stage, McVeigh received the death penalty, and was executed in 2001. Terry Nichols was subsequently convicted and sentenced to a life term for his part in the bombing plot.

While most people on both sides of the gun control issue behave within the legal confines of the system, a complete treatment of the gun control debate must recognize that some people view gun control advocates not only as mistaken in their interpretation of the Second Amendment, but anxious to wrest freedom away from average Americans who can depend only on themselves for self-protection. Indeed, the federal government is viewed as the great oppressor that, among other tyrannous acts, intends to disarm all Americans. This view, while highly implausible, apparently motivated McVeigh to take the use of force into his own hands.

See also: Black Talon Bullet; Brady Handgun Violence Prevention Act; Bureau of Alcohol, Tobacco, Firearms, and Explosives; Ruby Ridge; Second Amendment; *The Turner Diaries*; Waco, Texas, Raid.

Further Reading: Jonathan Karl, *The Right to Bear Arms: The Rise of America's Militia Movement* (New York: HarperCollins, 1995); Lou Michel and Dan Herbeck, *American Terrorist: Timothy McVeigh and the Oklahoma City Bombing* (New York: Regan Books, 2001).

Open Carry Movement

Aggressive advances in the gun rights movement, capped by two Supreme Court cases that recognized a personal, individual right to own guns for personal self-protection in the home (*District of Columbia v. Heller* in 2008), and that extended this right to the states (*McDonald v. Chicago* in 2010), emboldened gun rights advocates to more aggressively carry and display their guns. The open carry movement, advanced by zealous gun owners who want to openly carry holstered handguns in public places, staged various public events in 2009 and 2010 to advance their cause. These demonstrations reflected a schism in the gun rights movement, as the National Rifle Association (NRA) did not support these activities, and some in the gun carry movement feel that the NRA has become too conservative, cautious, and mainstream. A Web-based organization, Opencarry.org, formed in 2004, is dedicated to the public carrying of guns. It claimed 22,000 members in 2010. As of 2010, thirty-five states allow open gun carrying, 12 states require a permit for open carrying, and three states bar the practice.

National attention was drawn to the open carry movement when some opponents to President Barack Obama's health care reform initiative showed up at public meetings organized to address the issue with guns openly displayed in 2009. A few protestors also showed up at an Obama speaking event in Arizona with guns, including an AR-15 rifle. Such carrying was legal, but it also increased concerns about the president's safety. In 2010, gun carry advocates began showing up at businesses such as Starbucks coffee restaurants to demonstrate their support for open carrying. Even zealous gun activists like Alan Gottlieb of the Second Amendment Foundation expressed misgivings in 2010: "I'm all for open-carry laws, but I don't think flaunting it is very productive for our cause. It just scares people." Defenders of open carry argue that the action is legal in most places, is an expression of Second Amendment rights, and is beneficial for public safety.

The open carry movement has found little favor among the general public, because many feel intimidated by civilians openly carrying guns, and because of the belief that such open carrying does nothing to promote public safety, and is an unnecessary and intimidating action. Ironically, supporters of open carry say that one reason they have held open carry events is to build support for concealed carry laws by showing that people do feel uncomfortable with open carry. The open carry movement has focused particular efforts on California in hopes that it can push the state to make concealed carry easier.

See also: Concealed Carry Laws; *District of Columbia v. Heller* (2008); Gottlieb, Alan Merril; *McDonald v. Chicago* (2010); Second Amendment Foundation.

Further Reading: Opencarry.org Web site, www.opencarry.org; Vanessa O'Connell, "Gun Advocates Open Up a New Front," *Wall Street Journal,* April 19, 2010, 3; Ian Urbina, "Locked, Loaded, and Ready to Caffeinate," *New York Times*, March 7, 2010, A1.

Orlando, Florida, Shooting

On June 12, 2016, the city of Orlando, Florida, added its name to the list of municipalities— including Newtown, Connecticut (27 people killed), Virginia Tech in Blacksburg, Virginia (32 killed), and San Bernardino, California (14 killed)—that have experienced the trauma of a mass shooting. In Orlando, the shooter killed 49 people and wounded many others before law enforcement officers shot and killed him. The incident was the most deadly shooting in U.S. history.

In the early morning hours of June 12, a gunman, the 29-year-old sone of Afghan immigrants, Omar Mateen, who was born in Queens, New York, entered the Pulse, a gay nightclub. He was armed with an AR-15-type rifle and a handgun, which he had recently purchased legally from a gun shop. The gunman fired the first shots around 2:00 a.m., soon after which an armed security guard challenged the shooter. The first police officers to reach the scene joined the security guard in exchanging fire with the shooter, who moved deeper into the large area of the club, ultimately retreating into a bathroom where several patrons had gone to hide.

A siege began that did not end until 5:00 a.m. Early on, Mateen called 911 and calmly stated his allegiance to the Islamic State. As the siege continued, the gunman claimed he would set off explosives and that he was wearing an explosive vest. As the Mateen began shooting people in the restroom, the police decided to move in, first attempting to blow holes in the exterior wall and then using an armored BearCat (Ballistic Engineered Armored Response Counter Attack Truck) to penetrate the wall. Dozens of hostages fled through the hole before the gunman appeared, firing at police officers, several of whom returned fire, killing Mateen. Law enforcement officials found no explosives when they entered the building.

The carnage in Orlando led once again to attempts to explain why such events can occur and to consider possible ways to prevent such a tragedy. Officials quickly gained information about the shooter, who in 2013 the Federal Bureau of Investigation (FBI) placed on the terrorist watch list after his co-workers at G4S, a major private security company where he was employed, revealed that he had suggested he might have ties to terrorist organizations. The FBI interviewed Mateen twice and conducted record checks, witness interviews, and surveillance, but agents were unable to discover any conclusive evidence of terrorist associations and ended the investigation. A year later, the FBI placed Mateen on the terrorist watch list as agents investigated a possible link between him and an individual who became the first American suicide bomber in Syria, but again found no conclusive evidence. In addition to the possible ideological motive for the shooting rampage, officials discovered that Mateen had expressed strong objections to homosexuality.

The Orlando shooting resulted in renewed calls for additional gun control legislation, and Congress considered bills to extend background checks for firearm purchases to online and gun show sales, and to prohibit individuals on the terrorist watch list, who are kept from flying on commercial airlines, from purchasing firearms. The U.S. Senate rejected such legislative proposals, and the Republican leadership in the House of Representatives refused to consider gun control legislation. Democratic representatives, led by Congressman John Lewis (D-GA) staged a sit-in on the House floor, ultimately to no avail.

See also: San Bernardino, California, Shooting.

Further Reading: Lizette Alvarez and Richard Pérez-Peña, "Praising Isis, Gunman Attacks Gay Nightclub, Leaving 50 Dead in Worst Shooting on U.S. Soil," *New York Times* (June 13, 2016): A1; Marc Santora, "Last Call, and Shot Ring Out: In the Bathroom 'He Has Us,'" *New York Times* (June 13, 2016): A1; Jennifer Steinhauer, "Senate Blocks 4 Measures Proposed to Curb Gun Sales," *New York Times* (June 21, 3016): A12; richard Fausset, "House Gun Sit-In Evokes a Civil Rights-Era Scene," *New York Times* (June 26, 2016): 14

Rep. Xavier Becerra, D-Calif., attends a vigil on the House steps of the Capitol at which members held up pictures of the Orlando nightclub victims to mark the one-month anniversary of the shooting, July 12, 2016. *Photo By Tom Williams/CQ Roll Call; Getty Images*

P

Pacific Center for Violence Prevention (PCVP)

Located within the Trauma Foundation of San Francisco General Hospital, the Pacific Center for Violence Prevention (PCVP) was formed to reduce youth violence. The Trauma Foundation has engaged in a number campaigns to improve the safety of citizens, including advocacy of fire-safe cigarettes, mandatory seat belt laws, motorcycle helmet statutes, an increase in the liquor tax, regulation of alcohol advertising to prohibit demeaning images of women, and health care for battered women.

The Trauma Foundation began in 1973 as the Burn Council, an organization devoted to preventing burn injuries to children. The Council advocated such measures as requiring flame-resistant children's sleepwear. In 1979, the organization was expanded to deal with all injuries. Firearms were identified as one of the unsafe products for younger people that should be given attention. The Pacific Center, which has focused on gun control as one means of preventing violence especially among youth, is the policy headquarters of the Violence Prevention Initiative, a collaboration of community groups engaged cooperatively in local violence prevention. The Center offers various services to communities, including media and policy advocacy training and information resources.

The Pacific Center has established three major objectives. First, it supports a policy shift away from institutional confinement for youth who commit violent acts toward community-based crime prevention programs that regard youth as a resource to be developed. Second, the Center works to reduce the access youth have to alcohol and other drugs by increasing the excise tax on beer, limiting youth-oriented advertising of alcoholic products, and allowing local communities to regulate alcohol sales. Finally, the organization hopes to initiate policies to limit firearm possession among youth.

The Policy Center considers youth access to firearms, as well as firearms possession generally, a major contributor to high levels of violence in California and across the nation. The organization notes that in California, firearms have become the leading cause of death for those aged 1 to 19. In California, 80 percent of homicides involving youth are committed with firearms. Also of concern is the large number of nonfatal gun injuries.

The Center has supported several proposals to keep firearms away from youth. It promotes a total ban on the sale and possession of Saturday night specials, or junk guns, which are still produced in the United States even though the Gun Control Act of 1968 prohibited foreign imports. Although this proposal has experienced serious opposition in California, where several manufacturers are located, the Center strongly advocates such a ban, reporting that junk guns made in California are often used in crimes. The Center promotes home rule legislation that allows local communities to establish firearms limitations independent of state government. Gun rights organizations have strongly opposed such provisions, advocating instead state laws that preempt localities from approving gun control ordinances. The organization supports uniform penalties for carrying concealed weapons. In 1989, during the debate over an assault weapons ban, the Pacific Center, along with a coalition of health care workers and community leaders, campaigned for the bill's passage. The Pacific Center played a key role in the passage of five gun control bills in California in 1999. It also supported the state's ban on the sale of .50-caliber sniper rifles to civilians passed in 2004.

In working toward its goals, the Center collaborates with other organizations, including the Berkeley Media Studies Group, which assists with media advocacy training and news monitoring; the California Child Youth and Family Coalition, an organization concerned with the basic causes of violence; and the Urban Strategies Council, a group that examines the social factors affecting the level of violence in a community.

See also: Assault Weapons Ban; Concealed Carry Laws; Gun Control Act of 1968; Health Care Professionals; Saturday Night Special; Schools and Guns; Youth and Guns.

Further Reading: The Trauma Foundation at San Francisco General Hospital Web site, www.traumaf.org/.

Paladin Press

Paladin Press, headquartered in Boulder, Colorado, offers a list of books, DVDs, and video tapes on such controversial topics as weaponry and combat shooting, sniping, espionage, explosives, achieving revenge, and establishing a new identity. Paladin publishes a catalog, containing hundreds of titles, which is also available on the Internet. Among the listed categories most relevant to firearms and gun control are "exotic weapons," "firearms," "sniping," and "explosives and demolitions."

In 1970, Peder Lund and Robert K. Brown joined forces to establish Paladin Press, which had previously been known as Panther Publications. Lund and Brown decided on the new name, fearing that the company might otherwise be confused with the Black Panther Party, a radical African American group. During its first four years, Paladin limited its offerings primarily to government military manuals. When Brown left the company in 1974 to found *Soldier of Fortune* magazine, Lund expanded the publication list beyond military subjects to include how-to manuals dealing with such topics as identity change, bounty hunting, explosives, sniping, and martial arts.

Paladin offers several publications on firearms, some of which describe how to make guns at home. For instance, a description of *A Do-It-Yourself Submachine Gun* by Gerard Metral, states that, "You'll never have to worry about which submachine guns turn up on the banned-import list again. Now you can build your own simply by following the complete step-by-step plans and machinist's drawings." However, the description concludes by stating: "*Warning.* All BATF rules apply to the construction of this firearm. This book is presented for *academic study only.*" Advertisements for a series of books by Bill Holmes dealing with the home manufacture of firearms contain the same disclaimer. A similar disclaimer follows a depiction of *Full-Auto Conversion of the SKS Rifle* by "Powder Burns," which is described as containing "complete plans for putting together a fully automatic weapon 'powerful enough to make would-be tyrants tremble in their jackboots.'" In response to those who express reservations about publishing such how-to books, Lund has been quoted as saying, "I've never seen a man killed by a book."

Some of the advertised publications express an explicit anti-gun control position. Alan M. Rice's *Lethal Laws* asserts a relationship between a government's tendency to control the ownership of guns and its intentions to engage in genocide. In *Gun Control: Gateway to Tyranny*, Jay Simkin and Aaron Zelman argue that U.S. gun control legislation was inspired by gun laws in Nazi Germany. The authors compare the Gun Control Act of 1968 and Nazi laws to demonstrate "the fascist roots of American anti-gunners' progressive firearm confiscation policies."

The Paladin catalog describes Ragnar Benson's *Modern Weapons Caching* as a manual for hiding weapons from the authorities: "Firearms owners must literally take their weapons underground— bury them— or be prepared to have them confiscated." *Boston on Guns and Courage* by "Boston T. Party" is said to deal with such topics as which firearms to purchase, why the gun owner may not wish to apply for a concealed carry permit, and what guns are likely to be outlawed. The catalog also describes John Ross's novel, *Unintended Consequences*, which deals with the events surrounding a man's refusal to submit to "the increasingly heavy-handed tactics of the BATF."

See also: Black Panther Party; Bureau of Alcohol, Tobacco, Firearms, and Explosives; Concealed Carry Laws; Gun Control Act of 1968; *Soldier of Fortune.*

Further Reading: Paladin Press Catalog (Boulder, Colorado); Paladin Press Web site, www.paladin-press.com.

Palin, Sarah Louise Heath (1964–)

Alaska's first female governor rocketed to national fame overnight when she was tapped by 2008 Republican presidential nominee and Arizona Senator John McCain to serve as McCain's vice presidential running mate. The selection of the attractive, young, and vigorous Palin provided the McCain campaign with the initial boost it was looking for in his flagging campaign against Democratic presidential frontrunner Barack Obama. However, Palin's lack of experience and penchant for making bombastic and sometimes inaccurate statements soon proved to be more of a liability than an asset to the McCain campaign, which went down to defeat that November. Chief among Palin's conservative credentials were her love of hunting, ability to handle guns, and allegedly, even the ability to "field dress a moose."

Palin was born in Idaho, the third of four children, the child of a science teacher and a school secretary. While still young, Palin's family moved to Alaska. After graduating from high school in 1982, she attended four different colleges (one of them twice), eventually earning a degree in journalism in 1987. In 1984, she came in third in the Miss Alaska beauty pageant. Moving to Wasilla, Alaska, with her husband and high school sweetheart Todd, Palin's political career began with election to the Wasilla City Council, where she served from 1992–1996. That year, she was elected mayor of Wasilla, a position she held until 2002. After an unsuccessful run for lieutenant governor in 2002, she won election as Alaska's governor in 2006, making her both the youngest and first female governor in Alaskan history. After her unsuccessful vice presidential bid, she resigned as governor in early 2009, wrote a book, endorsed conservative candidates around the country, and became a commentator on the Fox News Channel.

Palin, a life member of the National Rifle Association (NRA), is a lifelong hunter, having shot her first rabbit at the age of 10. She speaks with pride about her use of guns, but earned the ire of naturalists and gun control supporters as governor by promoting the hunting of wolves from the air as a move to control the wolf population. She also supports the individualist view of the Second Amendment, opposes any ban on assault weapons, and favors gun safety education programs for young people. Palin also voiced admiration for the Alaskan Independence Party (AIP), a separatist group that supports Alaska's secession from the United States, and that has advocated a violent uprising against the federal government. Palin attended the AIP's annual convention in 2006, and spoke by videotape to the 2008 convention in which she urged the party to "keep up the good work." Her husband Todd was a registered party member from 1995–2002.

Palin also opposes abortion and sex education, favors the teaching of creationism in public schools and sexual abstinence before marriage, and also opposed environmental restrictions on oil drilling in Alaska and elsewhere. The mother of five, Palin's popularity among conservatives stoked speculation that she would seek the presidency on her own in 2012, but that effort never materialized. In 2016, she endorsed Donald J. Trump for president.

See also: National Rifle Association.

Further Reading: William J. Crotty, ed., *Winning the Presidency 2008* (Boulder, CO: Paradigm Publishers, 2009); Josh Horwitz, "Is Sarah Palin 'Mainstream' on Guns?" *The Huffington Post*, September 4, 2008, at www.huffingtonpost.com/josh-horwitz/is-sarah-palin-mainstream_b_124098.html; Sarah Palin, *Going Rogue: An American Life* (New York: HarperCollins, 2009).

Paul, Ron (1935–)

Ron Paul, a conservative Republican congressman from Texas and an avid supporter of the individualist interpretation of the Second Amendment guarantee of the right to keep and bear arms, has advocated the virtual elimination of restrictions on gun ownership for law-abiding citizens. Paul has championed several conservative causes, including abolition through constitutional amendment of personal income, estate, and gift taxes and a prohibition on federal government business activities that compete with private citizens. Paul has proposed a constitutional amendment authorizing state governments to prohibit destruction of the U.S. flag and empowering Congress to prohibit destruction of federally owned flags. In 1997, the congressman sponsored a bill that would have withdrawn the United States from the United Nations. Paul was sharply criticized that year for commenting in a televised interview that he feared being "bombed by the federal government at another Waco."

Ron Paul, a conservative Republican congressman from Texas, has advocated the virtual elimination of restrictions on gun ownership for law-abiding citizens. *Photo by David Carlyon; www.wikipedia.org*

An obstetrician and gynecologist, Paul received degrees from Gettysburg College and Duke University School of Medicine. After serving as a flight surgeon in the U.S. Air Force, he moved to Texas in 1968. Paul was first elected to the U.S. House of Representatives in 1976. He believes that the federal government should cease to play a role in education, leaving this function to state and local governments. A supporter of term limits, Paul did not run for reelection in 1984, choosing instead to return to his medical practice. In 1988, he ran for president as the Libertarian Party candidate. In 1996, Paul returned to the House of Representatives after wresting the party nomination from the Republican incumbent who had the support of the state and national Republican establishment.

In 1997, Paul sponsored a bill called the Second Amendment Restoration Act, which would repeal federal prohibitions on semiautomatic firearms and large capacity ammunition clips. The act would amend the federal criminal code and the Violent Crime Control and Law Enforcement Act of 1994, repealing prohibitions on "the manufacture, possession, transfer, and use of semiautomatic assault weapons and large capacity ammunition feeding devices." The act would acknowledge that the Second Amendment guarantees an individual's right to keep and bear arms, including semiautomatic firearms, and declare that Article I, section 8 of the U.S. Constitution, which enumerates the powers of Congress, does not grant Congress authority to enact gun control legislation.

Continuing his efforts to dismantle federal gun control legislation, in October 1997 Paul introduced a proposal, called the Second Amendment Protection Act, which would repeal the Brady Handgun Violence Prevention Act, amend provisions of the Internal Revenue Code regarding the taxation of machine guns, and eliminate the provisions of the Gun Control Act of 1968 that distinguish among firearms on the basis of sporting purposes. In 2008, Paul ran for the Republican nomination for the presidency, and while he was never among the top contenders for the nomination, his libertarian, antigovernment platform garnered considerable attention and raised an impressive campaign war chest, mostly from small donors through the Internet.

Wishing to establish a national right to carry a concealed weapon, Paul introduced a bill to provide for reciprocity among states in recognizing such a right. The legislation would establish that an individual who is not prohibited by federal law from possessing, transporting, shipping, or receiving a firearm, who has a valid state license to carry a concealed weapon, and "who is otherwise entitled to carry a concealed firearm in and pursuant to the law of the state of . . . residence" may carry a concealed firearm "in accordance with the terms of the license or with the laws of the state of the person's residence." Paul established the legal basis of the act in Article IV section 1 of the U.S. Constitution, which requires that each state give "full faith and credit" to the public acts, records, and judicial proceedings of every other state. Paul retired from Congress in 2013.

See also: Assault Weapons Ban; Brady Handgun Violence Prevention Act; Concealed Carry Laws; Gun Control Act of 1968; Libertarian Party; Second Amendment; United Nations; Waco, Texas, Raid.

Further Reading: Philip D. Duncan and Christine C. Lawrence, *CQ's Politics in America 2010: The 111th Congress* (Washington, DC: Congressional Quarterly, 2009); Congressman Ron Paul's Web site, http://paul.house.gov; Ron Paul political Web site, www.ronpaul.com.

Paul Revere Network (PRN)

The Paul Revere Network (PRN) was founded as an Internet Web page in August 1995 by Leroy Pyle, a former National Rifle Association (NRA) director and veteran of the San Jose, California, police force. The PRN is described as "a coast-to-coast network of committed grass-roots gun rights activists who rely upon computer bulletin board systems for their primary mode of communication." The organization considers the Second Amendment guarantee of the right to keep and bear arms to be the cornerstone of the Bill of Rights. Pyle is the director of the Network, which is headquartered in Chicago, Illinois. Regional coordinators are located in cities around the country. In addition to the regional coordinators, the PRN contains approximately 200 nodes, each of which contains large amounts of data on firearms, the Second Amendment, opinion pieces, legislative updates, newsletter articles, and information about local and regional activities. The PRN issues an occasional newsletter.

Pyle, a firearms expert and police gun safety training officer, testified before the California legislature's Public Safety Committee against banning assault weapons in the state. An assault weapons ban gained extensive support in California following the schoolyard shooting in Stockton. By speaking out against the ban, Pyle contradicted the position of San Jose police chief Joseph McNamara, a proponent of gun control. The PRN claims that gun control legislation has been ineffective in reducing crime and that greater gun ownership in the population contributes to lowering the incidence of crime. The Network holds that assault rifles are indistinguishable from sporting and hunting firearms, except for cosmetic features, and therefore bans are unwarranted limitations on the Second Amendment's right to keep and bear arms.

The PRN supports the "NEW NRA," in other words, a gun rights group unwilling to compromise on the issue of gun control. The Network expresses its attitude toward gun control organizations by declaring "No Negotiation with Terrorists!" Pyle believes that the Network gives Second Amendment activists an advantage over the gun control opposition. He expects that ultimately the Web site will facilitate supporters in the coordination of massive letter and telegram campaigns to contact public officials about firearms issues.

The organization is concerned about gun control proposals advanced at all levels of government, which it claims would place serious limitations on the rights of gun owners. The Network applauds gun owners who have demanded a "stronger NRA" and contacted their legislators. Local efforts are seen as the best way gun owners can "halt the erosion of their gun freedoms." The Network hopes to unite the various local and regional efforts and to enlist politically inactive gun owners through a computer bulletin board system.

See also: Assault Weapons Ban; National Rifle Association; Second Amendment; Stockton, California, Shooting.

Further Reading: Paul Revere Network Web site, www.paulrevere.org.

PAX

PAX works to create wide public support for social and political solutions to the problem of firearms violence against children and families. The organization generates attention through the mass media for the gun violence issue and encourages grassroots activism by demanding changes in policy. PAX was established in 1997 by Talmage Cooley and Daniel Gross. Gross serves as director and CEO of the organization. PAX numbers among its trustees and advisers a variety of celebrities, media people, and businesspeople.

A Wall Street trader from 1983 until 1993, Cooley left the world of finance to become a writer, director, and photographer. In 1995, he established The Gun Violence Project to develop media strategies to assist in the development of an anti-gun violence movement. In 1997, Cooley merged The Gun Violence Project with PAX. That year, Gross's brother Matthew, a rock singer, was wounded in the Empire State Building shooting. Following the incident Gross became involved in anti-gun violence efforts, making appearances on television and radio and writing about the need to curb gun violence. He resigned a position in an advertising firm to cofound PAX.

PAX notes a General Accounting Office (GAO) report indicating that in 60 percent of gun-related fatal accidents the firearm was located "near the home." PAX advocates that states pass laws to mandate that firearms owners keep guns locked and safely stored to prevent children from having access to weapons. Focusing on school violence, the organization refers to a Department of Education report that several thousand students are expelled in each school year for taking guns to school. PAX cites survey data indicating that over 80 percent of the U.S. population support legislation to make new handguns "childproof."

PAX recommends that parents familiarize themselves with the dangers of firearms, speak with their children about the dangers, and strive to keep them away from guns. Gun owners are advised to keep firearms locked and inaccessible to everyone but themselves. Those concerned about gun violence are encouraged to discover the position on gun control of their representatives in state legislatures and Congress; PAX suggests that individuals organize petition and letter-writing campaigns to lobby for proposals and take part in education programs to limit firearm violence. PAX supports the effort to have school children sign a pledge not to take a firearm to school and not to use a gun to settle disputes. The organization has produced and disseminated public service announcements about gun-related dangers, and promotes a "Speak Up" campaign to encourage students to speak up about the dangers of guns and violence.

See also: Empire State Building Shooting; Lautenberg, Frank R.; Schools and Guns; Schumer, Charles E.; Trigger Locks.

Further Reading: PAX Web site, www.paxusa.org.

Perpich v. Department of Defense (1990)

Although the decision in *Perpich v. Department of Defense* (496 U.S. 334, 1990) does not relate directly to the right to keep and bear arms, gun rights advocates consider that the U.S. Supreme Court's ruling in the case supports an individualist interpretation of the Second Amendment, and conclude that the Court's affirmation of congressional power over state militias argues against the pro-gun control position that the Second Amendment guarantees only a communal right of the states to establish militia organizations independent of the national government.

In presenting its decision, the Court examined the history of the militia system in the United States. In 1916, Congress enacted a statute requiring all members of National Guard organizations in the states to take a dual oath, obligating themselves to obey the president of the United States as well as the governor of the state. The legislation authorized the president to draft members of the Guard into federal service. Democratic President Woodrow Wilson used that power during World War I to call up troops. In 1933, Congress amended the 1916 act, creating two overlapping organizations: the several state National Guards and the National Guard of the United States. Since 1933, anyone enlisting in a state's National Guard simultaneously enlists in the National Guard of the United States.

While originally the president was empowered to order National Guard units to active duty only in periods of national emergency, in 1952 Congress authorized the president to order units to "active duty or active duty for training" without the emergency requirement. However, the law specified that such orders required gubernatorial consent. In 1985, the governor of California refused to agree to a training mission in Honduras for 450 California National Guard personnel. The following year, Congress responded by enacting the Montgomery Amendment, which stated that, "the consent of a Governor . . . may not be withheld (in whole or in part) with regard to active duty outside the United States, its territories, and its possessions, because of any objection to the location, purpose, type, or schedule of active duty."

The governor of Minnesota objected to the Montgomery Amendment, arguing that it violated the two militia clauses of the Constitution. The governor contended that, according to the traditional understanding, the militia may be employed only "to execute the Laws of the Union, suppress Insurrections and repel Invasions." The Court observed that members of the state National Guards "must keep three hats in their closets—a civilian hat, a state militia hat, and an army hat—only one of which is worn at any particular time." Situations may arise when state affiliation ceases and complete federal affiliation begins. Congress, which initially granted governors veto power over the use of state National Guard units in their respective states, has the authority to limit that power. Therefore, the Court concluded that the Montgomery Amendment does not violate the Constitution's militia clauses.

The governor contended that such an interpretation of the militia clauses would end in "nullifying an important state power that is expressly reserved in the Constitution." The Court responded that the Constitution simply recognizes federal supremacy in military affairs: "The Federal Government provides virtually all of the funding, the material, and the leadership for the State Guard units." The president's requiring a portion of a state guard to participate in a training exercise affects only slightly the overall guard unit in a state. In addition, the Court noted that Congress has passed legislation allowing a state to "provide and maintain at its own expense a defense force that is exempt from being drafted into the Armed Forces of the United States." Contrary to the claims of gun rights advocates in this case, gun control forces may use the Court's understanding that the states have maintained their unique position in sustaining the National Guard to argue for the communal interpretation of the Second Amendment.

See also: Militia Act of 1792; Second Amendment.

Further Reading: *Perpich v. Department of Defense,* 496 U.S. 334 (1990).

Physicians for Social Responsibility (PSR)

Physicians for Social Responsibility (PSR), a network of physicians and public health professionals founded in 1961 with national headquarters in Washington, D.C., develops strategies to decrease the dangers of nuclear weapons, environmental pollution, health care reform, and gun violence. The organization calls itself "the active conscience of American medicine." Adhering to an epidemiological model of gun violence, the PSR engages in developing a national violence prevention coalition to reduce the number of firearms and the level of domestic violence. The organization is active in recruiting interested people locally to provide information about violence and to persuade local, state, and national representatives to support violence-prevention legislation. The Chicago chapter of the PSR has developed a presentation and speakers' bureau that includes color slides showing the medical consequences of handgun violence, a speakers' guide, and training for speakers.

The PSR has taken stands on several public policy issues regarding firearms, supporting additional legislation and other actions the organization believes will decrease gun violence.

For instance, it supports legislation to limit handgun purchases to one per month to stop volume sales to underground dealers. In addition, just as consumer product safety regulations were instituted, such as child-resistant packaging for prescription drugs and air bags in automobiles, standards should be established for firearms safety and design. The organization has supported federal legislation to prevent foreign visitors from buying or carrying firearms while in the United States. Another favored piece of legislation would grant to the Bureau of Alcohol, Tobacco, Firearms, and Explosives (ATF) the authority to regulate the manufacture, distribution, and sale of firearms and ammunition, and subject guns to safety restrictions.

The PSR supports enactment of child access prevention (CAP), or safe storage, laws. Such laws are credited with preventing unauthorized use of firearms by minors. The organization advocates personalized gun technology that would prevent persons other than the gun owner from firing the weapon. If manufacturers do not introduce this technology voluntarily, state and national legislatures should approve legislation requiring the addition of such devices. The organization opposes the enactment of state concealed carry laws. Of greatest concern are "shall issue" laws that mandate the issuance of licenses virtually on demand to anyone not specifically prohibited from owning a firearm.

The PSR supports banning specific types of weapons. The organization advocates broadening the ban on the importation of junk guns, or Saturday night specials, that was instituted in the Gun Control Act of 1968. Not only foreign handguns, but domestically produced models should be subject to the ban. Claiming that "assault weapons are vectors of America's gun violence epidemic as surely as bacteria and viruses are vectors of infectious disease," the PSR supports reenactment of the assault weapons ban that lapsed in 2004. Estimating the costs of firearms deaths and injuries at tens of billions of dollars per year, the organization backs legislation to increase federal taxes on firearms. The additional revenue would be used to support victims of gun violence.

The PSR encourages physicians and other health care workers to inform families of the dangers of firearms to bring about greater numbers of gun-free homes. Concerned about the intensified marketing of firearms to women and arguing that guns do not offer the protection that gun manufacturers claim, the organization recommends that people not rely on firearms for self-protection.

See also: Assault Weapons Ban; Bureau of Alcohol, Tobacco, Firearms, and Explosives; Gun Control Act of 1968; Health Care Professionals; National Rifle Association; Saturday Night Special; Second Amendment; Women and Guns.

Further Reading: Physicians for Social Responsibility Web site, www.psr.org.

Police Executive Research Forum (PERF)

The Police Executive Research Forum (PERF), a group that represents those in leadership positions in municipal, county, and state law enforcement agencies, has taken stands in favor of several gun control proposals. Believing that the Gun Control Act of 1968 provided uniform national policy necessitated by the widely varying statutes among the states, PERF joined other law enforcement organizations to oppose provisions of the 1986 McClure-Volkmer Firearms Owners Protection Act that weakened the 1968 legislation. Since then PERF has supported firearms policies the organization believes will increase the safety of police officers. It also supports programs to reduce violent crime using such techniques as crime street mapping and various interdiction techniques.

The Forum began in 1975 when a small group of police executives from major cities met to discuss their concerns about policing. Two years later, it was incorporated as an organization dedicated to professionalizing policing at all levels of government. Based in Washington, D.C., the organization engages in and encourages research and public discussion to increase knowledge about law enforcement. Also emphasized are the encouragement of high ethical standards, integrity, responsibility, and accountability to the public. PERF receives support from government grants and contracts and from private organizations. The Forum supports the Senior Management Institute for Police (SMIP), a developmental program for current and future police executives.

Noting that keeping a loaded and unsecured handgun around children is "a tragedy waiting to happen," PERF supports the use of locks on handguns. The organization has backed such security devices since 1984, when it published guidelines for handgun safety that included a recommendation to owners to use trigger locks. The organization applauded the agreement between President Bill Clinton and representatives of several firearms companies to provide child safety mechanisms with newly manufactured handguns. Noting that from 1985 to 1994 the lives of over 2,000 police officers were saved by bulletproof vests, the Forum has supported legislation in Congress that would establish a grant program to assist local law enforcement agencies to purchase bulletproof vests for police officers. PERF has expressed support for the Brady Handgun Violence Prevention Act's criminal background check system for those wishing to purchase a handgun.

In a survey of 375 PERF members conducted in 1996, 92 percent of the respondents opposed legislation permitting the carrying of concealed weapons (CCW) laws, especially "shall issue" statutes that deny police officials discretion in granting permits. Members expressed doubt that concealed carry laws will reduce gun-related crime and feared that such laws threaten the safety of police officers. In addition to concern about "shall issue" CCW laws in general, PERF has objected to a legislative proposal that would exempt present and retired police officers from state laws that prohibit carrying concealed weapons. In 1997, John S. Farrell, legislative committee chairman for PERF and chief of police for Prince George's County, Maryland, presented reservations about such a law before the House Judiciary Committee's Subcommittee on Crime.

Farrell stated that although on some subjects a national policy is needed, the issue of CCW laws is best left to the individual states, especially provisions related to police officers carrying weapons. He expressed concern about former police officers being granted the right to carry a concealed weapon, raising questions about the responsibility for regular training and possible legal liability. Who would be held responsible for an off-duty police officer who misuses a weapon in another state? Even if the final ruling determines that no liability exists, a police agency may be faced with significant legal expenses defending itself against claims of responsibility for a police officer who misuses his or her firearm off-duty. Although many police officials express support for such a law, noting that police officers may be the target of retaliation while off-duty or even after retirement, PERF urged serious consideration of the potential dangers to police officers the legislation would pose. For instance, an officer faced with using a firearm may not have the other standard equipment carried by a uniformed officer. In addition, a police officer who uses a firearm while dressed in plain clothes may face an identification problem when approached by on-duty police.

See also: Brady Handgun Violence Prevention Act; Clinton, William Jefferson (Bill); Concealed Carry Laws; Firearms Owners Protection Act; Gun Control Act of 1968; McClure, James Albertas; Trigger Locks; Volkmer, Harold Lee.

Further Reading: Police Executive Research Forum Web site, www.policeforum.org.

Police Shootings

Police officers in the United States, unlike other developed nations, uniformly carry firearms, and have available sophisticated weapons beyond the mere handgun. The deadly firepower in the hands of law enforcement personnel calls for extensive training in the use of guns and the appropriate circumstances in which the weapons may be drawn and when they may be used.

Nonetheless, police officers have been criticized for unjustifiably shooting and killing individuals. News accounts of such events in several states have raised questions about law enforcement tactics as well as charges that police often use inappropriate force against minority group individuals. Of course, police officers face significant dangers, especially given the huge number of firearms—estimated at more than 300 million—in private hands in the United States, most in the hands of peaceful private citizens, but many possessed by those with criminal intent.

In 1989 the U.S. Supreme Court in Graham v. Connor (490 U.S. 386) established a standard for the use of force, stating that such use must be "objectively reasonable." However, the Court recognized that police officers must make quick decisions in ambiguous and volatile circumstances about the level of force that is appropriate. Some have argued that this standard has led to the use of deadly force far too often. One study determined that 30 percent of the 990 fatal police shootings in 2015 involved a person who did not have a firearm. In 9 percent of the cases, the person shot had no weapon, in 16 percent the person had a knife, and in 5 percent the person used an automobile as a weapon.

Although in some recent cases, police officers have been arrested on murder charges for the improper use of their weapon, in many situations, the use of deadly force met the Supreme Court standard, but nonetheless could be judged as avoidable. Such situations have been called "lawful but awful" outcomes. In 2016, the Police Executive Research Forum, a law enforcement policy organization, announced 30 principles intended to limit the number of such deadly encounters. The recommendations emphasize that police departments should develop a strategy for resolving incidents short of use force. The report recommends abandoning the so-called 21-foot rule, which directs officers to prevent individuals from approaching any closer to the officer.

The report also recommends that, when faced with a person carrying a knife, a better strategy would be to retreat and stay a safe distance from the person, rather than standing their ground, a strategy that would also apply to private citizens who carry concealed weapons for self-protection.

Controversial police shootings of African Americans continued to plague law enforcement across the nation. In July 2016, two incidents, one in Baton Rouge, Louisiana, and the other in Falcon Heights, Minnesota, in which black men were shot and killed by police officers, led to nationwide protests. In Dallas, Texas, a peaceful protest turned violent when a sniper, apparently angered by the shootings in previous days, shot and killed five police officers and wounded seven other officers along with two civilians. Other incidents of police officers being shot and killed added to the tension. The two types of police shootings—police shooting private individuals in questionable circumstances and private persons targeting police officers—combined with the questions of possible racial bias by some police officers and African American attitudes toward gun control. The long-standing support for gun control among blacks has been reported to be diminishing, and if so, one crucial factor may be that many African Americans not only perceive that police fail to protect their community, but that police unfortunately may be regarded at least in certain circumstances to pose a threat to minority communities.

See also: African Americans and Guns; Stand-Your-Ground Laws.

Further Reading: Al Baker, "Police Leaders Urge New Set of Standards," *New York Times* (January 30, 2016): A10; Chuck Wexler and Scott Thomason, "Making Policing Safer for Everyone," *New York Times* (March 2, 2016): A27

Potomac Institute

The Potomac Institute, located in Bethesda, Maryland, takes a contemporary liberal perspective on the issue of gun control in opposition to what it considers a joint conservative and libertarian position advocated by gun rights organizations. The Institute's motto is "It's not about guns . . . it's about citizenship," which emphasizes the role of citizens in a government-controlled militia rather than the individual right to possess firearms. The Institute advocates the registration of firearms, following what it considers the policy established by the Militia Act of 1792, which called for each citizen to be "enrolled" in the militia. The right to bear arms included a necessary obligation to serve the community.

The Institute claims that by registering all firearms the illegal trafficking in firearms could be significantly reduced primarily through the enforcement of local firearms regulations. Registration creates accountability in firearms ownership by connecting individuals to the uses to which their guns may be put. While the Institute regards as illegitimate the claims of gun rights advocates who assert a civil right to remain armed independent of the law, it also considers the agendas of gun control organizations ineffective in challenging the constitutional claims of pro-gun groups.

Among its activities, the Institute serves as a news service to report on gun violence and firearms policy, investigates and reveals the financial backing that gun rights groups provide for scholars, examines the background, objectives, and effectiveness of firearms legislation, analyzes the impact of current gun control strategies such as the public health approach, and encourages public debate of the gun control issue. The Institute holds that public health groups and gun control supporters must respond to the claim made by gun rights advocates that there is a right "to be armed outside the law."

The Institute rejects defenses of an individualistic right to keep and bear arms guaranteed in the Second Amendment, referring

Larry Pratt is executive director of Gun Owners of America and a strong supporter of the right to keep and bear arms. *Photo by Gage Skidmore; www.wikipedia.org*

to them as "pseudoscholarship" conducted by researchers who receive support from conservative foundations. According to the Institute, articles appearing in law journals have contributed "enormous respectability to gun lobby claims and posturing." The gun rights-supported doctrine of an armed populace is considered incompatible with a society ruled by law. In a broad ideological swipe at the pro-gun movement, the Institute claims that opposition to gun control can be seen as part of a right-wing reaction to New Deal reforms initiated by Democratic President Franklin Roosevelt's administration. Referring to the "libertarian fantasy" of individual sovereignty, the Institute contends that the gun rights agenda ultimately leads to support for anarchy.

While the Institute recognizes self-defense as a legitimate use of force, it contends that the National Rifle Association (NRA) exploits that claim to further the unacceptable position that individual sovereignty supports the right to possess arms unhindered by the government and as a potential means to oppose the government. The Institute sees no contradiction between the right to use firearms for self-defense and accountability to authority. Without legal controls, the individual possession of firearms could result in a domestic arms race that would fulfill the "anarchic libertarian fantasy" and facilitate gun interests' encouragement of gun ownership for self-defense purposes. The Institute holds that citizens may limit government coercion most effectively through the use of free institutions, not through a right outside the law to carry arms: "There can be no constitutional right to outflank this government with 'armed citizen guerrillas.'"

See also: Health Care Professionals; Libertarian Party; Militia Act of 1792; National Rifle Association; Second Amendment.

Further Reading: Potomac Institute Web site, www. potomac-inc.org.

Pratt, Larry (1942–)

Larry Pratt, founder and executive director of Gun Owners of America (GOA), has for years represented the more fervent segment of the gun rights movement. GOA was formed because Pratt and others believed that the National Rifle Association (NRA) was not tough enough in opposing gun laws. Pratt strongly opposes all gun control measures, including the Lautenberg Amendment (Domestic Violence Offender Gun Ban), which denies firearms ownership to anyone convicted of domestic violence, and the National Instant Check System (NICS) for those intending to purchase a firearm. He considers such measures intermediate steps toward the total banning of firearms. Pratt served as a Virginia state legislator and briefly as a Pat Buchanan campaign comanager during Buchanan's run for the Republican presidential nomination in 1996.

Pratt vehemently opposes any government regulation of firearms, arguing that the greatest murderers of the twentieth century were governments. Victims of government are most often unarmed citizens. Pratt declares that proposals to have the Consumer Product Safety Commission regulate firearms are unconstitutional, and violate what he considers the clear meaning of the Second Amendment. Pratt believes that firearms in the possession of private citizens provide a major deterrent to and defense against crime.

Contrary to gun control advocates who point to such incidents as the Empire State Building shooting in their push for more stringent legislation, Pratt claims that such tragedies can occur only because citizens are largely unarmed and thus present easy targets for predators. He observes that although the shooter in the Empire State Building incident purchased a firearm in Florida, he did not use it there. Pratt claims that a more lenient concealed carry law in that state deterred the man. He has suggested that Rodney King, the African American in California who was beaten by police, would have been at a greater advantage had he been armed to defend himself.

Pratt entered the political limelight in 1996 when he resigned as one of Pat Buchanan's campaign cochairpersons following news reports that he had spoken at meetings organized by white supremacists. One such meeting was held in Estes Park, Colorado, following the 1992 shoot-out between Randy Weaver and federal agents. Pete Peters, leader of Christian Identity, organized the meeting. It was also revealed that Pratt had appeared several times on Peters's radio talk show. Despite Buchanan's initial defense of Pratt against charges of associating with anti-Semitic groups, the GOA director left the campaign.

In his book, *Armed People Victorious*, published in 1990, Pratt defended the establishment of militias. He described efforts that were taken in Guatemala to develop armed civilian patrols and recommended that the United States reintroduce an armed citizenry for more effective defense. These Guatemalan militias were more widely known as "death squads" for their brutal and murderous tactics. Basing his advocacy of the right to bear arms not only on the Second Amendment but also on biblical interpretation, Pratt contended that scripture goes beyond establishing a right to keep and bear arms and mandates the carrying of weapons. In defending militias, Pratt argued that "virtually all militias are lawful," that no laws regulating militias are needed, and that Congress should not investigate militia groups.

Pratt also argues that the provision of the Brady Handgun Violence Prevention Act calling for an instant check system for those wishing to purchase a handgun amounts to a "massive scheme to register law-abiding gun owners." He has criticized the National Rifle Association (NRA) for failing to express concern about a system he believes involves registration "by its very design." Pratt argues that the system, meant to eliminate the five-day waiting period, violates existing law and the Second Amendment. Arguably, Pratt's more intense positions on firearms issues have inhibited more moderate gun rights advocates from compromising on gun control issues.

See also: Brady Handgun Violence Prevention Act; Empire State Building Shooting; Gun Owners of America; Lautenberg Amendment; National Instant Check System; National Rifle Association; Ruby Ridge; Second Amendment.

Further Reading: Gun Owners of America Web site, www.gunowners.org; Larry Pratt, letter to

Representative Bob Barr (May 23, 1997); Larry Pratt, "What Does the Bible Say About Gun Control?" (Springfield, VA: Gun Owners of America, n.d.); "Who Is Larry Pratt?" *New Republic* (March 11, 1996), 9.

Presbyterian Church (U.S.A.) (PCUSA)

Since the late 1960s, the Presbyterian Church (U.S.A.) (PCUSA), and its predecessor organizations have taken a resolute stand in favor of more stringent gun control regulations at the national and state levels. The General Assembly of the PCUSA called for "control [of] the sale and possession of firearms of all kinds." In 1976, the General Assembly reaffirmed this statement, but modified the resolution to exclude "shotguns and rifles used legitimately by sportsmen." At the 1988 meeting of the General Assembly, the Church again affirmed its position on gun control.

The PCUSA was formed in 1983 through a union of the Presbyterian Church in the United States. (PCUS), known as the "southern branch," and the United Presbyterian Church in the United States of America (UPCUSA), called the "northern branch." The Presbyterian church is generally considered a part of mainstream Christian churches and representative of their views. The Presbyterian Church in the United States has been noted for developing various factions and coalitions. In the 1920s, J. Gresham Machen, a conservative Presbyterian theologian, left Princeton Theological Seminary to found a more conservative wing of the Presbyterian Church. Contemporary theological descendants of Machen and the Westminster Theological Seminary that he founded are far less sympathetic to such social issues as gun control.

In 1990, the PCUSA General Assembly approved a more extensive statement on gun control, supporting "gun control at federal, state, and local levels as the most effective response to the present crisis of gun violence." The General Assembly called for the federal government to enact legislation to regulate the importation, manufacture, sale, and possession of firearms and ammunition by the general public, and suggested that legislation could include the registration and licensing of gun purchasers and owners; background checks to determine possible disqualifying circumstances, such as a criminal conviction; and waiting periods for those intending

to purchase firearms. The Assembly recommended "regulation of subsequent sale." The Church called for laws to be enacted at the state and local levels if federal legislation were delayed, a strategy that gun control advocates have pursued. Finally, the Assembly requested that government agencies at all levels provide "significant assistance" to victims of gun violence and their families. In recent years, the PCUSA has pursued a more narrow gun control agenda. In 2010, it focused on the problem of illegal gun sales and programs that have succeeded in stemming the illicit gun trade.

Further Reading: Presbyterian Church (U.S.A.) Web site, www.pcusa.org; Presbyterian Church (U.S.A.), Public Policy Statements of the Presbyterian Church (U.S.A.): "Gun Control" (Louisville, KY: PCUSA, 1996).

Presser v. Illinois (1886)

In *Presser v. Illinois* (116 U.S. 256, 1886), the U.S. Supreme Court heard an appeal from Herman Presser who was charged and convicted in 1879 of violating sections five and six of the Military Code of Illinois. The Code made it illegal for any group of individuals other than the organized volunteer militia of Illinois and U.S. troops to combine as a military organization or to parade with arms in any municipality of the state without first receiving a license from the governor.

Presser belonged to an organization called the *Lehr und Wehr Verein* (Education and Defense Society), which had been incorporated under the General Incorporation Laws of Illinois for the purpose of "improving the mental and bodily condition of its members, so as to qualify them for the duties of citizens of a republic." Among other activities, the members were to receive training in military exercises. In December 1879, Presser led a group of 400 members in a parade through the streets of Chicago. The members were armed with rifles and Presser, on horseback, carried a cavalry sword. The company of men had not received a license from the governor to parade as part of the state militia, was not a segment of either the organized state militia or the U.S. military, and had no official status under the national militia law.

After being found guilty of violating the Illinois Military Code, Presser appealed to the Supreme Court of Illinois, which affirmed the original decision. Presser then appealed the conviction to the U.S. Supreme Court on a writ of error. The plaintiff argued for the invalidity of the statute under which he was indicted and convicted, claiming that the Illinois legislature had wielded a power reserved to the national government under Article I, sections 8 and 10, and the Second Amendment of the U.S. Constitution. Presser also maintained that sections five and six of Article XI of the Military Code violated the protection against bills of attainder and ex post facto laws within Article I, section 9 of the U.S. Constitution (a claim the Court quickly dismissed), and the prohibition against states making laws abridging the privileges of U.S. citizens found in the Fourteenth Amendment to the U.S. Constitution.

The Court ruled that the sections of the Military Code of Illinois that forbade groups of individuals from associating as military organizations or to parade with arms in municipalities unless the organization has received authorization did not violate the right of the people to keep and bear arms. Although the Court indicated that states cannot prohibit people from keeping and bearing arms if such an action hindered the ability of the nation to maintain public security, it concluded that the sections at issue did not lead to that result.

The right to associate voluntarily as a military organization and to parade with arms independent of congressional or state legislative sanction fails as a claimed attribute of national citizenship. Because establishing a military organization and parading with arms are actions fundamentally under the control of government, no right to do so can be claimed without legal authorization. If this authority were denied to government, the Court reasoned, then the state would lack the ability to disperse groups intent on sedition and could not put down armed mobs about to riot.

Responding to Presser's claim that the articles at issue in the Code conflict with acts of Congress dealing with the organization of the militia, the Court stated that the purpose of these sections was to prohibit voluntary military groups with no legal authorization from organizing or parading with arms, and from obstructing the organization of the militia authorized by Congress. Therefore, these sections do not conflict with laws of Congress dealing with the militia. To the charge that the incorporation of the *Lehr und Wehr Verein* under the laws of Illinois constituted a license from the governor to parade, the Court stated that this was not a federal question and therefore was not an appropriate subject for a federal court ruling.

See also: Fourteenth Amendment; Militia Act of 1792; Second Amendment.

Further Reading: Robert J. Spitzer, *Gun Control: A Documentary and Reference Guide* (Westport, CT: Greenwood Press, 2009); *Presser v. Illinois*, 116 U.S. 256 (1886).

Printz v. United States (1997)

In *Printz v. United States* (521 U.S. 898, 1997), the U.S. Supreme Court held unconstitutional a provision of the Brady Handgun Violence Prevention Act that required chief law enforcement officers in local jurisdictions to conduct background checks on prospective handgun purchasers. Jay Printz, sheriff of Ravalli County, Montana, challenged the authority of the federal government to require him to assume a function of the national government, arguing that the federal mandate diverted critical resources from local law enforcement responsibilities. While invalidating mandated background checks, the Court left intact the law's five-day waiting period provision and the requirement that gun dealers submit to local authorities information about gun purchasers, with the proviso that any background check conducted by local officials must be voluntary. The provision of the law was found to be an unjustified use of Congress's power to regulate interstate commerce.

The background check requirement fell victim to the Court's increased concern for maintaining state sovereignty. In the 5 to 4 decision, Justice Antonin Scalia, speaking for the majority, stated that "Congress cannot compel the states to enact or enforce a federal regulatory program." The majority found no evidence in constitutional history for the claim that the national government may issue commands to state and local executive officials without the consent of the respective states.

The Court's decision was consistent with the 1995 ruling in *United States v. Lopez* in which the Court determined that Congress had exceeded its authority to regulate interstate commerce by banning guns within 1,000 feet of public schools. In the *Printz* ruling, the majority relied on the doctrine of dual sovereignty, holding that both the federal and state governments retain an inviolable realm of action independent of the other. What might otherwise by considered a legitimate power derived from the Necessary and Proper Clause of Article I, section 8 of the Constitution is invalid because the Brady law violates the constitutional system of state sovereignty.

In his dissent from the majority decision, Justice John Paul Stevens emphasized national concern over the role of handguns in violent crime. Congress should have the right to deal with a national emergency, enlisting the help of local officials. He compared the background check to a federal requirement that local police officers report to the federal government the names of missing children. Stevens further argued that the majority, intending to protect state sovereignty, ironically had invited the federal government to create a large new bureaucracy to administer the policy.

Gun control opponents hailed the decision as a victory for their side. They focused particularly on the separate opinion of Justice Clarence Thomas, who, although in the majority, went further than his colleagues in suggesting that the Second Amendment protection of the right to keep and bear arms limits the national government's authority to control guns. Supporters of the Brady law, who claimed the decision was only a minor setback, gave their attention to Justice Sandra Day O'Connor's opinion, also in the majority, that the Court's ruling did not spell the end of the objectives of the law, for local police may still voluntarily conduct background checks and Congress may legitimately provide financial help to local law enforcement agencies that continue the checks.

The decision had minimal impact on the operation of the Brady law, especially since the federal government was in the process of developing a national computerized system for conducting background checks that became operational in November 1998. The Court declined to rule on the appropriateness of the waiting period, the requirement that gun dealers provide information to government officials, or the law's relationship to the Second Amendment's right to bear arms.

See also: Brady Handgun Violence Protection Act; National Instant Check System; Second Amendment; State Laws, Appendix 2; *United States v. Lopez* (1995).

Further Reading: *Printz, Sheriff/Coroner, Ravalli County, Montana v. United States* (521 U.S. 898, 1997); Robert J. Spitzer, *Gun Control: A Documentary and Reference Guide* (Westport, CT: Greenwood Press, 2009).

Table 9
Causes of Injury Death by Manner of Death: United States, 2006

Motor Vehicles	24%
Poisonings	21%
Firearms	17%
Falls	12%
Suffocation	8%
Drowning, fire and burns, and cutting and piercing injuries	6%
Other	12%

Source: National Vital Statistics Reports, Vol. 57, No. 14, April 17, 2009, "Table 18: Number of Deaths, Death Rates, and Age-Adjusted Death Rates for Injury Deaths," pp. 89–90, accessed at http://www.cdc.gov/nchs/data/nvsr/nvsr57/nvsr57_14.pdf.

Product Liability Lawsuits

Gun control advocates argue that product liability lawsuits can provide opportunities to control the ill effects of firearms that legislative efforts have failed to bring about because of opposition from gun rights forces. They claim that the civil justice system can help reduce violence associated with firearms in two ways. First, firearms producers may be sued for defects in the design and manufacture of firearms and ammunition that lead to injuries to gun owners. Second, manufacturers and sellers of firearms may be held financially responsible for injuries or deaths because they sold firearms to individuals they should have known were highly likely to use the weapons illegally. Table 9 provides a breakdown of causes of injury deaths in the United States, indicating that firearms are the third most frequent cause of such deaths (behind motor vehicles and poisoning).

Several lawsuits indicated that the judicial systems at the state and national levels were more willing to entertain the possibility of product liability in the case of firearms. For instance, in 1979, the Supreme Court of Alaska affirmed a punitive damage award to a plaintiff who was injured by the Old Model Ruger single-action revolver. While loading the revolver, it slipped from his hand and fired, shooting him in the leg. Claims were made that there had been over 600 accidental discharges of the revolver, which was manufactured from 1953 to 1972. The Supreme Court of Alaska ruled that although the manufacturer was aware of the defective design and that injuries and deaths had resulted, production of the revolver continued.

A 1994 lawsuit in Texas involved the Remington Model 700 rifle. The plaintiff charged that the Remington Company knew that the rifle could fire without the trigger being pulled, but did not take steps to improve the design. The jury awarded the plaintiff $15 million in punitive damages. The manufacturers of Saturday night specials also have been the target of civil suits. Although gun rights advocates claim that such firearms can be excellent defensive weapons, others argue that they often fail to meet minimum safety and design standards. Of five California companies that manufacture such weapons, at least two have faced product liability lawsuits.

Lawsuits have been filed to recover damages from firearms manufacturers and sales outlets for injuries caused by so-called "high-risk" gun owners. A California gun store was sued for failing to conduct a sufficiently accurate identification of an assault weapon purchaser. The owner used the gun to shoot and kill a man, whose widow filed suit against the gun outlet. She recovered $400,000 in an out-of-court settlement.

Gun rights advocates, led by the National Rifle Association (NRA), won two major victories to halt such lawsuits. First, it spearheaded the enactment of "preemption" laws in many states around the country to prevent cities from bringing such lawsuits. Second and more important, the NRA logged a major victory for the gun industry when Congress enacted the Protection of Lawful Commerce in Arms Act of 2005, which provided legal immunity to gun manufacturers, distributors, dealers, and importers of firearms and ammunition, making the gun industry the only one exempted from such lawsuits. The immediate effect was to halt more than a dozen ongoing court cases in states around the country. A few lawsuits against gun manufacturers have proceeded, despite this law. For example, in 2016, the parents of children killed in the 2012 Sandy Hook elementary school shooting filed suit against Bushmaster Firearms, the company that produced the AR-15 rifle used by the shooter to kill 26 people at the school, claiming that the company bore responsibility for selling and marketing a military-type gun to civilians. A motion by the company's lawyers to dismiss the suit was rejected by the judge in the case.

See also: Clinton, William Jefferson (Bill); Consumer Product Safety; LaPierre, Wayne; National Rifle Association; Protection of Lawful Commerce in Arms Act of 2005; Remington, Eliphalet, II; Ruger, William Batterman (Bill); Sandy Hook elementary school shooting; Saturday Night Special.

Further Reading: Timothy D. Lytton,ed., *Suing the Gun Industry: A Battle at the Crossroads of Gun Control and Mass Torts* (Ann Arbor, MI: University of Michigan Press, 2006); Kristen Rand, *Lawyers, Guns, and Money: The Impact of Tort Restrictions on Firearms Safety and Gun Control* (Washington, DC: Violence Policy Center, 1996).

Project Exile

Project Exile, a joint federal and state government effort begun in Richmond, Virginia, charges felons found in possession of firearms with violation of federal firearms restrictions. Although recent years have seen a general nationwide drop in violent crime, Republican Governor James Gilmore attributed a significant drop in the Virginia murder rate to the initiation of Project Exile. The U.S. Attorney's Office in Richmond estimated that the number of gun deaths in Richmond declined 41 percent from the start of the Project in February 1997 until October 31, 1998.

Beginning in November 1998, Governor Gilmore, a member of the National Rifle Association (NRA), appeared in NRA print advertising praising Project Exile and stating that Virginia had "put politics aside" for a truly effective policy toward crime. The NRA considers Project Exile one way of reducing crime without restricting what it considers the rights of law-abiding gun owners and recommends that it be used nationwide, and the program is also supported by the Brady Campaign. The project adheres to the advice of many gun rights advocates, who have asserted that existing legislation should be strictly enforced against criminals.

The joint federal-state program was extended to Hampton Roads in December 1997 and to Norfolk early in 1998. The governor noted that through the federally supported program, 350 felons were arrested for illegal possession of firearms and 418 weapons had been confiscated. In October 1998, Governor Gilmore announced that the program would be expanded throughout the state as a way of punishing repeat offenders, recommending that the state Assembly pass the needed legislation. The state Assembly approved the legislation in March 1999 and Governor Gilmore signed it into law in April. Among its provisions, the law called for any person convicted of (1) possessing a firearm on school grounds, intending to use it or showing it in a threatening manner, (2) possessing a firearm after having been convicted of a violent felony, or (3) possessing a firearm while intending to sell drugs, shall be ineligible for probation and shall receive a minimum mandatory sentence of five years.

The governor pledged that Virginia law enforcement officials will prosecute repeat offenders "in a prompt and efficient manner." Other localities around the country adopted similar programs, including Atlanta, Georgia, Philadelphia, Pennsylvania, and Camden County, New Jersey. Baltimore, Maryland instituted the program in 2007 and reported a 30 percent drop in gun crimes over the next two years. However, some researchers have already concluded that enhanced sentencing laws have little effect on the rate of illegal firearm use, and the program has been criticized by gun extremist groups like the Gun Owners of America, and by civil rights groups concerned that this and similar programs unfairly target minority populations.

See also: National Rifle Association.

Further Reading: James Gilmore, "Project Exile for the Commonwealth," Office of the Governor Press Office, October 6, 1998, www.state.va.us/governor/ speech/exilesp.htm; "Project Exile's Crime success Has Others Following," February 25, 2010, WJZ TV, Baltimore, accessed at http://wjz.com/local/ Baltimore.Model.Decreasing.2.1520445.html.

Project Lifeline

Project Lifeline is an appendage of the Brady Center to Prevent Gun Violence (CPGV) and is sponsored by the Handgun Epidemic Lowering Plan (HELP) and Physicians for Social Responsibility (PSR), organizations of health care professionals striving to prevent firearm violence. Project Lifeline, begun in 1996, declared that it is not involved in government lobbying and does not promote a ban on handguns. The organization emphasizes three basic messages to discourage the ownership of firearms: (1) guns are the most

lethal means of violent injury; (2) handguns are responsible for the highest number of gun-related deaths and injuries; and (3) handgun injuries and deaths are preventable. The organization encourages health care professionals to educate the public regarding the dangers of handguns and possible preventive strategies to reduce deaths and injuries related to firearms. Advising parents to think carefully before allowing a firearm into the home, the organization claims that a child can more easily empty a handgun than a bottle of aspirin. The organization distributes a quarterly newsletter that keeps members informed about strategies for firearm injury prevention and about the experiences of various participants in the program.

Project Lifeline organized numerous national health-related organizations serving as partners, including the American Academy of Child and Adolescent Psychiatry, the American Academy of Pediatrics, the American Association of Public Health Physicians, and the American Public Health Association. Although the Project assesses no membership fees, organizations that become partners agree to distribute materials and individual members promise to offer public education regarding firearms in their local communities.

The Project, which discourages keeping firearms in the home, has publicized the claim that guns kept in the home are 43 times more likely to kill a member of the family or a friend than to kill an intruder, an assertion that gun rights advocates have vigorously challenged.

Noting that there are over 250 million privately owned firearms in the United States, the Project contends that the large difference in the rates between the United States and other nations is strongly related to the availability of guns.

See also: Physicians for Social Responsibility.

Further Reading: Brady Center Web site, www. bradycenter.org.

The Protection of Lawful Commerce in Arms Act of 2005

The National Rifle Association's top legislative priority in the early 2000s was the enactment of a federal law to protect the gun industry, and gun dealers, from litigation. For several decades, sporadic lawsuits had been filed against gun manufacturers seeking damages to compensate gun crime victims. The legal basis for such actions is the tort law principle that individuals or other entities can be held responsible for selling products that, while legal, needlessly or willfully exposes others to great risk of harm.

Litigants argued that handgun manufacturers knew that, because of their sales and distribution practices, a disproportionate number of their guns wound up in criminal hands, leading to claims of "negligent distribution practices." In addition, the failure of some companies to install simple and inexpensive safety features yielded additional legal charges. These lawsuits gained traction when a government report was released in 1999 revealing that in the previous three years, 0.3 percent of gun dealers were responsible for the sale of over 57 percent of gun crimes committed during this period. Clearly, some dealers were far more responsible in their sales practices than others.

Gun control foes decried this litigation, arguing that it was an abuse of the civil justice system that would only bankrupt gun manufacturers and pad lawyers' bank accounts, and that it amounted to backdoor gun control. Supporters argued that some in the gun industry were indeed culpable, and that they should be subject to the same civil law standards as rogue companies in other areas. NRA efforts were not limited to Congress, however. By 2005, 33 states had also passed laws barring such lawsuits by localities (called "preemption" laws).

In 2003, with support from the George W. Bush administration, momentum to provide federal liability protection finally resulted in the passage of a bill by the House of Representatives. The Senate was slower to act, but in March 2004 it was poised to approve the same bill, when gun control proponents, after failing to block the bill, managed to attach to it amendments to extend the assault weapons ban (by a 52-47 vote), slated to expire that September, to require background checks for all gun purchases at gun shows (closing the so-called "gun show loophole," by a 53-46 vote), and a measure to require safety locks to be sold with new handguns (approved 70-27). Infuriated, NRA leaders insisted that the bill be defeated rather than accept the "poison pill" amendments; within hours, it failed by a vote of 8-90.

The failure of the 108th Congress to enact the bill was remedied in the 109th. Fortified with an increase in Republicans in both houses, in July 2005, the Senate passed the measure by a vote of 65-31, partly thanks to key support from fourteen gun-sympathetic Democrats. The measure also got a lift when officials in the American military sent a letter to Congress in July saying that companies providing weapons to the military needed to be protected for national security reasons. The House passed the bill in October by a 283-144 vote. The bill passed with bipartisan support from 223 Republicans and 60 Democrats; voting against were 140 Democrats and four Republicans.

As passed and signed by the president, the Protection of Lawful Commerce in Arms Act of 2005 (P.L. 109-92) bars civil suits against gun manufacturers, distributors, dealers, and importers of firearms and ammunition, although it makes an exception for certain cases involving defective guns or expressly criminal behavior by manufacturers or dealers, as for example when a gun is knowingly sold to someone not legally entitled to own a gun. The immediate effect of the law was to halt more than a dozen ongoing cases in states around the country. The law did not affect cases that had already been resolved. The measure also included a requirement that handguns be sold with locks, and it barred the manufacture or importation of armor-piercing bullets. In the aftermath of winning this unique protection for the gun industry, other businesses lobbied Congress to win similar immunity. The law did not completely end such lawsuits, however. For example, family member of those killed in the 2012 Sandy Hook elementary school shooting filed a suit against Bushmaster Firearms, which produced a gun used by the shooter in that massacre.

See also: National Rifle Association; Product Liability Lawsuits; Sandy Hook elementary school shooting.

Further Reading: Timothy D. Lytton, ed., *Suing the Gun Industry: A Battle at the Crossroads of Gun Control and Mass Torts* (Ann Arbor, MI: University of Michigan Press, 2006); Robert J. Spitzer, *The Politics of Gun Control*, 6th ed. (Boulder, CO: Paradigm, 2015).

Protest Easy Guns (PEG)

Following the 2007 mass shooting at the Virginia Polytechnic Institute and State University (Virginia Tech) in Blacksburg, Virginia, in which a student killed 32 other students and faculty before killing himself, Abby Spangler organized a group of women in Alexandria, Virginia, to hold protests to express their anger over the accessibility of firearms to those who commit mass murder. In 2008 the organization, Protest Easy Guns (PEG), held a national lie-in that attracted thousands of individuals who participated in the protest. Since then, PEG reports that more than 125 lie-ins have been held in 32 states and the District of Columbia. The purpose of the lie-ins is to express concern for what the organization considers the lax firearm laws in the United States and to call for strengthening the laws in order to save lives. Participants lie down in public places for three minutes, the amount of time it is claimed to have taken for the Virginia Tech shooter to purchase a firearm.

The organization maintains a Facebook page, on which it comments regularly regarding firearm-related events. For instance, in 2016 the site expressed support for a California ballot initiative that would mandate state background checks for the sale of ammunition as well as firearms.

PEG's Website contains detailed information about organizing and scheduling a lie-in. The information includes a sample letter to be sent to prospective participants explaining the purpose of the protest and providing information about when the event will occur and how it will proceed. The site also encourages individuals to contact their congressional senators and representatives and specifies the organization's three basic objectives: to require background checks on all gun sales and transfers, not just those sold by federally licensed firearm dealers; to ban assault weapons and large-capacity ammunition magazines; and to pass federal legislation making gun trafficking a crime (straw purchasers—those who buy guns for others who cannot pass the criminal background check—would then be liable for prosecution beyond making false statements on the Bureaus of Alcohol, Tobacco, Firearms, and Explosives Form 4473, which each purchaser must complete before a purchase from a federally licensed firearms dealer can proceed).

PEG founder Abby Spangler continues to take part in protests in her home state of Virginia. When in fall 2015 a gun shop opened near Franklin Sherman elementary school in McLean, Spangler attended the protest opposing the proximity of the shop to the school. She emphasized PRG's campaign against easy access that criminals have to guns.

See also: Everytown for Gun Safety; Gun Trafficking.

Further Reading: Protest Easy Guns Website, www.protesteasyguns.com; Brigid Schulte, "The Moms Behind a Movement," *Washington Post* (July 3, 2008). www.washingtonpost.com/wp-dyn/content/article/2008/07/02/AR2008070201070_3.html; Danielle Grae, "Hundreds Protest As Gun Shop Opens Next to McLean Elementary School," *McClean Connection* (September 29, 2015). www.mcleanconnection.com/news/2015/sep/29/hundreds-protest-gun-shop-opens-next-mclean-elemen.

Q

Quilici v. Village of Morton Grove (1982)

In an appeal from the U.S. District Court for the Northern District of Illinois, Eastern Division, the U.S. Court of Appeals for the Seventh Circuit in *Quilici v. Village of Morton Grove* (695 F.2d 261, 1982) affirmed the decision of the district court that the Village of Morton Grove's Ordinance No. 81-11, which prohibits the possession of handguns within the borders of the village, is constitutional. In the ordinance, Morton Grove officials declared that the availability of firearms increased the probability of gun-related deaths and injuries and that handguns are strongly related to the commission of such crimes as homicide, assault, and armed robbery, and are responsible for accidental injuries and deaths.

Victor Quilici began his challenge of the ordinance in state court, but at the instigation of Morton Grove, the case was shifted to the federal court system and combined with two additional challenges to the ordinance. The plaintiffs claimed that the ordinance violated article I, section 22 of the state constitution of Illinois, which states that, "Subject only to the police power, the right of the individual citizen to keep and bear arms shall not be infringed." In addition, the claim was made that the ordinance violated the Second, Ninth, and Fourteenth Amendments to the U.S. Constitution.

Morton Grove held that section 22 of the state constitution guaranteed the keeping of some, but not all, firearms. The court of appeals agreed with the district court that the police power in Illinois justifies limiting the right to keep and bear arms. The court argued, first, that the state constitution grants the right to keep and bear arms, but not specifically handguns, and second, that although the constitutional framers intended handguns to be among those firearms conditionally protected, they also intended that local governments could employ their police power to restrict or prohibit the possession of handguns.

In response to the appellants' argument that allowing municipalities to exercise the police power to enact dissimilar gun control laws would lead to an absurd situation involving a crazy quilt of various ordinances across the state, the court declared that the state constitution allows home rule charters for local governments, permitting them to govern their own affairs as they deem appropriate in a wide number of areas, including regulation for protection of the public health, safety, morals, and welfare, and to tax and assume debt. Whether a wise policy or not, municipalities may set their own standards regarding gun control because the state constitution only prohibits a ban on all firearms. As long as the Morton Grove ordinance does not prohibit all firearms, it does not violate the provisions of the state constitution. In addition, the court noted that there exists empirical evidence that such legislation may lower the number of accidents and deaths attributed to handguns. The court of appeals concurred with the district court's ruling that the ordinance is intended to preserve the health and safety of Morton Grove residents, is a valid exercise of the municipal police power, and does not violate any rights guaranteed by the state constitution.

As for the Second Amendment, the court of appeals noted that this provision of the national Constitution, according to *Presser v. Illinois* (1886), is applicable to the national Congress and not state legislatures. The appellants argued that, given the large number of provisions of the Bill of Rights that have been determined to apply to the states via the Fourteenth Amendment, the Second Amendment has been implicitly made applicable to the states along with other rights. The court rejected this argument, noting that the U.S. Supreme Court has explicitly rejected the assumption that the entire Bill of Rights now applies to the states. The court associated the right to bear arms with the preservation of state militias. Arguing that individually owned handguns are not military weapons, they concluded that the national Constitution does not protect a right to keep and bear handguns.

The appellants argued that the Morton Grove ordinance violates the Ninth Amendment to the U.S. Constitution, which involves the protection of "certain rights" other than those enumerated in the constitution. The appellants had in mind an unwritten, fundamental right to own or possess firearms. The court rejected this idea, indicating that the Supreme Court has never identified any specific right protected by this amendment. The court concluded that the Morton Grove ordinance banning handguns is a proper exercise of the police power that violates neither article I, section 22 of the Illinois state constitution nor the Second, Ninth, or Fourteenth Amendments to the U.S. Constitution.

One justice filed a dissenting opinion, raising the potential difficulty of a hodgepodge of local ordinances applicable not only to local residents but also to those traveling through the local area. Such ordinances, the judge argued, were an undue limitation on the right to travel and interfered with commerce. The judge focused on a basic constitutional right to protect home and family, believing that the ordinance violates the fundamental right to "privacy in the home," limited, according to the judge, only by private, noncommercial activities, as long as the general welfare is not endangered. He concluded that the prohibition on handgun possession is not necessary to protecting the public welfare.

See also: Fourth Amendment; Morton Grove, Illinois; Ninth Amendment; *Presser v. Illinois* (1886); Second Amendment.

Further Reading: Robert J. Spitzer, *Gun Control: A Documentary and Reference Guide* (Westport, CT: Greenwood Press, 2009); *Quilici v. Village of Morton Grove*, 695 F.2d 261 (1982).

R

Reagan, Ronald (1911–2004)

Ronald Reagan, who served as U.S. president from 1981 to 1989, gained a reputation as an uncritical supporter of gun rights. In 1980, Reagan, a Republican, became the first presidential candidate to receive the official endorsement of the National Rifle Association (NRA). Although Reagan had narrowly escaped a 1981 assassination attempt in which his press secretary James Brady was critically wounded, in 1983 he became the first president to attend the NRA annual convention, where he pledged to support the goals of the organization. Reagan declared that the U.S. Constitution does not ordain the right to keep and bear arms, but states that the preexisting right to keep and bear arms shall not be infringed. The president, a life member of the NRA, promised that, "We will never disarm any American who seeks to protect his or her family from fear or harm."

The Republican platform on which Reagan campaigned in 1980 stated that the party supported the right of citizens to keep and bear arms, announced opposition to federal registration of firearms, and supported longer sentences for using firearms in the commission of a crime. The platform went on to advocate the repeal of provisions of the Gun Control Act of 1968 that "do not significantly impact on crime but serve rather to restrain the law-abiding citizen in his legitimate use of firearms." The 1984 platform on which Reagan ran for reelection stated that citizens should not be criticized for "exercising their constitutional rights." The 1980 platform foreshadowed the Firearms Owners Protection Act that was passed by Congress and signed by Reagan in 1986. However, the Reagan administration played a minimal role in the passage of the legislation.

In his first year as president, Reagan moved against the Bureau of Alcohol, Tobacco, and Firearms (ATF), the agency responsible for administering federal firearms legislation and one of the NRA's major targets. The president stated his intention to abolish the agency, shifting responsibilities to the Internal Revenue Service (IRS) and the Customs Service. Agents involved in explosives and arson regulation and enforcement would be transferred to the Secret Service. Although the NRA ultimately withdrew its support for the proposal to eliminate the ATF, the agency underwent budget cuts during the Reagan presidency.

Despite his staunch support for gun rights organizations, Reagan signed two gun control measures. In 1986, Reagan signed a bill banning so-called armor-piercing bullets (bullets composed of certain hard metals such as tungsten alloys, steel, or bronze). The NRA had raised no objections to this measure. In November 1988, he signed a bill that prohibited the production, importation, and sale of weapons composed primarily of plastic that could not be sensed by metal detectors. However, in May 1986, Reagan signed into law a more significant measure, the Firearms Owners Protection (McClure-Volkmer) Act, which significantly weakened the Gun Control Act of 1968 by, for instance, limiting the ATF's record-keeping authority and allowing resumption of mail-order ammunition sales.

After leaving office Reagan altered his stand on gun control legislation. In March 1991, on the tenth anniversary of the assassination attempt, he announced his support for the Brady Handgun Violence Prevention Act and urged Congress to pass the measure. He spoke to President George H. W. Bush at the White House, urging him to shift his position on the bill. In an article published in the *New York Times*, Reagan speculated that the attempt on his life might never have occurred if the Brady bill had been law in 1981. However, some on both sides of the gun control debate were quick to observe that the would-be assassin would not have been prevented from purchasing the weapon and that the waiting period would not have made any difference because the gun was purchased five months before the attempted assassination. In addition to supporting the Brady bill, Reagan argued in favor of a ban on assault weapons, and also criticized the NRA for its strident rhetoric critical of the ATF shortly before the Oklahoma City bombing (some of those killed were ATF agents). Although not the crucial factor in passage of further gun control legislation, Reagan's support added to the momentum of the pro-gun control forces.

See also: Brady Handgun Violence Prevention Act; Brady, James; Bureau of Alcohol, Tobacco, Firearms, and Explosives; Bush, George H. W.; Firearms Owners Protection Act; Gun Control Act of 1968; McClure, James Albertas; National Rifle Association; Volkmer, Harold Lee.

Further Reading: Gregg Lee Carter, *The Gun Control Movement* (New York: Twayne, 1997); Steven A. Holmes, "Gun Control Bill Backed by Reagan in Appeal to Bush," *New York Times* (March 29, 1991); Ronald Reagan, "Why I'm for the Brady Bill," *New York Times* (March 29, 1991); Robert J. Spitzer, *The Politics of Gun Control* (Washington, DC: CQ Press, 2008).

Remington, Eliphalet, II (1793–1861)

A gunsmith and firearms manufacturer, Eliphalet Remington II added significantly to the mystique of firearms in the United States. The Remington company provided military weapons to the United States during major conflicts and still produces rifles today. Throughout its existence, the company has attempted to diversify, engaging in the production of typewriters and sewing machines as well as firearms.

Remington's father, who built a forge after he moved to Staley Creek, New York, trained his son in blacksmithing. In August 1816, Remington manufactured his first rifle at his father's blacksmith shop. He traveled to Utica, New York, to have the barrel rifled, and when he returned,

Eliphalet Remington II was one of the foremost American gunmakers of the nineteenth century. *www.wikipedia.org*

Remington added the other essential parts of the weapon, including handmade screws and pins. Remington soon gained a reputation for gun making in New York. After four years, he had sold 200 gun barrels and complete rifles.

In 1828, Remington purchased 100 acres on the Mohawk River for an arms factory. When the building was completed in 1832, the new factory doubled the output of Remington's enterprise. With increased capacity, Remington began traveling to advertise his product. When his son Philo was old enough, Remington brought him into the business.

The war with Mexico in 1846 proved fortuitous for the Remington gun-making operation. When the John Griffiths Company of Cincinnati, Ohio, failed to meet a government contract to produce 5,000 muskets, Remington bought the contract. In 1847, the Remington company added to its business, filling a contract with the U.S. Navy.

In 1849, the company experimented with the handgun market, but no model it produced represented a serious challenge to Colt or Smith and Wesson. With the onset of the Civil War in

1861, Remington expanded the production plant in anticipation of what would amount to $30 million in government contracts. By the end of the war, the company was producing nearly 1,000 rifles per day. Remington, approaching 70 years of age, drove himself too hard in the early days of wartime production. He died in August 1861 and his son Philo succeeded him as company president.

Following the war, the company continued to diversify, producing agricultural implements. With surplus military rifles on the American market, the company sought foreign business, particularly with the French government, and had significant success selling the Rolling Block rifle. This rifle also became a preferred weapon among frontiersmen. In the 1870s, Remington produced other goods, including fire engines and steam trolley cars, none of which returned significant profits. The company introduced the typewriter in 1873, but when sales were disappointing, Philo sold this portion of the business to support the armory. Ironically, the typewriter enterprise subsequently proved profitable, while the Remington Company sank inexorably into bankruptcy.

In March 1888, Marcellus Hartley, founder of the Union Metallic Cartridge Company, participated in a buyout of Remington. Hartley became president of the newly renamed Remington Arms Company. Following Hartley's death in 1902, his grandson, Marcellus (Marcy) Hartley Dodge assumed control of the company. The company employed exhibitions to market its firearms and sponsored Annie Oakley's trick-shooting performances and other shooting events designed to attract and entertain prospective customers.

As World War I began in 1914, Remington geared up for war production. Both Great Britain and France signed contracts with the company. An agreement with Czar Nicholas II was nullified by the Russian Revolution of 1917, but the U.S. government ultimately agreed to purchase most of the rifles produced for the Russian sale. Remington produced nearly 70 percent of the rifles used by American forces in World War I. Following the war and the resulting fall in demand for new firearms, Remington diversified once more, introducing such products as knives and cash registers, but the company also responded to the increasing demand for hunting rifles and ammunition.

In 1933, Charles Davis assumed the office of company president. Despite the Depression, the new president succeeded in keeping the company in the black while at the same time increasing employee wages, establishing a standard 40-hour workweek, and introducing such innovations as a bonus plan and improved employee insurance. World War II brought another vast expansion in demand for rifles. In 1943, the number of workers was 20 times the number employed in 1939. Even though Remington planned for decreasing production over a year before the war's end, peace brought an oversupply of ammunition, an important component of production. The company quickly introduced new sporting-gun models, which continue to the present to be the primary focus of its firearms production.

See also: Colt, Samuel; Ruger, William Batterman (Bill); Smith and Wesson; Winchester, Oliver Fisher.

Further Reading: K. D. Kirkland, *America's Premier Gunmakers* (New York: Mallard, 1990); Wayne Van Zwoll, *America's Great Gunmakers* (Hackensack, NJ: Stoeger, 1992).

Reno, Janet (1938–)

Conservatives, gun rights organizations, and militia groups targeted President Bill Clinton's attorney general, Janet Reno, for her active support of gun control legislation. Stating in 1993 that youth violence was "the greatest single crime problem faced in America," Reno focused attention primarily on preventing firearm violence among youth, supporting various programs of the U.S. Department of Justice (USDOJ) intended to keep guns away from young people. She received severe criticism from pro-gun organizations for her approval of the Federal Bureau of Investigation (FBI) raid on the Branch Davidian headquarters in Waco, Texas, in 1993.

Reno received a B.S. in chemistry from Cornell University in 1960 and a law degree from Harvard Law School in 1963. She served as staff director of the judiciary committee of the Florida House of Representatives, contributing to a state constitutional revision that paved the way for a reorganized state court system. She was counsel for the Florida senate's criminal justice committee for the revision of the state criminal code. Reno was ultimately appointed state attorney for Dade County and was elected for successive terms in 1978, 1981, 1985, 1989, and 1991. President Clinton appointed her U.S. attorney general in 1993, making her the first woman to hold that position. As attorney general, Reno had a reputation for fierce independence from partisan considerations, a fact that made her unpopular in the White House. Nevertheless, she served for the full eight years of the Clinton presidency.

In 1994, Reno announced several DOJ youth grant programs, including efforts to upset the illegal firearms trade, to reduce youth demand for guns, and to make travel to school safer. The attorney general announced that such action was necessary to prevent gun use from becoming a normal part of the lives of youths. The crime bill approved that year included a federal ban on youth handgun possession, punishments for those selling guns to minors, and crime prevention programs aimed at youth.

When the Republicans won control of both houses of Congress in 1994, Reno and the president not only found it more difficult to push for new gun control initiatives, but had to fight attempts to repeal existing legislation. In 1996, the House of Representatives approved a repeal of the 1994 assault weapons ban. When the Senate considered the same measure, the attorney general stated publicly that such a repeal would be completely unjustified, claiming that the number of assault weapons associated with criminal activity had fallen 18 percent during the ban's first year of operation. Although the repeal ultimately failed, the president and the attorney general were even opposed by several Democrats in Congress.

Responding to a series of school shootings, Reno announced in June 1998 a renewed commitment to reducing youth violence through a number of initiatives, including limiting access to firearms. Regretting Congress's failure to pass legislation mandating safety locks for new handguns, Reno pledged to continue efforts to pass this legislation, which she termed a "commonsense, reasonable solution to make sure that guns are not accessible to children."

Reno announced a new advertising campaign developed through cooperation between the Office of Juvenile Justice and Delinquency Prevention in the Bureau of Justice Assistance and the National Crime Prevention Council. One purpose of the campaign is to inform parents of the risks that children face when an unlocked gun is kept in the home. The attorney general noted that school officials are encouraged to deal seriously with threats of violence and gang activity. After leaving office in 2001, she ran unsuccessfully in the

Democratic primary for governor of Florida in 2002.

See also: Assault Weapons Ban; Bureau of Alcohol, Tobacco, Firearms, and Explosives; Clinton, William Jefferson (Bill); Jonesboro, Arkansas, School Shooting; Littleton, Colorado, Columbine School Shooting; Schools and Guns; Trigger Locks; Waco, Texas, Raid.

Further Reading: Michael Isikoff, "NRA Fires Lobbyist Over Reno Rumor," *Washington Post* (March 1993), A1; Janet Reno, *News Conference, United States Department of Justice*, July 23, 1998.

Roberti-Roos Assault Weapons Act

In 1989, the California legislature passed the Roberti-Roos Assault Weapons Act, which became the first measure in the United States to prohibit the sale, possession, and manufacture of semiautomatic, military-style firearms. The assault weapons ban had heightened political significance because it was enacted despite major opposition from pro-gun organizations, particularly the National Rifle Association (NRA). During legislative consideration of the measure, the NRA enlisted the services of an ad agency that placed several newspaper and television advertisements criticizing the bill. The organization referred to the ban as "unworkable, inefficient, and money-wasting." Gun control supporters were encouraged by the bill's passage, looking forward to campaigns for legislation in other states and at the national level. Some of those active in the California battle were requested to support ban efforts in other parts of the country.

The Assault Weapons Act demonstrates the tendency of public officials to push for new gun control legislation immediately following a multiple murder incident involving the use of firearms. The campaign for an assault weapons ban began in fall 1988, gathering major support particularly in the Oakland and San Francisco areas. Various public officials, including police chiefs and prosecutors, held public hearings, conducted legal research, and assisted in preparing draft legislation. However, supporters of the ban admitted that the tragic murder of five schoolchildren in Stockton, California, by a man wielding a Chinese-made AK-47 semiautomatic rifle electrified the movement to work for passage. Supporters ultimately won the necessary votes in the California legislature for final passage.

The proposed ban, sponsored by Democrat David A. Roberti in the California Senate and Democrat Mike Roos in the Assembly, received support from leading public officials. Governor George Deukmejian, a conservative Republican who generally opposed additional gun control legislation, backed the assault weapons ban. Two other influential officials, Daryl F. Gates, Los Angeles police chief, and Sheriff Glen Craig of Sacramento County, came out in favor of the bill. Although similar bills in 1985 and 1986 had failed to gain legislative approval, the broad support of public officials and the groundswell of approval in the general public convinced enough legislators to support this measure.

The Assault Weapons Act banned over 20 specific assault weapons, including the AK-47, one of the more widely used weapons worldwide. The act allowed private citizens already legally in possession of assault weapons to keep them. However, owners were required to register the weapons. Because a ban in one state would have limited effect due to the possibility of weapons being brought into the state illegally, the legislation appeared to argue forcefully for the nationwide ban that was finally enacted in 1994. State actions like the Roberti-Roos Act have forced the NRA and other pro-gun groups to pay greater attention to state legislative actions nationwide.

See also: AK-47; Assault Weapons Ban; National Rifle Association; Stockton, California, Shooting.

Further Reading: Kristin A. Goss, *Disarmed: The Missing Movement for Gun Control in America* (Princeton, NJ: Princeton University Press, 2006).

Ruby Ridge

The unfortunate outcome of the standoff at Ruby Ridge, Idaho, in 1992 heightened suspicion of legal authority and led to the formation of militia groups that insisted upon the right to defend themselves with firearms, not only against criminals, but in opposition to the government. The events at Ruby Ridge incurred the special ire of gun organizations, for the case began with an illegal weapons charge against Randy Weaver. Before Weaver finally surrendered in August 1992, three people lay dead

from gunfire: a U.S. marshall and Weaver's wife and son.

Randy and Vicki Weaver became involved in the Christian Identity movement soon after their 1971 marriage in Cedar Rapids, Iowa. They adhered to a doctrine of white supremacy that claimed the United States had come under the control of ZOG, Zionist Occupied Government, an organization controlled by Jews who were carrying out a master plan to establish the New World Order. In 1983, Weaver moved his family from Iowa to Ruby Ridge, located in an isolated section of Idaho close to the Canadian border. He accumulated several weapons, including two semiautomatics, a rifle, a shotgun, a revolver, and a 9-mm. pistol. Although Weaver never joined a militia group, he and his wife periodically visited the Aryan Nations compound located 60 miles from their home. Weaver sold two sawed-off shotguns to an individual who was actually a government informant. After Weaver refused to accept a deal in which the federal government would drop the gun charges in return for his agreement to become an informant for the Federal Bureau of Investigation (FBI) against the white supremacist movement, he was indicted on the gun charge. When Weaver failed to appear for trial in February 1991, the Ruby Ridge standoff began.

For 17 months, U.S. marshals kept watch on the Weaver home. On August 21, 1992, marshals decided to conduct a surveillance of the area around the house. When Weaver's dog began to bark at the approaching lawmen, Weaver, his 14-year-old son Sam, and friend Kevin Harris went to investigate. When one of the marshals shot the dog, an exchange of gunfire began, leaving Sam Weaver and a deputy marshal dead. The following day a sharpshooter for the Federal Bureau of Investigation, operating under revised regulations to shoot at any armed man outside the house, fired at Harris, but hit and killed Vicki Weaver as she stood in the doorway holding her infant son. Both Harris and Weaver were wounded. Harris, needing medical assistance, surrendered on August 30, and Weaver came out the next day, thus ending the siege.

In 1994, Weaver was brought to trial for the murder of the deputy marshal and found innocent. A jury also acquitted him of the illegal gun-selling charges. His lawyer argued that Weaver had been entrapped by government officials who wanted to enlist Weaver as an informant. The defense argued that the government targeted Weaver for his unpopular beliefs and association with the Aryan Nations, a neo-Nazi organization. Weaver was convicted only of failing to appear at his February 1992 trial. Weaver ultimately received a $3.1 million out-of-court settlement from the federal government for the deaths of his wife and son.

In September 1995, Senator Arlen Specter, a Pennsylvania Republican, held hearings on the Ruby Ridge incident at which 62 witnesses testified. The committee's report criticized the FBI for a number of deficiencies, including the revised sharpshooter rules, poor intelligence gathering rules, and questionable internal investigations following the event. The FBI, which had assisted many Americans in their fight against hate groups, had suffered a blow to its reputation. The Bureau of Alcohol, Tobacco, and Firearms (ATF) was singled out by pro-gun organizations as particularly at fault. In a fund-raising letter, the National Rifle Association (NRA) compared the ATF agents to Nazi storm troopers. Former Republican President George H. W. Bush, upset by the NRA's intemperate language, resigned from the organization.

Although the general public had little sympathy for the racist beliefs of the Weavers and groups such as Aryan Nations, the failure of the FBI and the ATF to bring the situation to a peaceful conclusion harmed the reputation of two key agencies of the federal government. The inclusion of the gun rights issue heightened the postevent criticisms of government officials. This event, along with the Waco raid in 1993, motivated those who took part in the 1995 Oklahoma City bombing.

See also: Bureau of Alcohol, Tobacco, Firearms, and Explosives; Bush, George H. W.; National Rifle Association; Oklahoma City Bombing; Sawed-Off Shotgun; Waco, Texas, Raid.

Further Reading: Morris Dees, *Gathering Storm: America's Militia Threat* (New York: HarperCollins, 1996); Jonathan Karl, *The Right to Bear Arms: The Rise of America's New Militias* (New York: HarperCollins, 1995).

Ruger, William Batterman (Bill) (1916–2002)

Since the 1940s, Bill Ruger offered a wide variety of firearms to a receptive public. Ruger resembled the famed arms makers of the nineteenth century,

for his entrepreneurial abilities contributed to the construction of a firearms business on a par with those of his predecessors. Like Samuel Colt, he constructed firearms for mass distribution. Today anyone moderately familiar with guns has owned, or at least handled, a Ruger firearm.

When Ruger contracted scarlet fever at the age of 12, his father, Adolph, promised him that he would receive a Remington on his next birthday. Believing his father most likely meant a knife, Ruger was delighted when he received a Remington Model 12 pump gun. Thus began Ruger's great fascination with firearms. In his teens, he studied every gun he could acquire, and pored over issues of the *American Rifleman*. At 17, Ruger designed plans for a light machine gun. With resources obtained from a trust fund established by an aunt, he had an initial model made.

During the two years he attended the University of North Carolina, Ruger converted a lever-action rifle into a semiautomatic. A 1942 issue of the *American Rifleman* carried a report on his successful efforts. Impatient to continue his work with firearms, Ruger left college to seek a position with a gun company. He offered his machine gun design to Army Ordnance, but officials decided not to acquire it from Ruger. In 1939, he found a job at the Springfield Armory, but quickly became bored with the work, leaving the company in 1940. After returning to North Carolina, Ruger continued to work on a light machine-gun design for the military and took a position with Auto Ordnance Corporation, which was involved in producing the Thompson submachine gun. In 1946, unhappy about working for others, he began the Ruger Corporation in Southport, Connecticut.

The new business did not involve the production of firearms, but of tools such as screwdrivers and hand drills. The company did not do well and closed two years after its establishment. Alexander M. Sturm, a Yale Art School graduate, was impressed with Ruger's design for a high-quality but inexpensive. 22-semiautomatic pistol and decided to join the gun designer in a new business enterprise, investing $50,000 in the project. The new enterprise was named Sturm, Ruger and Company. The first model, resembling the German Luger, went into production in 1949. The gun, costing $37.50, was advertised in the *American Rifleman* and became an immediate success. Sturm put his artistic talents to work designing the trademark, a round red medallion with a hawk spreading its wings. When Sturm died in 1951 at the age of 29, Ruger changed the color of the medallion to black as a memorial. It has remained so ever since.

Ruger continued to produce new models that generally were well received. In 1951, the Mark Series I appeared, an upgrade of the original Ruger. In 1953, Ruger revealed the Single Six, a Colt-like six-gun. In 1955, Ruger introduced another successful sidearm, the single-action Blackhawk, which could be used for target shooting. Subsequent Blackhawks were released in 1956 (44 Magnum), 1959 (Super Blackhawk), 1965 (41 Magnum), and 1967 (30 Carbine). These weapons and others, including the Bearcat, a revolver with a four-inch barrel, became some of the most popular firearms in the United States. Ruger also produced long guns, including the Model 77, a bolt-action big game rifle similar to the Mauser.

Over the years Sturm Ruger has expanded its operations. The company opened the Pine Tree Casting Division in Newport, New Hampshire, a facility larger than the home office in Southport, Connecticut. Ruger also ran a plant in Prescott, Arizona. In the early 1990s, company assets were estimated at about $100 million. By the late 1980s, Ruger, who suffered from rheumatoid arthritis, allowed his two sons to assume management of the company's operations, although he continued to take part in the design of new firearms. During his lifetime, his firm produced over 20 million firearms.

See also: American Rifleman; Colt, Samuel; Remington, Eliphalet, II; Tommy Gun; Winchester, Oliver Fisher.

Further Reading: Sam Fadala, *Great Shooters of the World* (South Hackensack, NJ: Stoeger, 1990); Wayne Van Zwoll, *America's Great Gunmakers* (South Hackensack, NJ: Stoeger, 1992); R. L. Wilson, *Ruger and His Guns: A History of the Man, the Company and Their Firearms* (New York: Simon and Schuster, 1996).

Russia

Like the former Union of Soviet Socialist Republics (USSR), Russia maintains a strict policy regarding the availability of firearms and other weapons to private citizens. Gun rights advocates point out that despite stringent gun control in the former Soviet Union, the crime rate was high compared to nations such as Japan, which also has strict limitations on firearm ownership, suggesting that factors other than legal rules limiting firearm possession are involved in determining the level of crime and violence. Similar questions are raised about the effectiveness of present Russian firearms restrictions.

Generally, Russian law prohibits the ownership of handguns and fully automatic weapons. Exceptions are made for military officers who may be awarded a firearm for meritorious service. Private citizens may own shotguns and rifles if they acquire a license. Among the conditions that can disqualify a private citizen from owning a firearm are hospitalization for alcohol or drug abuse, felony conviction, two misdemeanor convictions, an illness or physical disability that prevents appropriate gun handling, and absence of a permanent address. The high cost of firearms discourages many from acquiring them. All firearms must be kept in a locked location and ammunition must be stored separately. Guns can be transported only if they have been disassembled. Roman V. Isaev, a commentator on Russian firearms laws, notes that this regulation renders firearms useless for self-defense outside the home. However, a shotgun may be kept at home for protection.

Included among prohibited weapons are armor-piercing, burning, or exploding ammunition. Weapons containing nerve agents, poisons, and other toxic gases are banned. Non-firearm weapons such as throwing knives and boomerangs, and any instrument that can be used as a club are prohibited, but private ownership of low-energy air guns is permitted. Although restrictions are placed on more powerful air guns, they are not strictly enforced. Sprays such as CS gas can be purchased without a license. Firearms cannot be equipped with silencers or night-vision devices and cannot be mailed. Carrying firearms and other weapons at political rallies and demonstrations is prohibited. To possess a firearm, a private citizen must be at least 18 years old. Smooth-bore firearms for hunting require a license. Rifled firearms may be acquired by professional hunters and those who have owned smooth-bore firearms for at least five years and have abided by the firearms regulations. Firearms must be registered within two weeks of purchase.

Registration involves a test firing of the weapon at a soft target to obtain a bullet sample that is kept on file in case of future criminal use. Licenses must be renewed every five years.

See also: Japan.

Further Reading: Roman V. Isaev, "Brief Summary: Russian Laws for Civilians" (n.d.), http://gunlab.com.ru/summary.html; Roman V. Isaev, "Excerpts from Russian Law on Weapons" (n.d.), http://gunlab.com.ru/excerpts.html.

S

Safety for Women and Responsible Motherhood (SWARM)

Safety for Women and Responsible Motherhood (SWARM), headquartered in Wheat Ridge, Colorado, describes itself as a nonpartisan organization "dedicated to winning for women and all peaceable citizens across the U.S. the legal right to defend themselves with a firearm—not just in the home, but where most crimes occur, on the street." Formed in 1994 by a group of women in Colorado, the organization claimed to have over 3,000 members across the nation by 1998. SWARM advertises itself as the "first women's profirearm lobby in America." SWARM, which has gained national media attention, considers itself a "powerful catalyst in returning the media to reality concerning guns." It has among its advisers David Kopel, a pro-gun rights author and member of the Independence Institute, a Colorado-based "think tank."

SWARM strives to change state firearms laws it considers unfair to women. While allowing target shooting and hunting, laws in some states make illegal the use of guns as a self-defense tool. The organization considers such restrictions especially unfair to women who are usually much lighter than potential attackers and hence are rendered defenseless without some means of defense. It considers the especially liberal Vermont concealed carry law a model to be copied by other states.

Among its goals, SWARM strives to obtain the right of "decent, peaceable citizens" to defend themselves, their families, and their communities with firearms. The organization encourages all states to adopt "shall-issue" carrying concealed weapons (CCW) laws that allow anyone who is not specifically prohibited from doing so (for instance, convicted felons) to possess and carry a firearm. SWARM supports concealed carry permits that are similar to a driver's license in that each state grants reciprocity to all others—a permit to carry in one state is recognized in all other states. SWARM promotes firearms safety and training courses to prepare women to use guns effectively for self-defense. Concerned about the causes of crime, the organization recommends reform of the welfare and criminal justice systems. To achieve its goals, SWARM is conducting a nationwide membership drive and is striving to develop state organizations dedicated to liberalizing CCW laws.

See also: Concealed Carry Laws; Independence Institute; Kopel, David B.; State Laws, Appendix 2; Women and Guns.

Further Reading: Safety for Women and Responsible Motherhood Web site, www.tcarlson.ca/swarm.txt.

San Bernardino, California, Shooting

The issues of firearm policy and terrorism solidly merged following the deadly shooting at the Inland Regional Center in San Bernardino, California, on December 2, 2015. At the time, the attack represented the worst mass shooting in nearly three years, and the deadliest terrorist assault since the September 11, 2001, suicide attack on the World Trade Center and the Pentagon.

A married couple, Syed Rizwan Farook and Tashfeen Malik, clothed in black barb, wearing masks, and armed with two .223-caliber assault rifles (one made by DPMS Panther Arms and the other an MM P15 Smith and Wesson) and two

9-mm semi-automatic pistols, entered the Regional Center where approximately 90 county health department workers were participating in a general education meeting and banquet. The shooters opened fire, killing fourteen people and wounding 21 others. Farook was employed by the health department as a health inspector. He attended the morning sessions, but left, leaving behind a jacket and other personal possessions at his seat, but in about a half hour, he returned with Malik. Both were shooting their weapons as they entered the meeting room, methodically killing and wounding Farook's co-workers.

The two shooters fled the Center in a rented SUV, but several hours later, when police stopped and surrounded the vehicle, a gun battle ensued and the suspects were killed. Although other motives for the shooting were considered, including the possibility of a workplace grudge, the Federal Bureau of Investigation quickly concluded that, because the two shooters had become proponents of radical Islam, their actions amounted to an act of terrorism.

Law enforcement officials discovered that the couple had accumulated thousands of rounds to ammunition and twelve homemade pipe bombs in their home. Farook was a U.S. citizen born in Illinois to Pakistani immigrant parents. He met Malik on a dating Web site. Farook had traveled several time to Saudi Arabia and went to Pakistan in 2014, returning with Malik, who had been granted a K-1 visa, a special 90-day entry permit for those planning to marry a U.S. citizen.

Law enforcement officials discovered that a third person not involved in the shooting, Enrique Marquez, a friend and former neighbor of Farook's, and a convert to Islam, had allegedly purchased the two assault rifles used in the attack. Farook himself allegedly purchased the two pistols legally. According to officials, Marquez revealed to them that in 2011 and 2012 Farook and Marquez had planned to launch an attack against students at Riverside City College and also to shoot drivers on California Route 91, a congested freeway. The two never carried out their plans.

After hearing of the shooting and that police had killed Farook and Malik, Marquez made a 911 call, stating that the shooters had used his guns in the attack, and then entered a hospital emergency room. Officials charged Marquez with conspiring to provide material support to terrorists for the earlier alleged plots. Marquez was also charged with lying on the gun purchase Form 4473, stating

that he was purchasing the guns for himself when he intended to provide them to Farook.

Gun control advocates referred to this event, like previous ones, as evidence for the need to strengthen firearm laws, especially tightening background checks, restricting the capacity of ammunition magazines, and banning assault weapons. Gun rights supporters tended to focus on the shooters as terrorists and the need for private individuals to arm themselves against such horrendous attacks. Many people apparently accepted the latter view, for firearm sales increased following the much-publicized shooting. Holiday purchases of firearms on Black Friday were reported to have set a record.

See also: Assault Weapons Ban; Large Capacity Ammunition Magazines; Orlando, Florida, Shooting.

Further Reading: Jennifer Medina, Richard Perez-Pena, Michael S. Schmidt, and Laurie Goodstein, "Arms Stockpile Is Found in Home of Two Suspects," *New York Times* (December 4, 2015): A1; Adam Nagourney, Ian Lovett, and Richard Perez-Pena, "California Rampage Leaves Chaos and Death," *New York Times* (December 3, 2015): A1; Fernanda Santos, "In Wake of Shootings, a Familiar Call to Arms Drives Latest Jump in Weapon Sales," *New York Times* (December 6, 2015): 30.

Sandy Hook School Shooting

On the morning of December 14, 2012, 20-year old Adam Lanza shot and killed his mother as she lay in bed asleep, using a gun she owned. Lanza had lived with his mother in her Newtown, Connecticut home, but had not spoken with her in two years, insisting that they communicate by email only. Lanza had exhibited significant mental health problems for many years, and among other things had been obsessed with stories of past mass shootings. All of the guns Lanza had in his possession on that day belonged legally to his mother, who had been an avid shooter. She had tried to interest her son in shooting as a way to bond with him.

After killing his mother, Lanza drove to nearby Sandy Hook Elementary School, taking four of his mother's guns with him. He entered the school, shooting out its glass front entrance, and proceeded into the building, where he shot and killed 20 elementary school children, as well

Family members who have lost loved ones to gun violence gather with members of Congress four days before the second anniversary of the shooting at Sandy Hook Elementary School. *Photo by Win McNamee/Getty Images*

as six adult teachers and staff using a Bushmaster XM15-E2S .223 caliber semi-automatic assault rifle along with several 30-bullet magazines. He fired 154 shots in less than five minutes. All of those killed were shot with the assault rifle, and each was shot at least three times. About a minute after the first police arrived, Lanza shot and killed himself with a Glock 10mm handgun. He also had another handgun with him, a Sig Sauer 9mm, which he did not fire. A 12-gauge semi-automatic shotgun was found in Lanza's car, but he did not use it in the killings. No motive for the attack was ever established.

The Sandy Hook shooting followed several other senseless mass shootings in previous months, yet the pointless, savage cruelty of such violence directed at children shocked the nation in a way recent past shootings had not. The last mass shooting to have a similarly traumatizing effect on the country was the 1999 Columbine High School shooting. For President Barack Obama, as for many newly mobilized because of this event, this was a watershed moment.

During his first term, Obama had largely avoided the gun issue, but after a convincing re-election campaign the previous month, bringing with it a renewed electoral mandate, and with his January 2013 inauguration and the State of the Union both in sight, Obama decided to move on the issue. Within days of the shooting, Obama appointed Vice President Joe Biden to head a task force to study the gun issue and make recommendations for change.

Within a month, the group presented its report, calling for universal background checks for gun purchases, restrictions on assault weapons and high capacity bullet magazines, mental health and school safety initiatives, increased funding for police protection in schools, and stronger measures to stop straw gun purchases and gun trafficking. In mid-January, Obama also issued nineteen executive orders to enhance and fund research on gun violence, improve federal gun trafficking databases, examine gun safety measures, and other steps involving federal agencies. Congress ultimately failed to enact Obama's legislative proposals.

In Connecticut, however, the state legislature enacted new gun measures in April 2013, including a ban on bullet magazines holding more than ten bullets, required background checks for private gun sales, including at gun shows, and expanded its existing assault weapons ban. It also appropriated additional money for school safety and mental health programs, and called for the creation of a state registry of dangerous offenders. The measures were strongly backed by Connecticut Governor Dannel Malloy (D).

Further Reading: *Final Report of the Sandy Hook Advisory Commission*, Presented to Governor Dannel Malloy, March 6, 2015, at http://www.shac.ct.gov/ SHAC_Final_Report_3-6-2015.pdf; Robert J. Spitzer, *The Politics of Gun Control*, 6th ed. (Boulder, CO: Paradigm Publishers, 2015).

Saturday Night Special

For many years, the banning of the Saturday night special has been one of the causes célèbres of the gun control movement. Although lacking in any precise definition, the term is generally used to refer to a small, inexpensive, low-quality, low-caliber handgun with little or no sporting value, but which is nonetheless effective at close range when used in a holdup or to settle an argument. Prior to the Gun Control Act of 1968 such weapons were imported into the United States in large numbers and were easily obtainable in stores or by mail order.

The term "Saturday night special" has disputed origins. John Ciardi, the noted master of the written word, observed in his *A Browser's Dictionary* (1980) that the term refers to weapons that quickly transport the victims of robberies and crimes of passion to hospital emergency rooms, especially during the Saturday night "rush hour."

This .38-caliber pistol is part of an easily concealable class of handguns known as Saturday night specials. *www. wikipedia.org*

Those who are unenthusiastic about gun control laws claim that the term was used in a derogatory way to characterize violent behavior among African Americans. Therefore, efforts to ban Saturday night specials in the 1960s and 1970s are regarded as examples of racial discrimination, an explanation that tends to oversimplify the train of events leading to passage of the 1968 legislation establishing limits on the importation of these weapons.

In 1961, Senator Thomas J. Dodd, Democratic senator from Connecticut and chairman of the Subcommittee on Juvenile Delinquency of the Senate Judiciary Committee, opened communications with the American firearms industry, the National Rifle Association (NRA), and other interested parties regarding the perceived problems of cheap handguns. The economy of Dodd's home state included firearms manufacturers who were concerned about the competition that cheap imported handguns represented.

Although the Gun Control Act of 1968 banned importation of Saturday night specials, a loophole in the law allowed the continued importation of parts for such handguns that could then be assembled in the United States. The domestic production of cheap handguns increased sixteenfold from 1968 to 1970. Therefore, rather than providing for a ban on the Saturday night special, the law established trade protection for the domestic handgun industry.

In the early 1970s, Democratic Senator Birch Bayh of Indiana, concerned with the continued importation of cheap handgun parts, introduced a bill that would prohibit the domestic production

and sale of cheap handguns that lacked any reasonable sporting purpose. The May 1972 attempted assassination of presidential candidate George Wallace, governor of Georgia, gave the Bayh bill momentum.

The national response was so intense that even the executive vice president of the NRA, Maxwell Rich, testified before a Senate committee that the NRA basically agreed that "crudely made and unsafe handguns" should be banned from the American market. The Senate passed the ban on Saturday night specials by a wide margin, but the bill never reached the floor for a vote in the House of Representatives. Rich's support of a cheap handgun ban was in part responsible for a subsequent movement in the NRA that resulted in his removal from leadership.

The failure of Congress to deal with cheap handguns moved the issue to the courts, where litigants claimed that gun manufacturers should be held responsible for the damage their products caused. In 1985, in *Kelley v. R.G. Industries, Inc.*, a case before the Maryland Court of Appeals, the court held a manufacturer of Saturday night specials responsible for the way in which they were used. Such suits were all but eliminated, however, when Congress enacted the Protection of Lawful Commerce in Arms Act of 2005, which provided legal immunity for the gun industry from such suits.

The Firearms Owners Protection Act of 1986, although essentially an anticontrol measure, introduced a ban on the importation of barrels for cheap handguns. As of 2008, eight states had some kind of legal ban on cheap handguns. Critics argue that a ban on Saturday night specials simply encourages criminals to use better weapons. From the perspective of gun control advocates, such a ban represents only one aspect of a larger program to limit the damage they attribute to firearms.

See also: Dodd, Thomas J.; Firearms Owners Protection Act; Gun Control Act of 1968; *Kelley v. R.G. Industries, Inc.* (1983); National Rifle Association; Protection of Lawful Commerce in Arms Act of 2005.

Further Reading: John Ciardi, *A Browser's Dictionary* (New York: Harper and Row, 1980); Lee Kennett and James La Verne Anderson, *The Gun in America: The Origins of a National Dilemma* (Westport, CT: Greenwood, 1975); Earl R. Kruschke, *Gun Control* (Santa Barbara, CA: ABC-CLIO, 1995).

Sawed-Off Shotgun

In the 1920s and 1930s, the sawed-off shotgun, like the machine gun, came to be regarded as a weapon whose use was confined solely to criminal activity, and therefore should be strictly controlled. A sawed-off shotgun is literally a shotgun with a barrel that has been sawed off, making it a formidable weapon at close range. Although this weapon became popular with gangsters in the 1920s, its history goes much further back. In 1898, the Winchester Company marketed a shotgun with a 20-inch barrel, touting it as a firearm that police could use to control riots. During World War I, the American army issued the weapon, termed a "trench gun," for use in hand-to-hand combat. The Germans protested its use, arguing that it violated the laws of war. The sawed-off shotgun's ultimate notoriety as a disreputable firearm developed after the war when gang members began to use it in criminal activities.

The sawed-off shotgun is legally defined as a shotgun with a barrel less than 18 inches in length from the breech to the muzzle, or less than 26 inches in overall length. Like an ordinary shotgun, the sawed-off version fires a shell containing as many as 400 small pellets. Some versions of the shotgun can contain two to five rounds, and some types used by police agencies contain 20 or more shells. It is an intimidating weapon that can coincide nicely with criminal intentions. At close distances, it can have savage effects and can be used quickly because it does not require deliberate aiming. It is easily concealed on the person, either in a holster, as used by the notorious bank robber Clyde Barrow, who developed a quick-draw technique; or kept beneath a coat, dangling by a cord hung from the neck.

By shortening the barrel, the shotgun was made virtually useless for hunting or any other legitimate purpose. The weapon's continued use in criminal activity sealed its fate in the 1934 National Firearms Act and the 1938 Federal Firearms Act, each of which banned the sale and possession of the weapon. During congressional hearings held prior to passage of the 1934 act, General M. A. Reckord, executive vice president of the National Rifle Association (NRA), expressed reservations about the legislation, but stated that the NRA had no objections to Congress's placing severe limitations on the ownership and sale of sawed-off shotguns and other "gangster-type" weapons.

In 1939, the Supreme Court, in a challenge to the National Firearms Act (*United States v. Miller*), ruled that the sawed-off shotgun was not protected by the Second Amendment because the defendant in the case was not a member of the militia when he was caught with the weapon, and that the federal government had the right to regulate it as a gangster weapon. It noted no relationship between this weapon and the preservation of a well-regulated militia. Some people have noted that U.S. military forces employed the sawed-off shotgun in combat in the Vietnam War, arguing that military use makes the weapon eligible for private ownership under the Supreme Court's interpretation of the Second Amendment in the *Miller* case. Some gun rights advocates have pointed to the potential defensive and deterrent use of the sawed-off shotgun by private citizens, thus raising questions about the long-standing claim that the only intended use of such a weapon is criminal. However, gun control advocates criticize this interpretation by noting that to allow civilian possession of weapons based on the premise that they have military use would allow civilians to own weapons from machine guns to howitzers and other battlefield weapons that have no place in civilian life.

See also: Federal Firearms Act of 1938; National Firearms Act of 1934; National Rifle Association; Second Amendment; *United States v. Miller* (1939).

Further Reading: Gregg Lee Carter, *The Gun Control Movement* (New York: Twayne, 1997); Lee Kennett and James La Verne Anderson, *The Gun in America: The Origins of a National Dilemma* (Westport, CT: Greenwood, 1975); Robert J. Spitzer, *Gun Control: A Documentary and Reference Guide* (Westport, CT: Greenwood Press, 2009).

Schools and Guns

Many Americans have expressed concern for the danger students and teachers face when youths take guns to school. Two major reasons are given to explain why students take guns to school: self-protection, and as a way of impressing fellow students. Various claims have been made regarding the number of guns taken to school each day. According to the U.S. Department of Education's National Center for Education Statistics, in 2013 5.2 percent of students reported carrying a weapon (including guns, knives, and clubs) to school within

Table 10
High School Students Reporting Carrying a Weapon on School Property on at Least 1 Day During the 30 Days Before the Survey, 1993–2013*

1993	1995	1997	1999	2001	2003	2005	2007	2009	2013
11.8%	9.8%	8.5%	6.9%	6.4%	6.1%	6.5%	5.9%	5.6%	5.2%

*Among weapon types (e.g. gun, knife, club), guns are mentioned in about a third of instances. Males are 4-5 times more likely to report weapons carrying than females.

Source: National Youth Risk Behavior Survey, U.S. Department of Health and Human Services, Centers for Disease Control and Prevention, Division of Adolescent and school Health, http://www.cdc.gov/HealthyYouth/yrbs/pdf/us_violenceschool_trend_yrbs.pdf; http://nces.ed.gov/programs/digest/d15/tables/dt15_231.40.asp

the previous 30 days. That represented a long-term decrease in school weapons carrying (in 1993, the number was 12 percent). Guns represented less than a third of all weapons reportedly carried to schools.

Usually following a violent incident, school districts have taken additional measures to prevent students from taking guns into school buildings. For instance, in 1993, following the deaths of two students, the Los Angeles Unified School District instituted a "zero-tolerance" policy that includes random gun sweeps in middle and high schools. In 1990, New York City began using metal detectors at schools with the greatest incidence of violence. Many schools in high-crime areas followed suit. Other districts enlisted police officers or security guards to serve as school "resource officers" to deter guns and crime, and adopted a variety of policies, practices, and procedures to thwart potential violent crime episodes. By the start of the twenty-first century, such measures were common at schools around the country, and are designed to keep schools "gun free."

A sea change occurred after the Columbine High School shooting in 1999. Thereafter, schools across the country dramatically increased monitoring and preventive activities to thwart gun and other crimes on school grounds. As Table 10 shows, weapons carrying has been generally declining in schools. The number of gun injuries and deaths at schools is both small and declining. A high of 45 shooting deaths at schools nationwide were reported in the 1992–1993 school year. During the 1998–1999 school year, the year of Columbine, 25 shooting deaths were reported (13 of those deaths were at Columbine). In 2013–2014, 13 school shooting deaths were reported nationwide. Given a nationwide school population of over 50 million students, the odds of a student

dying at school from a shooting are vanishingly small. Over the last twenty years, shooting deaths account for three-quarters of all violent school deaths. Statistically speaking school-age children are less likely to encounter crime at school than at home or on the streets.

Gun control supporters are concerned about what students learn about guns while in school. The Violence Policy Center has criticized the National Shooting Sports Foundation (NSSF) for creating educational materials that are distributed to public and private schools as a means of introducing students to firearms. The NSSF's board of directors has contained members from the firearms and ammunition industry (including Colt, Remington, and Smith and Wesson), hunting publications, and conservation groups. The Center cites NSSF communications that encourage the development of various school programs that may nurture future gun buyers. NSSF materials intended for use in grades 4 through 12 discuss hunting and wildlife management. The Center estimates that since 1980 the NSSF program has been distributed to thousands of schools. The Center, which is opposed to any encouragement given to youth to use firearms, recommends that a part of the Pittman-Robertson funds be used toward the health care costs caused by gun violence.

See also: Gun-Free Schools Act; Jonesboro, Arkansas, School Shooting; Kleck, Gary; Littleton, Colorado, Columbine School Shooting; National Shooting Sports Foundation; Stockton, California, Shooting; Violence Policy Center; Youth and Guns.

Further Reading: Bureau of Justice Statistics, *Indicators of School Crime and Safety: 2009* National Center for Education Statistics (Washington, DC:

U.S. Department of Justice, 2009); Vic Cox, *Guns, Violence, and Teens* (Springfield, NJ: Enslow, 1997); Dave Cullen, *Columbine* (New York: Twelve Books, 2009); "Starting Them Young: How the Firearms Industry and Gun Lobby are Targeting Your Children," *Violence Policy Center,* February 2016, *vpc.org.*

Schubert v. DeBard (1980)

The Court of Appeals of Indiana for the Third District ruled in *Joseph L. Schubert, Jr. v. Robert L. Debard, Indiana State Police Department* (398 N.E. 2d 1339, 1980) that Joseph Schubert had been arbitrarily denied the right to carry a handgun under Indiana law. Schubert applied in June 1975 for a permit to carry a handgun for self-protection. A state statute provided that an individual seeking such a license must apply to the chief of police or equivalent police officer in the municipality of residence, or to the sheriff of the county of residence. The officer shall then conduct an investigation to determine the applicant's "character and reputation" and ascertain the accuracy of information provided on the application. The information together with a recommendation shall then be forwarded to the superintendent of the Indiana State Police Department. If the law enforcement officer recommends to the superintendent that the request for a license be rejected, he shall provide reasons in writing for the recommendation. The superintendent may conduct a further investigation should he deem it necessary.

In providing evidence of his need to protect himself, Schubert offered two pieces of mail he received in 1975: a picture of a pig labeled with his name, and a letter demanding money that contained a death threat. Although Schubert suspected that his brother had sent the letters, he indicated that he had not spoken to his brother about them, nor had he contacted the police. He also reported that his brother had fired a rifle at the vehicle in which he was riding after a confrontation at their mother's home. Schubert believed that these incidents justified his application to carry a weapon for self-protection.

When Schubert's application was denied, he filed a petition for administrative review. Following the review, the superintendent of the Indiana State Police ruled that Schubert failed to demonstrate a proper reason for being granted a license and the permit was denied. Schubert then appealed to a trial court, claiming that his right to bear arms under the Indiana state constitution had been denied. The relevant provision within the constitution states that, "The people shall have a right to bear arms, for the defense of themselves and the State." A trial court upheld the superintendent's decision.

The Court of Appeals based its ruling on the appeal from the trial court decision on a previous decision (*Matthews v. State*, 1958) in which the state supreme court determined that the superintendent did not have the discretion to deny a license to an applicant who has met the conditions of the statute. In the Schubert case, the court determined that the status of the application was determined on the basis of the statutory authority of the superintendent to make a subjective evaluation of the need for self-defense. This authority, the court claimed, infringed on the constitutional right to bear arms. The court determined that Schubert's stated reason for wishing to obtain a license "stood unrefuted," and was an appropriate reason within the statute. Therefore, the case was returned to the lower court for a new hearing.

A judge dissenting from the majority opinion claimed that Superintendent DeBard had determined, in his appropriate role as factfinder, that Schubert's self-defense claim was not substantiated. The dissenting opinion further stated that should the present ruling set a precedent, the superintendent would have no choice but to grant licenses to carry handguns "to any 'proper' person who simply alleged a need for self-defense." While the judge admitted that there can be many "proper" persons, there may be only a few citizens who need to carry a handgun outside the home or business. Because the right to bear arms is not an absolute, those not satisfying the established standards for licensing could be denied the right. He expressed the opinion that Schubert's apparent need, considered psychological rather than actual, was not a satisfactory reason under the law to grant a license. The ultimate result of the majority decision, according to the dissenting judge, was to de-regulate handguns in the state of Indiana. However, statutory reasons for denying a license to bear a firearm still remained in effect.

See also: Concealed Carry Laws; State Laws, Appendix 2.

Further Reading: *Schubert v. DeBard*, 398 N.E. 2d 1339 (1980).

Schumer, Charles E. (1950–)

U.S. Senator Charles Schumer, Democrat from New York, has for many years been a major opponent of the legislative objectives of the National Rifle Association (NRA) and a supporter of stronger gun laws. During Democratic President Bill Clinton's first two years in office, Schumer, as a member of the U.S. House of Representatives, devoted his energies to winning passage of anticrime legislation. As chairman of the Crime Subcommittee of the House Judiciary Committee, he led the way in developing the anticrime bill that passed both houses of Congress in August 1994, which included the assault weapons ban. Although the bill contained provisions to appeal to conservatives as well as liberals, and the total budget authorization was reduced to win Republican support, a faction of the NRA ran an ad in *USA Today* referring to Schumer as "the criminal's best friend." Schumer stated that he wore the allegation as "a badge of honor."

Schumer received a B.A. degree in 1971 and a law degree in 1974 from Harvard University. He served as legislative aide to New York state assemblyman Stephen J. Solarz, a Democrat from Brooklyn, before himself winning Solarz's seat in the Assembly in 1974 following his mentor's move to the U.S. House of Representatives. In 1980, after two terms in the state legislature, Schumer won election to the U.S. House of Representatives. Generally considered a liberal, he has consistently received high ratings from the liberal Americans for Democratic Action and low ratings from the American Conservative Union.

Schumer backed the 1993 Brady Handgun Violence Prevention Act and the 1994 ban on certain types of assault weapons, a measure included in the 1994 Violent Crime Control and Law Enforcement Act. When Republicans took control of both houses of Congress following the 1994 election, Schumer became a major defender of past legislative accomplishments against Republican attempts to weaken or repeal legislation.

Following the April 1995 bombing of the Alfred P. Murrah Federal Building in Oklahoma City, Oklahoma, Schumer supported President Clinton's efforts to pass antiterrorism legislation. He strongly opposed an amendment by Representative Bob Barr, Republican of Georgia, that restricted the federal government's authority to prevent people associated with terrorist groups from entering the country and limited the government's ability to convict individuals accused of selling or trading guns that are subsequently used in a felony. Schumer blamed the NRA for what he considered a serious weakening of the legislation.

In July 1995, Schumer criticized hearings initiated by the Republican majority to investigate the actions of the Bureau of Alcohol, Tobacco, and Firearms (ATF) during the 1993 raid on the Branch Davidian encampment near Waco, Texas. He blamed the National Rifle Association for what he considered strong bias against the government agency. He claimed that the bias resulted from the NRA's long opposition to the organization that is primarily responsible for enforcing firearms legislation.

Claiming in 1996 that NRA contributions had played an important role in electing a Republican majority to Congress in 1994, Schumer charged that the House vote to repeal the assault weapons ban was a direct payment for the monetary support. He criticized Republican Speaker Newt Gingrich of Georgia for demonstrating special deference to the NRA. Schumer also charged the Republicans with engaging in partisan rivalry, claiming that

Senator Charles Schumer (D-NY) is a proponent of gun control legislation and a noted foe of the National Rifle Association. *http://schumer.senate.gov*

they wanted to deny the Democratic president a legislative victory. In 1998, Schumer won election to the U.S. Senate, defeating incumbent Republican Al D'Amato. He was easily reelected in 2004, 2010, and 2016. He continues in the Senate to support gun control and tough anti-terrorism and anticrime measures, playing a leading role in the advocacy of new gun measures in 2013 and 2016.

See also: Assault Weapons Ban; Barr, Bob; Brady Handgun Violence Prevention Act; Bureau of Alcohol, Tobacco, Firearms, and Explosives; Clinton, William Jefferson (Bill); National Rifle Association; Oklahoma City Bombing; Waco, Texas, Raid.

Further Reading: Robert J. Spitzer, *Guns across America: Reconciling Gun Rules and Rights* (New York: Oxford University Press, 2016); Charles Schumer Web site, http://schumer.senate.gov/.

(Dred) Scott v. Sandford (1857)

Gun rights advocates have cited a brief statement by Chief Justice Roger B. Taney in his majority decision in the case *Dred Scott v.Sandford* (60 U.S. [19 Howard] 393, 15 L.Ed. 691, 1857) that, some argue, gives credence to the claim that the Second Amendment protects the individual right of citizens to keep and bear arms. Taney rejected the claim that African Americans, either enslaved or free, have the rights of American citizens. Among the rights the chief justice insisted slaves could not enjoy was the right to keep and bear arms.

In 1834, Dred Scott, a slave, traveled with his owner, John Emerson, an army surgeon, from their home state of Missouri to Illinois. By this time Illinois had abolished slavery. Two years later, Emerson took Scott with him to Fort Snelling in the Louisiana territory, an area where slavery had been banned by the Missouri Compromise of 1820. In 1838, Scott returned with Emerson to Missouri. Following Emerson's death, a suit was brought on Scott's behalf in the Missouri state court system against Emerson's widow, claiming that Scott became free at the time he resided in a free territory. Although a lower court ruled in Scott's favor, the Missouri Supreme Court reversed the ruling in 1852, stating that Missouri law kept Scott a slave. In the meantime, ownership of Scott shifted to C.C. Chaffee, a Massachusetts abolitionist. Chaffee transferred ownership to his wife's brother,

John Sanford, a New York resident. Chaffee was friendly toward Scott's cause, and arranged for an attorney to file suit for Scott. On appeal from the state court, the U.S. Supreme Court heard the case in February 1856, and again the following December.

Seven justices, including Taney, joined in a majority decision that denied to Scott his claim of freedom. Packed within this emotionally charged decision, gun rights advocates claim to find evidence to support their position on the Second Amendment. Referring to "the inferior and subject condition of that race at the time the Constitution was adopted," Taney imagined the state of affairs should African Americans be received into citizenship. Being recognized as citizens in one state, they would have the right to enter any other state of their own volition, "singly or in companies," without the need for any special permission, "to stay there as long as they pleased, to go where they pleased at every hour of the day or night without molestation." African Americans would have "the full liberty of speech in public and in private . . . to hold public meetings upon political affairs, *and to keep and carry arms wherever they went*" (emphasis added).

If some African Americans had these rights guaranteed by the constitutional system to all citizens of the United States, while at the same time slavery continued for most African Americans, Taney assumed that "discontent and insubordination" would result, thus "endangering the peace and safety of the State." The "great men" of the slaveholding states could not have had this intention when taking part in framing the Constitution. Taney appears to have concluded that the Bill of Rights applied to the states as well as to the national government. No constitutional interpretation prior to ratification of the Fourteenth Amendment in 1868 would support such a position. Taney may have assumed that the Second Amendment did grant an individual right to keep and bear arms, or the reference could have been alluding to citizens carrying guns in connection with militia service. However, Taney improperly implied that the Bill of Rights limited the actions of states.

Gun control advocates in the twentieth century are unconvinced by the authority of Taney's statement, given its alarmist and offhand nature. Not all members of the Court's majority in 1857 agreed completely with Taney's decision. Modern gun control advocates find unconvincing any interpretation of the nature of the constitutionally protected right to keep and bear arms based on one justice's brief comment in a case that did not deal directly with the subject. Nonetheless, gun rights advocates today believe Taney's brief comments contribute to the credibility of their Second Amendment interpretation.

See also: African Americans and Guns; Black Codes; Fourteenth Amendment; Second Amendment.

Further Reading: Alan M. Gottlieb, "Gun Ownership: A Constitutional Right," *Northern Kentucky Law Review* 10 (1982), 113–40; *Scott v. Sanford*, 60 U.S. (19 Howard) 393, 15 L.Ed. 691 (1857).

Second Amendment

Gun rights advocates look to the Second Amendment to the U.S. Constitution as the fundamental support in their cause. This amendment states, "A well regulated Militia, being necessary to the security of a free State, the right of the people to keep and bear Arms, shall not be infringed." Although the issues arising over the interpretation of the Amendment have been many, two tend to predominate. First, does it protect a collective (in other words, state) right related to militia service, or an individual right, and second, assuming that it does in fact protect the right of individuals to keep and bear arms, does it apply to the states as well as the national government?

The Second Amendment was one of 12 constitutional amendments proposed and sent to the states for ratification by the First Congress in 1789. James Madison, a major architect of the Constitution, believed that the original document adequately protected citizens' rights. However, he agreed to propose to the First Congress amendments limiting government power to gain support for ratification from those who had qualms about the new government's powers. True to his promise, Madison submitted to Congress the amendments that would become the Bill of Rights. Ten of the 12 proposals were ratified by the required three-fourths of the state legislatures. The Second Amendment was ratified on December 15, 1791.

Gun rights advocates insist that the amendment protects two separate rights: first, the right to keep arms, and second, the right to bear arms.

If this is so, they argue, then the amendment cannot be referring simply to the right of states to stockpile weapons at armories. The people, taken individually, are the ones who have a need to keep arms in their homes for both self-protection as well as to maintain readiness against a threat to the public peace. Supporters indicate that when the word "people" is used elsewhere in the Bill of Rights, as in the First and Fourth Amendments, it refers to individuals. Therefore, consistency requires that the Second Amendment also be interpreted as protecting an individual's right.

Supporters of the collective or militia interpretation note that Madison's original proposal indicates his intent to provide a collective guarantee that states could maintain militias: "The right of the people to keep and bear arms shall not be infringed; a well armed and well regulated militia being the best security of a free country; but no person religiously scrupulous of bearing arms shall be compelled to render military service in person." Modifications were made in the final wording. First, "country" became "state," and "the best security of" became "necessary to." The guarantee that "religiously scrupulous" persons could not be compelled to serve in the military was dropped, owing to the concern that too many men would use this provision to avoid service. The amendment, according to this interpretation, as well as all of the debate in the First Congress about the amendment, deals solely with military questions, modifying the militia clause in Article I, section 8 of the original Constitution. Supporters of the individualist interpretation counter that the reference to the militia merely means that the individual's right to keep and bear arms is conducive to the maintenance of a well-regulated militia.

Supporters of the collective interpretation reject the claim that two rights are being protected: the right to keep and the right to bear arms. They claim that the phrase "to bear arms" has specific military reference, and can be taken as a synonym for waging war. The phrase cannot be separated, they argue, but might best be rendered as one connected process, to-keep-and-bear, which most appropriately refers to a militia maintaining an arsenal of weapons on a continuing basis. While gun rights supporters claim that "the people" refers to all citizens as actual or potential members of the militia, who are thereby guaranteed the right to keep and bear arms, opponents note that all citizens were never considered part of the militia. Only those of militia-eligible age (18-45) who have received appropriate training and have been received into a "well-regulated" militia as established under provisions of the Constitution can be considered a member of this portion of the people.

Some gun rights advocates claim that the militia extends beyond government-established militias, and argue that an individual's right to possess arms was intended to be a strong deterrent against a government that might attempt to violate the rights of citizens. In effect, they contend that the Constitution, through the Second Amendment, guarantees a right of armed rebellion against the government of the United States. Opponents respond that finding such a right in the Second Amendment contradicts the provision in the original Constitution, found in Article I, which calls for militias to be used to "suppress insurrections," and Article III, that defines and provides punishment for treason. No government would provide within its governing document the formal right to overthrow legally established institutions. Should a government become tyrannical, a right to revolution does not depend upon any legal provision within the governing document.

In *United States v. Cruikshank* (1876) and *Presser v. Illinois* (1886), the U.S. Supreme Court ruled that the Second Amendment did not apply to the states, but only to the national government. Gun rights advocates consider these nineteenth-century cases to be antiquated because many of the guarantees in the Bill of Rights, which originally limited the authority only of the national government, have since been interpreted to limit state governments as well. However, no previous case dealing with another provision of the Bill of Rights can automatically be argued to grant the claimed individual protection within the Second Amendment. The Supreme Court has followed a "selective incorporation" policy whereby specific rights have been determined on a case-by-case basis to apply to states through the Fourteenth Amendment.

In *United States v. Miller* (1939), a case involving the National Firearms Act of 1934, the Court upheld a conviction for illegal possession of a sawed-off shotgun, ruling that such a firearm does not fit the category of weapons commonly used in the militia. Gun rights advocates have concluded that, conversely, an individual has the right to possess any weapon that is actually employed by the militia. Opponents argue that such an interpretation would lead to a *reductio*

ad absurdum: the right of private citizens to possess a wide variety of weapons, including not only handguns and shotguns, but machine guns, grenade launchers, and antitank weapons, would be guaranteed as long as they were legitimate weapons of the militia.

Supporters of the individualist interpretation of the Second Amendment often refer to antecedent documents, such as the English Bill of Rights of 1689, which stated that Protestant subjects "may have arms for their defense and as allowed by law." They also appeal to common law within the American colonies that strongly suggests an individualist interpretation. Opponents argue that although such alternative sources as natural law, common law, and tradition may support a private right to own and employ firearms, the Second Amendment clearly has a military reference and hence cannot be used to defend such a private right. Gun rights advocates respond that a common law protection of the right to keep and bear arms is guaranteed through the Ninth Amendment.

In 2008, the Supreme Court rejected its past rulings, as well as nearly fifty lower federal court rulings, by ruling for the first time in history in *District of Columbia v. Heller* that the Second Amendment protected an individual's right to have a handgun for personal protection in the home. The court also went to great pains to say that most existing gun laws would be allowable under this ruling. From 2008 to 2016, nearly 1000 gun laws have been challenged as violating the Second Amendment, but nearly all of the laws have been upheld. The decision sparked great controversy, a fact reflected in the court's 5-4 vote. Historians in particular were sharply critical of the decision, saying that it distorted the history of the Second Amendment and of American gun habits. Two years later, the high court applied the Second Amendment to the states in *McDonald v. Chicago*, by the same 5-4 vote.

See also: District of Columbia v. Heller (2008); Fourteenth Amendment; Fourth Amendment; *McDonald v. Chicago* (2010); National Firearms Act of 1934; Ninth Amendment; *Presser v. Illinois* (1886); *United States v. Cruikshank* (1876); *United States v. Miller* (1939).

Further Reading: Saul Cornell, *A Well-Regulated Militia* (New York: Oxford University Press, 2006); Stephen Halbrook, *The Founders' Second Amendment*

(Chicago: Ivan R. Dee, 2008); Robert J. Spitzer, *Guns across America: Reconciling Gun Rules and Rights* (New York: Oxford University Press, 2015).

Second Amendment Committee (SAC)

The Second Amendment Committee (SAC) is a little-known organization based in Hanford, California, which takes an uncompromising stand in support of gun rights. SAC focuses much of its attention on the Second Amendment, which it calls the "keystone amendment" within the Bill of Rights, claiming that the right to keep and bear arms, being "unalienable" is incapable of being repealed. Gun rights are seen as predating the Constitution and as embedded in the common law tradition. The Committee sees such a close relationship between the Second Amendment and other freedoms guaranteed in the Bill of Rights that it claims if firearms are eliminated, private ownership of land will disappear, the use of automobiles will be restricted, the right to vote will be eliminated, states will be eradicated, and people will no longer have religious freedom.

Bernadine Smith founded SAC in 1984 to provide information to those seeking to protect a right to keep and bear arms. For many years, Smith has conducted a campaign against what she considers a plan to disarm individual citizens. Considering the United Nations a threat to individual rights, she has opposed U.S. membership in the international organization. Smith argues that the Second Amendment guarantees both a collective as well as an individual's right to keep and bear arms, claiming that reference to "the people" means all the people when applied to citizen militias and each person individually when applied to the individual's right to keep and bear arms.

According to the Committee, citizens must protect the right to possess firearms as an element of force they require to maintain control over a potentially despotic government, to protect themselves against the injustice and abuse of public officials, to defend liberty, and to secure the nation against foreign invasion.

Privately owned firearms are needed for protection against criminals because the police cannot protect the people and the police may require assistance from private citizens to keep the peace.

SAC considers itself, not the National Rifle Association (NRA), the major defender of gun rights. The organization disagrees with the policy of the NRA and the Citizens Committee for the Right to Keep and Bear Arms (CCRKBA) that involves supporting state preemption laws intended to prevent local communities from enacting firearms legislation more restrictive than state laws. The Committee fears that uniform state regulations establish a dangerous precedent for a federal preemption law that could grant to the national government extensive authority over the regulation of firearms.

The Committee argues that those state and federal government officials who support gun control have violated their oaths of office by failing to uphold the Second Amendment, which is a part of the Constitution they have pledged to defend. Any actions to bring about "the complete disarmament of the United States and the people within" are labeled "acts which are against the law" and "acts of insurrection, rebellion, sedition, or tyranny against the laws of the United States."

See also: Citizens Committee for the Right to Keep and Bear Arms; National Rifle Association; Second Amendment; United Nations.

Further Reading: Second Amendment Committee Web site, www.libertygunrights.com.

Second Amendment Foundation (SAF)

The Second Amendment Foundation (SAF) focuses on the constitutional right of individuals to keep and bear arms. Alan M. Gottlieb founded SAF in 1974 as a nonprofit corporation in the state of Washington. Since its founding, the organization has focused on ways to defend the right to keep and bear arms against advocates of firearms regulation. According to SAF literature, the organization is "dedicated to promoting a better understanding of the constitutional right of private citizens to keep and bear arms." SAF has headquarters in Bellevue, Washington (in a building named for James Madison, who introduced the proposal that ultimately became the Second Amendment), and has a publishing office in Buffalo, New York. The Foundation is administered by a board of trustees, of which Gottlieb is a member.

SAF supports several publications, including *Gun Week*, a publication devoted largely to news about efforts to protect the interests of gun owners and to counter the efforts of gun control advocates; *Women and Guns*, which focuses on women's right to bear arms; *Gun News Digest*, a quarterly publication advocating the right to bear arms; *SAF Reporter*, a quarterly newsletter; *Journal on Firearms and Public Policy*, an annual publication containing reprints of articles dealing with gun rights; and the *Gottlieb-Tartaro Report*, a monthly publication containing current information on gun issues from board members Gottlieb and Joseph P. Tartaro.

Since 1976, the Foundation has organized writers' conferences to encourage research on the right to keep and bear arms. The organization has sponsored or cosponsored training conferences, including the annual Gun Rights Policy Conference, legal conferences at universities, and leadership training conferences to prepare local activists. The Foundation employs various methods to make its message known to the general public. It distributes materials to high school and college students who are preparing class assignments on firearms issues and donates pro-gun works to public and school libraries. It also distributes position papers and commentaries on gun issues to media outlets. Representatives of the Foundation regularly appear on radio and television programs and contribute articles to newspapers and magazines. As one of the organization's major spokesmen, Gottlieb makes over 350 radio and television appearances each year.

The Foundation furthers the cause of gun rights by supporting cases in the courts and filing *amicus curiae* briefs advocating the right to keep and bear arms. Among its successful actions, the organization took part in a case overturning handgun bans in San Francisco, California, and New Haven, Connecticut, and in the Supreme Court cases of *District of Columbia v. Heller* (2008) that adopted the individualist view of the Second Amendment, and *McDonald v. Chicago* (2010), that applied the Second Amendment to the states. Other issues that have gained SAF's attention include carrying concealed weapons (CCW) license provisions that the organization considers unfair, and bans on firearms in several cities and states. For instance, the Foundation assisted in the successful court action to end restrictive CCW license policies in Los Angeles.

The organization refers those involved in gun suits to attorneys who have had experience in dealing with firearms cases.

SAF produces advertisements that are placed in newspapers and magazines, and runs radio commercials daily across the country. The Foundation occasionally funds television commercials that advocate gun rights. In its many publications, radio and television advertisements, and appearances by members, SAF places great emphasis on suggesting to the grassroots gun advocate strategies that can be followed to advance the right to keep and bear arms.

See also: Concealed Carry Laws; *District of Columbia v. Heller* (2008); Gottlieb, Alan Merril; *Gun News Digest*; Gun Rights Policy Conference; *Gun Week*; *McDonald v. Chicago* (2010); Second Amendment; Women and Guns; *Women and Guns Magazine*.

Further Reading: Alan M. Gottlieb and David Workman, *Assault on Weapons* (Bellevue, WA: Merril Press, 2009); Second Amendment Foundation Web site, www.saf.org; Peter Harry Brown and Daniel G. Abel, *Outgunned: Up Against the NRA* (New York: The Free Press, 2003).

Second Amendment Foundation v. City of Renton (1983)

In *Second Amendment Foundation v. City of Renton* (688 F.2d 596, 1983), the Court of Appeals of Washington upheld a city ordinance in Renton, Washington, which made it unlawful for a person within the city limits to carry a rifle, shotgun, or pistol in any place of business where liquor is sold by the drink. This ordinance applied to individuals whether or not they had a license or permit to carry a firearm, and regardless of whether the firearm was concealed.

Four residents of Renton, supported by the Second Amendment Foundation (SAF), sought an injunction against the new gun restrictions. They claimed that the ordinance violated the state constitutional provision that granted the right of citizens to bear arms both for individual defense and for the defense of the state. The only apparent limitation on the right to bear arms involved a prohibition on any individuals or groups to organize or maintain an armed organization. SAF also claimed that the ordinance violated the Second Amendment to the U.S. Constitution, which the organization interpreted as granting individuals the right to keep and bear arms.

After the Superior Court of King County, the original trial court, ruled in favor of the city of Renton, the SAF appealed the decision to the Court of Appeals. This court ruled that Renton acted appropriately when it passed the ordinance forbidding the carrying of firearms into bars. The court declared that while the state constitution did protect the individual's right to bear arms, that right is liable to reasonable regulation under the state's police power. The extent of regulation depends on a balance between the good consequences expected from the specific limitation placed on the right and the extent to which the regulation impedes the intention of the constitutional provision.

The court ruled that the ordinance reduced the danger of armed encounters among those who had been drinking while minimally reducing the right to keep and bear arms, concluding that "on balance, the public's right to a limited and reasonable exercise of police power must prevail against the individual's right to bear arms in public places where liquor is served." The court was careful to note that had the municipality of Renton established a blanket ban on the possession of handguns even though individuals held state permits, the ordinance would have violated the state constitution and laws. However, the actual ordinance was limited in that it applied to particular places as a means to protect the public welfare, an accepted function of local government.

The court compared Washington to other states with constitutional provisions regarding the right to bear arms, noting that in all states with such provisions, the right has never been considered absolute. In addition, in five states having constitutional provisions similar to Washington's, the right to bear arms has been considered open to limitations under the police power.

See also: Concealed Carry Laws; *Quilici v. Village of Morton Grove* (1982); Second Amendment; Second Amendment Foundation.

Further Reading: Mark A. Siegel, Nancy R. Jacobs, and Carol D. Foster, *Gun Control: Restricting Rights or Protecting People?* (Wylie, TX: Information Plus, 1991); *Second Amendment Foundation v. City of Renton*, 688 F.2d 596 (1983).

Second Amendment Sisters

In 2000, five women founded Second Amendment Sisters (SAS) in response to the Million Mom March that was held on Mother's Day, May 14, 2000, in Washington, D.C., at which an estimated 750,000 people met on the National Mall to support stronger limitations on firearms to keep guns away from children and criminals. In contrast to the Million Mom March, SAS is dedicated to the protection of the right to keep and bear arms and holds to the view that the Second Amendment protects all the other rights guaranteed in the Bill of Rights. SAS advocates the position that women have "the right to life," which the organization interprets as women's "basic human right to self-defense." SAS claims thousands of members and adherents in all 50 states and sees its role as a monitor of government activities and public officials and a resource for women wishing to receive training in firearms and self-protection.

The organization's Web site provides news stories about efforts to maintain the rights of gun owners. An October 2009 item, by Jennifer Coffey, National Coordinator and member of the New Hampshire House of Representatives, reported that the National Rifle Association (NRA), the Citizens Committee for the Right to Keep and Bear Arms (CCRKBA), and knife manufacturing companies defeated an attempt at the federal level to categorize nearly all knives that could be opened with one hand as switchblades and hence subject to restriction under federal law. In an August 2010 item, Kim Grady strongly criticized a proposal, attributed to the Humane Society of the United States (HSUS), that a nationwide ban on lead-shot ammunition be instituted. Grady claimed that lead shot was not as harmful to wildlife as the HSUS claimed, and that alternatives (copper and steel) would be far more expensive. Grady concluded by stating that "This latest ban attempt is the [HSUS's] attempt to take away our guns, point blank!"

The SAS Website advertises several books and DVDs related to firearms. Suzanna Hupp's autobiographical book, *From Luby's to the Legislature: One Woman's Fight Against Gun Control*, describes the 1991 shooting at a Killeen, Texas, restaurant where Hupp's mother and father and 22 other people were shot and killed, including the gunman. Following the shooting, Hupp became a vocal advocate of gun rights, was elected to the Texas legislature, and became a national speaker supporting the liberalizing of gun laws in several states to permit the concealed carrying of firearms. The site also advertises the DVD documentary produced by Jews for the Preservation of Firearms Ownership (JPFO), *True Americans Don't Tolerate "Gun Control" Laws* that supposedly exposes "the irresponsible, malicious, and criminal actions" of the Bureau of Alcohol, Tobacco, Firearms, and Explosives (ATF). Another advertised JPFO DVD, *Innocents Betrayed*, argues that governments historically have deprived citizens of the right to own firearms, and then have oppressed and killed them. To the recommendation that the United States should follow the policies of other nations that have instituted restrictive firearm policies, JPFO claims that 170 million "innocent, non-combatant men, women and children" lost their lives after the right to own firearms was abolished. Another advertised book by David Barton titled *The Second Amendment: Preserving the Inalienable Right of Individual Self-Protection* contains quotes from the constitutional framers about the importance of possessing firearms, and includes early laws and proposals for dealing with gun violence. The SAS site also advertises a fictional work by Matthew Bracken, *Enemies Foreign and Domestic*, which portrays a conspiracy to change Americans' view of gun rights by staging a shooting at a football stadium.

The national organization reportedly ceased operations in 2015, although state chapters continue to operate independently. For instance, the Massachusetts chapter conducts various events including shooting practice and informational meetings on concealed carry for women, and offers assistance to women in applying for a firearm permit. The organization has as its fundamental mission "To reach out to women and educate them on their basic human right of self-defense and the important role of the Second Amendment in protecting that right." Members of the organization pay an annual fee of $25.

See also: Women Against Gun Control; *Women and Guns* Magazine.

Further Reading: Humane Society of the United States, "The HSUS Calls for Nationwide Ban on Lead Shot after Study Findings" (November 10, 2008, www.humanesociety.org/news/press_releases/2008/11/hsus_calls_for_nationwide_ban_on_lead_shot_111008.html; Second Amendment Sisters Web site, http://www.2sisters.org; Second Amendment Sisters Massachusetts Chapter Website, www.2asistersma.org.

Shotgun News

See **Firearms News**

Sklar v. Byrne (1984)

Sklar v. Byrne (727 F.2d 633, 1984), a case that dealt with a Chicago, Illinois, ordinance prohibiting handgun registration after April 10, 1982, reinforced the state decision in the *Quilici v. Village of Morton Grove* (1981) case. Jerome Sklar, a handgun owner with a valid Illinois Firearms Identification Card, lived in Skokie, Illinois, when the Chicago ordinance was passed. Soon after April 10, 1982, Sklar moved to Chicago, where he discovered that the new law prevented him from registering his handgun. Therefore, he could not take the weapon with him to his new residence.

Sklar challenged the new firearms ordinance in court, arguing that Chicago had denied him the equal protection of the laws under the U.S. Constitution. Handgun owners living in Chicago before April 10, 1982, could maintain registration of their weapons, a right he was prevented from exercising. The U.S. District Court for the Northern District of Illinois ruled that the precedent affirmed in the *Quilici* decision required a conclusion that the Chicago ordinance did not violate Sklar's constitutional rights. In response to Sklar's claim that Chicago could have employed alternative and more effective means of protecting citizens from the damaging consequences of firearms, the court stated that it could not invalidate a law simply because judges concluded that other policies would result in better outcomes. Only if a law were judged "wholly arbitrary" could it face the possibility of invalidation. Because the city pursued a legitimate objective, limiting the right of registration to individuals who had registered their firearms by a certain date could be considered a nonarbitrary, and hence legitimate, exercise of government power.

The district court concluded that Sklar had not been denied equal protection under the U.S. Constitution. A policy-making body has the right to deal with a recognized harm piecemeal, and therefore the City of Chicago was not required to ban completely the registration of handguns. By passing an ordinance that limited handgun ownership to those already possessing a valid registration, "a notable first step toward limiting the havoc and mayhem caused by firearms could be made."

In his appeal to the U.S. Court of Appeals for the Seventh Circuit, Sklar argued that because he could not travel to Chicago without surrendering his weapon, the city ordinance also violated his right to travel freely. The Court of Appeals, upholding the lower court ruling, denied that the case involved any constitutional issue. Because the city council had concluded that the presence of firearms and ammunition were associated with crimes, deaths, and injuries in the city, it acted legitimately under the police power to protect the health and welfare of citizens.

Sklar further argued that the ordinance, by allowing some but not others to keep handguns, was arbitrary and unfair. The Court of Appeals rejected this argument, claiming that the grandfather clause allowing Chicago registrants to keep their handguns was a reasonable exception within the law. Although the city could have banned all handguns, the council had decided to make reasonable exceptions.

Sklar suggested that making a distinction based on qualifications for possessing a handgun constitutes a far more reasonable criterion for excluding some and not others from handgun registration. In a response similar to that given by the court of original jurisdiction, the Court of Appeals noted that the city council, as a political institution responding to many interests, could not be held to a standard of perfect consistency. A political body must be allowed the leeway to resolve a problem in the way it sees fit, which may mean only partial resolution of the difficulty. Provided that the city council devoted reasonable consideration to the question, the court should not impose its own substantive evaluation of what might constitute the best policy in a situation.

More than 25 years later, the U.S. Supreme Court in *McDonald v. Chicago* (2010) ruled that the restrictions Chicago had instituted on the possession of firearms violated the Second Amendment guarantee of an individual right to possess firearms.

See also: District of Columbia v. Heller (2008); *McDonald v. Chicago* (2010); *Quilici v. Village of Morton Grove* (1982).

Further Reading: Mark A. Siegel, Nancy R. Jacobs, and Carol D. Foster, eds., *Gun Control: Restricting Rights or Protecting People?* (Wylie, TX: Information Plus, 1991); *Sklar v. Byrne*, 727 F.2d 633 (1984).

Small Arms Review

The *Small Arms Review* (*SAR*), which began publication in October 1997, is devoted to firearms and gun accessories, such as machine guns, silencers, short-barreled shotguns, and other "exotic weapons," including flamethrowers, that are restricted by the National Firearms Act. The magazine was established to increase interest in automatic weapons at the same time that the national government was attempting to place greater limitations on such firearms. The editorial staff contends that the National Firearms Act (NFA) of 1934, which governs automatic weapons, is bad law and violates the U.S. Constitution. Nonetheless, *SAR* provides detailed information about abiding by the law in order to avoid legal problems with the Bureau of Alcohol, Tobacco, Firearms, and Explosives (ATF). *SAR* provides "NFA (National Firearms Act) collectors and historians, NFA leisure and competition shooters, military users, law enforcement personnel, and industry people" with information about various automatic weapons and reports on gun shows and shooting events involving the use of automatic weapons.

Chipotle Publishing produces the *Small Arms Review*, which deals with military small arms and collecting and focuses primarily on the United States. The company also publishes a sister periodical, *Small Arms Defense Journal*, which treats military arms and the arms industry from an international perspective.

Many of *SAR*'s columns contain information and commentary on firearms legislation, particularly the National Firearms Act of 1934 and the Gun Control Act (GCA) of 1968. Dan Shea, the magazine's editor in chief, writes an editorial column titled "SITREP" (Situation Report) that provides news and opinions on issues relevant to automatic weapons. In the October 2014 issue, Shea discussed what he considers the positive aspects of the Firearms Owners Protection Act— for instance, establishing the right of gun owners to travel legally through areas with more stringent firearm laws as long as their possession is legal at the starting and ending point of the travel and the firearms are locked. He praised the end to keeping ammunition record books, which he called pointless, "having helped solve no crimes and only been used to annoy and impede ownership." However, he commented that machine gun owners were net well served, and the law is "absolutely unconstitutional regarding automatic weapons."

In the column "Industry News," Robert M. Hausman reports on recent developments by firearms manufacturers and sales figures for various companies. In the March 2015 issue, Hausman discussed the disappointing sales figures for Ruger, the resulting production cuts, and the company's decreased earnings. He also referred to the economic problems that Colt faces. Hausmasn discussed approvingly the support that the Second Amendment Foundation and other groups were providing to four California gun dealers who had challenged the state's prohibition on displaying images of handguns, claiming that the ban violates the First Amendment guarantee of freedom of speech.

John Brown writes a column for the National Firearms Act Trade and Collectors Association (NFATCA) titled "NFATCA Report." In the January 2015 issue, Brown discussed changes in leadership at the Bureau of Alcohol, Tobacco, Firearms, and Explosives (ATF), expressing hope that the accommodating relationship between the NFATCA and the ATF can be reestablished with new leadership in the Bureau.

See also: Brady Handgun Violence Prevention Act; Bureau of Alcohol, Tobacco, Firearms, and Explosives; Concealed Carry Laws; Eddie Eagle; Gun Owners of America; Law Enforcement Alliance of America; National Firearms Act of 1934; National Instant Check System; National Rifle Association; Sawed-Off Shotgun.

Further Reading: *Small Arms Review* (Moose Lake Publishing, LLC, Henderson, Nevada); Web site, www.smallarmsreview.com.

Smart Guns

The call for smart, or personalized, guns, firearms engineered so that only the legitimate owner may fire it, demonstrates the lack of consensus on either side of the gun control issue. Smart guns, along with trigger locks, would appear to be a proposal that gun control groups would support, but some gun control advocates are suspicious, claiming that the introduction of smart guns, assuming a reliable technology becomes available, would have little preventive capacity for gun deaths and injuries in the United States. Because most firearms

deaths result from suicides and homicides, simply preventing someone other than the owner from using the weapon will not prevent such violent uses of handguns.

The Violence Policy Center (VPC) questions the availability of technology to make the smart gun feasible. The organization expresses concern because gun control advocates who are willing to entertain smart guns would need to depend on the firearms industry to develop the technology to make a system of personalization workable and available to gun owners. The VPC expresses skepticism about the motives of the firearms industry, which, the organization claims, is primarily interested in profits and limiting potential liability rather than improving gun safety. Therefore, the VPC resists the surface attractiveness of such mechanisms. Women, who demonstrate great concern for safety, may find the smart gun an attractive product, thus providing a new market for gun manufacturers. Gun control advocates claim that placing attention on smart gun technology could take attention away from other serious safety issues, such as the tendency of some handguns to fire without pulling the trigger when they are dropped or bumped. Therefore, the concern should be for establishing general safety standards.

Similar to gun rights advocates' arguments that gun locks may provide a false sense of security, some gun control supporters claim that personalized guns would give the impression that a firearm so equipped is safer than it actually is. Gun control advocates also express concern that the advocacy of smart guns creates the false impression that firearms can be beneficial for legitimate owners. Contrary to a fundamental stand taken by gun rights groups, they argue that firearms have little defensive value for private citizens. In contrast to the simple ban-no-ban dichotomy, smart guns would require a government bureaucracy to determine the suitableness of a particular technology and to oversee its implementation.

Comparing smart gun technology to putting filters on cigarettes, gun control supporters who advocate restricting firearm ownership express concern that manufacturers will be able to claim their products are far safer than they actually are. They claim that smart technology makes sense only for weapons used by law enforcement officers who run the risk of being shot by their own firearms that have been wrestled from them in a confrontation.

In 2002 New Jersey approved a law that would require handgun manufacturers to sell only "smart" handguns beginning three years after the technology has been perfected. Instead of focusing on the use of physical characteristics of the gun owner, such as fingerprint recognition, Don Sebastian of the New Jersey Institute of Technology has developed a "dynamic biometrics" system that measures the individual's unique pressure when squeezing the trigger. The system is reported to be 90 percent reliable, but in order to be usable it must approach 100 percent reliability before being put into use.

Gun rights supporters resist any proposal that imposes controls on the gun owner, especially when the requirement may in some way restrict the intended use of firearms. The reaction to smart guns, similar to gun locks, will be cautious, depending on whether their use is made mandatory for all, and the extent to which the technology is considered intrusive and unreliable. While some gun control supporters view smart guns as a possible strategy to expand the market for guns and to ward off more stringent safety measures, some gun advocates see them as a potential first step toward greater gun control that ultimately can result in confiscation.

Despite doubts about the reliability of existing technology and concerns among gun rights groups about possible government mandates, and boycotts of manufacturers and dealers that have attempted to introduce personalized firearms, technological development continues. In 2014 Ron Conway's Smart Tech Foundation awarded $1 million to 15 grantees that are developing smart-gun technology. A German company has developed a smart gun, the Armatix iP1, which can only be fired by a shooter wearing a special wristwatch. In 2015 Kai Kloepfer, a high school senior in Boulder, Colorado, developed a smart handgun that can be fired only if its recognizes the authorized user's fingerprint on the grip. In April 2016 President Barack Obama announced that the Justice and Homeland Security Departments will work to establish criteria for firearm manufacturers in moving toward selling smart gins to law enforcement agencies. Obama also announced the availability of grants to firearm manufacturers who engage in smart-gun development.

See also: Trigger Locks; Violence Policy Center; Women and Guns.

Further Reading: American Association for the Advancement of Science, "Smart Gun" (2010), www.sciencenetlinks.com/sci_update.php?DocID=254; National Rifle Association, " 'Smart' Guns" (2000), www.nraila.org/Issues/FactSheets/Read.aspx?id=38; Violence Policy Center, "The False Hope of the 'Smart' Gun" (1998), www.vpc.org/fact_sht/smartgun.htm; Michael D. Shear and Eric Lichtblau, "Obama Puts Weight Behind 'Smart-Gun' Technoloby, Fueling N.R.A. Objections," *New York Times* (April 30, 2016): A9; Nicholas Kristof, "Smart Guns Save Lives. So Where Are They?" *New York Times* (January 18, 2015): SR11; Grand Burmingham, "Silicon Valley Targets Smart Guns," *Newsweek* (April 12, 2016), www.newsweek.com/silicon-valley-targets-smart-guns-446523.

Smith and Wesson

Today the names Smith and Wesson elicit the image of powerful handguns. When Clint Eastwood, as movie character Dirty Harry, tells a suspect that "we" will arrest him, the suspect asks who "we" are. Eastwood responds: "Smith, Wesson, and me." The Smith and Wesson .44-Magnum handgun has achieved legendary status in American culture as "the most powerful handgun in the world." New police officers, impressed with the weapons, began carrying them, only to shift to a smaller, less "powerful" but more easily handled weapon.

Horace Smith (1808–1893) and Daniel Baird Wesson (1825–1906) established the Smith and Wesson company in the mid-nineteenth century. Smith began apprenticeship at the Springfield Armory in 1824 where his father had been working for some time. In 1842, he moved to Worcester, Massachusetts, where he worked for a tool-making firm. In the same year, having already demonstrated a keen interest in firearms, Wesson was indentured to his brother Edwin who operated a gun shop in Grafton, Massachusetts. By 1848, Wesson had learned the trade and he and his brother moved the operation to Hartford, Connecticut, renaming it the Wesson Rifle Company. After his brother's death in 1849, Wesson was forced to sell the estate.

In 1852, Smith and Wesson joined their independently developed talents to improve both ammunition and firearms. The two partners joined with Courtlandt Palmer to produce the Volcanic pistol, and developed the rimfire cartridge, considered a major advance in ammunition. In 1855, a group of investors, among them Oliver

Winchester, bought out the Smith and Wesson operation, giving it the name Volcanic Repeating Arms Company. Wesson stayed with the company, but Smith returned to Springfield. In 1856, Wesson left Volcanic to rejoin his old partner, forming the Smith and Wesson Revolver Factory. The firm prospered, especially from the manufacture and sale of ammunition. The Smith and Wesson Model 1 revolver and subsequent revisions proved very popular, and the Civil War boosted orders. In 1862, as the sole company that could legally produce cartridge revolvers, Smith and Wesson amassed orders that would take three years to fulfill.

In 1871, Smith, considerably older than his partner, sold out to Wesson. At that time the company received an order from the Russian government, and in 1873, pleased with the results, the Russian government ordered an additional 20,000 revolvers, called the Model 3 Russian Second Model. The Japanese government bought 5,000 of these handguns, and over 6,000 were sold commercially. That same year the Smith and Wesson company signed a contract with the U.S. government to deliver 3,000 Schofield revolvers. After the Schofield, the company produced the New Model 3, which stayed in production for many years.

In 1917, during World War I, Smith and Wesson obtained several contracts to deliver military revolvers. Joseph Wesson, the new company president, had become ill and management of the operation suffered. Therefore, the U.S. government assumed control of the company for the duration of the war. Following the war, the company perceived three potential impediments to its continued success: (1) the surplus of weapons that dampened sales for newly manufactured guns; (2) competition from imported weapons; and (3) a developing political movement lobbying for firearms controls.

The company survived the difficult Depression years of the 1930s to provide weapons during World War II. In 1946, Carl Hellstrom became the fifth president of the firm. Hellstrom avoided diversification, insisting that the company focus on gun production. During his administration, the company began producing the .44 Magnum. Hellstrom retained the presidency throughout the profitable 1950s, and was still president of the company when he died of a heart attack in 1963. When Smith and Wesson was offered a stock buyout, the company accepted. The new management insisted on product diversification and established an academy to train police officers.

By the 1990s, Smith and Wesson, unlike many gun manufacturers, was operating its facilities at near capacity, offering 187 variations of its assorted models. The company saw itself serving the interests of four categories of customers: hunters, competitive shooters, law enforcement officers, and the private person concerned with personal security. In 2010, the Smith and Wesson Holding Corporation received a contract from the Bureau of Alcohol, Tobacco, Firearms, and Explosives (ATF) to provide the M&P 40 pistol to federal agencies. Smith and Wesson estimated that the contract could amount to $40 million in sales during the next 10 years, which would contribute significantly to the company's financial health. In 2014, Smith and Wesson Holding Company acquired Batterfield Technologies of Columbia, Missouri, a hunting and shooting accessories distributor.

As Smith and Wesson's stock share price reportedly increased 36 percent in the first half of 2016, a new pro-gun control group composed of gays was established following the mass shooting at a gay night club in Orlando, Florida. The new organization targeted Smith and Wesson as well as Sturm, Ruger—the two largest firearms manufacturers in the United States—and the firms that invest in the companies. The group, called Gays Against Guns, noted that gun sales rise following mass shootings, and claimed that Smith and Wesson and other gun manufacturers have profited from tragic events.

See also: Colt, Samuel; Remington, Eliphalet, II; Winchester, Oliver Fisher.

Further Reading: "Smith and Wesson Awarded ATF Contract," http://ir.smith-wesson.com/phoenix.zhtml?c=90977&p=irol-newsArticle&ID=1470110&highlight=; Wayne Van Zwoll, *America's Great Gunmakers* (South Hackensack, NJ: Stoeger, 1992); Emily Palmer and Sarah Maslin Nir, "Gays Against Guns," *New York Times* (June 26, 2016), www.nytimes.com/live/gay-pride-parade-nyc-2016/gays.

Smith v. United States (1993)

In *Smith v. United States* (508 U.S. 223, 1993), the U.S. Supreme Court examined what activities may be regarded as the "use" of a firearm in the commission of a drug crime. A federal statute

[U.S.C. 924 (c) (1)] calls for mandatory prison sentences for a defendant who "during and in relation to . . . [a] drug trafficking crime uses . . . a firearm." A defendant who has used a firearm must be sentenced to five years in prison, and if the firearm is a machine gun or has been equipped with a silencer, the sentence is 30 years. Citing the dictionary definition of "use," the Court ruled that trading a firearm for drugs can count as a clear example of use within the wording of the statute. Although the dissenting justices wished to make a more definite distinction between the firing of a weapon and a firearm's involvement as an object for barter, the majority, led by Justice Sandra Day O'Connor, regarded a firearm as continually an instrument of deadly force.

Angus Smith traveled with a companion from Tennessee to Florida to purchase illegal drugs. He made a deal with an undercover policeman to receive two ounces of cocaine in return for a MAC-10 firearm, which had been converted to automatic mode capable of firing 1,000 rounds per minute. He was arrested and a federal grand jury indicted him for two drug trafficking crimes. The indictment also charged Smith with knowingly using the firearm and its silencer "during and in relation to a drug trafficking crime." Because the firearm in question had been converted to automatic operation, Smith was subject to a 30-year prison term. A jury convicted Smith on all charges.

The Court of Appeals for the Eleventh Circuit, which heard Smith's appeal, rejected his argument that the penalty established in 924 (c) (1) applies only to the use of a firearm as a weapon. Because another Court of Appeals had ruled that trading a gun in a drug transaction does not constitute a use of a firearm within the intention of the statute, the Supreme Court agreed to hear the case to resolve the disagreement. The Court noted that the prosecution had to satisfy two conditions: (1) prove that the defendant "used or carried a firearm" and (2) demonstrate that the use or carrying occurred "during and in relation to" a "crime of violence or drug trafficking crime."

Smith contended that a conviction required not only a demonstration that he used the firearm, but in addition that he used the firearm *as a weapon*. The Court observed that the words "as a weapon" appear nowhere in the statute. Although Smith appealed to what the average person would take "using a firearm" to mean, the Court ruled that the prevailing understanding does not preclude other meanings. The primary delimiter to the meaning

of use, according to the Court, is whether the use occurred "during and in relation to" an incident of illegal drug trafficking. Commenting that the meaning of a word such as "use" within a statute cannot be determined in isolation, the Court observed that the section of the federal statute dealing with forfeiture of firearms lists offenses involving the use of a firearm not only as a weapon, but also as "an item of barter or commerce." The majority held that Congress, when adding drug trafficking crimes to the statute in 1986, "employed the term 'use' expansively, covering both use as a weapon . . . and use as an item of trade or barter, as an examination of 924 (d) demonstrates."

The Court remarked further that Congress "was no doubt aware that drugs and guns are a dangerous combination," increasing the danger to the general public. The Court noted that in 1989, 80 percent of murders in Washington, D.C., were drug-related. In the *Smith* case, the firearm played an integral part in the drug transaction, which could not have proceeded without it. Therefore, finding no reason to believe that Congress did not intend a broader meaning of use, the Court upheld the lower court conviction.

Further Reading: *Smith v. United States*, 508 U.S. 223 (1993).

Soldier of Fortune

Soldier of Fortune (*SOF*) magazine opposes gun control in its own unique way, taking a survivalist attitude toward the purpose of firearms and other weapons. The magazine has an editorial policy that is "pro-military, pro-strong U.S. defense, pro-police, and pro-veteran," and that supports the individual right to keep and bear arms. The magazine promotes the view that the world is a dangerous place and that each individual must become aware of the need for national and personal defense. The publication contains articles about mercenary activities, unusual weapons, and military conditions around the world. The magazine's Web site contains several streaming videos dealing with arms training and military engagements around the world. The editorial page of each issue contains a disclaimer that states in part: "The data and products in this publication have not been tested or verified by *SOF*. Mention of a product in advertisement or text does not mean that it has been tested or approved by *SOF*. *SOF*, its agents, officers and employees accept no responsibility for the use of any products, equipment, editorial content, or for any results for use thereof obtained by persons using such data and disclaim all liability for any consequential injuries or damages."

Robert K. Brown, a retired Air Force lieutenant colonel who has served on the National Rifle Association (NRA) board of directors, publishes the magazine. He writes a column each month titled "Command Guidance," which sets the tone for each issue. Taking a conservative political stand, Brown has referred to former Representative Ron Dellums, Democrat from California, as being "as far left as one can be without having a likeness of Lenin tattooed on a visible body part." Referring to the "sissies of the Clinton Administration" and the "draft dodger" president, Brown labeled President Bill Clinton's policy toward women and homosexuals in the U.S. military one of "sissification." In the November 2010 issue, Brown commented on the controversy over plans to build a Muslim mosque near "Ground Zero," the location of the terrorist attacks in New York on September 11, 2001. He remarked that the construction would be offensive to the families of the victims, and called for a similar right for Christian groups to build a church in Mecca. Brown called "thumb suckers" those critics of the Vietnam War who maintain that the United States was opposing agrarian reform.

Like other pro-gun publications, *Soldier of Fortune* has targeted the Bureau of Alcohol, Tobacco Firearms, and Explosives (ATF) for severe criticism, labeling this government agency the "Gun Gestapo." *SOF* has claimed that the ATF could potentially interpret the Gun-Free Schools Act very broadly. The magazine has warned parents who educate their children at home that the Act, which prohibits the possession of a firearm in schools, could be applied to private homes where schooling occurs and thus firearms belonging to home-schooling families could be confiscated.

SOF contains columns that deal with political and military themes. Oliver North, retired Marine Corps lieutenant colonel, has written the column "Common Sense." In the November 2010 issue, North discussed foreign policy "snakes" that presidents have faced (for instance, Thomas Jefferson and the Barbary pirates, Franklin Delano Roosevelt and the Japanese attack on Pearl Harbor, and John F. Kennedy and the failed Bay of Pigs invasion), warning that President Barack Obama's administration has failed to recognize the foreign

policy dangers the United States faces. The November 2010 issue also contained Martin Bass's "Terrorism Sitrep," which presented a two-page world map highlighting events in various countries relevant to the U.S. struggle against terrorism. "Bulletin Board," which appears in each issue, contains several brief news items on such topics as terrorism, immigration, perceived threats to gun rights, and military policy.

The magazine contains advertising for many unconventional items. Its pages include several ads for locksmithing tools and instruction videos on the subject. Other ads tout martial arts training videos, "killing techniques," and the "Navy SEAL Fighting System." Paladin Press runs ads displaying books and videos on such topics as weapons building, dirty tricks, "how to live hidden and free," sniping and sharpshooting, and how to change identities. Although few firearm ads appear in the magazine, accessories such as gun grips and ammunition are featured, and articles review new weaponry. A section called the "Supply Depot" advertises a wide variety of items, including body armor, military equipment, and law enforcement supply catalogs. An advertisement index provides the page numbers where companies' ads appear.

Soldier of Fortune published it last print issue in April 2016 and is now offered only online. The Website contains reports on the military, terrorism, survival, the Second Amendment, and "Best of SOF" (articles from past issues).

See also: Bureau of Alcohol, Tobacco, Firearms, and Explosives; Clinton, William Jefferson (Bill); Gun-Free Schools Act; National Rifle Association; Paladin Press.

Further Reading: *Soldier of Fortune* (Mount Morris, Illinois); *SOF* Web site, www.sofmag.com.

Sonzinsky v. United States (1937)

In *Sonzinsky v. United States* (300 U.S. 506, 1937), the U.S. Supreme Court ruled on the constitutionality of section two of the 1934 National Firearms Act, which imposed a $200 annual license tax on firearms dealers. The law required firearms dealers to register with the Internal Revenue Service (IRS) in the district in which they conduct business and to pay the special excise tax. Importers or manufacturers were taxed $500 per year. The law defined a firearm as a shotgun or rifle with a barrel less than 18 inches long, or "any other weapon, except a pistol or revolver, from which a shot is discharged by an explosive, if capable of being concealed on the person, or a machine gun, and includes a muffler or silencer for any firearm." Section three of the act imposed a tax of $200 on the transfer of each firearm, but the Court did not consider the constitutionality of that provision in its decision.

Harold Sonzinsky was convicted in a federal district court in Illinois on two counts of violating the Federal Firearms Act. The defendant appealed the case to the Circuit Court of Appeals, which reversed one conviction, but affirmed the conviction for dealing in firearms without paying the special occupational tax. The U.S. Supreme Court decided to grant certiorari to consider the original conviction. Although Sonzinsky admitted that Congress could tax his firearms business, he protested that the assessment in question was not a genuine tax, but a penalty that Congress instituted to discourage traffic in certain types of weapons the government considered objectionable. Successive taxes imposed on dealers, manufacturers, importers, and purchasers amounted to a large penalty compared to the worth of the weapons involved, thus prohibiting trade in firearms. Sonzinsky further argued that the authority to regulate such weapons was reserved to the states.

The Court's decision did not rest on an interpretation of the Second Amendment, but rather on the taxing power of the federal government. The Court ruled that the National Firearms Act did not contain regulatory provisions related to the tax in such a way that the tax was primarily a means of enforcing the regulations. Section two contained no regulation other than the requirement to register as a firearms dealer, which assisted in the collection of revenues. Although Sonzinsky contended that the tax operated as a regulatory tool beyond the authority of Congress, the Court concluded that every tax is to some extent regulatory, imposing an "economic impediment" on the activity taxed in comparison to enterprises not taxed. The Court refused to infer the intentions of Congress in establishing the $200 special occupational tax: "We are not free to speculate as to the motives which moved Congress to impose it, or as to the extent to which it may operate to restrict the activities taxed." Because the tax was not accompanied by an "offensive regulation" and did in fact operate as a tax, the provision fell within the federal taxing power.

See also: Federal Firearms Act of 1938; National Firearms Act of 1934.

Further Reading: *Sonzinsky v. United States*, 300 U.S. 506 (1937).

Sporting Arms and Ammunition Manufacturers' Institute (SAAMI)

In 1926 the federal government requested that firearms and ammunition manufacturers establish the Sporting Arms and Ammunition Manufacturer's Institute (SAAMI) to develop and disseminate industry standards for firearms and ammunition, coordinate technical data, and promote safe use of firearms. The organization became a major representative for the interests of the firearms industry. SAAMI publishes more than 700 voluntary standards for firearms and ammunition quality and safety. The organization notes approvingly that in 1972 Congress exempted firearms and ammunition producers from the provisions of the Consumer Safety Protection Act. SAAMI observes that other products are exempted, including automobiles, boats, and aircraft, and opposes any change in the firearms and ammunition exemption, objecting to the call for the regulation of firearms as a consumer product.

The major U.S. firearms manufacturers are members of SAAMI, including North American Arms, Remington Arms, SIG SAUER, Taurus, Beretta USA, Browning Arms, Glock, Smith and Wesson, and Sturm Ruger.

The Technical Committee, a subgroup of SAAMI, conducts the major work of the Institute in establishing industry standards. Two Product Standards Task Forces, one for firearms and one for ammunition, develop product standards. The SAAMI Logistics and Regulatory Affairs Committee (SLARAC), engages in the development of guidelines for the safe transportation and distribution of products manufactured by member companies. The committee offers advice regarding the classification, labeling, and packaging of small arms ammunition and conducts tests to confirm the safety of storage and transportation practices for small arms ammunition. The SLARAC issued a video, *Sporting Ammunition and the Firefighter*, which assures firefighters that they have little to fear when stores of ammunition are involved in a fire. Ammunition is hard to ignite, no mass explosion will occur, and any bullets that may be fired are of low velocity.

SAAMI publicizes firearms safety as one of its major concerns. The Institute prepared *Firearms Safety Depends on You*, a booklet that firearms manufacturers include with each firearm produced. The organization also has distributed more than 15 million copies of the booklet "A Responsible Approach to Firearms Safety." SAAMI advises those who keep weapons in the home to abide by safe storage and handling methods. Among the Institute's ten firearm safety rules, firearm owners are urged always to keep firearms unloaded when not in use, don't rely on the firearm's safety, learn the mechanical and handling characteristics of the firearm before using it, use the correct ammunition, wear eye and ear protection, and point the muzzle in a safe direction.

SAAMI has cited estimates placing the number of defensive uses of firearms as high as 3.6 million per year, and has disseminated the claim that as many as 400,000 lives are saved each year through the use of firearms for self-defense. Citing John Lott's research, the organization emphasizes the deterrent effect of firearms. As for the risks of firearm ownership, the organization contends that dangers can be minimized through training and educational programs and safe handling and storage practices. According to SAAMI, the greatest danger of firearms exists outside the home and are associated with criminals on the streets.

In response to those who advocate additional gun control and the prohibition of certain types of firearms, SAAMI emphasizes that guns are "an acceptable, responsible, and desirable ingredient of our nation's heritage." In addition, the organization emphasizes the economic effects of the firearms and ammunition industry. Americans spend over $30 billion each year on hunting and shooting sports and the industry employs more than 986,000 people. Although this number of employees represents less than 1 percent of the nation's workforce, it is greater than all the people employed in both Wyoming and West Virginia. More than 1,100 manufacturers, 100 distributors, and 14,000 retailers are engaged almost totally in activities related to hunting and recreational shooting.

SAAMI has consultative status with the United Nations Economic and Social Council (ECOSOC) and provides input when the U.S. discusses arms control. In March 2013, when the U.N. was considering the Arms Trade Treaty (ATT), Richard Patterson, managing director of SAAMI, recommended against including ammunition regulation in the treaty, arguing that such a regulation is unworkable. He stated that "firearms in the hands of law-abiding citizens provide many positive benefits to society" and that "there is no validity to the assumption that more guns will equal more violence." Patterson recommended that the U.N. limit the scope of the ATT to fully automatic military weapons.

In October 2015 Patterson expressed disappointment that the ATT lacked consensus among the nations, but resulted instead from majority vote, with many participants opposed to the final result. He stated that only 40 percent of U.N. member states had officially ratified the treaty, representing no more than 30 percent of global arms exports.

See also: Accidents Involving Guns; Lott, John R., Jr.; Trigger Locks.

Further Reading: Sporting Arms and Ammunition Manufacturers' Institute Web site, www.saami.org.

Sporting Purposes Test

Pro-gun rights interests have expressed their concern about the sporting purposes test for the importation of firearms, which was originally included in the Gun Control Act of 1968. In the article "The 'Sporting Purposes' Time Bomb" (1999), gun rights advocate Richard L. Gaynes argued that through the use of the sporting purposes criterion in the Gun Control Act, the Bureau of Alcohol, Tobacco, and Firearms (ATF) "has effectively provided support to the Disarm America political agenda and greatly damaged the Second Amendment rights . . . in the name of fighting violent crime." Gun control advocates consider the test necessary to keep out of the country weapons they consider devoid of any legitimate purpose.

Section 925, subsection (d)(3) of the Gun Control Act states that "(d) The [Treasury] Secretary shall authorize a firearm or ammunition to be imported or brought into the United States or any possession thereof if the firearm or ammunition . . . (3) is of a type that does not fall within the definition of a firearm as defined in section 5845(a) [a machine gun] of the Internal Revenue Code of

1954 and is generally recognized as particularly suitable for or readily adaptable to sporting purposes, excluding surplus military firearms." In 1984, the Gun Control Act was amended by adding section (e) which states: "Notwithstanding any other provision of this title, the Secretary shall authorize the importation of, by any licensed importer, the following: (1) All rifles and shotguns listed as curios or relics by the Secretary pursuant to section 921(a)(13), and (2) All handguns, listed as curios or relics by the Secretary pursuant to section 921(a)(13), provided that such handguns are generally recognized as particularly suitable for or readily adaptable to sporting purposes."

Gaynes observed that, following the murder of children at a Stockton, California, school by a deranged gunman wielding a semiautomatic assault rifle, ATF officials formed a working group to establish a basis within the Gun Control Act of 1968 to prohibit the importation of certain types of firearms, to determine firearms evaluation standards on which to make such prohibitions, and "to prohibit the domestic manufacture and sale of certain firearms." The focus for establishing bans was the sporting purposes test. The ATF developed a list of physical characteristics of firearms (for instance, the capability of accepting detachable magazines, the presence of a flash suppressor, or the inclusion of a separate pistol grip) that could be used to determine the absence of a sporting purpose. Gaynes offered several criticisms of the sporting purposes test, faulting the ATF for failing to demonstrate the prevalent use of particular weapons in crimes. He charged that the ATF working group adopted a narrow interpretation of firearms to which the sporting purposes test would apply.

The group Jews for the Preservation of Firearms Ownership (JPFO) especially opposes the sporting purposes test, associating it with a weapons law passed in Nazi Germany in 1938. The German law also contained a sporting purposes exception, permitting licenses for firearms designed for hunting game. The JPFO is uncomfortable with the grant of authority to the Treasury secretary to determine which firearms have a sporting purpose because the Nazi law had a similar provision, granting to administrative officials and the courts the power to determine which firearms had a sporting purpose.

For gun control supporters, the sporting purposes test has none of the ominous significance attributed to it by pro-gun rights groups. Instead,

the test has provided a basis on which to limit the importation of weapons that are considered to have no legitimate use by sporting persons and therefore are thought to be likely candidates for criminal use. In 2004, Senator Dianne Feinstein expressed her concerns to the ATF about the reported importation of semiautomatic assault rifles that she asserted failed the sporting purposes test. Not long after, the Congress failed to renew the 1994 Assault Weapons Ban that had prohibited the sale of semiautomatic firearms to civilians.

Pro-gun rights advocates continue to criticize the sporting purposes test. Jeff Knox of the Firearms Coalition has labeled the sporting purposes test a violation of the Second Amendment. He states: "the right to arms enumerated in the Constitution is about self-defense and self-determination, not about trap and skeet or taking game." Knox has supported a bill the Representative Rob Bishop (R-UT) introduced that would replace the phrase "sporting purposes" with "lawful purposes" in the Gun Control Act of 1968.

See also: Bureau of Alcohol, Tobacco, Firearms, and Explosives; Gun Control Act of 1968; Jews for the Preservation of Firearms Ownership; Second Amendment; Stockton, California, Shooting.

Further Reading: Dianne Feinstein, "Senator Feinstein Questions Importation of Banned Assault Weapons into the U.S.," http://feinstein.senate. gov/04Releases/r-aft-assault.htm; Richard L. Gaynes, "The 'Sporting Purposes' Time Bomb," *Guns and Ammo* 43 (January 1999), 14–17, 94, 100; Jews for the Preservation of Firearms Ownership Web site, www.jpfo.org; Jeff Knox, "'Sporting Purpose' Language in Law: Unconstitutional," WND (July 2015), wnd.com/2015/07/ sporting-purpose-language-in-law-unconstitutional.

Stand Your Ground laws

American law has long struggled with competing principles regarding the justifiability of self-defense claims when one individual kills another in the name of self defense in a public place. One principle has held that, when confronted with a dire threat to personal safety, the individual so threated has a duty to avoid a confrontation by retreating as long as one can do so safely. A competing view supports the idea that, under at least some circumstances, individuals facing imminent serious harm or death are not obligated to retreat, but are instead entitled to "stand their ground" in a public place where they have a right to be, and meet force with force.

Values of individualism, anti-government sentiment, actual and mythical notions of behavior in America's unsettled western lands, and the "true man" doctrine all supported the notion that citizens have a right to meet force with force not only in their home, referred to as the Castle Doctrine, but even in public places – and without the need to retreat. The "true man" doctrine refers to individuals with clean legal records who have not run afoul of the law, or who are otherwise free from legal fault. The phrase is akin to a similar old fashioned expression, "good men and true," a phrase from the Middle Ages referring to those eligible to serve on a jury.

Several Supreme Court rulings have addressed the issue of self-defense. In Beard v. U.S. (1895), the Supreme Court overturned a lower court ruling upholding the conviction of a man, Babe Beard, who killed another by whom he felt threatened while the man was on Beard's property (although not in his house). In this instance, the high court decision rejected the notion that Beard had a duty to retreat from his own property. In Allen v. U.S. (1896), the Supreme Court concluded that a man attacked by another could defend himself lawfully, even to the extent of killing the other person, if he felt in danger of losing his life or suffering serious bodily harm "provided he use all the means in his power otherwise to save his own life or prevent the intended harm, such as retreating as far as he can. . . ." In 1921, the Supreme Court again took up a self-defense case in Brown v. U.S. In a decision written by Justice Oliver Wendell Holmes, the court overturned the conviction of a man who had killed another in a public place with whom he had had a longstanding feud. The trial judge had instructed the jury that the man had a duty to retreat before killing his assailant, and so convicted him. Appeals courts upheld the verdict.

In his opinion, Justice Holmes noted that "the failure to retreat is a circumstance to be considered with all the others" in order to reach a verdict. But, he continued, "Many respectable writers agree that if a man reasonably believes that he is in immediate danger of death or grievous bodily harm from his assailant he may stand his ground and that if he kills him he has

not exceeded the bounds of lawful self-defense." Unlike the Beard case, Brown was not on his own property, said Holmes, but nevertheless was "at a place where he was called to be, in the discharge of his duty." (Both men were working on the construction site of a federal post office facility.) In application, this ruling applied to the federal government, not the states.

Yet this view was not, and has not been universally embraced. At the start of the twentieth century, only nine states abandoned the safe retreat principle, but even in these nine, individuals making a stand your ground claim had to demonstrate that their actions were reasonable. Another fourteen states required individuals to establish that they faced "imminent" threats in confrontations in public places, and eleven states retained safe retreat. In recent decades, state laws did and do continue to be divided on the stand your ground versus safe retreat views of justifiable self-defense in public places. The Model Penal Code of the American Law Institute emphasizes safe retreat over physical confrontation, although the authors also recognize that more jurisdictions around the country have favored some version of standing one's ground as opposed to safe retreat.

In 2005, however, the direction of stand your ground laws took a turn when Florida adopted a new, beefed-up stand your ground law. It expanded the right of citizens to use deadly force in circumstances where individuals feeling threatened could "stand their ground" in a public place rather than first seek safe retreat, as Florida law had stipulated up to that time. The legislature acted rapidly, despite opposition from police and prosecutors. The law had been advanced by the National Rifle Association, and the effort in Florida was spearheaded by a former NRA president, Marion Hammer. With the subsequent endorsement of the American Legislative Exchange Council (ALEC), a business-funded group that advances conservative legislation on many subjects in the states, by 2012, twenty-six states had adopted similar laws, largely as the result of pressure from the NRA. Of these states, at least ten adopted laws pretty much identical to Florida's.

The significance of such laws was heightened by the spread of the concealed carry handgun movement. Since the 1980s, forty states have adopted laws to make it easier to obtain a permit to carry a concealed firearm. As of 2015, an estimated

11 million citizens had such permits (six states of the 40 require no permits). ALEC withdrew its support for stand your ground laws in 2012, however, after the adverse publicity surrounding the killing of an African American teenager, Trayvon Martin, by a neighborhood watch volunteer, George Zimmerman, in Florida. The case received extensive national publicity; Zimmerman was acquitted of murder, a verdict that provoked outrage among many.

Florida's 2005 law went significantly beyond similar past laws in other states because it gave to a person claiming self-defense "an absolute and irrebuttable presumption that an individual who kills or harms another. . .has acted in self-defense and cannot be prosecuted," according to the state law. Law enforcement must thus presume that an individual making a self-defense claim acted out of reasonable fear, a standard met by nothing more than the individual's claim to such a fear. Those claiming self-defense could also ask for a preliminary hearing to determine whether a criminal trial was justified; the standard at this hearing for dropping charges is lower than that in a criminal trial. In addition to eliminating the requirement that people feeling threatened in public places must first attempt safe retreat, these provisions changed the manner in which Florida's criminal justice system handles such cases. Fewer full police investigations have been conducted, and fewer criminal charges brought. Also, those who are successful in making a stand your ground claim are immunized from civil suits arising from the encounter. An investigation of the effects of the new Florida law found that it was administered in widely varying ways across the state, such that circumstances where persons were found not guilty in some jurisdictions were convicted in other cases involving virtually identical circumstances, and that most of the people who benefited from the law had prior criminal records. Several studies of the effects of these new, heightened stand your ground laws around the country found that they resulted in an increase in deaths and that they failed to suppress crime or produce any other societal benefit.

Further Reading: Andrew F. Branca, *The Law of Self Defense* (Maynard, MA: Andrew F. Branca, 2013); Richard Maxwell Brown, *No Duty to Retreat* (Norman, OK: University of Oklahoma Press, 1994); Robert J. Spitzer, *Guns across America: Reconciling Gun Rules and Rights* (New York: Oxford University Press, 2015)

Staples v. United States (1994)

In *Staples v. United States* (511 U.S. 600, 1994), the U.S. Supreme Court determined whether defendants had to know their actions were criminal (demonstration of *mens rea*) to find them guilty of the prohibited act. In this case, the offense involved a violation of a provision of the National Firearms Act of 1934 [section 5861 (d)], which bans the possession of certain unregistered firearms, including fully automatic weapons (machine guns). Gun rights advocates had a special stake in the outcome of the case because they feared that otherwise law-abiding citizens might be prosecuted for inadvertent violations of federal firearms laws.

Local police and Bureau of Alcohol, Tobacco, and Firearms (ATF) agents, having acquired a search warrant, inspected the home of the defendant, Harold E. Staples III, and discovered an AR-15 assault rifle. This rifle is a civilian, semiautomatic version of the M-16. The M-16 contains a selector switch that allows the operator to switch from semiautomatic to automatic fire. Although the AR-15 and the M-16 have interchangeable parts, the AR-15 has a metal stop on its receiver to prevent fully automatic fire. The metal stop on the defendant's AR-15 had been filed down and a selector switch and other M-16 parts had been installed. Suspecting that the weapon was capable of fully automatic fire, ATF agents arrested Staples for violating 5861 (d). ATF testing confirmed that the AR-15 could fire more than one shot with a single pull of the trigger.

At his district court trial, the defendant testified that he was unaware of the rifle's automatic fire capability, arguing that his ignorance of the firearm's characteristics should shield him from criminal liability for failing to register the weapon. However, the court denied his request to instruct the jury that the government must demonstrate that he knew of the fully automatic capability of the firearm. He was found guilty of failing to register an automatic weapon.

On appeal, the U.S. Supreme Court rejected the government's claim that Congress had not explicitly established criminal intent as a criterion for determining an offense. Justice Clarence Thomas, delivering the opinion for the Court, noted that in public welfare offenses involving especially dangerous objects, such as narcotics or hand grenades, demonstration beyond a reasonable doubt that a defendant has specific knowledge of a statutory prohibition is unnecessary to establish guilt. However, noting that "there is a long tradition of widespread lawful gun ownership by private individuals in this country," the Court declared that firearms in general do not fall into the category of dangerous products. The Court further stated that "even dangerous items can, in some cases, be so commonplace and generally available that we would not consider them to alert individuals to the likelihood of strict regulation." Even though firearms may potentially cause harm, they "can generally be owned in perfect innocence."

The Court noted that to accept the government position that owners of dangerous and regulated items have an obligation to "inquire at their peril into compliance with regulations" would lead to unacceptable results, such as making it a crime to operate an automobile with an inoperative emission control system. The Court argued that in the same way the government's position would impose criminal penalties on individuals whose ignorance of the capabilities of weapons in their possession "make their actions entirely innocent."

In accepting the applicability of *mens rea*, the Court noted the severe penalties associated with violation of 5861 (d), which include a prison sentence of up to 10 years. Where harsh penalties are imposed, it is usually assumed that defendants must know their actions are illegal. While not attempting to define those crimes that require a "mental element," the Court concluded that Congress did not intend to "make outlaws out of gunowners who were wholly ignorant of the offending characteristics of their weapons."

See also: Bureau of Alcohol, Tobacco, Firearms, and Explosives; National Firearms Act of 1934.

Further Reading: *Staples v. United States* (U.S. Supreme Court, Docket No. 92–1441, 1994).

State Firearms Preemption Laws

Responding to the policy enactments of local governments such as Morton Grove, Illinois, which in 1981 passed an ordinance banning handgun possession, gun rights groups lobbied state legislatures to enact firearms preemption laws. Preemption measures establish state control over the issue of gun regulation and forbid local governments from enacting more stringent ordinances. Gun rights supporters considered this issue at least as important as the establishment of

the right to carry concealed weapons. According to pro-gun rights interests, preemption laws prevent a confusing variety of local ordinances throughout a state. Local gun control measures, they argue, place gun owners in a difficult position. While crossing local jurisdiction lines within their state, they may confront widely varying ordinances regarding the right to possess and bear arms. According to the Law Center to Prevent Gun Violence, the fifty states are divided into three categories regarding preemption. First, five states (Connecticut, Hawaii, Massachusetts, New Jersey, and New York) do not have statutes expressly preempting local ordinances dealing with firearms and ammunition. Second, two states (California and Nebraska) have provisions preempting specific aspects of local regulation, but permit broad local regulation of firearms and ammunition. Third, the remaining 43 states severely limit the authority of local governments to regulate firearms and ammunition. With such laws in place, local governing units are prevented from engaging in policy making with regard to firearms restrictions, thus allowing pro-gun interests to concentrate their efforts in state legislatures and the national Congress. At the same time, pro-gun control groups are denied an arena to pursue their agenda.

The decision of the U.S. Court of Appeals for the Seventh Circuit in *Quilici v. Village of Morton Grove* (1982) let stand the local ordinance in Morton Grove, Illinois, banning handguns. The decision supported the argument that local governments are more suited to determine the special circumstances and needs of local citizens. Although generally holding to the conservative position that on many issues local control is preferable, pro-gun rights interests nonetheless argue that measures dealing with the regulation of firearms are more appropriately established at the state rather than the local level. Matters most often subject to local control, pro-gun groups argue, concern real property policies and matters that have minor or no effects on those traveling through a local jurisdiction. On the other hand, local gun regulation measures have potentially serious consequences for gun owners traveling with their weapon.

Associating the preemption issue with concealed carry permits, gun rights advocates hold that local ordinances limiting the right to carry weapons can nullify state-established concealed carry laws. They argue that such ordinances violate the constitutionally protected right to bear arms and the individual right of self-defense. Adding to the difficulty of complying with widely varying ordinances and their legal complexities, supporters of preemption laws argue that a citizen cannot be expected to know all the various ordinances in local jurisdictions across the state, and may not know when he or she has crossed from one jurisdiction to another.

Gun control advocacy groups respond that preemption laws do not allow for variations in local conditions that may require unique responses to the problem of gun violence and that allowing local government freedom of action can lead to innovative solutions to firearm-related violence.

See also: Kennesaw, Georgia; Morton Grove, Illinois; *Quilici v. Village of Morton Grove* (1982).

Further Reading: National Rifle Association, "Firearms Preemption Laws," www.nraila.org/Issues/FactSheets/Read.aspx?id=48; Second Amendment Foundation, "State Firearms Preemption Laws" (Bellevue, WA, n.d.); Law Center to Prevent Gun Violence, "Local Authority to Regulate Firearms," smartgunlaws.org/gun-laws/policy-areasother-laws/local-authority (accessed June 26, 2016).

State v. Boyce (1983)

The Oregon case, *State v. Boyce* (658 P.2d 577, 1983), continued the trend of state courts deciding that the right to keep and bear arms, although protected in the state constitution, is subject to reasonable limitations. The city of Portland, Oregon, had passed an ordinance that prohibited anyone from carrying a loaded weapon in a public place or from driving with such a weapon in an automobile. The ordinance specified that ammunition must be absent from the weapon's chamber, cylinder, clip, or magazine. Michael Boyce, who was found guilty of violating the ordinance, appealed the conviction to the state court of appeals, arguing that the law violated the provision in the Oregon constitution that guaranteed the right to bear arms for self-defense and the defense of the state.

Boyce referred to a 1980 decision (*State v. Kessler*) in which the Oregon State Supreme Court invalidated a state law that prohibited such weapons as switchblades and blackjacks. However, the appeals court refused to accept a direct correspondence between the two cases. While the law nullified by the Oregon Supreme Court forbade the very possession of certain weapons, the law at issue in *Boyce* had a more limited objective—to regulate possession in a restricted manner. The court ruled that such a limitation, if reasonable, could stand the test of constitutional validity.

The court commented that a government at times may pass legislation that affects a right guaranteed by the state or national constitution to assure the public safety, especially if the unlimited enjoyment of the right endangers the public welfare. Government is limited in that such restrictions must not unreasonably circumscribe the right. The court did not deny the right of individuals to protect themselves, a situation that may arise in public places. Individuals who find it necessary to defend themselves in such situations will be restricted in their right to self-defense to the extent that they must load the weapons. However, the court indicated that such an inconvenience is reasonable as a means of safeguarding the general public against possible acts of violence.

See also: State v. Kessler (1980).

Further Reading: Mark A. Siegel, Nancy R. Jacobs, and Carol D. Foster, *Gun Control: Restricting Rights or Protecting People?* (Wylie, TX: Information Plus, 1991); *State v. Boyce*, 658 P.2d 577 (1983).

State v. Kerner (1921)

The 1921 case, *State v. Kerner* (181 N.C. 574, 107 S.E. 222, 1921), involves an appeal by the state of North Carolina to reverse a lower court ruling that, due to the unconstitutionality of a statute prohibiting the carrying of a pistol, whether concealed or not, in public, the defendant was not guilty. The appeals court's decision focused on an interpretation of Article I, section 24 of the North Carolina state constitution, which reads, "The right of the people to keep and bear arms shall not be infringed. . . . Nothing herein contained shall justify the practice of carrying concealed weapons or prevent the legislature from enacting penal statutes against said practice." The court ultimately decided in Kerner's favor, ruling that the statute violated the provisions of the state constitution.

O. W. Kerner had been walking along the street when another individual accosted him. Kerner set down the packages he was carrying, went to his place of business to secure a pistol, and returned to the scene of the altercation with the weapon in open sight. He was arrested and indicted for violating Chapter 317, Public Laws 1919, which prohibited citizens of Forsyth County from carrying concealed weapons and required a permit to carry a weapon openly. Violation of the statute resulted in a misdemeanor charge. The court of original jurisdiction, concluding that the statute violated the constitutional guarantee of the right to bear arms, directed a verdict of not guilty. The state appealed the verdict.

The appeals court made the distinction between the "sacred right" to bear arms, and the "practice of carrying concealed weapons," which could be controlled to prevent assassinations and other "advantages taken by the lawless." The right to bear arms included the right to possess and carry a rifle, musket, shotgun, or pistol. The possession of any weapon in common use at the time the constitution was adopted could not be denied to citizens. However, the court rejected a constitutional right to carry and use more contemporary weapons, such as bombs dropped from a "flying machine," those used in submarines, or lethal gases.

The court concluded that the colonists successfully repulsed the British at Lexington in 1775 because the people had been "accustomed to bear arms." Similarly, the regular use of arms allowed pioneers to repulse Indian attacks and to defend the country at New Orleans during the War of 1812. The court revealed a contemporary interpretation of oppression, not in terms of government action, but the activities of powerful private groups. Corporations employing detectives or private police could intimidate and oppress the people, leaving them "completely at the mercy of these great plutocratic organizations," if they were denied the right to bear arms. Although a country often resorts to disarming the people when the use of force prevails, the court reasoned that the people should have the opportunity to "meet illegal force with legal force" to defend themselves.

The court recognized circumstances in which the right to bear arms could be limited, thus affirming the distinction between regulation and banning. Prohibitions on bearing firearms by those under the influence of alcohol were justified, as was the possession of deadly weapons in particular locations, such as church, polling places, or public assemblies, or to "inspire terror." Such limitations the court considered "mere regulations" unoffensive to the constitutional guarantee. In addition, the legislature could reasonably regulate the length of firearms to prevent their being concealed on the person.

Nonetheless, the basic right of the people to use firearms to protect themselves had to be guaranteed. The court objected especially to the statute at issue because it required citizens to apply to the municipal or superior court to receive permission to carry a firearm off their premises and mandated that a permit be purchased for each weapon. With such restrictions, the peaceful citizen would be at the mercy of the lawless should violent disorder occur. Because Kerner had acted to protect himself and his property, the appeals court ruled that the court of original jurisdiction acted properly when it determined that he was not guilty because the statute violated the state constitution.

See also: Concealed Carry Laws.

Further Reading: Earl R. Kruschke, *The Right to Keep and Bear Arms* (Springfield, IL: Charles C. Thomas, 1885); *State v. Kerner*, 181 N.C. 574, 107 S.E. 222 (1921).

State v. Kessler (1980)

The Court of Appeals of the state of Oregon, in *State v. Kessler* (Or. 614 P.2d 94, 1980), examined the right to bear arms for personal defense and protection of property. The case involved possession of a billy club, not a firearm, but the court's decision that having a club in the home is protected by the Oregon state constitution is relevant to firearms as well.

Randy Kessler had been engaged in an intermittent argument with his apartment manager. At first only verbal, the confrontation intensified into moderate physical violence, such as the defendant kicking the elevator door of the building. When the police came to arrest Kessler, they discovered two billy clubs in his apartment. He was charged with disorderly conduct and "possession of a slugging weapon." The defendant moved to dismiss the charge, arguing that no actual crime had been committed. The court denied the motion and found Kessler guilty as charged on both counts.

The defendant appealed the conviction to the Court of Appeals, asserting first of all that his actions did not constitute disorderly conduct, and second, that the statute under which he was charged for possession of a billy club violated Article I, section 27 of the Oregon state constitution by denying him the right to have a weapon for personal defense in the home. That section states that "The people shall have the right to bear arms for the defence [sic] of themselves, and the State, but the Military shall be kept in strict subordination to the civil power." The Oregon statute prohibited the possession of a "billy," but allowed police officers to carry a billy club, or "blackjack."

The court entered into an analysis of the origins of the state constitutional provision, which can be traced to other state constitutions drafted in the revolutionary war era and shortly thereafter. These state constitutions often included a bill of rights patterned after the English Bill of Rights of 1689. Like that document, the state constitutions guaranteed the right to bear arms and betrayed a general suspicion of standing armies, especially in peacetime. The court traced the right contained in the state constitution of Oregon directly to the Indiana constitution adopted in 1816, and determined that the phrase "for defence of themselves, and the State" probably derived from either the Kentucky constitution of 1799 or the Ohio constitution of 1802. This wording also appeared in the constitutions of Oregon and seven other states. The identical language notwithstanding, differing interpretations of its significance developed. The phrase was placed in these constitutions either to indicate a preference for a militia over a standing army, to provide for a curb on government abuse of authority, or to guarantee the right of personal defense.

The court noted that historically, the right to bear arms for personal defense and protection of property gained special significance in the United States due to the uncertainties of rural life in early America. The term "arms," the court argued, came to refer in state constitutions to all those objects that settlers used for personal as well as military defense, including guns, hatchets, swords, and knifes. The court concluded that more advanced weapons used in modern warfare were intended exclusively for military use and therefore their personal possession could not be justified as protected under the constitutional right of the individual to bear arms for purposes of self-defense. Therefore, although the legislature could limit the right to carry a concealed club in public, it could not institute a blanket prohibition on keeping a club in the home.

See also: Concealed Carry Laws.

Further Reading: Earl R. Kruschke, *The Right to Keep and Bear Arms* (Springfield, IL: Charles C. Thomas, 1985); *State v. Kessler*, Or. 614 P.2d 94 (1980).

State v. Rosenthal (1903)

In *State v. Rosenthal* (75 Vt. 295, 55 A. 610, 1903), the Appeals Court of Vermont heard the claim that the Rutland city ordinance that forbade the carrying within city limits of "any steel or brass knuckles, pistol, slung shot, stiletto, or weapon of similar character," or a concealed weapon, except with the permission of the mayor or chief of police, violated the state constitution that guaranteed the right to bear arms. The court ruled in favor of Andrew Rosenthal, stating that individuals have the right, under the state constitution, to bear arms for their defense.

Rosenthal was charged with carrying a loaded and concealed pistol within the city limits in violation of the city ordinance. The defendant argued that the statute under which he was charged, by forbidding the carrying of a pistol, was in violation of the state constitutional provision granting to the people of the state the right to bear arms for self-defense and defense of the state. The court determined that the city council had not been delegated the clear right to enact the restrictive ordinance, especially given the constitutional guarantee of the right of the people to bear arms.

The court placed prime importance on the intent involved in carrying a firearm. It pointed to a state statute prohibiting the carrying of a deadly weapon, whether in the open or concealed, with the *intention* of harming another person. A further provision banned the carrying of a deadly weapon while the person was "in attendance upon a school," and another section of state law penalized the intentional pointing of a firearm toward another individual, or the firing of a weapon toward another person, whether or not injury resulted. However, these limitations did not apply when firearms were used for self-defense or carried by an officer of the law in the conduct of his duty, or in the case of justifiable homicide. Therefore, an individual not associated with a school may bear a firearm, whether in the open or concealed, unless the *intent* of the bearer is to injure another person.

Relying on precedent, the court noted that a land owner could rightfully defend himself against assault from a trespasser, and therefore could employ reasonable force in deterring the trespasser.

If the land owner intended to employ a pistol solely for self-defense, then bearing the firearm should be judged lawful. In contrast, the city ordinance of Rutland forbade the carrying of a weapon for any purpose prior to acquiring permission in writing from the mayor or police chief and therefore the ordinance did not take into consideration the essential importance of the firearm bearer's intentions when determining whether an offense had occurred. Conversely, if a person acquired permission to carry a weapon, then even though the intent of carrying a weapon was to injure another person, there would be no violation of the ordinance. The ordinance prohibited the carrying of a weapon when the constitution and the laws of the state regarded such carrying as legal, but at the same time allowed the bearing of weapons when the general laws of the state considered it a crime. Therefore, the court determined that the city ordinance was contrary to the constitution and laws of the state.

See also: Concealed Carry Laws.

Further Reading: Earl R. Kruschke, *The Right to Keep and Bear Arms* (Springfield, IL: Charles C. Thomas, 1985); *State v. Rosenthal*, 75 Vt. 295, 55 A. 610 (1903).

Stevens v. United States (1971)

In *Stevens v. United States,* 440 F.2d 144, 149 (1971), the United States Court of Appeals for the Sixth Circuit upheld a provision of the Gun Control Act of 1968 [18 U.S.C. App. Section 1202 (a) (1)] that prohibits convicted felons from receiving, possessing, or transporting a firearm. In presenting its decision, the Appeals Court expressly rejected an individualist interpretation of the Second Amendment. The relevant portion of the statute states that "Any person who has been convicted by a court of the United States or of a State or any political subdivision thereof of a felony . . . and who receives, possesses, or transports in commerce or affecting commerce, after the date of enactment of this Act, any firearm shall be fined not more than $10,000 or imprisoned for not more than two years, or both."

Frank James Stevens appealed his conviction for violating this provision. In 1958, a Kentucky court found him guilty of armed assault with intent to rob, and in 1962 he was found guilty of voluntary manslaughter. Following passage of the Gun Control Act of 1968, Stevens was charged with possessing a 9-mm. Astra semiautomatic pistol. Not denying any of the facts in the prosecution's charge against him, Stevens argued that the conviction should be dismissed because the indictment did not assert, and the evidence did not demonstrate, that his possession of a firearm was "in commerce or affecting commerce." The appellant argued that the phrase "in commerce or affecting commerce" modified all three actions, "receives," "possesses," and "transports," while the government contended that the phrase applies only to "transports." The court's ruling that Stevens's position lacked credibility depended on the absence of a comma in the statute after the word "transports."

Independent of congressional intent, the appellant's argument could prevail only with a comma in place, which would indicate that the commerce phrase modified all three activities.

Recognizing Congress's determination that convicted felons who possess firearms pose a threat to interstate commerce, the court concluded that Congress has the constitutional authority to prohibit such possession. Congress reasonably considered the rate of recidivism and crimes such as bank robbery that impede commerce as relevant considerations in establishing the prohibition of gun ownership by felons. Stevens, twice convicted of a felony before being discovered in possession of a firearm, belonged to the class of individuals that Congress intended to deny the right to possess firearms. Although an individual case may appear to affect commerce remotely, the court declared that Congress need not wait until commerce has been severely interrupted before taking protective action.

While Stevens claimed that Congress had no authority under the Constitution to deny him the right of possessing a firearm, the court argued that the Second Amendment right to keep and bear arms refers to a state prerogative to maintain a militia, not to an individual right to bear arms. The court declared that no serious claim could be made that individuals have an explicit constitutional right to possess firearms and concluded that Congress has the authority, under the commerce clause of the Constitution, to limit firearms possession. The U.S. Supreme Court ruling in *District of Columbia v. Heller* (2008) ultimately controverted this appeals court interpretation of the Second Amendment by deciding that the amendment recognizes an individual right to keep and bear arms.

See also: Gun Control Act of 1968; Second Amendment.

Further Reading: *Stevens v. United States*, 440 F.2d 144, 149 (1971).

Stockton, California, Shooting

The Stockton, California, shooting at an elementary school, in which several children were killed and wounded, sparked a fresh surge toward gun control legislation that resulted in the passage of measures to limit the purchase and possession of assault rifles. On January 17, 1989, Patrick Purdy entered the schoolyard carrying a Chinese-made AK-47. Purdy was a drifter who had lived in Stockton, California, during his youth and had attended the school. He began shooting at the mostly Cambodian, Vietnamese, Chinese, and Hispanic children, killing five girls and wounding 29 others. Police estimated the shooter fired over 106 rounds in a matter of a few minutes. Purdy then took his own life with a pistol.

The previous August, Purdy had purchased the AK-47 from a gun dealer in Sandy, Oregon, for $349.95. At that time, only three states—Hawaii, Illinois, and Pennsylvania—required a waiting period to purchase a rifle or a shotgun. Purdy gave a false name on a federal form necessary for the purchase, which required each gun purchaser to state that he or she is not a convicted criminal, under indictment, a drug addict, or mentally ill. At that time, the federal government required no background check or waiting period to verify the information the purchaser had given. The dealer had to inform the Bureau of Alcohol, Tobacco, and Firearms (ATF) of the sale, and provide a description and serial number of the weapon and the type of identification presented at the time of purchase. Nonetheless, the purchaser's name was not provided to the ATF. An assault weapon containing a high-capacity ammunition magazine could be purchased as easily as a rifle or a shotgun. Following the Stockton shooting, supporters of more stringent gun control legislation moved quickly to enact measures to ban assault weapons. Within two weeks of the Stockton tragedy, bills were introduced into the California legislature to ban the manufacture, sale, and possession of various rifles and pistols. Senator Howard Metzenbaum, Democrat from

Ohio, introduced similar legislation in Congress. Twenty-seven additional states were considering a variety of measures to limit or ban assault weapons. Ironically, the general call for a ban led to significantly increased sales of AK-47s, presumably fueled by gun enthusiasts who wished to beat the deadline for the beginning of the prohibition.

Amid the overall momentum for new legislation, opponents of any ban argued that an attempt to prohibit particular weapons would not achieve its objective. They recommended instead that sentences for using firearms in a crime be increased and enforcement of bans on the ownership of guns by convicted criminals and the mentally unstable be tightened. Don B. Kates, a major opponent of gun control legislation, attempted to focus the debate on the more basic causes of violence in our society: socioeconomic and cultural factors such as poverty and broken families. He claimed that guns by themselves did not affect the crime rate, and to institute a general gun ban only succeeded in taking firearms away from "good citizens" who would not misuse the weapons and who needed the guns for their own protection.

Despite opposition from pro-gun rights groups, within a month of the school shooting the city councils of Stockton and Los Angeles had approved bans on the sale or possession of semiautomatic weapons equipped with a detachable magazine that could hold at least 20 rounds. The measures, which also banned sawed-off shotguns holding at least six shells, made any violation a misdemeanor punishable by six months in prison and a maximum fine of $1,000. The Los Angeles City Council approved an ordinance on February 7 by a unanimous vote and Mayor Tom Bradley signed the measure that same day.

Beginning February 10, 1989, Senator Metzenbaum held hearings on banning a number of assault weapons, at which a teacher at the Stockton school described the shooting in vivid detail. Although progress toward a ban did not proceed as quickly on the national level, public outrage at the shooting led steadily toward limitations on assault weapons. Even former Republican President Ronald Reagan, who had strongly opposed gun control, expressed his cautious support for a ban on assault weapons.

The Stockton shooting for a time put gun rights groups at a disadvantage in the struggle over gun control. Arguments about the defensive advantages of firearms and the underlying causes of gun violence in the United States did not sway the public away from the perception that a horrible person had killed and injured many children, and the instrument he used with frightening efficiency was an assault weapon.

See also: AK-47; Assault Weapons Ban; Bureau of Alcohol, Tobacco, Firearms, and Explosives; Kates, Don B.; Reagan, Ronald; Roberti-Roos Assault Weapons Act.

Further Reading: Wilbur Edel, *Gun Control: Threat to Liberty or Defense Against Anarchy?* (Westport, CT: Praeger, 1995); Don B. Kates, "The Hopelessness of Trying to Disarm the Kinds of People Who Murder," *Bridges* (Fall/Winter 2005), 313–330; *New York Times*, January 19, 1989, B6; January 28, 1989, 1; February 4, 27; March 3, 20.

Stop Handgun Violence (SHV)

Stop Handgun Violence (SHV) was established in 1995 by businessmen and women concerned about the high number of firearms-related deaths in the United States. The founders were especially alarmed that children were the victims of firearm violence. Troubled by several school shootings in 1997 and 1998, SHV called for greater efforts to reduce the access youth have to firearms. Headquartered in Newton, Massachusetts, SHV has participated in public awareness campaigns, educational programs, and community outreach to inform the public about the dangers of firearms. To finance media presentations, the organization has conducted fund-raising events, such as benefit concerts, educational house parties, and t-shirt sales, and appeals for donations on the organization's Web site.

SHV focuses its public awareness campaigns on highly emotional individual cases of firearms-related deaths, especially among young people. As its first project, the organization constructed a large "tribute wall" facing the Massachusetts Turnpike. Motorists could read the message, "The cost of handguns keeps going up. Fifteen kids killed every day." The pictures of 15 children under age 19 appeared below the message. The organization claims that in the twenty years since the billboard was installed, the number of gun-related deaths in Massachusetts declined from 309 in 1994 to 213 in 2013.

After twenty years, SHV announced that the billboard would be removed because the land on which it was constructed had been sold. Until a new location could be acquired, the organization planned to construct more than two dozen smaller digital billboards would be constructed, which contain the message, "We're No Anti-Gun. We're Pro-Life. Massachusetts Gun Laws Save Lives." Believing that the use of trigger locks is an important step in preventing firearms accidents, especially those involving children, organization members have worked to establish community-based trigger lock distribution programs. Such programs have been conducted in Massachusetts cities as well as in New Hampshire, Maine, and Miami, Florida. Another project has involved the development of a school curriculum geared to prevent firearm accidents among young people.

SHV worked with Massachusetts state legislators to pass a gun safety bill that became law in July 1998. The law is considered the most comprehensive gun control legislation in the country. SHV states that it has supported mandated gun safety training and child access prevention, background checks for private gun sales, consumer protection guidelines for firearms sold in Massachusetts, and a ban on the sale of assault weapons and large capacity ammunition magazines (more than ten rounds). The organization reports that since 1994, gun injuries and gun accidents in Massachusetts have declined by 50 percent and 56 percent, respectively. SHV hopes to expand its agenda to the national level, advocating firearms training, gun licensing, and registration.

The organization is a strong advocate of the regulation of firearms by the Consumer Product Safety Commission in the same manner in which Massachusetts has come to regulate guns as consumer products. The organization supports one-gun-a-month legislation that would limit an individual to purchasing just one handgun in a 30-day period, and advocates the application of personalization (smart gun) technology to firearms so that only the intended user may fire a gun.

In January 2016 SHV co-founder John Rosenthal attended President Barack Obama's announcement at the White House that his administration would expand background checks to apply to more private gun dealers, add FBI and ATF agents to perform background checks, and use federal gun purchases to influence the way in which the firearm industry conducts business.

See also: Accidents Involving Guns; Assault Weapons Ban; Jonesboro, Arkansas, School Shooting; Littleton, Colorado, Columbine School Shooting; Schools and Guns; Trigger Lock; Youth and Guns.

Further Reading: Stop Handgun Violence, Inc., Web site, www.stophandgunviolence.org; "Major Accomplishments" (SHV, 1998); "National Solutions to Gun Violence" (SHV, 1998).

Straw Purchases

Although the Brady Handgun Violence Prevention Act, which took effect in 1994, established at first a five-day waiting period to conduct background checks on prospective purchasers of firearms, and subsequently a computerized instant check system that could clear a person within minutes, or at most within 72 hours, those not qualified to purchase a gun might use a "straw purchaser" to obtain the weapon. A straw purchaser is a person who buys a firearm for someone who is not qualified to do so, such as a convicted felon or a juvenile. The National Shooting Sports Foundation (NSSF) states that a straw purchase occurs "when a buyer uses an intermediary (the 'straw man') to purchase a firearm(s) from a licensed firearms dealer. The purpose is to hide the true identity of the actual purchaser of the firearm(s). Straw purchases are a felony violation of the Gun Control Act of 1968 for both the straw purchaser (who can be charged with lying on Federal Form 4473) and the actual possessor. Frequently, the actual purchaser is a prohibited person under federal law." One question on Form 4473 asks if the person completing the form is the actual buyer of the firearm, and the form further cautions that if the person is not the actual buyer, the dealer cannot transfer the firearm to that person. It is a violation of the law when a straw purchaser responds "yes" to the question.

In 2008 Mayors Against Illegal Guns (MAIL) issued a report on straw purchases titled *Inside Straw Purchasing*, which was based on research conducted by the James Mintz Group. Interviews were conducted with licensed firearms dealers and those who have made straw purchases. The report notes that gun traffickers often choose someone they already know, such as a relative or a girlfriend, to make the purchase. Those making straw purchases receive anywhere from $20 to $100 per gun. From an examination of more than 1,000

gun-related prosecutions the report concluded that in 60 percent of straw purchases, the straw purchaser and the actual purchaser entered the store together. Often the actual purchaser indicated to the straw purchaser which firearm to purchase, and money exchanged hands in the store. Frequently the trafficker has the straw purchaser buy less expensive guns because the profit from resales is higher.

There is evidence that some gun dealers know when a straw purchase is being made, but, undoubtedly considering the profit to be made, continue with the sale. When some gun store employees were interviewed for the MAIL study, they reported having attempted to stop straw purchases, but were overruled by the store manager. Other interviews revealed that gun dealers sometimes assisted customers with a straw purchase. However, the report noted that many gun stores recognize a straw purchaser and refuse to complete the sale. The signs of a straw purchase include a man selecting a gun that a woman then tries to purchase; two people in the store exchanging money for the purchase; payment being made in cash, and with small bills (possibly from drug sales); and people making a purchase who appear intoxicated.

The NSSF, in cooperation with the Bureau of Alcohol, Tobacco, Firearms, and Explosives (ATF), developed a training program for licensed firearms dealers titled "Don't Lie for the Other Guy." The ATF distributes copies of the Federal Firearms Regulations Reference Guide to licensed dealers and gun show promoters, and provides a supplemental online guide.

Advocates for strengthening the National Instant Criminal Background Check System (NICS) support making a straw purchase a separate crime punishable by imprisonment. Presently a straw purchaser is only guilty of making a false statement on Form 4473.

See also: Bureau of Alcohol, Tobacco, Firearms, and Explosives; National Shooting Sports Foundation; United States-Mexico Illegal Gun Trade.

Further Reading: Bureau of Alcohol, Tobacco, Firearms and Explosives, "Federal Firearms Regulations Reference Guide Learning Theater," www.atf.gov/training/firearms/ffl-learning-theater (accessed November 8, 2010); Mayors Against Illegal Guns, *Inside Straw Purchasing* (April 2008), www.mayorsagainstillegalguns.org/dounloads/ pdf/ inside-straw-purchases.pdf; National Shooting Sports Foundation, "Straw Purchase," www.nssf.org/ newsroom/factsheets/straw-purchase.cfm (accessed November 8, 2010).

Student Pledge Against Gun Violence

The Student Pledge Against Gun Violence, coordinated by Mary Lewis Grow (who also is a board member of Citizens for a Safer Minnesota) and headquartered in Northfield, Minnesota, involves a campaign to have students pledge not to use firearms in anger. The Student Pledge states, "I will never bring a gun to school; I will never use a gun to settle a dispute; and I will use my influence with my friends to keep them from using guns to settle disputes. My individual choices and actions, when multiplied by those of young people throughout the country, will make a difference. Together, by honoring this pledge, we can reverse the violence and grow up in safety." Each fall since 1996 the pledge movement has sponsored a Day of National Concern about Young People and Gun Violence that reaches students around the country.

In 1996, Grow originated the idea of the Student Pledge and the Day of National Concern during a meeting with Bill Bradley, Democratic senator from New Jersey. Bradley introduced a Senate resolution calling for a Day of National Concern and the national distribution of the Student Pledge. In 1997, Senators Patty Murray, Democrat from Washington, and Dirk Kempthorne, Republican from Idaho, in a demonstration of bipartisan support for the Day of National Concern, sponsored a similar resolution. Each year the resolution passed by unanimous consent. On November 6, 1997, President Bill Clinton issued a proclamation calling for the observance of that day as one of concern for young people.

Various groups, including the American Federation of Teachers, the National School Boards Association, the National Parent Teachers Association, the American Academy of Pediatrics, and the U.S. Attorneys Network have endorsed the Student Pledge. For the 1998 Day of National Concern, various organizations cooperated in publicizing the event. The United Way of America sent packets to 600 chapters, the National Education Association distributed materials to its local organizations, and the American Federation

of Teachers reported on the Student Pledge in its newsletter. Several cities, including New York, Philadelphia, Boston, Chicago, and Washington, D.C., distributed Pledge materials to local schools. Programs in various states emphasized the dangers of firearms to youth, often presenting personal accounts of firearms violence.

Organizers of the Student Pledge campaign encourage parents, community groups, and religious organization to take part in the National Davy of Concern. Teachers are asked to initiate special activities, such as art projects and writing assignments. Social studies teachers are encouraged to invite an emergency room physician to speak to students at an all-school assembly about the special problems involved in treating gunshot wounds. Other suggested speakers included the police chief, a respected athlete, and elected officials, or a community leader. Another suggestion is to ask someone who has lost a relative to gun violence, or a survivor of a gunshot wound, to speak to students. The organizers recommend the use of children's books to convey the message that carrying firearms is dangerous. In the context of several highly publicized school shootings, many prominent pubic officials agreed to take part in encouraging young people to sign the Student Pledge.

In February 2015, Grow wrote an opinion piece for the *New York* Times in which she urged an expansion of the category of person prohibited from purchasing a firearm to include those on the terrorist (no fly) watch list. Grow states that since the Pledge began in 1996, "more than 10 million young people nationwide have participated in the program." The twenty-first annual Day of Concern was held on October 19, 2016.

See also: Clinton, William Jefferson (Bill); Handgun Control, Inc.; Mothers Against Violence in America; National Education Association; Physicians for Social Responsibility.

Further Reading: Mary Lewis Grow, "Security Alert: Gun Show Loopholes," *Minneapolis-St. Paul Star Tribune* (January 24, 2010), www.startribune.com/ opinion/commentary/82443812.html; Student Pledge Against Gun Violence Web site, www.pledge.org.

Sugarmann, Josh (1960–)

For many years, Josh Sugarmann, executive director of the Violence Policy Center (VPC), has been a vocal critic of the National Rifle Association (NRA), firearms manufacturers and dealers, and the gun rights movement generally. Sugarmann served as a press officer for Amnesty International USA and communications director for the National Coalition to Ban Handguns before establishing the VPC. He writes a column about firearms issues for the *Huffington Post*, an online newspaper. Sugarmann's presence in the news media and his aggressive style have made him a well-known figure on all sides of the gun control and gun rights debate. In 1992, Sugarmann published *National Rifle Association: Money, Firepower, and Fear*, in which he examined the development of the NRA from its founding in 1871 as an organization promoting marksmanship to its development in the twentieth century into a highly influential national interest group. He focused not only on the political maneuvering of the organization, but also on the internal strife of the 1970s that brought to prominence staunch supporters of an absolutist understanding of the Second Amendment.

In 2002 Sugarmann published *Every Handgun Is Aimed at You: The Case for Banning Handguns*, in which he argues for his long-held position that handguns are a major threat to the health and welfare of the nation. Sugarmann argues that more moderate policies, such as licensing gun owners, registering guns, and introducing additional safety features such as trigger locks—often referred to by other organizations concerned about gun violence as "reasonable" or "common sense" measures—will not lead to the desired reduction in the number of people killed and injured by firearms each year. The key to reducing firearm-related violence, Sugarmann argues, is the elimination of handguns, which, according to the data he presents, are responsible for the majority of firearm-related deaths and injuries each year. His argument that such a policy would face no valid constitutional challenge came to naught when, six years after Sugarman's book was published, the U.S. Supreme Court in *District of Columbia v. Heller* (2008) ruled that the Second Amendment guarantees the right of individuals to possess firearms in the home, and especially handguns, for self-defense.

Following the subsequent Supreme Court decision in *McDonald v. Chicago* (2010), in which the Court invalidated a Chicago restriction on the ownership of firearms, Sugarmann commented that the winners in the decision were the gun lobby and gun manufacturers, and the losers were "America's communities and the victims of gun violence."

He predicted that the decision would result in "an inevitable tide of frivolous pro-gun litigation" that would force state and local governments to "expend scarce resources to defend long-standing, effective public safety laws." Sugarmann also has been a vocal critic of the policy change that allows the carrying of firearms in national parks, a change he attributes to National Rifle Association lobbying.

In other commentary on firearms, Sugarmann has used data from various sources to indicate the dangers of firearms. For instance, in arguing that firearms are more a threat to women than a means of self-defense, he presents data from the Federal Bureau of Investigation's (FBI) Supplementary Homicide Report to highlight the number of women killed by men (1,817 in 2008). Sugarmann notes that in those cases in which the type of weapon was determined (1,662), 52 percent involved firearms, and 71 percent of the firearms homicides involved handguns. He concludes that "Guns can easily turn domestic violence into domestic homicide." Sugarmann also targets state concealed carry laws, pointing out that from May 2007 to July 2010, "concealed carry holders have killed at least 175 individuals—including nine law enforcement officers—in 26 states."

Although Sugarmann uses the interpretation of crime data to demonstrate his position on the dangers of firearms, in his arguments against gun rights groups and firearms manufacturers, he often cites the motives of self-interest, profit, and political influence to explain the strong pro-gun rights position. While the National Rifle Association and other gun rights groups claim that Sugarmann's more extreme gun control advocacy actually represents the true agenda of those who advocate more moderate measures, in response, Sugarmann portrays the National Rifle Association as a right-wing organization that ultimately offers encouragement to extremist groups.

Sugarmann has commented that as the number of mass shootings (defined as an incident in which a gunman kills at least three victims) has remained high, firearms rarely used in defense against criminals. For instance, he cites the 2013 study by the Violence Policy Center, using data from the Federal Bureau of Investigation (FBI) Uniform Crime Reporting (UCR) Program's Supplementary Homicide Report (SHR) and data from the Bureau of Justice Statistics National Crime Victimization Survey (NCVS) that identified just 211 justifiable homicides involving a private citizen. According to the study, from 2012 to 2014, "less than one percent of victims of attempted or completed violent crimes used a firearm, and only 0.2 percent of victims of attempted or completed property crimes used a firearm."

Sugarmann criticizes the firearm industry and the NRA for encouraging adults to familiarize children with firearms. He argues that tragic results happen too often when children as young as five or six are granted access to firearms. Sugarmann has also reported that black men and women are at greater risk of being victims of gun violence. He cites a Violence Policy Center study, which reported that although African Americans compose 13 percent of the population, 50 percent of homicide victims are black.

See also: Concealed Carry Laws; *District of Columbia v. Heller* (2008); National Rifle Association; Trigger Locks; Violence Policy Center.

Further Reading: Josh Sugarmann, "Coming Soon to a National Park Near You: Guns, Guns, Guns!" *Huffington Post* (February 11, 2010), www. huffingtonpost.com; Sugarmann, "McDonald Gun Case: More Deaths, Unending Litigation," *Huffington Post* (June 28, 2010); Sugarmann, "Murders by Concealed Handgun Permit Holders: 52 Convictions or Suicides and Counting," *Huffington Post* (July 1, 2010); Sugarmann, "Top Ten Most Murderous States for Women Killed by Men," *Huffington Post* (October 26, 2010); Violence Policy Center, "National Rifle Association—Embracing Tea Partiers and Anti-Government Rhetoric—Meets in Charlotte, NC"; Josh Sugarmann, "Why Does the Gun Lobby Encourage Small Children to Handle Guns?" Huffington Post (March 11, 2016), huffingtonpost.com/josh-sugarmann/why-does-the-gun-lobby-en_b_9440156. html; Josh Sugarmann, "The Gun Violence Epidemic Impacts Black Americans the Most," Huffington Post (March 24, 2016), huffingtonpost.com/josh-sugarmann/the-gun-violence-epidemic_b_9540258/ html; Josh Sugarmann, "Guns Are Rarely Use in Self-Defense," Huffington Post (April 26, 2016), huffingtonpost.com/josh-sugarmann/guns-are-rarely-used-in-s_b_9774008.html.

Suicide

Pro-gun control groups have pointed to the prevalence of suicide involving guns as a reason for further legislation limiting the availability of firearms. Data indicate that guns are more frequently involved in suicides than in homicides. Evidence is also marshaled to demonstrate that gun suicide attempts are successful more often than other common methods of self-destruction, such as hanging, carbon monoxide poisoning, and drowning. The argument over gun control and suicide revolves around the interpretation of often inadequate statistical research and the attempt to determine whether gun availability itself contributes to a higher suicide rate. For instance, gun rights supporters argue that individuals are not more prone to suicide simply because they possess firearms. However, David Hemenway has cited research indicating a statistically significant relationship between the availability of firearms in the home and adolescent suicides. Hemenway also notes that those areas in the United States where gun ownership is higher have higher rates of suicide.

Researchers disagree about whether stricter legislation would result in fewer suicides (or fewer successful attempts) overall. If guns were not as readily available, would other methods simply be substituted? Gun control opponents argue that prospective suicides have a number of means available to them and therefore the unavailability of guns would not affect the total number of people who commit suicide. Therefore, while limiting gun availability might reduce the number of suicides in that category, the overall suicide rate would remain largely unchanged. As Gary Kleck has commented, "Few people would argue . . . that it is a worthwhile goal of public policy merely to shift suicides from one method to another, without producing any net reduction in the total number of suicides." Much depends on the actual availability of other methods, the preferences for a method by those making the attempt (some might be committed to one method and would not initiate the act if it were not available), and the seriousness of intent. Perhaps those using less lethal methods do so because their resolve is less certain than those using firearms. Therefore, if guns were less available, the resolve of those who would otherwise choose this method would lead them to use equally lethal means.

Suicide among young people is an especially troubling problem. While the suicide rate for all age groups increased slightly from 1950 to 1980, the rate for adolescents tripled. Suicide has become the third most common cause of death among children and the second most common cause among older teenagers. In *The Politics of Gun Control* (2015), Robert Spitzer cited a study of adolescent suicide in Chicago that reported large numbers of suicides among the children of law enforcement officers. Although the availability of guns may have only a modest effect on the overall suicide rate, there is evidence that such availability may have a far greater impact on the adolescent suicide rate.

By 2014, the overall suicide rate in the United States had reached the highest rate in almost 30 years. In 2014, 42,773 people died from suicide. According to a National Institutes of Health study, the percentage of suicides committed with a gun fell in the period 1999 to 2014, from 37 percent to 31 percent for women, and from 62 percent to 55 percent for men. Although the suicide rates for men and women has narrowed, men still commit suicide at a rate 3.6 times greater than women. Of all the gun-related deaths each year, about two-thirds (20,000) are suicides, and approximately 85 percent of suicide attempts with a firearm are successful. Attempts using drug overdoses are successful less than 3 percent of the time. About half of the suicides in 2013 involved the use of a gun. In order to reduce the rate of successful suicides among youth, many have recommended that gun owners secure their weapons in safes or lock boxes in order to prevent youth access. State licensing laws for firearms may also deter the impulsive purchase of guns by those contemplating suicide.

See also: Kleck, Gary; Youth and Guns.

Further Reading: Gregg Lee Carter, *The Gun Control Movement* (New York: Twayne, 1997); David Hemenway, *Private Guns, Public Health* (Ann Arbor, Michigan: University of Michigan Press, 2004); Gary Kleck, *Point Blank: Guns and Violence in America* (New York: Aldine de Gruyter, 1991); Robert J. Spitzer, *The Politics of Gun Control*, 6th ed. (Boulder, CO: Paradigm, 2015); Elizabeth P. Aronson and Maxwell T. Smith, "Guns, Suicide, and Suicide Prevention," in Glenn H. Utter, ed., *Guns and Contemporary Society* (Santa Barbara, CA: Praeger, 2016): vol. 2, 145-184; Sabrina Tavernise, "Sweeping Pain As Suicides Hit a 30-Year High," *New York Times* (April 22, 2016): A1.

Sullivan Law

In 1911, the New York State legislature, responding to a popular outcry against street violence in New York City, passed the Sullivan Dangerous Weapons Law (named after Timothy Sullivan, a senator in the New York state legislature), the most stringent gun control legislation up to that time. For 50 years, the law stood as the model for such legislation. It required individuals to acquire a license to possess or carry a concealable weapon and made it a felony to carry a firearm small enough to be concealed on the person. Because the law contained a provision making it illegal for aliens to possess firearms "in any public place," opponents of gun control legislation have pointed to the Sullivan law as an example of the ulterior motives behind, and hence the illegitimacy of, such measures.

Although the 1911 law applied to the entire state of New York, state legislators had New York City in mind when passing the measure. In the1870s, New York City politicians first began to consider proposals to regulate the carrying of concealed handguns. The responses of many resemble more recent opposition to gun control: only law-abiding citizens would be affected, thus decreasing their ability to defend themselves against criminals. Although the Board of Aldermen approved an ordinance in 1877 that required a permit to carry a concealed weapon, it was not effectively enforced. The Board of Aldermen approved another concealed weapons ordinance in 1905 that raised the penalties for violations.

As in more recent years, many shocking newspaper accounts of firearms violence moved New York politicians toward further legislation. In 1910, a disgruntled former public employee shot and seriously wounded Mayor William J. Gaynor. Newspapers covered the mayor's long recovery and frequently printed articles dealing with gun violence. Notable city residents formed a citizens committee that called for stronger legislation. As gun violence gained increasing public visibility, politicians were drawn to the issue. Timothy D. "Big Tim" Sullivan, a Tammany politician recently elected to the state senate, promised to introduce a bill to regulate the purchase, possession, and carrying of concealed weapons. In January 1911, after David Graham Phillips, a popular novelist, was shot and killed on a New York City sidewalk, the concern for concealed weapons increased considerably. A report issued shortly thereafter indicating that gun homicides had risen nearly 50 percent in the previous year gave legislators further incentive to act.

When the state senate held hearings, the only people who spoke against the new legislation were hardware merchants from New York City and lobbyists representing small arms manufacturing firms. The overwhelming sentiment was in favor of passing a more restrictive measure. New York City's judges, police officials, and magistrates almost without exception supported passage. A mood of optimism regarding the possible beneficial results of new legislation pervaded the legislature and New York newspapers. Sullivan declared, "If this bill passes, it will do more to carry out the commandment thou shalt not kill and save more souls than all the talk of all the ministers and priests in the state for the next ten years." With virtually no organized opposition, the bill passed by overwhelming majorities in both houses of the state legislature.

Among its provisions, the legislation made carrying an unlicensed firearm a felony, mandated a permit to possess a concealable firearm, and required that pistols be sold only to those who presented a permit for possessing or carrying a weapon. Anyone selling a firearm was required to keep records of sales, identifying the purchaser by name, age, occupation, and residence, and reporting the caliber, make, model, and manufacturer's number of the firearm. The law made a misdemeanor of the sale, loan, lease, or gift to a person under 16 years old of any firearm, air gun, or spring gun. Any unlawful weapons seized were to be destroyed or made useless by the chief law enforcement officer of the jurisdiction. The law applied to other weapons, making it a misdemeanor to make or have made, or sell or give "a blackjack, bludgeon, sandbag, sandclub, billy, sl[i]ngshot, metal knuckles, etc. to any other person."

The expectation that the new legislation would certainly reduce the number of homicides appeared to be substantiated by initial reports. The Coroner's Report for 1912 indicated that the number of firearm suicides had declined by 40 percent compared with the previous year. However, the number of homicides actually increased from 1910 to 1912, suggesting the difficulty that has existed ever since in attempting to interpret data regarding the effects of gun control legislation.

After the initial euphoria had subsided, objections began to arise. The National Rifle Association (NRA) complained that the law made it difficult for an "honest man" and "good citizen" to acquire a pistol. Many questioned the Sullivan Law's constitutionality, but it survived court challenges. The law is still in effect, despite many attempts at repeal. It has been amended many times, but the fundamental purpose has remained constant. Many claim that the law has done little to reduce crime in New York City, while others argue that the crime rate would have been even higher without it. Some note that New York residents have found it easy to transport guns from other jurisdictions with more lenient gun regulations and therefore advocate more stringent national legislation. Following the U.S. Supreme Court decisions in *District of Columbia v. Heller* (2008) and *McDonald v. Chicago* (2010), speculation arose about the possible fate of the Sullivan Law in the courts.

See also: Concealed Carry Laws; *Districtof Columbia v. Heller* (2008); *McDonald v. Chicago* (2010); National Rifle Association.

Further Reading: Lee Kennett and James LaVerne Anderson, *The Gun in America: The Origins of a National Dilemma* (Westport, CT: Greenwood, 1975); *New York Times* (May 17, 1911), 12, (August 29, 1911), 5, (August 30, 1911), 6; Josh Sugarmann, *The National Rifle Association: Money, Firepower and Fear* (Washington, DC: National Press, 1992).

Survivalism

Survivalism involves the belief that world or national social, economic, and political systems will collapse in the foreseeable future, leaving each individual, or groups of individuals, to fend for themselves, including providing for personal security and defense. Since the September 11, 2001 terrorist attacks, survivalist movements have emphasized the need to prepare for a major cataclysm. The right to keep and bear arms has been a major concern of survivalists, who believe that firearms represent an important ingredient for living through the anticipated conflagration. Among the possible sources of the expected disruption are natural disasters, famine and disease, terrorist attacks, economic collapse and resulting civil unrest, global warfare, government disintegration or tyranny, and class, race, or religious conflict.

Although survivalist groups tend to differ in the emphasis they place on firearms and other weapons, guns remain an important ingredient in many survival scenarios because those who have prepared for the worst may have to defend themselves against those who have not. Because firearms are often considered crucial to surviving a variety of perceived dangers, many survivalists react strongly against those who advocate gun control, considering them threats to the security of the nation and enemies of the Bill of Rights. The Survival and Self-Reliance Studies Institute (SSRSI), formerly known as the Rocky Mountain Survival Group (RMSG), has taken a relatively moderate position on the possession and use of firearms, holding that the right to keep and bear arms includes rifles, pistols, and shotguns that are commonly used by military forces, but accepts limitations on the right to possess cannons, mines, tanks, and other weapons capable of causing mass destruction. More recently, SSRSI appears to have been reduced to a Facebook page, with little evidence of activity.

Meg Raven, who has been associated with the SSRSI, has encouraged careful thought before deciding to carry a firearm and emphasizes safe usage and maintenance, but claims that most firearms owners fail the safety criterion. Professional snipers and expert hunters possess the virtues of self-control and patience that the average shooter does not have. Raven notes that those not prepared to shoot a human being may have the weapon taken away from them and advises that they would be safer not acquiring guns and concentrating instead on "nonviolent methods of escape and evasion." Nonetheless, despite these cautions, the basic survivalist logic calls for some means of defense, and firearms are the most available solution.

Raven identifies five distinct types of survivalist groups. The first are called "low impact, back-to-nature" organizations that intend to rely on the natural environment for survival. They emphasize such skills as botany, meteorology, holistic medicine, and plant cultivation. The second, "primitive skills" groups, focus on developing nontechnological skills and are often associated with religious organizations such as the Quakers and the Amish. The third, "high-tech" groups, expect to depend on advanced technology to support them during a catastrophe. Finally, paramilitary groups concentrate on collecting firearms and conducting military training. Raven does not consider them true survivalists, labeling them "borderline terrorists" that law enforcement organizations are justified in suppressing. Raven believes that "positive action/combined skills" groups have the best strategy, which involves integrating the views of the previous four.

Several enterprises concentrate on providing services to survivalists. Some offer storable food supplies, such as Survival Gear Source, which offers 72-hour survival kits, water purification products, medical supplies, and other emergency supplies. 2012 Supplies. com focuses on more extensive disaster scenarios, offering assistance in preparing for a major catastrophe. The site provides information about recent disasters, including earthquakes, hurricanes, and tornados. Consumertronics sells publications in all areas of survivalism, including items on homemade explosives, firearms, booby traps, and self-defense. Another Website devoted to survivalism is Survivalist.com, with Eric Cassano as the webmaster. The site contains varied topics relevant to survivalism, including emergency preparation, food storage, wilderness survival, bomb shelters, survival kits, water storage, first aid, self-defense, guns, weapons cashing, and militias. The site contains links to several firearm manufacturers.

See also: Gritz, James (Bo); Self-Defense.

Further Reading: Consumertronics Website, www.consumertronics.net; Survival and Self-Reliance Studies Institute Website, www.ssri.org; Survival Gear Source Web site, www.survivalgearsource.com; 2012 Supplies Web site, www.2012supplies.com; Survivalist Website, www.survivalist.info.

Switzerland

While gun rights supporters argue that Switzerland's experience with firearms confirms their opposition to gun control in the United States, gun control advocates conclude that the Swiss case supports their call for more stringent gun control legislation. Gun supporters note the widespread availability of guns in Switzerland—more than 3.4 million 8 million—a country that has a very low crime rate. In 2002, Switzerland had just 213 homicides, 68 of which were firearms-related. The Swiss homicide rate in 2010 was .05 per 100,000 population, compared to a rate of 5.0 per 100,000 in the United States. Some suggest that the Swiss culture is primarily responsible for the low crime rate in a nation with extensive private gun ownership. However, gun control proponents point to the extensive regulations the federal and canton governments impose on firearms ownership.

Swiss attitudes toward weapons were forged in a 200-year revolutionary battle for independence that ended in 1499 when Emperor Maximilian of Hapsburg finally granted Switzerland complete autonomy. In the following centuries, the country defended its independence against invaders, relying upon a militia composed of all able-bodied male citizens who, until the late nineteenth century, provided their own weapons. Switzerland maintained neutrality in conflicts among various European powers, but many Swiss, having acquired military training, became mercenaries and served in foreign armies. From the thirteenth to the twentieth centuries, citizenship was closely associated with weapons possession and service in the militia, which meant that women were traditionally excluded from political participation long after they had won political rights in other Western democracies. Today, women have the same rights as men, including the right to possess firearms.

All able-bodied males must complete military service. Men between the ages of 21 and 32 serve as frontline troops, devoting three weeks each year to training. Servicemen traditionally have been expected to keep a rifle, ammunition, and other equipment in their homes. Men aged 33 to 42 serve in the equivalent of the U.S. National Guard and participate in brief periods of training. Men in their 40s serve as a reserve force, receiving infrequent training. After leaving military service, each citizen may keep his rifle. The army sells various other weapons, including machine guns, howitzers, and antiaircraft guns, to private citizens.

Although gun control organizations emphasize the registration requirements imposed by the Swiss federal government and the various cantons, gun rights advocates indicate that such controls are minimal. Long gun purchases require no special procedures, but a purchase certificate from a cantonal authority is needed to acquire a military-size handgun. A certificate is routinely issued to anyone who is not disqualified due to criminal activity or mental instability. Switzerland has no significant limitations on the purchase of any firearms, and no registration requirements for gun purchases or restrictions on carrying long guns. The government only registers fully automatic long guns.

The high concentration of firearms in Switzerland appears to present a minimal crime problem. The incidence of murder is approximately 15 percent of the rate in the United States. Those more sympathetic to the gun rights cause suggest that the low crime rate may be explained in part by the awareness potential

violent criminals have that possible victims are trained in armed and unarmed defense and may possess a firearm. However, Switzerland has a high suicide rate (17.5 per 100,000 population in 2006 compared to a U.S. rate of approximately 11 per 100,000), with firearms involved in nearly one-quarter of the total.

The relatively high suicide rate as well as violent incidents involving firearms (for instance, the murder of 14 people in the cantonal parliament of Zug in 2001) has led to calls for additional restrictions on the possession of firearms. Such events were responsible in part for new gun control laws that were enacted in 1996 and that established a system of registration and uniform national standards requiring police authorization to purchase firearms. In a 2008 agreement in the Swiss parliament, soldiers actively serving may not keep ammunition at home. In February 2009, the Social Democratic Party along with several pacifist organizations began an initiative to require army weapons to remain in barracks rather than allowing soldiers to take them home, and to establish national gun registration. The initiative also would prohibit individuals from owning automatic weapons and pump-action shotguns. Given the long tradition of militia soldiers keeping firearms at home, the initiative has been controversial. Opponents of the initiative have argued that laws are already sufficiently restrictive, while supporters have contended it is reasonable to expect that guns be kept in an arsenal. In June 2010, the parliamentary House of Representatives urged voters to reject the initiative and it was defeated in February 2011, with 56 percent of voters rejecting the proposal.

Subsequent mass shootings—in 2013 a gunman in Lucerne killed four people and wound six others, and a man killed three women and wounded two men in a southern village, and in 2015 a gunman in a northern village killed four people before shooting and killing himself—led the central government to take some measures, such as enhancing the sharing of information among regional gun registries, Swiss attitudes toward firearm ownership likely will assure continuing lenient gun policies

See also: Australia; Israel; Japan.

Further Reading: Catherine Foster, "Nations Around World Try to Get a Grip on Guns," *Christian Science*

Monitor (May 15, 1996), 1, 10–11; "Parliament Rejects Tougher Gun Laws" (June 18, 2010), www. swissinfo.ch/eng/ politics/Parliament_rejects_ tougher_gun_laws. html?cid=9126536; David B. Kopel, *The Samurai, the Mountie, and the Cowboy: Should America Adopt the Gun Controls of Other Democracies?* (Buffalo, NY: Prometheus, 1992);

Library of Congress, "Firearms-Control legislation and Policy: Switzerland," loc.gov/law/help/firearms-control/Switzerland.php (accessed August 15. 2016); Saura Secorun Palet, "Why Neutral Switzerland Has So Many Guns," *USA Today* (July 8, 2014), www.usatoday/story/news/world/2014/07/08/ ozy-switzerland-guns/12357435.

T

Taggants

Bombing incidents, particularly at the World Trade Center in New York in 1993, the Alfred P. Murrah Federal Building in Oklahoma City in 1995, and the Centennial Olympic Park in Atlanta in 1996, and more recent terrorist threats, such as the 2001 "shoe bomber" and the 2009 "Christmas day bomber" attempts to destroy passenger planes, have increased calls for federal legislation requiring the inclusion of chemical tags, or "taggants," in materials that can be used to produce explosives. Such taggants also could be included in black and smokeless powder for the identification of gun users. National Rifle Association (NRA) officials have expressed skepticism regarding the use of taggants, arguing on the basis of a 1980 study that such additions could destabilize gunpowder. The Antiterrorism and Effective Death Penalty Act of 1996 contained a provision to fund a six-month study of taggants to be conducted by the Treasury Department, but the NRA and other organizations lobbied successfully to exclude gunpowder from the study.

In the early 1970s, Richard G. Livesay developed the first tags, which were tiny particles approximately a tenth of a millimeter in diameter consisting of layers of colored melamine plastic, a chemically inert substance likely to survive an explosion. Distinctive layering permits identification of the manufacturer, the production date, and the distributor of the explosive. Fluorescent materials included in the taggant assisted in detection. The magnetized taggants, when placed over a magnet, reveal their unique color coding. This type of taggant, called Microtaggant, is produced by Microtrace, a company that has sold its product primarily to Switzerland, where since 1980 all explosives have been tagged. From 1984 to 1996, the Swiss reportedly used Microtaggants to solve more than 500 bombing cases.

More recently, researchers have developed another type of taggant—nonradioactive heavy-isotope variations of molecules already present in the explosives. These isotopes of hydrogen, carbon, nitrogen, and oxygen vary only in atomic weight from materials already in the explosive. Potentially millions of distinct codes can be written as identifiers of specific explosive compounds. Identifying the tags requires relatively sophisticated laboratory analysis. Two companies, Microtrace of Minneapolis, Minnesota, and Isotag (which in 2002 merged with Biocode to form Authentix of Addison, Texas) provide isotope tags for many business firms for such products as shampoo, paint, gasoline, perfume, and glue to protect brand name products from counterfeiting and dilution. Taggant producers recommend the use of their products for materials employed in the production of explosives, such as flammable liquids, black powder, smokeless powder, fireworks powders, ammonium nitrate fertilizer, and fuel oil.

Manufacturers demonstrate less enthusiasm for taggants. The Institute of Makers of Explosives (IME) contends that the inclusion of taggants is still too expensive. Although the precise cost is difficult to determine, the IME notes that the 1994 estimated cost of one taggant, mesh Microtaggant, was $326 per pound, which for the mining industry by itself would amount to approximately $750 million per year. The processing costs of all high explosives could reach as high as $520 million, which, the IME estimates, would double the cost to customers. To prevent contamination of taggants from one batch to another, manufacturers maintain that the production line would have to be cleaned thoroughly after each run, thus further increasing costs. Because explosives must meet emission and contamination standards, the addition of taggants would require retesting to assure that they continue to meet government standards. However, more recent isotope taggants may obviate the concern about the older plastic version. The IME notes that taggants must survive an explosion, and discovering taggants could be a very difficult process. Complicating the procedure is the likelihood that other taggants from legitimate uses during construction could contaminate the scene of the explosion. Unlike identification taggants, the IME supports detection taggants, which allow for determing the presence of an explosive before detonation and can be added to explosives without jeopardizing the effectiveness of the materials.

According to supporters of taggants, their extensive use in Switzerland demonstrates the safety of such materials. However, the IME argues that the Swiss program is significantly different from that proposed in the United States, which would be implemented on a much larger scale. Record-keeping by chemical manufacturers and retail store owners may prove burdensome. In the case of powder-containing bullets, retail outlets would have to determine the name of each purchaser and maintain the records. Policy makers are left to decide whether the objective of apprehending those who have committed crimes using explosive materials and deterring such crimes is worth the financial costs involved. The IME argues that placing taggants in commercially manufactured explosives may actually impede the investigation of a bombing, and countries, such as Israel and Germany, that have experienced significant terrorist incidents, have not adopted a taggant project.

See also: National Rifle Association; Oklahoma City Bombing; Switzerland.

Further Reading: Institute of Makers of Explosives, "Taggant History and Background" (January 2005), www.ime.org/dynamic.php?page_id=66; Institute of Makers of Explosives, "Taggants in Explosives" (January 2016), www.ime.org/uploads/public/Issues%20Briefs%20-2016/Taggants%20lr%20Explosives.pdf; Michael Kramer, "Without a Clue: Why Congress Balks at a Method for Tracing Bombs," *Time* 148 (August 12, 1996), 27; Robert F. Service, "NRC Panel Enters the Fight Over Tagging Explosives," *Science* 275 (January 24, 1997), 474–75; Corinna Wu, "Tagged Out: New Markers for Explosives May Lay Old Safety Questions to Rest," *Science News* 150 (September 14, 1996), 168–69; Peter Overb y, "'Taggants' in Gunpowder Might Have Helped Identify Bombers" (April 24, 2013), National Public Radio, http://npr.org/2013/04/21/178858037/taggants-in-gunpowder-might-have-helped-identify-bombers.

Texas Tower Shooting

The Texas Tower shooting, which occurred at the University of Texas at Austin in August 1966, initiated public discussion regarding the dangers of firearms and provided a rationale for Democratic President Lyndon Johnson and the national Congress to push for gun control legislation, which was approved two years later. A lone gunman climbed to the observation deck of the university tower, called the Main Building, lugging a trunk containing several firearms, ammunition, food and water, and other provisions. For 80 minutes, Charles J. Whitman, a 25-year-old architectural student, sprayed bullets from all sides of the University of Texas landmark.

A Marine Corps veteran, Whitman had received two rifleman ratings, "marksman" and "sharpshooter." Whitman shot and killed his mother and stabbed his wife to death the night before the tower shooting. That morning he purchased a .12-gauge semiautomatic shotgun at a Sears store and cut off a portion of the stock and barrel. He also carried into the tower a 6-mm. Remington rifle with a telescopic sight, a Remington .35-caliber reconditioned Army carbine, a .357 magnum pistol, a 9-mm. Luger pistol, and a Bowie knife. Following the shooting, police found three rifles and two Derringers in his home.

His first victim at the tower was the elevator attendant, who was shot at her position at the visitors' register. Dragging the trunk to the observation platform, Whitman was in position to begin shooting just before noon. He succeeded in killing 12 people and wounding 33 others. The killing rampage ceased only when Romero Martinez, an off-duty policeman, made his way up the tower and shot Whitman six times with his service revolver and once with a shotgun. The final death toll, including Whitman and his wife and mother, was 15 people. An autopsy conducted soon after the event revealed that the gunman had a brain tumor, which might have contributed to the young man's rage.

President Johnson announced the day following the shooting that easy access to firearms must be given some of the blame for the incident. He urged Congress to take prompt action on a gun control bill that had been languishing in Congress, claiming that the bill would help prohibit the sale of firearms to those who were not qualified to possess or use them. Senator Thomas Dodd, Democrat of Connecticut, the bill's major sponsor, also saw some remedy for this kind of act with passage of the pending legislation.

Gun control opponents maintained their resistance to new legislation, arguing that the tower shooting had no relevance at all to either a judgment on guns as such or on their use for marksmanship training. They further argued that additional legislation would not have prevented Whitman from committing his horrendous acts of violence. Not until 1968, with further public reaction against gun violence, particularly following the assassinations of Robert Kennedy and Martin Luther King, Jr., did Congress approve the first significant piece of gun control legislation in 30 years.

See also: Dodd, Thomas J.; Gun Control Act of 1968; Sawed-Off Shotgun.

Further Reading: Gary M. Lavergne, *A Sniper in the Tower: The Charles Whitman Murders* (Denton, TX: University of North Texas Press, 1997); *New York Times*, August 2, 1966, 1, 15; August 3, 1966, 1.

Third Way

Third Way, headquartered in Washington, D.C., is a think tank that presents moderately progressive policy positions in a number of issue areas. The organization's policy agenda includes an economic focus on growth and the welfare of the middle class, an emphasis on elaborating shared values in the American culture, pursuing a reasoned approach to national security, and implementing clean energy solutions. Third Way issues publications on legislative proposals and major political issues, and conducts public opinion research. Jonathan Cowan, cofounder and president of Third Way, also established and managed Americans for Gun Safety, an organization that merged with Third Way. Therefore, it is not surprising that firearms policy is one of the issue areas in which the organization has expressed views and made recommendations.

Third Way advocates a seven-step strategy for progressives to "take back the Second Amendment." In other words, progressives are asked to distinguish themselves from liberals who deny that the Second Amendment guarantees an individual's right to possess firearms (survey data are cited indicating that less than 10 percent of voters believe the Second Amendment does not protect such a right), as well as from those conservatives who hold to an absolutist position on the Second Amendment and claim that all liberals want to deny citizens the right to own a gun. According to Third Way, the first step progressives should take is to establish a public position on the issue rather than try to avoid it entirely. Second, progressives should "own" the Second Amendment; in other words, support the individual's right in engaging in any debate about firearms. The third step is to redefine the issue as one of gun safety rather than gun control. Fourth, progressives should demand energetic application of existing gun laws. Fifth, they should use moderate language when advocating firearm policies. Sixth, rather than allowing the opposition to define their position, progressives should speak directly to gun owners about issues of concern. Finally, "implement your gun plan and watch the gun votes roll in." Third Way summarizes this approach by recommending three basic actions: support the Second Amendment; advocate the closing of the gun show loophole that allows non-licensed individuals to sell firearms at gun shows and elsewhere without a background check; and call for the vigorous enforcement of existing firearms laws.

Third Way has taken a strong position against the continuation of the Tiahrt Amendment, a rider attached to Justice Department appropriations since fiscal year 2004 that, among its restrictions on the Bureau of Alcohol, Tobacco, Firearms, and Explosives (ATF), prohibits the Bureau from divulging crime gun trace data. The organization argues that the amendment succeeded only in helping criminals by restricting the access of state and local law enforcement officers to gun trace information. With regard to the gun show loophole, the organization notes that, according to the ATF, gun shows are the second most frequent source of firearms that are linked to illegal gun investigations. Third Way argues that an effort to close the loophole would not conflict with the U.S. Supreme Court's *District of Columbia v.*

Heller (2008) or *McDonald v. Chicago* (2010) decisions in which the Court interpreted the Second Amendment as protecting an individual's right to possess firearms.

Although Third Way has found significant improvements in the National Instant Check System (NICS) intended to prevent ineligible people from purchasing firearms, major deficiencies in the system remain. Particularly, states frequently fail to include in computerized records those "adjudicated as a mental defective or . . . committed to a mental institution." With regard to concealed carry (CCW) laws, Third Way opposes any effort at the federal level to pass legislation that would require states to recognize the CCW licenses of any other state, supporting instead the right of states and localities to determine CCW policies.

In January 2016 the organization strongly supported President Barack Obama's announcement regarding more than a dozen executive actions to increase the effectiveness of federal firearms laws. Third Way selected four of these policy announcements as especially significant. First, the organization agreed that the definition of what constitutes being "engaged in the business" of selling firearms needed to be clarified, which involves requiring law enforcement to examine in each case the seller's behavior, including the frequency of sales, whether guns sold are still in original packaging, and time between original purchase and re-sale.

Second, Third Way supported President Obama's order that the Social Security Administration should provide to the NICS information on people who lack "the capacity to contract for themselves or manage their own affairs" and hence are prohibited from purchasing a firearm. Third Way also applauded the president for easing legal restriction on health professional regarding submission of mental health records to the NICS.

Finally, the organization supported the president's call for the departments of Defense, Justice, and Homeland Security to review the progress of smart gun technology and its use in improving gun safety. The government departments are to determine when the technology has met the federal government's requirements. This action could have significant consequences for development of smart gun technology because the federal government is the largest purchaser of firearms in the United States.

See also: Concealed Carry Laws; Gun Show Loophole; National Instant Check System; Tiahrt Amendment.

Further Reading: Third Way Web site, http://www. thirdway.org; Sarah Trumble, "Explaining the President's Executive Actions on Guns" (January 6, 2016), thirdway.org/memo/explaining-the-presidents-executive-actions-on-guns.

Thompson, Linda (1952–2009)

In the two years following the federal government attack on the Branch Davidian compound in Waco, Texas, in 1993, Linda Thompson, founder of the American Justice Federation and advocate of extreme militia politics, energetically disseminated materials claiming the existence of a vast government conspiracy to destroy the militia movement and take control of the country. Thompson was identified as the most vocal person in making the Waco event a rallying cry for the militia and patriot movements. Thompson produced two videotapes, *Waco: The Big Lie* and *Waco: The Big Lie Continues*, in which she claimed that government tanks used flamethrowers against the Branch Davidian compound during the attack of April 19, 1993. Thompson and her husband Al attributed the 1995 Oklahoma City bombing to a government plot to encourage a backlash against the militia movement. They expressed a similar skepticism about highly visible acts of gun violence that occurred just as Congress was considering new gun control legislation.

Before Thompson became involved in the militia movement, she worked as a civil rights attorney in her native Georgia. The events at Randy Weaver's cabin at Ruby Ridge, Idaho, in 1992 altered her view of government. Six months later, soon after the siege at the Davidian compound had begun, Thompson traveled to Waco to offer her legal services to David Koresh, the leader of the Davidians. After a disagreement with another Koresh supporter, she left, but returned two weeks later to call for militant action to support the Davidians. Following the raid, Thompson began her campaign against a government she claimed was guilty of murderous activities.

On April 19, 1994, the first anniversary of the raid on the Branch Davidian compound, Thompson sent registered letters to each member of the U.S. House of Representatives and the Senate. Her "ultimatum" made a number of demands, including a complete government investigation of the Waco siege, repeal of the Fourteenth Amendment and of the Brady Handgun Violence Prevention Act, which imposed a waiting period and background check on those wanting to purchase a handgun. If Congress did not act by September 19, 1994, she declared that its members would be branded traitors, tried by a people's court, and executed. She identified herself as the acting adjutant general of the Unorganized Militia of the United States of America. At rallies across the country, Thompson advocated trials for leading government officials like Attorney General Janet Reno and Secretary of the Treasury Lloyd Bentsen, who had ultimate responsibility for the Bureau of Alcohol, Tobacco, and Firearms (ATF), the agency in charge of enforcing federal gun control legislation.

Thompson called for militias to travel to Washington, D.C., on September 19, armed, in uniform, and ready to take members of Congress into custody, try them for their crimes, and execute them. When militia organizations failed to respond to her call, Thompson canceled the event, saying that she never intended to carry out her threats. The self-proclaimed leader of the American militia movement had lost her credibility even among the more extreme militia organizations. In July 1994, she was arrested for attempting to use her car to block a bus loaded with supporters of Democratic President Bill Clinton's health care plan. Her car contained a .45-caliber pistol, a derringer, and an assault rifle, along with nearly 300 rounds of ammunition. She was arrested once again, in May 1995, for carrying a concealed firearm into the Marion County, Indiana, prosecutor's office.

Thompson took the gun rights argument that firearms are necessary for citizens to protect themselves from their own imminently oppressive government to its most extreme level. The ultimate oppressor, the United Nations, supposedly already had secret forces in the United States and was preparing for the final takeover. The telltale signs of such a force were the alleged black helicopters of an invading force that flew over her house to maintain surveillance on her activities. Within this paranoid scenario, gun control legislation fit neatly into a grander scheme to enslave the American people. Therefore, such legislation became not just a policy to be considered unwise and possibly unconstitutional, but part of a declaration of war by a government on its people. Not even the more radical groups were willing to accept Thompson's

perception of reality, at least publicly, much less to act on that perception.

In 1997 Thompson underwent gastric bypass surgery at Duke University. She suffered harmful side effects from the procedure and underwent reconstructive surgery for her stomach and esophagus. Hence her activities for the America Justice Federation were suspended. She continued to experience a great deal of discomfort and in 2009 she overdosed on pain medication and died.

See also: Brady Handgun Violence Prevention Act; Bureau of Alcohol, Tobacco, Firearms, and Explosives; Clinton, William Jefferson (Bill); Fourteenth Amendment; Oklahoma City Bombing; Reno, Janet; Ruby Ridge; United Nations; Waco, Texas, Raid.

Further Reading: Morris Dees, *Gathering Storm: America's Militia Threat* (New York: Harper Collins, 1996); Alex Heard, "The Road to Oklahoma City," *The New Republic* 212 (May 15, 1995), 15–20; Jonathan Karl, *The Right to Bear Arms: The Rise of America's New Militias* (New York: HarperCollins, 1995); Jason Vest, "Leader of the Fringe," *The Progressive* 59 (June 1995); 28–29; Maryanne Vollers, "The White Woman from Hell," *Esquire* 124 (July 1995), 50–51; "Attorney Linda Capps (Thompson) Abrams Obituary" (May 12, 2009), Paulding.com/forum/topic/208225-attorney-linda-capps-thompson-abrams.

Tiahrt Amendment

In 2003, Representative Todd Tiahrt (R-KS) was successful in attaching an amendment to the Justice Department appropriations for fiscal year 2004 that placed restrictions on the information the Bureau of Alcohol, Tobacco, Firearms, and Explosives (ATF) could provide to state and local government agencies or generally make public to organizations and individuals. Over the objections of such groups as the Violence Policy Center and the Brady Campaign to Prevent Gun Violence, the Tiahrt amendment was added to appropriations bills each subsequent fiscal year. Prior to passage of the first Tiahrt amendment, various groups claimed the right to receive information about gun traces from the ATF under the Freedom of Information Act (FOIA). In 2002, a federal court ruled that the ATF interpreted too broadly the law enforcement exemption to the FOIA by withholding information that the city of Chicago had requested from the Firearms Tracing System database. City officials wanted the information to establish a basis for lawsuits against firearms manufacturers and dealers. Undoubtedly the National Rifle Association (NRA), concerned about any perceived threat to the right to keep and bear arms, and also concerned for the interests of firearms manufacturers and dealers, played a key role in having the amendment placed in the Justice Department appropriation.

The Tiahrt amendment contains three basic restrictions. First, it strictly limits the authority of the ATF to comply with FOIA requests for the release of crime trace data, and disallows the use of such data in lawsuits that victims of crime may bring against gun manufacturers and dealers. Second, the amendment formalized the George W. Bush administration's policy of deleting National Instant Criminal Background Check System (NICS) records after 24 hours. Finally, the amendment prohibits the ATF from activating its proposed policy of mandating that firearms dealers perform annual audits in order to keep track of inventories (the Brady Center to Prevent Gun Violence estimates that in 2007 more than 30,000 guns remained unaccounted for at licensed firearm dealers).

Critics of the amendment charged that the restrictions prevented state and local officials from using gun trace data to investigate corrupt gun dealers and traffickers and to suspend or revoke the license of a gun dealer who has broken the law. Opponents also noted that keeping NICS records no longer than 24 hours makes it difficult to discover any falsification of records and to identify straw purchasers. In addition, the amendment does not allow the ATF to require inventory checks, which reduces the chances of discovering illegal firearm sales.

The NRA defends the Tiahrt amendment, arguing that the purpose of the gun trace system is not to gather data for statistical analysis but to assist law enforcement agencies to determine the line of ownership for individual firearms. In addition, the NRA states that guns are traced for reasons other than involvement in crimes, such as traffic violations, and therefore trace data can be misleading. The organization contends that law enforcement agencies still can access trace information in connection with a genuine criminal investigation or prosecution. The NRA claims that the ATF and the Fraternal Order of Police (FOP) oppose release of trace data in

order not to compromise current law enforcement investigations. The organization lobbied Congress to have the restrictions on gun trace data made permanent and Congress complied in 2000 for the 2007 acquisitions bill.

Critics supported revisions to the Tiahrt amendment, which in 2009 led to the reestablishment of greater access to gun trace data for state and local law enforcement and of the authority of agencies to share trace data with each other. However, organizations critical of the amendment are concerned that other provisions remain in place, such as the mandate to delete NICS background check information within 24 hours. Also, the ATF still does not have the authority to require dealers to conduct inventory checks for lost or stolen guns, and state and local officials are prohibited from using the data to rescind the license of a gun dealer who has broken the law.

President Barack Obama, following the 2008 election, pushed unsuccessfully to repeal the Tiahrt Amendment, and in 2013 a group of 43 Democrats in the U.S. House of Representatives urged the Obama administration to remove the amendment from the budget. However, Republicans and some pro-gun rights Democrats in both the House and the Senate made any repeal effort extremely unlikely.

See also: Brady Campaign to Prevent Gun Violence; Bureau of Alcohol, Tobacco, Firearms, and Explosives (ATF); Mayors Against Illegal Guns; National Rifle Association; Straw Purchases; Violence Policy Center.

Further Reading: Brady Center to Prevent Gun Violence, "The Tiahrt Amendment," www.bradycampaign.org/legislation/gunlobbybacked/Tiahrt (accessed September 3, 2010); James V. Grimaldi and Sari Horwitz, "Industry Pressure Hides Gun Traces, Protects Dealers From Public Scrutiny," *The Washington Post* (October 23, 2010), www.washingtonpost.com/wp-dyn/content/article/2010/10/23/AR2010102302996.html; Mayors Against Illegal Guns, "The Tiahrt Amendments," www.mayorsagainstillegalguns.org/html/federal/tiahrt.shtml; Violence Policy Center, "Restrictions Imposed on the Release of Crime Gun Trace Data by the 'Tiahrt Amendment' Are a Substantive Change in the Freedom of Information Act," www.vpc.org/fact_sht/Tiahrt110FOIA.fs.pdf (accessed September 3, 2010); Bill Wrigley, "House Democrats Urge

Obama, OMB to Repeal Amendment Prohibiting Gun Tracking," *Huffington Post* (March 26, 2013), huffingtonpost.com/2013/03/26/house-democrats-tiahrt-amendment_n_2958341.html; National Rifle Association, Institute for Legislative Action, "The Tiahrtr Amendment On Firearms Traces: Protecting Gun Owners' Privacy and Law Enforcement Safety" (January 15, 2013), nraila.org/articles/20130115/the-tiahrt-amendment-on-firearms-traces-protecting-gun-owners-privacy-and-law-enforcement-safety.

Tommy Gun

The Tommy gun exemplified lawlessness and gangsterism that characterized much of the 1920s and early 1930s. Attempts to isolate particular types of weapons as "criminal," independent of who owns them, can be attributed to a general negative reaction to the Tommy gun and its use in criminal activity during this era of American history. Colonel John M. Thompson developed the weapon during World War I for use by American troops. To distinguish it from larger and heavier automatic weapons used at the time, Thompson called the weapon a submachine gun. The Thompson submachine gun, or Tommy gun, fired .45-caliber bullets without interruption with one pull of the trigger.

Following the war, Thompson attempted to market his submachine gun as a police weapon, but police departments showed little interest. The national government also exhibited a lukewarm response. In 1926, the Treasury Department had only four Tommy guns. As demand for the weapon failed to increase, the price dropped from $225 to $50. Colt originally manufactured 15,000 guns, but by 1925 only 3,000 had been sold. Desperate to increase sales, dealers looked for customers wherever they could find them. The Irish Republican Army placed a large order, but the federal government subsequently seized the shipment.

Chicago gangsters determined the Tommy gun's fate. Historians claim that the Joe Saltis and Frank McErlane gang, which controlled the Southwest Side of Chicago, first introduced the submachine gun for criminal purposes. However, others claim that the Tommy gun, also known in underworld slang as the "Chicago Piano," was first used in 1926 to murder two gunmen for the O'Donnell gang, Jim Doherty and Tom Duffy, and assistant state's attorney William H. McSwiggin. Others speculate that the notorious Chicago gangster Al Capone pulled the trigger. In 1927, the gun appeared in Philadelphia and in 1928 New York gangsters had acquired the weapon. The crime wave of the 1930s brought nationwide notoriety to the submachine gun, which had become the preferred weapon of such notorious outlaws as Pretty Boy Floyd and Ma Barker. The Tommy gun possessed advantages that attracted outlaws and gang members. It was an uncomplicated weapon, weighed just eight and one-half pounds, and could fire a withering hail of bullets, approaching 1,000 rounds per minute. Also, the gun was conveniently available by mail order.

The Tommy gun became so closely associated with criminal activity that it was commonly regarded as a firearm that no respectable, law-abiding citizen would want to possess. During Democratic President Franklin Roosevelt's first administration, the criminal use of this firearm, along with such other weapons as the sawed-off shotgun, instigated the call for gun regulation. The 1934 National Firearms Act regulated the sale of machine guns, establishing taxation and regulation

The Thompson machine gun, or Tommy gun, became widely used in 1928. *www.wikipedia.com*

of the interstate sale or transfer of the weapons. The legislation focused almost exclusively on so-called "gangster weapons" such as the Tommy gun, leaving handguns and other weapons largely unregulated.

With government controls on the sale of firearms, gangsters sought alternative ways of acquiring the Thompson submachine gun. A black market developed, with the price of the weapon significantly higher than the original $225 price tag. Nonetheless, the new controls had some effect, and despite loopholes, the criminal use of submachine guns subsided.

Ever since restrictions were placed on the sale and ownership of the Tommy gun and other automatic weapons, gun rights advocates have protested that they possess a constitutional right to own such firearms. The controversy continues, with gun rights groups, including more zealous elements within the National Rifle Association (NRA), calling for repeal of restrictions on the private ownership of machine guns. In November 2010, a full-page advertisement appeared in Texas newspapers for a souvenir semiautomatic version of the Thompson submachine gun in honor of the Texas Rangers. Touting the gun as "the ultimate crime fighting tool," no mention was made of the criminal associations that led to the legal restrictions placed on the weapon.

See also: National Firearms Act of 1934; National Rifle Association; Sawed-Off Shotgun.

Further Reading: "America Remembers Presents the Texas Ranger Tribute Thompson," *Houston Chronicle* (November 2, 2010), A7; Bill R. Davidson, *To Keep and Bear Arms* (New Rochelle, NY: Arlington House, 1969); Lee Kennett and James La Verne Anderson, *The Gun in America: The Origins of a National Dilemma* (Westport, CT: Greenwood, 1975); Carl Sifakis, *Encyclopedia of American Crime* (New York: Facts on File, 1982).

The Trace

The Trace is an organization composed of journalists devoted to providing media coverage of the various aspects of guns in the United States. The organization's editorial team admits a basic viewpoint that the rates of firearm-related deaths and injuries are too high. The organization was established in order to remedy what the editors believe is a dearth of information on the subject, a situation for which the National Rifle Association (NRA) and other gun rights organizations are responsible because, The Trace argues, these gun rights groups have lobbied Congress successfully to limit government-funded research on the subject and to limit the availability of gun-related crime data to police agencies and the general public. Because gun rights organizations have multiple media outlets to present their policy positions, The Trace contends that the group is meant to correct the imbalance in the debate over firearm violence and gun control.

The Trace is a nonprofit organization registered as a 501c3 group under the Internal Revenue Service code. Its headquarters are located in New York City. In 2015, Michael Bloomberg, former mayor of New York, and Everytown for Gun Safety provided initial funding to initiate the organization. *Huffington Post* co-founder Ken Lerer, venture capitalist Nick Hanauer, and the Joyce Foundation also have supported the organization. James Burnett, former editor of *The New Republic* magazine, serves as the editorial director. Among the news stories that The Trace has issued include congressional action on gun control, involvement of the NRA in election campaigns, the problem of illegal guns, Supreme Court rulings on gun control and gun rights, the history of firearms and gun control, and data on the rates of gun violence.

Following the mass shooting at a nightclub in Orlando, Florida, which was categorized as a terrorist act, The Trace reported on the Federal Bureau of Investigation's terrorist watch list, the policy of prohibiting those on the list from boarding commercial airline flights, and the proposal to extend the prohibition to purchasing firearms. The Trace presented both sides of the issue.

The NRA's Institute for Legislative Action (ILA) responded to the establishment of The Trace, commenting that the "fanatically anti-gun" Michael Bloomberg and other "anti-gun" individuals and groups have funded an organization that the ILA claimed is intended to "gin up 'news' or biased 'analyses'" to support "whichever draconian law is Bloomberg's favorite flavor of the day at the national or state level." In contrast to the NRA-ILA perception of The Trace, Burnett stated that the organization's participating journalists will solicit the views of conservatives, Republican elected officials, and gun rights supporters in order to engage in objective reporting.

See also: Americans for Responsible Solutions; Bloomberg, Michael; Everytown for Gun Safety.

Further Reading: The Trace Web site, https://thetrace.org; Michael Calderone, "The Trace, Bloomberg-Backed Journalism Startup, Tackles Gun Violence 'Epidemic,'" *Huffington Post* (June 16, 2016). huffingtonpost.com/2015/06/16/the-trace-bloomberg-guns_n_7581446.html; National Rifle Association-Institute for Legislative Action, "The Trace: Just Another Effort to Mislead America" (June 18, 2015). www.nralia.org/articles/20150626/the-trace-just-another-effort-to-mislead-america.

Trigger Locks

In 1997, mandatory trigger locks on handguns became a prominent issue in the gun control debate. In his State of the Union Address in January, President Bill Clinton advocated legislation to require newly manufactured handguns to be sold with such devices, also called "child safety locks." Some gun rights advocates demonstrated immediate skepticism, claiming that such devices were not the most effective way to ensure the safety of children. Instead, education and training efforts such as the National Rifle Association's (NRA) Eddie Eagle program could best prevent the gun accidents that prompted the proposal. Citing long-term data, opponents of such a measure claimed that education had already significantly reduced the number of accidents Each year involving children.

The Clinton administration attempted to attach an amendment to a juvenile justice reform measure mandating trigger locks and various other proposals were considered in each house of Congress. In the Senate, an amendment softened the gun lock provision to require that gun dealers simply make gun locks available to customers who wished to purchase them. In October 1997, following meetings of representatives of the Sporting Arms and Ammunition Manufacturers' Institute (SAAMI), the American Shooting Sports Council (ASSC), and executive and legislative branch officials, some gun manufacturers agreed to provide gun locking devices. On October 9, representatives of firearms manufacturing companies, including Richard Feldman, who was the executive director of the ASSC, and officials from Beretta, Glock, H&R 1871, Heckler and Koch, O.F. Mossberg and Son, SIG Arms, Smith and Wesson, and Taurus stood with President Clinton in the Rose Garden

for the annual "Top Cop" award ceremony. At the ceremony, Richard Feldman of the ASSC stated that "within the coming year, most major handgun manufacturers will institute company policies of providing safety devices with all handguns shipped in the United States," and President Clinton in his comments focused on the importance of protecting children from firearm violence. Other companies not represented expressed their intention to support the agreement.

The NRA had opposed the negotiations with the Clinton Administration about gun locks. Following the announced agreement, Wayne LaPierre, NRA executive vice president, sent a letter to the participating companies in which he claimed that their decision was a serious error. Tanya Metaksa, executive director of the NRA's Institute for Legislative Action (ILA), insisted that the "one-size-fits-all" gun lock option would not work and that the most effective way of dealing with the gun accident problem was through "effective safety strategies." Charlton Heston, NRA first vice president, submitted a letter to the *New York Times* stating that he supported the agreement, but still thought that education was the most important factor in gun safety and that a loaded gun provided the best protection against criminal assault. Some pro-gun control forces also expressed reservations about the agreement. For instance, Sarah Brady, director of Handgun Control, Inc., congratulated President Clinton for gaining a concession from gun manufacturers, but indicated that much still needed to be done to improve firearm safety.

Representatives of Sturm, Ruger and Company cast doubt on the significance of the agreement. In open letters, Sturm, Ruger emphasized that the company believed proper instruction had led to the lowest level of gun accidents in the twentieth century. The company stated that by taking part in the agreement, it was only continuing a policy that was begun 10 years before—to ship pistols in lock boxes with a padlock, a practice that was expanded to most of the handguns the company manufactured. The letters also expressed doubts about the safety of trigger locks, opting instead for the company's lockable boxes.

In the meantime, gun manufacturers and gun accessory companies advertised various types of trigger locks in gun magazines. Taurus began equipping its handguns with a locking device that appeared to avoid the safety criticisms leveled against other products, ensuring that the weapon would not fire as the owner disengaged the lock. The Taurus system involved a mechanism integral to the firearm that locked the hammer with a special key. Of importance to gun rights advocates, the owner could use the locking system as he or she wished, thus avoiding the perception of government mandate and preserving freedom of choice.

Other proposals at the national and state levels were made in an effort to provide for safer handguns, particularly in the presence of children. Some advocated devices that would only allow the owner to disengage the lock, so-called "user-sensitive" locking devices. However, gun advocates continue to claim that such mechanisms should never substitute for education and "common sense," arguing that if gun owners rely on them too much, trigger locks may actually lead to more accidents. Various companies sell locking devices, and firearms manufacturers include a trigger lock with each new gun. States such as California and Massachusetts have instituted trigger lock provisions, but the U.S. Supreme Court decision in *District of Columbia v. Heller* (2008) raise questions about whether, given the recognized defensive function of firearms, gun owners can be required to keep handguns locked.

In 2005 the U.S. Congress included in the Protection of Lawful Commerce in Arms Act a provision that required any licensed firearms importer, manufacturer, or dealer to provide the purchaser with a secure gun storage or safety device. The law [18 U.S.C. §921(a) (34)] defines such a device as once that either prevents the firearm from operating without first being deactivated; is included in the design of the firearm and prevents its operation by anyone who does not have legitimate access; or a "safe, gun safe, gun case, lock box, or other device" for storing a firearm that can be unlocked only by a key, a combination, or other means. The legislation does not apply to private transfers, and those purchasing a firearm are not required to use the device.

Eleven states have passed laws mandating locking devices. Massachusetts has the most stringent requirement: all firearms are to be stored in a locked location. California, Connecticut, and New York require firearms to be secured with a locking device if the residence includes someone who is prohibited from possessing firearms. The remaining seven states—Illinois, Maryland, Michigan, New Jersey, Ohio, Pennsylvania, and Rhode Island—have varying requirements.

See also: Accidents Involving Guns, Brady Campaign to Prevent Gun Violence; Brady, Sarah; Clinton, William Jefferson (Bill); Consumer Product Safety; *District of Columbia v. Heller* (2008); Eddie Eagle; Heston, Charlton; Institute for Legislative Action; Metaksa, Tanya K.; National Rifle Association; Product Liability Lawsuits; Smart Guns; Smith and Wesson; Sporting Arms and Ammunition Manufacturers' Institute.

Further Reading: James Jay Baker, "Gun Legislation," *Shooting Times* (January 1998), 10–13; Richard Feldman, *Ricochet: Confessions of a Gun Lobbyist* (Hoboken, NJ: John Wiley and Sons, 2008); News Briefs, "Reports Confuse Clinton, Industry Gun Lock Deal," *Gun News Digest* (Winter 1997–1998),8–9; Staff Report, "Taurus Security System: Internal Mechanism Locks Revolver," *Gun World* (February 1998), 79–81; Law Center to Prevent Gun Violence, "Safe Storage and Gun Locks," www.smartgunlaws. org/gun-laws/policy-areas/consumer-child-safety/ safe-storage-gun-locks (accessed July 14, 2016).

Tucson, Arizona Shooting, 2011

On the morning of January 8, 2011, Arizona Democratic Representative Gabrielle Giffords convened a "Congress on Your Corner" constituent meet-and-greet in front of a local supermarket in Tucson. As she was speaking with constituents, a twenty-two-year-old man with a recent history of mental disorders walked up to Giffords after weaving his way through the crowd of people around her, pointed a 9-mm Glock 19 handgun a couple of feet from her head, and pulled the trigger. The bullet passed through her head, but, miraculously, she not only survived but also showed immediate and dramatic improvement in the days and weeks that followed. After shooting Rep. Giffords, 22-year old Jared Lee Loughner proceeded to empty the thirty-one-bullet magazine, killing six people and wounding thirteen others. When he stopped to insert a second bullet magazine, a diminutive sixty-one-year-old woman snatched a second, bullet-filled magazine he had dropped on the floor from his grasp, and several bystanders proceeded to restrain the man. Among those killed were a federal judge who had stopped by after church to speak with Giffords, a nine-year-old girl interested in visiting with her congressional representative, and a Giffords staff member.

As the shooting unfolded, an armed bystander, Joe Zamudio, heard the commotion and ran to

Makeshift memorial at the site of the January 8, 2011 shooting in Tucson, Arizona. *Photo by Steve Karp; www.wikimedia.org*

the scene. "I had my gun in my hand," he said later. The first person he encountered was holding a gun, but it turned out that that person wasn't the shooter, but the man who had taken the gun away from the shooter. Zamudio didn't shoot the heroic bystander; instead, he wound up keeping his own gun in its holster because, in the confused few seconds, he "didn't want to be confused as a second gunman."

In the years leading up to the shooting, Loughner had displayed ever more erratic behavior, accelerating after he was evicted from Pima Community College for threatening behavior in 2010. After the shooting, he was diagnosed with schizophrenia, and was found to be increasingly delusional. Loughner pled guilty in 2012 and was sentenced to seven consecutive life prison terms, plus 140 years, without possibility of parole. While his parents took a gun away from him as his behavior deteriorated, he was able to obtain a handgun legally.

Both Giffords and her husband, Mark Kelly – a retired Navy captain and former astronaut – are gun owners. Yet both were motivated by the shooting, and the 2012 Sandy Hook elementary school shooting, to form a group called Americans for Responsible Solutions in 2013, a 501(c)(4) advocacy organization. It also has a separate political action committee. According to them, while they respect and support Second Amendment rights, they also support what they call commonsense protections from gun violence. Through their organization, they press for stronger gun laws, in part working with the Obama administration, and contribute money to the political campaigns of pro-gun safety candidates. After serving three terms in Congress, Giffords retired from her seat in 2012.

In testimony before Congress in 2013 in support of several bills supported by President Barack Obama, including one to limit the capacity of bullet magazines, Kelly testified that if the shooter had been limited to 10-round bullet magazines, fewer people would have been shot, including a nine-year-old girl killed at the scene with the thirteenth bullet he fired, because he was stopped when he changed magazines after emptying the 33-round magazine he obtained legally.

Recommended Readings: Robert J. Spitzer, *The Politics of Gun Control,* 6th ed. (Boulder, CO: Paradigm Publishers, 2015); Dennis Wagner, "Records Detail Shooter's Agitation Before Ariz. Rampage," *USA Today,* March 27, 2013, at http://www.usatoday.com/story/news/nation/2013/03/27/gabby-giffords-shooting-records/2024589/

The Turner Diaries

The Turner Diaries, a novel by William Pierce (1933–2002), a former college instructor at Oregon State University, was first published in 1978 under the pseudonym "Andrew Macdonald." The novel has been blamed for inspiring members of militia organizations to acts of terrorism. Supporters have called *The Turner Diaries* "the book most hated by the gun control crowd," whereas critics have labeled the book "a blueprint for Nazi terror," an "explicit terrorism manual," and "the bible of the racist right." The cover depicts a man and woman firing a pistol and automatic weapon. Originally available only through the National Alliance and other right-wing groups, the novel was republished in 1996 by Barricade Books, a New York publishing house that printed 50,000 copies. In addition, the book was made available on audiocassette. Pierce published a sequel, *Hunter* (second edition, 1998), which portrays a drive-by shooter who murders interracial couples.

The book is a fictional account of violent acts committed in the 1990s by a racist and anti-Semitic underground military group called the "Organization." Prior to the revolutionary tumult, Congress outlaws private ownership of guns, and crime rates soar, with predatory groups wandering at will looking for victims. Members of the Organization take matters into their own hands, retrieving weapons and explosives that have been secretly stored away. Various terrorist acts are depicted, including a mortar attack on the Capitol building and the bombing of public utilities and communication networks. The Organization gains power in the United States and ultimately in the world, killing members of minority groups.

Timothy McVeigh, the convicted bomber of the Murrah Federal Building in Oklahoma City in 1995, avidly promoted the book. He reportedly sent copies to friends, encouraging them to read the novel, and sold the book at guns shows. One friend testified that when he heard of the Oklahoma City bombing, he was reminded of a similar event in the novel and informed the Federal Bureau of Investigation (FBI) about his suspicions. In the novel, Organization members steal ammonium nitrate fertilizer from a farm-supply warehouse, mix it with heating oil, and load bags of the explosive material in a stolen truck. At 9:15 in the morning they explode the truck at the FBI building in Washington, D.C. McVeigh reportedly mailed portions of *The Turner Diaries* to his sister, who burned them after hearing about the Oklahoma City bombing. Police found a passage from the book in the car McVeigh drove on the day of the bombing. The passage stated in part that "[politicians and bureaucrats] learned today that not one of them is beyond our reach. They can huddle behind barbed wire and tanks in the city, or they can hide behind the concrete walls and alarm systems of their country estates, but we can still find them and kill them." Critics charge that other acts of violence by paramilitary organizations were inspired by the novel.

Pierce acknowledged that his book may have had some influence on those involved in the Oklahoma City bombing, but commented that the incident was not politically relevant because the perpetrators lacked sustained organization. He stated in 1996 that he did not approve of the bombing because the country was not yet ready for revolution. The book still can be found for sale at gun show book displays and is available at Amazon.com. That subsequent terrorist attacks such as the Boston marathon bombing have occurred is perhaps less the direct inspiration of the novel than the widespread recognition of similar methods by terrorist groups and radicalized individuals.

See also: Oklahoma City Bombing.

Further Reading: Anti-Defamation League, "The Turner Diaries" (2005), www.archive.adl.org/learn/ext_us/turner.diaries.html; William Pierce ("Andrew Macdonald"), *Hunter,* 2nd ed. (Hillsborough, WV: National Vanguard Books, 1998); William Pierce ("Andrew Macdonald"), *The Turner Diaries* (New York: Barricade Books, 1996).

U

Umpqua Community College Shooting, 2015

On October 1, 2015, 26-year old Christopher Harper-Mercer shot and killed nine people, and wounded nine others, in an attack at Umpqua Community College in Roseburg, Oregon. Wearing body armor, Harper-Mercer entered an English classroom – one in which he had been enrolled – where he herded the students together, asking some of them if they were Christians before shooting them, although he shot both Christians and non-Christians. As police arrived at the scene, the man was wounded by police when he leaned out a window, whereupon he killed himself. Police recovered six guns and considerable additional ammunition from the scene: five handguns and one long gun (which was not fired). Eight more guns were found at the man's apartment. In all, the shooter had 14 guns, all legally obtained either by him or by family members within the previous three years. As an enrolled student at the college, he had taken classes in English and Theater. Harper-Mercer served in the Army for a month in 2008, but was discharged. According to writings he left behind, he had studied past mass shootings, exhibited anger and resentment toward African Americans and about his generalized feelings of isolation, and planned to kill police along with others. His family said that he suffered from long-term mental health problems. He lived with his mother, and the two of them often shot at gun ranges.

During the Umpqua shooting, student and military veteran John Parker was carrying his handgun (concealed carry is allowed on Oregon campuses) as the mass shooting there unfolded. Parker thought about intervening, but decided against, because he thought a SWAT team might confuse him with the attacker. Oregon allows citizens with gun permits to carry guns on college campuses, but they may be restricted from carrying them into buildings, which was the policy at Umpqua.

Further Reading: FBI, "A Study of Active Shooter Incidents in the United States Between 2000 and 2013," U.S. Department of Justice, September 16, 2013; Sara Sidner, et al., "Oregon Shooting: Gunman Was Student in Class where he Killed 9," CNN, October 2, 2015 at http://www.cnn.com/2015/10/02/us/oregon-umpqua-community-college-shooting/

Undetectable Firearms Act

The Undetectable Firearms Act of 1988, also known as the Terrorist Firearms Detection Act, banned the manufacture, importation, possession, receipt, and transfer of plastic and ceramic guns that are undetectable by magnetometers and X-ray machines in airports and other public places. The act specified that a firearm must contain a minimum of 3.7 ounces of metal to make it detectable.

When Congress began consideration of a ban on plastic weapons, the National Rifle Association (NRA) expressed its opposition. In Senate hearings, an NRA representative labeled proposed legislation a "Trojan horse" intended to compromise the gun ownership rights of law-abiding citizens. The organization claimed that simply because terrorists might employ a product does not justify denying its use to the general public. Gun supporters claimed that the new weapons, which were not yet in production, had definite advantages over existing firearms. They would be lighter and more easily used, and would not rust. However, supporters of a ban defined the issue not as one of gun control, but of safety, for the guns were considered a major threat to the security of citizens if they could not be detected by standard equipment.

In February 1988, Vice President George H. W. Bush brought the issue into the national headlines. Participating in a debate among candidates for the Republican nomination for president sponsored by Gun Owners of New Hampshire, Bush showed the audience a small .22-caliber plastic pistol lent to him by the Treasury Department. While reiterating his support for the right of citizens to bear arms, he stated that Congress must deal with new firearms that are virtually undetectable by existing devices. The audience showed its approval and the other candidates quickly agreed with Bush, indicating widespread support for legislation banning plastic guns.

However, Senator James A. McClure, Republican of Idaho, one of the original authors of the Firearms Owners Protection Act, had introduced a weakened measure as an alternative to the one sponsored by Senators Strom Thurmond, Republican of South Carolina, and Howard Metzenbaum, Democrat of Ohio. McClure's proposal, supported by the NRA, would ban guns made entirely of plastic, but would allow the production of firearms with minimum amounts of metal. The NRA expressed its concern that the Thurmond-Metzenbaum legislation would lead to a ban on some existing weapons. Police organizations objected to the McClure proposal, claiming that the standard would allow the production of guns that could not be detected by existing devices.

Representatives of 12 police organizations met with Republican President Ronald Reagan's Attorney General, Edwin Meese, who had expressed his support for the alternative measure. Although the Justice Department initially indicated that advances in electronic equipment would improve the ability to detect weapons, thus obviating the need for stricter standards, the Reagan administration ultimately agreed to change its position and support the more restrictive provisions. In discussions among representatives of the Justice, Treasury, and Transportation Departments and a Law Enforcement Steering Committee representing law enforcement organizations, a compromise level of 3.7 ounces of metal was reached. When the NRA was assured that no existing gun would be banned under this standard, the organization dropped its opposition to the measure.

With all concerned groups supporting the same principle, the House of Representatives and the Senate passed slightly different versions of the bill in May 1988. The final legislation, approved by both houses in October and signed by President Reagan in November 1988, required all guns to set off metal detectors at a level equivalent to a firearm containing 3.7 ounces of stainless steel, or to be detectable by X-ray machines. In 1998 Congress renewed the Act for an additional five years, and in 2003 Congress approved a ten-year renewal. In 2013 Senator Charles Schumer, arguing that some plastic guns still could pass through screening undetected, proposed a revised version of the Act that would mandate non-detachable metal parts to firearms. The National Rifle Association strongly objected to any expansion in the law and so Congress renewed the legislation for another ten years without changes.

Richard Feldman, former lobbyist for the now disbanded American Shooting Sports Council, has noted that the Glock 17—the Austrian-manufactured handgun that was the original focus of controversy—always could be detected by airport or building security X-ray machines and that the controversy revolved around the political motives of gun control and gun rights groups alike.

See also: Bush, George H. W.; Firearms Owners Protection Act; McClure, James Albertas; National Rifle Association; Reagan, Ronald.

Further Reading: Richard Feldman, *Ricochet: Confessions of a Gun Lobbyist* (New York: John Wiley and Sons, 2008); *New York Times* (February 3, 1988), 21A; (March 15, 1988), 20A; (April 27, 1988), 19A; (May 26, 1988), 25A; Library of Congress, "Bill Summary and Status, 108th Congress (2003–2004, H.R. 3348), http://thomas.loc.gov/cgi-bin/bdquery/z? d108:h.r.03348; Josh Sugarmann, *National Rifle Association: Money, Firepower and Fear* (Washington, DC: National Press, 1992);(December 3, 2013); Rebecca Leber, "This Is the Only Gun Safety Bill That Passed Congress This Year," Think Progress (December 10, 2013), www.thinkprogress.org/justice/2013/12/10/303696/congress-undetectable-guns; National Rifle Association, "NRA Statement on the Reauthorization of the 'Undetectable Firearms Act,' HR 3626," www.nraila.org/articles/20131203/nra-statement-on-the-reauthorization-of-the-undetectable-firearms-act-hr-3626.

United Kingdom

Both pro- and anti-gun control groups in the United States have used Great Britain's experience with firearms to argue for their respective positions. Gun rights advocates note that the Magna Carta, signed by King John in 1215, granted rights and freedoms to free men, including the possession of arms for defense and protection against government tyranny. However, over the centuries the British government did not follow a consistent policy on the right to keep and bear arms, at times taking steps to protect, and at other times to limit, that right.

In 1819, Parliament, fearful of civil unrest, passed the "Six Acts," which included a ban on drilling and training in the use of arms and an authorization to search and seize weapons in private homes. In 1903, Parliament, like other European legislatures, passed legislation (the Pistol Act) in reaction to violent crime and the perceived threat of insurrection that arose from the social and economic pressures of industrialization. The Firearms Act was passed in 1920, and in 1937 economic and political unrest combined with international instability led to further firearms legislation in the United Kingdom and other European countries. After World War II, such laws were strengthened even further. In 1988, an additional statute placed even more restrictions on firearms ownership. Subsequently, the British Parliament acted to ban all handguns and many Britons have advocated a complete prohibition on all firearms.

Those on both sides of the gun control debate have disputed the success of gun control policy in the United Kingdom, where even prior to the call for a gun ban, strict regulations had been enacted. Gun control supporters argue that the relatively low homicide rate in Great Britain can be attributed to the country's stringent gun control legislation, while opponents attribute this phenomenon to cultural factors. Advocates of the defensive use of firearms suggest that the inability of the average Briton to deter crime through gun ownership can help to explain the high rate of robbery in Great Britain—criminals have little to fear from their victims.

By the early 1990s, British gun regulations required all firearms owners to have licenses for their weapons and to register them. Identification of the person seeking a permit must be established, including photographs and the verification of another individual who knows the applicant. To receive a permit, applicants must not have any criminal record, mental problems, or history of drug or alcohol abuse. The applicant must have sufficient reason to own a firearm, which cannot include defense of the home or personal protection. A weapon must be stored in a secure place, and the applicant must have a safe location to shoot the weapon. Purchasers of long guns, including shotguns, must acquire a police certificate. Possessing a firearm with criminal intent could lead to a maximum punishment of life imprisonment, and simple illegal possession can bring a three-year sentence. Although traditionally British police have not carried firearms, in recent years that practice has been modified. Some police are now regularly armed and others can be quickly provided with weapons to meet extraordinary dangers. Still, the use of firearms by police is generally considered a last resort, limited to situations where such use can prevent the loss of life.

Warning against hasty conclusions from cross-national comparisons, Gary Kleck, in *Targeting Guns: Firearms and Their Control* (1997), criticized the association of lower rates of violence in Great Britain with more stringent gun legislation, a relationship that Kleck considered spurious. Kleck noted that in 1919, when British gun laws were far less strict, the homicide rate for England and Wales was 0.8 per 100,000, while the rate for the United States in the same year was 9.5, or 11.9 times as great as Great Britain. The homicide rate in the United States in the period 1983 to 1986 was 7.59 per 100,000, 11.3 times as great as the British rate of 0.67. Kleck concluded that after more than six decades of stricter gun laws in Great Britain, the difference between British and American homicide rates actually declined slightly, implying that more stringent gun regulations had no effect on the homicide rate. However, hidden within that finding may be other factors such as a low rate of gun ownership in Great Britain that extends from 1919 to the present, and the enactment of many gun control laws in the United States at all levels of government.

Proposals for even more severe gun restrictions surfaced after the 1996 shooting of 16 schoolchildren and their teacher in the Scottish town of Dunblane. The call from the British public for additional gun control measures was far more extensive than has occurred in the United States in similar circumstances. In 1997, Parliament approved firearms legislation that outlawed handguns larger than .22 caliber. Handguns of .22 caliber or less must be stored at gun clubs. The legislation granted police greater discretion in licensing procedures and required all people who use a handgun to have a license. In addition, strict controls were placed on expanding ammunition and mail-order sales of firearms. These additional controls notwithstanding, in June 2010 Derrick Bird, a 52-year-old Whitehaven cab driver, shot and killed his twin brother and the family lawyer before starting on a shooting spree that left 12 dead and as many wounded. The gunman finally shot and killed himself. Bird held licenses for a shotgun and a .22-caliber rifle, the two firearms he used in the shootings.

Gun rights supporters cite data indicating that the 1997 legislation has been a failure. For instance, they point out that the violent crime rate in the United Kingdom doubled from 1997 to 2001 and that the probability of being mugged in London increased to six times that of New York City. Also mentioned is that 53 percent of burglaries in England, but only 13 percent in the United States, occur when occupants are home, leading to the conclusion that in the United States, burglars fear armed residents. However, in 1997 Franklin Zimring reported that assaults in New York result in 11 times more deaths than in London and that 81 percent of assaults in London, compared to 13 percent in New York, did not involve a weapon. Nigel Morris noted in 2009 that the number of firearm-related deaths in the United Kingdom had dropped to its lowest level in 20 years. Undoubtedly, factors other than implementation of the 1997 firearms law in the United Kingdom contributed to increased incidents of crime, especially when it is noted that firearm ownership was already very low before its passage.

The more stringent firearms laws notwithstanding, commentators note that large numbers of guns are still in present in the United Kingdom, and mass shootings still occur, as happened in 2010 when a 52-year-old taxi driver, who possessed two rifles, killed twelve people in Cumbria in northern England. However, data indicate that the overall rate of deaths from firearms has decreased somewhat, from 0.42 per 100,000 population in 1996 to 0.22 per 100,000 population in 2013. Similarly, the firearm homicide rate declined from 0.14 in 1996 to 0.04 per 100,000 in in 2013. Also, the suicide rate per 100,000 declined from 0.23 in 1996 to 0.17 in 2013.

See also: Kleck, Gary; Zimring, Franklin

Further Reading: Wilbur Edel, *Gun Control: Threat to Liberty or Defense Against Anarchy?* (Westport, CT: Preager, 1995); Tony Jingo, "The UK Gun Ban," *Associated Content* (July 16, 2009), www.associatedcontent.com/article/1950860/the_uk_gun_ban.html?cat=17; Gary Kleck, *Targeting Guns: Firearms and Their Control* (New York: Aldine De Gruyter, 1997); David B. Kopel, *The Samurai, the Mountie, and the Cowboy: Should America Adopt the Gun Controls of Other Democracies?* (Buffalo, NY: Prometheus, 1992); Ben McConville and Jennifer Quinn, "Rampage Motive Still Unknown," *Houston Chronicle* (June 4, 2010), A15; Stryker McGuire, "The Dunblane Effect: Horror From the Massacre Prompts a Ban on Handguns," *Newsweek* 128 (October 28, 1996), 46; Nigel Morris, "Britain Records 18% Fall in Gun Deaths," *The Independent* (January 8, 2009), www/independent.co.uk/news/uk/crime/britain-records-18-fall-in-gun-deaths-1232069.html; Pacific Center for Violence Prevention, "Handgun Ban Becomes Law," www.pcvp.org/firearms (1998); Gordon Witkin, "A Very Different Gun Culture: Britain Plans a Near Total Ban on Handguns," *U.S. News and World Report* 121 (October 28, 1996), 44; Franklin E. Zimring, *Crime Is Not the Problem: Lethal Violence in America* (New York: Oxford University Press, 1997); Peter Wilkinson, "Dunblane: How UK School Massacre Led to Tighter Gun Control," Cable News Network (December 17, 2012), www.cnn.com/2012/12/17/world/europe/dunblane-lessons/index.html; Philip Alpers, "United Kingdom—Gun Facts, Figures and the Law," International Firearm Injury Prevention and Policy, www.gunpolicy.org/firearms/region/united-kingdom (accessed July 16, 2016).

United Nations (UN)

In recent years, United Nations (UN) agencies have investigated the possibility of international initiatives to control the world market in small arms. UN agencies express concern that while trade in major weapons has declined, the spread of small arms has continued apace throughout the world. Those UN agencies that have been involved in discussions to propose controls on light weapons include the Disarmament Commission, the Panel of Governmental Experts on Small Arms, and the Economic and Social Council's Commission on Crime Prevention and Criminal Justice. Many participants support international agreements

The United Nations (Manhattan headquarters pictured here) has raised concerns among American gun rights groups with its recent efforts to explore the possibility of international initiatives to control the world market in small arms. *www.wikimedia.org*

to control private arms trading, limit smuggling activities, and increase the security of police and military arms caches. However, these investigations raised concerns among gun rights organizations that multinational agreements might result in increased restrictions on gun ownership in the United States.

In 1995, the Economic and Social Council, spurred by financial support from Japan, launched a global study of firearm ownership and use. The purpose of the study was to gain information about civilian possession of firearms, the use of firearms in crime, and the effectiveness of existing firearms regulations in approximately 50 countries. James Hayes of the Firearms Control Task Group of the Canadian Department of Justice became coordinator for the project. The UN Center for International Crime Prevention prepared the report *International Study on Firearm Regulation*.

In May 1996, the UN Commission on Crime Prevention and Criminal Justice met in Vienna, Austria, to discuss summary information from the multicountry survey, which included

data about gun-related accidents and suicides, transnational illicit trafficking in firearms, and regional legislative efforts. A report from the secretariat included such possible action as making recommendations to governments about creating a database to facilitate sharing information worldwide about firearms and initiating cooperation among nations to control illegal firearms trafficking. Policy proposals included the destruction of small weapons remaining at the end of an armed conflict, the introduction of a technologically sophisticated marking system to facilitate tracing of firearms, and establishing a global registry of firearms licenses.

Gun rights organizations have strongly criticized these initiatives, as well as what they consider inappropriate deliberative procedures within UN agencies. They fear that UN agreements could result in gun licensing and registration requirements imposed on the United States. Gun rights advocates refer to the UN treaty to ban landmines to illustrate the potential dangers of a firearms agreement for the United States, whose request for an exemption to keep landmines along the Korean demilitarized zone was rejected.

The National Rifle Association (NRA) obtained recognition as a nongovernmental organization to participate in various UN deliberations on the issue of gun control. In April 1998, Tanya Metaksa, then head of the NRA's Institute for Legislative Action (ILA), addressed a meeting of the UN Commission on Crime Prevention and Criminal Justice held in Vienna, Austria. Metaksa denounced various proposals to regulate firearms, contending that they went far beyond attempts to prevent illicit international arms trading and would seriously restrict the rights of law-abiding firearms owners. Responding to the exclusion of NRA representatives from certain UN agency meetings, Metaksa recommended a commitment to democratic processes within UN agencies and institutions. She urged an "open meeting" and "public records" policy for the UN, which would ensure greater access for pro-gun organizations like the NRA/ILA.

In December 2000, the UN General Assembly adopted the United Nations Convention Against Transnational Organized Crime, and in May 2001, the Assembly endorsed one of the agreements associated with the Convention, a Protocol Against the Illicit Manufacturing of and Trafficking in Firearms, Their Parts and Components and Ammunition. According to the protocol, signatory states would establish policies to eliminate illegal firearms manufacturing, trace existing illegal weapons, and prosecute offenders; collaborate with other nations in stopping the illegal manufacture and trafficking of firearms; regulate the export and import of firearms; and share information about illegal firearms with other nations. The United States signed the Convention in December 2000 and it was sent, along with two other protocols, to the U.S. Senate in February 2004 for ratification. The Senate Foreign Relations Committee held hearings in June 2004, but took no further action.

Assurances that such agreements are intended to fight organized crime and to reduce rampant violence around the world notwithstanding, many gun rights advocates claimed that the stated goal of restricting the illegal gun trade was only the surface objective of the protocol, and that the ultimate purpose was to disarm ordinary citizens. In 2005, a working group continued to develop a draft international treaty for tracing "Illicit Small Arms and Light Weapons," and subsequent meetings have been held. Assisting in the effort is the International Action Network on Small Arms (IANSA), which was established in 1998 as a coalition of approximately 800 nongovernmental organizations to support the regulation of the distribution and use of small arms and light weapons. The IANSA and its director, Rebecca Peters, have been strongly criticized by gun rights groups such as the NRA and its executive vice president, Wayne LaPierre.

In a November 2010 mailing, Alan M. Gottlieb, chairman of the Citizens Committee for the Right to Keep and Bear Arms (CCRKBA), asked supporters to sign and return a petition, "Don't let the UN take our Guns," which CCRKBA would then submit to U.S. Senate majority leader Harry Reid. Gottlieb said that he hoped to deliver at least 600,000 petitions and stated that "Gun owners are facing another emergency as gun banners and America haters are again trying to use the United Nations to disarm law-abiding citizens." Gottlieb referred to a report to the UN Secretary General on the activities of the Commission on Crime Prevention and Criminal Justice that he claimed would require hunters to store their firearms in sports clubs and would permit only smooth-bore firearms or shotguns for personal defense. Gottlieb asked supporters to send a donation along with the signed petition.

UN consideration of an Arms Trade Treaty (ATT) initiated strong opposition from the NRA and other gun rights organizations in the United States. The NRA campaigned for the removal of civilian firearm ownership from the treaty, but the organization concluded that its recommendation was not heeded, although the treaty's Preamble recognizes "the legitimate trade and lawful ownership, and use of certain conventional arms for recreational, cultural, historical, and sporting activities, where such trade, ownership, and use are permitted by law."

The UN General Assembly approved the Treaty on April 2, 2013, and U.S. Secretary of State John Kerrey signed the document at the UN headquarters in New York City on September 25, 2013. However, U.S. ratification would not officially occur until the Senate approved the treaty by a two-thirds vote, which is an unlikely outcome. The NRA, in its continuing opposition to the Treaty, claimed that U.S. firearms policy could still be subject to international control through trade restrictions that could be imposed if the United States did not meet the provisions of the treaty.

See also: Canada; Institute for Legislative Action; Japan; Metaksa, Tanya K.; National Rifle Association; United States-Mexico Gun Trade.

Further Reading: Ronald Bailey, "Global Gun Grabbers," *Weekly Standard* (February 23, 1998), 19–20; Marjorie Ann Browne, "The United Nations and 'Gun Control,'" Congressional Research Service (April 7, 2005); Robert M. Hausman, "Arms Ban Strategies Disclosed at UN Meeting," *Gun News Digest* (Spring 1998), 28–30; Wayne LaPierre, *The Global War on Your Guns: Inside the UN Plan To Destroy the Bill of Rights* (Nashville, TN: Thomas Nelson, 2006); Helen Metaksa, "Metaksa Tells UN Commission on Crime to Open Closed Doors," *Gun Week* (June 20, 1998), 5; United Nations, "United Nations Global Study Begun on Civilian-Owned Firearms, Small Arms Trafficking, Firearms Re; United Nations Arms Trade Treaty, www.un.org/disarmament/ATT; National Rifle Association, "International and United Nations Gun Control," www.nraila.org/issues/internationalun-gun-control-issues (accessed August 1, 2016); Henry B. Sirgo, "U.S. Import and Export of Firearms," in Glenn H. Utter, ed., Guns and Contemporary Society (Santa Barbara, CA: Praeger, 2016): vol. 2, 51-74.

United States Concealed Carry Association (USCCA)

The establishment of the United States Concealed Carry Association is clearly the result of the expansion in recent years of some form of concealed carry laws in all fifty states. In addition, many states, by passing so-called stand-your-ground laws, have expanded the right of self-defense in public places by eliminating the duty to retreat before resorting to the use of deadly force. Tim Schmidt established the organization in 2003 to offer education and self-defense training to those carrying a concealed weapon. The USCCA also offers self-defense insurance coverage, called "Self-Defense Shield," that provides legal and other assistance to those who fire a weapon in self-defense. The USCCA offers four levels of insurance coverage: Silver ($300,000), Gold ($575,000), and Platinum ($1,100,000). The cost of the insurance is $13 per month for Silver, $22 per month for Gold, and $30 per month for Platinum.

The USCCA, in encouraging individuals to purchase one of the insurance plans, conducts the "Gun-a-Day Giveaway," which offers to prospective enrollees a chance to win a new firearm. Rather than giving the actual gun, the organization sends each winner a check for the manufacturer's suggested retail price of the firearm.

Those involved in a shooting incident who are covered by the USCCA insurance program will receive funds to help post bail and to retain an attorney experienced in the law of self-defense. If the case goes to trial, insured members will receive compensation for lost wages. Even with passage of stand-your-ground laws in many states, the USCCA still claims that "the deck is stacked against the responsible gun owner." Schmidt refers to "crooked defense attorneys who bring civil damage cases against those who have used a firearm in self-defense and on behalf of the criminal aggressor." Therefore, the organization claims that the insurance program is crucial to enduring the legal and emotional aftermath of a shooting incident.

Schmidt repeatedly emphasizes that those carrying concealed weapons should be responsibly armed. Those who fail to act responsibly, Schmidt argues, harm the image of "respectable firearm-owning civilians." Those carrying concealed weapons must act appropriately when they take potentially deadly action, knowing in advance when force may be used justifiably and legally. The USCCA offers online training programs and DVDs such as "Home Security and Home Defense" and "Developing a Personal Protection Plan." The organization also distributes Concealed Carry Magazine and an online weekly newsletter, Concealed Carry Report as well as broadcasts on Armed American Radio and Armed American Television. The organization advises: "Don't do anything stupid, careless, or reckless," and know the law when it come to the legal use of self-defense.

The USCCA strongly supports concealed carry, but expresses doubts about the open carry of firearms, which, the organization argues, leaves the carrier at a disadvantage because criminals are allowed the opportunity to take steps to target and disarm an individual carrying a weapon openly.

See also: Castle Doctrine; Self-Defense; Stand-Your-Ground Laws.

Further Reading: United States Concealed Carry Association Website, www.usconcealedcarry.com; Tim Schmidt, *Guns, Freedom, and the American Dream: The Story of Tim Schmidt and the USCCA* (West Bend, WI: Delta Defense, 2015).

United States Conference of Mayors (USCM)

Since 1968, the United States Conference of Mayors (USCM) has advocated various gun control policies. In 1994, the Conference adopted a resolution calling for several gun control measures, including a ban on the manufacture, sale, and possession of all semiautomatic weapons and component parts; a requirement to register all newly purchased and transferred firearms and the imposition of a registration fee; expansion of the Brady Handgun Violence Prevention Act background check to all firearms sales; a tightening of federal gun dealer licensing provisions; an increase in taxes on ammunition and firearms sales; a ban on armor-piercing and hollow-point ammunition; and the destruction of all firearms confiscated by law enforcement agencies.

The USCM was established in 1932 as a nonpartisan organization of mayors representing cities with populations of 30,000 or more. The Conference strives "to aid the development of effective national urban policy, strengthen federal-city relationships, ensure that federal policy meets urban needs, and provide mayors with leadership and management tools of value in their cities." An executive committee and an advisory board develop and guide policies and programs, and the executive director, who is appointed by the executive committee, serves as the chief administrative officer. An annual conference is held each June.

In 1998, the USCM took active steps to initiate gun control provisions at the local, state, and national levels. In March, Chicago Mayor Richard M. Daley, president of the Conference, and Fort Wayne, Indiana, Mayor Paul Helmke, the vice president (who in 2006 became president of the Brady Campaign to Prevent Gun Violence), met with Sarah and Jim Brady in a Capitol Hill press conference to announce proposed legislation to require all handguns sold to be equipped with safety locks. The Chicago City Council had just adopted an ordinance requiring that all handguns registered, sold, or transferred must be equipped with safety mechanisms, such as trigger locks, to prevent unauthorized use, especially by children, and load indicators showing whether weapons contain ammunition.

The 1998 USCM annual conference formed a mayoral task force that initiated discussions with gun manufacturers about measures that could be taken to make firearms safer and keep them out of the hands of criminals. Philadelphia Mayor Ed Rendell, chair of the task force, called for passage of a national Straw Purchaser Enforcement Act to prevent the sale of large quantities of handguns to one person who then sells them to those prohibited from owning firearms. He asked the firearms industry to take precautions to prevent the stealing of guns from manufacturing plants and called for ammunition manufacturers to buy back armor-piercing bullets from retail outlets that still have them in stock.

In August 1998, Rendell, four other mayors, and representatives of the National Association of Counties met with Richard Feldman and others from the American Shooting Sports Council in St. Louis, Missouri, to discuss possible steps to reduce gun violence. The group discussed placing greater restrictions on selling firearms at gun shows and proposed legislation to limit individuals to purchasing one handgun a month. Rendell, who was scheduled to testify before a special Senate hearing on September 2 regarding restrictions on gun sales, invited the manufacturers to accompany him. However, Feldman later declined the request. Rendell testified at the hearing and several other

members of the gun violence task force submitted letters supporting the proposed legislation.

The mayors of several cities initiated another strategy, filing lawsuits against firearms manufacturers and gun dealers to recover the medical and legal costs of violent crimes. In October 1998, New Orleans Mayor Marc H. Morial announced a lawsuit against 15 manufacturers, 3 trade associations, and several local pawnshops and gun dealers, and in November, Mayor Daley of Chicago announced a lawsuit against 12 gun shops in the suburbs surrounding Chicago, 22 gun manufacturers, and 4 gun distributors. Following the announcement, Daley wrote to USCM executive director J. Thomas Cochran, encouraging other cities to consider filing similar suits. The Chicago lawsuit involved the claim that gun manufacturers had become a "public nuisance" by oversupplying gun shops outside the city's jurisdiction, intending that the handguns would be sold to city residents. In the article "Gun Shy" (1998), gun researcher John R. Lott, Jr., questioned such lawsuits, claiming that the economic benefits derived from the defensive use of firearms far outweigh the costs cities are attempting to recover. In early 1999, several other cities, including Boston, San Francisco, and Bridgeport, Connecticut, were taking steps to develop lawsuits against firearms manufacturers. Rendell proposed a simultaneous filing by up to 100 cities. To counter this strategy, gun interests began lobbying efforts to have state legislatures and Congress limit the authority of local jurisdictions to file such suits. In 2005, Congress passed the Protection of Lawful Commerce in Firearms Act, which prohibited lawsuits against firearms manufacturers and dealers for crimes committed with firearms they produced and sold. The law also mandated that handguns be sold with child safety locks.

In April 2009, the USCM submitted an *amicus curiae* brief to the U.S. Court of Appeals for the Seventh Circuit in support of Chicago's restrictions on firearms ownership. Lawrence Rosenthal, professor of law at Chapman University in Orange, California, prepared the brief, in which he argued that the Fourteenth Amendment does not apply the Second Amendment to state and local governments and emphasized that gun control laws play a crucial role in municipalities' efforts to fight crime. The U.S. Supreme Court ultimately ruled in *McDonald v. Chicago* (2010) that state and local governments are bound by the Second Amendment protection of an individual's right to possess firearms. Also in 2009, USCM president Greg Nickels, mayor of Seattle, Washington, joined other mayors in opposing the Thune Amendment to the National Defense Authorization Act for FY 2010 that would have mandated that states recognize the concealed carry permits of all other states. The U.S. Senate defeated the amendment in July 2009.

At the 78th annual meeting in 2010, the Conference approved a resolution supporting a declaration signed by mayors from 50 major cities worldwide who met in April 2010 in Chicago at the Sixth Annual Richard J. Daley Global Cities Forum. The mayors at the forum concluded that illegal firearms in cities results in "unacceptable levels of human, social and economic damage" and are subverting efforts to improve safety and the quality of life in cities. The mayors agreed to ask their national governments to take action to cooperate in dealing with global gun trafficking and firearm violence; called on the United States to lead the way by establishing greater regulation of the firearms industry and by enforcing strict regulation of gun trafficking; pledged to pursue restitution from the gun industry through their legal systems for damages caused by trafficking in illegal guns; and agreed to demand that the news media report more thoroughly on the international gun trade.

At the June 2015 annual meeting, the USCM approved a resolution supporting laws that prohibit individuals "convicted of domestic violence crimes, including violent misdemeanors, or subject to final domestic violence restraining orders from acquiring or possessing firearms." The resolution also strongly opposed state firearm preemption laws that authorize lawsuits against local officials who institute policies to reduce gun violence. The resolution expressed opposition to proposals to permit teachers and non-security school employees to carry firearms in the public schools, stating that trained law enforcement officers and professional security personnel are best able to protect children and teachers.

Following the June 2016 mass shooting in Orlando, Florida, in which a gunman killed 49 people, USCM president Stephanie Rawlings-Blake, mayor of Baltimore, Maryland, issued a statements condemning the shooting, praising the responding police officers, and calling for action to reduce "the unacceptable level of gun violence."

See also: American Shooting Sports Council; Brady Handgun Violence Prevention Act; Brady, James; Brady, Sarah; Gun Shows; Lott, John R.; Straw Purchases; Trigger Locks.

Further Reading: Richard Feldman, *Ricochet: Confessions of a Gun Lobbyist* (New York: John Wiley and Sons, 2008); "Local Gun Laws Tested in Federal Courts," *U.S. Mayor Newspaper* (May 11, 2009), http://usmayors.org/usmayornewspaper/document/05_11_09/pg7_local_gun_law.asp; John R. Lott, Jr., "Gun Shy: Cities Turn from Regulation to Litigation in Their Campaign Against Guns," *National Review* 50 (December 21, 1998), 46–48; Roberto Suro, "Targeting Gun Makers with a Cigarette Strategy," *Washington Post National Weekly Edition* 16 (January 4, 1999), 30; "Thune Concealed Gun Amendment Defeated in Senate," *U.S. Mayor* Newspaper (July 27, 2009), http://usmayors. org/ usmayornewspaper/documents/07_27_09/ pg1_thune. asp; United States Council of Mayors, "Resolution in Support of the Collective Agreement on Gun Violence Signed by Mayors Assembled at the 2010 Richard J. Daley Global Cities Forum, Chicago, Illinois" (June 2010), www.usmayors.org/resolutions/78th_ Conference/ adoptedresolutionsfull.pdf.

United States Practical Shooting Association (USPSA)

The United States Practical Shooting Association (USPSA), a promoter of the sport of defensive shooting in various scenarios using handguns to shoot rapidly and with accuracy, conducts the Open and Limited National Championships each year and sponsors Steel Challenge championships. The organization is affiliated with the International Practical Shooting Confederation (IPSC) and sends the United States shooting team to the IPSC World Shoot every three years. The USPSA distributes *Front Sight*, a bimonthly magazine containing articles and features on the various aspects of practical shooting, including improvement of competitive skills, reloading, practical shooting accessories, future matches, and views on practical shooting. The organization includes rifle and shotgun competitions in its practical shooting program.

Based on the adult Steel Challenge competitions, the organization sponsors the Scholastic Steel Challenge, which offers those aged 12 through 20 the opportunity to take part in "speed steel," a family-oriented competitive sport. Trained adult coaches provide support and training in how to handle and fire handguns safely. The USPSA states that the program provides "a safe action packed competition, one that both neophyte and experienced shooters will enjoy." The organization also has established a program, First Shots, that is offered at the Steel Challenge World Shoot to introduce novices to the sport.

The organization previously distributed *In Touch*, a newsletter that frequently contained articles expressing the leadership's concern about various gun control efforts. In the February 1998 issue, Keith Milberger, Area 4 Director, discussed the lack of unity in the USPSA and other pro-gun organizations, in contrast to the singleness of purpose he perceived in pro-gun control groups. Milberger claimed that Handgun Control, Inc. (which in 2001 became the Brady Campaign to Prevent Gun Violence) had been successful because it possessed a specific focus. He complained that pro-gun supporters seemed unable to agree on anything except that "the gun grabbers" are succeeding and no effective opposition was being mustered against them. Milberger suggested that to defend shooting sports, all members must "get along and work together or they just need to go."

The newsletter referred to potential problems resulting from allowing minor children to participate in shooting matches and the bad publicity generated by such "left-wing, anti-gun" news anchors as Dan Rather and Tom Brokaw. The organization reported that it was developing policies to be adopted by the board of directors that were intended to "prevent any legal disaster that may befall us as well as any foreseeable personal disaster associated with a junior program." Proposed guidelines would include a statement holding a parent or guardian responsible for the safety of a minor and requiring a parental presence when a minor is armed and shooting. Given that gun control organizations opposed the involvement of minor children in shooting events, the USPSA at the time was sensitive to the possibility that any accident would not only lead to legal action, but also could result in limitations on the sport.

Like many other pro-gun rights organizations, the USPSA campaigned against the 1997 ballot initiative in the state of Washington that would have placed limitations on the ownership of handguns. The organization's newsletter stated that the proposal "originated in the White House" and predicted that if the measure was successful in Washington, members could expect similar initiatives in their own states. Members were advised to call legislators, write letters to local newspapers, and contact friends and acquaintances in Washington to offer assistance. The ballot measure ultimately failed.

Nelson, Area 2 Director, noted that the organization could find itself in a "Catch 22" circumstance when it discovered that a member legally should not be handling firearms, but have no way of excluding such a person without exposing the organization to a lawsuit. Nelson expressed frustration that the organization had no effective means of abiding by provisions of the Brady Handgun Violence Prevention Act.

See also: Brady Campaign to Prevent Gun Violence; Brady Handgun Violence Prevention Act; International Defensive Pistol Association; Youth and Guns.

Further Reading: United States Practical Shooting Association Website, www.uspsa.org.

United States v. Cruikshank (1876)

In *United States v. Cruikshank* (92 U.S. 542, 1876), the U.S. Supreme Court made its first major ruling on the Second Amendment right to keep and bear arms. The final decision limiting the right to bear arms was based on the Supreme Court's refusal to recognize that the Fourteenth Amendment protected the rights of American citizens from state action. The defendants were found guilty in federal district court of violating the sixth section of the Force Act of 1870 by conspiring to deprive two black men (Levi Nelson and Alexander Tillman) of their rights guaranteed by the First and Second Amendments to the U.S. Constitution to freedom of speech and assembly, and to bear arms. A circuit court of appeals overruled the district court, after which U.S. officials appealed the decision to the U.S. Supreme Court.

Among the various counts in the indictment, the defendants were charged with joining together with the intent to "injure, oppress, threaten, and intimidate" two citizens of African descent and "persons of color," with the objective of preventing their exercise of the right to assemble with others "for a peaceable and lawful purpose." Also included in the indictment was the charge that the defendants wished to prevent the exercise of "the right to keep and bear arms for a lawful purpose."

The Court stated that for the case to be placed under the statute, the rights that were violated must be ones granted by the Constitution or laws of the United States. If this were not the case, the criminal charges were not indictable by any act of Congress. The federal government was established for specific purposes, and could not grant or secure for citizens any right that the Constitution did not place under its jurisdiction. The Court understood national powers narrowly as only those powers expressly delegated to the national government.

Regarding the right of assembly, the Court ruled that it existed prior to the adoption of the U.S. Constitution and was not a right granted to the people by that document. The states had the obligation to protect this right, but the national government had no duty to require states to fulfill such an obligation. The First Amendment, protection of the right of assembly only limits the power of the national government. For the people to enjoy its continued operation, they must appeal to the states.

The Court ruled similarly on the charge that the defendants hindered the right of the two African Americans to bear arms for a lawful purpose. Again, the Court stated that this right was not granted by the U.S. Constitution, nor was it dependent on the Constitution for its continued existence. Although the Second Amendment stated that the right to bear arms shall not be infringed, this meant, according to the Court, simply that Congress shall not place limitations on this right. Only the powers of the national government are restricted by this amendment. The people must look to the legal actions of the states, or what the Court termed the "internal police," to protect them against a violation of this right by fellow citizens.

With regard to the argument that the Fourteenth Amendment prohibits states from depriving any person of life, liberty, or property without due process of law, the Court ruled that this amendment contributed nothing to the rights that one citizen has against another, but offers an "additional guarantee" against the invasion by state governments of the rights that every member of society already has. Nothing was added to the rights any citizen possessed under the Constitution. The Court claimed that the duty of protecting citizens fell originally on the states, and that duty had not changed. The Fourteenth Amendment only guaranteed that states could not deny rights mentioned within it, and the power of the national government ended at that point.

The Court ruled that the Civil Rights Act of 1866, intended to protect citizens of the United States against discrimination on the basis of race, color, or previous condition of servitude, did not apply in this case because the charges of violating the rights of citizens did not indicate that such violation was due to the race or color of the victims.

See also: African Americans and Guns; Fourteenth Amendment; Second Amendment.

Further Reading: Earl R. Kruschke, *The Right to Keep and Bear Arms: A Continuing American Dilemma* (Springfield, IL: Charles C. Thomas, 1985); Mark A. Siegel, Nancy R. Jacobs, and Carol D. Foster, eds., *Gun Control: Restricting Rights or Protecting People?* (Wylie, TX: Information Plus, 1991).

United States v. Emerson (2001)

Contrary to previous decisions of U.S. courts of appeals, the U.S. Court of Appeals for the Fifth Circuit in *United States v. Emerson* (270 F.3d 203, 2001) ruled that the Second Amendment to the U.S. Constitution guarantees a right of individuals to keep and bear arms. The *Emerson* decision involved a challenge to the constitutionality of a federal statute, 19 U.S.C. § 922 (g) (8) (C) (ii), that prohibited a person subject to a court order involving threatened physical force against a domestic partner or child from transporting firearms or ammunition across state lines. Timothy Joe Emerson's wife had obtained a temporary injunction against Emerson, which was to remain in effect until a final divorce decree. While the injunction was still in effect, Emerson was charged with the possession of a pistol "in and affecting interstate commerce." The U.S. District Court for the Northern District of Texas granted Emerson's motion to dismiss the indictment in part because the statute violated the Second Amendment guarantee of a right to keep and bear arms.

The government appealed the dismissal to the Fifth Circuit Court of Appeals, which reversed the dismissed indictment and returned the indictment to the district court for trial. However, the appeals court judges presented an argument that the Second Amendment guarantees an individual's right to possess firearms, but a right, similar to the First Amendment right to free speech, that is not unlimited. The court presented three possible interpretations of the Second Amendment. The first is the "states' rights" or "collective rights" interpretation, which holds that each state has the right to maintain an armed militia. The second contends that any individual's right to possess firearms must be associated with active participation in an organized state militia. The final interpretation, and the one with which the court agreed, is that the Second Amendment guarantees the right of individuals to possess and carry firearms.

The court's decision took the view that the U.S. Supreme Court decision in *United States v. Miller* (1939) did not support the collectivist interpretation of the Second Amendment, but instead held to the understanding that the National Firearms Act's reference to a shotgun with a sawed-off barrel "less than eighteen inches in length" is not one of the "Arms" the Second Amendment prohibits government from infringing the rights of individuals to keep and bear. The court's examination of the history and wording of the Second Amendment, including the meaning of "the people," "bear arms," and the preamble's statement that "A well-regulated militia, being necessary to the security of a free State," led to the conclusion that the amendment protects an individual right. However, the court recognized that exceptions could be made to that right, such as that minors and felons could be kept from possessing firearms. In the case of Emerson, the court concluded that the injunction was "minimally" sufficient to deprive Emerson of the right to keep and bear arms. In another seven years, the U.S. Supreme Court, in the justices' first ruling since *Miller* on the Second Amendment, would follow similar reasoning to find the District of Columbia's restrictive gun statute unconstitutional because it violated an individual right to possess firearms guaranteed in the Second Amendment.

See also: District of Columbia v. Heller (2008); National Firearms Act of 1934; Second Amendment; *United States v. Miller* (1939).

Further Reading: *United States v. Emerson*, United States Court of Appeals for the Fifth Circuit (270 F.3d 203, 2001).

United States v. Freed (1971)

The issues brought before the U.S. Supreme Court in *United States v. Freed* (401 U.S. 601, 1971) involved the frequent concerns expressed by gun rights advocates that gun control measures violate not only the Second Amendment but also infringe on the protection against self-incrimination guaranteed in the Fifth Amendment and in addition lead to the punishment of a law-abiding individual who unknowingly breaks the law. In the *Freed* case, the defendants were charged with possessing and conspiring to possess hand grenades that had not been registered according to the provisions of federal firearms legislation.

The Supreme Court had previously held unconstitutional a portion of the National Firearms Act under the self-incrimination clause of the Fifth Amendment. The law levied a tax on certain classes of firearms that were used for unlawful purposes and provided for giving information about such weapons and their illegal owners to state and local government officials. In response to the Court's ruling, Congress amended the law to require only the lawful manufacturers and importers of firearms to register them. The amended law mandated that persons transferring weapons at issue identify themselves, describe the weapons, and provide the names and addresses of the persons to whom the weapons are transferred, along with their photograph and fingerprints. No information received by the federal government can be used against a registrant in a criminal proceeding dealing with a violation of the law that occurred before or concurrently with the application filing or registration. No information may be shared with other federal agencies or with state and local government officials.

Despite the amendments to the law, the defendants in the *Freed* case argued that the law compelled self-incrimination and that the law infringed on due process by omitting a specific knowledge of the law. In addition, the defendants maintained that the fingerprints and photograph requirement could lead to future incrimination. They argued that registering under federal law would have incriminated them under California law, which outlaws possession of hand grenades. The district court granted the defendants' motion to dismiss the case, arguing that the amended act, like the original legislation, violated the protection against self-incrimination.

Hearing the case on direct appeal, the U.S. Supreme Court reversed the lower court decision, concluding that the amended act presents no realistic possibility of violating the self-incrimination clause of the Fifth Amendment. The court observed that the transferor makes the potentially incriminating statements, not the person receiving the weapon. Although the law requires the receiver's fingerprints and photo, the process makes the recipient the lawful possessor of the weapon. Noting that the defendants asserted that the self-incrimination clause protects a person against past and present as well as future violations, the Court ruled that the clause cannot be stretched to supply "insulation for a career of crime about to be launched."

With regard to the defendants' scienter claim (that they lacked knowledge of the law they were accused of violating), the Court noted that the statute does not require demonstration of intent or knowledge that the hand grenades were unregistered, but simply makes it unlawful for a person "to receive or possess a [controlled] firearm which is not registered to him." The only knowledge necessary was that the thing possessed was a firearm. The Court did not consider the claimed lack of knowledge a disqualifying circumstance, noting that "one would hardly be surprised to learn that possession of hand grenades is not an innocent act." They are "highly dangerous offensive weapons," presenting a hazard to the public similar to that posed by narcotics.

See also: National Firearms Act of 1934; Second Amendment.

Further Reading: *United States v. Freed*, 401 U.S. 601 (1971).

United States v. Lopez (1995)

The U.S. Supreme Court, in *United States v. Lopez* (115 U.S. 1624, 1995), affirmed the reversal of the conviction of Alphonso Lopez, Jr., by the Court of Appeals for the Fifth Circuit. Lopez had been found guilty in the U.S. District Court for the Western District of Texas of violating the Gun-Free School Zones Act of 1990. Congress had made it a federal crime for an individual knowingly to possess a firearm within a public, parochial, or private school, or within a zone extending 1,000 feet from the grounds of a school. In disallowing this gun control measure, the Court majority did not base its decision on the Second Amendment, but relied instead on an interpretation of Congress's commerce power.

On March 12, 1992, Lopez, a student, was discovered bearing a concealed .38-caliber handgun and ammunition at Edison High School in San Antonio, Texas. He was arrested for violating a state statute prohibiting possession of a firearm on school grounds. When federal officials indicted Lopez for violation of the Gun-Free School Zones Act, the state officials dismissed charges. Despite Lopez's objection at his trial that the federal statute violated the U.S. Constitution, he was found guilty.

The majority decision of the Supreme Court involved a determination of the extent to which Congress may use the commerce power. The Court identified three areas that fall within Congress's constitutional power to regulate commerce: (1) activities involving channels of interstate commerce; (2) instrumentalities of, and persons or things in, interstate commerce; and (3) activities that have a "substantial relation" to interstate commerce. The Court rejected the first two categories as possible justifications of the commerce clause in this circumstance. Therefore, if the Gun-Free School Zones Act were to be held constitutional, it would need to be judged as regulating an activity that has a substantial effect on interstate commerce.

The Court determined that the statute deals with criminal activity and therefore has nothing to do with commerce or economic enterprise and has no essential relation to maintaining the regulation of an economic activity. Therefore, precedents established under the commerce power do not apply to the act. The elements of the statute demonstrate no relation between firearm possession and interstate commerce. The Court decided that the act represented a break with the previous constitutional standards for national firearms legislation.

The government argued that the considerable costs of violent crime spread beyond state boundaries, especially through the costs of insurance; that violent crime restricts people's disposition to travel to certain areas of the country; and that an educational process hindered by violence contributes to a less productive population. In rejecting these arguments, the Court reasoned that similar arguments could be employed to justify federal government involvement in a variety of areas, thus granting to it a wide police power traditionally determined to reside with the states.

In a dissenting opinion, Justice Stephen Breyer, joined by Justices John Paul Stevens, David Souter, and Ruth Bader Ginsberg, relied on three principles: the power to regulate commerce includes the ability to regulate local activities to the extent that they affect interstate commerce; ascertaining the effect of an activity requires considering not one action of an individual, but the effect of all related cases; and the granting of latitude to Congress in the determination of a connection between interstate commerce and an activity considered for regulation. Breyer argued that Congress could establish a reasonable link between education and the health of the national economy.

Although the Lopez decision did not alter precedents established by the Supreme Court regarding the Second Amendment, it did indicate that the Court had become less willing to allow Congress to intervene in new policy areas unless such intervention is narrowly based on the constitutional powers delegated to the national legislature.

See also: Gun-Free Schools Act; Schools and Guns; Second Amendment.

Further Reading: Alpheus Thomas Mason and Donald Grier Stephenson, Jr., *American Constitutional Law*, 11th ed. (Upper Saddle River, NJ: Prentice-Hall, 1996); *United States v. Lopez* (115 U.S. 1624, 1995).

United States v. Miller (1939)

Based on a challenge to the National Firearms Act of 1934, *United States v. Miller* (307 U.S. 174, 1939) involved an appeal by two individuals who had been convicted of transporting an unregistered sawed-off shotgun across state lines. The defendants based their challenge on the claim that the National Firearms Act, in restricting their right to bear arms, violated the Second Amendment to the U.S. Constitution and that the act could not be justified under Congress's commerce power.

The defendants, Jack Miller and Frank Layton, were indicted in a federal district court in Arkansas for unlawfully transporting a double-barrel 12-gauge shotgun having a barrel less than 18 inches long. They allegedly transported the weapon from Claremore, Oklahoma, to Siloam, Arkansas, but had not registered the weapon as required under the National Firearms Act. The defendants, not disputing the facts of the case, claimed that the section of the law under which they were charged was not a revenue measure but rather sought to

appropriate the police power retained by the states. The district court ruled that section 11 of the act violated the Second Amendment protection of the right to keep and bear arms.

The U.S. Supreme Court, receiving the case directly, first decided that the regulation of firearms could be encompassed under Congress's federal taxing power. The Court declared that the Second Amendment, according to its manifest purpose, assured the preservation of an effective militia in the states as provided for in Article 8 of the Constitution. The Court discovered no evidence demonstrating that a shotgun with "a barrel of less than eighteen inches in length" had at the time of the decision any connection to the maintenance of a well-regulated militia.

The Court related the Second Amendment to the power granted to Congress within the body of the original Constitution to make provision for activating the militia if needed to enforce national law, suppress insurrections, and repel invasions. Congress was to establish policy regarding the organization, arms provision, and discipline of the militia, and for administering the portion of the militia that may be called into national service. The Court viewed the Second Amendment guarantee as a method of assuring that the effectiveness of militia forces would be continued. Citizens had a constitutionally protected right to bear arms when such a right could be associated with militia service.

Later commentators on the case would contend that the Second Amendment guaranteed the possession of any weapon that has some connection to the national defense. However, subsequent federal court decisions did not support this view. Otherwise, individuals could legitimately claim the constitutional right to possess not only sawed-off shotguns (which were used in the Vietnam War), but a long list of other weapons from bazookas to nuclear weapons. Many supporters of restrictions on the ownership and use of firearms argued that the *Miller* decision supported a communal interpretation of the Second Amendment and thus that the right of individuals to possess firearms could be limited and even prohibited.

However, the U.S. Supreme Court, in *District of Columbia v. Heller* (2008), claimed that *Miller* did not refute an individualist understanding of the Second Amendment. Justice Antonin Scalia in his majority opinion argued that the Court in *Miller* did not decide that Miller and Layton could not rely on Second Amendment protection because they were bearing arms for nonmilitary use, but because "the *type of weapon at issue* was not eligible for Second Amendment protection." Justice Scalia quoted from the decision: "In the absence of any evidence tending to show that the possession or use of a [short-barreled shotgun] at this time has some reasonable relationship to the preservation or efficiency of a well regulated militia, we cannot say that the Second Amendment guarantees the right to keep and bear *such an instrument*" (Justice Scalia's emphasis). Scalia concludes that "We therefore read *Miller* to say only that the Second Amendment does not protect those weapons not typically possessed by law-abiding citizens for lawful purposes, such as short-barreled shotguns." Therefore, the Supreme Court decision in *Heller* employed the *Miller* ruling to support the position that the Second Amendment protects an individual (but not unlimited) right to keep and bear arms.

See also: District of Columbia v. Heller (2008); *McDonald v. Chicago* (2010); National Firearms Act; Sawed-Off Shotgun; Second Amendment; *United States v. Warin* (1976).

Further Reading: *District of Columbia v. Heller* (2008); *United States v. Miller*, 307 U.S. 174 (1939); Nicholas J. Johnson, "*Heller* as *Miller*: Court Decisions Dealing with Firearms," in Glenn H. Utter, ed., *Guns and Contemporary Society* (Santa Barbara, CA: Praeger, 2016): vol. 1, 83-102.

United States v. One Assortment of 89 Firearms (1984)

The U.S. Supreme Court, in *United States v. One Assortment of 89 Firearms* (465 U.S. 354, 1984), decided that federal authorities may proceed with the seizure of firearms even when the owner has been acquitted of criminal charges related to their possession, basing its decision on an interpretation of a section of the Gun Control Act of 1968 [18 U.S.C. 924 (d)], which provides for the seizure and forfeiture of firearms "involved in or used or intended to be used in, any violation of the provisions of this chapter." The decision overruled a precedent set in *Coffey v. United States* (1886).

In 1977, following a Bureau of Alcohol, Tobacco, and Firearms (ATF) raid on his home to seize a store of firearms, Patrick Mulcahey was charged with knowingly engaging in the firearms

trade without a license, thus violating federal law (18 U.S.C. 922). At the trial, Mulcahey admitted to buying and selling firearms without a license, but argued that federal agents had entrapped him into the illegal activities. The jury returned a verdict of not guilty. Following the acquittal, the U.S. government began action to gain forfeiture of the seized firearms. Mulcahey attempted to stop the forfeiture, arguing that the criminal action had already settled the matter in his favor, but the district court ruled that the firearms were subject to forfeiture.

The United States Court of Appeals for the Fourth District by a narrow margin reversed the lower court decision, arguing that the forfeiture proceeding was fundamentally criminal and punitive and therefore violated the constitutional guarantee against double jeopardy. The court ruled that the forfeiture action was based on the same information presented in the criminal case and therefore could not arrive at a ruling that contradicted the original decision. The court based its ruling on the Supreme Court's decision in *Coffey v. United States* (1886), which held that forfeiture action against distilling equipment could not proceed because the owner had been acquitted of charges related to the equipment.

The U.S. Supreme Court rejected the basis for the Court of Appeals decision, thus overruling the Coffey decision. Chief Justice Warren Burger, presenting the majority opinion, stated that "an acquittal on criminal charges does not prove that the defendant is innocent; it merely proves the existence of a reasonable doubt as to his guilt." The acquittal in the criminal case did not preclude a possible action in which the "preponderance of the evidence" could demonstrate that Mulcahey had conducted an unlicensed firearms business, and therefore that the relevant firearms should be forfeited according to section 924 (d) of the Gun Control Act.

The Court concluded that Congress, in establishing the forfeiture procedure, intended it as a "remedial civil action," not a criminal sanction. The purpose of section 924 (d) was to discourage unregulated trade in firearms and to prevent the trade of firearms "that have been used or intended for use outside regulated channels of commerce." By attempting to keep "potentially dangerous weapons" away from unlicensed dealers through the forfeiture provision, Congress had remedial, not punitive, goals in mind. The forfeiture process against the seized firearms did not constitute a criminal proceeding, and therefore the constitutional guarantee against double jeopardy does not apply.

Following the decision, gun rights groups, fearing a general confiscation of firearms, lobbied for changes in the Gun Control Act of 1968 that would provide greater assurance to gun owners acquitted in criminal proceedings that they would have appropriate procedures available to them to require the return of any seized firearms. The Firearms Owners Protection Act of 1986 provided such procedures to gun owners. Nonetheless, more recent federal forfeiture policies have again raised concerns among gun rights advocates about possible firearms seizures.

See also: Bureau of Alcohol, Tobacco, Firearms, and Explosives; Firearms Owners Protection Act; Gun Control Act of 1968; Second Amendment.

Further Reading: *United States v. One Assortment of 89 Firearms,* 465 U.S. 354 (1984).

United States v. Powell (1975)

In *United States v. Powell* (423 U.S. 87,1975), the U.S. Supreme Court examined the constitutionality of a federal statute (18 U.S.C. 1715) that prohibits the mailing of pistols, revolvers, and "other firearms capable of being concealed on the person," to determine whether the law applied to weapons such as sawed-off shotguns, which were considerably larger than handguns. The defendant, Josephine M. Powell, who was convicted of sending a sawed-off shotgun through the mail, claimed that the statute was so vague in its application as to be unconstitutional and that the law did not cover sawed-off shotguns. A Court of Appeals overturned the original conviction, arguing that the vagueness of the statute violated the Due Process Clause of the Fifth Amendment to the U.S. Constitution.

The U.S. Supreme Court, in deciding the Powell case, first dealt with the defendant's claim that the phrase "other firearms capable of being concealed on the person" does not apply to sawed-off shotguns but only to pistols and revolvers. Rejecting this contention, the Court argued that it would be justified in narrowing the scope of the statute only if there were evidence of congressional intent beyond the wording of the law. The Court observed that the stated purpose of the statute

was "to avoid having the Post Office serve as an instrumentality for the violation of local laws which prohibited the purchase and possession of weapons," noting that local laws would more likely ban sawed-off shotguns than pistols and revolvers. The Court concluded that the defendant's narrow interpretation of the statute did not correspond to Congress's objective of making the acquisition of concealable weapons more difficult and therefore a jury could legitimately find that a 22-inch sawed-off shotgun was a "firearm capable of being concealed on the person."

Although recognizing that statutory vagueness can be a basis for overturning a conviction, the Court held that such a situation did not apply in this case. The Court commented that the relevant law "intelligibly forbids a definite course of conduct: the mailing of concealable firearms" and therefore gave "adequate warning" to the defendant that mailing a 22-inch sawed-off shotgun was a violation of the law. The language of the statute was sufficient to provide notice to potential violators of what weapons were prohibited from mailing.

The Court of Appeals had argued that the "person" to which the statute refers may vary in physical characteristics to such an extent that what is a concealable weapon for one individual is not for another. Did the statute refer to the person mailing the firearm, the person receiving the weapon, or the average person? The Supreme Court responded that the commonsense meaning of "person" as an average individual "garbed in a manner to aid, rather than hinder, concealment of the weapons" most fairly represents the intentions of Congress.

See also: Concealed Carry Laws; Sawed-Off Shotgun.

Further Reading: *United States v. Powell,* 423 U.S. 87 (1975).

United States v. Rene Martin Verdugo-Urquidez (1990)

Although the subject of *United States v. ReneMartin Verdugo-Urquidez* (494 U.S. 259, 1990) had nothing to do with gun control laws, the decision involved an interpretation of what "the people" means in various sections of the Constitution. According to gun rights advocates, the Supreme Court decision provides substantial support for an individualist interpretation of "the people" in the Second Amendment to the U.S. Constitution. The justices joining in the ruling noted that "the people" refers to "a class of persons who are part of a national community or who have otherwise developed sufficient connection with this country to be considered part of that community." The Court indicated that this definition applies not only to the Fourth Amendment, the focus for the decision, but also to the First, Second, Ninth, and Tenth Amendments.

The case had to do with the constitutionality of a search and seizure involving a non-U.S. citizen who resided outside the territory of the United States. The U.S. Drug Enforcement Agency (DEA) suspected that Rene Martin Verdugo-Urquidez, a citizen and resident of Mexico, was a leader of a drug-smuggling organization in Mexico. The DEA obtained a warrant for his arrest in August 1985, and in January 1986 Mexican police officials transported Verdugo-Urquidez to the U.S. Border Patrol station in Calexico, California, where he was arrested by U.S. marshals. Following the arrest, DEA officials decided to pursue a search of Verdugo-Urquidez's residences in Mexicali and San Felipe, Mexico, to acquire evidence of the defendant's illegal drug activities. In cooperation with Mexican officials, a search was conducted, revealing certain incriminating evidence.

The defendant claimed that the evidence had been acquired illegally because the DEA had not obtained a search warrant. The U.S. district court concluded that the Fourth Amendment protection against unwarranted searches and seizures applied in this case. The U.S. Court of Appeals for the Ninth Circuit affirmed the lower court decision, after which U.S. officials appealed the rulings to the U.S. Supreme Court.

The Supreme Court reversed the lower court rulings, arguing that the relevant portion of the Fourth Amendment, which states that "The right of the people to be secure in their persons, houses, papers, and effects, against unreasonable searches and seizures, shall not be violated, and no Warrants shall issue, but upon probable cause, supported by oath or affirmation, and particularly describing the place to be searched, and the persons or things to be seized," protects specifically "the people of the United States." The Court ruled that "the people" was a "term of art" used in certain portions of the Constitution to refer to a "person" or the "accused," as in the Fifth and Sixth Amendments

involving criminal procedure. The term "people" refers to a class of persons that composes the national community. Those who have developed a sufficient connection with the nation may also be include in "the people." In the specific case, Verdugo-Urquidez, a citizen of Mexico who only entered the United States as a criminal defendant, did not satisfy the conditions to be considered a part of "the people" qualified to receive Fourth Amendment protections.

Gun rights supporters focused on the Court's mention of the Second Amendment, along with other portions of the Bill of Rights, as protecting the right of the people as a class of persons closely associated with the American community. In the Second Amendment, "the right of the people to keep and bear arms" is protected. Gun rights supporters emphasized this brief mention of the Second Amendment because they saw this as a promising foreshadowing of future Supreme Court rulings regarding the right to keep and bear arms. When the Court in the *Verdugo-Urquidez* case referred to a similar use of the term "people" in both the First Amendment, where rights definitely refer to those of individuals, and the Second Amendment, supporters hoped that the corporate notion of the people, as those involved in organized militias within states, would be rejected in favor of a more individualistic interpretation of the Second Amendment.

However, the *Verdugo-Urquidez* decision did not necessarily support the position of gun rights advocates. The Court's notion of the people as a class of persons who are part of the national community or have a close connection to the country could still be interpreted as a collective right exercised by the states in the formation of militia units. All that the Court ruled in the present case was that Verdugo-Urquidez lacked sufficient connection to the United States to be considered part of "the people" as mentioned in the Fourth Amendment.

Even if the ruling indicated a willingness to view the Second Amendment right to keep and bear arms in the same way as the First Amendment guarantees of freedom of speech and press, just four Supreme Court justices adhered to such a notion (Chief Justice William Rehnquist and associate justices Byron White, Sandra Day O'Connor, and Antonin Scalia). Two other justices (Anthony Kennedy and John Paul Stevens) supported the ruling, but issued concurring opinions that declined to accept the idea of "the people" presented in the opinion written by Rehnquist. Three justices (William J. Brennan, Thurgood Marshall, and Harry Blackmun) dissented. Therefore, a minority of the Court adhered to the notion of "the people" and its application to the Second Amendment as well as to the First and Fourth Amendments. Nonetheless, eighteen years later, with alterations in the makeup of the Court, a majority ruled that the Second Amendment does recognize the right of individuals to keep and bear arms.

See also: District of Columbia v. Heller (2008); Fourteenth Amendment; Fourth Amendment; Ninth Amendment; Second Amendment.

Further Reading: Alan M. Gottlieb, *The Rights of Gun Owners* (Bellevue, WA: Merril Press, 1991); *United States v. Rene Martin Verdugo-Urquidez*, 494 U.S. 259 (1990).

United States v. Tot (1942)

Frank Tot was tried in federal district court for unlawful possession of a firearm under a provision of the Federal Firearms Act of 1938 and found guilty. The act made it unlawful for anyone convicted of a violent crime "to receive any firearm or ammunition which has been shipped or transported in interstate or foreign commerce."

In September 1938, Tot was arrested at his Newark, New Jersey, home on a warrant charging that he had stolen cigarettes from an interstate shipment. Federal officers making the arrest found a .32-caliber Colt Automatic pistol at his residence. After his arrest, Tot requested that the pistol be returned to him and that the fact of its possession not be admitted at his trial, contending that officers had obtained it in violation of his Fourth Amendment guarantee against unreasonable searches and seizures. The court denied all of Tot's motions. In *United States v. Tot* (131 F.2d 261, 1942), the U.S. Court of Appeals for the Third Circuit, ruling that the admission of the firearm into evidence was constitutional, upheld Tot's conviction. First, the defendant had offered to produce the gun himself. Second, the U.S. Supreme Court had previously ruled that law enforcement officers may seize without a search warrant during a lawful arrest any weapons and other objects that could be used to assist the suspect in escaping from custody. Therefore, the court ruled that Tot

could not legitimately claim any violation of Fourth Amendment rights against unwarranted search and seizure of the gun.

Tot also claimed the Federal Firearms Act violated the Second Amendment to the U.S. Constitution. In response to this contention, the court affirmed that this Amendment, unlike First Amendment guarantees, does not apply to the rights of individuals (an interpretation that the U.S. Supreme Court ultimately overturned in *District of Columbia v. Heller*, 2008). Rather, the Amendment was adopted to protect states in their right to maintain militia organizations against interference from the national government. The Court indicated that Americans at the time wished to avoid the English experience under James II, when armed forces were lodged among a defenseless population. Many state constitutions adopted similar measures that, according to the court, supported this interpretation of the Second Amendment. In addition, the court referred to the common law tradition, which never treated the right to bear weapons as absolute, observing that regulation of the right to bear arms can be found in much earlier times, such as the Statute of Northampton in 1328.

The court dealt with the constitutionality of a provision that depends upon presumptive evidence, since it appears to violate the basic principle that a person is innocent until proven guilty. The notion of presumptive evidence seems to place the burden of proof on the defendant who is challenged to demonstrate his or her innocence in the face of assumed guilt. Citing precedent, the court ruled that the legislature may provide for the presumption of one fact from evidence of another, thus shifting the burden of proof without denying due process to the accused. The Court observed that the gun in question had crossed state lines at least twice; it was originally shipped from Connecticut, the state of manufacture, to Illinois, and ultimately to New Jersey where it was found in Tot's possession.

The court then faced directly the question of the time at which Tot received the weapon. The statute went into effect on July 30, 1938. The trial judge had instructed the jury to presume that the gun was shipped in interstate commerce if the jury determined that Tot had obtained the weapon after the date the statute went into effect. At the trial, the only evidence presented for the defense was the testimony of Tot and his wife and sister; but jurors apparently did not believe their testimony. The defendant had the opportunity to present his evidence as to the time when he acquired the weapon. If, contrary to the actual outcome, he had been believed, this would have established that the defendant came into possession of the weapon prior to passage of the statute.

The court noted that the legislation has a limited scope, dealing only with objects classified as firearms, and with a narrow group of people already convicted of violent crimes. In addition, the objective of the Federal Firearms Act, to protect society against violent individuals armed with dangerous weapons, can be considered fundamental to established government. The court recognized that the national government can appropriately assist in the accomplishment of this objective. Therefore, the court concluded that the means provided in the act to achieve the objective, while demanding, were not so arbitrary as to determine that Congress exceeded its authority.

See also: Federal Firearms Act of 1938; Fourth Amendment; Second Amendment.

Further Reading: *United States v. Tot*, 131 F.2d 261 (1942).

United States v. Warin (1976)

The U.S. Court of Appeals for the Sixth Circuit, in *United States v. Warin* (530 F.2d 103, 1976), affirmed the U.S. District Court's judgment that Francis J. Warin had knowingly possessed a firearm—a 9-mm. prototype submachine gun—that he had not registered in the National Firearms Registration and Transfer Record as required under the National Firearms Act of 1934 as amended by the Gun Control Act of 1968. Warin, an engineer and designer of firearms, worked for a company that developed weapons for the government. He made the 9-mm. submachine gun, which was of standard military design. Warin testified at the original trial that he had built the firearm to test and refine it for possible sale to the government as an improvement on military weapons then in use. He had not registered it as required by law.

A member of the Ohio "sedentary militia," Warin argued that the Second Amendment to the U.S. Constitution protected his right to possess a weapon that can be used by the armed forces of the United States. Basing his argument on *United States v. Miller* (1939), Warin argued that as a member of the sedentary militia, he could possess a

weapon with military capability, and therefore the relevant provision of the National Firearms Act was unconstitutional.

Disagreeing with Warin's contention, the court ruled that when the U.S. Supreme Court in *Miller* determined that "a shotgun having a barrel of less than eighteen inches in length" had no reasonable connection to the maintenance of a well-regulated militia, the Court did not state that the Second Amendment is an absolute guarantee of the right to possess any weapon appropriate for military use. Citing the opinion in *Cases v. United States* (1942), the Court concluded that in *Miller* the Supreme Court made its ruling on the basis of the facts of that case, and was not establishing a broad ruling about the right to bear arms. The development of weaponry since World War II might be taken to indicate that only the most primitive of weapons could be regulated under the Warin decision. However, this would be an unacceptable conclusion in a time of nuclear weapons and other highly sophisticated instruments of destruction.

The court asserted that the Second Amendment clearly protected a collective, not an individual, right, and applied solely to the right of states to support a militia, not to an individual's right to bear arms. Therefore, an individual cannot legitimately claim to possess an unlimited constitutional guarantee to possess a firearm. In addition, Warin's membership, along with all adult citizens of Ohio, in the sedentary militia, did not confer on him the right under the Second Amendment to possess a submachine gun.

Citing *United States v. Tot* (1942), the court indicated that even when applicable, the Second Amendment did not confer an absolute right against congressional regulation of firearms. Going back as far as the fourteenth century, common law has not treated the bearing of weapons as an absolute right. Supreme Court rulings indicate that even First Amendment rights are not considered absolute, for such rights must be applied to achieve both liberty as well as an orderly life. Without an organized society where limitations may be placed on individual action, liberty would be lost to "unrestrained abuses." Further, regulation of firearms can be justified by Congress's taxing power and the commerce power.

The court rejected Warin's further argument that regulation of the manufacture of certain types of firearms was unconstitutional. The appeals court affirmed the district court's refusal to consider this argument because Warin was not charged with violating any law concerning the manufacture of firearms, but solely with the possession of an unregistered submachine gun. The court also agreed with the lower court regarding the argument that the statute under which Warin was charged violated the Ninth Amendment. The Court was not persuaded that possession of an unregistered submachine gun could be considered a fundamental right guaranteed in this amendment. Even though the U.S. Supreme Court majority in *District of Columbia v. Heller* (2008) subsequently recognized an individual right to keep and bear arms, the Court appeared to agree with the *Warin* decision to the extent that such a right is subject to limitation.

See also: Cases v. United States (1942); *District of Columbia v. Heller* (2008); Gun Control Act of 1968; *McDonald v. Chicago* (2010); National Firearms Act of 1934; Ninth Amendment; Second Amendment; *United States v. Miller* (1939); *United States v. Tot* (1942).

Further Reading: *United States v. Warin*, 530 F.2d 103 (1976).

United States-Mexico Gun Trade

As the drug cartel-related violence in Mexico increased in 2008 and 2009, reports surfaced that firearms purchased in the United States had been used in many of the violent incidents. As David Ogden, Deputy U.S. Attorney General, commented, "The drugs flow north into our communities— and contribute to violence here and harm public health and safety—and we know weapons from the United States flow south and are used in these violent attacks." In 2008, the Mexican government asked ATF agents to trace the source of more than 7,500 firearms left at crime scenes in Mexico. In that year, more than 6,200 people were killed in drug-related violence. One ATF report noted that more than 328 guns worth an estimated $352,000 were traced from crime scenes in Mexico to gun dealers in Houston, Texas.

The ownership of firearms in Mexico is generally illegal, so drug cartels reportedly have established ties in the United States with U.S. citizens, termed "straw purchasers," who can pass the criminal background check to purchase weapons. During a Bureau of Alcohol, Tobacco, Firearms, and Explosives (ATF) four-month antidrug cartel operation (called the "Gun Runner

Impact Team") in the Houston area, the federal government announced that Houston was a primary source for firearms that ultimately were used in criminal activities in Mexico. One hundred ATF agents who came to Houston from other locations around the nation investigated 700 requests from the Mexican government to trace firearms from crime scenes to those who purchased the weapons in the United States.

Because federal law prohibits the government from establishing a database of gun owners, ATF agents in the 2009 operation ran on-site inspections of gun dealer records and visited the homes of people whose gun purchases ended up in Mexico. One case involved a small-town Texas police officer who purchased rifles and left them in his unlocked car, where they were supposedly stolen the same day as the purchase. The officer did not make the theft known to authorities and reportedly visited Mexico the day after the purchase. Inspections of approximately 1,100 licensed firearms dealers led to 77 warnings and the revocation of one license. Investigators often charged those suspected of purchasing firearms for drug cartel members with making a false statement on the official application when they declared that they were purchasing the guns for themselves.

In October 2009, the U.S. Justice Department announced that guns purchased in Houston-area stores had been traced to at least 55 murders of police officers, gangsters, and innocent civilians in Mexico. The Justice Department announced that the 2009 operation resulted in the seizure of more than 141,000 rounds of ammunition and 443 firearms. In April 2010, as the illegal gun trade continued, Mexican President Felipe Calderón criticized the failure of the United States to monitor sufficiently the approximately 10,000 gun shops close to the U.S.-Mexico border.

A report commissioned by the House Foreign Affairs Subcommittee on the Western Hemisphere and conducted by the Government Accountability Office (GAO) disclosed that from 2004 to 2009, 87 percent of guns left at crime scenes in Mexico that could be traced to the original owners were purchased in the United States. According to the GAO report, in addition to the legal restriction on gathering data on weapons purchases in the United States, other difficulties that federal government agents faced included coordination problems among the various law enforcement agencies and widespread corruption in the Mexican government. The GAO estimated that 39 percent of guns smuggled into Mexico originated in Texas, 20 percent in California, 10 percent in Arizona, and 31 percent in other states. The National Shooting Sports Foundation agreed to initiate an effort to emphasize to gun dealers and buyers that purchasing a firearm for someone legally prohibited from doing so is a felony.

In response to reports about the U.S.-Mexico gun trade, Alexa Fritts, speaking for the National Rifle Association (NRA), commented that the problem was a Mexican one and thus required a Mexican solution, and that the United States should enforce existing firearms laws, not pass new ones. On the other side of the gun control debate, Paul Helmke of the Brady Campaign to Prevent Gun Violence stated that "Anyone who wanted to outfit their private army could do so very easily in this country." Kristin Rand of the Violence Policy Center issued a report in April 2009 stating that, on the basis of records from 21 federal prosecutions in Arizona, California, Nevada, and Texas from February 2006 to February 2009, 42 percent of the guns identified were semiautomatic assault weapons and 18 percent were "armor-piercing handguns."

Despite reports of increased law enforcement activities along the U.S.-Mexico border to stem the flow of drugs into the United States and guns into Mexico, a September 2010 Justice Department report identified lack of intelligence sharing by ATF agents with the Department of Homeland Security's Office of Immigration and Customs Enforcement (ICE) as a "significant weakness" in the Border Liason Program to limit firearms trafficking. In addition, the Barack Obama administration had difficulty placing someone in nomination to head the ATF, an organization that faced serious opposition among gun rights groups. Dewey Webb, director of the Houston division of the ATF, commented in October 2009 that "As long as we are the cheapest, easiest place to buy guns, they'll keep doing it. . . . These cartels want the best and newest available."

Reports from Mexico in November 2010 revealed that drug cartel gangs sometimes have ten times the ammunition of government forces. Unlike firearms, ammunition purchases in the United States do not require a background check. Weapons recovered from cartel members included assault rifles, machine guns, and antitank rockets. U.S. and Mexican authorities estimated that 90 percent of assault rifles are smuggled into Mexico from the United States; but other weapons, including hand grenades, enter Mexico from Central America. In an attempt to stem the flow of firearms from the United States to Mexico, in December 2010 the ATF proposed that gun dealers near the U.S. border with Mexico be required to report to the agency within five consecutive business days any sales of two or more semiautomatic rifles greater than .22-caliber that have detachable magazines. Chris Cox of the National Rifle Association's Institute for Legislative Action criticized the proposal, calling it an attempt to establish a national gun registry.

In October 2009 the ATF's Phoenix, Arizona, field division initiated the project Operation Fast and Furious to trace firearm from straw purchasers to their ultimate destination in Mexico. However, ATF agents ultimately lost track of the firearms, some of which were found at the scene when in 2010 a U.S. border patrol agent was killed. This failed operation led to a congressional investigation and embarrassment for President Barack Obama's administration. It appears that neither the United States nor Mexico has succeeded in dealing adequately with the cross-border gun trade. It has been recommended that greater communication and coordination between the two sovereign national law enforcement agencies would be required to discover strategies to combat more effectively the illegal trade.

See also: Bureau of Alcohol, Tobacco, Firearms, and Explosives; Mexico; National Shooting Sports Foundation; Straw Purchases.

Further Reading: Michael Isikoff, "The ATF's Big Hole," *Newsweek* (April 26, 2010), 11; Tim Johnson, "In Mexico, Cartels Winning the Arms Race," *Houston Chronicle* (November 21, 2010), A34; Dane Schiller, "U.S. Slow to Stop Gun Traffickers, Report Says," *Houston Chronicle* (June 19, 2009), A1; Dane Schiller, "Hunting for Guns, a House at a Time," *Houston Chronicle* (July 1, 2009), A1; Dane Schiller, "Guns Bought Here Tied to 55 Slayings in Mexico," *Houston Chronicle* (October 2, 2009), A1; Violence Policy Center, "Mexican Gun Traffickers Easily Obtain Military-Style Weapons from U.S. Civilian Gun Market, New Analysis of Federal Criminal Court Records Confirms" (April 2009), www.vpc.org/ press/0904indict.htm; Jason C. Sides, James M. Vanderleeuw, and Joanna Melissa Joseph, "The Failure of 'Operation Fast and Furious' and the Complexity of Firearms Trafficking into Mexico," in Glenn H. Utter, ed., *Guns and Contemporary Society* (Santa Barbara, CA: Praeger, 2016): vol. 1, 197-220.

V

Violence Policy Center (VPC)

Established in 1988, the Violence Policy Center (VPC) is a Washington-based organization that conducts research on violence associated with firearms. In 1994, the Center joined with the Firearms Policy Project in supporting more stringent controls on the possession of handguns. Josh Sugarmann, executive director of the Center, has commented that few people have a true understanding of the gun control issue, arguing that the success of the National Rifle Association (NRA) and other pro-gun organizations stems in part from the lack of knowledge gun control organizations have about the issue. Therefore, the organization strives to be an alternative source of information to pro-gun groups. The VPC has criticized the premier gun control organization, Handgun Control, Inc. (HCI), and its successor, the Brady Campaign to Prevent Gun Violence, for accepting the NRA's major premise that not handguns, but handguns in the wrong hands, result in violence. The Center considers the NRA's well-known saying, "Guns don't kill, people do," as virtually identical to the Brady Campaign's motto, "Working to keep handguns out of the wrong hands" (the 1993 Brady Handgun Violence Prevention Act, which established a mandatory background check before a person can purchase a handgun, conforms to this viewpoint).

According to the VPC, keeping handguns from the "wrong hands," in other words, from minors, criminals, alcoholics, drug users, and the mentally incompetent, does not address some major causes of gun violence. The simple availability of firearms can lead to violence. As Sugarmann has stated, "the 'right hands' have a nasty tendency to turn into the 'wrong hands.'" The organization holds that a major difficulty with guns derives from their use in suicides and homicides involving family members and acquaintances. The Center has criticized the standard sorts of gun control measures advocated by the Brady Campaign, such as mandating the use of gun locks and instituting waiting periods before permitting the purchase of a firearm. The VPC rejects the potential efficacy of other gun control measures, such as licensing, registration, safety training, or mandatory sentencing for those who use firearms in the commission of a crime. Legal handgun possession leads to major suffering without providing their owners with any significant self-defense advantage.

In effect, the VPC agrees with the NRA that waiting periods and background checks have extremely limited consequences for handgun violence, and that banning multiple handgun sales to the same person and mandatory trigger locks would have minimal influence on the reduction of violence associated with firearms. However, the agreement ends when the Center strongly advocates the banning of handguns, which the organization has contended is the only way to deal with the problems of guns so widely available in the United States. According to the VPC, guns are a public health problem associated with a system of distribution that has allowed weapons to pervade society. However, with recent U.S. Supreme Court decisions (*District of Columbia v. Heller*, 2008, and *McDonald v. Chicago*, 2010) that recognize a right of individuals to own and bear firearms, especially for self-defense, the VPC's position on handguns is highly unlikely to be instituted at any level of government.

The organization distributes information on such subjects as assault weapons; strategies to reduce firearms violence; various studies of women and guns, including an analysis of justifiable homicides committed by women and persuasive techniques employed by the firearms industry to appeal to potential female buyers; analyses of the firearms industry; firearms manufacturers in the United States; federally licensed firearms dealers; guns and terrorism; drive-by shootings; the danger of .50-caliber rifles; explosives; cases of homicides committed by those with permits to carry concealed weapons; and case studies of felons granted the right to own firearms despite the restrictions of federal firearms laws.

In 2016 the VPC issued several reports on current gun policy issues, including data on black homicide victimization, the ways in which the firearms industry targets children as potential future gun purchasers, the danger to public safety posed by firearms silencers, the use of high-capacity magazines in mass shootings, and an analysis of Hispanic victims of lethal firearms violence. Earlier reports have dealt with murder-suicide, the trafficking of foreign-made assault weapons from the United States to Mexico, the decline of firearm ownership in the United States, and gun-related justifiable homicides and non-fatal self-defense.

The VPC monitors the NRA and the gun industry, criticizing their activities and policy positions. The organization is especially critical of gun manufacturers and gun rights organizations for their attempts to market firearms to children. The VPC advocates regulating firearm like other consumer products. The organization does not take a position of smart, or personalized, guns, holding that any consideration of such technology should determine what possible risks could be involved in its use. Although supporters claim that smart gun technology would prevent the deaths of children, the VPC notes that in 2014, of 586 fatal accidental shootings, just 74 were children under 18 years old.

See also: Brady Campaign to Prevent Gun Violence; Concealed Carry Laws; Gun Culture; National Rifle Association; Trigger Locks; Women and Guns.

Further Reading: Josh Sugarmann, *Every Handgun Is Aimed at You* (New York: New Press, 2002); Josh Sugarmann, *National Rifle Association: Money, Firepower and Fear* (Washington, DC: National Press, 1992); Violence Policy Center Web site, www.vpc.org.

Violence Prevention Research Program (VPRP)

The Violence Prevention Research Program (VPRP), located at the University of California at Davis, focuses its research efforts on the causes, nature, and prevention of violence. Garen J. Wintemute, who practices emergency medicine at the UC Davis Medical Center in Sacramento and is professor of emergency medicine at the UC Davis School of Medicine, serves as the Program's director. He has been a consultant for several organizations, including the National Institute of Justice, the World Health Organization (WHO), the U.S. Centers for Disease Control and Prevention (CDC), and the American Red Cross. Wintemute has engaged in a number of studies under the auspices of the Program that deal with the nature and prevention of violence and the development of strategies to prevent violent behavior. Magdalena Cerdá serves as the Program's associate director and is the vice chancellor's Endowed Chair in Violence Prevention and associate professor in the Department of Emergency Medicine. Her research deals with the causes, effects, and prevention of violence. The Program has focused on the issue of gun violence from a health care perspective, which has drawn criticism from those less willing to identify guns as an independent variable in the determination of the causes of violence. Wintemute's recent research has dealt with the use of epidemiological evidence in understanding and preventing gun violence. He has called for increased government funding for firearm research.

Research supported by the Program concentrates on guns as a significant ingredient in violent criminal behavior. According to a VPRP report, illegal gun use adversely affects the lives of more than one million Americans each year, making the illegal use of firearms a "raging epidemic." Program-backed research focuses on acquiring greater information about firearms: the types that are more likely to be used in crime, the manufacturers, the users, the uses, where they are acquired (especially for illegal purposes), and where they are more prevalently used. The Program is conducting research on such topics as the prediction of criminal behavior, the efficacy of background checks and waiting periods for prospective purchasers of firearms, and the factors contributing to firearm violence.

In 2009, the Program published a report, prepared by Wintemute, that examines the role of gun shows as economic, social, and cultural events, as well as an unregulated source of firearms for criminal use. The report is based on data that researchers collected from 78 gun shows in 19 states, most of which were held from 2005 to 2008. While federally licensed firearms dealers constitute a large majority (as much as two-thirds) of gun show sales, unlicensed sales make up the remainder. The report notes that private party sales at gun shows constitute a small portion of all gun sales in the United States, and that licensed retailers are likely to be the main source at gun shows of firearms used in crimes. Although a major policy proposal has been to close the "gun show loophole" by requiring all such sales to be subject to background checks and record-keeping, the report suggests that a more effective alternative would be to institute the regulation of all private party gun sales.

Due to the disproportionate involvement of youth in illegal gun activity, the Program has recommended efforts to keep guns away from young people. Also recommended is an aggressive program of gun tracing to discover the source of firearms. Legal purchases that find their way into the illegal gun market (so-called straw purchases) and direct channels from manufacturers were identified as important sources to investigate. Because a large proportion of firearms are obtained through the illegal market, police officials must be able to penetrate this enterprise to prosecute those involved.

Because theft is an important source of weapons used in crimes, gun owners and dealers should become involved in antitheft programs. Among the actions recommended to firearm owners are keeping serial numbers, locking guns away, and reporting any gun thefts. The Program advocates greater authority for police to destroy confiscated firearms, an action that may conflict with current federal law regarding a gun owner's right to repossess a confiscated weapon. Another recommended policy involves removing firearms from homes where domestic violence is likely to take place. As part of that recommendation, police officers should ask whether firearms are present when they are investigating incidents of domestic violence.

See also: Health Care Professionals; Straw Purchases; Trigger Locks; Wintemute, Garen J.; Youth and Guns.

Further Reading: Don B. Kates, Henry E. Schaffer, John K. Lattimer, Geroge B. Murray, and Edwin H. Cassem, "Bad Medicine: Doctors and Guns," in David B. Kopel, ed., *Guns: Who Should Have Them?* (New York: Prometheus, 1995); E. Robinson-Haynes and Garen J. Wintemute, *Gun Confiscations: A Case Study of the City of Sacramento in 1995* (Sacramento, CA: Violence Prevention Research Program, 1997); Violence Prevention Research Program Web site, http://web.ucdmc.ucdavis.edu/ vprp; Garen J. Wintemute, *Inside Gun Shows: What Goes On When Everybody Thinks Nobody's Watching* (Sacramento, CA: Violence Prevention Research Program, 2009).

Violent Crime Rate

In 1994, after several decades of seeming relentless increases, the violent crime rate began to fall, prompting questions about both the possible success of gun control legislation and the need for additional controls, as well as the success of concealed carry laws. From 1992 to 1996, the number of violent crimes declined 13 percent. The Federal Bureau of Investigation (FBI) released data in May 1998 indicating that violent crime had dropped an additional 5 percent during 1997. The number of murders decreased from 24,526 in 1993 to 19,645 in 1996, representing a 20-percent drop. The murder rate had declined from 9.5 to 7.4 per 100,000 residents. Franklin Zimring reports that from 1990 to 2000, crime rates in all categories experienced a decline: homicide by 39 percent, rape 22 percent, aggravated assault 24 percent, robbery 44 percent, burglary 41 percent, auto theft 37 percent, and larceny 23 percent.

Gordon Witkin, writing for *U.S. News and World Report* in May 1998, provided an analysis of possible explanations for the notable decline in violent crime. Some social scientists have suggested that an improved economy and low unemployment made crime a less appealing activity. However, although economic conditions may be related to robbery offenses, the murder rate, a category that declined dramatically, is far less likely to vary with economic conditions. While others suggested that organized youth activity and other crime prevention programs contributed to the drop, these sorts of initiatives have often been judged ineffective. Many analysts suggested that the increasing number of people held in prisons helped to explain the drop in crime. The rate of incarceration increased dramatically after 1974 and the number of people held in federal, state, and local jails rose from 744,000 in 1985 to more than 1.7 million in 1997. When those convicted of crimes reside in jail, they obviously cannot commit additional crimes, at least in the greater society.

Larger police forces and improved police procedures have also been credited with declining rates of violent crime. A notable example is New York City, where improved policing has been suggested as the reason for a dramatic decline in the number of murders from 1,946 in 1993 to 983 in 1996. Houston, which experienced a 58 percent drop in the murder rate, had added 1,400 new police officers since 1991. Although recognizing that the previously mentioned factors may have contributed to a portion of the decline in violent crime, Witkin ultimately focused on the crack cocaine trade that spread across the country beginning in 1985–86. Criminologists speculate that associated with the crack trade were large numbers of young people acting as street sellers. These youth, who carried drugs and money with them, felt compelled to carry handguns to protect themselves from robberies. As the crack trade began to subside in the early 1990s, so did the murder rate.

Although guns often play an important role in the commission of violent crimes, Gary Kleck, in *Targeting Guns: Firearms and Their Control* (1997), cautioned against arriving at hasty conclusions. He highlighted three observations: (1) there are over 200 million (currently estimated to be 300 million) guns in the United States, (2) the level of violence is high, and (3) a large proportion of homicides are committed with firearms. However, it is inappropriate, he argued, to infer a causal relationship between a higher level of gun ownership in the United States and a corresponding higher violence rate. Kleck suggested that, in fact, high rates of violence could cause high levels of gun ownership (for defensive use). Nevertheless, firearms are used in a high proportion of homicide cases.

In the case of the crack trade explanation, the ownership of guns by a specific group of people engaged in criminal activity is hypothesized to be the reason for a higher violent crime rate. Correspondingly, a decline in the crack trade, and hence in the number of people carrying guns, leads to a decline in the murder rate. Whether the murder rate would have been lower if gun control measures could have kept firearms out of the hands of those engaged in criminal activity has been a matter for debate.

The decline in violent crime notwithstanding, the United States still has an exceptionally high rate of violent crime compared to many other developed nations. Therefore, gun control advocates continue to press for additional measures to curb gun-related violence, while gun rights advocates proclaim that guns are a primary means for citizens to protect themselves from, and to deter, violent crime. Reports in 1998 indicated that at least a portion of the decline in violent crime was attributable to intentional underreporting of crime in certain cities such as Philadelphia, New York, Atlanta, and Boca Raton, Florida. Law enforcement officials speculated that recent data indicating a decline in crime rates pressured police commanders to demonstrate even further declines, especially when such data are linked to promotions and pay raises.

As Zimring notes, in the last three years of the 1990s (1997–2000), the crime rate in seven categories each decreased by double digits, whereas in the first three years of the twenty-first century, crime rates remained fairly stable overall, with a continuing decrease in aggravated assault (minus 8.9 percent) and an increase in auto theft (5.2 percent). Changes in all other categories were less than one percent. In 2007, Zimring speculated that the decline in the level of various crimes ended at the turn of the century. However, more recent data suggest that the "great crime decline" may not be over, even with an economic downturn that traditionally is associated with higher crime rates.

The Bureau of Justice Statistics, U.S. Department of Justice, reported in 2015 that "There was no significant change in the overall rate of violent crime, defined as rape or sexual assault, robbery, aggravated assault, and simple assault, from 2013 (23.2 victimizations per 1,000 persons age 12 or older) to 2014 (20.1 per 1,000)." From 2013 to 2014, there was no statistically significant change "in the rate of serious violence, domestic violence, intimate partner violence, violence resulting in an injury, and violence involving a firearm." With regard specifically to firearms, the U.S. Department of Justice reported no significant change in the rate of nonfatal firearm violence (1.3 per 1,000 in 2013 adn1.7 per 1,000 in 2014).

See also: Kleck, Gary; Youth and Guns; Zimring, Franklin.

Further Reading: Gary Kleck, *Targeting Guns: Firearms and Their Control* (New York: Aldine De Gruyter, 1997); Gordon Witkin, "The Crime Bust,"

U.S. News & World Report 124 (May 25, 1998), 28–33, 36–37; Franklin E. Zimring, *The Great American Crime Decline* (New York: Oxford University Press, 2007); Jennifer L. Truman and Lynn Langton, "Criminal Victimization, 2014," www.bjs.gov/content/pub/pdf/cv14/pdf (accessed July 28, 2016).

Virginia Tech Shooting

On April 16, 2007, Virginia Tech, a university of more than 30,000 students located in Blacksburg, Virginia, experienced a deadly shooting rampage when a student, Seung-Hui Cho, killed 32 students and faculty before shooting and killing himself. Cho had purchased a .22-caliber handgun at a pawnbroker's shop and a 9-mm. pistol at a gun shop in February and March 2007. He used 15-round magazines in the 9-mm. pistol. The production, but not the distribution, of such magazines had been prohibited by the assault weapons ban of 1994, but in 2004Congress allowed the ban to expire. Cho first shot and killed two students in a dormitory in the early morning, and more than two hours later, he killed 30 others in a classroom building, where he had chained some of the doors to prevent escape.

Although Cho did not have an arrest record, he had exhibited belligerent behavior. His instructors in the English department became concerned about his unsociable demeanor and disturbing writings. One professor became so concerned that she threatened to quit if Cho were not removed from her class. In 2005, two female students complained to campus police about unwanted telephone calls and text messages. After the second incident, campus police took Cho into custody when another student informed them that Cho appeared to be suicidal. After Cho was taken to a behavioral health center for evaluation, a judge declared that he was a danger to himself; but rather than ordering hospitalization, the judge recommended outpatient treatment. Although Cho remained a student at Virginia Tech in 2006, he continued to show signs of mental problems. He submitted two plays that dealt with themes of extreme violence and sexuality. Despite Cho's mental health problems, he was never committed involuntarily to a mental institution, and therefore was still able to pass background checks required to purchase the two handguns he used in the shooting rampage. Kristin Rand of the Violence Policy Center commented that if Virginia had adopted the guidelines established in federal law, Cho would have failed the background check. In any event, there was no general call for additional limitations on firearms that could prevent such tragedies from happening in the future, in part due to the strong political influence that the National Rifle Association and other gun rights groups have at the national and state levels, as witnessed by the number of more lenient concealed carry laws that states have instituted.

As with other shooting events, those on both sides of the gun rights debate commented on the Virginia Tech Shooting. However, the reactions in this case tended overall to be muted. Josh Horwitz, executive director of the Coalition to Stop Gun Violence, noted that this shooting may have been one that additional legislation could not have prevented. Immediately following the shooting, the National Rifle Association (NRA) issued a brief statement of sympathy for the families of the victims. However, other gun rights organizations asserted that allowing faculty, students, and staff to carry guns on campus would deter such crimes. David Burnett, president of Students for Concealed Carry on Campus, claimed that the Virginia Tech shooting was an example of why those who are licensed to carry concealed firearms should be allowed to have guns on campus. At the time, two states, Colorado and Utah, permitted concealed weapons on college campuses. Richard Feldman, former political director for the NRA, although critical of that organization's emphasis on fundraising, sided with those who label as inadvisable policies intended to maintain a "gun-free" campus.

Perhaps a more stringent adherence to the Crime Awareness and Campus Security Act of 1990 (amended in 1992, 1998, 2000, and 2008), also known as the Jeanne Clery Act, named for the 19-year-old Lehigh University student who was raped and murdered in a campus dormitory, could have contained the violence. Among the provisions of the Clery Act were the requirements that educational institutions participating in federal student financial aid programs publish a yearly report of campus security policies and crime data from the previous three years, and provide prompt warnings to the campus community about crime threats. After the Virginia Tech shooting, some students complained that the campus police had waited too long before informing them about the first shooting. In 2010, the U.S. Department of Education announced that the university had violated federal campus security laws when campus officials delayed notifying students about the danger.

See also: Binghamton, New York, Shooting; *Bowling for Columbine*; Coalition to Stop Gun Violence; Gun-Free Schools Act; National Rifle Association; Schools and Guns; Violence Policy Center.

Further Reading: Richard Feldman, *Ricochet: Confessions of a Gun Lobbyist* (New York: Wiley, 2008); Christine Hauser and Anahad O'Connor, "Virginia Tech Shooting Leaves 33 Dead," *New York Times* (April 16, 2007), www.nytimes. com/2007/04/16/us/16cnd-shooting.html?_r=1; Titania Kumeh, "Do Guns and College Mix?" *Mother Jones* (September 2010), http://motherjones. com/mojo/2010/09/guns-college-university-texas-texas-concealed-carry; Security on Campus, Inc., "Complying With the Jeanne Clery Act," www. securityoncampus.org/index.php?option=com_content &view=article&id=271&Item=60; Will Sullivan, "An Uphill Climb for Gun Laws: A New Debate, Perhaps, But the Same Old Politics," *U.S. News and World Report* (April 30, 2007), 46–47.

Volkmer, Harold Lee (1931–2011)

Harold Volkmer, Democratic congressman from Missouri and longtime supporter of gun rights, worked for years to bring about passage of the Firearms Owners Protection Act of 1986, also known as the McClure-Volkmer Act. When Senator James A. McClure, Republican of Idaho, began backing the legislation in the Senate, Volkmer had already worked for several years to repeal major portions of the Gun Control Act of 1968. He first introduced a version of the Firearms Owners Protection Act in 1978, and played a key role in the bill's final passage in the House eight years later.

Volkmer attended Saint Louis University and received a law degree from the University of Missouri School of Law in Columbia in 1955. He served as assistant attorney general of Missouri in 1955 and, after a stint in the U.S. Army, established a private practice in Hannibal, Missouri, in 1958. He was prosecuting attorney for Marion County from 1960 to 1966 and served in the Missouri State House of Representatives from 1967 to 1976. Volkmer won election to the U.S. House of Representatives in 1976 and soon thereafter established himself as a major critic of the Gun Control Act of 1968.

Volkmer charged that the Bureau of Alcohol, Tobacco, and Firearms (ATF) was misapplying the law to the detriment of innocent gun owners. He believed that the law made criminals out of law-abiding citizens who inadvertently violated provisions of the act. Rather than harassing law-abiding citizens, Volkmer wanted to require the ATF to focus its energies on those who violated the law through criminal activities. He included in the legislation provisions intended to protect citizens against the confiscation of property. The only weapons subject to seizure by law enforcement officials would be those actually involved in a crime. If charges were not filed within 120 days, the confiscated weapons were to be returned to the owners, and if the accused was acquitted, the law would require return of the seized firearms. If the government failed to return such weapons, the bill provided for the payment of attorney fees to a claimant in any lawsuit to obtain release of the firearms. The legislation also decreased federal controls on the interstate sale of long gun s and ammunition.

Although the Firearms Owners Protection Act passed the Senate in July 1985, by spring 1986 the bill was still in the House Judiciary Committee, where chairman Peter Rodino, Democrat of New Jersey, refused to take action. In April, Volkmer filed a discharge petition to release the bill from the Judiciary Committee. Infrequently attempted and even less frequently successful, a discharge petition requires the signatures of a majority of the House members (218) to bypass a committee and put a bill on the calendar for consideration by the whole House. When Volkmer's discharge petition received 200 signatures and appeared headed for a majority, the Judiciary Committee quickly released a compromise measure. Despite the conspicuous disapproval of a coalition of police organizations, the Volkmer bill, strongly supported by gun rights organizations, was substituted for the compromise bill.

After 1986, Volkmer witnessed some of the political fallout of his pro-gun bill. The McClure-Volkmer Act was a limited victory for gun rights interests because it galvanized gun control supporters to work harder to pass more stringent gun control legislation. During Volkmer's tenure in the House, Congress passed the Brady Handgun Violence Prevention Act, the Undetectable Firearms Act, and the assault weapons ban. Volkmer served in the House until January 1997, when he left after being defeated by his Republican opponent, Kenny Hulshof, in the November 1996 election. After leaving Congress, Volkmer was elected to the National Rifle Association (NRA) board of directors, a position he held until 2009. From 1998 to 2001, Volker was a lobbyist for the NRA's Institute for Legislative Action (ILA). He served on the NRA executive council until his death in 2011. At the time of his death, Volkmer was involved in reviewing a legal case for the NRA's Civil Rights Defense Fund.

See also: Assault Weapons Ban; Brady Handgun Violence Prevention Act; Bureau of Alcohol, Tobacco, Firearms, and Explosives; Firearms Owners Protection Act; Gun Control Act of 1968; McClure, James Albertas; Undetectable Firearms Act.

Further Reading: Earl R. Kruschke, *Gun Control* (Santa Barbara, CA: ABC-CLIO, 1995); Robert Spitzer, *The Politics of Gun Control*, fourth edition (Washington, DC: CQ Press, 2008); Josh Sugarmann, *National Rifle Association: Money, Power and Fear* (Washington, DC: National Press, 1992).

Waco, Texas, Raid

The Waco, Texas, raid by federal law enforcement officials against David Koresh's Branch Davidian compound occurred less than one year after the tragedy at Ruby Ridge, Idaho, in which two members of Randy Weaver's family and a federal marshal were killed during a standoff with federal agents. Each event began with an allegation of violating federal firearms statutes. The Branch Davidians were accused of converting AR-15 semiautomatic rifles into machine guns, which are illegal under federal law. When the standoff ended on April 19, 1993, at least 80 people had lost their lives, including members of the religious cult as well as law enforcement officers. The Waco raid galvanized militia movements, which believed that the federal government had declared war on the American people. Pro-gun rights groups took the opportunity to challenge the federal government's motives and tactics in enforcing gun control legislation.

Members of the Branch Davidians, a religious sect, were convinced that the apocalypse was imminent and believed their leader, David Koresh, a 33-year-old erstwhile rock-and-roll band member, was the second Messiah. Approximately 130 Branch Davidians were living at the compound situated just seven miles northeast of Waco. Bureau of Alcohol, Tobacco, and Firearms (ATF) officials were concerned over the group's alleged stockpiling of illegal firearms and were considering how to serve an arrest warrant on Koresh and search the headquarters for illegal weapons with a minimum of disturbance.

On the morning of February 28, 1993, despite warnings that the Branch Davidians had received advance warning of a raid, 100 ATF agents jumped from cattle trailers and headed for the complex.

Gunfire began as the agents attempted to enter the compound. When the shooting stopped, four ATF agents and six Branch Davidians, including Koresh's 2-year-old daughter, had been killed. The government then began a siege that lasted 51 days. More than 700 law enforcement officers from various jurisdictions, including the Federal Bureau of Investigation (FBI), the ATF, the Waco police, the National Guard, and the Texas Rangers, took part in the extended standoff. Although the FBI successfully negotiated the release of 20 children, Koresh and his followers refused to surrender.

The FBI cut off electricity, used loudspeakers to play discordant music, and kept searchlights on the building during the night. None of these tactics appeared to create any dissension in the religious group or bring about any significant defections. Basing her decision on alleged child abuse among the Branch Davidians, Attorney General Janet Reno ordered an assault on the compound. Early on the morning of April 19, two tanks drove into the wall, and shot tear gas into the building. However, the occupants still refused to leave. Around noon, smoke was seen coming from the windows, and soon the building was in flames. The government claimed that the Davidians had started the fires, but others insisted firing the tear gas had ignited the flames. Seventy-five people died in the fire, including 20 children.

The ATF took the brunt of criticism from many quarters, including pro-gun rights organizations like the National Rifle Association (NRA), which raised the fear that agents of the federal government were attempting to strip all Americans of their right to bear arms. Militia groups concluded they had gained additional evidence that the federal government had declared war on them. Members of Congress were highly critical of the government agencies involved in the raid. The head of the ATF resigned under pressure from the Treasury Department, and those responsible for the operation were demoted.

Because of the Waco raid, April 19 took on special significance for militia members and gun rights advocates. It was on that day in 1775 that the battles of Lexington and Concord occurred. British soldiers attempting to destroy a store of arms at Lexington engaged a group of Minutemen, American militiamen who were defending the towns. Contemporary militia members believed that just as the April 19, 1775, event had begun a revolutionary war, so would the April 19, 1993, raid against the Davidians begin a new revolution. In 1995, Timothy McVeigh chose this date to bomb the Alfred P. Murrah Federal Building in Oklahoma City, Oklahoma, to continue the revolutionary symbolism.

See also: American Revolution; Bureau of Alcohol, Tobacco, Firearms, and Explosives; Minutemen, Revolutionary; National Rifle Association; Oklahoma City Bombing; Reno, Janet; Ruby Ridge.

Further Reading: Morris Dees, *Gathering Storm: America's Militia Threat* (New York: HarperCollins, 1996); Jonathan Karl, *The Right to Bear Arms: The Rise of America's New Militias* (New York: HarperCollins, 1995).

Washington, D.C.

Advocates as well as opponents of gun control have pointed to Washington, D.C., the nation's capital, to bolster their respective positions regarding restrictions on firearms. In 1976, the District of Columbia came under the limitations imposed by the Firearm Control Regulations Act, which prohibited any new acquisition of handguns as well as semi-automatic firearms capable of using a detachable ammunition magazine with a capacity of more than 12 rounds. The only handguns that could be possessed were those registered before September 23, 1976 and reregistered by February 5, 1977. The District required a permit to purchase a rifle or shotgun from a licensed dealer in the District. Criteria for such purchases included minimum age (21), physical fitness, knowledge of safe gun use, and no criminal record. Owners of registered firearms had to keep them unloaded and disassembled or locked away unless being used for

recreational purposes or when kept at a business. The penalty originally established for violating the firearms law was 10 days in jail and a $300 fine, but in 1981 the punishment was increased to a $1,000 fine and one year in jail.

Gun control supporters claimed that the homicide rate in the District declined 25 percent from 1968 to 1987 (from 13.0 to 9.7) and estimated that 500 homicides were prevented in that time period. In the adjacent states of Maryland and Virginia, which did not have such stringent regulations, the monthly gun-related homicide rates experienced a more modest decline (from 5.8 in 1968 to 5.4 in 1987). However, the rate for the District remained considerably higher than for the two neighboring states despite the stricter firearms regulations. Those who questioned the effectiveness of gun control legislation noted that the murder rate in the District remained the highest in the country. In addition, 85 percent of such cases in the District, compared to 68.3 percent of cases nationwide, were firearm-related.

In response to such criticisms, gun control supporters presented two arguments. First, the murder rate for the District possibly was lower than it would have been without stringent gun control; and second, because surrounding states had far less stringent restrictions on the purchase and possession of firearms, individuals could easily acquire guns elsewhere and transport them into the District. The July 1998 shooting at the Capitol Building highlighted the dilemmas of enforcing firearms restrictions locally. The assailant, who killed two security officers at the visitors' entrance, brought the weapon with him into the District.

The shooting did not lead to a call for more gun control legislation. Attempts to pass legislation concentrated, for instance, on keeping firearms away from children and would have had no effect on the murder of the two security officers. Those on both sides of the gun control debate stated that little could have been done to prevent the shooting. Bob Walker, then president of Handgun Control, Inc., admitted that more gun control legislation would not have kept the assailant from obtaining a handgun. Bill Powers, spokesman for the National Rifle Association (NRA), declared that existing laws did not keep firearms away from the shooter, who violated restrictions on bringing firearms into the District and taking guns onto the Capitol grounds.

A number of District residents initiated court challenges to the city's strict firearm restrictions, and in 2008, the U.S. Supreme Court in *District of Columbia v. Heller* ruled that by prohibiting the possession of handguns, the District had violated the Second Amendment which, the Court majority decided, protects an individual right to keep and bear arms for self-defense. Following the decision, the District city council established a handgun registration policy that required those possessing handguns to provide fingerprints and to permit the police department to conduct ballistics tests. The District also maintained a ban on semiautomatic pistols. Dick Heller, who successfully challenged the city's handgun ban in 2008, also filed suit against the new regulations, claiming that they are too restrictive and too onerous. In March 2010, when the federal district court judge ruled the new provisions constitutional, Stephen P. Halbrook, Heller's attorney, stated that the ruling likely would be appealed.

In July 2014 a federal judge invalidated the District's ban on carrying firearm in public. The District council quickly passed an ordinance to allow residents as well as visitors who have a concealed carry license in their home state, to carry concealed firearms. The council passed the measure unanimously, although some members expressed their displeasure with the new policy even though it placed strict limitations on acquiring a concealed carry license.

Gun right supporters quickly challenged the new policy. In September 2015, a three-judge panel of the U.S. Court of Appeals for the District of Columbia Circuit upheld six of the ten regulations that were being challenged. One judge, Karen Henderson, stated that she would have allowed all ten regulations. The court ruled that the District could require long gun registration, that applicants could be required in person, be fingerprinted and photographed, and pay a fee. Also, applicants could be required to complete a firearms safety and training course. The court invalidated the statue's requirement that a gun owner reapply for a permit every three years, struck down a provision that applicants pass a test on local gun laws and that applicants register just one handgun in a 30-day period, and overruled a requirement that applicants bring their firearms with them for registration.

Although the ruling supported many of the restrictions that the District imposed on gun registration and carrying, gun rights supporters undoubtedly will continue their efforts in the District and in the nation generally to challenge limits on gun ownership and carrying.

See also: District of Columbia v. Heller (2008); Brady Campaign to Prevent Gun Violence; National Rifle Association; Trigger Locks; Violent Crime Rate.

Further Reading: *District of Columbia v. Heller* (2008); Stephen P. Halbrook, "Second-Class Citizenship and the Second Amendment in the District of Columbia," *George Mason University Civil Rights Law Journal* (1995), 105–78; C. Loftin, et al., "Effects of Restrictive Licensing of Handguns on Homicide and Suicide in the District of Columbia," *New England Journal of Medicine* 325 (December 5, 1991), 1615–20; Kathleen Maguire and Ann L. Pastore, eds., *Bureau of Justice Statistics Sourcebook of Criminal Justice Statistics 1997* (Washington, DC: U.S. Government Printing Office, 1998); Lawrence Hurley, "Washington, D.C. Gun Laws Partly Upheld by U.S. Court" (September 18, 2015), reuters.com/article.us-districtofcolumbia-guns-idUSKCN0RI1ZL20150918.

Washington, D.C., Navy Yard Shooting

Several issues, including mental health screening, security at government facilities, and the overall question of gun control and gun rights, were raised by the shooting at the Washington, D.C., Navy Yard on September 16, 2013, in which a lone gunman killed twelve workers and wounded four others.

Law enforcement officials identified Aaron Alexis, a former Navy reservist, as the shooter. A consulting firm based in Florida had hired him to conduct subcontracting work at the naval facility, assisting in updating military computer systems. Alexis had begun working there during the summer. Two days before the incident, Alexis visited a shooting range in Virginia where he rented a rifle, purchased ammunition, and used the practice range. The range reportedly ran a background check on Alexis, which resulted in no disqualifying information. He also purchased a shotgun from a gun shop in Virginia, a weapon he apparently used in the shooting.

While in the Navy, Alexis was issued a secret-level security clearance classification, which he maintained as an employee of The Experts, a Hewlett-Packard subcontractor, after the company ran background checks and received confirmation from the Pentagon that he had security clearance.

On the morning of September 16, Alexis arrived at the Navy Yard and walked to the Naval Sea Systems Command headquarters building, where he had been working the previous week. He opened the door with his security card, carrying a bag that is believed to have contained a disassembled shotgun. He then entered a bathroom where he assembled the gun. He went to the fourth floor where he could look down on the atrium where employees were gathered for breakfast and coffee, and began shooting down at those gathered there, as well as across to the facing walkways. When security officers began returning fire, Alexis went to the stairway and moved to other levels, continuing to fire his weapon. He shot a security officer and took his firearm. After searching for several minutes, police officers confronted the shooter in a hallway and returned fire, killing him.

Of major concern following the shooting was Alexis's mental state in the weeks before he began the deadly rampage. He had complained to Veterans Administration doctors that he was suffering from insomnia. On August 7, in Newport, Rhode Island, Alexis called police to tell them that voices were annoying him and that they were using microwaves to keep him from sleeping. When police informed the Navy about the episode, his employer withdrew his classified status, but just for two days.

The shooter's mental status indicated the many complexities of evaluating the mental condition of an individual when the appraisal may depend on the willingness or ability of the individual to respond truthfully to questions. Following the shooting, Federal Bureau of Investigation agents discovered a note from the shooter claiming that for the previous three months he had been receiving low frequency radio waves. But during that time he had denied experiencing any anxiety or other symptoms of mental instability. When doctors questioned him about his emotional state, Alexis denied being under any emotional stress, was not suffering from anxiety or depression, nor was he having thoughts of suicide or aggression. A doctor concluded that his continuing to work for the Defense Department presented no problem. When treating a patient for a condition like insomnia, health care officials are legally prohibited from contacting that person's family or friends to assist in the evaluation the person's mental state and must depend on what the patient is willing to reveal.

See also: Background Checks; Brady Handgun Violence Prevention Act

Further Reading: CBS Evening News, "Navy Yard Gunman's Doctor Before Rampage: 'No Problem There'" (January 31, 2014). www.cbsnews.com/news/navy-yard-gunmans-doctor-before-rampage-no-problem-there; CBS Evening News, "The Washington Navy Yard Shooting As It Happened" (October 31, 2013). www.cbsnews.com/news/the-washington-navy-yard-shooting-as-it-happened; Helen Cooper, "Pentagon Review Says Navy Yard Rampage Was Preventable," *New York Times* (March 19, 2014): A13; Barbara Starr, Catherine E. Shoichet, and Pamela Brown, "12 Victims Slain in Navy Yard Shooting Rampage; Dead Suspect ID'd" (September 16, 2013). www.cnn.com/2013/09/16/us/dc-navy-yard-gunshots/index.html.

Watts, Shannon (1973–)

Shannon Watts is a former communications executive and public relations specialist, and mother of five, who engineered the creation of a new gun safety organization, Moms Demand Action for Gun Sense in America. The day after the Sandy Hook Elementary School shooting in December 2012, Watts was sufficiently shocked and outraged that she decided to take action by creating a Facebook page calling for a march on Washington, D.C. A few days later, Watts was contacted by five women in New York City, who formed the first chapter of the Moms group. While the women lacked political experience, they attempted to model their organization on Mothers Against Drunk Driving (MADD), also a grassroots organization that organized in the 1980s to enact tougher laws against drunk driving. The organization says that it supports Second Amendment rights, but also that the cost of gun violence, especially against women and children, calls for more aggressive action by the government and concerned citizens. On average, eight children a day are killed by guns, and women are often the victim of gun violence at the hands of abusive spouses or other partners. Surveys have reported that in about 40 percent of homes with guns and children in them, at least one gun is not properly stored or secured, inviting the possibility of an accidental gun shooting, suicide attempt, or theft.

Word spread largely via the internet, and within two years, the organization claimed 200,000 members from all across the country, including chapters in every state in the Union. Realizing that prospects for change at the national level in Congress were little to none, they sought to utilize pre-existing public support for stronger gun measures, and specifically to apply economic pressure to businesses that allowed customers to carry guns in their places of business. One of the first such target was the coffee chain Starbucks, which allowed open gun carry in its stores (even in states with liberal gun carrying laws, businesses are generally allowed to bar carrying if they post a sign saying so on their doors). In 2013, the Moms group called for a "skip Starbucks" on Saturdays action, urging participants to take pictures of themselves to post having coffee in non-Starbucks places. Gun carriers in some places attempted to confront protesting mothers, but the effort was a public relations disaster for gun carriers, and a few months later, Starbucks announced that it would no longer allow gun carrying in its establishments nationwide. The success of this effort resulted in similar high profile protests or boycotts against companies including Chipotle's, Chili's, Sonic America's Drive-In restaurants, Target, Kroger, and Panera, among others. They also focused attention on states where the law allows gun carrying in schools and bars.

At the end of 2013, the Moms group merged with former New York City Mayor Michael Bloomberg's organization, then called Mayors Against Illegal Guns, to form Everytown for Gun Safety. Yet they retained their own identity and distinctive grassroots approach.

Further Reading: Mark Follman, "These Women Are the NRA's Worst Nightmare," *Mother Jones,* September/October 2014; Kristin A. Goss, *Disarmed: The Missing Movement for Gun Control in America* (Princeton: Princeton University Press, 2006); http://momsdemandaction.org/

Whitney, Eli (1765–1825)

The Militia Act of 1792 to establish a militia system in the United States, an act in 1798 to dispense weapons from the U.S. arsenals to the states, and an 1808 law to advance funds to states to finance militias provided the economic initiative to supplement Eli Whitney's inventive genius. By innovating the manufacturing process, Whitney was able to provide large numbers of muskets to the national and state governments in the early years of the nineteenth century. The federal government in the late eighteenth and early nineteenth centuries wanted to get guns into the hands of militia members and the regular military, and Whitney's work with standardized production increased the capacity to fulfill that policy goal.

Whitney's fame rests primarily on his invention of the cotton gin in 1792, a device that made the production of cotton more profitable. Although the invention is credited with reshaping the whole economy of the South, the inventor gained little economically from his efforts. He shifted his attention to another enterprise—the manufacture of firearms. In January 1798, Whitney signed a contract with the national government to produce 10,000 muskets. He planned to manufacture the arms through a procedure that amounted to an early version of a system of interchangeable parts and mass production. Whitney put immense effort and time into developing the process, for at the time there existed neither the necessary machinery or the skilled labor. He built a manufacturing plant, called Mill Rock, outside New Haven, Connecticut, using the funds invested by local residents to make the required tools and machines.

In October 1808, Whitney negotiated an agreement to produce 2,000 muskets for the New York State militia. At the same time, he pressed for a second contract with the federal government. In 1810, he obtained a contract to deliver 700 muskets, and the following year committed himself to producing 700 more. As the War of 1812 approached, Whitney anticipated the need for additional weapons. He signed a contract with the secretary of war to deliver 15,000 muskets by the end of 1820.

Callender Irvine, commissary general of purchases for the federal government, discouraged Whitney's completion of the contract, hoping to end the gun maker's agreement with the federal government. Irvine, wanting the U.S. War Department to adopt a musket in which he had a personal interest, endeavored to maintain control over government procurement policies. Conflicts over payment and inspection standards delayed production. In 1814, Whitney appealed directly to Secretary of State James Monroe and in 1815 wrote to President James Madison. Through his direct appeals to officials at the highest levels of government, Whitney achieved a satisfactory resolution to the conflict over arms production.

In 1822, Whitney entered a third contract with the federal government, agreeing to deliver 15,000 additional muskets. During this time, Whitney introduced innovative tools, such as a milling machine, to improve the production process.

Before Whitney's death late in 1824, his son, Eli, Jr., assumed management of the Mill Rock arms works, but lacked the ingenuity of his father. The factory became just one of many producers of arms. Not until the twentieth century did textbooks begin to recognize Whitney either as the inventor of the cotton gin or as an innovator in the production of firearms.

See also: Colt, Samuel; Militia Act of 1792; Remington, Eliphalet, II; Ruger, William Batterman (Bill); Smith and Wesson; Winchester, Oliver Fisher.

Further Reading: Constance McLaughlin Green, *Eli Whitney and the Birth of American Technology* (Boston: Little, Brown, 1956); Wayne Van Zwoll, *America's Great Gunmakers* (South Hackensack, NJ: Stoeger, 1992).

Winchester, Oliver Fisher (1810–1880)

Many people regard early gun makers as heroic contributors to the establishment of the nation and none has gained a higher status than Oliver Fisher Winchester. To this day, the Winchester retains its reputation as the rifle that conquered the American West. By the end of western expansion, the Winchester company had become the foremost manufacturer of long guns. However, Winchester himself bore no resemblance to the rugged individual of the old West, for before entering the firearms business, he was a successful shirt salesman.

Samuel Winchester, Oliver's father, died the year after the birth of Oliver and his twin brother in Boston, Massachusetts. From the age of 7, Winchester worked on local farms, which limited his schooling to winter months. At 14, he was apprenticed to a carpenter who taught him construction skills. In 1834, Winchester entered the dry goods business, opening a men's store in Baltimore. In June 1855, Winchester, at the age of 45, joined a group of 40 businessmen to form and incorporate the Volcanic Repeating Arms Company, which bought out Smith, Wesson, and Palmer a month later. Although he held a minimal number of stock shares, Winchester was elected the company's director. The company was relocated from Norwich to New Haven, Connecticut. The poor performance of the Volcanic firearm forced Winchester and

Oliver Winchester, maker of the rifle that "conquered the American West." *www.wikipedia.org*

company president Nelson Gaston to secure loans through personal mortgages. After Gaston's death, Winchester became president. In February 1857, Volcanic was declared bankrupt, and the next month Winchester was able to purchase all company assets for $40,000 and became the company's president and treasurer.

In 1858, Winchester asked B. Tyler Henry to modify the Volcanic rifle, and early in 1860, anticipating the Civil War, Winchester wrote to the U.S. government, requesting the military adoption of the Henry repeater. Like so many prophets of technology, Winchester predicted that major changes would result from the company's new rifle: "Probably it will modify the art of war; possibly it may revolutionize the whole science of war." However, Christopher Spencer received the major government contracts to supply the Union army with repeating rifles during the Civil War.

Following the war, pioneers moving west overwhelmingly chose the Winchester Model 1866, preferring its larger cartridge capacity and quickness. They found it an excellent weapon for defense against the dangers of the wilderness. When Nelson King solved a nagging problem with the ammunition magazine, Winchester dominated the market and Spencer's company could not survive. Customers chose the $50 Henry over the war-surplus Spencer, which sold for $7. The Model 1866 was so popular that it came to be known simply as "the Winchester." Throughout the 1870s, Winchester did well, making arms deals with foreign countries such as Turkey. With the Hotchkiss rifle (subsequently named the Model 1883), Winchester believed that the government contract that so far eluded the company could now be acquired. The Hotchkiss received superior ratings in tests conducted in 1878, but poor workmanship on the first shipment killed the deal. Winchester died in December 1880, and his son, whom he had expected to assume the presidency of the company, died of tuberculosis a few months later.

Concentrating on the civilian market, around the turn of the century the Winchester Company introduced "missionary" salesmen, entertainers who would not only make arms deals for the company, but would put on trick shot demonstrations to attract customers. Adolph (Ad) Topperwein, a circus performer since he was six years old, and his wife "Pinky" conducted tours on behalf of Winchester. At this time, Winchester produced other successful models, including the 94, which today is the rifle most often associated with Winchester.

During World War I, the Winchester company made large commitments to produce military arms. However, following the war, the drop in demand and inefficient production standards left the company $17 million in debt. Winchester had to borrow $3 million to pay taxes on wartime profits. Efforts in the 1920s to diversify and to open retail stores failed to raise the company out of debt. In January 1931, hit hard by the Great Depression, the company was forced into bankruptcy. After reorganization, the introduction of the Model 70, which became for the modern sportsman what the Winchester 66 had been for the post-Civil War settlers, improved the financial status of the company. World War II brought renewed government contracts.

In more recent times Winchester has gone through additional reorganizations, especially in 1984 when the company filed for bankruptcy under Chapter 11. In 1987, five investors bought the company. By the 1990s, managers had moved Winchester toward more aggressive sales strategies to maintain a share of the market. Winchester continues to sell a line of rifles and shotguns and various other products, including ammunition, hunting apparel, and promotional items.

See also: Colt, Samuel; Remington, Eliphalet, II; Ruger, William Batterman (Bill); Smith and Wesson; Winchester, Oliver Fisher.

Further Reading: K. D. Kirkland, *America's Premier Gunmakers* (New York: Mallard, 1990); Winchester Repeating Arms Web site, http://winchesterguns.com; Wayne Van Zwoll, *America's Great Gunmakers* (South Hackensack, NJ: Stoeger, 1992).

Wintemute, Garen J. (1951–)

Garen J. Wintemute, is a professor of emergency medicine in the department of epidemiology and preventive medicine, director of the Violence Prevention Research Program at the University of California at Davis, and Inaugural Susan P. Baker-Stephen P. Teret Chair in Violence Prevention. He has gained the critical attention of pro-gun rights groups and social science firearms researchers for his research on firearms and the gun manufacturing industry. Wintemute has published research findings dealing with accidental shootings involving children, types of weapons used in suicides, hospital costs of firearm injuries, and firearms used in fatal shootings of law enforcement officers. Wintemute's 1994 study of southern California handgun manufacturers focused on what many gun control advocates consider the continuing problem of inexpensive handguns, or Saturday night specials, which Wintemute claims are disproportionately used in violent crime. In 2009, Wintemute issued the results of a study of gun shows that involved the gathering of information from 78 shows in 19 states primarily between 2005 and 2008.

Wintemute received an undergraduate degree in biology from Yale University in 1973 and an M.D. from the University of California in 1977. In 1983, he was awarded a Master of Public Health degree from Johns Hopkins University. That year he became assistant professor of family practice at the University of California at Davis. In 1988, he was appointed director of the university's Family Practice Inpatient and Outpatient Services. An emergency room doctor, Wintemute became interested in firearm research when he realized that standard medical care was saving as many gunshot victims as possible and that any further improvements had to be made in the area of violence prevention.

Wintemute advocates the treatment of firearms as consumer products that should be subject to design, performance, safety, and reliability standards. He is especially concerned about U.S. manufacturers of inexpensive handguns. Wintemute has called the group of California companies (mostly belonging to the same family) that manufacture such weapons the "Ring of Fire." He has expressed unease about the availability of cheap handguns that are more powerful, more reliable, more accurate, and more easily used than previous models.

Wintemute is concerned that, to increase sales, gun manufacturers have targeted new customers, particularly women. He contends that manufacturers lack a sense of responsibility for what happens to the firearms they produce. Wintemute believes that the Bureau of Alcohol, Tobacco, Firearms, and Explosives (ATF) lacks the authority necessary to control firearms trafficking. Because the ATF is forbidden by law to keep a registry of firearms, the agency has a difficult task of tracing firearms used in crimes.

In a study of 88 unintentional shooting deaths of children in California from 1977 through 1983, Wintemute noted that 53 of the cases involved a child shooting another child. In 40 percent of these cases, the shooter was another family member. In 21 of the 88 shootings there was evidence that the child did not know the gun was loaded. In 1988, Wintemute participated in a California study of 5,360 authorized handgun purchasers between the ages of 21 and 25. He concluded that purchasers with a previous criminal history were more likely to acquire inexpensive handguns. Purchasers with no criminal history who acquired inexpensive handguns were nearly twice as likely to be charged with a crime of violence than purchasers of other types of handguns. Wintemute contends that these findings support other information indicating that cheap handguns are used disproportionately in the commission of crimes.

In 2016 Wintemute coauthored an article in *Epidemiological Review* which argues that gun-related assaults, suicides, and unintentional injuries represent a tremendous strain on public health, concluding that greater investment in research is required to deal successfully with gun violence. In another coauthored article, which appeared in the *Western Journal of Emergency Medicine*, Wintemute and colleagues call for lifting the congressional prohibition on firearms research.

See also: Bureau of Alcohol, Tobacco, Firearms, and Explosives; Saturday Night Special; Violence Prevention Research Program.

Further Reading: Garen Wintemute, *Inside Gun Shows: What Goes On When Everybody Things Nobody's Looking* (Sacramento, CA: Violence Prevention Research Program, 2009); Garen Wintemute, *Ring of Fire: The Handgun Makers of Southern California* (Sacramento, CA: Violence Prevention Research Program, 1994); Garen Wintemute, Carrie A. Parham, Mona A. Wright, James J. Beaumont, and Christiana M. Drake, "Weapons of Choice: Previous Criminal History, Later Criminal Activity, and Firearm Preference among Legally Authorized Young Adult Purchasers of Handguns," *Journal of Trauma Injury, Infection ,and Critical Care* 44 (January 1998) 155–160; Garen Wintemute, S. P. Teret, J. Kraus, M. A. Wright, and G. Bradfield, "When Children Shoot Children: 88 Unintended Deaths in California," *Journal of the American Medical Association* 257 (1987), 3107–09; D. W. Webster, M Cerdá, G. J. Wintemute, and P. J. Cook, "Epidemiological Evidence to Guide the Understanding and Prevention of Gun Violence," *Epidemiological Review* 38 2016): 1-4; M. E. Betz, M. L. Ranney, and G. J. Wintemute, "Frozen Funding on Firearm Research: 'Doing Nothing Is No Longer a Solution,'" *Western Journal of Emergency Medicine* (January 14, 2016): 91-93.

Women Against Gun Violence (WAGV)

In 1993 Ann Reiss Lane, the Los Angeles, California, police commissioner, and Betty Friedan, a noted feminist advocate, organized a national conference that focused on gun violence as a health concern and a women's issue. Women Against Gun Violence (WAGV) grew out of that conference. Lane remains the organization's chair emeritus. Margot Bennett currently serves and the organization's executive director.

Headquartered in Los Angeles, California, WAGV conducts educational campaigns that emphasize "the human, financial and public health consequences of gun violence." Distinguishing the organization from what WAGV calls traditional strategies for opposing gun violence, which it says is limited to advocating public policy change, the organization emphasizes gun violence as a women's issue that can be confronted through violence prevention efforts at the community level.

WAGV maintains a speakers bureau consisting of adults and youth who have lost family members and friends to gun violence or have themselves survived gun violence. The organization conducts a campaign against billboard movie advertisements that graphically depict gun violence. WAGV works to have such public advertising moved away from schools and high-crime areas. WAGV advises parents to ask neighbors if they have guns in the home and whether they have taken appropriate safety measures to secure the weapons. The organization has cooperated with the Los Angeles School Police Department to distribute gun locks to gun owners and to issue information about the importance of safely storing firearms. Among the brochures that WAGV distributes are "Talking With Your Children About Guns," "Ask Your Neighbors About Guns," and "Lock It Up," which are printed in English as well as Spanish.

The organization participates in several events during the year. In August 2016, WAGV participated in the "Disarm Hate" rally at the National Mall in Washington, D.C., and in September 2016 the organization hosted a symposium on guns and suicide in which experts on suicide and gun violence discussed ways of reducing the lethal means of committing suicide. Also in September, WAGV co-produced the Concert Across America to End Gun Violence, which was held in 68 cities across the country.

WAGV invites local organizations to host a showing of two documentary films, "Making a Killing: Greed, Guns, and the NRA," and "Under the Gun," hosted by television personality Katie Couric. Each year, WAGV hosts the Courageous Leader Awards Brunch, at which the organization recognizes the contributions individuals have made to reducing gun violence.

See also: Million Mom March; Mothers Against Violence in America; National SAFE KIDS Campaign; Protest Easy Guns; Student Pledge Against Gun Violence.

Further Reading: Women Against Gun Violence Website, www.wagv.org.

Women and Guns

Traditionally, women and guns have been compared to oil and water: Annie Oakley and other notable exceptions notwithstanding, they simply do not mix. In 1934, when the National Rifle Association (NRA) successfully opposed the inclusion of handgun control measures in the National Firearms Act, the General Federation of Women's Clubs, representing 2 million members, reproached the NRA and approved a resolution calling, unsuccessfully, for the passage of the original bill. Sixty years later, results of a 1994 national survey conducted by the National Institute of Justice (NIJ) indicated that 42 percent of men, but only 9 percent of women owned guns. In 1995, employing General Social Survey data, Tom Smith and Robert Smith found no evidence that gun ownership among women was increasing. Smith and Smith estimated that less than 12 percent of women own a firearm, and less than eight percent own a handgun. They noted that gun ownership was higher among married women residing outside large cities and was related to hunting rather than concerns for self-defense. A 2005 Gallup poll suggested a moderate increase in gun ownership for both genders, with 47 percent of men and 13 percent of women reporting that they personally own a firearm.

In the early 1990s, self-protection became a motivation to own a gun for women who were fearful of being victims of violent crime. Of the respondents in the 1994 NIJ survey, 41 percent of males, but 67 percent of females indicated that their primary purpose in possessing a gun was for protection against crime. At the same time, pro-gun rights organizations began a more serious effort to persuade growing numbers of women to become members and to convince them of the defensive value of gun ownership. Perceiving a growing market among women concerned about personal protection, dealers at gun shows and gun shops began to carry pink-colored handguns and all the accompanying paraphernalia, including holsters and hunting gear. Especially popular among women has been Smith and Wesson's Lady Smith revolver. In response to this increased interest by women in owning and learning to use firearms, women's magazines such as *Glamour*, *Ms.*, and *Vogue* printed articles questioning the value of gun ownership for women.

The NRA established the "Refuse to Be a Victim" program, which involved two initiatives. First, the NRA created a Web site that women could access to receive information about seminars in their local area that provide information about self-defense techniques for women. The organization then set up a self-defense seminar for women. Anti-gun feminists responded skeptically to this program, charging that the NRA was primarily concerned with increasing membership in what previously had been a largely untapped segment of the population. Gun control advocates also claimed that the firearms industry, which had saturated the male market, had been searching for new customers and had found them in women. Sarah Brady, chair of Handgun Control, Inc. (subsequently the Brady Campaign to Prevent Gun Violence) claimed that pro-gun advocates were cynically manipulating fear of crime among women to enlist new converts to their cause. "Refuse to Be a Victim" seminars were criticized for focusing on crimes committed by persons unknown to the victim, when the most common violent crime against women is rape and assault by a boyfriend or husband.

The NRA and other pro-gun advocates have presented gun ownership as an issue of choice, thus co-opting a major feminist theme often associated with the major feminist issue of reproductive rights. In response to the strong opposition to women owning firearms, pro-gun advocates contend that gun ownership should be, like other choices, a decision to be made by the individual woman. Pro-gun advocates, including some feminists, argue that gun ownership in the face of continuing violence represents a way that women can take control of their lives and can also act as a deterrent to the types of violent crimes that women now fear.

In response to the arguments for choice, pro-gun control feminists contend that the NRA offered no support for state legislative measures to authorize police to confiscate guns of men who assault women or who violate restraining orders. Opponents also suggest that a woman who purchases a gun would more likely have it used against her by a male living with her than use it to protect herself. In addition, the limited training women receive in the use of firearms may be insufficient to ensure their effective use. Those critical of gun ownership note that 16 percent of police officers who are murdered are shot with their own guns, despite the extensive training they receive in firearm use. However, the specter still remains of the woman, faced with a threatening boyfriend or husband or stranger, who, had she possessed the means of defense, might be alive today. Pro-gun rights advocates, considering themselves "pro-choice," criticize anti-gun feminists for attempting to deny individual women the right to take control of their own lives. The call not to be a victim has strong appeal for women concerned about their own safety.

The organization Women Against Gun Control (WAGC) was established in 1994 largely through the efforts of Janalee Tobias, who served as the organization's president. WAGC held the position that any limitation on the right of law-abiding citizens to own firearms prevents women from defending themselves in a dangerous environment. The organization applauded the passage of laws that allow the carrying of concealed weapons. When still active, WAGC's Website contained a pledge for women that included five items: to vote, to believe in and defend the Second Amendment, to act safely and responsibly when handling guns, to reject the claim that guns cause crime, and to impose bodily harm on others only in self-defense.

Among the sources of information that are available for women is The Well Armed Woman (TWAW), an LLC (limited liability company) established by Carrie Lightfoot to offer to women instruction in firearms, products designed especially for women, and a community with which women can identify. Lightfoot founded and is the chairwoman of the board for TWAW Shooting Chapters Inc., a nonprofit organization with 310 chapters in 49 states that claims a membership of more than 10,000. Members of the chapters meet regularly to practice shooting and learn safe gun handling.

Gun rights advocate Mary Zeiss Stange (2016) notes that, although many more men than women are gun owners and more women than men support gun control, from 2001 to 2013, female gun ownership in the United States increased by 85 percent. Concern for self-protection certainly still motivates women to acquire firearms, but the first decade of the 21st century saw a more than 50 percent increase in women's participation in target shooting and a 41.8 percent increase in women hunters. Stange comments that many feminists, when confronted with the prospect of becoming a gun owner, once responded "Guns? But Why?" now reply "Guns? Why not?"

See also: Brady Campaign to Prevent Gun Violence; Brady, Sarah; National Firearms Act of 1934; National Rifle Association; *Women and Guns* Magazine.

Further Reading: Joseph Carroll, "Gun Ownership and Use in America" (Gallup Poll, November 22, 2005), www.gallup.com/poll/20098/

gun-ownership- use-america.aspx; George Flynn and Alan Gottlieb, *Guns for Women: The Complete Handgun Buying Guide for Women* (Bellevue, WA: Merril, 1988); Ann Jones, "Living with Guns," *Ms.* (May/June 1994), 38–44; Ellen Neuborne, "Cashing In on Fear," *Ms.* (May/June 1994), 46–50; Paxton Quigley, *Armed and Female* (New York: St. Martin's, 1989); Tom W. Smith and Robert J. Smith, "Changes in Firearms Ownership among Women, 1980–1994," *Journal of Criminal Law and Criminology* 86 (Fall 1995), 133–145; Mary Zeiss Stange, "Arms and the Woman: A Feminist Reappraisal," in David B. Kopel, ed., *Guns: Who Should Have Them?* (Amherst, NY: Prometheus, 1995); Mary Zeiss Stange, "A Big Bang for 'the Little Woman:' Firearms and Feminism in Contemporary America," in Glenn H. Utter, ed., *Guns and Contemporary Society* (Santa Barbara, CA: Praeger, 2016): vol. 2, 263-289.

Women and Guns Magazine

Established in 1989, *Women and Guns* magazine (*WG*) is published every other month by the Second Amendment Foundation. Julianne Versnel Gottlieb serves as the publisher and Peggy Tartaro is the executive editor, who writes the editorial in each issue. *WG* contains many of the same types of articles that appear in other gun publications, including reviews of new products, such as handguns, gun locks, and gun safes. The magazine profiles gun manufacturers' product lines, such as American Derringer's series of small handguns. American Derringer is even more attractive because the company's president is a woman (Elizabeth Saunders). The magazine especially emphasizes self-protection themes. While gun rights advocates see *WG* as a key avenue for providing women the opportunity to become acquainted with their right to bear arms and to gain information about topics relevant to women, proponents of gun control claim the magazine is another example of the attempt by gun manufacturers to open a new market among women.

Closely associated with *Women and Guns* magazine has been the Women's Firearm Network, a Website established by computer graphics and design specialists Keeva Segal and Carole Walsh. Apparently no longer active, the Website was described as "dedicated to making firearms and self-defense information available to women everywhere. We feature info on guns, rifles, handguns, shotguns, hunting, self-defense, and more." Articles appearing on the site covered such topics as women taking responsibility for self-defense, support for the Second Amendment, and responses to gun control supporters.

In her column, "From the Editor," Tartaro touches on various political trends relevant to gun owners and the issue of gun control. The emphasis on self-defense is clear in a "News" column, which presents accounts of successful uses of firearms to thwart crime. The media are taken to task for focusing on incidents, such as the 1991 Kileen, Texas, shooting in which a gunman opened fire in a cafeteria, killing 22 people and injuring 23 others, and the 1989 Stockton, California, schoolyard shooting, while deemphasizing the successful use of firearms to prevent other possible incidents.

"Defensive Strategies," a column by Lyn Bates, a contributing editor, explores the sometimes complex circumstances of self-defense. In one issue, Bates introduced two scenarios, asking which of three options the reader would choose in each case. The reader was asked to consider not only whether the use of a firearm is justified, but if it is worth risking the consequences, which could involve criminal charges, expenditures for legal assistance, and lawsuits. The author mentioned three situations in which the gun owner should not hesitate to act: (1) when under deadly attack, (2) when being stalked by a killer, and (3) when family members are in serious danger. In all situations, Bates asserted, it is better to be armed than not.

In the January-February 2015 issue, Bates discusses the Federal Bureau of Investigation's report that active shooter incidents increased from 2000 to 2013, with 160 occurring during that time period. In some of those cases, private citizens were able to stop the shooter. Bates advises that. Although the probability of confronting an active shooter "are vanishingly small," if a person does, "the best response is a trained and armed one. Don't just carry; get the training you need to be certain of your ability to deal with an active shooter."

In another issue (May-June 2015) Bates recounts an incident in Springdale, Arkansas, armed young men attempted to rob a pawnshop. The two proprietors, an elderly woman and man, were armed and successfully resisted the would-be robbers. Bates provides an exciting account of the events and concludes with pieces of advice: know the law in your home state, particularly regarding crimes against property (as in this case) as opposed to crimes against a person. She concludes: "The most important thing is: have a gun with you that you can access quickly and use reliably."

Firearms are not the only weapons that *WG* encourages women to consider for self-protection. In an article by R. K. Campbell titled "Edged Weapon Options for Personal Protection," women were informed that even when in possession of a gun, they should consider carrying a knife as well. If a person cannot carry a gun, she has even greater use for a knife. Campbell noted that most types of knives are legal, inexpensive, easily purchased, and not dependent on one's physical strength. Women were advised to practice "slashing, striking, saber strikes and reverse slashes."

The column, "Legally Speaking" by Karen L. MacNutt, a contributing editor and consulting attorney for the Second Amendment Foundation, the NRA, and the Gun Owners' Action League, explores the legal implications of self-protection. In each issue, Karen L. MacNutt offers answers to legal questions regarding gun rights. In one issue, MacNutt discussed appropriate responses to verbal threats. She noted that "you may not use deadly force, nor should you display deadly force, if you are verbally threatened." Otherwise, the gun owner may risk a charge of assault with a deadly weapon. However, assault upon the gun owner would justify the use of deadly force as a self-defense measure. In the September/October 2010 issue, MacNutt reviewed the U.S. Supreme Court ruling in *McDonald v. Chicago* and offered her own thoughts on the decision and its implications for gun ownership.

In the January/February 2015 issue, MacNutt presents a basic description of the U.S. court system, distinguishing between the 50 state court systems and the federal system. With regard to firearms statutes, MacNutt cautions that individuals are governed by the laws of the state in which they reside; for instance, whereas Vermont has a very permissive policy on carrying a concealed weapon, Massachusetts has enacted very strict policies. She describes the legal process for taking a case to the courts—from state trial courts to state appeals courts and the possibly (on national constitutional grounds) to the federal court system and perhaps ultimately to the U.S. Supreme Court. In the May-June 2015 issue, MacNutt discusses the tendency for eyewitness accounts to be inaccurate and the reasons why this occurs, even though people sincerely believe they are providing a true account of events. Memory can also be influenced by suggestion from others. MacNutt emphasizes that data from studies about eyewitness accounts have significant consequences for defense attorney in criminal trials.

See also: Gun Owners' Action League; National Rifle Association; Second Amendment Foundation; Stockton, California, Shooting; Women and Guns.

Further Reading: *Women and Guns* (Second Amendment Foundation, Buffalo, NY); *Women and Guns* Web site, www.womenshooters.com.

Y

Youth and Guns

Gun control advocates have focused much of their attention on gun violence among children and adolescents. They note that gunshot wounds are more likely to kill teenage males than all natural causes combined. From 1983 to 1995, the proportion of gun homicides in which juveniles used guns rose from 55 percent to 80 percent. Marian Wright Edelman, president of the Children's Defense Fund, notes that in 2007, 3,042 children and teenagers died in shootings, of which 1,499 were African American. Edelman also notes that nearly 20 percent of high school students in 2007 reported carrying a weapon, and 5 percent reported carrying a gun. These data are reflected in a 1993 Louis Harris poll, in which 35 percent of children from 6 to 12 years old said they feared for their lives because of gun violence.

Some people have advocated the introduction of greater safety measures to curb youth injury and death due to firearms. For instance, in 1997 Democratic President Bill Clinton called for mandatory safety devices on guns to prevent accidents involving children. Although some argue for more stringent gun control legislation, others contend that such legislation would have little effect on the overall level of gun possession and usage by youth. Gun researcher Gary Kleck has argued against mandating certain gun safety measures, claiming that they miss the true problem of gun violence. He noted that just 18 percent of accidental deaths from gun shots involved children 12 years of age or younger. He also claimed that few young children have the strength to pull the trigger on the average handgun. Because children are seldom involved in gun accidents, Kleck argued that various safety devices cannot have a significant effect on the overall fatal gun accident (FGA) rate among young children.

Existing laws forbid juvenile purchases of handguns from retail stores or pawnshops; federal law restricts crossing state lines to purchase guns; theft of guns is illegal; transfer of stolen property is against the law; firing a gun inside the city limits is widely banned; and bearing a weapon on school property is legally prohibited. Those who oppose further gun control legislation conjecture that better enforcement of the law could result in improved compliance. Although Joseph Sheley and James Wright, in their 1995 study of youth and firearms, conceded that more severe criminal penalties could have some positive effect in reducing gun violence, they concluded that the extent of the problem and the lack of resources have kept existing laws from having their intended effect. Although controlling the supply of ammunition has also been suggested as a means of limiting gun violence, some, noting the experience with the illegal drug trade, argue that a black market for ammunition would spring up quickly to meet the demand.

Sheley and Wright further argued that stiff new penalties would place the worst youth offenders in prison, but would ultimately prove futile because new offenders would soon replace those who have been taken off the streets. However, this objection appears not to take into account the possible deterrent effect of harsher treatment of offenders. The recent decline in arrests for murder may have a number of causes, but one of them could be that a criminal justice system that has incarcerated larger numbers of offenders has deterred others from committing similar violent crimes.

Stuart Greenbaum (1997) emphasized the promising results of selected enforcement programs such as the Kansas City Gun Experiment, which targeted a limited area within the city to be patrolled intensively by police officers to disrupt the illegal gun trade. Greenbaum also emphasized programs that educate youth to the dangers of firearms, including the introduction of gun safety curricula in the public schools. To reduce juvenile gun possession, he noted that youth must be convinced they can cope with their environment without carrying weapons. However, Sheley and Wright observed that one of the major reasons youths carry weapons, at least in the inner city, is out of a perceived need for self-protection, whether or not they are involved in the drug trade or in gang activities. They painted a grim picture of life for such youth, who have developed a "siege mentality." They fear for their safety and believe that carrying a gun is a reasonable step for them to take to remain safe and ultimately to preserve their lives. When living in disintegrating neighborhoods where police protection may be very low, or virtually nonexistent and where schools are chaotic, carrying a gun offers a feeling of empowerment.

Sheley and Wright emphasized that gun possession as well as drug use and gang activity are all symptoms of a larger social breakdown. Assuming the legitimacy of this conclusion, others recognize that solving these larger problems will take a long and committed effort. In the meantime, schools and law enforcement agencies are thrust back into the struggle to find methods of controlling the instruments of violence. However, gun rights groups and gun magazines, concerned about passing on the culture of firearms to the next generation, emphasize introducing youth to the legitimate value of firearms in various sports.

The National Association of School Psychologists (NASP) reports that from 1981 to 2010, 112,711 infants, children, and teens were killed by firearms. The NASP also notes that 1,659 teenagers who committed suicide in 2010, 40 percent of them used a firearm. The organization also reports that the availability of firearms at home is associated with an increased risk of youth suicide. The Center for Injury Research and Prevention at Children's Hospital in Philadelphia, Pennsylvania, has disclosed that in 2013, 1,670 children died from gunshot wounds and 9,718 were injured.

In 2015, Ziming Zuan and David Hemenway reported their analysis of data from the Youth Risk Behavior Survey of students in grades nine through twelve in 2007, 2009, and 2011. Ziming and Hemenway rated each state's gun laws on a scale from 0 to 100, with higher scores indicating

more restrictive gun laws. Among their findings, the authors discovered a 10-point rise in the gun law score corresponded to a 9 percent lower chance of youth gun carrying. They also reported that from 1999 to 2013, an average of 15,000 young people ages 12 to 19 died each year from three causes: unintentional injuries, homicide, and suicide. Of homicides, 83 percent were gun-related, and of suicides, 45 percent involved a firearm.

See also: Clinton, William Jefferson (Bill); Kleck, Gary; Schools and Guns; Trigger Locks.

Further Reading: Marian Wright Edelman, "Gun Violence and Children: Have We No Shame or Respect for Child Life?" *The Huffington Post* (September 7, 2010), www.huffingtonpost. com/ marian-wright-edelman/gun-violence-and-children_b_708038.html; Stuart Greenbaum, "Kids and Guns: From Playgrounds to Battlegrounds," *Juvenile Justice* 3 (September 1997), 3–10; Gary Kleck, *Targeting Guns* (New York: Aldine de Gruyter, 1997); David B. Kopel, "Children and Guns," in David B. Kopel, ed., *Guns: Who Should Have Them?* (Amherst, NY: Prometheus, 1995), 309–406; Joseph F. Sheley and James D. Wright, *In the Line of Fire: Youth, Guns, and Violence in Urban America* (New York: Aldine de Gruyter, 1995); Centers of Disease Control, "Youth Violence Facts at a Glance" (2012), www.cdc.gov/ViolencePrevention/pdf/yv-datasheet-a. pdf; National Association of School Psychologists, "Youth Gun Violence Fact Sheet," www.nasponline. org/Documents/Resources%20and%20Publications/ Handouts/Safety%20and%20Crisis/Youth_Gun_ Violence_Fact_Sheet.pdf (accessed August 6, 2016); Ziming Zuan and David Hemenway, "State Gun Law Environment and Youth Gun Carrying in the United States," *Journal of the American Medical Association Pediatrics* (2015), DOI: 10.1001/ jamapediatrics.2015.2116.

Youth Crime Gun Interdiction Initiative (YCGII)

The Bureau of Alcohol, Tobacco, and Firearms (ATF) began the Youth Crime Gun Interdiction Initiative (YCGII) in 1996 as a pilot program to identify and disrupt the illegal supply of firearms to youth. The YCGII was an expansion of the Juvenile Firearms Trace Initiative begun in 1993 and was intended to supplement the gun trafficking efforts of the ATF by focusing on youth and gun-related crime. Although the YCGII received limited funding from the U.S. Department of the Treasury ($1.175 million in fiscal 1996 and $2.49 million in fiscal 1997), the initiative addressed what many consider the serious problem of gun violence committed by those under 25 years of age. The Initiative traced recovered crime guns through the National Tracing Center and engaged in analyses of crime gun data to identify trends involving the characteristics of recovered firearms.

Seventeen cities, including Atlanta, Georgia; Cleveland, Ohio; Memphis, Tennessee; San Antonio, Texas; and Washington, D.C. first joined the YCGII effort. Ten of the sites were cities that already received funding from the Office of Community Oriented Policing Services (COPS) for initiatives to control juvenile crime. The National Institute of Justice (NIJ) had research activities already underway in three other sites. The municipal governments of all 17 cities expressed their commitment to address the problem of armed youth crime.

During the first year of operation, more than 36,000 firearms were traced in the initial 17 sites. After the first year, 10 additional cities, including Chicago, Detroit, Miami, and Philadelphia, were added to the initiative. Cities selected included those with populations over 250,000 that had a high rate of gun-related violent crimes committed by youths and juveniles, and cities with a population over 100,000 that the U.S. attorney general had included in the Special Cities Project because violent crime had increased each year from 1993 to 1996. By 2000, the number of local governments involved in the program had increased to 50.

The police departments in the participating cities signed a memorandum of understanding," agreeing to trace all recovered firearms. The YCGII was committed to coordinating federal and state court prosecutions of illegal firearms trafficking involving youth. The Initiative used the services of Project LEAD, the computerized illegal firearms trafficking information system maintained by the ATF. The YCGII provided each site with a laptop computer capable of operating the Project LEAD software, which facilitated ongoing analyses of trace information on illegal firearms.

The ATF expected that the initiative would prove a valuable tool for controlling violent crime, especially because the population of juveniles was projected to increase significantly in the coming years, producing what was termed a "demographic crime bomb." Because firearms used in crimes committed by juveniles had a briefer "time to crime" (the time in days from initial purchase to criminal use), there was a greater probability that attempts to trace such weapons would end successfully.

The YCGII trace analysis reports provided basic information about crime guns and their users. Data analyses indicated that 4 of every 10 guns that law enforcement officials recovered could be traced to individuals aged 24 and younger, and eight out of ten guns recovered from youths and juveniles were handguns. The initiative reported that guns diverted from federally licensed firearms dealers contributed to the availability of firearms on the black market. The YCGII concluded from its analyses that law enforcement agencies could increase their capacity to reduce the rate of armed crimes through sharing crime gun information with other communities through the program.

Anthony A. Braga and Peter L. Gagliardi (2013) report that the YCGII, which not long is functioning, generated national and municipal-level gun trace reports more complete than the ATF's current state-level crime gun summaries that, they claim, "do not provide more rigorous and detailed analyses of crime gun sources, trends, and patterns."

See also: Bureau of Alcohol, Tobacco, Firearms, and Explosives; National Tracing Center; Youth and Guns.

Further Reading: Bureau of Alcohol, Tobacco, Firearms, and Explosives, "Youth Crime Gun Interdiction Initiative Report 2000," www.atf.gov/publications/historical/ycgii-report-2000.html; Anthony A. Braga and Peter L. Gagliardi, "Enforcing Federal Laws Against Firearms Traffickers," in Daniel W. Webster and Joh S. Vernick, eds., *Reducing Gun Violence in America* (Baltimore, MD: John Hopkins University Press, 2013): 143-154.

Z

Zimring, Franklin E. (1942–)

Franklin E. Zimring, William G. Simon Professor of Law and chair of the Criminal Justice Research Program, Institute for Legal Research, at the University of California at Berkeley, has conducted research on the causes and control of firearms violence. He published the first study of death rates from gun versus knife attacks and in 1968–69 served as director of research for the Task Force on Firearms of the National Violence Commission. Zimring adheres to the concept of instrumentality, that "a conflict is more likely to be lethal if a lethal weapon is at hand." He holds that if the death rate due to violence is a major problem, then handguns are a major part of that problem.

Zimring received a B.A. from Wayne State University in 1963 and a J.D. from the University of Chicago in 1967. From 1968 to 1969, Zimring served as director of research for the Task Force on Firearms, National Commission of the Causes and Prevention of Violence. He served as Llewellyn Professor of Law and director of the Center for Studies in Criminal Justice at the University of Chicago before joining the faculty at the University of California at Berkeley in 1985. Zimring has coauthored books with Gordon Hawkins dealing with penal confinement, drug control policy, and capital punishment. In 1987, he published *The Citizen's Guide to Gun Control*. Zimring has served as a member of the MacArthur Foundation Research Program on Adolescent Development and Juvenile Justice, the Center for Gun Policy and Research at the Johns Hopkins University, the Violent and Serious Juvenile Offender Project of the National Council on Crime and Delinquency, the National Policy Committee of the American Society of Criminology, and the National Academy of Sciences Panel on Violence.

Zimring notes that firearm injury reduction might be viewed in the same way as attempts to reduce auto crashes, or, alternatively, like efforts to eliminate smoking as a hazardous activity. Although efforts to improve traffic safety led to successful strategies to improve automobiles and highways, Zimring identifies a key weakness in applying the traffic safety model to firearms: because firearms are designed to be lethal, it is extremely difficult to devise a safe handgun. But Zimring identifies one crucial area of correspondence between firearms and automobiles: just as there are accident-prone individuals (for instance, those who drink and drive), there are people predisposed to violent conflict.

In 1997, Zimring coauthored with Hawkins *Crime Is Not the Problem*, which challenged traditional understandings of crime in Western nations. Zimring argued that the United States does not have a greater crime problem, or even a greater violence problem than other nations, but does have a greater lethal violence problem. Rates of nonviolent crime in the United States are comparable to, and sometimes lower than, rates in other countries. However, the rate of lethal violence is far greater in the United States than in other Western nations. Zimring has commented that in 1990, although the probability of being a victim of robbery or burglary was about equal in New York City and London, the chances of being killed during a robbery or burglary were 54 times greater in New York. Explaining the gap, Zimring noted that while 81 percent of assaults in London occurred without the use of a weapon, only 13 percent of reported cases in New York involved no weapon.

Zimring claims that most killings in the United States are unrelated to criminal activity and therefore "get tough on crime" campaigns fail to distinguish between lethal violence and other crimes. Not only is the rate of deadly violence disproportionately high in the United States, but 70 percent of all killings are committed with firearms. Given the high level of lethal violence compared to other countries, Zimring recommends that lawmakers respond specifically to this problem, which in a high proportion of cases involves firearms. Zimring notes that in the 1990s an extensive decrease in crime rates occurred, but at the same time events such as the Columbine high school shooting also took place, leading to a focus on violence "without a differentiating criminal identity." He has commented that the distinction often used by gun rights supporters between the legitimate and criminal use of firearms became less clear-cut "when good people's guns went to school." Recognizing that many policy proposals have been made to reduce the death rate due to firearms, such as closing the so-called gun show loophole and instituting waiting periods for purchasing a firearm, Zimring concludes that any one measure likely will not lead to a significant reduction in violent deaths.

In 2015 Zimring, with Brittany Arsiniega, published an article on killings of, and by police, a publication that presaged the subsequent controversial and highly publicized events in Dallas, Texas, Baton Rouge, Lousiana, and other cities in which police officers were specifically targeted

See also: United Kingdom; Violent Crime Rate.

Further Reading: Thomas B. Cole, "Franklin E. Zimring on Law and Firearms," *Journal of the American Medical Association* 275 (June 12, 1996), 1709; D. Lyn Hunter, "An Empiricist Tackles Crime," *Berkeleyan* (October 16, 2002), www.berkeley.edu/news/berkeleyan/2002/10/16_empir.html; Franklin E. Zimring, "Continuity and Change in the American Gun Debate" (UC Berkeley Public Law and Legal Theory Working Paper Series, April 12, 2001), http://papers.ssrn.com/paper.taf?abstract_id=266680; Franklin E. Zimring, *The Great American Crime Decline* (New York: Oxford University Press, 2007); Franklin E. Zimring and Gordon Hawkins, *Crime Is Not the Problem: Lethal Violence in America* (New York: Oxford University Press, 1997); Franklin E. Zimring and Brittany Arsiniega, "Trends in Killings of an by Police: A Preliminary Analysis," *Ohio State Journal of Criminal Law* 13 (Fall 2015): 247-264.

PRIMARY DOCUMENTS

The 25 original documents in this section are arranged chronologically, and span more than 200 years. They include political debates, court cases, acts of law, and contemporary articles on both sides of gun control v. gun rights. They are designed to offer an historical reference point and broader understanding of the complicated issues that surround this ongoing debate.

The Federalist Papers were 85 essays, numbered consecutively, that were written in 1787 and 1788 and published in newspapers to persuade the country to adopt the new Constitution by explaining and defending its provisions. The papers were initially authored under the fictional name "Publius," but were in fact written by Alexander Hamilton, James Madison, and John Jay. The papers reprinted below discuss in detail concerns related to federal versus state power in relation to militias, standing armies, and arms.

Federalist Paper 24

The Powers Necessary to Common Defense Further Considered for the Independent Journal To the People of the State of New York:

To THE powers proposed to be conferred upon the federal government, in respect to the creation and direction of the national forces, I have met with but one specific objection, which, if I understand it right, is this, that proper provision has not been made against the existence of standing armies in time of peace; an objection which, I shall now endeavor to show, rests on weak and unsubstantial foundations.

It has indeed been brought forward in the most vague and general form, supported only by bold assertions, without the appearance of argument; without even the sanction of theoretical opinions; in contradiction to the practice of other free nations, and to the general sense of America, as expressed in most of the existing constitutions. The proprietory of this remark will appear, the moment it is recollected that the objection under consideration turns upon a supposed necessity of restraining the LEGISLATIVE authority of the nation, in the article of military establishments; a principle unheard of, except in one or two of our State constitutions, and rejected in all the rest.

A stranger to our politics, who was to read our newspapers at the present juncture, without having previously inspected the plan reported by the convention, would be naturally led to one of two conclusions: either that it contained a positive injunction, that standing armies should be kept up in time of peace; or that it vested in the EXECUTIVE the whole power of levying troops, without subjecting his discretion, in any shape, to the control of the legislature.

If he came afterwards to peruse the plan itself, he would be surprised to discover, that neither the one nor the other was the case; that the whole power of raising armies was lodged in the LEGISLATURE, not in the EXECUTIVE; that this legislature was to be a popular body, consisting of the representatives of the people periodically elected; and that instead of the provision he had supposed in favor of standing armies, there was to be found, in respect to this object, an important qualification even of the legislative discretion, in that clause which forbids the appropriation of money for the support of an army for any longer period than two years a precaution which, upon a nearer view of it, will appear to be a great and real security against the keeping up of troops without evident necessity.

Disappointed in his first surmise, the person I have supposed would be apt to pursue his conjectures a little further. He would naturally say to himself, it is impossible that all this vehement and pathetic declamation can be without some colorable pretext. It must needs be that this people, so jealous of their liberties, have, in all the preceding models of the constitutions which they have established, inserted the most precise and rigid precautions on this point, the omission of which, in the new plan, has given birth to all this apprehension and clamor.

If, under this impression, he proceeded to pass in review the several State constitutions, how great would be his disappointment to find that TWO ONLY of them[1] contained an interdiction

---

[1] This statement of the matter is taken from the printed collection of State constitutions. Pennsylvania and North Carolina are the two which contain the interdiction in these words: "As standing armies in time of peace are dangerous to liberty, THEY OUGHT NOT to be kept up." This is, in truth, rather a CAUTION than a PROHIBITION. New Hampshire, Massachusetts, Delaware, and Maryland have, in each of their bils of rights, a clause to this effect: "Standing armies are dangerous to liberty, and ought not to be raised or kept up WITHOUT THE CONSENT OF THE LEGISLATURE"; which is a formal admission of the authority of the Legislature. New York has no bills of rights, and her constitution says not a word about the matter. No bills of rights appear annexed to the constitutions of the other States, except the foregoing, and their constitutions are equally silent. I am told, however that one or two States have bills of rights which do not appear in this collection; but that those also recognize the right of the legislative authority in this respect. http://www.yale.edu/lawweb/avalon/federal/fed24.htm

of standing armies in time of peace; that the other eleven had either observed a profound silence on the subject, or had in express terms admitted the right of the Legislature to authorize their existence.

Still, however he would be persuaded that there must be some plausible foundation for the cry raised on this head. He would never be able to imagine, while any source of information remained unexplored, that it was nothing more than an experiment upon the public credulity, dictated either by a deliberate intention to deceive, or by the overflowings of a zeal too intemperate to be ingenuous. It would probably occur to him, that he would be likely to find the precautions he was in search of in the primitive compact between the States. Here, at length, he would expect to meet with a solution of the enigma. No doubt, he would observe to himself, the existing Confederation must contain the most explicit provisions against military establishments in time of peace; and a departure from this model, in a favorite point, has occasioned the discontent which appears to influence these political champions.

If he should now apply himself to a careful and critical survey of the articles of Confederation, his astonishment would not only be increased, but would acquire a mixture of indignation, at the unexpected discovery, that these articles, instead of containing the prohibition he looked for, and though they had, with jealous circumspection, restricted the authority of the State legislatures in this particular, had not imposed a single restraint on that of the United States. If he happened to be a man of quick sensibility, or ardent temper, he could now no longer refrain from regarding these clamors as the dishonest artifices of a sinister and unprincipled opposition to a plan which ought at least to receive a fair and candid examination from all sincere lovers of their country! How else, he would say, could the authors of them have been tempted to vent such loud censures upon that plan, about a point in which it seems to have conformed itself to the general sense of America as declared in its different forms of government, and in which it has even superadded a new and powerful guard unknown to any of them? If, on the contrary, he happened to be a man of calm and dispassionate feelings, he would indulge a sigh for the frailty of human nature, and would lament, that in a matter so interesting to the happiness of millions, the true merits of the question should be perplexed and entangled by expedients so unfriendly to an impartial and right determination. Even such

a man could hardly forbear remarking, that a conduct of this kind has too much the appearance of an intention to mislead the people by alarming their passions, rather than to convince them by arguments addressed to their understandings.

But however little this objection may be countenanced, even by precedents among ourselves, it may be satisfactory to take a nearer view of its intrinsic merits. From a close examination it will appear that restraints upon the discretion of the legislature in respect to military establishments in time of peace, would be improper to be imposed, and if imposed, from the necessities of society, would be unlikely to be observed.

Though a wide ocean separates the United States from Europe, yet there are various considerations that warn us against an excess of confidence or security. On one side of us, and stretching far into our rear, are growing settlements subject to the dominion of Britain. On the other side, and extending to meet the British settlements, are colonies and establishments subject to the dominion of Spain. This situation and the vicinity of the West India Islands, belonging to these two powers create between them, in respect to their American possessions and in relation to us, a common interest. The savage tribes on our Western frontier ought to be regarded as our natural enemies, their natural allies, because they have most to fear from us, and most to hope from them. The improvements in the art of navigation have, as to the facility of communication, rendered distant nations, in a great measure, neighbors. Britain and Spain are among the principal maritime powers of Europe. A future concert of views between these nations ought not to be regarded as improbable. The increasing remoteness of consanguinity is every day diminishing the force of the family compact between France and Spain. And politicians have ever with great reason considered the ties of blood as feeble and precarious links of political connection. These circumstances combined, admonish us not to be too sanguine in considering ourselves as entirely out of the reach of danger.

Previous to the Revolution, and ever since the peace, there has been a constant necessity for keeping small garrisons on our Western frontier. No person can doubt that these will continue to be indispensable, if it should only be against the ravages and depredations of the Indians. These garrisons must either be furnished by occasional detachments from the militia, or by permanent corps in the pay of the government. The first is impracticable; and if practicable, would be pernicious. The militia would not long, if at all, submit to be dragged from their occupations and families to perform that most disagreeable duty in times of profound peace. And if they could be prevailed upon or compelled to do it, the increased expense of a frequent rotation of service, and the loss of labor and disconcertion of the industrious pursuits of individuals, would form conclusive objections to the scheme. It would be as burdensome and injurious to the public as ruinous to private citizens. The latter resource of permanent corps in the pay of the government amounts to a standing army in time of peace; a small one, indeed, but not the less real for being small. Here is a simple view of the subject, that shows us at once the impropriety of a constitutional interdiction of such establishments, and the necessity of leaving the matter to the discretion and prudence of the legislature.

In proportion to our increase in strength, it is probable, nay, it may be said certain, that Britain and Spain would augment their military establishments in our neighborhood. If we should not be willing to be exposed, in a naked and defenseless condition, to their insults and encroachments, we should find it expedient to increase our frontier garrisons in some ratio to the force by which our Western settlements might be annoyed. There are, and will be, particular posts, the possession of which will include the command of large districts of territory, and facilitate future invasions of the remainder. It may be added that some of those posts will be keys to the trade with the Indian nations. Can any man think it would be wise to leave such posts in a situation to be at any instant seized by one or the other of two neighboring and formidable powers? To act this part would be to desert all the usual maxims of prudence and policy.

If we mean to be a commercial people, or even to be secure on our Atlantic side, we must endeavor, as soon as possible, to have a navy. To this purpose there must be dock-yards and arsenals; and for the defense of these, fortifications, and probably garrisons. When a nation has become so powerful by sea that it can protect its dock-yards by its fleets, this supersedes the necessity of garrisons for that purpose; but where naval establishments are in their infancy, moderate garrisons will, in all likelihood, be found an indispensable security against descents for the destruction of the arsenals and dock-yards, and sometimes of the fleet itself.

PUBLIUS.

Federalist Paper 25

The Same Subject Continued (The Powers Necessary to the Common Defense Further Considered) To the People of the State of New York:

IT MAY perhaps be urged that the objects enumerated in the preceding number ought to be provided for by the State governments, under the direction of the Union. But this would be, in reality, an inversion of the primary principle of our political association, as it would in practice transfer the care of the common defense from the federal head to the individual members: a project oppressive to some States, dangerous to all, and baneful to the Confederacy.

The territories of Britain, Spain, and of the Indian nations in our neighborhood do not border on particular States, but encircle the Union from Maine to Georgia. The danger, though in different degrees, is therefore common. And the means of guarding against it ought, in like manner, to be the objects of common councils and of a common treasury. It happens that some States, from local situation, are more directly exposed. New York is of this class. Upon the plan of separate provisions, New York would have to sustain the whole weight of the establishments requisite to her immediate safety, and to the mediate or ultimate protection of her neighbors. This would neither be equitable as it respected New York nor safe as it respected the other States. Various inconveniences would attend such a system. The States, to whose lot it might fall to support the necessary establishments, would be as little able as willing, for a considerable time to come, to bear the burden of competent provisions. The security of all would thus be subjected to the parsimony, improvidence, or inability of a part. If the resources of such part becoming more abundant and extensive, its provisions should be proportionally enlarged, the other States would quickly take the alarm at seeing the whole military force of the Union in the hands of two or three of its members, and those probably amongst the most powerful. They would each choose to have some counter-poise, and pretenses could easily be contrived. In this situation, military establishments, nourished by mutual jealousy, would be apt to swell beyond their natural or proper size; and being at the separate disposal of the members, they would be engines for the abridgment or demolition of the national authcrity.

Reasons have been already given to induce a supposition that the State governments will too naturally be prone to a rivalship with that of the Union, the foundation of which will be the love of power; and that in any contest between the federal head and one of its members the people will be most apt to unite with their local government. If, in addition to this immense advantage, the ambition of the members should be stimulated by the separate and independent possession of military forces, it would afford too strong a temptation and too great a facility to them to make enterprises upon, and finally to subvert, the constitutional authority of the Union. On the other hand, the liberty of the people would be less safe in this state of things than in that which left the national forces in the hands of the national government. As far as an army may be considered as a dangerous weapon of power, it had better be in those hands of which the people are most likely to be jealous than in those of which they are least likely to be jealous. For it is a truth, which the experience of ages has attested, that the people are always most in danger when the means of injuring their rights are in the possession of those of whom they entertain the least suspicion.

The framers of the existing Confederation, fully aware of the danger to the Union from the separate possession of military forces by the States, have, in express terms, prohibited them from having either ships or troops, unless with the consent of Congress. The truth is, that the existence of a federal government and military establishments under State authority are not less at variance with each other than a due supply of the federal treasury and the system of quotas and requisitions.

There are other lights besides those already taken notice of, in which the impropriety of restraints on the discretion of the national legislature will be equally manifest. The design of the objection, which has been mentioned, is to preclude standing armies in time of peace, though we have never been informed how far it is designed the prohibition should extend; whether to raising armies as well as to KEEPING THEM UP in a season of tranquillity or not. If it be confined to the latter it will have no precise signification, and it will be ineffectual for the purpose intended. When armies are once raised what shall be denominated "keeping them up," contrary to the sense of the Constitution? What time shall be requisite to ascertain the violation? Shall it be a week, a month, a year? Or shall we say they may be continued as

long as the danger which occasioned their being raised continues? This would be to admit that they might be kept up IN TIME OF PEACE, against threatening or impending danger, which would be at once to deviate from the literal meaning of the prohibition, and to introduce an extensive latitude of construction. Who shall judge of the continuance of the danger? This must undoubtedly be submitted to the national government, and the matter would then be brought to this issue, that the national government, to provide against apprehended danger, might in the first instance raise troops, and might afterwards keep them on foot as long as they supposed the peace or safety of the community was in any degree of jeopardy. It is easy to perceive that a discretion so latitudinary as this would afford ample room for eluding the force of the provision.

The supposed utility of a provision of this kind can only be founded on the supposed probability, or at least possibility, of a combination between the executive and the legislative, in some scheme of usurpation. Should this at any time happen, how easy would it be to fabricate pretenses of approaching danger! Indian hostilities, instigated by Spain or Britain, would always be at hand. Provocations to produce the desired appearances might even be given to some foreign power, and appeased again by timely concessions. If we can reasonably presume such a combination to have been formed, and that the enterprise is warranted by a sufficient prospect of success, the army, when once raised, from whatever cause, or on whatever pretext, may be applied to the execution of the project.

If, to obviate this consequence, it should be resolved to extend the prohibition to the RAISING of armies in time of peace, the United States would then exhibit the most extraordinary spectacle which the world has yet seen, that of a nation incapacitated by its Constitution to prepare for defense, before it was actually invaded. As the ceremony of a formal denunciation of war has of late fallen into disuse, the presence of an enemy within our territories must be waited for, as the legal warrant to the government to begin its levies of men for the protection of the State. We must receive the blow, before we could even prepare to return it. All that kind of policy by which nations anticipate distant danger, and meet the gathering storm, must be abstained from, as contrary to the genuine maxims of a free government. We must expose our property and liberty to the mercy of foreign invaders, and invite them by our weakness to seize the naked and defenseless prey, because we are afraid that rulers, created by our choice, dependent on our will, might endanger that liberty, by an abuse of the means necessary to its preservation.

Here I expect we shall be told that the militia of the country is its natural bulwark, and would be at all times equal to the national defense. This doctrine, in substance, had like to have lost us our independence. It cost millions to the United States that might have been saved. The facts which, from our own experience, forbid a reliance of this kind, are too recent to permit us to be the dupes of such a suggestion. The steady operations of war against a regular and disciplined army can only be successfully conducted by a force of the same kind. Considerations of economy, not less than of stability and vigor, confirm this position. The American militia, in the course of the late war, have, by their valor on numerous occasions, erected eternal monuments to their fame; but the bravest of them feel and know that the liberty of their country could not have been established by their efforts alone, however great and valuable they were. War, like most other things, is a science to be acquired and perfected by diligence, by perseverance, by time, and by practice.

All violent policy, as it is contrary to the natural and experienced course of human affairs, defeats itself. Pennsylvania, at this instant, affords an example of the truth of this remark. The Bill of Rights of that State declares that standing armies are dangerous to liberty, and ought not to be kept up in time of peace. Pennsylvania, nevertheless, in a time of profound peace, from the existence of partial disorders in one or two of her counties, has resolved to raise a body of troops; and in all probability will keep them up as long as there is any appearance of danger to the public peace. The conduct of Massachusetts affords a lesson on the same subject, though on different ground. That State (without waiting for the sanction of Congress, as the articles of the Confederation require) was compelled to raise troops to quell a domestic insurrection, and still keeps a corps in pay to prevent a revival of the spirit of revolt. The particular constitution of Massachusetts opposed no obstacle to the measure; but the instance is still of use to instruct us that cases are likely to occur under our government, as well as under those of other nations, which will sometimes render a military force in time of peace essential to the security of the society, and that it is therefore improper in this respect to control the legislative discretion. It also teaches us, in its application to the United States, how little the rights of a feeble government are likely to be respected, even by its own constituents. And it teaches us, in addition to the rest, how unequal parchment provisions are to a struggle with public necessity.

It was a fundamental maxim of the Lacedaemonian commonwealth, that the post of admiral should not be conferred twice on the same person. The Peloponnesian confederates, having suffered a severe defeat at sea from the Athenians, demanded Lysander, who had before served with success in that capacity, to command the combined fleets. The Lacedaemonians, to gratify their allies, and yet preserve the semblance of an adherence to their ancient institutions, had recourse to the flimsy subterfuge of investing Lysander with the real power of admiral, under the nominal title of vice-admiral. This instance is selected from among a multitude that might be cited to confirm the truth already advanced and illustrated by domestic examples; which is, that nations pay little regard to rules and maxims calculated in their very nature to run counter to the necessities of society. Wise politicians will be cautious about fettering the government with restrictions that cannot be observed, because they know that every breach of the fundamental laws, though dictated by necessity, impairs that sacred reverence which ought to be maintained in the breast of rulers towards the constitution of a country, and forms a precedent for other breaches where the same plea of necessity does not exist at all, or is less urgent and palpable.

PUBLIUS.

http://www.yale.edu/lawweb/avalon/federal/fed25.htm

The debates in the First Congress provide the most direct evidence regarding the intentions and meaning of what eventually became the Second Amendment; the Senate met in secret at the time, so no official record of debate was kept. The reference in an early version of the amendment to the militia composed of the body of the people has raised questions about who was being referenced. When the phrase the body of the people *is taken by itself, it suggests the entire population of the country. Yet it was inserted as an operational definition of militia:* A well regulated militia, composed of the body of the people *and did not include elderly men, for example, or those with physical infirmities that prevented them from serving in the militia. Thus, while militia service was an important civic right or civic responsibility, it was different from some of the other rights expressed in the Bill of Rights, such as free speech or freedom of assembly, which were not limited to subgroups of the population based on traits like physical fitness or age (leaving aside those adults who were not granted full rights earlier in the country's history, including women and African Americans). The debate in the First Congress also confronted the longstanding fear of standing armies. The new Constitution gave Congress control over both, but many in Congress, such as Elbridge Gerry, wanted the country to maintain a strong and active militia to serve as a potential counterbalance to a standing army. But the subject that prompted the most debate was whether to include an express exemption from military service for those who had religious objections to military service (those religiously scrupulous). All of the debate regarding the Second Amendment pertained to military matters and militia service.*

U.S. House of Representatives Debate over the Second Amendment, excerpts

The Congressional Register, August 17, 1789

The house went into a committee of the whole, on the subject of amendments. The 3rd clause of the 4th proposition in the report was taken into consideration, being as follows; ?A well regulated militia, composed of the body of the people, being the best security of a free state; the right of the people to keep and bear arms shall not be infringed, but no person, religiously scrupulous, shall be compelled to bear arms.?

Mr. Gerry ? This declaration of rights, I take it, is intended to secure the people against the mal-administration of the government; if we could suppose that in all cases the rights of the people would be attended to, the occasion for guards of this kind would be removed. Now, I am apprehensive, sir, that this clause would give an opportunity to the people in power to destroy the constitution itself. They can declare who are those religiously scrupulous, and prevent them from bearing arms. What, sir, is the use of a militia? It is to prevent the establishment of a standing army, the bane of liberty. Now it must be evident, that under this provision, together with their other powers, congress could take such measures with respect to a militia, as make a standing army

necessary. Whenever governments mean to invade the rights and liberties of the people, they always attempt to destroy the militia, in order to raise an army upon their ruins. This was actually done by Great Britain at the commencement of the late revolution. They used every means in their power to prevent the establishment of an effective militia to the eastward. The assembly of Massachusetts, seeing the rapid progress that administration were making, to divest them of their inherent privileges, endeavored to counteract them by the organization of the militia, but they were always defeated by the influence of the crown.

Mr. Seney ? Wished to know what question there was before the committee, in order to ascertain the point upon which the gentleman was speaking?

Mr. Gerry ? Replied, that he meant to make a motion, as he disapproved of the words as they stood. He then proceeded, No attempts that they made, were successful, until they engaged in the struggle which emancipated them at once from their thralldom. Now, if we give a discretionary power to exclude those from militia duty who have religious scruples, we may as well make no provision on this head; for this reason he wished the words to be altered so as to be confined to persons belonging to a religious sect, scrupulous of bearing arms.

Mr. Jackson ? Did not expect that all the people of the United States would turn Quakers or Moravians, consequently one part would have to defend the other, in case of invasion; now this, in his opinion, was unjust, unless the constitution secured an equivalent, for this reason he moved to amend the clause, by inserting at the end of it "upon paying an equivalent to be established by law."

Mr. Smith, (of S.C.) ? Enquired what were the words used by the conventions respecting this amendment; if the gentleman would conform to what was proposed by Virginia and Carolina, he would second him: He thought they were to be excused provided they found a substitute.

Mr. Jackson ? Was willing to accommodate; he thought the expression was, "No one, religiously scrupulous of bearing arms, shall be compelled to render military service in person, upon paying an equivalent."

Mr. Sherman ? Conceived it difficult to modify the clause and make it better. It is well-known that those who are religiously scrupulous of bearing arms, are equally scrupulous of getting substitutes or paying an equivalent; many of them would rather die than do either one or the other ? but he did not see an absolute necessity for a clause of this kind. We do not live under an arbitrary government, said he, and the states respectively will have the government of the militia, unless when called into actual service; beside, it would not do to alter it so as to exclude the whole of any sect, because there are men amongst the quakers who will turn out, notwithstanding the religious principles of this society, and defend the cause of their country. Certainly it will be improper to prevent the exercise of such favorable dispositions, at least while it is the practice of nations to determine their contests by the slaughter of their citizens and subjects.

Mr. Vining ? Hoped the clause would be suffered to remain as it stood, because he saw no use in it if it as amended so as to compel a man to find a substitute, which, with respect to the government, was the same as if the person himself turned out to fight.

Mr. Stone ? Enquired what the words "Religiously scrupulous" had reference to, was it of bearing arms? If it was, it ought so to be expressed.

Mr. Benson ? Moved to have the words "But no person religiously scrupulous shall be compelled to bear arms" struck out. He would always leave it to the benevolence of the legislature ? for, modify it, said he, as you please, it will be impossible to express it in such a manner as to clear it from ambiguity. No man can claim this indulgence of right. It may be a religious persuasion, but it is no natural right, and therefore ought to be left to the

discretion of the government. If this stands part of the constitution, it will be a question before the judiciary, on every regulation you make with respect to the organization of the militia, whether it comports with this declaration or not? It is extremely injudicious to intermix matters of doubt with fundamentals. I have no reason to believe but the legislature will always possess humanity enough to indulge this class of citizens in a matter they are so desirous of, but they ought to be left to their discretion.

The motion for striking out the whole clause being seconded, was put, and decided in the negative, 22 members voting for it, and 24 against it.

Mr. Gerry ? Objected to the first part of the clause, on account of the uncertainty with which it is expressed: a well-regulated militia being the best security of a free state, admitted an idea that a standing army was a secondary one. It ought to read "a well regulated militia, trained to arms," in which case it would become the duty of the government to provide this security, and furnish a greater certainty of its being done.

Mr. Gerry's motion not being seconded, the question was put on the clause as reported, which being adopted.

Mr. Burke ? Proposed to add to the clause just agreed to, an amendment to the following effect: "A standing army of regular troops in time of peace, is dangerous to public liberty, and such shall not be raised or kept up in time of peace but from necessity, and for the security of the people, nor then without the consent of two-thirds of the members present of both houses, and in all cases the military shall be subordinate to the civil authority." This being seconded.

Mr. Vining ? Asked whether this was to be considered as an addition to the last clause, or an amendment by itself? If the former, he would remind the gentleman the clause was decided; if the latter, it was improper to introduce new matter, as the house had referred the report specially to the committee of the whole.

Mr. Burke ? Feared that what with being trammelled in rules, and the apparent disposition of the committee, he should not be able to get them to consider any amendment; he submitted to such proceeding because he could not help himself.

Mr. Hartley ? Thought the amendment in order, and was ready to give his opinion of it. He hoped the people of America would always be satisfied with having a majority to govern. He never wished to see two-thirds or three-fourths required, because it might put it in the power of a small minority to govern the whole union.

The question on Mr. Burke's motion was put, and lost by a majority of 13.

The Congressional Register, August 20, 1789

Mr. SCOTT objected to the clause in the sixth amendment, "No person religiously scrupulous shall be compelled to bear arms." He said, if this becomes part of the constitution, we can neither call upon such persons for services nor an equivalent; it is attended with still further difficulties, for you can never depend upon your militia. This will lead to the violation of another article in the constitution, which secures to the people the right of keeping arms, as in this case you must have recourse to a standing army. I conceive it is a matter of legislative right altogether. I know there are many sects religiously scrupulous in this respect: I am not for abridging them of any indulgence by law; my design is to guard against those who are of no religion. It is said that religion is on the decline; if this is the case, it is an argument in my favour; for when the time comes that there is no religion, persons will more generally have recourse to these pretexts to get excused.

Mr. BOUDINOT said that the provision in the clause or something like it appeared to be necessary. What dependence can be placed in men who are conscientious in this respect? Or what justice can there be in compelling them to bear arms, when, if they are honest men, they would rather die than use them. He then adverted to several instances of oppression in the case which occurred during the [revolutionary] war. In forming a militia we ought to calculate for an effectual defence, and not compel characters of this description to bear arms. I wish that in establishing this government we may be careful to let every person know that we will not interfere with any person's particular religious profession. If we strike out this clause, we shall lead such persons to conclude that we mean to compel them to bear arms.

Mr. VINING and Mr. JACKSON spoke upon the question. The words 'in person' were added after the word 'arms', and the amendment was adopted.

Source: http://www.constitution.org/mil/militia_debate_1789.htm

The Uniform Militia Act, passed by Congress one year after the adoption of the Bill of Rights, reveals in considerable detail what the country's leaders meant by the concept of militia at a time when it was still considered to be the backbone of the American military. Congress required the militias to be organized according to military principles; membership was limited not only to white males, but to those between eighteen and forty-five who were fit for service, underscoring the fact that white males over the age of forty-five, and the infirm, were excluded from militias, even though they were eligible to exercise other rights and freedoms; they were to provide their own arms and other military accessories (since neither the states nor the national government could be relied on to provide weapons and the like); and the militias were to be put to any use specified by the government. Thus, militias were not to be privately formed or operated, nor were they to be used against the government (except by the federal government against a state in rebellion or chaos). The Uniform Militia Act provided a very detailed list of items that militia-eligible men were required to obtain, at their own expense, including a musket, a bayonet, spare flints (these made the necessary spark to ignite the gun powder to fire the gun), a knapsack, twenty-four cartridges and more. For all of this, however, the Act included no penalties against states or men who did not comply—another compromise owing to continued tensions between Federalists and Anti-Federalists—and the terms of this Act, along with similar state enactments, were largely ignored.

The Uniform Militia Act of 1792, 1 U.S. Stat. 271

CHAP. XXXIII.-An Act more effectually to provide for the National Defence by establishing an Uniform Militia throughout the United States.

SECTION I. Be it enacted by the Senate and House of Representatives of the United States of America in Congress assembled, That each and every free able-bodied white male citizen of the respective states, resident therein, who is or shall be of the age of eighteen years, and under the age of forty-five years (except as is herein after excepted) shall severally and respectively be enrolled in the militia by the captain or commanding officer of the company, within whose bounds such citizen shall reside, and that within twelve months after the passing of this act. And it shall at all times hereafter be the duty of every such captain or commanding officer of a company to enrol every such citizen, as aforesaid, and also those who shall, from time to time, arrive at the age of eighteen years, or being of the age of eighteen years and under the age of forty-five years (except as before excepted) shall come to reside within his bounds; and shall without delay notify such citizen of the said enrolment, by a proper non-commissioned officer of the company, by whom such notice may be proved. That every citizen so enrolled and notified, shall, within six months thereafter, provide himself with a good musket or firelock, a sufficient bayonet and belt, two spare flints, and a knapsack, a pouch with a box therein to contain not less than twenty four cartridges, suited to the bore of his musket or firelock, each cartridge to contain a proper quantity of powder and ball: or with a good rifle, knapsack, shot-pouch and powder-horn, twenty balls suited to the bore of his rifle, and a quarter of a pound of powder; and shall appear, so armed, accoutred and provided, when called out to exercise, or into service, except, that when called out on company days to exercise only, he may appear without a knapsack. That the commissioned officers shall severally be armed with a sword or hanger and espontoon, and that from and after five years from the passing of this act, all muskets for arming the militia as herein required, shall be of bores sufficient for balls of the eighteenth part of a pound. And every citizen so enrolled, and providing himself with the arms, ammunition and accoutrements required as aforesaid, shall hold the same exempted from all suits, distresses, executions or sales, for debt or for the payment of taxes.

SEC. 2. And be it further enacted, That the Vice President of the United States; the officers judicial and executive of the government of the United States; the members of both Houses of Congress, and their respective officers; all custom-house officers with their clerks; all post officers, and stage drivers, who are employed in the care and conveyance of the mail of the post-office of the United States; all ferrymen employed at any ferry on the post road; all inspectors of exports; all pilots; all mariners actually employed in the sea service of any citizen or merchant within the United States; and all persons who now are or may hereafter be exempted by the laws of the respective states, shall be, and are hereby exempted from militia duty, notwithstanding their being above the age of eighteen, and under the age of forty-five years.

SEC. 3. And be it further enacted, That within one year after the passing of this act, the militia of the respective states shall be arranged into divisions, brigades, regiments, battalions and companies, as the legislature of each state shall direct; and each division, brigade and regiment, shall be numbered at the formation thereof; and a record made of such numbers in the adjutant-general's office in the state; and when in the field, or in service in the state, each division, brigade and regiment shall respectively take rank according to their numbers, reckoning the first or lowest number highest in rank. That if the same be convenient, each brigade shall consist of four regiments; each regiment of two battalions; each battalion of five companies; each company of sixty-four privates. That the said militia shall be officered by the respective states, as follows: To each division, one major-general and two aids-de-camp, with the rank of major; to each brigade, one brigadier-general, with one brigade inspector, to serve also as brigade-major, with the rank of a major; to each regiment, one lieutenant-colonel commandant; and to each battalion one major; to each company one captain, one lieutenant, one ensign, four sergeants, four corporals, one drummer and one fifer or bugler. That there shall be a regimental staff, to consist of one adjutant and one quartermaster, to rank as lieutenants; one paymaster; one surgeon, and one surgeon's mate; one sergeant-major; one drum-major, and one fife-major.

SEC. 4. And be it further enacted, That out of the militia enrolled, as is herein directed, there shall be formed for each battalion at least one company of grenadiers, light infantry or riflemen; and that to each division there shall be at least one company of artillery, and one troop of horse: there shall be to each company of artillery, one captain, two lieutenants, four sergeants, four corporals, six gunners, six bombadiers, one drummer, and one fifer. The officers to be armed with a sword or hanger, a fusee, bayonet and belt, with a cartridge-box to contain twelve cartridges; and each private or matross shall furnish himself with all the equipments of a private in the infantry, until proper ordnance and field artillery is provided. There shall be to each troop of horse, one captain, two lieutenants, one cornet, four sergeants, four corporals, one saddler, one farrier, and one

trumpeter. The commissioned officers to furnish them-selves with good horses of at least fourteen hands and an half high, and to be armed with a sword and pair of pistols, the holsters of which to be covered with bearskin caps. Each dragoon to furnish himself with a serviceable horse, at least fourteen hands and a half high, a good saddle, bridle, mailpillion and valise, holsters, and a breast-plate and crupper, a pair of boots and spurs, a pair of pistols, a sabre, and a cartouche-box, to contain twelve cartridges for pistols. That each company of artillery and troop of horse shall be formed of volunteers from the brigade, at the discretion of the commander-in-chief of the state, not exceeding one company of each to a regiment, nor more in number than one eleventh part of the infantry, and shall be uniformly clothed in regimentals, to be furnished at their own expense; the colour and fashion to be determined by the brigadier commanding the brigade to which they belong.

SEC. 5. And be it further enacted, That each battalion and regiment shall be provided with the state and regimental colours by the field officers, and each company with a drum and fife, or bugle-horn, by the commissioned officers of the company, in such manner as the legislature of the respective states shall direct.

SEC. 6. And be it further enacted, That there shall be an adjutant-general appointed in each state, whose duty it shall be to distribute all orders from the commander-in-chief of the state to the several corps; to attend all public reviews when the commander-in-chief of the state shall review the militia, or any part thereof; to obey all orders from him relative to carrying into execution and perfecting the system of military discipline established by this act; to furnish blank forms of different returns that may be required, and to explain the principles on which they should be made; to receive from the several officers of the different corps throughout the state, returns of the militia under their command, reporting the actual situation of their arms, accoutrements, and ammunition, their delinquencies, and every other thing which relates to the general advancement of good order and discipline: all which the several officers of the divisions, brigades, regiments, and battalions, are hereby required to make in the usual manner, so that the said adjutant-general may be duly furnished therewith: from all which returns he shall make proper abstracts, and lay the same annually before the commander-in-chief of the state.

SEC. 7. And be it further enacted, That the rules of discipline, approved and established by Congress in their resolution of the twenty-ninth of March, one thousand seven hundred and seventy-nine, shall be the rules of discipline to be observed by the militia throughout the United States, except such deviations from the said rules as may be rendered necessary by the requisitions of this act, or by some other unavoidable circumstances. It shall be the duty of the commanding officer at every muster, whether by battalion, regiment, or single company, to cause the militia to be exercised and trained agreeably to the said rules of discipline.

SEC. 8. And be it further enacted, That all commissioned officers shall take rank according to the date of their commissions; and when two of the same grade bear an equal date, then their rank to be determined by lot, to be drawn by them before the commanding officer of the brigade, regiment, battalion, company, or detachment.

SEC. 9. And be it further enacted, That if any person, whether officer or soldier, belonging to the militia of any state, and called out into the service of the United States, be wounded or disabled while in actual service, he shall be taken care of and provided for at the public expense.

SEC. 10. And be it further enacted, That it shall be the duty of the brigade-inspector to attend the regimental and battalion meetings of the militia composing their several brigades, during the time of their being under arms, to inspect their arms, ammunition, and accoutrements; superintend their exercise and manoeuvres, and introduce the system of military discipline before described throughout the brigade, agreeable to law, and such orders as they shall from time to time receive from the commander-in-chief of the state; to make returns to the adjutant-general of the state, at least once in every year, of the militia of the brigade to which he belongs, reporting therein the actual situation of the arms, accoutrements, and ammunition of the several corps, and every other thing which, in his judgment, may relate to their government and the general advancement of good order and military discipline; and the adjutant-general shall make a return of all the militia of the state to the commander-in-chief of the said state, and a duplicate of the same to the President of the United States.

And whereas sundry corps of artillery, cavalry, and infantry now exist in several of the said states, which by the laws, customs, or usages thereof have not been incorporated with, or subject to the general regulations of the militia:

SEC. 11. Be it further enacted, That such corps retain their accustomed privileges, subject, nevertheless, to all other duties required by this act, in like manner with the other militia.

APPROVED, May 8, 1792.

Source: http://www.constitution.org/mil/mil_act_1792. htm

The Supreme Court's Presser *case arose when Herman Presser was convicted of violating a state law that made it illegal for individuals to combine as a private military organization or to parade without first receiving a license to do so. Presser and his group violated the law when they paraded, armed, through the streets of Chicago without a license. Presser challenged the conviction, partly on Second Amendment grounds. In its ruling, the Supreme Court upheld Presser's conviction. It also said that the Second Amendment did not apply to the states, a position that the court maintained until 2010. Beyond that, the court discussed at length the meaning of the term "militia" as it appears in the Second Amendment, and in other parts of the Constitution, rejecting the ideas that citizens may lawfully create their own, private militias, or that there is any private citizen right to own or carry weapons under the Second Amendment. Only the government has the power to create militias. The* Presser *court also said that citizens could not form their own private militias (what today are called paramilitary groups), as only the government has authority over military organizations.*

Presser v. State of Illinois, 116 U.S. 252 (1886)

Mr. Justice Woods delivered the opinion of the court:

Herman Presser, the plaintiff in error, was indicted on September 24, 1879, in the criminal court of Cook county, Illinois, for a violation of the following sections of article 11 of the Military Code of that state (Act May 28, 1879; Laws 1876, 192):

"Sec. 5. It shall not be lawful for any body of men whatever, other than the regular organized volunteer militia of this state, and the troops of the United States, to associate themselves together as a military company or organization, or to drill or parade with arms in any city or town of this state, without the license of the governor thereof, which license may at any time be revoked: and provided, further, that students in educational institutions, where military science is a part of the course of instruction, may, with the consent of the governor, drill and parade with arms in public, under the superintendence of their instructors, and may take part in any regimental or brigade encampment, under command of their military instructor; and while so encamped shall be governed by the provisions of this act. They shall be entitled only to transportation and subsistence, and shall report and be subject to the commandant of such encampment: Provided, that nothing herein contained shall be construed so as to prevent benevolent or social organizations from wearing swords.

Sec. 6. Whoever offends against the provisions of the preceding section, or belongs to, or parades with, any such unauthorized body of men with

arms, shall be punished by a fine not exceeding the sum of ten dollars, ($10,) or by imprisonment in the common jail for a term not exceeding six months, or both."

The indictment charged in substance that Presser, on September 24, 1879, in the county of Cook, in the state of Illinois, "did unlawfully belong to, and did parade and drill in the city of Chicago with, an unauthorized body of men with arms, who had associated themselves together as a military company and organization, without having a license from the governor, and not being a part of, or belonging to, 'the regular organized volunteer militia' of the state of Illinois, or the troops of the United States."

A motion to quash the indictment was overruled. Presser then pleaded not guilty, and, both parties having waived a jury, the case was tried by the court, which found Presser guilty and sentenced him to pay a fine of $10.

The bill of exceptions taken upon the trial set out all the evidence, from which it appeared that Presser was 31 years old, a citizen of the United States and of the state of Illinois, and a voter; that he belonged to a society called the *Lehr und Wehr Verein*, a corporation organized April 16, 1875, in due form, under chapter 32, Revised Statutes of Illinois, called the General Incorporation Laws of Illinois, "for the purpose," as expressed by its certificate of association, "of improving the mental and bodily condition of its members so as to qualify them for the duties of citizens of a republic. Its members shall, therefore, obtain, in the meetings of the association, a knowledge of our laws and political economy, and shall also be instructed in military and gymnastic exercises;" that Presser, in December, 1879, marched at the head of said company, about 400 in number, in the streets of the city of Chicago, he riding on horseback and in command; that the company was armed with rifles, and Presser with a cavalry sword; that the company had no license from the Governor of Illinois to drill or parade as a part of the militia of the state, and was not a part of the regular organized militia of the state, nor a part of troops of the United States, and had no organization under the militia law of the United States. The evidence showed no other facts. Exceptions were reserved to the ruling of the court upon the motion to quash the indictment, to the finding of guilty, and to the judgment thereon. The case was taken to the Supreme Court of Illinois, where the judgment was affirmed. Thereupon Presser brought the present writ of error for a review of the judgment of affirmance.

The position of the plaintiff in error in this court was that the entire statute under which he was convicted was invalid and void because its enactment was the exercise of a power by the legislature of Illinois forbidden to the states by the Constitution of the United States. The clauses of the Constitution of the United States referred to in the assignments of error were as follows:

Article 1, 8. "The Congress shall have power . . . to raise and support armies; . . . to provide for calling forth the militia to execute the laws of the Union, suppress insurrections, and repel invasions; to provide for organizing, arming, and disciplining the militia, and for governing such part of them as may be employed in the service of the United States, reserving to the states, respectively, the appointment of the officers, and the authority of training the militia, according to the discipline prescribed by congress; . . . to make all laws which shall be necessary and proper, for carrying into execution the foregoing powers," etc.

Article 1, 10. "No state shall, without the consent of congress, keep troops . . . in time of peace."

Art. 2 of Amendments. "A well regulated militia being necessary to the security of a free State, the right of the people to keep and bear arms shall not be infringed."

The plaintiff in error also contended that the enactment of the fifth and sixth sections of article 11 of the Military Code was forbidden by subdivision 3 of section 9 of article 1, which declares "no bill of attainder or ex post facto law shall be passed," and by article 14 of Amendments, which provides that "no state shall make or enforce any law which shall abridge the privileges or immunities of citizens of the United States, nor

shall any state deprive any person of life, liberty, or property without due process of law."

The first contention of counsel for plaintiff in error is that the Congress of the United States having, by virtue of the provisions of article 1 of section 8, above quoted, passed the act of May 8, 1792, entitled "An Act More Effectually to Provide for the National Defense by Establishing an Uniform Militia Throughout the United States," (1 St. 271,) the act of February 28, 1795, "To Provide for Calling Forth the Militia to Execute the Laws of the Union, Suppress Insurrections, and Repel Invasions," (1 St. 424,) and the Act of July 22, 1861, "To Authorize the Employment of Volunteers to Aid in Enforcing the Laws and Protecting Public Property," (12 St. 268,) and other subsequent Acts, now forming "Title 16, The Militia," of the Revised Statutes of the United States, the legislature of Illinois had no power to pass the act approved May 28, 1879, "To Provide for the Organization of the State Militia, entitled the Military Code of Illinois," under the provisions of which (sections 5 and 6 of article 11) the plaintiff in error was indicted.

The argument in support of this contention is, that the power of organizing, arming, and disciplining the militia being confided by the Constitution to Congress, when it acts upon the subject, and passes a law to carry into effect the constitutional provision, such action excludes the power of legislation by the state on the same subject.

It is further argued that the whole scope and object of the Military Code of Illinois is in conflict with that of the law of Congress. It is said that the object of the act of Congress is to provide for organizing, arming, and disciplining all the able-bodied male citizens of the states, respectively, between certain ages, that they may be ready at all times to respond to the call of the nation to enforce its laws, suppress insurrection, and repel invasion, and thereby avoid the necessity for maintaining a large standing army, with which liberty can never be safe, and that, on the other hand, the effect if not object of the Illinois statute is to prevent such organizing, arming, and disciplining of the militia.

The plaintiff in error insists that the Act of Congress requires absolutely all able-bodied citizens of the state, between certain ages, to be enrolled in the militia; that the Act of Illinois makes the enrollment dependent on the necessity for the use of troops to execute the laws and suppress insurrections, and then leaves it discretionary with the governor by proclamation to require such enrollment; that the Act of Congress requires the entire enrolled militia of the state, with a few exemptions made by it and which may be made by state laws, to be formed into companies, battalions, regiments, brigades, and divisions; that every man shall be armed and supplied with ammunition; provides a system of discipline and field exercises for companies, regiments, etc., and subjects the entire militia of the state to the call of the president to enforce the laws, suppress insurrection, or repel invasion, and provides for the punishment of the militia officers and men who refuse obedience to his orders. On the other hand, it is said that the state law makes it unlawful for any of its able-bodied citizens, except 8,000, called the Illinois National Guard, to associate themselves together as a military company, or to drill or parade with arms without the license of the Governor, and declares that no military company shall leave the state with arms and equipments without his consent; that even the 8,000 men styled the Illinois National Guard are not enrolled or organized as required by the Act of Congress, nor are they subject to the call of the President, but they constitute a military force sworn to serve in the military service of the state, to obey the orders of the Governor, and not to leave the state without his consent; and that, if the state act is valid, the national act providing for organizing, arming, and disciplining the militia is of no force in the state of Illinois, for the Illinois act, so far from being in harmony with the act of Congress, is an insurmountable obstacle to its execution.

We have not found it necessary to consider or decide the question thus raised as to the validity of the entire Military Code of Illinois, for, in our opinion, the sections under which the plaintiff in error was convicted may be valid, even if the other sections of the act were invalid. For it is a settled rule "that statutes that are constitutional in part only will be upheld so far as they are not in conflict with the Constitution, provided the allowed and prohibited parts are separable." Packet Co. v. Keokuk, 95 U.S. 80 ; Penniman's Case, 103 U.S. 714, 717; Unity v. Burrage, Id. 459. See, also, Trade-Mark Cases, 100 U.S. 82.

We are of opinion that this rule is applicable in this case. The first two sections of article 1 of the Military Code provide that all able bodied male citizens of the state between the ages of 18 and 45 years, except those exempted, shall be subject to military duty, and be designated the "Illinois State Militia," and declare how they shall be enrolled and under what circumstances. The residue of

the Code, except the two sections on which the indictment against the plaintiff in error is based, provides for a volunteer active militia, to consist of not more than 8,000 officers and men, declares how it shall be enlisted and brigaded, and the term of service of its officers and men; provides for brigade generals and their staffs, for the organization of the requisite battalions and companies and the election of company officers; provides for inspections, parades, and encampments, arms and armories, rifle practice, and courts-martial; provides for the pay of the officers and men, for medical service, regimental bands, books of instructions and maps; contains provisions for levying and collecting a military fund by taxation, and directs how it shall be expended; and appropriates $25,000 out of the treasury, in advance of the collection of the military fund, to be used for the purposes specified in the Military Code.

It is plain from this statement of the substance of the Military Code that the two sections upon which the indictment against the plaintiff in error is based may be separated from the residue of the Code, and stand upon their own independent provisions. These sections might have been left out of the Military Code and put in an act by themselves, and the act thus constituted and the residue of the Military Code would have been coherent and sensible acts. If it be conceded that the entire Military Code, except these sections, is unconstitutional and invalid, for the reasons stated by the plaintiff in error, these sections are separable, and, put in an act by themselves, could not be considered as forbidden by the clauses of the Constitution having reference to the militia, or to the clause forbidding the states, without the consent of Congress, to keep troops in time of peace. There is no such connection between the sections which prohibit any body of men, other than the organized militia of the state and the troops of the United States, from associating as a military company and drilling with arms in any city or town of the state, and the sections which provide for the enrollment and organization of the state militia, as makes it impossible to declare one, without declaring both, invalid.

This view disposes of the objection to the judgment of the Supreme Court of Illinois, which judgment was in effect that the legislation on which the indictment is based is not invalid by reason of the provisions of the Constitution of the United States which vest Congress with power to raise and support armies, and to provide for calling out, organizing, arming, and disciplining the militia, and governing such part of them as may be employed in the service of the United States, and that provision which declares that "no state shall, without the consent of Congress, . . . keep troops . . . in time of peace."

We are next to inquire whether the fifth and sixth sections of article 11 of the Military Code are in violation of the other provisions of the Constitution of the United States relied on by the plaintiff in error. The first of these is the Second Amendment, which declares: "A well regulated militia being necessary to the security of a free State, the right of the people to keep and bear arms shall not be infringed."

We think it clear that the sections under consideration, which only forbid bodies of men to associate together as military organizations, or to drill or parade with arms in cities and towns unless authorized by law, do not infringe the right of the people to keep and bear arms. But a conclusive answer to the contention that this amendment prohibits the legislation in question lies in the fact that the amendment is a limitation only upon the power of Congress and the national government, and not upon that of the states. It was so held by this court in the case of U. S. v. Cruikshank, 92 U.S. 542 , 553, in which the Chief Justice, in delivering the judgment of the court, said that the right of the people to keep and bear arms "is not a right granted by the Constitution. Neither is it in any manner dependent upon that instrument for its existence. The Second Amendment declares that it shall not be infringed, but this, as has been seen, means no more than that it shall not be infringed by Congress. This is one of the amendments that has no other effect than to restrict the powers of the national government, leaving the people to look for their protection against any violation by their fellow-citizens of the rights it recognizes to what is called in City of New York v. Miln, 11 Pet. the 'powers which relate to merely municipal legislation, or what was perhaps more properly called internal police,' 'not surrendered or restrained' by the Constitution of the United States.". . .

It is undoubtedly true that all citizens capable of bearing arms constitute the reserved military force or reserve militia of the United States as well as of the states, and, in view of this prerogative of the general government, as well as of its general powers, the states cannot, even laying the constitutional provision in question out of view,

prohibit the people from keeping and bearing arms, so as to deprive the United States of their rightful resource for maintaining the public security, and disable the people from performing their duty to the general government. But, as already stated, we think it clear that the sections under consideration do not have this effect.

The plaintiff in error next insists that the sections of the Military Code of Illinois, under which he was indicted, are an invasion of that clause of the first section of the Fourteenth Amendment to the Constitution of the United States which declares: "No state shall make or enforce any law which shall abridge the privileges or immunities of citizens of the United States."

It is only the privileges and immunities of citizens of the United States that the clause relied on was intended to protect. A state may pass laws to regulate the privileges and immunities of its own citizens, provided that in so doing it does not abridge their privileges and immunities as citizens of the United States. The inquiry is therefore pertinent: What privilege or immunity of a citizen of the United States is abridged by sections 5 and 6 of article 11 of the Military Code of Illinois?

The plaintiff in error was not a member of the organized volunteer militia of the State of Illinois, nor did he belong to the troops of the United States or to any organization under the militia law of the United States. On the contrary, the fact that he did not belong to the organized militia or the troops of the United States was an ingredient in the offense for which he was convicted and sentenced. The question is, therefore: Had he a right as a citizen of the United States, in disobedience of the state law, to associate with others as a military company, and to drill and parade with arms in the towns and cities of the state?. . .

We have not been referred to any statute of the United States which confers upon the plaintiff in error the privilege which he asserts. The only clause in the Constitution which, upon any pretense, could be said to have any relation whatever to his right to associate with others as a military company, is found in the First Amendment, which declares that "Congress shall make no laws . . . abridging . . . the right of the people peaceably to assemble and to petition the government for a redress of grievances." This is a right which it was held in U. S. v. Cruikshank, above cited, was an attribute of national citizenship, and, as such, under the protection of, and guaranteed by, the United States. But it was held in the same case that the right peaceably to assemble was not protected by the clause referred to, unless the purpose of the assembly was to petition the government for a redress of grievances.

The right voluntarily to associate together as a military company or organization, or to drill or parade with arms, without, and independent of, an act of Congress or law of the state authorizing the same, is not an attribute of national citizenship. Military organization and military drill and parade under arms are subjects especially under the control of the government of every country. They cannot be claimed as a right independent of law. Under our political system they are subject to the regulation and control of the state and federal governments, acting in due regard to their respective prerogatives and powers. The Constitution and laws of the United States will be searched in vain for any support to the view that these rights are privileges and immunities of citizens of the United States independent of some specific legislation on the subject.

It cannot be successfully questioned that the state governments, unless restrained by their own constitutions, have the power to regulate or prohibit associations and meetings of the people, except in the case of peaceable assemblies to perform the duties or exercise the privileges of citizens of the United States, and have also the power to control and regulate the organization, drilling, and parading of military bodies and associations, except when such bodies or associations, are authorized by the militia laws of the United States. The exercise of this power by the states is necessary to the public peace, safety, and good order. To deny the power would be to deny the right of the state to disperse assemblages organized for sedition and treason, and the right to suppress armed mobs bent on riot and rapine. . . .

The argument of the plaintiff in error that the legislation mentioned deprives him of either life, liberty, or property without due process of law, or that it is a bill of attainder or ex post facto law, is so clearly untenable as to require no discussion.

It is next contended by the plaintiff in error that sections 5 and 6 of article 11 of the Military Code, under which he was indicted, are in conflict with the acts of Congress for the organization of the militia. But this position is based on what seems to us to be an unwarranted construction of the sections referred to. It is clear that their object was to forbid voluntary military associations, unauthorized by law, from organizing or drilling and parading with arms in the cities or towns of the state, and not to interfere with the organization, arming and drilling of the militia under the authority of the acts of Congress. If the object and effect of the sections were in irreconcilable conflict with the acts of Congress, they would of course be invalid. But it is a rule of construction that a statute must be interpreted so as, if possible, to make it consistent with the Constitution and the paramount law. . . . If we yielded to this contention of the plaintiff in error, we should render the sections invalid by giving them a strained construction, which would make them antagonistic to the law of Congress. We cannot attribute to the legislature, unless compelled to do so by its plain words, a purpose to pass an act in conflict with an act of Congress on a subject over which Congress is given authority by the constitution of the United States. We are, therefore, of opinion that, fairly construed, the sections of the Military Code referred to do not conflict with the laws of Congress on the subject of the militia.

The plaintiff in error further insists that the organization of the *Lehr und Wehr Verein* as a corporate body, under the general corporation law of the state of Illinois, was in effect a license from the Governor, within the meaning of section 5 of article 11 of the Military Code, and that such corporate body fell within the exception of the same section "of students in educational institutions where military science is a part of the course of instruction." In respect to these points we have to say that they present no federal question. It is not, therefore, our province to consider or decide them. . . .

All the federal questions presented by the record were rightly decided by the Supreme Court of Illinois. Judgment affirmed.

Source: http://caselaw.lp.findlaw.com/scripts/getcase.pl? na vby=case&court=us&vol=116&page=252

The Militia Act of 1903, also known as the Dick Act, named after Rep. Charles Dick (R-Ohio), the member of Congress who sponsored the legislation, finally modernized the old and mostly obsolete federal militia laws. The new law distinguished between the organized militias, which henceforth would be known as the National Guard, and the "reserve militia," a synonym for the general militias or unorganized militias. Aside from reserving to Congress the option of calling up the reserve militia should the need arise, no other provision was made for the latter, as national military emergencies were and are met by drafting men into the professional military forces rather than activating the militias. Most of the rest of this law provided for federal arming, training, and drilling of the National Guard, requiring these units to conform to federal military standards and organization, sweeping aside eighteenth century requirements that militiamen arm themselves. Federal funding for Guards also increased dramatically.

The Militia Act of 1903 PL 33; 32 Stat. 775

CHAP. 196.—An Act To promote the efficiency of the militia, and for other purposes. Public Law No. 33; 32 Stat. 775

Be it enacted by the Senate and House of Representatives of the United States of America in Congress assembled, That the militia shall consist of every able-bodied male citizen Of the respective States Territories, and the District of Columbia, and every able-bodied male of foreign birth who has declared his intention to become a citizen, who is more than eighteen and less than forty-five years of age, and shall be divided into two classes—the organized militia, to be known as the National Guard of the State, Territory, or District of Columbia, or by such other designations as may be given them by the laws of the respective States or Territories, and the remainder to be known as the Reserve Militia.

SEC. 2. That the Vice-President of the United States, the officers, judicial and executive, of the Government of the United States, the members and officers of each House of Congress, persons in the military or naval service of the United States, all custom-house officers with their clerks, postma8tera and persons employed by the United States in the transmission of the Militia. ferrymen employed at any ferry on a post road, artificers and workmen employed in the armories and arsenals of the United States, pilots, mariners actually employed in the sea service of any citizen or merchant within the United States, and all persons who are exempted by the laws of the respective States or Territories shall be exempted from militia duty, without regard to age: *Provided*, That nothing in this Act shall be construed to require or compel any member of

any well-recognized religious sect or organization at present organized and existing whose creed forbids its members to participate in war in any form, and whose religious convictions are against war or participation therein, in accordance with the creed of said religious organization, to serve in the militia or any other armed or volunteer force under the jurisdiction and authority of the United States.

SEC. 3. That the regularly enlisted, organized, and uniformed active militia in the several States and Territories and the District of Columbia who have heretofore participated or shall hereafter participate in the apportionment of the annual appropriation provided by section sixteen hundred and sixty-one of the Revised Statutes of the United States, as amended, whether known and designated as National Guard, militia, or otherwise, shall constitute the organized militia. The organization, armament, and discipline of the organized militia in the several States and Territories and in the District of Columbia shall be the same as that which is now or may hereafter be pre8cribed for the Regular and Volunteer Armies of the United States, within five years from the date of the approval of this Act: *Provided*, That the President of the United States, in time of peace, may by order fix the minimum number of enlisted men in each company, troop, battery, signal corps, engineer corps, and hospital corps: *And provided further*, That any corps of artillery, cavalry and infantry existing in any of the States at the passage of the Act of May eighth, seventeen hundred and ninety-two, which, by the laws, customs or usages of the said States have been in continuous existence since the passage of said Act under its provisions and under the provisions of Section two hundred and thirty-two and Sections sixteen hundred and twenty-five to sixteen hundred and sixty, both inclusive, of Title sixteen of the Revised Statutes of the United States relating to the Militia, shall be allowed to retain their accus-tomed privileges, subject, nevertheless, to all other duties required by law in like manner as the other Militia.

SEC. 4. That whenever the United States is invaded, or in danger of invasion from any foreign nation or of rebellion against the authority of the Government of the United States, or the President is unable, with the other forces at his command, to execute the laws of the Union in any part thereof, it shall be lawful for the President to call forth, for a period not exceeding nine months, such number of the militia of the State or of the States or Territories or of the District of Columbia as he may deem necessary to repel such invasion, suppress such rebellion, or to enable him to execute such laws, and to issue his orders for that purpose to such officers of the militia as he may think proper.

SEC. 5. That whenever the President calls forth the militia, of any State or Territory or of the District of Columbia to be employed in the service of the United States, he may specify in his call the period for which such service is required, not exceeding nine months, and the militia so called shall continue to serve during the term so specified, unless sooner discharged by order of the President.

SEC. 6. That when the militia of more than one State is called into the actual service of the United States by the President he may, in his discretion apportion them among such States or Territories or to the District of Columbia according to representative population.

SEC. 7. That every officer and enlisted man of the militia who shall be called forth in the manner hereinbefore prescribed and shall be found fit for military service shall be mustered or accepted into the United States service by a duly authorized mustering officer of the United States: *Provided, however*, That any officer or enlisted man of the militia who shall refuse or neglect to present himself to such mustering officer upon being called forth as herein prescribed shall be subject to trial by court-martial, and shall be punished as such court-martial may direct.

SEC. 8. That courts-martial for the trial of officers or men of the militia, when in the service of the United States, shall be composed of militia officers only.

SEC. 9. That the militia, when called into the actual service of the United States, shall be subject to the same Rules and Articles of War as the regular troops of the United States.

SEC. 10. That the militia, when called into the actual service of the United States, shall, during their time of service, be entitled to the same pay and allowances as are or may be provided by law for the Regular Army.

SEC. 11. That when the militia is called into the actual service of the United States, or any portion of the militia is accepted under the provisions of this Act, their pay shall commence from the day of their appearing at the place of company rendezvous. But this provision shall not be construed to authorize any species of expenditure previous to arriving at such places of rendezvous which is not provided by existing laws to be paid after their arrival at such places of rendezvous.

SEC. 12. That there shall be appointed in each State, Territory and District of Columbia, an Adjutant-General, who shall perform such duties as may be prescribed by the laws of such State, territory, and District, respectively and make returns to the Secretary of War, at such times and in such form as he shall from time to time prescribe, of the strength of the organized militia, and also make such reports as may from time to time be required by the Secretary of War. That the Secretary of War shall, with his annual report of each year, transmit to Congress an abstract of the returns and reports of the adjutants-general of the States, Territories, and the District of Columbia with such observations thereon as he may deem necessary for the information of Congress.

SEC. 13. That the Secretary of War is hereby authorized to issue, on the requisitions of the governors of the several States and Territories, or of the commanding general of the militia of the District of Columbia, such number of the United States standard service magazine arms, with bayonets, bayonet scabbards, gun slings, belts, and such other necessary accouterments and equipments as are required for the Army of the United States, for arming all of the organized militia in said States and Territories and District of Columbia, without charging the cost or value thereof, or any which have been issued since December first, nineteen hundred and one, or any expense connected therewith, against the allotment to said State, Territory, or District of Columbia, out of the annual appropriation provided by section sixteen hundred and sixty-one of the Revised Statutes, as amended, or requiring payment therefor, and to exchange, without receiving any money credit therefor, ammunition, or parts thereof, suitable to the new arms, round for round, for corresponding ammunition suitable to the old arms theretofore issued to said State, Territory, or District by the United States: *Provided*, That said rifles and carbines and other property shall be receipted for and shall remain the property of the United States and be annually accounted for by the governors of the States and Territories as now required by law, and that each State, Territory, and District shall, on receipt of the new arms, turn in to the Ordnance Department of the United States Army, without receiving any money credit therefor, and without expense for transportation, all United States rifles and carbines now in its possession.

To provide means to carry into effect the provisions of this section, the necessary money to cover the cost of exchanging or issuing the new arms, accouterments, equipments, and ammunition to be exchanged or issued hereunder is hereby appropriated out of any moneys in the Treasury not otherwise appropriated.

SEC. 14. That whenever it shall appear by the report of inspections, which it shall be the duty of the Secretary of War to cause to be made at least once in each year by officers detailed by him for that purpose, that the organized militia of a State or Territory or of the District of Columbia is sufficiently armed, uniformed, and equipped for active duty in the field, the Secretary of War is authorized, on the requisition of the governor of such State or Territory, to pay to the quartermaster-general thereof, or to such other officer of the militia of said State as the said governor may designate and appoint for the purpose, so much of its allotment out of the said annual appropriation under section sixteen hundred and sixty-one of the Revised Statutes as amended as shall be necessary for the payment, subsistence, and transportation of such portion of said organized militia as shall engage in actual field or camp service for instruction, and the officers and enlisted men of such militia while so engaged shall be entitled to the same pay, subsistence, and transportation or travel allowances as officers and enlisted men of corresponding grades of the Regular Army are or may hereafter be entitled by law, and the officer so designated and appointed shall be regarded as a disbursing officer of the United States, and shall render his accounts through the War Department to the proper accounting officers of the Treasury for settlement, and he shall be required to give good and sufficient bonds to the United States, in such sums as the Secretary of War may direct,

faithfully to account for the safe-keeping and payment of the public moneys so intrusted to him for disbursement.

SEC. 15. That the Secretary of War is hereby authorized to provide for participation by any part of the organized militia of any State or Territory on the request of the governor thereof in the encampment, maneuvers, and field instruction of any part of the Regular Army at or near any military post or camp or lake or seacoast defenses of the United States. In such case the organized militia so participating shall receive the same pay, subsistence, and transportation as is provided by law for the officers and men of the Regular Army, to be paid out of the appropriation for the pay, subsistence, and transportation of the Army: *Provided*, That the command of such military post or camp and of the officers and troops of the United States there stationed shall remain with the regular commander of the post without regard to the rank of the commanding or other officers of the militia temporarily so encamped within its limits or in its vicinity.

SEC. 16. That whenever any officer of the organized militia shall, upon recommendation of the governor of any State, Territory, or general commanding the District of Columbia, and when authorized by the President, attend and pursue a regular course of study at any military school or college of the United States such officer shall receive from the annual appropriation for the support of the Army the same travel allowances, and quarters, or commutation of quarters, to which an officer of the Regular Army would be entitled if attending such school or college under orders from proper military authority, and shall also receive commutation of subsistence at the rate of one dollar per day while in actual attendance upon the course of instruction.

SEC. 17. That the annual appropriation made by section sixteen hundred and sixty-one, Revised Statutes, as amended, shall be available for the purpose of providing for issue to the organized militia any stores and supplies or publications which are supplied to the Army by any department. Any State Territory, or the District of Columbia may, with the approval of the Secretary of War, purchase for cash from the War Department, for the use of its militia, stores, supplies, material of war, or military publications, such as are furnished to the Army, in addition to those issued under the provisions of this Act, at the price at which they are listed for issue to the Army, with the cost of transportation added, and funds received from such sales shall be credited to the appropriations to which they belong and shall not be covered into the Treasury, but shall be available until expended to replace therewith the supplies sold to the States and Territories and to the District of Columbia in the manner herein provided.

SEC. 18. That each State or Territory furnished with material of war under the provisions of this or former Acts of Congress shall, during the year next preceding each annual allotment of funds, in accordance with section sixteen hundred and sixty-one of the Revised Statutes as amended, have required every company, troop, and battery in its organized militia not excused by the governor of such State or Territory to participate in practice marches or go into camp of instruction at least five consecutive days, and to assemble for drill and instruction at company, battalion, or regimental armories or rendezvous or for target practice not less than twenty-four times, and shall also have required during such year an inspection of each such company, troop, and battery to be made by an officer of such militia or an officer of the Regular Army.

SEC. 19. That upon the application of the governor of any State or Territory furnished with material of war under the provisions of this Act or former laws of Congress, the Secretary of War may detail one or more officers of the Army to attend any encampment of the organized militia, and to give such instruction and information to the officers and men assembled in such camp as may be requested by the governor. Such officer or officers shall immediately make a report of such encampment to the Secretary of War, who shall furnish a copy thereof to the governor of the State or Territory.

SEC. 20. That upon application of the governor of any State or Territory furnished with material of war under the provisions of this Act or former laws of Congress, the Secretary of War may, in his discretion, detail one or more officers of the Army to report to the governor of such State or Territory for duty in connection with the organized militia. All such assignments may be revoked at the request of the governor of such State or Territory or at the pleasure of the Secretary of War.

SEC. 21. That the troops of the militia encamped at any military post or camp of the United States may be furnished such amounts of ammunition for instruction in firing and target practice as may be prescribed by the Secretary of War, and such instruction in firing shall be carried on under the direction of an officer selected for that purpose by the proper military commander.

SEC. 22. That when any officer, noncommissioned officer, or private of the militia is disabled by reason of wounds or disabilities received or incurred in the service of the United States he shall be entitled to all the benefits of the pension laws existing at the time of his service, and in case such officer noncommissioned officer, or private dies in the service of the United States or in returning to his place of residence after being mustered out of such service, or at any time, in consequence of wounds or disabilities received in such service, his widow and children, if any, shall be entitled to all the benefits of such pension laws.

SEC. 23. That for the purpose of securing a list of persons specially qualified to hold commissions in any volunteer force which may hereafter be called for and organized under the authority of Congress, other than a force composed of organized militia, the Secretary of War is authorized from time to time to convene boards of officers at suitable and convenient army posts in different parts of the United States, who shall examine as to their qualifications for the command of troops or for the performance of staff duties all applicants who shall have served in the Regular Army of the United States, in any of the volunteer forces of the United States, or in the organized militia of any State or Territory or District of Columbia, or who, being a citizen of the United States, shall have attended or pursued a regular course of instruction in any military school or college of the United States Army, or shall have graduated from any educational institution to which an officer of the Army or Navy has been detailed as superintendent or professor pursuant to law after having creditably pursued the course of military instruction therein provided. Such examinations shall be under rules and regulations prescribed by the Secretary of War, and shall be especially directed to ascertain the practical capacity of the applicant. The record of previous service of the applicant shall be considered as a part of the examination. Upon the conclusion of each examination the board shall certify to the War Department its judgment as to the fitness of the applicant, stating the office, if any, which it deems him qualified to fill, and, upon approval by the President, the names of the persons certified to be qualified shall be inscribed in a register to be kept in the War Department for that purpose. The persons so certified and registered shall, subject to a physical examination at the time, constitute an eligible class for commissions pursuant to such certificates in any volunteer force hereafter called for and organized under the authority of Congress, other than a force composed of organized militia, and the President may authorize persons from this class, to attend and pursue a regular course of study at any military school or college of the United States other than the Military Academy at West Point and to receive from the annual appropriation for the support of the Army the same allowances and commutations as provided in this Act for officers of the organized militia: *Provided*, That no person shall be entitled to receive a Commission as a second lieutenant after be shall have passed the age of thirty; as first lieutenant after he shall have passed the age of thirty-five; as captain after he shall have passed the age of forty; as major after he shall have passed the age of forty-five; as lieutenant colonel after be shall have passed the age of fifty, or as colonel after be shall have passed the age of fifty-five: *And provided further*, That such appointments shall be distributed proportionately, as near as may be, among the various States contributing such volunteer force: *And provided*, That the appointments in this section provided for shall not be deemed to include appointments to any office in any company, troop, battery, battalion, or regiment of the organized militia which volunteers as a body or the officers of which are appointed by the governor of a State or Territory.

SEC. 24. That all the volunteer forces of the United States called for by authority of Congress shall, except as hereinbefore provided, be organized in the manner provided by the Act entitled "An Act to provide for temporarily increasing the military establishment of the United States in time of war, and for other purposes," approved April twenty-second, eighteen hundred and ninety-eight.

SEC. 25. That sections sixteen hundred and twenty-five to sixteen hundred and sixty, both included, of title sixteen of the Revised Statutes, and section two hundred and thirty-two thereof, relating to the militia, are hereby repealed.

SEC. 26. That this Act shall take effect upon the date of its approval.

Approved, January 21, 1903.

Source: Statutes at Large

The National Firearms Act was the first significant modern national gun control law. Enacted in large part as a response to rising criminal and gang activity, the law barred gangster-type weapons, including sawed-off shotguns (the possession of which by two men led to the 1939 Supreme Court case of U.S. v. Miller; see page 437), machine guns, and silencers. It also required that new guns be stamped with unique, identifying serial numbers, a practice that would be a boon to law enforcement efforts to track guns used in crimes. The law used the federal government's power to tax to restrict these weapons as there was concern that the courts might reject a regulatory effort based on Congress's power to regulate interstate commerce. The steep fees imposed by the law proved effective. Aside from a few thousand licensed dealers, the law has successfully kept weapons like machine guns out of civilian hands. The terms of this law are administered by the Bureau of Alcohol, Tobacco, Firearms, and Explosives (ATFE).

The National Firearms Act of 1934
PL 73-474; 48 Stat. 1236

To provide for the taxation of manufacturers, importers, and dealers in certain firearms and machine guns, to tax the sale or other disposal of such weapons, and to restrict importation and regulate interstate transportation thereof. Be it enacted by the Senate and House of Representatives of the United States of America in Congress assembled, That for the purposes of this Act-

(a) The term "firearm" means a shotgun or rifle having a barrel of less than eighteen inches in length, or any other weapon, except a pistol or revolver, from which a shot is discharged by an explosive if such weapon is capable of being concealed on the person, or a machine gun, and includes a muffler or silencer for any firearm whether or not such firearm is included within the foregoing definition.

(b) The term "machine gun" means any weapon which shoots, or is designed to shoot, automatically or semi automatically, more than one shot, without manual reloading, by a single function of the trigger.

(c) The term "person" includes a partnership, company, association, or corporation, as well as a natural person.

(d) The term "continental United States" means the States of the United States and the District of Columbia.

(e) The term "importer" means any person who imports or brings firearms into the continental United States for sale.

(f) The term "manufacturer" means any person who is engaged within the continental United States in the manufacture of firearms, or who otherwise produces therein any firearm for sale or disposition.

(g) The term "dealer" means any person not a manufacturer or importer engaged within the continental United States in the business of selling firearms. The term "dealer" shall include wholesalers, pawnbrokers, and dealers in used firearms.

(h) The term "interstate commerce" means transportation from any State or Territory or District, or any insular possession of the United States (including the Philippine Islands), to any other State or to the District of Columbia.

(i) The term "Commissioner" means the Commissioner of Internal Revenue.

(j) The term "Secretary" means the Secretary of the Treasury.

(k) The term "to transfer" or "transferred" shall include to sell, assign pledge, lease, loan, give away, or otherwise dispose of.

SEC 2. (a) Within fifteen days after the effective date of this Act, or upon first engaging in business, and thereafter on or before the 1st day of July of each year, every importer, manufacturer, and dealer in firearms shall register with the collector of internal revenue for each district in which such business is to be carried on his name or style, principal place of business, and places of business in such district, and pay a special tax at the following rates: Importers or manufacturers, $500 a year; dealers, other than pawnbrokers, $200 a year; pawnbrokers, $300 a year. Where the tax is payable on the 1st day of July in any year it shall be computed for one year; where the tax is payable on any other day it shall be computed proportionately from the 1st day of the month in which the liability to the tax accrued to the 1st day of July following.

(b) It shall be unlawful for any person required to register under the provisions of this section to import, manufacture, or deal in firearms without having registered and paid the tax imposed by this section.

SEC. 3. (a) There shall be levied, collected, and paid upon firearms transferred in the continental United States a tax at the rate of $200 for each firearm, such tax; to be paid by the transferor, and to be represented by appropriate stamps to be provided by the Commissioner, with the approval of the secretary; and the stamps herein provided shall be affixed to the order for such firearm, hereinafter provided for. The tax imposed by this section shall be in addition to any import duty imposed on such firearm.

(b) All provisions of law (including those relating to special taxes, to the assessment, collection, remission, and refund of internal revenue taxes, to the engraving, issuance, sale, accountability, cancellation, and distribution of tax-paid stamps provided for in the internal-revenue laws, and to penalties) applicable with respect to the taxes imposed by section 1 of the Act of December 17, 1914, as amended (U.S.C., Supp. VII, title 26, secs. 1040 and 1383), and all other provisions of the internal-revenue laws shall, insofar as not inconsistent with the provisions of this Act, be applicable with respect to the taxes imposed by this Act.

(c) Under such rules and regulations as the Commissioner, with the approval of the Secretary, may prescribe, and upon proof of the exportation of and firearm to any foreign country (whether exported as part of another article or not) with respect to which the transfer tax under this section has been paid by the manufacturer, the Commissioner shall refund to the manufacturer the amount of the tax so paid, or, if the manufacturer waives all claim for the amount to be refunded, the refund shall be made to the exporter.

SEC. 4. (a) It shall be unlawful for any person to transfer a firearm except in pursuance of a written order from the person seeking to obtain such article, on an application form issued in blank in duplicate for that purpose by the Commissioner. Such order shall identify the applicant by such means of identification as may be prescribed by regulations under this Act: Provided, That, if the applicant is an individual, such identification shall include fingerprints and a photograph thereof.

(b) The Commissioner, with the approval of the Secretary, shall cause suitable forms to be prepared

for the purposes above mentioned, and shall cause the same to be distributed to collectors of internal revenue.

(c) Every person so transferring a firearm shall set forth in each copy of such order the manufacturer's number or other mark identifying such firearm, and shall forward a copy of such order to the Commissioner. The original thereof with stamps affixed, shall be returned to the applicant.

(d) No person shall transfer a firearm which has previously been transferred on or after the effective date of this Act, unless such person, in addition to complying with subsection (c), transfers therewith the stamp-affixed order provided for in this section for each such prior transfer, in compliance with such regulations as may be prescribed under this act for proof of payment of all taxes on such firearms.

(e) If the transfer of a firearm is exempted from the provisions of this Act as provided in section 13 hereof, the person transferring such firearm shall notify the Commissioner of the name and address of the applicant, the number or other mark identifying such firearm, and the date of its transfer, and shall file with the Commissioner such documents in proof thereof as the Commissioner may by regulations prescribe.

(f) Importers, manufacturers, and dealers who have registered and paid the tax as provided for in section 2(a) of this Act shall not be required to conform to the provisions of this section with respect to transactions in firearms with dealers or manufacturers if such dealers or manufacturers have registered and have paid such tax, but shall keep such records and make such reports regarding such transactions as may be prescribed by regulations under this Act.

SEC. 5. (a) within sixty days after the effective date of this act every person possessing a firearm shall register, with the collector of the district in which he resides, the number or other mark identifying such firearm, together with his name address, place where such firearm is usually kept, and place of business or employment, and, if such person is other than a natural person, the name and home address of an executive officer thereof: Provided, That no person shall be required to register under this section with respect to any firearm acquired after the effective date of, and in conformity with the provisions of, this Act.

(b) Whenever on trial for a violation of section 6 hereof the defendant is shown to have or to have had possession of such firearm at any time after such period of sixty days without having registered as required by this section such possession shall create a presumption that such firearm came into the possession of the defendant subsequent to the effective date of this act, but this presumption shall not be conclusive.

SEC. 6. It shall be unlawful for any person to receive or possess any firearm which has at any time been transferred in violation of section 3 or 4 of this Act.

SEC. 7. (a) Any firearm which has at any time been transferred in violation of the provisions of this act shall be subject to seizure and forfeiture, and (except as provided in subsection (b)) all the provisions of internal-revenue laws relating to searches, seizures, and forfeiture of unstamped articles are extended to and made to apply to the articles taxed under this Act, and the persons to whom this Act applies.

(b) In the case of the forfeiture of any firearm by reason of a violation of this Act: No notice of public sale shall be required; no such firearm shall be sold at public sale; if such firearm is in the possession of any officer of the United states except the Secretary, such officer shall deliver the firearm to the Secretary; and the Secretary may order such firearm destroyed or may sell such firearm to any State, Territory, or possession (including the Philippine Islands), or political subdivision thereof, or the District of Columbia, or retain it for the use of the Treasury department or transfer it without charge to any Executive department or independent establishment of the Government for use by it.

SEC. 8. (a) Each manufacturer and importer of a firearm shall identify it with a number or other identification mark approved by the Commissioner, such number or mark to be stamped or other placed thereon in a manner approved by the Commissioner.

(b) It shall be unlawful for anyone to obliterate, remove, change, or alter such number or other identification mark. Whenever on trial for a violation of this subsection the defendant is shown to have or to have had possession of any firearm upon which such number or mark shall have been obliterated, removed, changed, or altered, such possession shall be deemed sufficient evidence to authorize conviction unless the defendant explains such possession to the satisfaction of the jury.

SEC. 9. Importers, manufacturers, and dealers shall keep such books and records and render such returns in relation to the transactions in firearms

specified in this Act as the Commissioner, with the approval of the Secretary, may by regulations require.

SEC. 1O. (a) No firearm shall be imported or brought into the United States or any territory under its control or jurisdiction (including the Philippine Islands) except that, under regulations prescribed by the Secretary, any firearm may be so imported or brought in when (1) the purpose thereof is shown to be lawful and (2) such firearm is unique or of a type which cannot be obtained within the United States or such territory.

(b) It shall be unlawful (1) fraudulently or knowingly to import or bring any firearm into the United States or any territory under its control or jurisdiction (including the Philippine Islands), in violation of the provisions of this Act; or (2) knowingly to assist in so doing; or (3) to receive, conceal, buy, sell, or in any manner facilitate the transportation, concealment or sale of any such firearm after being imported or brought in, knowing the same to have been imported or brought in contrary to law. Whenever on trial for a violation of this section the defendant is shown to have or to have had possession of such firearm, such possession shall be deemed sufficient evidence to authorize conviction unless the defendant explains such possession to the satisfaction of the jury.

SEC. 11. It shall be unlawful for any person who is required to register as provided in section 5 hereof and who shall not have so registered, or any other person who has not in his possession a stamp-affixed order as provided in section 4 hereof, to ship, carry, or deliver any firearm in interstate commerce.

SEC. 12. The Commissioner with the approval of the Secretary, shall prescribe such rules and regulations as may be necessary for carrying the provisions of this Act into effect.

SEC. 13. This Act shall not apply to the transfer of firearms (1) to the United States Government, any State, Territory, or possession of the United States, or to any political subdivision thereof, or to the District of Columbia; (2) to any peace officer or any Federal officer designated by regulations of the Commissioner; (3) to the transfer of any firearm which is unserviceable and which is transferred as a curiosity or ornament.

SEC. 14. Any person who violates or fails to comply with any of the requirement of this Act shall, upon conviction, be fined not more than $2,000 or be imprisoned for not more than five years, or both, in the discretion of the court.

SEC. 15. The taxes imposed by paragraph (a) of section 600 of the Revenue Act of 1926 (U.S.C., Supp. VII, title 26, sec. 1120) and by section 610 of the Revenue Act of 1932 (47

Stat. 169, 264), shall not apply to any firearm on which the tax provided by section 3 of this Act has been paid.

SEC. 16. If any provision of this Act, or the application thereof to any person or circumstance, is held invalid, the remainder of the Act, and the application of such provision to other persons or circumstances shall not be affected thereby.

SEC. 17. This Act shall take effect on the thirtieth day after the date of its enactment.

SEC. 18. This Act may be cited as the "National Firearms Act."

Approved, June 26, 1934.

Source: U.S. Code Congressional and Administrative News

Two men, Jack Miller and Frank Layton, were indicted for violating the National Firearms Act of 1934 that barred transport of a saw-off shotgun (a weapon modified by gangsters by cutting off part of the barrel to increase a shotgun's lethality) across state lines. The law regulated the interstate transport of such weapons as sawed-off shotguns and machine guns by imposing a large tax on their interstate transport. They appealed their indictment through the federal courts, arguing that the law violated their Second Amendment right to keep and bear such a firearm. They also argued that the federal tax power applied to such weapons amounted to an improper attempt by the federal government to usurp the state police power (meaning the power belonging to the states to control criminal conduct). Reversing a lower federal court ruling, the Supreme Court ruled unanimously against Miller and Layton, saying that the Second Amendment only came in to play when citizens were serving in a government organized and regulated militia, and that there was no citizen right to keep and bear arms aside from this purpose. Most of the decision is devoted to a painstaking description of the history of militias, emphasizing that any law-based right to have firearms was always linked to the amendment's obvious purpose of ensuring an effective militia as described in Article I, section 8 in the Constitution.

United States v. Miller, 307 U.S. 174 (1939)

Argued March 30, 1939.
Decided May 15, 1939.

Appeal from the District Court of the United States for the Western District of Arkansas. Mr. Gordon Dean, of Washington, D.C., for the United States.

No appearance for appellees.

Mr. Justice McREYNOLDS delivered the opinion of the Court.

An indictment in the District Court Western District Arkansas, charged that Jack Miller and Frank Layton "did unlawfully, knowingly, wilfully, and feloniously transport in interstate commerce from the town of Claremore in the State of Oklahoma to the town of Siloam Springs in the State of Arkansas a certain firearm, to-wit, a double barrel 12-gauge Stevens shotgun having a barrel less than 18 inches in length, bearing identification number 76230, said defendants, at the time of so transporting said firearm in interstate commerce as aforesaid, not having registered said firearm as required by Section 1132d of Title 26, United States Code, 26 U.S.C.A. 1132d (Act of June 26, 1934, c. 757, Sec. 5, 48 Stat. 1237), and not having in their possession a stamp-affixed written order for said firearm as provided by Section 1132c, Title 26, United States Code, 26 U.S.C.A. 1132c (June 26, 1934, c. 757, Sec. 4, 48 Stat. 1237) and the regulations issued under authority of the said Act of Congress known as the 'National Firearms Act' approved June 26, 1934, contrary to the form of the statute in such case made and provided, and against the peace and dignity of the United States."

A duly interposed demurrer alleged: The National Firearms Act is not a revenue measure but an attempt to usurp police power reserved to the States, and is therefore unconstitutional. Also, it offends the inhibition of the Second Amendment to the Constitution—"A well regulated Militia, being necessary to the security of a free State, the right of the people to keep and bear Arms, shall not be infringed."

The District Court held that section 11 of the Act violates the Second Amendment. It accordingly sustained the demurrer and quashed the indictment.

The cause is here by direct appeal. Considering Sonzinsky v. United States (1937), 300 U.S. 506, 513, and what was ruled in sundry causes arising under the Harrison Narcotic Act—United States v. Jin Fuey Moy (1916), 241 U. S. 394; United States v. Doremus (1919), 249 U. S. 86, 94; Linder v. United States (1925), 268 U. S. 5; Alston v. United States (1927), 274 U. S. 289; Nigro v. United States (1928), 276 U. S. 332—the objection that the Act usurps police power reserved to the States is plainly untenable.

In the absence of any evidence tending to show that possession or use of a "shotgun having a barrel of less than eighteen inches in length" at this time has some reasonable relationship to the preservation or efficiency of a well regulated militia, we cannot say that the Second Amendment guarantees the right to keep and bear such an instrument. Certainly it is not within judicial notice that this weapon is any part of the ordinary military equipment or that its use could contribute to the common defense. . . .

The Constitution as originally adopted granted to the Congress power- "To provide for calling forth the Militia to execute the Laws of the Union, suppress Insurrections and repel Invasions; To provide for organizing, arming, and disciplining, the Militia, and for governing such Part of them as may be employed in the Service of the United States, reserving to the States respectively, the Appointment of the Officers, and the Authority of training the Militia according to the discipline prescribed by Congress.". . . With obvious purpose to assure the continuation and render possible the effectiveness of such forces the declaration and guarantee of the Second Amendment were made. It must be interpreted and applied with that end in view.

The Militia which the States were expected to maintain and train is set in contrast with Troops which they were forbidden to keep without the consent of Congress. The sentiment of the time strongly disfavored standing armies; the common view was that adequate defense of country and laws could be secured through the Militia—civilians primarily, soldiers on occasion.

The signification attributed to the term Militia appears from the debates in the Convention, the history and legislation of Colonies and States, and the writings of approved commentators. These show plainly enough that the Militia comprised all males physically capable of acting in concert for the common defense. "A body of citizens enrolled for military discipline." And further, that ordinarily when called for service these men were expected to appear bearing arms supplied by themselves and of the kind in common use at the time.

Blackstone's Commentaries, Vol. 2, Ch. 13, p. 409 points out ?that king Alfred first settled a national militia in this kingdom? and traces the subsequent development and use of such forces.

Adam Smith's Wealth of Nations, Book V. Ch. 1, contains an extended account of the Militia. It is there said: "Men of republican principles have been jealous of a standing army as dangerous to liberty." "In a militia, the character of the labourer, artificer, or tradesman, predominates over that of the soldier: in a standing army, that of the soldier predominates over every other character; and in this distinction seems to consist the essential difference between those two different species of military force."

"The American Colonies In The 17th Century," Osgood, Vol. 1, ch. XIII, affirms in reference to the early system of defense in New England—

"In all the colonies, as in England, the militia system was based on the principle of the assize of arms. This implied the general obligation of all adult male inhabitants to possess arms, and, with certain exceptions, to cooperate in the work of defence." "The possession of arms also implied the possession of ammunition, and the authorities paid quite as much attention to the latter as to the former." "A year later [1632] it was ordered that any single man who had not furnished himself with arms might be put out to service, and this became a permanent part of the legislation of the colony [Massachusetts]."

Also "Clauses intended to insure the possession of arms and ammunition by all who were subject to military service appear in all the important enactments concerning military affairs. Fines were the penalty for delinquency, whether of towns or individuals. According to the usage of the times, the infantry of Massachusetts consisted of pikemen and musketeers. The law, as enacted in 1649 and thereafter, provided that each of the former should be armed with a pike, corselet, head-piece, sword, and knapsack. The musketeer should carry a 'good fixed musket,' not under bastard musket bore, not less than three feet, nine inches, nor more than four feet three inches in length, a priming wire, scourer, and mould, a sword, rest, bandoleers, one pound of powder, twenty bullets, and two fathoms of match. The law also required that two-thirds of each company should be musketeers."

The General Court of Massachusetts, January Session 1784 (Laws and Resolves 1784, c. 55, pp. 140, 142), provided for the organization and government of the Militia. It directed that the Train Band should "contain all able bodied men, from sixteen to forty years of age, and the Alarm List, all other men under sixty years of age, ..." Also, "That every non-commissioned officer and private soldier of the said militia not under the controul of parents, masters or guardians, and being of sufficient ability therefor in the judgment of the Selectmen of the town in which he shall dwell, shall equip himself, and be constantly provided with a good fire arm, &c."

By an Act passed April 4, 1786 (Laws 1786, c. 25), the New York Legislature directed: 'That every able-bodied Male Person, being a Citizen of this State, or of any of the United States, and residing in this State, (except such Persons as are herein after excepted) and who are of the Age of Sixteen, and under the Age of Forty-five Years, shall, by the Captain or commanding Officer of the Beat in which such Citizens shall reside, within four Months after the passing of this Act, be enrolled in the Company of such Beat. . . . That every Citizen so enrolled and notified, shall, within three Months thereafter, provide himself, at his own Expense, with a good Musket or Firelock, a sufficient Bayonet and Belt, a Pouch with a Box therein to contain not less than Twenty-four Cartridges suited to the Bore of his Musket or Firelock, each Cartridge containing a proper Quantity of Powder and Ball, two spare Flints, a Blanket and Knapsack; . . . ."

The General Assembly of Virginia, October, 1785 (12 Hening's Statutes c. 1, p. 9 et seq.), declared: "The defense and safety of the commonwealth depend upon having its citizens properly armed and taught the knowledge of military duty."

It further provided for organization and control of the Militia and directed that "All free male persons between the ages of eighteen and fifty years," with certain exceptions, "shall be inrolled or formed into companies." "There shall be a private muster of every company once in two months."

Also that "Every officer and soldier shall appear at his respective muster-field on the day appointed, by eleven o'clock in the forenoon, armed, equipped, and accoutred, as follows: . . . every non-commissioned officer and private with a good, clean musket carrying an ounce ball, and three feet eight inches long in the barrel, with a good bayonet and iron ramrod well fitted thereto, a cartridge box properly made, to contain and secure twenty cartridges fitted to his musket, a good knapsack and canteen, and moreover, each non-commissioned officer and private shall have at every muster one pound of good powder, and four pounds of lead, including twenty blind cartridges; and each sergeant shall have a pair of moulds fit

to cast balls for their respective companies, to be purchased by the commanding officer out of the monies arising on delinquencies. Provided, That the militia of the counties westward of the Blue Ridge, and the counties below adjoining thereto, shall not be obliged to be armed with muskets, but may have good rifles with proper accoutrements, in lieu thereof. And every of the said officers, non-commissioned officers, and privates, shall constantly keep the aforesaid arms, accoutrements, and ammunition, ready to be produced whenever called for by his commanding officer. If any private shall make it appear to the satisfaction of the court hereafter to be appointed for trying delinquencies under this act that he is so poor that he cannot purchase the arms herein required, such court shall cause them to be purchased out of the money arising from delinquents."

Most if not all of the States have adopted provisions touching the right to keep and bear arms. Differences in the language employed in these have naturally led to somewhat variant conclusions concerning the scope of the right guaranteed. But none of them seem to afford any material support for the challenged ruling of the court below.

In the margin some of the more important opinions and comments by writers are cited. We are unable to accept the conclusion of the court below and the challenged judgment must be reversed. The cause will be remanded for further proceedings.

Reversed and remanded.

MR. JUSTICE DOUGLAS took no part in the consideration or decision of this cause.

FOOTNOTES OMITTED

Source: http://www.cs.cmu.edu/afs/cs/usr/wbardwel/public/ nfalist/miller.txt

This essay by gun rights author Alan Korwin offers a compilation of his opinion of the positive uses and purposes of guns.

The Noble uses of Firearms

Plus: Gun hatred and a gun-free world

By Alan Korwin

In the great din of the national firearms debate it's easy to lose sight of the noble and respectable place firearms hold and have always held in American life. While some gun use in America is criminal and despicable, other applications appeal to the highest ideals our society cherishes, and are enshrined in and ensured by the statutes on the books:

- Protecting your family in emergencies
- Personal safety and self defense
- Preventing and deterring crimes
- Detaining criminals for arrest
- Guarding our national borders
- Preserving our interests abroad
- Helping defend our allies
- Overcoming tyranny
- International trade
- Emergency preparedness
- Commerce and employment
- Historical preservation and study
- Obtaining food by hunting
- Olympic competition
- Collecting
- Sporting pursuits
- Target practice
- Recreational shooting

News reports, by focusing almost exclusively on criminal misuse of firearms, create the false impression that firearms and crime are directly linked, when in fact almost all guns never have any link whatsoever to crime. The media, while claiming to be unbiased, judiciously ignore stories concerning justifiable homicide in legitimate self defense, which occur almost daily according to the FBI.

A reasonable person should object to the media's mearly total silence on the effect the firearms industry has on jobs in the manufacturing sector, contributions to the tax base, capital and investments, scientific advances, national trade and balance of payments, ballistics, chemistry, metallurgy, and, of course, the enjoyment of millions of decent people who use firearms righteously.

Some people associate guns with crime, fear and danger, and want them to go away. Those who associate guns with liberty, freedom, honor, strength and safety understand the irreplaceable role firearms play in our lives.

Source: www.gunlaws.com/noble.htm

CRS Report for Congress
Received through the CRS Web
The United Nations and "Gun Control"

Marjorie Ann Browne
Specialist in International Relations
Foreign Affairs, Defense, and Trade Division

Summary

Since the mid-1990s, some sources have stated that the United Nations is trying to disarm the world by taking control of all guns, including in particular, guns held by private citizens in the United States. U.N. member states have discussed problems associated with increasing numbers of firearms throughout the world in various U.N. organs and subsidiary bodies. These discussions have been directed towards illegal manufacture and trafficking in firearms. This report summarizes the results of these considerations in two central U.N. venues—the criminal arena and the arms control and disarmament arena. U.S. representatives have participated in these discussions, usually pointing out this country's interest in protecting the Second Amendment rights of U.S. citizens to own guns. U.S. representatives have also expressed concern that the increasing quantities of illegally manufactured and trafficked firearms that are contributing, to rising levels of crime, violence, and conflict are also accessible to terrorists. This report will be updated as events warrant.

Over the past several years, United Nations member governments have discussed issues related to firearms and guns, in two different U.N. venues— the crime prevention arena and the arms control and disarmament arena. Both aimed at reducing the level of illegal and illicit firearms moving across borders as a way of reducing crime, violence, and conflict. Some observers have characterized these discussions as part of an overall "U.N." plan to impose gun control in the United States. This report provides a brief overview of U.N. activities in the area of firearms and small arms and light weapons.

A United Nations Plan
for Gun Control?

Accusations that the United Nations has a gun control plan have circulated since the mid-1990s. The headlines found on the Internet referred to the "global gun grab." the U.N. coming for your guns, "The 40-year gun grab," and "The United Nations Wants to Take Your Gun?"

The number of comments increased during 2001 as the U.N. Conference on the Illicit Trade in Small Arms and Light Weapons in all Its Aspects took place in New York in July. For example, an article in NewsMax.corn on April 27. 2001. reporting on the position of the National Rifle Association, began in the following way:

> The U.N. is after Americans' Second Amendment gun rights—it wants gun ownership banned in the U.S., and it's not going to stop until it gets its way.

> That's the warning from the National Rifle Association's Wayne LaPierre, who reveals that "for the first time in the history of the world, a United Nations conference has set its sights on global disarmament— disarming citizens worldwide— including you and me."

***

> "The bottom line is that international gun banners want every gun every single gun worldwide—to be under U.N. and government control." warns LaPierre. "And that includes your rifle, your shotgun, your handgun, and even family heirlooms that have been handed down from generation to generation."[2]

U.N. General Assembly adoption in May 2001 of a Protocol Against the Illicit Manufacturing of and Trafficking in Firearms, Their Parts and Components and Ammunition in the crime venue also provoked commentary such as the following by Tom DeWeese at American Policy Center in June 2001:

> On Thursday. May 31st, the United Nations General Assembly approved a gun control treaty that calls on all nations to work together "to prevent, combat and eradicate the illicit manufacturing of and trafficking in firearms, their parts and components. and ammunition."

The public face of the treaty is the lie that it is supposed to make it easier to crack down on illegal gun trafficking by helping authorities trace the global movement of all new weapons. *** The small print of this treaty no doubt contains a raft of other restrictions and requirements that will have the effect of disarming ordinary citizens everywhere. The result will be that only UN forces and governments will have guns. This spells doom for freedom anywhere in the world.[3]

Citations to more recent comments can be found in the footnote below.[4]

Crime

Initial discussions by U.N. member states started as early as 1995 within the U.N. Commission on Crime Prevention and Criminal Justice under the heading "Measures to Regulate Firearms." The Commission sought to identify the parameters of the presence of firearms worldwide, the relationship between firearms presence and crime, and the extent of national firearms legislation. In 1995, it recommended the preparation of a study on firearm regulation. Based on information provided by U.N. member nations,. including the United States, the U.N. Center for International Crime Prevention, on request of the U.N. Economic and Social Council, prepared an *International Study on Firearm Regulation* and set up a database on the regulation offirearms.[5] This work was not funded

out of the U.N. reuular budget but from voluntary contributions of Governments, including Australia, Canada. and Japan.

On July 28, 1998, the U.N. Economic and Social Council adopted a resolution recommending that nation states work towards "elaboration of an international instrument to combat the illicit manufacturing of and trafficking in firearms, their parts and components and ammunition" within the context of a United Nations convention against transnational organized crime. This resolution had been recommended to the Council by the April 1998 meeting of the U.N. Commission on Crime Prevention and Criminal Justice. On December 9, 1998, the U.N. General Assembly, without a vote, adopted Resolution 53/111, by which the Assembly decided to draft a "comprehensive international convention against transnational organized crime," including an international instrument to combat "the illicit manufacturing of and trafficking in firearms, their parts and components and ammunition."

In December 2000, the U.N. General Assembly adopted and opened for signature a United Nations Convention Against Transnational Organized Crime. One of the four protocols associated with this Convention, but not completed in time to be adopted and opened for signature in December was a Protocol Against the Illicit Manufacturing of and Trafficking in Firearms, Their Parts, and Components and Ammunition. The U.N. General

---

[1]These may be found at the following wvebsites: *Global Gun Grah*, by Thomas R. Fddlem. The New American, November 22, 1999, at [http://www.thene wamerican.com]; U.N. *coming for your guns. Private groups, governments team up to restrict use, ownership of firearms*: World Net Daily, December 7, 1999, at [http://www.mikene w.com/un_guns.html]; *The 40 year gun grab. '60s disarmament plan still going strong, say U.N critics*. World Net Daily. December 13, 1999, at [http://www.mikene w.com:/gun_grab .html]; and *The United Nations Wants to Take Your Gun!* at [http://www.getusout.org/guns].

[2]*U.N. wants Global Gun Ban*, NewsMax.com, April 27. 2001, at [http://www.newsmax.com]. Wayne LaPierre is the Executive Vice President and Chief Executive Officer of the National Rifle Association.

[3]UN Seeks Global Gun Control; The West is Being Systematically Disarmed. by Tom DeWeese. American Policy Center. June 4.2001, at [http://americanpolic y.org/un/globalguncontrol.htm]. Other comments can be found at *United Nations Attack on Gun Ownership*. The Phyllis Schlafly Report, v. 34, no. 11, June 2001, at [http://www.eagleforum.org/psr/2001/ june0l.shtml]; U.N. *Summit for Worldwide Gun Control Begins*, by Robert Villa for NewsMax.com, July 9, 2001, at [http://www.newsmax. com]; *Gunningforyourgun rights* by Michael Scardaville. July 11, 2001, Heritage Foundation Views 2001, at [http://www. heritage.org/views/2001/ed071101b.html]; and *U.N. Gun Control*, by Oliver North, July 13, 2001, at [http://www.townhall.com/ columnists/ollienorth/prinon20010713.shtm1].

[4]*Gun-Ban Shenanigans at the UN* by James Bovard, January 2002, at [http://www.fff.org/freedom/fd0201e.asp] ; *U.N. vs. Guns. An international gun-control fight*. by John R. Lott Jr., July 11, 2003. at National Review Online, [http://www. nationalreview. com]; and Remarks by Chris W. Cox, Executive Director. NRA-ILA, at the 2004 Annual Meeting, April 22, 2004, at [http:// www.nraila.org/News/Read/Speeches.aspx?ID=31]

[5]For information on the Study, see [http://www.uncjin.org/Statistics/firearms/]. The Commission recommendation was approved by the U.N. Economic and Social Council in its Resolution 1995/27.

Assembly adopted this Protocol on May 31, 2001. Under this Protocol, states parties would be expected to:

- enact laws to eradicate the illegal manufacture of firearms, including tracing existing illicit weapons and prosecuting offenders;
- cooperate to prevent. combat, and eradicate the illegal manufacture and trafficking of firearms;
- tighten controls on the export and import of firearms: and
- exchange information about illicit firearms.

The U.N. Convention was signed by the United States on December 13, 2000, and transmitted to the Senate, along with two protocols, on February 23, 2004 (108'h Congress, 2"ᵈ Session, Senate Treaty Document 108-16). The Senate Foreign Relations Committee held hearings on June 17, 2004, with no further action. The United States took no action on the firearms protocol, neither signing it nor transmitting it to the Senate.

Preceding this U.N. action was adoption in 1997 by the Twenty-Fourth Special Session of the General Assembly of the Organization of American States of the Inter- American Convention Against Illicit Manufacturing and Trafficking of Firearms, Ammunition, Explosives, and other Related Materials. The United States signed this Convention on November 11, 1997; it was transmitted to the Senate on June 9, 1998 (105ᵗʰ Congress, 2ⁿᵈ Session. Senate Treaty Document 105-49). Hearings have not been held. According to the State Department, the Preamble to this treaty

> makes clear that the Convention is intended to address the problem of transnational trafficking in firearms, and is not meant to regulate the internal firearms trade of the States Parties. The Preamble expressly recognizes, for example, that the Convention "does not commit States Parties to enact legislation or regulations pertaining to firearms ownership, possession or trade of a wholly domestic character. . . ."[6]

Arms Control and Disarmament; Conflict Control

A second venue for United Nations discussion of firearms and guns as early as 1994 was provided by the U.N. Disarmament Commission which set up a Special Panel of Governmental Experts on Small Arms. The U.N. General Assembly, in December 1998, decided to convene the United Nations Conference on the Illicit Trade in Small Arms and Light Weapons in All Its Aspects which was held in New York, July 9 to 20, 2001. This Conference produced a Program of Action to Prevent, Combat and Eradicate the Illicit Trade in Small Arms and Light weapons in All Its Aspects, but not a treaty. On July 9, 2001, then U.S. Under Secretary of State for Arms Control and International Security Affairs John R. Bolton, in a statement to the Conference, noted that

> Small arms and light weapons, in our understanding, are the strictly military arms— automatic rifles, machine guns, shoulder-fired missile and rocket systems, light mortars—that are contributing to continued violence and suffering in regions of conflict around the world. We separate these military arms from firearms such as hunting rifles and pistols, which are commonly owned and used by citizens in many countries. As U.S. Attorney General John Ashcroft has said. "just as the First and

> Fourth Amendments secure individual rights of speech and security respectively, the Second Amendment protects an individual right to keep and bear arms." The United States believes that the responsible use of firearms is a legitimate aspect of national life. Like many countries, the United States has a cultural tradition of hunting and sport shooting. We. therefore, do not begin with the presumption that all small arms and light weapons are the same or that they are all problematic. It is the illicit trade in military small arms and light weapons that we are gathered here to address and that should properly concern us.[7]

Under way in early 2005 are negotiations by an Open-Ended Working Group on Tracing Illicit Small Arms and Light Weapons aimed at a draft international instrument (treaty) for the "timely and reliable identification" and tracing of illicit small arms and light weapons. The second meeting was held January 24 to February 4, 2005, with a third substantive session scheduled for June 6 to 17, 2005. This meeting is scheduled to be followed by the Second Biennial Meeting of States to Consider the Implementation of the U.N. Program of Action to Prevent, Combat and Eradicate the

---

[6]I05th Congress, 2d Session. Senate. Treaty Doc. 105-49, p. v.

[7]Statement to the U.N. Conference, July 9, 2001, by John R. Bolton. USUN Press Release #104 (01). See [http://www. un.int/ usa/01_104.htm]. Third paragraph on page 1.

Illicit Trade in Small Arms and Light Weapons in All its Aspects at the National, Regional and Global Levels, held July 1 1-15, 2005.[8] The first biennial meeting took place in 2003. Finally, a Review Conference for the 2001 Program of Action is scheduled for 2006.[9]

In a related development, the U.N. Security Council has also discussed the issue of small arms and light weapons, the proliferation of which contributes to and "exacerbates conflict, hinders economic and social development, fuels crime and terrorism, and contributes to the continued destabilization of war- torn societies."[10] In its latest statement, the Council "recognized that the dissemination of illicit small arms and light weapons has hampered the peaceful settlement of disputes, fuelled such disputes into armed conflicts and contributed to the prolongation of such armed conflicts." The Council encouraged "international and regional cooperation in identifying the origin and transfer of small arms and light weapons in order to prevent their diversion, in particular, to Al Qaeda and other terrorist groups." It welcomed the "ongoing efforts by [the] open- ended working group . . . to negotiate an international instrument to enable States to identify and trace, in a timely and reliable manner, illicit small arms and light weapons . . . " The Council also called on all Member States to "enforce all Security Council resolutions on sanctions, including those imposing arms embargoes...and to bring their own domestic implementation into compliance with the Council's measures on sanctions."[11]

Concluding Observations

While U.N. bodies have adopted resolutions and a "firearms protocol," these efforts have focused on the availability of firearms manufactured and obtained illegally and on the use or misuse of these firearms in the criminal arena, including for organized crime, and/or to facilitate the spread of or prolongation of conflict. During meetings and negotiations in U.N. bodies, U.S. representatives have focused on the need to combat organized crime and to reduce out-of-control violence and conflict by limiting the availability of firearms, light weapons, and small arms that contribute to and aggravate these situations. They have made it clear that the reduction of crime and conflict is a primary goal of the United States. They have supported U.S. Second Amendment rights of citizens to firearms. As the experience with the OAS Convention and the U.N. Protocol illustrates, any international treaties in this area would not bind the United States unless these documents were acted on favorably by the U.S. Senate, if the President decided to transmit the treaty to the Senate for its consideration.

Source: http://fpc.state.gov/documents/organization/4545.pdf

---

[8]See the text of the latest (2004) U.S. report on implementation of the program of action at [http://disarmament2.un.org/cab/saltw-nationalreports. html]

[9]See [http://disarmament2.un.org/cab/salw.html] and [http://disarmament2.un.org/cab/salw-oewg.html] for further information on small arms and light weapons.

[10]Statement by Ambassador Stuart Holliday, U.S. Alternate Representative for Special Political Affairs to the United Nations, on Small Arms/Light Weapons. in the Security Council, January 19, 2004. USUN Press Release #06 (04). See [http:// www. un.int/usa/04print_006.htm]

[11]Presidential Statement by the President of the U.N. Security Council, S/PRST/2005/7, February 17, 2005.

This law represented the culmination of political efforts to give legal protection to gun manufacturers and dealers from a rising tide of lawsuits filed against them by several cities, states, and individuals who held the industry at least partly responsible for gun violence. The Protection of Lawful Commerce in Arms Act barred civil suits against gun and ammunition manufacturers, distributors, dealers, trade associations, and importers, making narrow exception for cases involving defective guns or expressly criminal behavior by those otherwise protected, as, for example, when a gun is knowingly sold to someone not legally eligible. The law stopped over a dozen then-pending lawsuits around the country. In addition, the law required that handguns be sold with locks, and barred the manufacture or import of armor-piercing bullets. This unprecedented legal immunity for the gun industry prompted other businesses to lobby Congress for similar protection.

S.397

One Hundred Ninth Congress of the United States of America At The First Session

Begun and held at the City of Washington on Tuesday, the fourth day of January, two thousand and five

An Act

To prohibit civil liability actions from being brought or continued against manufacturers, distributors, dealers, or importers of firearms or ammunition for damages, injunctive or other relief resulting from the misuse of their products by others.

Be it enacted by the Senate and House of Representatives of the United States of America in Congress assembled,

SECTION I. SHORT TITLE.

This Act may be cited as the "Protection of Lawful Commerce in Arms Act".

SEC. 2. FINDINGS; PURPOSES.

(a) FINDINGS.—Congress finds the following:

(1) The Second Amendment to the United States Constitution provides that the right of the people to keep and bear arms shall not be infringed.

(2) The Second Amendment to the United States Constitution protects the rights of individuals, including those who are not members of a militia or engaged in military service or training, to keep and bear arms.

(3) Lawsuits have been commenced against manufacturers, distributors, dealers, and importers of firearms that operate as designed and intended, which seek money damages and other relief for the harm caused by the misuse of firearms by third parties, including criminals.

(4) The manufacture, importation, possession, sale, and use of firearms and ammunition in the United States are heavily regulated by Federal, State, and local laws. Such Federal laws include the Gun Control Act of 1968, the National Firearms Act, and the Arms Export Control Act.

(5) Businesses in the United States that are engaged in interstate and foreign commerce through the lawful design, manufacture, marketing, distribution, importation, or sale to the public of firearms or ammunition products that have been shipped or transported in interstate or foreign commerce are not, and should not, be liable for the harm caused by those who criminally or unlawfully misuse firearm products or ammunition products that function as designed and intended.

(6) The possibility of imposing liability on an entire industry for harm that is solely caused by others is an abuse of the legal system, erodes public confidence in our Nation's laws, threatens the diminution of a basic constitutional right and civil liberty, invites the disassembly and destabilization of other industries and economic sectors lawfully competing in the free enterprise

system of the United States, and constitutes an unreasonable burden on interstate and foreign commerce of the United States.

(7) The liability actions commenced or contemplated by the Federal Government, States, municipalities, and private interest groups and others are based on theories without foundation in hundreds of years of the common law and juris-prudence of the United States and do not represent a bona fide expansion of the common law. The possible sustaining of these actions by a maverick judicial officer or petit jury would expand civil liability in a manner never contemplated by the framers of the Constitution, by Congress, or by the legislatures of the several States. Such an expansion of liability would constitute a deprivation of the rights, privileges, and immunities guaranteed to a citizen of the United States under the Fourteenth Amendment to the United States Constitution.

(8) The liability actions commenced or contemplated by the Federal Government, States, municipalities, private interest groups and others attempt to use the judicial branch to circumvent the Legislative branch of government to regulate inter-state and foreign commerce through judgments and judicial decrees thereby threatening the Separation of Powers doctrine and weakening and undermining important principles of federalism, State sovereignty and comity between the sister States.

(b) PURPOSES.—The purposes of this Act are as follows:

(1) To prohibit causes of action against manufacturers, distributors, dealers, and importers of firearms or ammunition products, and their trade associations, for the harm solely caused by the criminal or unlawful misuse of firearm products or ammunition products by others when the product functioned as designed and intended.

(2) To preserve a citizen's access to a supply of firearms and ammunition for all lawful purposes, including hunting, self-defense, collecting, and competitive or recreational shooting.

(3) To guarantee a citizen's rights, privileges, and immunities, as applied to the States, under the Fourteenth Amendment to the United States Constitution, pursuant to section 5 of that Amendment.

(4) To prevent the use of such lawsuits to impose unreasonable burdens on interstate and foreign commerce.

(5) To protect the right, under the First Amendment to the Constitution, of manufacturers, distributors, dealers, and importers of firearms or ammunition products, and trade associations, to speak freely, to assemble peaceably, and to petition the Government for a redress of their grievances.

(6) To preserve and protect the Separation of Powers doctrine and important principles of federalism, State sovereignty and comity between sister States.

(7) To exercise congressional power under article IV, section 1 (the Full Faith and Credit Clause) of the United States Constitution.

SEC. 3. PROHIBITION ON BRINGING OF QUALIFIED CIVIL LIABILITY ACTIONS IN FEDERAL OR STATE COURT.

(a) In general.—A qualified civil liability action may not be brought in any Federal or State court.

(b) Dismissal of pending actions.—A qualified civil liability action that is pending on the date of enactment of this Act shall be immediately dismissed by the court in which the action was brought or is currently pending.

SEC. 4. DEFINITIONS.
In this Act:

(1) Engaged in the business.—The term "engaged in the business" has the meaning given that term in section 921(a)(21) of title 18, United States Code, and, as applied to a seller of ammunition, means a person who devotes time, attention, and labor to the sale of ammunition as a regular course of trade or business with the principal objective of livelihood and profit through the sale or distribution of ammunition.

(2) Manufacturer.—The term "manufacturer" means, with respect to a qualified product, a person who is engaged in the business of manufacturing the product in interstate or

foreign commerce and who is licensed to engage in business as such a manufacturer under chapter 44 of title 18, United States Code.

(3) Person.—The term "person" means any individual, corporation, company, association, firm, partnership, society, joint stock company, or any other entity, including any governmental entity.

(4) Qualified product.—The term "qualified product" means a firearm (as defined in subparagraph (A) or (B) of section 921(a) (3) of title 18, United States Code), including any antique firearm (as defined in section 921(a) (16) of such title), or ammunition (as defined in section 921(a)(17)(A) of such title), or a component part of a firearm or ammunition, that has been shipped or transported in interstate or foreign commerce.

(5) Qualified civil liability action.—

(A) In general.—The term "qualified civil liability action" means a civil action or proceeding or an administrative proceeding brought by any person against a manufacturer or seller of a qualified product, or a trade association, for damages, punitive damages, injunctive or declaratory relief, abatement, restitution, fines, or penalties, or other relief, resulting from the criminal or unlawful misuse of a qualified product by the person or a third party, but shall not include—

(i) an action brought against a transferor convicted under section 924(h) of title 18, United States Code, or a comparable or identical State felony law, by a party directly harmed by the conduct of which the transferee is so convicted;

(ii) an action brought against a seller for negligent entrustment or negligence per se;

(iii) an action in which a manufacturer or seller of a qualified product knowingly violated a State or Federal statute applicable to the sale or marketing of the product, and the violation was a proximate cause of the harm for which relief is sought, including—

(I) any case in which the manufacturer or seller knowingly made any false entry in, or failed to make appropriate entry in, any record required to be kept under Federal or State law with respect to the qualified product, or aided, abetted, or conspired with any person in making any false or fictitious oral or written statement with respect to any fact material to the lawfulness of the sale or other disposition of a qualified product; or

(II) any case in which the manufacturer or seller aided, abetted, or conspired with any other person to sell or otherwise dispose of a qualified product, knowing, or having reasonable cause to believe, that the actual buyer of the qualified product was prohibited from possessing or receiving a firearm or ammunition under subsection (g) or (n) of section 922 of title 18, United States Code;

(iv) an action for breach of contract or warranty in connection with the purchase of the product;

(v) an action for death, physical injuries or property damage resulting directly from a defect in design or manufacture of the product, when used as intended or in a reasonably foreseeable manner, except that where the discharge of the product was caused by a volitional act that constituted a criminal offense, then such act shall be considered the sole proximate cause of any resulting death, personal injuries or property damage; or

(vi) an action or proceeding commenced by the Attorney General to enforce the provisions of chapter 44 of title 18 or chapter 53 of title 26, United States Code.

(B) Negligent entrustment.—As used in subparagraph (A)(ii), the term "negligent entrustment" means the supplying of a qualified product by a seller for use by another person when the seller knows, or reasonably should know, the person to whom the product is supplied is likely to, and does, use the product in a manner involving unreasonable risk of physical injury to the person or others.

(C) Rule of construction.—The exceptions enumerated under clauses (i) through (v) of subparagraph (A) shall be construed so as not to be in conflict, and no provision of this Act shall be construed to create a public or private cause of action or remedy.

(D) MINOR CHILD EXCEPTION.—Nothing in this Act shall be construed to limit the right of a person under 17 years of age to recover damages authorized under Federal or State law in a civil action that meets 1 of the requirements under clauses (i) through (v) of subparagraph (A).

(6) Seller.—The term "seller" means, with respect to a qualified product—

(A) an importer (as defined in section 921(a)(9) of title 18, United States Code) who is engaged in the business as such an importer in interstate or foreign commerce and who is licensed to engage in business as such an importer under chapter 44 of title 18, United States Code;

(B) a dealer (as defined in section 921(a)(11) of title 18, United States Code) who is engaged in the business as such a dealer in interstate or foreign commerce and who is licensed to engage in business as such a dealer under chapter 44 of title 18, United States Code; or

(C) a person engaged in the business of selling ammunition (as defined in section 921(a)(17)(A) of title 18, United States Code) in interstate or foreign commerce at the wholesale or retail level.

(7) state.—The term "State" includes each of the several States of the United States, the District of Columbia, the Commonwealth of Puerto Rico, the Virgin Islands, Guam, American Samoa, and the Commonwealth of the Northern Mariana Islands, and any other territory or possession of the United States, and any political subdivision of any such place.

(8) Trade association.—The term "trade association" means—

(A) any corporation, unincorporated association, federation, business league, professional or business organization not organized or operated for profit and no part of the net earnings of which inures to the benefit of any private shareholder or individual;

(B) that is an organization described in section 501(c)(6) of the Internal Revenue Code of

1986 and exempt from tax under section 501(a) of such Code; and

(C) 2 or more members of which are manufacturers or sellers of a qualified product.

(9) Unlawful misuse.—The term "unlawful misuse" means conduct that violates a statute, ordinance, or regulation as it relates to the use of a qualified product.

SEC. 5. CHILD SAFETY LOCKS.

(a) Short title.—This section may be cited as the "Child Safety Lock Act of 2005".

(b) PURPOSES.—The purposes of this section are—

(1) to promote the safe storage and use of handguns by consumers;

(2) to prevent unauthorized persons from gaining access to or use of a handgun, including children who may not be in possession of a handgun; and

(3) to avoid hindering industry from supplying firearms to law abiding citizens for all lawful purposes, including hunting, self-defense, collecting, and competitive or recreational shooting.

(c) Firearms safety.—

(1) Mandatory transfer of secure gun storage or safety device.—Section 922 of title 18, United States Code, is amended by inserting at the end the following: "(z) secure gun storage or safety device.—

"(1) In general.—Except as provided under paragraph (2), it shall be unlawful for any licensed importer, licensed manufacturer, or licensed dealer to sell, deliver, or transfer any handgun to any person other than any person licensed under this chapter, unless the transferee is provided with a secure gun storage or safety device (as defined in section 921(a)(34)) for that handgun.

"(2) Exceptions.—Paragraph (1) shall not apply to—

"(A)(i) the manufacture for, transfer to, or possession by, the United States, a department or agency of the United States, a State, or a department, agency, or political subdivision of a State, of a handgun; or

"(ii) the transfer to, or possession by, a law enforcement officer employed by an entity referred to in clause (i) of a handgun for law enforcement purposes (whether on or off duty); or

"(B) the transfer to, or possession by, a rail police officer employed by a rail carrier and certified or commissioned as a police officer under the laws of a State of a handgun for purposes of law enforcement (whether on or off duty);

"(C) the transfer to any person of a handgun listed as a curio or relic by the Secretary pursuant to section 921(a)(13); or

"(D) the transfer to any person of a handgun for which a secure gun storage or safety device is temporarily unavailable for the reasons described in the exceptions stated in section 923(e), if the licensed manufacturer, licensed importer, or licensed dealer delivers to the transferee within 10 calendar days from the date of the delivery of the handgun to the transferee a secure gun storage or safety device for the handgun.

"(3) Liability for use.—

"(A) In general.—Notwithstanding any other provision of law, a person who has lawful possession and control of a handgun, and who uses a secure gun storage or safety device with the handgun, shall be entitled to immunity from a qualified civil liability action.

"(B) Prospective actions.—A qualified civil liability action may not be brought in any Federal or State court.

"(C) Defined term.—As used in this paragraph, the term 'qualified civil liability action'—

"(i) means a civil action brought by any person against a person described in subparagraph (A) for damages resulting from the criminal or unlawful misuse of the handgun by a third party, if—

"(I) the handgun was accessed by another person who did not have the permission or authorization of the person having lawful possession and control of the handgun to have access to it; and

"(II) at the time access was gained by the person not so authorized, the handgun had been made inoperable by use of a secure gun storage or safety device; and

"(ii) shall not include an action brought against the person having lawful possession and control of the handgun for negligent entrustment or negligence per se."

(2) Civil penalties.—Section 924 of title 18, United States Code, is amended—

(A) in subsection (a)(1), by striking "or (f)" and inserting "(f), or (p)"; and

(B) by adding at the end the following: "(p) Penalties relating to secure gun storage or safety device.—

"(1) In general.—

"(A) suspension or revocation of license; civil penalties.—With respect to each violation of section 922(z)(1) by a licensed manufacturer, licensed importer, or licensed dealer, the Secretary may, after notice and opportunity for hearing—

"(i) suspend for not more than 6 months, or revoke, the license issued to the licensee under this chapter that was used to conduct the firearms transfer; or

"(ii) subject the licensee to a civil penalty in an amount equal to not more than $2,500.

"(B) Review.—An action of the Secretary under this paragraph may be reviewed only as provided under section 923(f).

"(2) Administrative remedies.—The suspension or revocation of a license or the imposition of a civil penalty under paragraph (1) shall not preclude any administrative remedy that is otherwise available to the Secretary.".

(3) Liability; evidence.—

(A) Liability.—Nothing in this section shall be construed to—

(i) create a cause of action against any Federal firearms licensee or any other person for any civil liability; or

(ii) establish any standard of care.

(B) Evidence.—Notwithstanding any other provision of law, evidence regarding compliance or noncompliance with the amendments made by this section shall not be admissible as evidence in any proceeding of any court, agency, board, or other entity, except with respect to an action relating to section 922(z) of title 18, United States Code, as added by this subsection.

(C) Rule of construction.—Nothing in this paragraph shall be construed to bar a governmental action to impose a penalty under section 924(p) of title 18, United States Code, for a failure to comply with section 922(z) of that title.

(D) Effective date.—This section and the amendments made by this section shall take effect 180 days after the date of enactment of this Act.

SEC. 6. ARMOR PIERCING AMMUNITION.

(a) Unlawful acts.—Section 922(a) of title 18, United States Code, is amended by striking paragraphs (7) and (8) and inserting the following:

"(7) for any person to manufacture or import armor piercing ammunition, unless—

"(A) the manufacture of such ammunition is for the use of the United States, any department or agency of the United States, any State, or any department, agency, or political subdivision of a State;

"(B) the manufacture of such ammunition is for the purpose of exportation; o"(C) the manufacture or importation of such ammunition is for the purpose of testing or experimentation and has been authorized by the Attorney General;

"(8) for any manufacturer or importer to sell or deliver armor piercing ammunition, unless such sale or delivery—

"(A) is for the use of the United States, any department or agency of the United States, any State, or any department, agency, or political subdivision of a State;

"(B) is for the purpose of exportation; or

"(C) is for the purpose of testing or experimentation and has been authorized by the Attorney General;".

(b) Penalties.—Section 924(c) of title 18, United States Code, is amended by adding at the end the following:

"(5) Except to the extent that a greater minimum sentence is otherwise provided under this subsection, or by any other provision of law, any person who, during and in relation to any crime of violence or drug trafficking crime (including a crime of violence or drug trafficking crime that provides for an enhanced punishment if committed by the use of a deadly or dangerous weapon or device) for which the person may be prosecuted in a court of the United States, uses or carries armor piercing ammunition, or who, in furtherance of any such crime, possesses armor piercing ammunition, shall, in addition to the punishment provided for such crime of violence or drug trafficking crime or conviction under this section—

"(A) be sentenced to a term of imprisonment of not less than 15 years; and

"(B) if death results from the use of such ammunition—

"(i) if the killing is murder (as defined in section 1111), be punished by death or sentenced to a term of imprisonment for any term of years or for life; and

"(ii) if the killing is manslaughter (as defined in section 1112), be punished as provided in section 1112.".

(c) Study and report.—

(1) Study.—The Attorney General shall conduct a study to determine whether a uniform standard for the testing of projectiles against Body Armor is feasible.

(2) Issues to be studied.—The study conducted under paragraph (1) shall include—

(A) variations in performance that are related to the length of the barrel of the handgun or center-fire rifle from which the projectile is fired; and

(B) the amount of powder used to propel the projectile.

(3) Report.—Not later than 2 years after the date of enactment of this Act, the Attorney General shall submit a report containing the results of the study conducted under this sub-section to—

(A) the chairman and ranking member of the Committee on the Judiciary of the Senate; and

(B) the chairman and ranking member of the Committee on the Judiciary of the House of Representatives.

Speaker of the House of Representatives. Vice President of the United States and President of the Senate.

The mass shooting on the campus of Virginia Tech State University in 2007 raised troubling questions about how a man with a history or mental disorders was able to legally purchase two handguns. This report prepared by the Congressional Research Service (CRS), the research arm of Congress, addresses that and related questions.

Congressional Research Service

Memorandum   August 1, 2007

TO: Senator Tom Coburn
                  Attention: Hendrik Van Der Vaart

FROM: William J. Krouse (7-2225)
                  Specialist in Domestic Security Domestic
                  Social Policy Division

SUBJECT: Virginia Tech Tragedy, Analysis of the NICS Improvement
                  Amendments Act of 2007, and Possible Issues for Congress

Per your request, this memorandum provides an overview of the tragedy that transpired on the campus of the Virginia Polytechnic Institute and State University (Virginia Tech) on April 16, 2007, with a focus on why a disqualifying record on the shooter, Seung-Hui Cho (sung-wee joh), was not forwarded to the Federal Bureau of Investigation (FBI) for inclusion in the National Instant Criminal History Background Check System (NICS) even though he had been adjudicated as a mental defective. In addition, this memorandum includes an analysis of the NICS Improvement Amendments Act of 2007 (H.R. 2640), a bill that includes provisions designed to improve information sharing between state and local authorities and the FBI on persons known to be disqualified from possessing a firearm. Finally, the memorandum breaks out several possible issues for Congress regarding this bill.

April 16ᵗʰ, 2007, Virginia Tech

On April 16, 2007, a mass shooting occurred on the campus of Virginia Tech, in which 32 persons were shot to death, before the shooter reportedly took his own life with a single shot to the temple.[1] On that day, according to Virginia State Police, a rescue call was received at 7:20 a.m. from West Ambler Hall, and the campus police arrived within 2 minutes, finding Emily Hilscher and Ryan Clark shot to death on the fourth floor.[2] At 9:42 a.m., the campus police received a 911 call, reporting shots fired in Norris Hall.[3] Police responded, but the doors of Norris Hall had been chained and locked from the inside.[4] Eventually, a side door was breached by shooting through a dead bolt and cutting the chains with a bolt cutter.[5] By that time, however, more than 50 students, staff, and faculty were either injured or killed.[6]

---

[1]Kristen Gelineau, "Medical Examiner: Virginia Tech Gunman Died of Gunshot Wound to Head, Caused More Than 100 Wounds," *Associated Press Worldstream*, Apr. 22, 2007.

[2]Virginia State Police, "Virginia Tech Investigation—Final Press Briefing," Apr. 25, 2007.

[3]Ibid.

[4]Ibid.

[5]Ibid.

[6]Ibid.

The shooting spree in Norris Hall lasted an estimated 9 minutes and an estimated 170 shots were fired, or about one shot every three seconds.[7] According to preliminary statements by a Virginia medical examiner, over 100 wounds were inflicted on the shooter's victims.[8] At the crime scene, a 9mm Glock 19 and .22 caliber Walther P22 were recovered.[9] Such firearms routinely come equipped with 15-round and 10-round magazines, respectively.[10] In addition, up to 17 magazines[11] were reportedly recovered, including unused ammunition. Some of those magazines reportedly may have been of the extended variety, meaning that they could hold more than 15 or 10 rounds,[12] but law enforcement sources have not verified those reports. Nevertheless, for the Glock 19, extended magazines are available that can accommodate up to 33 rounds. Such magazines are referred to as "extended," because they extend for several inches below the butt of the pistol handle.

The shooter was Seung-Hui Cho, a 23 year-old, Virginia Tech student from Centreville, Virginia.[13] Cho had reportedly immigrated legally to the United States from South Korea and[3] was still a legal permanent resident at the time of the shootings.[14] Initially, authorities were4 unsure of Cho's identity as his face was disfigured from his self-inflicted gun shot. His identity was reportedly determined when authorities matched fingerprints on the two handguns used in the shootings with the fingerprint file in his immigration records.[15]

As Cho had no criminal arrest record, nor was there any federal record of his court-ordered outpatient care for psychiatric reasons in December 2005, Cho's handgun purchases in February and March 2007 were not impeded by criminal background checks that are required under federal law.[16]

---

[7]Kristen Gelineau, "Police: Va. Tech Bloodbath Lasted 9 Min.," *Associated Press Online*, Apr. 6, 2007.

[8]"Virginia-Tech Autopsies," *Broadcast News*, Apr. 22, 2007.

[9]Neither handgun would have been considered a semiautomatic assault weapon, which were banned from further production in the United States from September 30, 1994 through September 30, 2004. A similar ban on large capacity ammunition feeding devices, however, would have arguably prevented a federally licensed firearms dealer from selling a newly manufactured pistol, like the Glock 19, with a magazine (ammunition feeding system) that could accommodate more than 10 rounds (see note 12 below). For further information, see CRS Report RL32585, *Semiautomatic Assault Weapons Ban*, by William J. Krouse.

[10]Jerry Markon and Sari Horwitz, "Va. Tech Killer's Motives Pursued; Some Action During Rampage Still a Mystery," *Washington Post*, Apr. 26, 2007, p. A01.

[11]According to the National Rifle Association, a magazine is a device for holding ammunition ready for loading into the chamber of a repeating firearm. See National Rifle Association of America, *NRA Firearms Fact Book*, 3 rEd., 1989, p. 306. Such devices are often self-contained, spring-d loaded, and detachable.

[12]For ten years (September 30, 1994—September 30, 2004), magazines with capacities of over 10 rounds were banned from further production in the United States, and from importation, unless those magazines had been manufactured before September 30, 1994. Under federal law, magazines with capacities of greater than 10 rounds were defined as large capacity ammunition feeding devices. In the 106 tCongress, following the Columbine shootings (April 20, 1999), the House adopted anh amendment offered by Representative Henry Hyde during consideration of H.R. 2122 that would have banned the importation of those devices, but that bill was not passed, largely because of the gun show provisions included in the bill. Earlier, the Senate had adopted a similar import ban provision as an amendment offered by Senator Dianne Feinstein to S. 254, a bill that would have required background checks for all firearms transfers at gun shows. The Senate passed S. 254, but the bill was returned to the Senate by the House when it was determined that the bill violated the prerogative of the House to originate all measures concerning taxes and tariffs, because the import ban provisions would have an impact on tariffs. The Senate later amended the text of S. 254 to a House- passed juvenile justice bill (H.R. 1501), without the importation ban. Conference negotiations on this measure were never concluded, however, and the bill did not become law. For further information on the taxes and tariffs origination issue, see CRS Report RL31399, *The Origination Clause of the U.S. Constitution: Interpretation and Enforcement*, by James V. Saturno.

[13]Kristen Gelineau, "Medical Examiner: Virginia Tech Gunman Died of Gunshot Wound to Head, Caused More Than 100 Wounds," *Associated Press Worldstream*, Apr. 22, 2007.

[14]Beverly Lumpkin, "Assailant in Gun Rampage Was Permanent Legal Immigrant; Lived in United States for 14 Years," *Associate Press Worldstream*, Apr. 17, 2007.

[15]Ned Potter, David Schoetz, Richard Esposito, and Pierre Thomas, "Killer's Note: 'You Caused Me to Do This,'" *ABC News*, Apr. 17, 2007.

[16]Brigid Schulte and Sari Horwitz, "Weapons Purchases Aroused No Suspicion; Pawnshop, Dealer Supplied Firearms," *Washington Post*, Apr. 18, 2007, p. A13.

Cho had attempted to obliterate (file off) the serial numbers on the firearms.[17] Bureau of Alcohol, Tobacco, Firearms and Explosives (ATF) agents, however, were able to raise those serial numbers and trace those firearms to the federally licensed dealers who had sold him those firearms.[18] The dealers' transaction records identified Cho as the buyer of those firearms.[19]

Cho's Behavior Called to the Attention of Campus Police

In the fall and winter of 2005, Cho's behavior was called to the attention of Virginia Tech authorities. In October, faculty complained to a department chair and Associate Dean of Students about Cho's in-class behavior and disturbing writings. In late November, two female students complained to campus police that Cho was harassing them.[20] In December, at the request of the campus police, a mental health clinician evaluated Cho's mental state, and a district court magistrate issued a temporary detention order on Cho.[21] Next, a psychologist evaluated Cho, and a special justice certified him to be a danger to himself and others.[22] Cho, however, was not involuntarily committed to inpatient care in a psychiatric ward.[23] Instead, based upon the psychologist's recommendation, Cho was ordered to receive outpatient care, but reportedly he did not comply with the court order.[24]

Faculty and Student Complaints About Cho

In October 2005, Virginia Tech English Department faculty were disturbed by Cho's writings and behavior in class.[25] Cho's creative writing instructor, poet Nikki Giovanni, had him removed from her class, following an altercation during which she confronted him for photographing the legs of female students with his cell phone.[26] Professor Lucinda Roy, then chair of the English department, described Cho's demeanor as "arrogant" with an "underlying tone of anger."[27] In addition, other English department faculty found Cho's writings disturbing. In one creative writing class, Cho's fellow students refused to analyze his writings, because of their violent and profane imagery.[28] In another class, the instructor found his writings so disturbing that she contacted the Associate Dean of Students, but the Dean's options were reportedly limited as there was no prior record of problems with Cho.[29]

---

[17]Adam Geller, "Virginia Tech Says Gunman In Nation's Deadliest Shooting Was Student From S. Korea," *Associated Press Worldstream*, Apr. 17, 2007. It is notable that Cho's possession of firearms with serial numbers that had been "removed, obliterated or altered" was a violation of federal law (18 U.S.C. §922(k)), punishable by a fine and imprisonment of not more than 5 years (18 U.S.C. §924(a)(1)(B)).

[18]Michael J. Sullivan, "Gun-Trace Date Shared—Prudently," *Boston Herald*, May 2, 2007.

[19]Under 18 U.S.C. §923(g)(1)(A), federal firearm licensees (dealers, manufacturers and importers) must keep records at their place of business on the importation, production, receipt, sale or other disposition of firearms that are part of their inventory. Under 18 U.S.C. §923(g)(4), licensees must transfer their records to the next owner, when they sell or pass on their business. If they go out of business, their records must be transferred to the Attorney General within 30 days. ATF stores these out-of-business records at the National Tracing Center in Martinsburg, West Virginia. These records are indexed by serial number. They are digitally copied for ease of retrieval and microfilmed for evidentiary purposes—digital copies are not acceptable in court.

[20]Ned Potter and David Schoetz, "Va. Tech Killer Ruled Mentally Ill by Court; Let Go After Hospital Visit," *ABC News,* Apr. 18, 2007.

[21]Ibid.

[22]Ibid.

[23]Ibid.

[24]Brigid Schulte and Chris L. Jenkins, "Cho Didn't Get Court-Ordered Treatment," *Washington Post*, May 7, 2007, p. A01.

[25]Shaila Dewan and Marc Santora, et al., "Officials Knew of Troubled State of Killer in '05," *New York Times*, Apr. 19, 2007, p. 1.

[26]Ibid.

[27]Ibid.

[28]Ibid.

[29]Ibid.

On November 27, 2005, Cho came to the attention of the Virginia Tech campus police when a female student complained that he was making unwanted and "annoying" approaches towards her in person and over the phone.[30] That student declined to press any charges against him; but less than two weeks later, a second female student complained that Cho was sending her unwanted instant messages.[31] On December 13, 2005, campus police met with Cho and warned him to leave those students alone.[32] Cho reportedly emailed an acquaintance and intimated that he was contemplating suicide, who in turn informed police of his despondency.[33]

Temporary Detention Order

On December 13, 2005, the Virginia Tech campus police took Cho into custody because of a report that he was contemplating suicide. A mental health clinician, Kathy Godbey, from the New River Valley Community Services Board[34] evaluated Cho's mental state. Based on Ms. Godbey's evaluation, a Montgomery County District Court Magistrate, Elinor E. Williams,[35] issued a temporary detention order (TDO) on Cho.[36] On the TDO, Ms. Godbey indicated that Cho was possibly "mentally ill and in need of hospitalization," and "an imminent danger to self or others as result of mental illness, or is so seriously mentally ill as to be substantially unable to care for self, and is incapable of volunteering or unwilling to volunteer for treatment."[37] The TDO authorized the Virginia Tech campus police to detain Cho for 24 hours and transport him to the Carilion St. Albans Behavioral Center in Radford, Virginia, for psychiatric evaluation.[38]

Certification for Involuntary Commitment

Officer Howard O. Lucas, of the Virginia Tech campus police, filed a Virginia Department of Mental Health petition for proceedings for certification for involuntary admission to a public or privately licensed mental health facility.[39] That notarized form was also signed by mental health clinician, Ms. Godbey, on December 13, 2007.[40] On the next day, a psychologist, Dr. Roy Crouse, at the Carilion St. Albans Behavioral Center, evaluated Cho's "mental symptoms" and noted the following observations on the petition:

---

[30]Ned Potter and David Schoetz, "Va. Tech Killer Ruled Mentally Ill by Court; Let Go After Hospital Visit," *ABC News*, Apr. 18, 2007.

[31]Ibid.

[32]Brigid Schulte and Chris L. Jenkins, "Cho Didn't Get Court-Ordered Treatment," *Washington Post*, May 7, 2007, p. A01.

[33]Ibid.

[34]According to the Virginia Association of Community Services Boards, Inc., there are about 40 community service boards/behavioral health authorities (CSB/BHAs) in Virginia. These CSB/BHAs provide community-based mental disability services. They receive both federal and state funding. For further information, go to [http://www.vacsb.org/ aboutVACSB.asp].

[35]Magistrate Elinor E. Williams serves the Montgomery County, Virginia, General District Court. That court hears civil and traffic cases involving amounts under $10,000 as well as suits involving misdemeanor crimes; preliminary hearings on felonies; and commitments for the mentally ill. For further information, go to [http://www.montva.com/ departments/courts/distcourt/].

[36]According to the Virginia Department of Medical Assistance Services, Temporary Detention Orders (TDOs) are obtained and issued for persons who are in imminent danger to themselves and others as a result of mental illness or are so seriously mentally ill that they cannot care for themselves and are incapable or unwilling to volunteer for treatment. Under Virginia state law, the duration of TDOs cannot exceed 48 hours prior to commitment hearings unless the 48 hours terminates on Saturday, Sunday, a legal holiday, or there are unusual circumstances (e.g., inclement weather or custody issues). For further information, see [http://www.dmas.virginia.gov/rcp-temporary_detention_order.htm].

[37]For a copy of the temporary detention order dated December 13, 2005, go to [http://news.findlaw.com/nytimes/docs/vatech/seunghui2005ord.html].

[38]Ibid.

[39]For a copy of the petition, go to [http://news.findlaw.com/nytimes/docs/vatech/seunghui2005ord.html].

[40]Ibid.

Affect is flat and mood is depressed. He denies suicidal ideation. He does not acknowledge symptoms of a thought disorder. His insight and judgement are normal.[41]

On the petition, Dr. Crouse also answered several other questions about Cho's mental health regarding whether he had attempted suicide or homicide, undergone previous psychiatric care, or had alcoholic or drug habits.[42] The answers to all of those questions were negative.[43]

Following Dr. Crouse's evaluation, on December 14, 2006, Special Justice Paul M. Barnett certified on the petition that Cho presented "an imminent danger to himself as a result of mental illness."[44] As an alternative to involuntary hospitalization, however, Justice Barnett approved of Dr. Crouse's recommendation that Cho undergo outpatient treatment. Cho, however, reportedly did not comply with the court order and did not undergo outpatient treatment.[45]

Cho's Adjudication Was Not Forwarded to FBI

Cho arguably met the ATF definition of "adjudicated as a mental defective,"[46] but he was not involuntarily hospitalized under Virginia state law. As a consequence, the state of Virginia did not forward a disqualifying firearms transfer and possession record on Cho to the FBI for inclusion in NICS.[47]

National Instant Background Check System (NICS)

Background checks are conducted on applicants for both handgun and long gun transfers between Federal Firearms Licensees (FFLs) and the general public through NICS. While the FBI handles background checks entirely for some states, other states serve as full or partial points of contact (POCs) for background check purposes. In POC states, FFLs contact a state agency, and the state agency contacts the FBI for such checks.[48] Virginia is a POC state for all firearm background checks.[49]

Prohibited Persons

Under current federal law, there are nine classes of persons prohibited from possessing or receiving firearms or ammunition: (1) persons convicted in any court of a crime punishable by imprisonment for a term exceeding one year; (2) fugitives from justice; (3) drug users or addicts; (4) persons adjudicated as "mental

---

[41]Ibid.

[42]Ibid.

[43]Ibid.

[44]Ibid.

[45]Brigid Schulte and Chris L. Jenkins, "Cho Didn't Get Court-Ordered Treatment," *Washington Post*, May 7, 2007, p. A01.

[46]Under 27 CFR 478.11, the term "adjudicated as mental defective" includes a determination by a court, board, commission, or other lawful authority, that a person, as a result of marked subnormal intelligence, or mental illness, incompetency, condition, or disease: (1) is a danger to himself or others; or (2) lacks the mental capacity to manage his own affairs. The term also includes (1) a finding of insanity by a court in a criminal case; and (2) those persons found incompetent to stand trial or found not guilty by reason of lack of mental responsibility pursuant to articles 50a and 72b of the Uniform Code of Military Justice, 10 U.S.C. 850a, 876(b).

[47]The Governor of Virginia has reportedly issued an executive order to close what many people have characterized as a loophole in the law. See Commonwealth of Virginia, Office of the Governor, Governor Timothy M. Kaine, Press Release, "Governor Kaine Issues Executive Order Expanding Background Checks for Gun Purchases; Attorney General McDonnell Provides Legal Advice for Expedited Solution, Database to Include Involuntary Outpatient Mental Health Treatment," Apr. 30, 2007. Available at [http://www.governor.virginia.gov/MediaRelations/NewsReleases/ viewRelease.cfm?id=399].

[48]In 13 states, state agencies serve as full POCs and conduct background checks for both handgun and long gun transfers. In eight states, state agencies serve as partial POCs for handgun transfers and/or handgun permits. In those partial POC states, checks for long gun transfers are conducted entirely through the FBI. In the 30 non-POC states, the District of Columbia, and five territories (Guam, Samoa, Northern Mariana Islands, Puerto Rico, and the Virgin Islands), FFLs contact the FBI directly to conduct background checks through NICS for both handgun and long gun checks.

[49]For a FBI NICS Participation Map, go to [http://www.fbi.gov/hq/cjisd/nics.htm]. Last visited on May 18, 2007.

defectives" or committed to mental institutions; (5) unauthorized immigrants and most nonimmigrant visitors; (6) persons dishonorably discharged from the Armed Forces; (7) U.S. citizenship renunciates; (8) persons under court-order restraints related to harassing, stalking, or threatening an intimate partner or child of such intimate partner; and (9) persons convicted of misdemeanor domestic violence.[50] It is also prohibited for any person to transfer firearms or ammunition to any person, whom they know or have reasonable cause to believe is prohibited from possessing firearms.[51] Legal permanent residents are eligible to possess firearms on the same basis as citizens in the United States.

Relief from Disabilities

Federal law authorizes the Attorney General to consider applications from prohibited persons for relief from disqualification.[52] Since FY1993, however, Congress has attached an appropriations rider on the ATF salaries and expenses account that prohibits the expenditure of any funding under that account to process such applications.[53]

NICS-Queried Databases of Disqualifying Records

NICS queries three databases to determine firearms transfer/possession eligibility. They include the National Crime Information Center (NCIC), the Interstate Identification Index (III), and the NICS index. The NICS index includes six categories of disqualifying records for persons who (1) have been dishonorably discharged from the U.S. Armed Forces, (2) have been adjudicated mental defectives or committed to mental institutions, (3) are known to be controlled substance abusers, (4) have renounced their U.S. citizenship to a State Department consular officer, (5) are known to be in an illegal immigration status, or (6) have been previously denied firearm transfers. The III includes criminal history records for persons arrested and convicted of felonies and misdemeanors.[54] The NCIC includes law enforcement "hot files" on information that is of immediate importance and applicability to law enforcement officials. Some of these "hot files" include information on (1) wanted persons (fugitives), (2) persons subject to domestic abuse restraining orders,[55] (3) deported felons, (4) persons in the U.S. Secret Service protective file, and (5) foreign fugitives, among others.

According to the Department of Justice, Bureau of Justice Statistics (BJS), in calendar year 2005, the FBI and state POCs conducted background checks on 8,277,873 firearms applications, and rejected 131,916 of those applications (1.6%).[56] Of those rejections, 72,423 (55%) were rejected for felony indictment/convictions and other criminal histories.[57] Domestic violence misdemeanor convictions accounted for 14,899 (11.3%) rejections.[58] Domestic violence restraining orders accounted for 5,483 (4.2%) rejections.[59] Mental illness or disability records accounted for 2,290 (1.7%) rejections.[60]

---

[50] 18 U.S.C. §922(g).

[51] 18 U.S.C. §922(d).

[52] 18 U.S.C. §925(c).

[53] The FY1993 appropriations rider was included in P.L. 102-393, 106 Stat. 1731.

[54] The Bureau of Justice Statistics has reported that, as of March 1, 2003, 25 states had fully automated their criminal history records, and 24 states had partially automated those records. Nonetheless, 93% of criminal history records maintained by state criminal history repositories are automated, but about 4.8 million or 7% are not. See U.S. Department of Justice, Bureau of Justice Statistics, *Survey of Criminal History Information Systems, 2003, A Criminal Justice Information Policy Report*, NCJ 210297, Feb. 2006, 58 pp.

[55] According to the FBI, there were nearly 970,000 state-generated protection orders in NCIC as of December 31, 2006.

[56] U.S. Department of Justice, Office of Justice Programs, *Background Checks for Firearm Transfers*, 2005, NCJ 214256, Nov. 2006, p. 5.

[57] Ibid.

[58] Ibid.

[59] Ibid.

[60] Ibid.

NICS Mental Defective File

As of December 2006, the NICS index included over 159,000 state-contributed mental defective records.[61] According to the FBI, 22 states report persons "adjudicated as mental defective" to the NICS.[62] Some states, however, decline to report persons adjudicated mentally defective to the FBI because of state mental health, patients' rights, and privacy laws that prohibit the disclosure of those records.[63] Other states may not be able to report such persons to the FBI because mental health "databanks" that would include such records are not maintained.[64] Virginia has contributed over 80,000 records to the NICS index mental defective file, more than any other state.[65] In addition, the state of Michigan has contributed over 71,000 files to the NICS mental defective file. Hence, Virginia and Michigan have contributed roughly 65% of the mental defective records in NICS. It is also notable that some states opt to place persons adjudicated mentally defective in the NICS denied persons file.[66] As of May 31, 2007, the NICS index included nearly 140,000 federally-contributed mental defective records—nearly all of those records were contributed by the Department of Veterans Affairs.

Loophole in the NICS?

The 1968 Gun Control Act prohibited any person who "has been adjudicated mental defective or has been committed to a mental institution" from receiving firearms or ammunition.[67] Enforcing this and subsequent provisions has been problematic, however. As alluded to above, state laws often prevent authorities from giving the FBI and other law enforcement agencies mental health information that is considered confidential. With the enactment of the Brady Handgun Violence Prevention Act of 1993 (P.L. 103-159),[68] requiring background checks for firearm transfers between federally licensed firearm dealers and non-licensed persons, these legal circumstances have been described by some gun control advocates as a "loophole" in the law.[69] Jim Kessler, a spokesperson for Americans for Gun Safety, recently remarked that "the system [NICS] barely works at all, particularly when it has to do with mental illness."[70] More recently, on May 10, 2007, the House Oversight and Government Reform Subcommittee on Domestic Policy held a hearing on "lethal loopholes: deficiencies in state and federal gun purchase laws."

Governor Kaine's Executive Order

On April 30, 2007, Virginia Governor Timothy M. Kaine issued Executive Order Number 50 that requires state officials to include the "names of individuals found dangerous and ordered to undergo involuntary mental health treatment" in the Central Criminal Records Exchange (central database), the state database that is accessed to determine firearms transfer and possession eligibility.[71] The Virginia Generally Assembly

---

[61]Federal Bureau of Investigation, *National Instant Criminal Background Check System (NICS): NICS Operations 2005*, Jan. 2006.

[62]Federal Bureau of Investigation National Press Office, "Response to Inquiries on the FBI's National Instant Criminal Background Check System," Apr. 19, 2007, available at [http://www.fbi.gov/pressrel/pressrel07/nics041907.htm].

[63]For New York state, for example, see Section 33.13 of the Mental Health Law, which addresses the rights of patients and confidentiality of mental health records.

[64]Donna M. Norris, M.D., et al., "Firearms Laws, Patients, and the Roles of Psychiatrists," *American Journal of Psychiatry*, 163:8, Aug. 2006, p. 1394.

[65]Ibid.

[66]According to the FBI, the NICS denied persons file included over 344,000 records as of December 31, 2006.

[67]P.L. 90-618, 82 Stat. 1220, Oct. 22, 1968 (18 U.S.C. §922(h)(4)).

[68]107 Stat. 1536, Nov. 30, 1993.

[69]"Armed and Dangerous," *CBS News, 60 Minutes*, Apr. 29, 2007, available at [http://www.cbsnews.com/stories/2007/04/27/60minutes/main2735294.shtml].

[70]Ibid.

[71]Commonwealth of Virginia, Office of the Governor, Governor Timothy M. Kaine, Press Release, "Governor Kaine Issues Executive Order Expanding Background Checks for Gun Purchases; Attorney General McDonnell Provides Legal Advice for Expedited Solution, Database to Include Involuntary Outpatient Mental Health Treatment," Apr. 30, 2007.

reportedly made changes to Va. Code Section 37.2-819 in 2005, which require mental health adjudications be reported to the central database.[72] The language of those changes apparently were recently interpreted by the State Attorney General to authorize the inclusion of persons ordered by Virginia courts to undergo outpatient mental health treatment in the central database.[73] Nonetheless, the sharing of mental health records remains an issue for many other states and illustrates the legal complexities that often accompany such information sharing with law enforcement for the purposes of gun control.

Report to the President

On June 13, 2007, the U.S. Departments of Health and Human Services, Education, and Justice reported to President George W. Bush on the issues raised by the Virginia Tech tragedy.[74] Among other things, those departments reported that critical information sharing on persons prohibited from possessing firearms was hindered by substantial obstacles. The report noted:

> In addition to federal laws that may affect information sharing practices, such as the Health Insurance Portability and Accountability Act (HIPAA)[75] Privacy Rule and the Family Education Rights and Privacy Act (FERPA),[76] a broad patchwork of state laws and regulations also [have an] impact how information is shared on the state level. In some situations, those state laws and regulations are more restrictive than federal laws.[77]

The report included the observation that there were differing interpretations of federal and state privacy laws that have resulted in confusion and impeded appropriate information sharing.[78] At the same time, the report underscored that such information sharing on individuals ought to be predicated on "recognizing when individuals pose a threat to themselves or others, and when intervention to pre-empt the threat is appropriate."[79]

To ensure that accurate and complete information on prohibited persons is appropriately provided to federal and state officials, the report recommends that state and local governments address the legal and financial barriers to submitting the relevant disqualifying information to the FBI for inclusion in NICS.[80] The report also calls upon the Departments of Health and Human Services and Education to develop guidance that clarifies what information can be shared legally under HIPAA and FERPA.[81] In addition, the report calls upon the Department of Justice, through the FBI and ATF, to encourage state and federal agencies to share appropriate information with the FBI for inclusion in NICS.[82]

Congressional Hearings

The Senate Homeland Security and Governmental Affairs Committee and the House Homeland Security Committee have held oversight hearings on college campus safety and security in the wake of the Virginia Tech tragedy on April 23 and May 17, 2007, respectively. While the issues stemming from this tragedy are manifold, these hearings focused on three overarching issues:

---

[72]Ibid.

[73]Ibid.

[74]U.S. Department of Health and Human Services, U.S. Department of Education, and U.S. Department of Justice, *Report to the President on Issues Raised by the Virginia Tech Tragedy*, June 13, 2007, 22 pp. Available at [http://www. usdoj.gov/opa/pr/2007/June/vt_report_061307.pdf].

[75]P.L. 104-191.

[76]P.L. 93-579.

[77]Ibid., p. 7.

[78]U.S. Department of Health and Human Services, et al, *Report to the President on Issues Raised by the Virginia Tech Tragedy*, June 13, 2007, p 7.

[79]Ibid.

[80]Ibid., p. 10.

[81]Ibid., p. 8.

[82]Ibid., p. 11.

- How do colleges and universities notify students, faculty, and staff during emergencies like the April 16th shootings?[83]
- As the shooter had exhibited disturbing behavior that was previously noted by university officials, and he was deemed by several health care professionals to be a possible danger to himself and others, how are such individuals with mental health issues handled at the university level?
- When is it the responsibility of educational and health care officials to warn others when they believe an individual could be a danger to themselves or others?

While the first two issues are beyond the scope of this memorandum, the last is directly relevant. Indeed, witnesses at both hearings noted that there were possible constraints placed on university officials under HIPAA and FERPA that affected their ability to identify, share, and receive information on possible threats posed by students suffering from mental illness.[84]

HIPAA governs health information, while FERPA protects the confidentiality of student records and defines under what circumstances parents can have access to student information and grades. While both statutes include provisions that authorize the release of information for health and safety emergencies, these statutes may have been inadvertently constructed so that some health care information is not covered under either law in certain instances. For example, HIPAA specifically exempts educations records covered under FERPA from coverage under HIPAA.

However, FERPA does not cover medical information about a[85] student that is made or maintained by a health care professional and kept inside a clinic. Once that information is released by the health care professional or clinic, however, it is then subject to FERPA. Consequently, health care information may not be covered under FERPA or HIPAA during such time as it remains under the control of the health care professional or clinic. How this possible gap in coverage played out in the months leading up to the Virgina Tech tragedy is unknown. Nevertheless, as did the *Report to the President* (described above), witnesses at those hearings noted that these statutes posed possible constraints to appropriate information sharing in regard to persons who could be a danger to themselves or others.[86]

Mental Health Records and Confidentiality

In the past, proposals made by Representative McCarthy to improve information sharing and NICS background checks have been opposed by some mental health advocates.[87] Michael Faenza, who was formerly president of the National Mental Health Association, recently opined that "We feel that people with mental

---

[83]On June 20, 2007, the Senate Committee on Health, Education, Labor, and Pensions ordered reported with amendments the Higher Education Amendments of 2007 (S. 1642). This bill would amend the Higher Education Act (HEA) to require institutions of higher education (IHEs) to disclose to all current students and staff, as well as applicants for enrollment or employment, the institution's policies and procedures related to campus emergency response and evacuation procedures, including the use of electronic and cellular communication (if appropriate). More specifically, S. 1642 would require that these policies include procedures to notify the campus community in a timely manner in the event of a "significant" emergency or dangerous situation occurring on campus that poses an immediate threat to the health and safety of students or staff. Under S. 1642, IHEs would also be required to publicize their emergency response and evacuation procedures on an annual basis, specifically to students and staff, and to test their emergency response and evacuation procedures annually.

[84]See statements of Dr. Russ Federman, Director of Counseling and Psychological Services, Department of Student Health, University of Virginia, to Senate Committee on Homeland Security and Governmental Affairs, April 23, 2007, and David Rainer, Associate Vice Chancellor, NC State University, to House Committee on Homeland Security, May 17, 2007.

[85]Under 45 CFR 160.103, protected health information excludes identifiable health information in (1) education records covered under FERPA, as amended, and (2) records described in 20 USC 1232g(a)(4)(B)(iv).

[86]Indeed, Representative Tim Murphy has introduced the Mental Health Security for America's Families in Education Act of 2007 (H.R. 2220), which would amend FERPA to allow an educational agency or institution to disclose to a parent or legal guardian when a student who is their dependent has exhibited behavior that demonstrates that he poses a significant risk or harm to himself or to others.

[87]National Association of Social Workers, "Government Relations Action Alert: Contact Your U.S. Senators to Push for Necessary Modifications to S. 2826/H.R. 4757, Our Lady of Peace Act of 2002," Oct. 16, 2002. Available at [https:// www.naswdc. org/advocacy/alerts/2002/101602_lady.asp], last visited on May 18, 2007.

illness should not have special restrictions regarding firearms; [and] . . . when we're talking about intruding on the medical privacy of a class of people in this country that are already discriminated against, that is really a step in the wrong direction."[88] Mental health advocates reportedly continue to oppose Representative McCarthy's proposal to provide greater access to disqualifying mental health records, arguing that being labeled a "criminal" will discourage people from seeking mental health care.[89]

The confidentiality of individually identifiable medical (including mental health) information is protected by a set of federal standards commonly referred to as the HIPAA privacy rule.[90] The privacy rule attempts to balance the health privacy rights of patients with the legitimate needs of various individuals and entities for access to such information. The rule gives patients the right of access to their medical records and prohibits health plans and health care providers from using or disclosing health information without the individual's written authorization except as expressly permitted or required by the rule. For routine health care operations, including treatment and payment, plans and providers may use and disclose health information without the patient's authorization and with few restrictions.

The HIPAA privacy rule also permits the disclosure of health information without a patient's authorization in certain circumstances and for various specified activities, consistent with other applicable laws and regulations. For example, disclosures may be made to law enforcement officials pursuant to a warrant, subpoena, or order issued by a judicial officer, or pursuant to a grand jury subpoena.[91] Consistent with applicable law and standards of ethical conduct, health information may also be disclosed if the health care provider believes it is necessary to prevent or lessen a serious or imminent threat to the health or safety of a person or the public. Any such disclosure must be to a person reasonably able to prevent or lessen the threat.[92]

The HIPAA privacy rule, however, does not preempt state health care privacy laws that may be more restrictive. The U.S. Surgeon General addressed the issue of the confidentiality of mental records in a 1999 report on the state of mental health in the United States.[93] Chapter 7 of that report, entitled the "Current State of Confidentiality Law," discussed the complicated framework of "federal and state constitutional, statutory, regulatory, and case law" that governs the confidentiality of mental health records. The report underscored that there was "no national standard for the confidentiality of health care information in general and mental health information in particular." Nevertheless, the rationale for maintaining the confidentiality of these records is based upon values of (1) reducing the stigma associated with mental health, (2) fostering trust with patients, and (3) protecting the privacy of patients. On the other hand, it was noted that it is often necessary to disclose mental health records to law enforcement for a variety of purposes, such as criminal investigations or to prevent persons from harming themselves or others.

The continuing tension between federal and state law with regard to the privacy of mental health records (including those held by university health care officials) was possibly a significant factor in the events leading up to the Virginia Tech mass shooting.

NICS Improvement Amendments Act of 2007

Overview of the Bill's Provisions

The NICS Improvement Amendments Act of 2007 (H.R. 2640) was introduced by Representative Carolyn McCarthy and co-sponsored by Representative John Dingell. Among other things, this proposal would amend

---

[88]"Armed and Dangerous," *CBS News, 60 Minutes*, Apr. 29, 2007.

[89]Those advocates counter that Congress should authorize and appropriate additional funding for substance abuse and mental health services administered by the Department of Health and Human Services. See Shawn Zeller, "Mental- Health Advocates Dig In Against Watch-List Legislation," *CQ Weekly—Vantage Point*, Apr. 30, 2007.

[90]The privacy rule was developed pursuant to section 264 of HIPAA (P.L. 104-191). The rule is codified in 45 C.F.R. Parts 160 and 164. For more information, see CRS Report RS20500, *Medical Records Privacy: Questions and Answers on the HIPAA Privacy Rule*.

[91]45 C.F.R. 164.512(f).

[92]45 C.F.R. 164.512(j).

[93]U.S. Department of Health and Human Services, *Mental Health: A Report of the Surgeon General*, 1999. Available at [http://www.surgeongeneral.gov/library/mentalhealth/home.html#forward].

and strengthen a provision of the Brady Handgun Violence Prevention Act that requires federal agencies to provide, and the Attorney General to secure, any government records with information relevant to determining the eligibility of a person to receive a firearm for inclusion in the National Instant Criminal Background Checks System. To remain eligible for the optimum amount of federal justice assistance grants, H.R. 2640 would require states to make available to the Attorney General certain records that would disqualify persons from acquiring a firearm, particularly those records that relate to convictions for misdemeanor crimes of domestic violence and to persons adjudicated as mentally defective.

H.R. 2640 would also require those states, as well as federal agencies, to establish administrative procedures under which a person who has been adjudicated mentally defective could apply to have one's firearms possession and transfer eligibility restored. Finally, H.R. 2640 would authorize appropriations for grant programs to assist states, courts, and local governments in establishing or improving such automated record systems. This bill reportedly reflects a compromise between groups favoring and opposing greater gun control. The compromise bill would allow persons adjudicated mentally defective to apply for relief from disabilities to regain eligibility to possess a firearm if it could be demonstrated that, based upon the prohibited person's record and reputation, it would not be likely that they would act in a manner dangerous to public safety. H.R. 2640 passed the House on June 13, 2007.

Federal Records on Mentally Defective Persons

Electronic Transfer of Federally Held Disqualifying Records

H.R. 2640 would amend the Brady Handgun Violence Prevention Act (P.L. 103-159, sec. 103(e)) regarding the Attorney General's authority to secure from any department or agency of the U.S. government information on persons who are prohibited from possessing or receiving a firearm under federal (18 U.S.C. §§922(g) or (n)) or state law. The bill would require those departments or agencies to (1) furnish "electronic versions" of that information quarterly; (2) update, correct, modify, or remove those records as required to maintain their timeliness, if those records are stored in any databases that are maintained or made available to the Attorney General, and (3) inform the Attorney General of any record changes so NICS could also be updated to reflect those changes. Furthermore, the bill would require the Attorney General to submit to Congress an annual report on the compliance of each U.S. department or agency that possesses such disqualifying records.

DHS Records on Illegal Immigrants and Certain Nonimmigrants

For inclusion in NICS, H.R. 2640 would require the Secretary of Homeland Security to provide the Attorney General with information on persons who are ineligible to possess a firearm under federal law on a quarterly basis. It would also require the Secretary to provide information on illegal immigrants and certain nonimmigrants who subsequently change their status so that they are no longer ineligible to possess firearms so that information could be removed from NICS.[94]

System Safeguards and Requirements

Regarding any information submitted or maintained in NICS, H.R. 2640 would require the Attorney General to ensure that information be kept accurate and confidential and that obsolete and erroneous names be removed from NICS and destroyed in a timely manner. It also requires the Attorney General to work with the states to develop computer systems that would electronically notify the Attorney General when a court order has been issued, lifted, or otherwise removed, or when a person has been adjudicated as mentally defective or committed to a mental institution.

---

[94]The Comprehensive Immigration Reform Act of 2007 (S. 1348) included a provision (sec. 231) that would have required the Secretary of Homeland Security to provide the FBI with the following information for inclusion in the NCIC: (1) aliens for whom a final order of removal had been issued; (2) aliens who had accepted, or had been granted, voluntary departure, or who had violated the terms of that voluntary departure; (3) aliens who had been confirmed to be unlawfully present by an immigration officer; and (4) aliens who have had their visas revoked.

Prohibited Inclusion of Certain Mental Heath Records

H.R. 2640 would prohibit any department or agency of the U.S. government from providing the Attorney General with any record regarding mental health adjudications, determinations, or commitments, if (1) those actions have been set aside or expunged, or the person has otherwise been fully released or discharged from all mandatory treatment, supervision, or monitoring; (2) the person in question has been found by a court, board, commission or other lawful authority to no longer suffer from a mental health condition; or (3) there are no findings that the person in question is a danger to oneself or others, or lacks the mental capacity to manage one's own affairs, and the underlying medical finding is based solely on disability.

Administrative Relief from Disabilities

H.R. 2640 would require each department or agency of the U.S. government that makes adjudications or determinations related to mental health that impinges upon eligibility to posses or receive firearms to establish a process by which a person who is the subject of such an adjudication or determination may apply for relief from that disability. (In this sense, the disability is the person's ineligibility to transfer or possess a firearm under 18 U.S.C. §922(d)(4) or (g)(4).) The bill sets out further that such "relief and review" would be made available according to standards outlined in 18 U.S.C. §925(c).[95] For persons who are granted relief from disability under this bill, or who are the subject of mental health records that this bill would prohibit from being turned over to the Attorney General, the underlying events that were the basis for those records would be deemed not to have occurred for the purposes of determining firearms transfer and possession eligibility under federal law.

NICS Records Prohibition

H.R. 2640 would prohibit the inclusion in NICS of any record of an adjudication, determination, or commitment related to a person's mental health, if those judgements do not include a finding that the person in question is a danger to oneself or to others, or that the person lacks the mental capacity to manage one's own affairs. This prohibition would be effective on the date of enactment and would apply to names and other information submitted before, on, or after that date. It would build upon the earlier provision that would prohibit any department or agency from submitting such a record to the Attorney General.

NCHIP and State Matching Grant Waiver

Waiver of State Matching Grant

Beginning three years after the date of enactment, H.R. 2640 would allow states to receive a waiver of the 10% match requirement for grants awarded under the National Criminal History Improvement Program (NCHIP; 42 U.S.C. §14601) if a state provides the Attorney General with at least 90% of state-collected information that would disqualify persons from possessing or receiving a firearm (e.g., criminal history records, court-issued restraining orders, and certain mental health records).[96] Under the bill, the waiver of the match requirement could not exceed two years.

State Estimates of the Number of Disqualifying Records

For purposes of receiving the waiver, H.R. 2640 would require each state to submit to the Attorney General a reasonable estimate of the number of "records" for which that state has jurisdiction that would

---

[95]Section 925(c) requires the Attorney General to consider applications from persons seeking relief from their ineligibility to acquire, receive, transfer, ship, transport, or possess firearms. Under this process, the Attorney General is required to consider the applicant's record and reputation, and determine whether the applicant would (will) not be likely to act in a dangerous manner that would be contrary to the public interest. If denied, the applicant can file an appeal in the U.S. district court for the district of residence. The U.S. district court has the discretion to admit additional evidence where a failure to admit such evidence would result in a miscarriage of justice. For FY1993 and every year thereafter, however, Congress has attached an appropriations rider on the ATF salaries and expenses account that prohibits the expenditure of any funding under that account to process such applications.

[96]That information is defined under section 102(c) of H.R. 2640.

prohibit persons from possessing or receiving a firearm under 18 U.S.C. §922(g) or §922(n). Such estimates would be based upon a method determined by the Attorney General. A state's best estimate would be used to determine a state's eligibility for an NCHIP matching grant waiver under section 103 of this bill (as described above), and a loss of Byrne Justice Assistance Grant (JAG) funding for not providing graduated amounts of disqualifying records under section 104 of this bill (as described below).[97] Under H.R. 2640, moreover, a state would be *ineligible* to receive any NCHIP funding if it failed to provide an estimate of the disqualifying records for which it would be responsible within 180 days of the bill's enactment.

Definition of Record

Under H.R. 2640, "record" is defined as: (1) a record that identifies a person arrested for a felony, and for which a record of final disposition is available electronically or otherwise; (2) a record that identifies a person for whom an arrest warrant has been issued that is valid under the laws of the state involved; (3) a record that identifies a person who is an "unlawful user" of, or "addicted" to, a controlled substance[98] and whose record is not protected from disclosure to the Attorney General under any provision of state or federal law; (4) a record that identifies a person who has been adjudicated mentally defective or committed to a mental institution[99] and whose record is not protected from disclosure to the Attorney General under any provision of state or federal law; (5) a record that is electronically available and that identifies a person who is subject to a court- issued restraining order;[100] or (6) a record that is electronically available and that identifies a person convicted in any court of a misdemeanor crime of domestic violence.[101]

State Compliance Parameters

To determine state compliance for purposes of awarding the NCHIP state matching grant waiver, H.R. 2640 would require the Attorney General to assess the total percentage of records provided by the state concerning any event within the previous 30 years that would prohibit a person from possessing or receiving a firearm under 18 U.S.C. §922(g) or §922(n). The bill would also require states to endeavor to provide all records concerning persons who are prohibited from possessing or receiving a firearm under 18 U.S.C. §922(g) or §922(n), regardless of the time that has elapsed since the disqualifying event.

State Records in NICS

To be eligible for certain grants administered by the Department of Justice, H.R. 2640 would require states to make electronically available to the Attorney General certain disqualifying information on persons ineligible to possess or receive a firearm for inclusion in NICS. It would also require the states to update, correct, modify, or remove those records when appropriate to reflect changing eligibility status in any database maintained by the federal or state governments from which information is submitted to NICS, and to notify the Attorney General of those changes. In addition, to remain eligible for the NCHIP matching grant waiver, H.R. 2640 would require states to certify to the Attorney General every two years that at least 90% of disqualifying records have been made available to the Attorney General electronically regardless of age. (*N.B.*, it is unclear why this requirement would be necessary if states are only eligible for the waiver for a 2 year period under H.R. 2640.)

---

[97]Under section 104 of H.R. 2640, states would face a loss of 3% of JAG funding for not providing at least 60% of disqualifying records within three years of enactment, and a possible loss of 5% of JAG funding for not providing at least 90% of records within five years of enactment.

[98]H.R. 2640 sets out that the terms "unlawful user" and "addicted" are to be defined by the regulations implementing 18 U.S.C. §922(g)(3), as in effect on the date the bill is enacted.

[99]H.R. 2640 sets out that the term "adjudicated mental defective" has the same meaning as defined in regulations implementing 18 U.S.C. §922(g)(4), as in effect on the date the bill is enacted.

[100]18 U.S.C. §922(g)(8).

[101]18 U.S.C. §921(a)(33).

Misdemeanor Crimes of Domestic Violence

For inclusion in NICS, H.R. 2640 would require states to provide the Attorney General with disqualifying records on persons convicted of a misdemeanor crime of domestic violence, including information specifically describing the offense, section or subsection of the criminal code, and relationship between the offender and victim.

Mentally Defective Adjudications and Privacy

For inclusion in NICS, H.R. 2640 would require states to provide the Attorney General with disqualifying records on persons adjudicated mentally defective or those committed to mental institutions. Regarding such records, the bill would require the Attorney General to work with states, local law enforcement, and the mental health community to establish regulations and protocols to protect the privacy of individuals whose records are in the system. It also requires the Attorney General to expeditiously develop those regulations and protocols and meet with any mental health group that expresses concern about those proposed protocols and regulations.

Attorney General Reporting Requirement

Not later than January 31 of each year, H.R. 2640 would require the Attorney General to report to the Senate and House Judiciary Committees on the progress of states in automating the databases that contain records that disqualify individuals from possessing or receiving firearms under federal law and providing those records electronically for inclusion in NICS.

State Assistance Implementation

In a manner consistent with the NCHIP program, H.R. 2640 would authorize the Attorney General to make grants to states and Indian tribal governments, in conjunction with units of local government and state and local courts, to establish or upgrade information and identification technologies for firearms eligibility determinations. The bill would reserve up to 5% of grant funding for Indian tribal governments, including tribal judicial systems. The bill would authorize that grants be used to (1) create electronic systems that would provide accurate and up-to-date information on persons prohibited from possessing or receiving firearms, including court dispositions and record corrections; (2) enhance state capabilities to perform NICS checks; (3) improve the accuracy and timeliness of criminal history records accessed by NICS; (4) improve the accuracy and timeliness of mental defective adjudication records that are used solely by the FBI for NICS checks; (5) improve the accuracy and timeliness of court-issued restraining orders and misdemeanor domestic violence convictions that are accessed by NICS; and (6) collect and analyze data needed to demonstrate state compliance with this bill.

As a condition of eligibility for NCHIP grants, the bill would require states to establish a relief from disabilities program for persons who are the subject of adjudicated mental defective records. States would also be required to specify the projects funded by such grants, and states that use such funding for other purposes would be liable to the Attorney General for the full amount of the grant received.

For these purposes, H.R. 2640 would authorize funding to be appropriated in the amount of $250 million for each fiscal year FY2008 through FY2010. The bill would also permanently prohibit the FBI from charging a fee for NICS background checks.[102]

Reduced JAG Funding for Noncompliance

By January 31 of each year, H.R. 2640 would require the Attorney General to submit to the Senate and House Committees on the Judiciary a report on the progress of the states in automating the databases that include disqualifying records for the purposes of determining eligibility to posses or receive firearms and providing that information to the Attorney General. The bill would authorize to be appropriated such funds as may be necessary to the Department of Justice to meet this reporting requirement.

---

[102]Since FY1999, Congress has included a provision in the Department of Justice appropriations bill that would prohibit the collection of any fee by the FBI for such background checks.

Beginning three years after the bill is enacted, H.R. 2640 would allow the Attorney General to withhold up to 3% of the funding available to a state under the JAG program[103] for a two year period if that state provides less than 60% of disqualifying records for which the state is responsible. The bill would require the Attorney General, after the two-year period expired, to withhold 5% of JAG funding available to a state if the state provides less than 90% of the disqualifying records for which it has jurisdiction. The bill would allow the Attorney General to waive this requirement if a state could provide substantial evidence, as determined by the Attorney General, that the state was making a reasonable effort to comply with the requirements of sections 102 and 103 of the bill. H.R. 2640 would also allow funding that is not allocated to states for failing to comply with the requirements of the bill to be reallocated to states that do comply.

State Relief from Disabilities Requirement and Federal Grants

H.R. 2640 would require states to establish relief from disabilities programs to remain eligible for JAG funding that would allow an individual to apply to the state for relief from the disability imposed by federal law. [104] Such a program would permit a person who has been adjudicated mentally defective or committed to a mental institution to apply to a state for relief from disabilities. The bill requires that, in accordance with the principles of due process, a state court, board, commission, or other lawful authority tasked with making relief determinations would consider the prohibited person's record and reputation, and whether the person would be likely to act in a manner dangerous to public safety, before granting relief. The bill would require states to permit a person denied relief to petition a state court of appropriate jurisdiction for a *de novo* judicial review of the denial. If relief is granted, the bill would require that the matter of the adjudication or commitment be deemed not to have occurred for the purposes of determining person's eligibility to posses or receive a firearm.

Federal Assistance and Improving Access to Disqualifying Records

H.R. 2640 would require the Director of the Bureau of Justice Statistics (BJS) to study and evaluate NICS operations, including compilations and analyses of the operations and records systems of the agencies and organizations that provide disqualifying records and support to the FBI, as part of NICS background check operations. The bill would also require that the BJS Director report to Congress annually by January 31 the state estimates of accessible disqualifying records. Regarding the collection, maintenance, automation, and transmittal of disqualifying records, the bill would require further that the BJS Director report to Congress annually by January 31 the best practices of each state participating in the NCHIP program. For those purposes, H.R. 2640 includes an authorization for appropriations of the amounts necessary to complete those reports and related studies and evaluations for each fiscal year FY2008 through FY2010.

Improving Court Systems and the Transmittal of Dispositions

H.R. 2640 would authorize the Attorney General to make NCHIP grants to states to improve court systems to improve the automation and timely transmittal of case dispositions and improve criminal history records, including domestic violence misdemeanor convictions, restraining orders, and mental health adjudications and commitments. Of such grants for court systems, the bill would require that 5% of grant funding be reserved for Indian tribal governments and judicial systems. To remain eligible for such NCHIP grant funding under

---

[103]The House-passed bill includes in a parenthetical cite to 42 U.S.C. 3756 as the provision of the JAG program from which funding should be reduced. This provision, however, only authorizes about $40 million, of which $20 million goes to states for the purposes of counterterrorism. The bulk of JAG funding to states is authorized under 42 U.S.C. 3755.

[104]It is unclear whether the relief program required under the bill would be available to individuals to appeal state prohibitions. It is noteworthy that, under 18 U.S.C. 927, it is stated that it is not the intent of Congress for any provision of the Gun Control Act (GCA) of 1968, as amended, to conflict with any state law, unless there is a "direct and positive conflict" between a GCA provision and a state law.

H.R. 2640, states would be required to certify to the Attorney General that a disabilities relief program had been implemented. To improve court systems, the bill would authorize to be appropriated $125 million for each fiscal year FY2008 through FY2010.

GAO Audit

H.R. 2640 would require the Government Accountability Office to conduct an audit of the expenditure of all funds appropriated for criminal history record improvement under section 106(b) of the Brady Handgun Violence Prevention Act (P.L. 103-159) and report to Congress the findings of the audit six months after the date of enactment.

Possible Issues for Congress

H.R. 2640 enjoys wide support. If enacted, however, the bill could generate several issues for Congress regarding possibly unaddressed gaps in federal law, harmonizing federal and state law, establishing databases on persons adjudicated mentally defective, providing for possibly strong precedents for future changes in federal firearms law, and increasing competition for scarce resources.

Unaddressed Gaps in Federal Law

Under H.R. 2640, within three years of enactment, states would have to sort out state laws and regulations (privacy and other relevant laws) that impede critical information sharing with the FBI of records on persons adjudicated to be mental defective in order to remain eligible for the optimal amount of justice assistance grants. As reported to the President, however, there were and are differing interpretations of federal and state privacy laws that have resulted in confusion and impeded appropriate information sharing. H.R. 2640, however, does not address possible gaps in the privacy and information sharing provisions in federal health care and education law, namely HIPAA and FERPA.

State Mentally Defective Adjudications Databases

To comply with H.R. 2640, some states would have to establish databases going back at least 30 years on mental defective adjudications, as they do not currently exist. Establishing such databases may be difficult and costly. Some states may choose to incur cuts in their federal justice assistance grants rather than establish databases for which, up until the possible enactment of this bill, they may have seen no need.

Possible Strong Precedent to Widen Disabilities Relief

H.R. 2640 would also require states and federal agencies that provide such disqualifying information to the FBI for inclusion in NICS to establish an appeals process by which persons who have been adjudicated mental defective could apply to have their guns rights restored (relief from disabilities). As described above, an annual ATF appropriations rider has prevented that agency from considering such appeals from any prohibited person generally. If enacted, the relief from disabilities provisions in H.R. 2640 could serve as a strong precedent to strip this rider from the ATF appropriations.

DOJ Validation of State Self Assessments Could be Complicated

As described above, beginning three years after the date of enactment, H.R. 2640 would allow states to receive a waiver of the 10% match requirement for grants awarded under the National Criminal History Improvement Program if a state provides the Attorney General with at least 90% of state- collected information that would disqualify persons from possessing or receiving a firearm (e.g., criminal history records, court-issued restraining orders, and certain mental health records). Under the bill, the waiver of the match requirement could not exceed two years. In addition, H.R. 2640 would allow the Attorney General to withhold up to 3% of JAG funding available to a state annually for a two year period if that state provides less than 60% of disqualifying records for which the state is responsible. The bill would require the Attorney General, after the two-year period expired, to withhold 5% of JAG funding available to a state annually if the state provides less than 90% of the disqualifying records for which it has jurisdiction.

Under H.R. 2640, however, the NCHIP matching grant waiver and the JAG reductions would largely be based upon state self-assessments of what the bill would require to be turned over to the Attorney General. Determining the validity of such self assessments may be difficult, however. Under current practice, moreover, there is significant lag time in such assessments. For example, the last assessment of state criminal history records was published by the Bureau of Justice Statistics in 2006 for calendar year 2003.[105] Requiring the Department of Justice to validate state-produced, realtime assessments of such matters for the purposes of grant allocations could be complicated and there may not currently be underlying reporting processes and procedures to produce such assessments. Establishing them could be costly.

Increased Authorizations v. Downward Trending Appropriations

H.R. 2640 includes two authorizations for increased appropriations for the NCHIP program. To improve state and local records on persons prohibited from possessing firearms, H.R. 2640 would authorize funding to be appropriated in the amount of $250 million for each fiscal year FY2008 through FY2010. To improve court systems that feed into state and local criminal justice systems and other databases of disqualified persons, the bill would authorize to be appropriated $125 million for each fiscal year FY2008 through FY2010. Hence, H.R. 2640 would authorize appropriations of up to $375 million annually for the next three years to improve information sharing on disqualified persons.

For the last twelve years, Congress has provided a total of $505 million for NCHIP, or an annual average of $42 million. While the yearly appropriations have oscillated between the $79 million provided for FY1995 and the $11 million for FY2006, funding for NCHIP has trended downward in recent years as monies previously allocated for crime prevention have been increasingly dedicated to homeland security and counterterrorism. Consequently, securing increased appropriations for NCHIP that would adequately support state efforts under H.R. 2640 could be difficult.

Source: NICS Improvement Act by CRS

---

[105]U.S. Department of Justice, Office of Justice Programs, Bureau of Justice Statistics, *Survey of State Criminal History Information Systems 2003*, Feb. 2006, NCJ 210297, 58 pp.

Many returning military veterans face difficulties readjusting to civilian life, especially those suffering from mental difficulties such as post-traumatic stress disorder (PTSD). In a letter to the acting head of the Department of Veterans Affairs, Oklahoma Republican Senator Tom Coburn expresses his concern that many veterans may be improperly deprived of their Second Amendment right to own a gun if their names are included in the government's gun background check system.

COMMITTEE ON INDIAN AFFAIRS

COMMITTEE ON HOMELAND SECURITY
AND GOVERNMENT AFFAIRS

RANKING MEMBER

Subcommittee on Federal Financial
Management, Government
Information and International Security

United States Senate

Senator Tom Coburn, MD
Russell Senate Office Building,
Room 172
Washington, DC 20510-3604
Phone: 202-224-5754
Fax: 202-224-6008

October 16, 2007

COMMITTEE ON HEALTH, EDUCATION,
LABOR, AND PENSIONS

COMMITTEE ON THE JUDICIARY

RANKING MEMBER

Subcommittee on Human Rights and
the law

Gordon H. Mansfield
Acting Scretary
U.S. Department of Veterans Affairs 810 Vermont Avenue, NW
Washington, DC 20420

Acting Secretary Mansfield,

I know that we are in complete agreement that our veterans deserve the best healthcare and mental health treatment possible and that, in so doing, there should be no threat that they will lose their Constitutional rights in the process. Earlier this year I was informed that the VA submitted the names of some 83,000 veterans to the Department of Justice's National Criminal Instant Background Check System (NICS) in 1998. 1 was shocked to learn that veterans who had served their country could have their Second Amendment rights jeopardized in this way.

I have subsequently learned that this was not an isolated incident and it has happened on numerous other occasions. In fact, the VA continues to send the names of approximately 1,000 additional veterans to the Department of Justice every month. The Congressional Research Service estimates that this has resulted in approximately 140,000 Veterans being added to the list in total.

This situation is concerning to me as the vast majority of these veterans have committed no crime but, should they continue to own a firearm, they could unknowingly be in violation of 18 U.S.C 922 (g)(4) and can be prosecuted under 18 U.S.C. 924 (a)(2). This could result in fines and up to a ten year prison sentence. Also, this determination, as well as the forwarding of veterans' information to the Department of Justice, would come before these veterans have been given their right to appeal to the Board of Veterans' Appeals, the Court of Appeals for Veterans Claims, or the Federal Circuit.

Your General Counsel's office has stated that this determination and the forwarding of names to the DoJ has nothing to do with whether the veteran has been adjudicated to be a "danger to him/ herself or others." The only determining factor is whether a Veteran can manage his or her own financial affairs. I am concerned that, by placing these 140,000 veterans' on the NICS list, veterans have been permanently barred from purchasing or possessing any kind of firearm by your agency and, of further alarm, without notifying them of their placement on the list.

I am certainly understanding of the fact that some veterans could be debilitated to the point that such cataloguing is necessary, but we should ensure this process does not entangle the vast majority of our combat veterans who simply seek to readjust to normal life at the conclusion of their tours. I am troubled by the prospect of veterans refusing necessary treatment and the benefits they are entitled to. As I'm sure you would agree we cannot allow any stigma to be associated with mental healthcare or treatment of Traumatic Brain Injury-.

I look forward to working with you to restore the rights of those veterans who have been unfairly added to the NICS list, and I respectfully request that you share with me your plans to prevent the release of more veterans' names without due process.

Sincerely,
Tom A. Coburn. M.D.
United States Senator

Source: Coburn letter to Secretary Mansfield

The Tiahrt Amendments, named for their original sponsor, U.S. Representative Todd Tiahrt (R-KS), are provisions attached to federal spending bills that make it harder for law enforcement officers to aggressively pursue criminals who buy and sell illegal guns by restricting access to government gun data. Since it was formed in 2006, Mayors Against Illegal Guns has been fighting to reform the Tiahrt Amendments.

The Tiahrt Amendments

In 2007, hundreds of mayors joined with 30 national and state law enforcement organizations to wage a campaign against the Tiahrt restrictions. The campaign's efforts helped to defeat proposals that would have made the restrictions even worse, and also secured certain improvements to the Tiahrt Amendments in the FY 2008 appropriations bill. In 2009, mayors and police chiefs successfully pushed revisions to the Tiahrt language in the FY 2010 appropriations bill, which restored full access to crime gun trace data for state and local law enforcement.

Read the May 7, 2009 Statement of the Mayors Against Illegal Guns Co-Chairs on the Tiahrt reforms in the FY 2010 appropriations bill.

While the changes made in 2007 and 2009 are a step in the right direction, many of the anti-police provisions in the Amendments remain in place. For example, the Tiahrt provisions still block ATF from requiring gun dealers to conduct inventory checks to detect loss and theft, which law enforcement says is a dangerous back channel source for criminals who are in the market for illegal guns.

How Tiahrt Harms Law Enforcement: While some components of the Tiahrt Amendments were improved in 2007 and 2009, several damaging provisions continue to tie the hands of law enforcement:

- **NICS background check records are still destroyed within 24 hours:** The Tiahrt Amendments require the Justice Department to destroy the record of a buyer whose NICS background check was approved within 24 hours. This makes it harder to catch law-breaking gun dealers who falsify their records, and it makes it more difficult to identify and track straw purchasers who buy guns on behalf of criminals who wouldn't be able to pass a background check.
- **ATF still does not have the power to require dealer inventory checks to detect lost and stolen guns:** While dealers must notify ATF if they discover that guns from their inventories have been lost or stolen, the Tiahrt Amendments prevent ATF from requiring gun dealers to conduct annual physical inventory checks to detect losses and thefts. ATF reported that in 2007 it found 30,000 guns missing from dealer inventories based on its inspection of just 9.3% of gun dealers.
- **State and local authorities are still restricted from using trace data to fully investigate corrupt gun dealers and traffickers:** While the FY 2010 appropriations language restores full access to crime gun trace data for state and local law enforcement, the Tiahrt Amendments continue to restrict what state and local law enforcement can do with trace data they have gathered. For example, state and local law enforcement are still prohibited from using trace data in civil proceedings to suspend or revoke the license of a gun dealer who was caught breaking the law.

The Campaign Against the Tiahrt Amendments: The coalition's campaign against the Tiahrt Amendments has secured incremental but important improvements to the Tiahrt Amendment restrictions. Key FY 2010 Improvements to the Tiahrt Amendments:

- **Full Police Access to Crime Gun Trace Data:** The FY 2010 budget removes the restriction that limits access to federal crime gun trace data to state and local police investigations of individual crimes. That restriction prevents them from investigating the broader criminal networks that may be behind those crimes. The new language enables state and local law enforcement to have full access to ATF's gun trace database to analyze gun trafficking patterns.
- Prior to this change, state and local law enforcement could only access crime gun trace data in connection with an individual investigation.
- **Freedom to Share Data Between Agencies:** Law enforcement agencies and prosecutors are

now explicitly authorized to share with each other any trace data they acquire connected to their criminal investigations.

- Prior to this change, it was unclear whether law enforcement agencies were permitted to share gun trace data with each other.
- **Authorization to Release Limited Public Reports:** ATF is now allowed to release limited statistical reports using aggregate gun trace data to analyze firearm trafficking. The scope of these reports, however, remains significantly less extensive than reports published prior to the enactment of the Tiahrt Amendments.

- Prior to this change, ATF was prohibited from releasing reports using trace data to examine illegal gun trafficking patterns.
- ATF released reports in late 2007 and 2008 that, for each state, listed which other states were the top sources of guns recovered by law enforcement. These reports provided no information about which dealers were top sources of interstate crime guns.

View the ATF reports

Source: www.mayorsagainstilleguns.org/html/federal/tiahrt. shtml

Noah Smith is a professor of finance who offers a different take on curtailing gun violence. In his view, the country's protracted war on drugs is a chief culprit. End that, he argues, and watch gun deaths plummet.

Single Best Anti-Gun-Death Policy? Ending the Drug War

by Noah Smith

This is not a column against gun control. Gun control is a good idea. The assault-weapons ban is a good idea. So are background checks, stricter licensing agreements, and greater efforts to keep guns out of the hands of minors. A prohibitive tax on ammunition? There's another good idea finally getting attention it deserves, after being suggested by comedian Chris Rock a decade ago.

But much of the gun-policy commentary that has come in the wake of the tragic Newtown massacre is misdirected. Stringent gun-control measures are unlikely to turn the United States into a peaceful gun-free society like Japan. In addition, much of the hysteria over "rising gun deaths" is badly misplaced, since the violent-crime rate and the murder rate have both been declining since the early 1990s. If we really, truly want to reduce gun deaths, there is a much better way to do it than the gun-control measures.

The Impossible Dream: Zero-Gun America

Having lived in Japan, I've known for many years how peaceful it is. Women can (and often do) walk down the street at night alone in a big city without fear of attack. Fights are rare, and murders rarer. And much, though not all, of this is due to the fact that Japan doesn't allow people to own guns. If you think Japan is a special case, check out Germany, France, and other gun-free countries.

But to become like Japan, banning gun sales wouldn't be enough. We'd have to actually confiscate all the guns that Americans now have. This is because guns are very durable; they last many, many years. The United States has far more guns per 100 people than any other country (88.8 in 2007, compared to 58.2 for second-place Serbia). It would take many decades for a gun sale ban to reduce that number to rich-country averages.

Nor is there any certainty that marginal reductions in gun ownership would bring matching reductions in the murder rate. Brazil, for example, has a murder rate more than four times as high as the U.S., with less than 10% of the gun ownership that we have. In other words, it's possible that appreciably reducing gun murders might require a truly *huge* (and unrealistic) reduction in gun ownership.

Now, if the U.S. banned gun ownership, and confiscated all the guns that people currently own, it would probably be very effective. But this is almost certainly politically infeasible, and if somehow the 14th Amendment were repealed and this law were passed, it would cause violent civil unrest. Additionally, lots of people could hide their guns. The effort required to confiscate them would be likely to turn our country into a police state.

So universal gun confiscation is out.

The Gun Numbers To Focus On

Any gun control we enact will have a limited effect. But this should not be cause for despair. Much of the recent hysteria over gun deaths is misplaced.

A lot of people have been citing a recent report, "American Gun Deaths to Exceed Traffic Fatalities by 2015." The article shows that gun deaths in America are slowly rising, and now stand at 32,000 per year — a staggering toll. Now, 32,000 deaths per year is a lot of death, and I'd never minimize that. But what the article's authors fail to mention is that gun murders comprise less than a third of that total — about 9,000 per year in recent years. With accidental gun deaths steady at around 500-600 per year, the bulk of those 32,000 "gun deaths" are suicides.

In fact, murder by gun has been falling steadily since the early 1990s. Some of that is due to improvements in emergency medicine, but most is a result of the overall decline in violent crime that America has enjoyed over the last two decades. The fact that overall gun deaths has risen since 2000, despite the fall in murders, suggests that increased gun suicide has accounted for more than 100% of the increase in gun deaths. Obviously, suicide is a tragedy, and I don't want to minimize it. But people aren't panicking over suicide, they're panicking over murder, and gun-related murder is on the way down.

Of course, 9,000 gun deaths a year is still a lot. Still more than other rich countries, still a disgrace, still far too many! But people who have been watching the round-the-clock coverage of the Newtown massacre need to understand that "mass killings" of the Newtown type account for a very small percent of that 9,000. Most of those 9,000 gun murders are of the more mundane, but no less deadly variety — drive-by shootings, gang wars, personal quarrels, and other easily comprehensible crimes.

And if we really care about those 9,000 souls who are shot to death each year, there is an extremely effective policy that we could enact right now that would probably save many of them.

I'm talking about ending the drug war.

A Drug-War Policy, Not A Gun Policy

Reliable statistics on the number of drug-related murders in the United States are hard to come by. A 1994 Department of Justice report suggested that between a third and a half of U.S. homicides were drug-related, while a recent Center for Disease Control study found that the rate varied between 5% and 25% (a 2002 Bureau of Justice report splits the difference). Part of this variance is that "drug-related" murders are hard to define. There are murders committed by people on drugs, murders committed by addicts to get money for drugs, turf-war murders by drug suppliers, and murders committed by gangs whose principal source of income is drug sales.

But very few would argue that the illegal drug trade is a significant cause of murders. This is a straightforward result of America's three-decade-long "drug war." Legal bans on drug sales lead to a vacuum in legal regulation; instead of going to court, drug suppliers settle their disputes by shooting each other. Meanwhile, interdiction efforts raise the price of drugs by curbing supply, making local drug supply monopolies (i.e., gang turf) a rich prize to be fought over. And stuffing our overcrowded prisons full of harmless, hapless drug addicts forces us to give accelerated parole to hardened killers.

Ending the drug war would involve reducing all of these incentives to murder. Treating addicts in hospitals and rehab centers, instead of sticking them in prisons, would reduce demand for drugs, lowering the price and starving gangs of income while reducing their incentive to wage turf wars. Decriminalization would relieve pressure on our prison system, allowing us to focus on keeping violent people off the streets instead of pointlessly punishing drug users for destroying their own health. And full legalization of recreational marijuana — which is already proceeding quickly among the states, but is still foolishly opposed by the Obama administration — is an obvious first step.

In other words, yes, gun control is good. BUT don't expect it to be a panacea for America's gun violence problem. If we really want to save some of those 9,000 people, we need to end the self-destructive, failed drug policies that have turned us into a prison state and turned many of our cities into war zones.

source: www.theatlantic.com

New York Times health columnist Jane Brody examines the problem of guns and children from a public health point of view. While the number of such deaths is relatively small as compared with total annual gun deaths, children are the most vulnerable part of the population, and these deaths and injuries are highly preventable.

Keeping Guns Away From Children

By Jane E. Brody

I doubt that our forebears who ratified the Second Amendment in 1791 ever imagined how carelessly and callously firearms would be used centuries later. Witness the senseless slaughter of 20 innocent children and 6 adults last month in Newtown, Conn. As a mother of two and grandmother of four, I can't imagine a more painful loss.

If you are as concerned as I am about the safety of your children and grandchildren, consider that it may be time for a grass-roots movement, comparable to Mothers Against Drunk Driving, to help break the stranglehold the National Rifle Association seems to have on our elected officials. Do you really want, as the association proposed, an armed guard in every school?

The Connecticut massacre occurred just two months after the American Academy of Pediatrics issued a new policy statement on firearm-related injuries to children. Murder and accidental shootings were not the academy's only concerns. "Suicides among the young are typically impulsive," the statement noted, "and easy access to lethal weapons largely determines outcome."

In an article published online last month in The New England Journal of Medicine, Dr. Judith S. Palfrey, a pediatrician at Boston Children's Hospital, and her husband, Dr. Sean Palfrey, also a pediatrician in Boston, highlighted the shocking statistics.

Every day in the United States, 18 children and young adults between the ages of 1 and 24 die from gun-related injuries. That makes guns the second leading cause of death in young people — twice the number of deaths from cancer, five times the deaths from heart disease and 15 times the deaths from infections.

Dr. Judith S. Palfrey has seen this heartbreak up close. "My niece, who was sad about something, might be alive today if she hadn't had such easy access to a handgun at age 18," she told me.

The United States has the dubious distinction of leading high-income countries in firearm homicides, suicides and unintentional deaths among young people. Among American children ages 5 to 14, an international study showed that firearm suicide rates were six times higher, and death rates from unintentional firearm injuries 10 times higher, than in other high-income countries.

Innocent Victims

The Palfreys said they were haunted by the death of one of their patients, a 12-year-old boy who went on an errand for his mother and was caught in the cross-fire of a gun battle. The boy had shortly before written a letter to his mother expressing his desire to become a doctor.

And Dr. Sean Palfrey recalls "with horror" picking up a loaded .22-caliber rifle, at age 11 or 12, and threatening his baby sitter with it. "This scared the hell out of me and remains seared in my memory. I could have killed this person."

In explaining why he had a gun, he said, "I'm a great-grandson of Theodore Roosevelt, who was a hunter as well as a naturalist, and when I grew up guns were an acceptable part of youth. I took target practice and was an N.R.A. member myself as a child. We had guns for hunting, not automatic weapons that can shoot hundreds of rounds within seconds."

Now, he said, "I do all my shooting with a camera. This is not the same world it was when the Second Amendment was written. Guns have to be removed so that they can't be accessed by those who are immature, impulsive or mentally ill."

In their article, the Palfreys pointed out that "little children explore their worlds without understanding danger, and in one unsupervised moment, an encounter with a gun can end in fatality." School-age children who see guns used on television, in movies or video games "don't necessarily understand that people who are really shot may really die," they said.

Among teenagers, who may fight over girlfriends or sneakers, or have their judgment impaired by drugs or alcohol, "a fistfight may cause transient injuries, but a gunfight can kill rivals, friends, or innocent bystanders," the pediatricians wrote. Among depressed adolescents, they said, "less than 5 percent of suicide attempts involving drugs are lethal, but 90 percent of those involving guns are."

Preventing Access

In a 2006 study of gun-owning Americans with children under age 18, 21.7 percent stored a gun loaded, 31.5 percent stored one unlocked, and 8.3 percent stored at least one gun unlocked and loaded. And in households with adolescents ages 13 to 17, firearms were left unlocked 41.7 percent of the time.

These are accidents, or worse, waiting to happen, and the pediatrics academy reiterated its earlier recommendations that pediatricians talk to parents about guns in the home and their safe storage, and follow up by distributing cable locks.

To limit unauthorized access to guns, the academy recommended the use of trigger locks, lockboxes, personalized safety mechanisms, and trigger pressures that are too high for young children.

Still, the academy emphasized, "the safest home for a child or adolescent is one without firearms."

The Palfreys said that when one of their colleagues asked a mother about guns in her home, she responded, "Why, yes, I have a loaded gun in the drawer of my bedside table." It was only then the woman realized that this could be a danger to her child, Dr. Judith Palfrey said.

The academy also called for restoring the federal ban, in effect from 1994 to 2004, on the sale of assault weapons to the general public. None of the many attempts to renew it have succeeded in Congress.

The Supreme Court ruled in 2010, in the case of McDonald v. the City of Chicago, that the due process clause of the Fourteenth Amendment applied to provisions of the Second Amendment, and prevented states and localities from restricting citizens' right to bear arms. The academy stated that the ruling "set the stage for Second Amendment legal challenges to local and state gun laws, including laws requiring the safe storage of firearms and trigger locks, as well as laws aimed at protecting children from firearms."

In 2011, Florida passed legislation that raised First Amendment questions by forbidding doctors to ask families about guns in the home. Although a permanent injunction against the law was issued, Gov. Rick Scott has appealed the ruling. At the federal level, wording introduced into the Affordable Care Act restricts collection of data on guns in the home.

source: www.blogs.nytimes.com

Political commentator William Saletan urges gun control advocates to maintain their focus on what, he says, matters most: keeping guns out of the hands of people who everyone agrees should not have them. Yes, guns are dangerous, Saletan notes, but they're here to stay, so avoid demonizing them in the political struggle over gun laws.

Goon Control: Don't Regulate Guns. Regulate Who Can Get Them.

by William Saletan

To beat the NRA, don't focus on guns. Focus on keeping them away from dangerous people.

This weekend, a task force set up by President Obama after the Sandy Hook massacre will finalize its proposals to reduce gun violence. The deliberation involves some big strategic decisions. *Slate*'s Jacob Weisberg has one good piece of advice: Treat gun control as a health issue, not a moral issue. I have another: Target people, not guns.

For the most part, Americans don't blame criminal shootings on firearms. They blame the shooters—a bunch of crooks and wackos regarded as wholly unrelated to normal gun owners—and whoever passed the weapons to them. That's one reason why a New York newspaper's map of homeowners with handgun permits provoked so much outrage: It implies that owning a firearm is presumptively creepy or dangerous. The gun lobby relies on this bias in public opinion and argues that guns don't kill people; people kill people. Every time some guy shoots up a school or mall, the National Rifle Association calls for more security and more prosecution of thugs.

These arguments work because, to begin with, gun owners are far more likely to vote based on this issue than gun-control sympathizers are. That skews the polling math. To convince politicians that it's advantageous to embrace a gun restriction, you need more than majority support. You need something more like two-thirds support. Proposals to restrict the capacities of guns or ammunition (which I've endorsed) don't get that kind of support. What gets that support are proposals to restrict *who* can buy firearms.

Look at media polls taken since Sandy Hook. In a *Washington Post*/ABC News survey, 52 percent of respondents supported a ban on

semiautomatic handguns, and 59 percent favored a ban on high-capacity clips. Only 27 percent endorsed a general prohibition on handguns. A Pew Research Center poll got almost the same results: 56 percent of respondents favored a ban on armor-piercing bullets, and 53 percent supported a ban on high-capacity clips, while pluralities opposed a ban on semiautomatic guns (49 to 44 percent) or on handguns generally (67 to 28 percent).

But when the conversation turns to restrictions aimed at people, the numbers soar. In a CNN/ORC poll taken shortly after Sandy Hook, respondents opposed, by 52 to 48 percent, "limiting the number of guns an individual can own." They endorsed bans on high-capacity clips and on "semi-automatic assault guns, such as the AK-47," by 62 to 37 percent. But when they were asked about background checks and denying guns to "certain people, such as convicted felons or people with mental health problems," the support numbers shot up above 90 percent.

Gallup finds the same pattern. Even after Sandy Hook, its respondents opposed a ban on handguns by a record margin, 74 to 24 percent. They opposed a ban on "semi-automatic guns known as assault rifles," 51 to 44 percent. They favored a ban on high-capacity clips, 62 to 35 percent. But again, the support numbers jumped above 90 percent when they were asked about mandatory background checks at gun shows. The results of a survey taken by Public Policy Polling for Daily Kos are almost identical.

Gun-control groups don't advertise this gap, but their polls reflect it. Three years ago, the Brady Center To Prevent Gun Violence commissioned a survey by Lake Research Partners. "A majority of Americans oppose people carrying loaded guns openly in public," said the press release. But the fine print showed that only 52 percent backed this proposal, and even the released survey report didn't divulge the question. Mayors Against Illegal Guns gets better poll numbers because the questions it asks and its reports focus on who should be disqualified from access to firearms, not on gun owners or carriers in general. Look at the data it released six months ago:

> 74 percent of NRA members and 87 percent of non-NRA gun owners support requiring criminal background checks of anyone purchasing a gun. 79 percent of NRA members and 80 percent of non-NRA gun owners support requiring gun retailers to perform background checks on all employees … 75 percent of NRA members believe concealed carry permits should only be granted to applicants who have not committed any violent misdemeanors, including assault. … 68 percent of NRA members believe permits should only be granted to applicants who do not have prior arrests for domestic violence. … The NRA rank and file also supports barring people on terror watch lists from buying guns (71 percent) …

When MAIG surveyed Americans after the 2011 Tucson, Ariz., shooting, 58 percent endorsed a ban on high-capacity magazines. The group didn't even mention that finding in its press release. Instead, it highlighted proposals for background checks and data coordination to prevent terrorists, drug abusers, and mentally ill people from buying guns, all of which scored above 85 percent.

The NRA knows these ideas target its weakness. On Thursday, after its meeting with the White House task force, the organization issued a statement alleging that the task force "spent most of its time on proposed restrictions on lawful firearms owners—honest, taxpaying, hardworking Americans. … We will not allow law-abiding gun owners to be blamed for the acts of criminals and madmen."

Fine, then. Let's talk about how to keep guns away from the criminals and madmen. You NRA boys don't have a problem with that, do you?

source: www.slate.com

Historians Sweeney and Cornell seek to correct the historical record regarding the original meaning of the Second Amendment's right to bear arms: it was about militias, national defense, and individual obligations by citizens to their government, not personal self-defense.

All Guns Are Not Created Equal

By Kevin M. Sweeney and Saul Cornell

Few debates in the recent past have been as contentious as the one surrounding the history of gun ownership. Once again, as the nation considers gun violence, gun rights, and gun regulation, we return to early America to shed light on the meaning of the Second Amendment. When more than a decade ago the historian Michael A. Bellesiles wrote a controversial book claiming that Americans at the time of the Second Amendment's ratification owned few guns and were not particularly skilled at using them, he triggered a firestorm of controversy. That revisionist thesis was soon discredited for its dishonest use of historical evidence, leaving largely unchallenged the suspect counternarrative put forth by some legal scholars and the National Rifle Association.

The latter mythical history, which the U.S. Supreme Court majority swallowed whole in *District of Columbia v. Heller* (2008) when it ruled that the "Second Amendment protects an individual right to possess a firearm," goes something like this: In early America, all adult males owned firearms; those privately owned guns armed the militia; the Second Amendment was meant to ensure an individual's right to own firearms for self-defense and as protection against tyranny. But the actual historical record is much more complicated—and more interesting.

Data from probate inventories, militia rolls, and colonial census returns reveal that private gun ownership was quite common during the 1600s, and though it declined in cities and along the coast during the later 1700s, it remained widespread in most rural areas. Generally, colonists preferred to own fowlers, Indian trade guns, and fusils (light muskets) well suited to birding, hunting, and pest control, and not heavier military-style muskets. Essentially these weapons were in purpose closer to a modern shotgun or a .22 rifle than an M-16 assault rifle. A distinct minority of colonists, mostly urban residents, owned pistols that had a limited range and limited military uses.

Self-defense was not the issue; national defense was.

During the second half of the 18th century, colonial governments and then revolutionary state governments concluded that lighter personal firearms were no longer adequate for soldiers in the field or militiamen at musters. Governments wanted their soldiers and militiamen armed like British Regulars, who carried the Brown Bess, a heavy, large-caliber smoothbore military musket that fired lead balls weighing about an ounce each and was equipped with a steel ramrod and 17-inch bayonet. But in New York, government reports show, some colonial militiamen were "so indigent" that they couldn't "purchase their proper arms," and in Georgia, "many" in the militia were "unable to purchase arms."

The shift in requirements created problems during the Revolutionary War. To deal with the problem, a number of states distributed to their militiamen thousands of publicly owned military muskets equipped with steel ramrods and bayonets, but inadequate supplies, losses, and wastage made the task of providing the desired type of firearms nearly impossible.

By the time the fighting had ended, state militias lacked adequate firearms, which became a continuing problem and source of discontent. In Virginia, the former wartime governor Thomas Jefferson wrote that the "law requires every militia-man to provide himself with arms usual in regular service," but that "in the lower parts of the country they are entirely disarmed. In the middle country a fourth or fifth part of them may have such firelocks as they had provided to destroy the noxious animals which infest their farms."

In Pennsylvania, militiamen remained dependent on publicly supplied muskets. Late in 1787, they protested when the state recalled their firearms to clean them and possibly redistribute them to exposed frontier counties. It is also telling that in 1786-87, the Massachusetts uprising that came to be known as Shays' Rebellion led to a climactic confrontation at the national arsenal in Springfield as both sides sought to control its store of 7,000 military muskets.

In the late 1780s, many state militias no longer appeared to be capable of ensuring what the Second Amendment would call the "security of a free State" without improved organization, better training, and thousands of publicly supplied military muskets with bayonets. Americans were not worried that agents of the new federal government would come, door to door, to take away their squirrel guns, trade guns, fowlers, and pistols. Nor was the problem that concerned them the disarmament of some imaginary "people's militia" or "civilian militia"—rhetorical terms found in the *Heller* decision that have no historical basis.

Instead, the very real danger was that the existing state militias would be disarmed by simple federal inaction.

Anti-Federalists such as George Mason wanted reassurance that, "in case the general government should neglect to arm and discipline the militia there should be an express declaration, that the state governments might arm and discipline them." It was in that context that the Second Amendment emerged and was ratified in 1791.

So what does all of that say about the current debate over the regulation of firearms and the meaning of the Second Amendment?

The first point is that, even in the 18th century, not all guns were created equal. Today all 18th-century muzzle-loading, single-shot firearms appear to be ineffective and antiquated. But members of the founding generation saw them differently, making distinctions concerning the size and use of firearms just as we do today.

Second, not all private arms—especially pistols—were militia arms, and not all militia arms were private arms, by the late 1700s.

Third, the assumption by the majority in *Heller* that the Second Amendment gave handguns constitutional protection because "the American people have considered the handgun to be the quintessential self-defense weapon" fails to meet the self-proclaimed standard of those jurists seeking to recover the Constitution's original meaning. According to the originalists, a document's words mean what the average rational man on the street thought they meant at the time. The ruling makes sense only if you believe that Dirty Harry was the typical American in 1791.

Fourth, despite Justice Anthony Kennedy's observation during oral arguments in *Heller* that the authors of the Second Amendment were worried about defending themselves against "grizzlies and things like that," references to hunting, in general, and bears, in particular, were rather rare in the debates over the Constitution and the Second Amendment. One could say they were almost as rare as encountering a grizzly bear east of the Ohio River. Protecting or banning firearms that would be the equivalent of today's shotguns and .22s was not really an issue at the time.

Finally, the Second Amendment really was about the militia. The need for it grew out of the Constitution's grant of power to the federal government for "organizing, arming, and disciplining" the state militias and the continuing need to equip them with military-style muskets.

The Second Amendment sought to reassure anti-Federalists rhetorically, but not substantively. Critics and concerned state officials feared that actions or, more likely, inactions by the federal government would frustrate efforts to supply the nation's 13 state militias—the equivalent of today's National Guard—with the period's equivalent of the M-16. Self-defense was not the issue; national defense was.

Those who crafted and ratified the Second Amendment were dealing with very different issues from those we face today. We need to move our discussions about guns beyond claims rooted in a debate over securing military muskets to arm the militia. At the same time, it is useful to be aware that even in the 18th century, citizens and lawmakers made distinctions concerning the appropriate uses of different types of firearms.

source: http://chronicle.com

In the aftermath of the Sandy Hook elementary school shooting in 2012 and a nationwide call for stronger gun laws, National Rifle Association vice president and CEO Wayne LaPierre argued against new gun laws as both ineffective and a violation of Second Amendment Rights. In this article, he emphasizes the importance of guns for personal self-protection from society's dangers.

Stand and Fight

by Wayne LaPierre

Before I tell you how the NRA and our members are going to Stand And Fight politically and in the courts, let's acknowledge that all over this country, tens of millions of Americans are already preparing to Stand And Fight to protect their families and homes. These good Americans are prudently getting ready to protect themselves. It has always been sensible for good citizens to own and carry firearms for lawful protection against violent criminals who prey on decent people.

During the second Obama term, however, additional threats are growing. Latin American drug gangs have invaded every city of significant size in the United States. Phoenix is already one of the kidnapping capitals of the world, and though the states on the U.S./Mexico border may be the first places in the nation to suffer from cartel violence, by no means are they the last.

The president flagrantly defies the 2006 federal law ordering the construction of a secure border fence along the entire Mexican border. So the border today remains porous not only to people seeking jobs in the U.S., but to criminals whose jobs are murder, rape, robbery and kidnapping. Ominously, the border also remains open to agents of al Qaeda and other terrorist organizations. Numerous intelligence sources have confirmed that foreign terrorists have identified the southern U.S. border as their path of entry into the country.

When the next terrorist attack comes, the Obama administration won't accept responsibility. Instead, it will do what it does every time: blame a scapegoat and count on Obama's "mainstream" media enablers to go along.

A heinous act of mass murder—either by terrorists or by some psychotic who should have been locked up long ago—will be the pretext to unleash a tsunami of gun control. No wonder Americans are buying guns in record numbers right now, while they still can and before their choice about which firearm is right for their family is taken away forever.

After Hurricane Sandy, we saw the hellish world that the gun prohibitionists see as their utopia. Looters ran wild in south Brooklyn. There was no food, water or electricity. And if you wanted to walk several miles to get supplies, you better get back before dark, or you might not get home at all.

Anti-gun New York City Mayor Michael Bloomberg had already done everything he could to prevent law-abiding New Yorkers from owning guns, and he has made sure that no ordinary citizen will ever be allowed to carry a gun. He even refused to allow the National Guard into the city to restore civil order because Guardsmen carry guns!

Meanwhile, President Obama is leading this country to financial ruin, borrowing over a trillion dollars a year for phony "stimulus" spending and other payoffs for his political cronies. Nobody knows if or when the fiscal collapse will come, but if the country is broke, there likely won't be enough money to pay for police protection. And the American people know it.

Hurricanes. Tornadoes. Riots. Terrorists. Gangs. Lone criminals. These are perils we are sure to face—not just maybe. It's not paranoia to buy a gun. It's survival. It's responsible behavior, and it's time we encourage law-abiding Americans to do just that.

Since the election, millions of Americans have been lining up in front of gun stores, Cabela's and Bass Pro Shops exercising their freedom while they still have it. They are demonstrating they have a mass determination to buy, own and use firearms. Millions of Americans are using market forces like never before to demonstrate their ardent support for our firearm freedoms. That's one of the very best ways we can Stand And Fight.

Inevitably, the anti-gun media and the gun-ban lobbies are demonizing the purchase of firearms. They call us "extremists" because we wonder whether we will be able to buy a semi-auto in three years or, even in some states, later this year. That's despite the fact that President Obama long ago made clear that he wants to ban them all!

The media try to make rank-and-file Americans feel guilty about buying a gun. The enemies of freedom demonize gun buyers and portray us as social lepers. But we know the truth. We know that responsible gun ownership exemplifies what is good and right about America.

Responsible Americans realize that the world as we know it has changed. We, the American people, clearly see the daunting forces we will undoubtedly face: terrorists, crime, drug gangs, the possibility of Euro-style debt riots, civil unrest or natural disaster.

Gun owners are *not* buying firearms because they anticipate a confrontation with the government. Rather, we anticipate confrontations where the government isn't there—or simply doesn't show up in time.

To preserve the inalienable, individual human right to keep and bear arms—to withstand the siege that is coming—the NRA is building a four-year communications and resistance movement. The enemies of the Second Amendment will be met with unprecedented defiance, commitment and determination. We will Stand And Fight.

First, we are going to devise legal capability like never before. I fervently hope that President Obama does not get to appoint another anti-gun Supreme Court justice like Sonia Sotomayor or Elena Kagan. But he probably will, and we must meet that challenge. His chances of appointing a replacement for one of the five pro-rights justices in the 5-4 *Heller* and *McDonald* majorities are high. And there's no doubt he is going to appoint a huge number of new judges to lifetime positions in the lower federal courts.
YOUR GUN RIGHTS ARE UNDER CONSTANT ATTACK!

source: http://dailycaller.com

Gun and sporting enthusiast David Fellerath speaks for many gun owners in enjoying gun ownership but having disdain for the National Rifle Association, the nation's largest gun lobbying group. In this article, he explains why.

I own guns. But I hate the NRA.

by David Fellerath

Some time after I bought my first gun, I got a robocall from the National Rifle Association, asking me to join. After the customary "Please stay on the line…" from a pleasant but earnest voice, I recoiled from the barkings of an angry-sounding man.

Did I know that Barack Hussein Obama and European leaders are meeting on American soil right now, at this very moment, to plot the confiscation of my guns?

The caller continued with his insinuations of an imminent United Nations plot against America, but before I could be handed off to a live operator, I hung up the phone.

I was amused, and then insulted, that someone would think I was dumb enough to fall for such a pitch. But the sad truth is that there are enough people willing to open their checkbooks to make such a noxious fundraising appeal worthwhile.

The NRA claims to have five million dues-paying members (though there's some reason to believe this figure is inflated). That sounds formidable, until one considers that there are approximately 50 million adults who own firearms. Still, the organization has successfully positioned itself as the singular representation of gun owners. For decades they've worked to defend and expand access to firearms in spite of polls showing that most Americans, including gun owners, favor laws that would limit access in various reasonable ways (even three-quarters of NRA households favor background checks prior to private gun sales). But when a U.S. congresswoman was shot in the face, the NRA made certain that no law was passed that would have made her safer. There's no doubt that the NRA does have some grass-roots support, but it's smaller than we think. The NRA does not represent all gun owners, and it certainly doesn't represent me.

If I hate the NRA so much, why did I buy a gun at 37? As a meat eater with no particular desire to become a vegetarian, I wanted to confront the fact

of killing animals for food. Once I took up hunting, I discovered that I relished the time I spent off the grid. Some might scratch this itch with a weekend camping trip. I chose to trudge into the woods before dawn, often in freezing temperatures, to keep a silent vigil in the trees as the morning light begins to filter through the branches. I rarely see a deer. Such a contemplative, frequently fruitless endeavor isn't for everyone, but it suits me.

My guns are long guns, intended for hunting and skeet shooting. Relatively few crimes are committed with hunting weapons, which are designed to shoot animals, not humans. (In fact, knives are more commonly used to commit murder than long guns.) Meanwhile, the death toll from handguns is staggering, especially when we remember that the majority of gun deaths are suicides.

But as crucial as this distinction between hunting guns and handguns is, that fact that I am among America's gun owners puts my conscience to the test, particularly when horrific, random and widely reported violence tears at the fabric of my own community, and my own social network.

Last Feb. 10 in Chapel Hill, N.C., 15 miles from my home in Durham, three young Americans of Middle Eastern descent were murdered by a home invader. The killer was their neighbor, notorious and feared around the apartment complex for flashing his perfectly legal concealed handgun. Without his weapon, he would have been an angry but perhaps harmless, crank. With it, he snuffed out three lives in a matter of seconds. The deaths affected our community profoundly — everyone seemed to know someone who knew the victims.

Handgun apologists see nothing wrong with this killer possessing both a gun and a carry permit, because he had no prior record. In the moral reasoning that NRA has honed to soundbite perfection, it was his choice to commit a crime. *The gun didn't shoot itself.*

While we North Carolinians reel from the killing of Deah Shaddy Barakat, Yusor Mohammad Abu-Salha and Razan Mohammad Abu-Salha, our legislators continue to chip away at gun laws, an anti-business, anti-faith agenda that has forced shopkeepers, restaurateurs, barkeeps, schoolmasters and clergy to post "no-gun" signs on their doors.

The NRA and its adherents want us to bristle with alertness to danger, keeping a loaded gun within reach at all times. But where is the concern for people who want to live without fear of guns entering their lives? The three students in Chapel Hill could not make this choice. They were in the shelter of their own homes, but random, shocking violence found them anyway.

In the mid-1990s, I went to New Orleans for the wedding celebration of a charismatic young couple committed to filmmaking and music, community health care, veganism and spreading joy everywhere they went. I knew them only slightly, but I was there as a guest of a close mutual friend. It was a joyous, slightly unhinged all-night affair with costumes, music and a parade that ended at the banks of the Mississippi. It was unforgettable for the right reasons, and it's unforgettable for a horrific reason.

One morning in 2007, as she let the cat out before daybreak, the bride, Helen Hill, faced the scenario that gun nuts dream about. As she stepped outside early one morning, she came face-to-face with an intruder. She had time only to scream a warning to her husband and child. Then she was dead.

Gun advocates will say that if she'd owned a gun, she would have survived. But in truth, the only way she possibly could have survived was to live in her own home with a gun on her hip, like a character in a Mad Max movie. To conjure such an image of this particular woman is obscene. Only a suspicious and hostile person would choose to live this way.

I agree with the NRA on one point: Tightening controls on gun ownership will not eliminate gun violence. And it may not do much to address the psychopathology of young men who commit mass murder. Timothy McVeigh and the Tsarnaev brothers committed their crimes with bombs, while

Adam Lanza, with no criminal record, inexplicably stole his mother's guns, murdered her, and headed off to Sandy Hook Elementary School.

But by filtering out at least some people who are poor candidates for responsible ownership, gun control will reduce the steady bloodletting of everyday life in our cities, a pervasive environment of danger that police departments around the country have decried, calling for greater handgun controls.

Rather than being our American birthright, gun ownership should be a privilege earned after thorough examination and training, like driving a car. But in 21st-century America, arms-bearing is an inalienable right, thanks to 27 anachronistic words of a constitution ratified in an 18th-century world of slow-loading muskets.

But something interesting has happened in the wake of the racially motivated massacre of nine African Americans in Charleston, S.C: Republican politicians in the South have found that it isn't so hard to push for removing the Confederate flag from public places, and here in North Carolina, license plates. Like public acceptance of gay marriage, this development was once unthinkable. Could gun policy face the same disruption?

There are some signs that this could occur. Thanks to the decline in hunting and in violent crime, the percentage of homes with guns has been waning steadily since the 1970s. In 2014, the figure was reported to be 31 percent. Although there are believed to be about 300 million guns in the United States, they seem to be concentrated in fewer, undoubtedly more fervent hands: aging hands, perhaps. Millennials and guns? Not so much.

The Charleston massacre probably won't result in gun reform, but its survivors have challenged the NRA's bleak, seething worldview by suggesting that kindness can be the dominant mood of our public life. By offering perhaps premature forgiveness to the young man who killed their loved ones with a legally purchased Glock semiautomatic, they have shown us the possibility of living a more open, less timid existence. They imagine a world of joy, community and shelter, not fear, hatred and violence.

source: www.washingtonpost.com

One of the most frequently cited reasons for allowing civilians to carry guns is the possibility that they might be able to stop serious crimes, such as mass shootings. Political scientist Robert J. Spitzer argues that this idea is mostly a myth.

Arming everyone is not the answer: 'Good guys with guns' rarely help

By Robert J. Spitzer

As the shooting rampage unfolded outside the Inland Regional Center in San Bernardino, where 14 were killed and 21 wounded, a businessman who worked across the street, Glenn Willworth, grabbed his legally owned handgun and walked toward the building. According to CNN, he "was able to draw a bead on the shooters," but chose not to fire because of the chaos of the moment. During the Planned Parenthood shooting in Colorado Springs, a man approached police at the scene with a handgun and an ammunition vest, offering his assistance. The police asked him to leave, cautioning that wearing a gun and vest was a bad idea.

During the Umpqua Community College shooting, student and veteran John Parker was carrying his handgun (concealed carry is allowed on Oregon campuses) as the mass shooting there unfolded. Parker thought about intervening, but decided against, because he thought a SWAT team might confuse him with the attacker.

Most people can readily imagine themselves suddenly in the middle of a real-life shooting situation. If only I had a gun in my hand at that moment, one thinks, I could stop the attacker. The spread of concealed handgun carrying comes from just such scenarios. But real life is often very different from imagined scenarios or Hollywood movies.

For one thing, civilians with guns are amateurs, not professionals. Even police, trained professionals who carry firearms as part of their job and who undergo systematic training, may react adversely under live fire. A 10-year study of New York City police who discharged their weapons in the line of duty found that they hit their intended targets less than a third of the time. Similar studies of other police departments reported even lower numbers. In 2012, police who confronted a gunman at the Empire State Building shot nine bystanders.

Second, like the fog of war, a live-fire event is chaotic and usually occurs rapidly. The San Bernardino shooting unfolded in less than four minutes. An armed, well-meaning civilian might be taken for a perpetrator. An armed civilian would likely add to the chaos, might shoot another innocent or wind up a casualty by injecting herself into the line of fire — of police or of the perpetrator — instead of running or hiding. Third, if civilians are regularly carrying guns to work or elsewhere in anticipation of trouble, that means more guns that can be lost, stolen, fired accidentally, used in a suicidal act, or that transform a routine argument into a lethal encounter. Examples of all of these things abound.

Even in the case of the police, many of the unjustified police shootings that have dominated recent news occurred at least in part because police relied too readily on their guns to resolve a dispute.

To be sure, armed civilians have stopped shooters — but not many. A 2012 FBI study of 160 "active shootings" over 13 years (ones where "both law enforcement personnel and citizens have the potential to affect the outcome") found that most were stopped by the shooter, whether by suicide, flight or just ceasing to fire.

A quarter ended by police gunfire. Only five of the shootings (3%) were stopped by non-police with guns: four by security guards, one by an armed civilian. On the other hand, 21 of the shootings were stopped by unarmed civilians.

When these numbers are weighed against the costs of armed civilians, it's hard to produce a sane justification for civilian arming and carrying as policy, especially given that these terrible attacks constitute less than 1% of all gun homicides annually.

Once we invite civilian amateurs to carry with them readily accessible, easy-to-use lethal force, we not only second-guess the police, we pander to fear, not facts — especially since there are many ways to improve safety aside from arming.

An armed society isn't a polite society, it's a terrified society.

source: www.nydailynews.com

In many areas of the economy, businesses take the lead to change or reform their practices. Harvard Business School faculty member Robert Dolan turns the spotlight on gun manufacturers, offering a specific blueprint for how they can more responsibly market and sell their products to reduce unnecessary harm.

Gun Manufacturers Need to Lead Change, Not Just Follow the Law

by Robert Dolan

For some, guns are a great business. In the three years since December 2012 (the date of the Sandy Hook killings) the U.S.-based "Big 3" — Ruger, Remington, and Smith & Wesson — collectively generated over $2 billion in gross profits as they sold about 45% of guns in the U.S. Investors also did well: A $100 investment in Ruger in late 2010 was worth $443 in late 2015, while the equivalent investment in the S&P 500 yielded only $163 over that time frame.

But for many, guns are also a deadly business. From the time of Sandy Hook (20 children and 6 adults killed with a Remington assault rifle) to San Bernardino three years later (14 killed with Remington and Smith & Wesson assault rifles), mass killings have occurred about once a week in the United States. And as troubling as these killings are, they represent less than 1% of the 30,000 annual firearm deaths in the United States, a number that includes accidents and suicides. Gun violence is a daily threat to millions of Americans.

Gun control is a vigorous topic of debate, and it promises to remain so throughout the current U.S. presidential election. Debate-producing proposals on curbing gun violence have come from many corners, including the White House.

Absent from much of the discussion, and President Obama's recent Executive Order in particular, is any role for the gun manufacturers. When it comes to guns getting into the wrong hands, the President's executive order frames it as a dealer issue to be addressed by expanding the capability of the Bureau of Alcohol, Tobacco and Firearms (ATF). When it comes to technological development for safer guns, it is a task assigned to the Departments of Defense, Justice and Homeland Security — not to the U.S. based firms who have been designing and manufacturing guns since the Civil War. So it's natural to ask: Where are the gun manufacturers?

To understand why they're absent from any discussions of gun safety, you have to both grasp how the gun industry works — and go back about a decade to a landmark piece of legislation.

None of the "Big 3" sell guns directly to consumers. Ruger sells exclusively to a small set of wholesalers, each of which are licensed by the federal government. Remington sells to both federally licensed wholesalers and directly to some federally licensed retailers (Walmart being its largest retail account). In each case, the company uses this buffer of its distribution structure as a disclaimer of any responsibility for the ultimate use of their weapons. For example, in the wake of Sandy Hook where one of its Bushmaster assault rifles was used for all 26 killings, company management issued a statement saying the company: "…does not sell weapons or ammunition directly to consumers, through gun shows or otherwise. Sales are made only to federally licensed firearms dealers in accordance with applicable laws and regulations."

Statements like this seem to suffice as legal protection for manufacturers due to the 2005 passage of the *Protection of Lawful Commerce in Firearms Act*, which the National Rifle Association referred to as its "number one legislative priority and a monumental victory for the Association…" The Act grants broad immunity to manufacturers, distributors, dealers, and even industry trade associations. No action can be brought as long as the product functioned "as designed and intended" and there is no evident negligence. Since the act's passage, no case has been successfully brought against a gun manufacturer. So without the threat of litigation, the manufacturers' stance has been to protect the status quo – no matter how unhealthy that status quo is to the public.

"Obey the law" is generally good business advice. But gun manufacturers, guided by senior leaders trained at some of the best business schools in the country, are quite capable of more. It's worth remembering Peter Drucker's famous distinction: "management is doing things right; leadership is doing the right thing." Good management is an ample supply at the gun manufacturers. For example, Ruger's new product development process is "doing things right." It is the stuff of marketing textbooks – extensive market research driving product design and "jury testing" of the final gun design prior to market release. Similarly, Remington's brand building is done right. Its claim to creating a "portfolio of category-defining brands" (e.g. Bushmaster rifles) and substantial "brand equity" is justified.

Alongside its ability to "do things right," leading manufacturers have stated their aspirations. The "Ruger Vision," for example, claims a 60-year history as "a model of corporate and community responsibility." Remington promises to focus on "creating sustainable value for all" and adopts "society" as a stakeholder of the company. Thus, there seems an aspiration to also "do the right things."

So what would true Drucker-style leadership look like from gun companies highly competent in "doing things right," companies that truly have the best interests of society at the forefront? I see at least three steps to take.

Step one is for manufacturers to adopt the role of steward for the entire gun marketing system, all the way to the buyer. This would include not only efficient distribution within the legal channel but directing meaningful effort to minimize the flow of guns from legal to illegal channels.

There's already a model that could be learned from and expanded. Since 2000, there has been a small joint effort between the National Shooting Sports Foundation and the Bureau of Alcohol, Tobacco and Firearms called "Don't Lie for the Other Guy," publicizing the penalty in assisting in a straw purchase. However, this program is largely symbolic rather than substantive, as it is executed in only one city per year – it was Nashville's turn in 2015. The symbolism is important though, showing that government and gun industry cooperation is possible.

A program like this needs investment on a scale that only Big 3 profits could provide. Would this investment increase gun sales? Probably not. Is it what a "model of corporate and community responsibility" would do? Yes.

Step two is to monitor and stop selling to "problem" dealers. Currently, any dealer has to be federally licensed, and gun manufacturers have said that's good enough for them. While the most extensive study is a bit dated, it showed that 1% of dealers accounted for 57% of guns illegally possessed or used in a crime. The ATF does have some limited power to revoke a license. The gun manufacturers, however, have better data than anyone on dealer performance and are in the best position to quickly stop supplying them if disproportionate numbers of their guns are used in criminal activity.

Step three is to put some portion of the research and development spend — about $25 million in 2015 for the Big 3 — in technology-enabled gun safety to direct a new generation of guns to consumers. Even the NRA does not oppose "smart" gun development, as long as "conventional" guns are still available. And in all likelihood, a good number of the 300 million-plus guns are in the hands of law abiding people who would value increased safety in the form of decreased likelihood of use by an unauthorized person or accidental discharge. The makers of the guns are best suited to the technological challenges of retrofitting existing guns to enhance safety. This is a potential added-profit opportunity.

Is there any basis for optimism regarding all of this? Is it possible that manufacturers will do more than check to see if the entity they are selling to is federally licensed? The one mention of the manufacturers in the White House January 2016 Fact Sheet on the Executive Order is that "the Administration will engage with manufacturers… to explore what more they can do." Ruger, for its part, has said "we stand ready to participate in any constructive way to add our knowledge and technical expertise to what is emerging as one of the most critical debates of our time." The company also noted that "the firearms debate has sunk into a public relations game, replete with personal attacks on anyone who disagrees with someone else's opinion….it is time that decent citizens toned down the rhetoric against each other." So, perhaps there is room for guarded optimism.

There is, of course, a difference between a manufacturer like Ruger standing ready and actually doing something. A reluctance to move from passive to active may be understandable given the fate of the last manufacturer to actively engage in forging new rules on gun marketing and safe-gun technology investments. Smith and Wesson's

2000 agreement with the Clinton Administration on managing distribution and researching "safer" guns inspired NRA scorn and a consumer boycott driving a 95% decline in its stock price. No manufacturer will be able to "do things right" for its shareholders while also "doing the right thing" for society without engaging with the NRA in a productive way. Ruger's regular financial support of the NRA, its steadfast support for the Second Amendment, and recent appointment of a past president of the NRA to its board of directors indicate alignment of the manufacturer and the trade association — but it's unclear if that's progress in the spirit of a safer America.

All of these ideas are from an industry outsider, albeit one who has studied the gun industry in-depth from a management perspective. No doubt, if the leaders in charge of the top gun manufacturers asked "how can we maintain our values, serve our shareholders, and reduce the amount of chaos on the streets?," they would produce fruitful ideas that outsiders like me cannot possible see. Ruger, Remington, and Smith & Wesson understand the customer, the gun marketing system, present manufacturing capabilities, and future technological possibilities better than anyone. Society deserves to have that knowledge put to use in reducing the amount of gun violence in the country.

source: https://hbr.org

In 2005, Congress enacted a law giving special legal protection to the gun industry from lawsuits. Historian Joyce Lee Malcolm argues in this article that judges are going beyond the law by giving credence to claims of those who would seek to bring lawsuits against gun manufacturers for gun violence.

Judicial Nullification Continues: Connecticut Judge Defies Law Prohibiting Suits Against Gun Manufacturers

by Joyce Lee Malcolm

The decision of Connecticut judge Barbara Bellis to ignore federal law by permitting gun manufacturers to be sued for criminal use of a gun is part of a disturbing pattern. The affirmation of a Second Amendment right of individuals to be armed seems to be provoking otherwise sober-minded judges to nullify U.S. Supreme Court decisions and now federal law.

In the landmark case District of Columbia v. Heller [PDF] (2008), for example, the Supreme Court affirmed the individual's right to keep and bear those weapons in common use for self-defense and other lawful purposes. Two years later in McDonald v. City of Chicago [PDF], the court incorporated the Second Amendment protection, finding the right to be armed "fundamental to our scheme of ordered liberty and system of justice." Nevertheless writing for the Seventh Circuit Court of Appeals in Friedman and Illinois State Rife Association v. City of Highland Park five years after McDonald, Judge Frank Easterbrook upheld Highland Park's ban on "assault weapons" which it defined as any semi-automatic rifle taking a large capacity magazine and sporting certain cosmetic features. The city branded these guns "dangerous and unusual." Since these firearms are among the most popular hunting rifles and used safely by millions of Americans, Easterbrook thought "it better to ask whether the regulation bans weapons that were in common use at the time of ratification and [relying on the 1939 case United States v. Miller] weapons that have `some reasonable relationship to the preservation or efficiency of a well regulated militia.'" Both arguments—that the Second Amendment protects only weapons in use at the time of ratification and weapons related to militia use—were explicitly and emphatically rejected by the Supreme Court in Heller and

McDonald. In Heller Justice Scalia found the argument that only Eighteenth-Century weapons were protected "bordering on the frivolous" noting "[w]e do not interpret constitutional rights that way" while he characterized that interpretation of Miller as a "startling reading." Judge Manion, the dissenter in Friedman, was amazed his two colleagues came "not to bury Miller but to exhume it. To that end," he wrote, their opinion "surveys the landscape of firearm regulations as if Miller were still the controlling authority and Heller were a mere gloss on it." Regrettably the Supreme Court refused to hear the case and Highland Park's ban stands.

Last year the justices of the Supreme Judicial Court of Massachusetts in a unanimous opinion again defied the Supreme Court's Second Amendment rulings. In Caetano v. Massachusetts [PDF] the justices upheld their state's ban on the stun gun Ms. Caetano had brandished to protect herself because stun guns did not exist when the Second Amendment was ratified. If they had somehow overlooked Justice Scalia's dismissal of that interpretation in Heller, Justice Alito writing for the majority in McDonald v. City of Chicago was clear: "The Court has held that the Second Amendment extends, *prima facie*, to all instruments that constitute bearable arms, even those that were not in existence at the time of the founding." Can the members of the highest Massachusetts court read? The Caetano case was appealed to the US Supreme Court where, by 8 to 0, the Court found the Massachusetts law unconstitutional. In a concurring opinion Alito and Thomas wrote, "Although the Supreme Judicial Court professed to apply Heller, each step of its analysis defied Heller's reasoning."

Now we find Connecticut Judge Barbara Bellis permitting a law suit against gun manufacturers to go forward despite a federal law banning such suits. A bit of history is in order. In the late 1990s individuals and municipalities began suing gun manufacturers holding them responsible when guns they produced were used in violent crime. More than twenty law suits were launched, beginning with New Orleans in 1998. Chicago sued 22 gun manufacturers for $433 million dollars arguing the gun companies were "a public nuisance." Boston sued 31 named defendants for millions of dollars in compensation for the salaries and even the pensions of police, firemen, and medical personnel, claiming the companies were marketing an unsafe product and failed to keep guns from the hands of criminals. The advertised aim was to force the companies to include more safety modifications but the more fundamental goal was to drive them into bankruptcy. Then Housing Secretary Andrew Cuomo warned the companies they would face "death by a thousand cuts." Eliot Spitzer, New York's attorney general, threatened if Glock did not settle the state's claim, "your bankruptcy lawyers will be knocking at your door."

Law suits, however frivolous, are expensive to fight and companies that manufacture properly made legal products are not responsible for their misuse unless they sell them to dealers or individuals who they have reason to know may employ them for criminal ends. No one would hold a car manufacturer liable for a fatal accident caused by a purchaser. Apart from a few cases that settled, the courts dismissed all the law suits. The Boston suit, meant to be the first to go to trial, was withdrawn in 2002, the mayor claiming it was too expensive to proceed.

Finally, in 2005 Republicans in Congress joined by 60 Democrats passed the Protection of Lawful Commerce in Arms Act. The law shields licensed manufacturers, dealers, and sellers of firearms or ammunition and trade associations from any civil action "resulting from the criminal or unlawful misuse" of a firearm or ammunition. Seeking to hold "an entire industry for harm that is solely caused by others," the statute stated, "is an abuse of the legal system." The 2005 law contains some six common-sense exceptions such as evidence that the product was defective or that a weapon was knowingly sold to an individual intent on using it for criminal purposes.

The Connecticut suit brought by the parents of nine victims of the 2012 Sandy Hook massacre does not fall under any of the law's exceptions. Defendants are accused of producing a weapon unfit for civilian use and selling it to a person known to pose a risk. Since the gun was sold to the shooter, Adam Lanza's, mother and is a model used by millions of civilians, the arguments are clearly false. Further the manufacturer, Bushmaster, had no reason to know the circumstances of the sale. The judge did not rule on the merits but allowing the suit to go forward violated the law. We expect judges to ensure the law is followed, not circumvented to achieve a result they favor. Bellis has failed in that fundamental duty.

source: http://jurist.org

Lawyer Eric Ruben argues against Janet Lee Malcolm by saying that judges have not overstepped their authority when they have agreed to hear court challenges against gun manufacturers. Even the 2005 federal law protecting gun manufacturers from liability claims includes exceptions to allow for court challenges under some circumstances.

Exaggerated Claims of "Judicial Nullification" in Gun Cases

by Eric Ruben

Eight years after the Supreme Court struck down a handgun ban in District of Columbia v. Heller, Second Amendment law has not developed the way gun advocates hoped. They expected that popularly enacted gun laws would fall like dominoes. But lower courts for the most part have repeatedly upheld restrictions that stopped short of handgun bans, consistent with Heller's careful signal that the opinion left plenty of room for reasonable regulations. That result is deeply dissatisfying to the advocates, who have resorted to a tired attack on the courts for what the National Rifle Association called a "pervasive pattern of stubborn resistance." Given that the Supreme Court has had over 60 opportunities to correct lower court rulings in Second Amendment cases, but has chosen to do so only once, this critique is increasingly strained.

In an attempt to show just how rebellious judges have been, historian Joyce Lee Malcolm opens a new line of attack in her recent JURIST commentary. Malcolm asserts that the "disturbing pattern" of "nullification" is seen not only in Second Amendment cases, but also in a case brought against a gun manufacturer by the families of the children shot and killed at Sandy Hook:

> The decision of Connecticut judge Barbara Bellis to ignore federal law by permitting gun manufacturers to be sued for criminal use of a gun is part of a disturbing pattern. The affirmation of a Second Amendment right of individuals to be armed seems to be provoking otherwise sober-minded judges to nullify U.S. Supreme Court decisions and now federal law.

This novel allegation is both baseless and misleading about just how obstructive the federal immunity statute has been. Far from ignoring industry immunity, courts have applied it repeatedly, giving the firearm industry a free

pass no other business enjoys, let alone one that manufactures a lethal product like the assault rifle used to spray 154 bullets in under five minutes in Newtown, Connecticut.

If the Sandy Hook defendant did not sell guns, the parents of the slain children would be entitled to make a case. If the case lacked merit under ordinary liability principles, they would lose; otherwise, they would win. But as Malcolm concedes, firearm manufacturers are different—industry lobbyists in 2005 secured immunity from liability at the expense of gun victims in a federal statute called the Protection of Lawful Commerce in Arms Act (PLCAA).

As a result, only two cases against gun dealers have fit into one of PLCAA's narrow exceptions and reached a jury since the federal immunity benefit was granted to the industry. Needless to say, this hardly reflects what Malcolm characterizes as a "disturbing pattern" of judicial defiance.

Indeed, even the claim of judicial "nullification" in the Sandy Hook case is demonstrably unfounded and belies a misrepresentation of the case's procedural posture. According to Malcolm, Bellis "ignor[ed] federal law by permitting gun manufacturers to be sued." But, as a practical matter, the immunity statute does not prevent a gun manufacturer from "be[ing] sued." Rather, as interpreted by numerous courts, it provides the gun manufacturer with a defense against many types of claims after they are sued.

In fact, Bellis has not even ruled whether immunity applies in the case, so Malcolm's argument is a red herring. Although Bellis rejected the gun manufacturers' motion to dismiss in April, she did not rule on immunity [PDF]. Perhaps the confusion is that a federal motion to dismiss would be a procedural vehicle for raising and deciding the issue. This case is pending in Connecticut state court, however, where Bellis will await a separate "motion to strike" to consider whether the gun maker is immune from liability.

The sad reality is that the Sandy Hook plaintiffs — like all gun violence victims — face an uphill battle because of PLCAA. At a minimum, however, the plaintiffs deserve a thoughtful determination whether, among other things, the civilian marketing and sale of the assault rifle constituted a "negligent entrustment," an exception in the statute, in which case immunity would not apply and the case could proceed.

No basis exists to assert a "disturbing pattern" of judges "nullifying" the federal law providing firearm industry immunity. More relevant than arguing about whether courts have heeded the immunity statute — they have — is considering whether it is just to slam the courthouse.

Eric Ruben is a fellow at the Brennan Center for Justice at the New York University School of Law, where his work focuses on Second Amendment jurisprudence.

Source: Reprinted with permission from Brennan Center for Justice, www.brennancenter.org

Despite nearly unanimous opposition from college and university campus personnel, a few states have enacted laws allowing civilians to carry guns on state-operated campuses. College professor Javier Auyero argues against these laws, saying that the presence of guns is incompatible with a university environment.

Guns on Campus Make Colleges Less Safe

by Javier Auyero

Last year, Gov. Greg Abbott of Texas signed SB 11, also known as the "campus carry" law. The law allows licensed holders to carry concealed handguns in university buildings and classrooms, extending the reach of a previous law that permitted concealed handguns on university grounds. The law goes into effect Aug. 1, 2016 for Texas public colleges and universities, and a year later for community colleges. How will this law affect life on campus?

> Sure I dread vigilantes, but what I worry about even more is the effect that the presence of guns will have on teaching and learning.

To answer this question, let me go back to the debate that took place in the Texas Legislature last year. The debate – if we can call it that – was not about logical, evidence-based arguments, but guided by the interests and ideological commitments of the state legislators and the organizations that support them. Had it been about logic or evidence, the reasons put forward by William H. McRaven, the chancellor of the University of Texas and a former Navy SEAL, and Art Acevedo, chief of the Austin Police Department – both of whom know a thing or two about the subject – would have been heeded. They both opposed the new legislation with a similar argument: Allowing concealed weapons on campuses will create "less-safe" environments. When there are more guns around, there is more risk – it's as simple as that.

Allowing guns in classrooms (against the will of the overwhelming majority of professors, staff and students) will not only increase risk but, as has been argued elsewhere, will stifle classroom debates – an essential component of learning. It will furthermore irredeemably hurt the national and international reputation of the flagship University of Texas at Austin and other Texas universities. Reputations take a notoriously long time to build, but a short time to destroy.

Do I dread the potential presence of young vigilantes – because, let's not be euphemistic about it, "vigilante" is the right word for the people (mostly men) who will carry concealed guns – in my classroom? Certainly. But I don't want to concede an inch to fear mongers: University campuses are some of the safest places in the United States. What I do fear, what I am truly scared of, is that we will get used to the presence of guns. I fear that sharing a classroom with students "packing heat" will stop shocking us as it now does, and that we will become something other than what we are: Women and men committed to teaching and learning in environments where everybody can freely express his or her ideas.

source: www.nytimes.com

Mother and gun owner Amanda Collins draws on her own experience as a victim of a violent crime to argue for civilian gun carrying on college campuses.

Why I Would Have Liked to Have My Weapon With Me in College

by Amanda Collins

In college eight years ago, I was raped in a parking garage only feet from the campus police office.

I could see the police cruisers parked for the night as this stranger raped me, pistol to my head. I knew no one was coming to help me.

> I should not have to hand over my safety to a third party. Laws that prohibit campus carry turn women like me into victims.

At the time of my attack, I had a Nevada concealed carry permit. But in Nevada, permit holders are not allowed to carry firearms on campuses. As someone who obeys the law, I left my firearm at home when I went to school. The law that was meant to safeguard me – the gun-free zone – only guaranteed I would be defenseless.

Eventually the man was caught, tried and convicted – not just for using a gun in gun-free zone, but also for raping two other women and murdering one. My attacker was not a student, nor did he have a concealed-carry weapon permit.

I still wonder what would have been different if I'd had my weapon that night. But here's the truth:

I feel certain that I would have been able to stop the attack. Not only that, but two other rapes would have been prevented and three young lives would have been saved, including my own.

Any survivor of rape can understand that the young woman I was when I walked into the parking garage that night was not the same woman who left. My life has never been the same. Campus carry would have saved my family and me a great deal of untold torment.

My case is a perfect example. Despite law enforcement's best efforts, they can't be everywhere at once. All I wanted was a chance to effectively defend myself. The choice to participate in one's own defense should be left to the individual, not mandated by the government. I should not have to hand over my safety to a third party. Laws that prohibit campus carry turn women like me into victims.

source: www.nytimes.com

APPENDIX 1

State Constitutional Gun Rights Provisions

Forty-five states have constitutional provisions dealing with the right to keep and bear arms. The constitutions of five states—California, Iowa, Maryland, Minnesota, and New Jersey—contain no such provision. The following listing presents the relevant wording of state constitutions.

Alabama: Every citizen has a right to bear arms in defense of himself and the state. Any restriction on this right shall be subject to strict scrutiny. No citizen shall be compelled by any international treaty or international law to take an action that prohibits, limits, or otherwise interferes with his or her fundamental right to keep and bear arms in defense of himself or herself and the state, if such treaty or law, or its adoption, violates the United States Constitution (art. 1, sec. 26).

Alaska: A well-regulated militia being necessary to the security of a free state, the right of the people to keep and bear arms shall not be infringed. The individual right to keep and bear arms shall not be denied or infringed by the state or political subdivision of the State (art. 1, sec. 19).

Arizona: The right of the individual citizen to bear arms in defense of himself or the State shall not be impaired, but nothing in this section shall be construed as authorizing individuals or corporations to organize, maintain, or employ an armed body of men (art. 2, sec. 26).

Arkansas: The citizens of this State shall have the right to keep and bear arms for their common defense (art. 2, sec. 5).

Colorado: The right of no person to keep and bear arms in defense of his home, person and property, or in aid of the civil power when thereto legally summoned, shall be called in question; but nothing herein contained shall be construed to justify the practice of carrying concealed weapons (art. 2, sec. 13).

Connecticut: Every citizen has a right to bear arms in defense of himself and the state (art. 1, sec. 15).

Delaware: A person has the right to keep and bear arms for the defense of self, family, home and State, and for hunting and recreational use (art. 1, sec. 20).

Florida: The right of the people to keep and bear arms in defense of themselves and of the lawful authority of the state shall not be infringed, except that the manner of bearing arms may be regulated by law (art. 1, sec. 8).

Georgia: The right of the people to keep and bear arms shall not be infringed, but the General Assembly shall have power to prescribe the manner in which arms may be borne (art. 1, sec. 1, para. 8).

Hawaii: A well regulated militia being necessary to the security of a free state, the right of the people to keep and bear arms shall not be infringed (art. 1, sec. 15).

Idaho: The people have the right to keep and bear arms, which right shall not be abridged; but this provision shall not prevent the passage of laws to govern the carrying of weapons concealed on the person nor prevent passage of legislation providing minimum sentences for crimes committed while in possession of a firearm, nor prevent the passage of legislation providing penalties for the possession of firearms by a convicted felon, nor prevent the passage of any legislation punishing the use of a firearm. No law shall impose licensure, registration or special taxation on the ownership or possession of firearms or ammunition. Nor shall any law permit the confiscation of firearms, except those actually used in the commission of a felony (art. 1, sec. 11).

Illinois: Subject only to the police power, the right of the individual citizen to keep and bear arms shall not be infringed (art. I, sec. 22).

Indiana: The people shall have a right to bear arms, for defense of themselves and the State (art. I, sec. 32).

Kansas: The people have the right to bear arms for their defense and security; but standing armies, in time of peace, are dangerous to liberty, and shall not be tolerated, and the military shall be in strict subordination to the civil power (Bill of Rights, sec. 4).

Kentucky: All men are, by nature, free and equal, and have certain inherent and inalienable rights, among which may be reckoned: . . . the right to bear arms in defense of themselves and of the State, subject to the power of the

General Assembly to enact laws to prevent persons from carrying concealed weapons (art.1, sec. 1, para.7).

Louisiana: The right of each citizen to keep and bear arms shall not be infringed. Any restriction on this right shall be subject to strict scrutiny (art. I, sec. 4).

Maine: Every citizen has a right to keep and bear arms and this right shall never be questioned (art. I, sec. 16).

Massachusetts: The people have a right to keep and bear arms for the common defence [sic]. And as, in times of peace, armies are dangerous to liberty, they ought not to be maintained without the consent of the legislature; and the military power shall always be held in an exact subordination to the civil authority, and be governed by it (pt. I, art. 17).

Michigan: Every person has a right to keep and bear arms for the defense of himself and the state (art. 1, sec. 6).

Mississippi: The right of every citizen to keep and bear arms in defense of his home, person, or property, or in aid of the civil power when thereto legally summoned, shall not be called in question, but the legislature may regulate or forbid carrying concealed weapons (art. 3, sec. 12).

Missouri: That the right of every citizen to keep and bear arms, ammunition, and accessories typical to the normal function of such arms, in defense of his home, person, family and property, or when lawfully summoned in aid of the civil power, shall not be questioned. The rights guaranteed by this section shall be unalienable. Any restriction on these rights shall be subject to strict scrutiny and the state of Missouri shall be obligated to uphold these rights and shall under no circumstances decline to protect against their infringement. Nothing in this section shall be construed to prevent the general assembly from enacting general laws which limit the rights of convicted violent felons or those adjudicated by a court to be a danger to self or others as result of a mental disorder or mental infirmity (art. 1, sec. 23).

Montana: The right of any person to keep or bear arms in defense of his own home, person, and property, or in aid of the civil power when thereto legally summoned, shall not be called in question, but nothing herein contained shall be held to permit the carrying of concealed weapons (art. 2, sec. 12).

Nebraska: All persons are by nature free and independent and have certain inherent and inalienable rights: among those are life, liberty, the pursuit of happiness, and the right to keep and bear arms, for security or defense of self, family, home, and others, and for lawful common defense, hunting, recreational use, and all other lawful purposes, and such rights shall not be denied or infringed by the state or any subdivision thereof. To secure these rights, and the protection of property, governments are instituted among people, deriving their just powers from the consent of the governed (art. 1, sec. 1).

Nevada: Every citizen has the right to keep and bear arms for security and defense, for lawful hunting and recreational use and for other lawful purposes (art. 1, sec. 11, para. 1).

New Hampshire: All persons have the right to keep and bear arms in defense of themselves, their families, their property, and the state (part 1, art. 2a). . . . No person, who is conscientiously scrupulous about the lawfulness of bearing arms, shall be compelled thereto. (part 1, art. 13)

New Mexico: No law shall abridge the right of the citizen to keep and bear arms for security and defense, for lawful hunting and recreational use and for other lawful

purposes, but nothing herein shall be held to permit the carrying of concealed weapons. No municipality or county shall regulate, in any way, an incident of the right to keep and bear arms. (art. 2, sec. 6).

New York: A well-regulated militia being necessary to the security of a free state, the right of the people to keep and bear arms cannot be infringed (New York Civil Rights Law, art. 2, sec. 4).

North Carolina: A well regulated militia being necessary to the security of a free State, the right of the people to keep and bear arms shall not be infringed; and, as standing armies in time of peace are dangerous to liberty, they shall not be maintained, and the military shall be kept under strict subordination to, and governed by, the civil power. Nothing herein shall justify the practice of carrying concealed weapons, or prevent the General Assembly from enacting penal statutes against that practice (art. 1, sec. 30).

North Dakota: All individuals are by nature equally free and independent and have certain inalienable rights, among which are those of enjoying and defending life and liberty; acquiring, possessing and protecting property and reputation; pursuing and obtaining safety and happiness; and to keep and bear arms for the defense of their person, family, property, and the state, and for lawful hunting, recreational, and other lawful purposes, which shall not be infringed (art. 1, sec. 1).

Ohio: The people have the right to bear arms for their defense and security; but standing armies, in time of peace, are dangerous to liberty, and shall not be kept up; and the military shall be in strict subordination to the civil power (art. I, sec. 4).

Oklahoma: The right of a citizen to keep and bear arms in defense of his home, person, or property, or in aid of the civil power, when thereunto legally summoned, shall never be prohibited; but nothing herein contained shall prevent the Legislature from regulating the carrying of weapons (art. 2, sec. 26).

Oregon: The people shall have the right to bear arms for the defence [sic] of themselves, and the State, but the Military shall be kept in strict subordination to the civil power (art. 1, sec. 27).

Pennsylvania: The right of the citizens to bear arms in defense of themselves and the State shall not be questioned (art. 1, sec. 21).

Rhode Island: The right of the people to keep and bear arms shall not be infringed (art. 1, sec. 22).

South Carolina: A well regulated militia being necessary to the security of a free State, the right of the people to keep and bear arms shall not be infringed. As, in times of peace, armies are dangerous to liberty, they shall not be maintained without the consent of the General Assembly. The military power of the State shall always be held in subordination to the civil authority and be governed by it. No soldier shall in time of peace be quartered in any house without the consent of the owner nor in time of war but in the manner prescribed by law (art. 1, sec. 20).

South Dakota: The right of the citizens to bear arms in defense of themselves and the state shall not be denied (art. 6, sec. 24).

Tennessee: That the citizens of this State have a right to keep and to bear arms for their common defense; but the Legislature shall have power, by law, to regulate the wearing of arms with a view to prevent crime (art. 1, sec. 26).

Texas: Every citizen shall have the right to keep and bear arms in the lawful defense of himself or the State; but the Legislature shall have power, by law, to regulate the wearing of arms, with a view to prevent crime (art. 1, sec. 23).

Utah: The individual right of the people to keep and bear arms for security and defense of self, family, others, property, or the state, as well as for other lawful purposes shall not be infringed; but nothing herein shall prevent the legislature from defining the lawful use of arms (art. 1, sec. 6).

Vermont: That the people have a right to bear arms for the defence [sic] of themselves and the State--and as standing armies in time of peace are dangerous to liberty, they ought not to be kept up; and that the military should be kept under strict subordination to and governed by the civil power (chap. 1, art. 16).

Virginia: That a well regulated militia, composed of the body of the people, trained to arms, is the proper, natural, and safe defense of a free state, therefore, the right of the people to keep and bear arms shall not be infringed; that standing armies, in time of peace, should be avoided as dangerous to liberty; and that in all cases the military should be under strict subordination to, and governed by, the civil power (art. 1, sec. 13).

Washington: The right of the individual citizen to bear arms in defense of himself, or the state, shall not be impaired, but nothing in this section shall be construed as authorizing individuals or corporations to organize, maintain or employ an armed body of men (art. 1, sec. 24).

West Virginia: A person has the right to keep and bear arms for the defense of self, family, home, and state, and for lawful hunting and recreational use (art. 3, sec. 22).

Wisconsin: The people have the right to keep and bear arms for security, defense, hunting, recreation or any other lawful purpose (art. 1, sec. 25).

Wyoming: The right of citizens to bear arms in defense of themselves and of the state shall not be denied (art. 1, sec. 24).

APPENDIX 2

State Concealed Carry Policies

This table presents basic information about state concealed carry laws. First, states have adopted either "may issue" or "shall issue" concealed carry measures. In "may issue" states, state and local authorities can exercise wider discretion over who may receive a concealed carry license, taking into account such factors as employment that requires greater security, or good character. In "shall issue" states, authorities are required to grant a concealed carry license to anyone who is not specifically prohibited from carrying a weapon, such as those who have been convicted of a felony. A few states do not require a license to carry a concealed firearm and hence are neither "may issue" nor "shall issue" states. States vary with regard to the amount of training required before being granted a license and what courses fulfill the requirement. Most states call for a minimum amount of training hours to receive a concealed carry license, but some states do not mandate any training at all. States also vary widely regarding the recognition of the concealed carry licenses of other states, called reciprocity. In tandem with concealed carry laws, several states have enacted stand-your-ground laws, a controversial policy that extends the Castle Doctrine–which recognizes the right of a person to defend their home (including the use of deadly force) against intruders–to public places. When individuals are in a public place where they have a right to be, they may defend themselves with force, including lethal force, when they feel threatened, and are not required to attempt retreating from the encounter. While the specific policies of states vary, stand-your-ground laws provide immunity from prosecution and from civil liability for those using deadly force in self-defense. "Duty to retreat" states call for individuals in public places to seek a safe avenue of retreat from a threatening situation before the use of force may be justified. Finally, states are distinguished by the level of state control over local government laws dealing with firearms; whether state governments can overrule, or preempt, local ordinances that may place additional restrictions on the possession and carrying of firearms beyond those that the state has established.

STATE	SHALL ISSUE/ MAY ISSUE	TRAINING REQUIRED	RECIPROCITY[1]	STAND-YOUR-GROUND	PREEMPTION[2]
Alabama	Shall	None	22 states	Yes	Broad
Alaska	None	Complete a course	All states	Yes	Broad
Arizona	Shall	Complete a course	All states	Yes	Broad
Arkansas	Shall	Complete course	32 states	Yes	Broad
California	May	Course not to exceed 16 hours	None	Yes	Limited
Colorado	Shall	Various means	27 states	No	Broad
Connecticut	May	Complete an approved course	None	No	None
Delaware	May	Complete a course	18 states	No	Broad
Florida	Shall	Complete a course	33 states	Yes	Broad
Georgia	Shall	None	23 states	Yes	Broad
Hawaii	May	Required for purchase permit	None	No	None
Idaho	Shall	Demonstrate familiarity with firearm	All states	No	Broad
Illinois	Shall	At least 16 hour course	None	No	Broad
Indiana	Shall	None	All states	Yes	Broad
Iowa	Shall	Completion of a course	None	Yes	Broad
Kansas	Shall	8-hour course	22 states	Yes	Broad
Kentucky	Shall	Completion of a course	All states	Yes	Broad
Louisiana	Shall	Completion of a course	32 states	Yes	Broad
Maine	Shall	Completion of a course	5 states	Yes	Broad
Maryland	May	16-hour course	None	No	Broad
Massachusetts	May	Completion of a course	None	No	None
Michigan	Shall	8-hour course	All states	Yes	Broad
Minnesota	Shall	Completion of a course	15 states	No	Broad
Mississippi	Shall	None*	24 states	Yes	Broad
Missouri	Shall	8-hour course	All states	No	Broad
Montana	Shall	Completion of a course	40 states	Yes	Broad
Nebraska	Shall	Completion of a course	29 states	No	Limited
Nevada	Shall	Completion of a course	10 states	No	Broad
New Hampshire	No license required	None	21 states	Yes	Broad
New Jersey	May	Completion of a course	None	No	None
New Mexico	Shall	Completion of a course	19 states	No	Broad
New York	May	Varies by county	None	No	None
North Carolina	Shall	Completion of a course	32 states	Yes	Broad
North Dakota	Shall	Completion of a course	26 states	Yes	Broad
Ohio	Shall	12-hour course	20 states	No	Broad
Oklahoma	Shall	8-hour course	All states	Yes	Broad
Oregon	Shall	Completion of a course	None	No	Broad
Pennsylvania	Shall	None	24 states	Yes	Broad
Rhode Island	May	Demonstrate firing proficiency	None	No	Broad
South Carolina	Shall	Completion of a course	17 states	Yes	Broad
South Dakota	Shall	None	All states	Yes	Broad
Tennessee	Shall	Completion of a course	All states	Yes	Broad
Texas	Shall	Completion of a course	40 states	Yes	Broad
Utah	Shall	Completion of a course	All states	Yes	Broad

STATE	SHALL ISSUE/ MAY ISSUE	TRAINING REQUIRED	RECIPROCITY[1]	STAND-YOUR-GROUND	PREEMPTION[2]
Vermont	No license required	None	Permits not required	No	Broad
Virginia	Shall	Completion of a course	26 states	No	Broad
Washington	Shall	None	10 states	No	Broad
West Virginia	Shall	Completion of a course	19 states	Yes	Broad
Wisconsin	Shall	Completion of a course	None	Yes	Broad
Wyoming	May	Completion of a course	29 states	Yes	Broad

[1]The number in each cell is the number of other states whose concealed carry licenses are recognized by that state.

[2]There are three categories for preemption: (1) None: the state government has no authority to preempt local gun ordinances; (2) Limited: state government has restricted authority to overrule local government ordinances; (3) Broad: state government has wide latitude in preempting local government restrictions.

Sources: National Rifle Association, Institute for Legislative Action, "Guide to Right-to-Carry Reciprocity and Recognition," www.standeyo.com/news_files/Firearms/State_Reciprocity.guide.pdf; Legal Center to Prevent Gun Violence, http://smartgunlaws.org/category/state-concealed-weapons-permitting.

APPENDIX 3

List of Organizations

Listed below are names and contact information of organizations involved in gun rights and gun control issues.

Academics for the Second Amendment
Joseph E. Olson, President
P.O. Box 131254
St. Paul, MN 55113

American Academy of Pediatrics
141 Northwest Point Boulevard
Elk Grove Village, IL 60007-1098
(847) 434-4000
www.aap.org

American Bar Association
321 North Clark Street
Chicago, IL 60654-7598
(312) 988-5000
www.abanet.org

American Civil Liberties Union
125 Broad Street, 18th Floor
New York, NY 10004-2400
www.aclu.org

American Jewish Congress
115 57th Street, Suite 11
New York, NY 10022
(212) 879-4500
www.ajcongress.org

Americans for Democratic Action
1625 K Street NW, Suite 102
Washington, DC 20006
(202) 785-5980
www.adaction.org

Americans for Responsible Solutions
PO Box 15642
Washington, D.C. 20003
Americansforresponsiblesolutions.org

Arming Women Against Rape and Endangerment
P.O. Box 242
Bedford, MA 01730-0242
(781)893-0500
www.aware.org

Association for Women's Self-Defense Advancement
556 Route 17 North, Suite 7-209
Paramus, NJ 07652
(201) 794-2153
www.awsda.org

British American Security Information Council
110 Maryland Avenue NW, Suite 205
Washington, DC 20002
(202) 546-8055
www.basicint.org

Bureau of Alcohol, Tobacco, Firearms, and Explosives
99 New York Avenue NE
Washington, DC 20226
(202) 648-79080
www.atf.gov

CarryConcealed.net
20993 Foothill Boulevard #202
Hayward, CA 94541
www.carryconcealed.net

Center for the Study and Prevention of Violence
Institute of Behavioral Science
University of Colorado at Boulder
483 UCB
Boulder, CO 80309
www.colorado.edu/cspv

Central Conference of American Rabbis
355 Lexington Avenue
New York, NY 10017
(212) 972-3636
http://ccarnet.org

Children's Defense Fund
25 E. Street NW
Washington, DC 20001
(800) 233-1200
www.childrensdefense.org

Citizens Committee for the Right to Keep and Bear Arms
Liberty Park
12500 N.E. Tenth Place
Bellevue, WA 98005
(425) 454-4911
www.ccrkba.org

Coalition to Stop Gun Violence
1424 L Street NW, Suite 2-1
Washington, DC 20036
(202) 408-0061
www.csgv.org

Congress of Racial Equality
817 Broadway, 3rd Floor
New York, NY 10003
(212) 598-4000
www.core-online.org

Constitutional Accountability Center
1200 18th Street NW, Suite 1002
Washington, DC 20036
(202) 296-6889

Doctors for Responsible Gun Ownership
Claremont Institute
937 West Foothill Boulevard, Suite E
Claremont, CA 91711
(909) 621-6825
https://drgo.us

Educational Fund to End Handgun Violence
1424 L Street NW, Suite 2-1
Washington, DC 20005
(202) 408-0061
www.csgv.org

Everytown for Gun Safety
PO Box 4184
New York, NY 10163
Everytown.org

Firearms Coalition
P.O. Box 3313
Manassas, VA 20108
(703) 753-0424
www.firearmscoalition.org

Firearms Owners Against Crime
P.O. Box 14
Presto, PA 15142
(412) 221-3346
www.foac-pac.org

Fraternal Order of Police
701 Marriott Drive
Nashville, TN 37214
(615) 399-0900
www.fop.net

Gun Owners' Action League
37 Pierce Street, P.O. Box 567
Northboro, MA 01532
(508) 393-5333
www.goal.org

Gun Owners of America
8001 Forbes Place, Suite 102
Springfield, VA 22151
(703) 321-8585
http://gunowners.org

**Harborview Injury Prevention
and Research Center**
325 Ninth Avenue, Box 359960
Seattle, WA 98104
(206) 744-9430
http://depts.washington.edu/hiprc

Heartland Institute
19 South LaSalle Street #903
Chicago, IL 60603
(312) 377-4000
www.heartland.org

Independence Institute
13952 Denver West Parkway, Suite 400
Golden, CO 80401
(303) 279-6536
www.i2i.org

Injury Free Coalition for Kids
722 West 168th Street, Room 821 H-1
Columbia University New York, NY 10032
(212) 342-0514
www.injuryfree.org

Institute for Legislative Action, NRA
11250 Waples Road
Fairfax, VA 22030 &
(800) 392-8683
www.nraila.org

International Association of Chiefs of Police
515 North Washington Street
Alexandria, VA 22314
(703) 836-6767
www.theiacp.org

International Brotherhood of Police Officers
159 Burgin Parkway
Quincy, MA 02169
(617) 376-0220
www.ibpo.org

International Defensive Pistol Association
2232 CR 719
Berryville, AR 72616
(870) 545-3886
www.idpa.com

Izaak Walton League of America
707 Conservation Lane
Gaithersburg, MD 20878
(301) 548-0150
www.iwla.org

**Jews for the Preservation of Firearms
Ownership**
P.O. Box 270143
Hartford, WI 53027
(262) 673-9745
www.jpfo.org

John Birch Society
P.O. Box 8040
Appleton, WI 54913
(920) 749-3780
www.jbs.org

**Johns Hopkins Center for Gun Policy and
Research**
624 North Broadway Baltimore,
MD 21205-1996
(410) 955-7982
http://www.jhsph.edu/gunpolicy

Law Enforcement Alliance of America
5538 Port Royal Road Springfield, VA 22151
(703) 847-2677
www.leaa.org

Legal Action Project (Brady Center)
1225 Eye Street NW, Suite 1100
Washington, DC 20005
(202) 289-7319
www.bradycenter.org

Law Center to Prevent Gun Violence
268 Bush Street, Suite 5555
San Francisco, CA 94104
(415) 433-2062 smartgunlaws.org

Libertarian Party
2600 Virginia Avenue NW, Suite 200
Washington, DC 20037
(202) 333-0008
www.lp.org

Mayors Against Illegal Guns
everytown.org

Mennonite Central Committee
21 South 12th Street, P.O. Box 500
Akron, PA 17501
(717) 859-1151
www.mcc.org

Militia of Montana
P.O. Box 1486
Noxon, MT 59853
(406) 847-2735
www.militiaofmontana.com

Moms Demand Action for Gun Sense in America
Momsdemandaction.org

National Association of Federally Licensed Firearms Dealers
2400 East Las Olas Boulevard, No. 397
Fort Lauderdale, FL 33301
(954) 467-9994
www.amfire.com

National Association of Police Organizations
317 South Patrick Street
Alexandria, VA 22314
(703) 549-0775
www.napo.org

National Association of School Psychologists
4340 East-West Highway, Suite 402
Bethesda, MD 20814
(301) 657-0270
www.nasponline.org

National Center for Injury Prevention and Control
4770 Buford Highway NE, MS F-63
Atlanta, GA 30341-3717
(800) 232-4636
www.cdc.gov/injuy/index.html

National Center for Policy Analysis
601 Pennsylvania Avenue, Suite 900
Washington, DC 20004
(202) 220-3082
www.ncpa.org

National Crime Prevention Council
2001 Jefferson Davis Highway, Suite 901
Arlington, VA 22202
(202) 466-6272
www.ncpc.org

National Education Association
1201 16th Street NW
Washington, DC 20036-3290
(202) 833-4000
www.nea.org

National Firearms Association of Canada
P.O. Box 52183
Edmonton, Alberta
Canada T6G 2T5
(780) 439-1394
www.nfa.ca

National Muzzle Loading Rifle Association
State Road 62, Maxine Moss Drive
Friendship, IN 47021
(812) 667-5131
www.nmlra.org

National Organization of Black Law Enforcement Executives
4609-F Pinecrest Office Park Drive
Alexandria, VA 22312-1442
(703) 658-1529
www.noblenational.org

National Rifle Association
11250 Waples Mill Road
Fairfax, VA 22030 &
(800) 392-8683

National SAFE KIDS Campaign
1301 Pennsylvania Avenue NW, Suite
100Washington, DC 20004-1707
(202) 662-0600
www.safekids.org

National School Safety Center
6617 Smoketree Avenue
Oak Park, CA 91377
(805) 373-9977
www.schoolsafety.us

National Shooting Sports Foundation
11 Mile Hill Road
Newtown, CT 06470
(203) 426-1320
www.nssf.com

National Tracing Center
99 New York Avenue NE
Washington, DC
(202) 648-7080
www.atf.gov

Paul Revere Network
(312) 482-9910
www.paulrevere.org

Physicians for Social Responsibility
1875 Connecticut Avenue NW, Suite 1012
Washington, DC 20009
(202) 667-4260
www.psr.org

Police Executive Research Forum
1120 Connecticut Avenue NW,
Suite 930
Washington, DC 20036
(202) 466-7820
www.policeforum.org

Potomac Institute for Policy Studies
901 North Stuart Street, Suite 200
Arlington, VA 22203
(703) 525-0770
www.potomacinstitute.org

Presbyterian Church (U.S.A.)
100 Witherspoon Street
Louisville, KY 40202
(800) 728-7228
www.pcusa.org

Professional Gun Retailers Association
2620 Alamanda Court
Fort Lauderdale, FL 33301
(954) 467-9994
www.amfire.com

Second Amendment Committee
P.O. Box 1776
Hanford, CA 93232
(209) 584-5209
www.libertygunrights.com

Second Amendment Foundation
James Madison Building
12500 North East Tenth Place
Bellevue, WA 98005
(425) 454-7012
www.saf.org

Second Amendment Sisters
900 RR 620S
Suite C-101, Box 228
Lakeway, TX 78734
www.secondamendmentsisters.com

Southern Poverty Law Center
400 Washington Wvenue
Montgomery, AL 36104
(334) 956-8200
www.splcenter.org

Sporting Arms and Ammunition Manufacturers' Institute Flintlock Ridge Office Center
11 Mile Hill Road
Newtown, CT 06470-2359
(203) 426-1320
www.saami.org

Stop Handgun Violence
One Bridge Street
Newton, MA 02458
(617) 243-8174
www.stophandgunviolence.com

Student Pledge Against Gun Violence
112 Nevada Street
Northfield, MN 55057
(507) 645-5378
www.pledge.org

Third Way
1025 Connecticut Avenue NW, Suite 501
Washington, DC 20036
(202) 384-1700
www.thirdway.org

United States Conference of Mayors
1620 Eye Street NW
Washington, DC 20006
(202) 293-7330
www.mayors.org

United States Practical Shooting Association
P.O. Box 811
Sedro-Woolley, WA 98284
(360) 855-2245
www.uspsa.org

Violence Policy Center
1730 Rhode Island Avenue NW, Suite 1014
Washington, DC 20036
(202) 822-8200
www.vpc.org

Violence Prevention Research Program
Western Fairs Building
University of California, Davis
2315 Stockton Boulevard
Sacramento, CA 95817
(916) 734-3539
http://web.ucdmc.ucdavis.edu/vprp

Women's Firearm Network
Shooters, P.O. Box 990
One Court Street
Exeter, NH 03833
(603) 778-4720
www.womenshooters.com

BIBLIOGRAPHY

Ahern, Jerry. *CCW: Carrying Concealed Weapons, How to Carry Concealed Weapons and Know When Others Are*. Chino Valley, AZ: Blacksmith Corp., 1996.

Anderson, Jack. 1996. *Inside the NRA*. Beverly Hills, CA: Dove Books.

Apel, Lorelei. *Dealing with Weapons at School and at Home*. New York: Rosen Publishing Group, 1996.

Ayoob, Massad F. *In the Gravest Extreme: The Role of the Firearm in Personal Protection*. Concord, NH: Police Bookshelf, 1980.

_____. *Gunproof Your Children: Handgun Primer*. Concord, NH: Police Bookshelf, 1986.

Barrett, Paul M. *Glock: The Rise of America's Gun*. Broadway Books, 2013.

Bartone, John C. *Guns, the National Rifle Association, and Consumers as Armed Citizens*. Washington, DC: ABBE, 1994.

_____. *Guns and Their Importance to Americans Facing Crimes of Threat, Harm, and Property Invasion*. Washington, DC: ABBE, 1996.

Baum, Dan. *Gun Guys*. New York: Knopf, 2013.

Beckelman, Laurie. *Gun Control: You Decide*. Parsippany, NJ: Crestwood House, 1999.

Bellesiles, Michael. *Arming America: The Origins of a National Gun Culture*. New York: Alfred A. Knopf, 2000.

Berands, Neal. *Gun Control*. San Diego: Lucent Books, 1992.

Bijlefeld, Marjolijn. *Gun Control Debate: A Documentary History*. Westport, CT: Greenwood, 1997.

Bird, Chris. *The Concealed Handgun Manual: How to Choose, Carry, and Shoot a Gun in Self Defense*. San Antonio: Privateer Publications, 1998.

Bogus, Carl T., ed. *The Second Amendment in Law and History*. New York: New Press, 2002. Brennan, Jill W. *Gun Control in the 1990s*. Kettering, OH: PPI, 1996.

Brown, Peter Harry, and Daniel G. Abel. 2003. *Outgunned: Up Against the NRA*. New York: The Free Press.

Bruce, John M. and Clyde Wilcox, eds. *The Changing Politics of Gun Control*. Lanham, MD: Rowman and Littlefield, 1998. Burbick, Joan. *Gun Show Nation: Gun Culture and American Democracy*. New York: The New Press, 2006.

Bureau of Alcohol, Tobacco, and Firearms. *Federal Firearms Regulations Reference Guide*. Washington, DC: U.S. Government Printing Office, 1995.

_____. *State Laws and Published Ordinances_Firearms*, 21st ed. Washington, DC: U.S. Government Printing Office, 1998.

Carlson, Jennifer. *Citizen-Protectors*. New York: Oxford University Press, 2015.

Carter, Gregg Lee. *The Gun Control Movement*. New York: Twayne, 1997.

_____, ed. *Guns in American Society*. 3 vols. Santa Barbara, CA: ABC-CLIO, 2012.

_____. *Gun Control in the United States*. Santa Barbara, CA: ABC-CLIO, 2017.

Charles, Patrick J. *The Second Amendment: The Intent and Its Interpretation by the States and the Supreme Court*. Jefferson, NC: McFarland, 2009.

Cook, Philip, and Jens Ludwig. *Gun Violence: The Real Costs*. New York: Oxford University Press, 2000.

_____, and Kristin A. Goss. *The Gun Debate: What Everyone Needs to Know*. New York: Oxford University Press, 2014.

Cornell, Saul. *Whose Right to Bear Arms Did the Second Amendment Protect?* Boston: Bedford/St. Martin's, 2000.

_____. *A Well Regulated Militia*. New York: Oxford University Press, 2006.

_____, and Nathan Kozuskanich, eds. *The Second Amendment on Trial*. Amherst, MA: University of Massachusetts Press, 2013.

Cottrol, Robert J., ed. *Gun Control and the Constitution: Sources and Explorations on the Second Amendment*. New York: Garland, 1994.

Cox, Vic. *Guns, Violence and Teens*. Enslow, 1997.

Cozic, Charles P. *The Militia Movement*. San Diego: Greenhaven, 1997.

_____, and Carol Wekesser, eds. *Gun Control*. San Diego: Greenhaven, 1992. Cullen, Dave. *Columbine*. New York: Twelve, 2009.

Davidson, Osha Gray. *Under Fire: The NRA and the Battle for Gun Control*. Iowa City: University of Iowa Press, 1998.

DeConde, Alexander. *Gun Violence in America*. Boston: Northeastern University Press 2001.

DeBrabander, Firmin. *Do Guns Make Us Free?* New Haven, CT: Yale University Press, 2015.

Dekker, Virginia M. *Guns and Firearms: Index of New Information with Social, Medical, Psychological and Legal Implications*. Washington, DC: ABBE, 1995.

Devour, Cynthia D. *Kids and Guns*. Minneapolis: Abdo and Daughters, 1994.

Diaz, Tom. *Making a Killing: The Business of Guns in America*. New York: New Press, 1999.

_____. *The Last Gun*. New York: The New Press, 2013.

Dizzard, Jan E., Robert Merrill Muth, and Stephen P. Andrews, Jr., eds. *Guns in America: A Reader*. New York: New York University Press, 1999.

Doherty, Brian. *Gun Control on Trial: Inside the Supreme Court Battle over the Second Amendment*. Washington, D.C.: Cato Institute, 2008.

Dolan, Edward F. and Margaret M. Scariano. *Guns in the United States*. Danbury, CT: Franklin Watts, 1994. Edel, Wilbur. *Gun Control: Threat to Liberty or Defense Against Anarchy?* Westport, CT: Praeger, 1995. Fadala, Sam. *Great Shooters of the World*. South Hackensack, NJ: Stoeger, 1990.

Feldman, Richard, *Ricochet: Confessions of a Gun Lobbyist*. New York: Wiley, 2007.

Flynn, George and Alan Gottlieb. *Guns for Women: The Complete Handgun Buying Guide for Women*. Bellevue, WA: Merril, 1988.

Freedman, Warren. *The Privilege to Keep and Bear Arms: The Second Amendment and Its Interpretation*. New York: Quorum, 1989.

Fuller, Sharon. *The Gun Control Debate: An Update*. Upland, PA: DIANE Publishing, 1995.

Giffords, Gabrielle, and Mark Kelly. *Enough: Our Fight to Keep America Safe from Gun Violence*. New York: Scribner, 2014.

Goss, Kristin A. *Disarmed: The Missing Movement for Gun Control in America*. Princeton: Princeton University Press, 2006.

Gottfried, Ted. *Gun Control: Public Safety and the Right to Bear Arms*. Brookfield, CT: Millbrook, 1993. Gottlieb, Alan M. *Gun Rights Fact Book*. Bellevue, WA: Merril, 1989.

_____. *The Rights of Gun Owners*. Bellevue, WA: Merrill, 1991.

_____. *Politically Correct Guns*. Bellevue, WA: Merril, 1996.

_____. *The Gun Grabbers: Who They Are, How They Operate, Where They Get Their Money*, Reissue ed. Bellevue, WA: Merril, 1998.

Gottlieb, Alan M. and David B. Kopel. *Things You Can Do to Defend Your Gun Rights*. Bellevue, WA: Merril, 1993.

_____. *More Things You Can Do to Defend Your Gun Rights*. Bellevue, WA: Merril, 1995.

Haag, Pamela. *The Gunning of America*. NY: Basic Books, 2016.

Halbrook, Stephen P. *That Every Man Be Armed*. Oakland, CA: The Independent Institute, 1984.

_____. *Firearms Law Deskbook: Federal and State Criminal Practice*. New York: Clark Boardman Callaghan, 1995.

_____. *The Founders' Second Amendment*. Chicago: Ivan R. Dee, 2008.

Harcourt, Bernard E., ed. *Guns, Crime, and Punishment in America*. New York: NYU Press, 2003.

_____. *Language of the Gun: Youth, Crime, and Public Policy*. Chicago: University of Chicago Press, 2006.

_____. *Gun Control in the Third Reich*. Oakland, CA: The Independent Institute, 2013.

Hamilton, Neil A. *Militias in America*. Santa Barbara, CA: ABC-CLIO, 1996.

Hemenway, David. *Guns and the Constitution: The Myth of Second Amendment Protection for Firearms in America*. Northampton, MA: Aletheia, 1995.

_____. *Private Guns, Public Health*. Ann Arbor, MI: University of Michigan Press, 2004. Henderson, Harry. *Gun Control*. New York: Facts on File, Inc., 2000.

Henigan, Dennis A. *Lethal Logic: Exploding the Myths That Paralyze American Gun Policy*. Washington, D.C.: Potomac Books, 2009.

Homsher, Deborah. *Women and Guns: Politics and the Culture of Firearms in America*. Armonk, NY: M.E. Sharpe, 2001. Hook, Donald D. *Gun Control: The Continuing Debate*. Bellevue, WA: Merril, 1992.

Horwitz, Joshua, and Casey Anderson. 2009. *Guns, Democracy, and the Insurrectionist Idea*. Ann Arbor: University of Michigan Press, 2009.

Kates, Don B. and Gary Kleck, eds. *The Great American Gun Debate: Essays on Firearms and Violence*. San Francisco: Pacific Research Institute for Public Policy, 1997.

Kelly, Caitlin. *Blown Away: American Women and Guns*. New York: Pocket Books, 2004.

Kennet, Lee and James La Verne Anderson. *The Gun in America: The Origins of a National Dilemma*. Westport, CT: Greenwood, 1975.

Kleck, Gary. *Point Blank: Guns and Violence in America*. New York: Aldine De Gruyter, 1991.

_____. *Targeting Guns: Firearms and Their Control*. New York: Aldine De Gruyter, 1997.

Kopel, David B. *The Samurai, the Mountie, and the Cowboy: Should America Adopt the Gun Controls of Other Democracies?* Buffalo, NY: Prometheus, 1992.

_____, ed. *Guns: Who Should Have Them?* Amherst, NY: Prometheus, 1995.

Korwin, Alan, with Michael P. Anthony. *Gun Laws of America*. Phoenix: Bloomfield, 1997.

Krushke, Earl R. *The Right to Keep and Bear Arms: A Continuing American Dilemma*. Springfield, IL: Charles C. Thomas, 1985.

_____. *Gun Control: A Reference Handbook*. Santa Barbara, CA: ABC-CLIO, 1995.

Kyle, Chris. *American Gun: A History of the U.S. in Ten Firearms*. NY: William Morrow, 2013.

Landau, Elaine. *Armed America: The Status of Gun Control*. Parsippany, NJ: Julian Messner, 1991. LaPierre, Wayne R. *Guns, Crime, and Freedom*. Washington, DC: Regnery, 1994.

_____, and James Jay Baker. *Shooting Straight: Telling the Truth About Guns in America*. Washington, D.C.: Regnery, 2002.

Larosa, Benedict D. *Gun Control*. San Antonio: Candlestick, 1997.

Larson, Erik. *Lethal Passage: The Story of a Gun*. New York: Vintage, 1995. Levine, Herbert M. *Gun Control*. Chatham, NJ: Raintree Steck-Vaughn, 1997. Lott, John R., Jr. *The Bias Against Guns*. Washington, D.C.: Regnery, 2003.

_____. *More Guns Less Crime: Understanding Crime and Gun Control Laws,* 3rd ed. Chicago: University of Chicago Press, 2010.

Ludwig, Jens, and Philip Cook, eds. *Evaluating Gun Policy*. Washington, D.C.: Brookings, 2003. MacNutt, Karen. *Ladies Legal Companion*. Boston: MacNutt Art Trust, 1993.

Mahon, John K. *History of the Militia and the National Guard*. New York: Macmillan, 1983.

Malcolm, Joyce Lee. *To Keep and Bear Arms: The Origins of an Anglo-American Right*. Cambridge, MA: Harvard University Press, 1994.

_____. *Guns and Violence: The English Experience*. Cambridge, MA: Harvard University Press, 2004.

May-Hayes, Gila. *Effective Defense: The Woman, The Plan, The Gun*. Onalaska, WA: FAS Books, 1994.

McClurg, Andrew J., David B. Kopel, and Brannon P. Denning, eds. *Gun Control and Gun Rights*. New York: NYU Press, 2002.

Melzer, Scott. *Gun Crusaders: The NRA's Culture War*. NY: NYU Press, 2009.

Miller, Maryann. *Working Together Against Gun Violence*, Revised ed. New York: Rosen, 1997.

Miniter, Frank. *The Future of the Gun*. Washington, D.C.: Regnery, 2014.

Moore, James. *Very Special Agents*. Urbana: University of Illinois Press, 2001.

Murray, James M. *Fifty Things You Can Do about Guns*. San Francisco: Robert D. Reed, 1994.

National Research Council. *Firearms and Violence*. Washington, D.C.: National Academy of Sciences, 2005.

Neaderland, Louise Odes. *The Case for Gun Control*. Brooklyn, NY: Bone Hollow Arts, 1994. Nisbet, Lee, ed. *The Gun Control Debate: You Decide*. Amherst, NY: Prometheus, 1991.

O'Sullivan, Carol. *Gun Control: Distinguishing Between Fact and Opinion*. San Diego: Greenhaven, 1990. Pontonne, S., ed. *Gun Control Issues*. Commack, NY: Nova Science, 1996.

Pratt, Larry. *Safeguarding Liberty: The Constitution and Citizen Militias*. Franklin, TN: Legacy Communications, 1995.

Prothrow-Stith, Deborah. *Deadly Consequences: How Violence Is Destroying Our Teenage Population and a Plan to Begin Solving the Problem*. New York: HarperCollins, 1991.

Quigley, Paxton. *Armed and Female: Twelve Million American Women Own Guns, Shouldn't You?* New York: St. Martin's, 1993.

Ragnar, Benson. *Modern Weapons Caching: A Down to Earth Approach to Beating the Government Gun Grab*. Boulder, CO: Paladin, 1990.

Robin, Gerald D. *Violent Crime and Gun Control*. Cincinnati: Anderson, 1991. Roleff, Tamara L., ed. *Gun Control*. San Diego: Greenhaven, 2007.

Sawyer, C.W. *Firearms in American History 1600-1800*. Watchung, NJ: Albert Saifer, 1987.

Schulman, J. Neil. *Stopping Power: Why 70 Million Americans Own Guns*. Santa Monica, CA: Synapse-Centurion, 1994.

_____. *Self Control Not Gun Control*. Santa Monica, CA: Synapse-Centurion, 1995.

Sheley, Joseph F. and James D. Wright. *In the Line of Fire: Youth, Guns, and Violence in Urban America*. New York: Aldine De Gruyter, 1995.

Siegel, Mark A., Nancy R. Jacobs, and Carol D. Foster, eds. *Gun Control: Restricting Rights or Protecting People?* Wylie, TX: Information Plus, 1991.

Simkin, Jay, and Aaron S. Zelman. *Gun Control_Gateway to Tyranny: The Nazi Law 18 March 1938.* Milwaukee: Jews for the Preservation of Firearms Ownership, 1992.

Simkin, Jay, Aaron S. Zelman, and Alan M. Rice. *Lethal Laws: 'Gun Control' Is the Key to Genocide.* Milwaukee: Jews for the Preservation of Firearms Ownership, 1994.

Sinclair, Beth, Jennifer Hamilton, Babette Gutmann, Julie Daft, and Dee Bolcik, *Report on State Implementation of the Gun-Free Schools Act_School Year 1996-97.* Washington, DC: U.S. Department of Education, 1998.

Spitzer, Robert J. *The Right to Bear Arms.* Santa Barbara, CA: ABC-CLIO, 2001.

_____. *Gun Control: A Documentary and Reference Guide.* Westport, CT: Greenwood Press, 2009.

_____. *Saving the Constitution from Lawyers: How Legal Training and Law Reviews Distort Constitutional Meaning.* New York: Cambridge University Press, 2008.

_____. *Gun Control: A Documentary and Reference Guide.* Westport, CT: Greenwood, 2009.

_____. *Guns across America: Reconciling Gun Rules and Rights.* New York: Oxford University Press, 2015.

_____. *The Politics of Gun Control*, 6th ed. Boulder, CO: Paradigm Publishers, 2015.

Squires, Peter. *Gun Crime in Global Contexts.* New York: Routledge, 2014.

Stroud, Angela. *Good Guys with Guns.* Chapel Hill, NC: University of North Carolina Press, 2015.

Sugarmann, Josh. *Every Handgun Is Aimed at You: The Case for Banning Handguns.* New York: The New Press, 2001.

_____. and Kristen Rand. *Cease Fire: A Comprehensive Strategy to Reduce Firearms Violence.* Washington, DC: Violence Policy Center, 1997.

Tita, George, et al. *Reducing Gun Violence.* Santa Monica, CA: RAND Corporation, 2003. Tonso, William R., ed. *The Gun Culture and Its Enemies.* Bellevue, WA: Merril, 1990.

Torr, James D., ed. *Gun Violence.* San Diego, CA: Greenhaven Press, 2002.

Truby, J. David. *Zips, Pipes, and Pens: Arsenal of Improvised Arms.* Boulder, CO: Paladin, 1993.

Turley, Windle and James E. Rooks. *Firearms Litigation: Law, Science, and Practice.* New York: John Wiley and Sons, 1994. Tushnet, Mark V. *Out of Range: Why the Constitution Can't End the Battle Over Guns.* New York: Oxford University Press, 2007.

Utter, Glenn H., ed. *Guns and Contemporary Society,* 3 vols. (Santa Barbara, CA: ABC-CLIO, 2016).

Uviller, H. Richard, and William G. Merkel. *The Militia and the Right to Arms.* Durham, NC: Duke University Press, 2002. Van Zwoll, Wayne. *America's Great Gunmakers.* South Hackensack, NJ: Stoeger, 1992.

Vizzard, William J. *In the Cross Fire: A Political History of the Bureau of Alcohol, Tobacco and Firearms.* Boulder, CO: Lynne Rienner, 1997.

_____. *Shots in the Dark: The Policy, Politics, and Symbolism of Gun Control.* Lanham, MD: Rowman and Littlefield, 2000.

Waldman, Michael. *The Second Amendment: A Biography.* New York: Simon & Schuster, 2014.

Waters, Robert A. *The Best Defense: True Stories of Intended Victims Who Defended Themselves With a Firearm,* Nashville, TN: Cumberland House, 1998.

Webster, Daniel W., and Jon S. Vernick. *Reducing Gun Violence in America.* The Johns Hopkins University Press, 2013.

Weir, William. *A Well Regulated Militia: The Battle Over Gun Control.* North Haven, CT: Archon, 1997. Whitman, Neil. *Gun Control War.* Kettering, OH: PPI, 1995.

Whitney, Craig R. *Living With Guns: A Liberal's Case for the Second Amendment.* NY: Public Affairs, 2013.

Wills, Garry. *A Necessary Evil.* New York: Simon and Schuster, 1999.

Wilson, R.L. *Ruger and His Guns: A History of the Man, the Company and Their Firearms.* New York: Simon and Schuster, 1996.

Windlesham, Lord. 1998. *Politics, Punishment, and Populism.* New York: Oxford University Press.

Winkler, Adam. *Gun Fight: The Battle Over the Right to Bear Arms in America.* New York: W.W. Norton, 2011.

Wintemute, Garen. *Ring of Fire: The Handgun Makers of Southern California.* Sacramento, CA: Violence Prevention Research Program, 1994.

Wright, James D. and Peter H. Rossi. *Armed and Considered Dangerous: A Survey of Felons and Their Firearms.* New York: Aldine De Gruyter, 1994.

Zimring, Franklin E., and Gordon Hawkins. *The Citizen's Guide to Gun Control.* New York: Macmillan, 1987.

_____. *Crime Is Not the Problem: Lethal Violence in America.* New York: Oxford University Press, 1997.

INDEX